THE

Month-By-Month
Gardening Guide

English-language edition published in 2022 by
Timber Press, Inc.
The Haseltine Building
133 S.W. Second Avenue, Suite 450
Portland, Oregon 97204-3527
timberpress.com

Text and cover design by Vincent James
Cover Illustration by Nina Montenegro
Illustration credits appear on page 404

ISBN 978-1-64326-141-6
Printed in China on paper from responsible sources
Catalog records for this book are available from the
Library of Congress and the British Library.

THE
Month-By-Month
Gardening Guide

Daily Advice for Growing Flowers, Vegetables,
Herbs & Houseplants

FRANZ BÖHMIG
Translated by Michael Ashdown

Timber Press
Portland, Oregon

FOREWORD

With his informative and easy-to-understand tips, Franz Böhmig laid the foundation for this book more than 50 years ago. Since then, it has become an established standard reference work: the 28th edition was an anniversary edition, and the book was then revised further with the 29th edition, which featured a greater emphasis on nature and environmental conservation. We now present the 30th edition, translated into English for the first time.

Nearly 1400 tips and a wealth of sound advice will help gardening enthusiasts plan more attractive gardens, try their hand at growing new vegetable species, and take special maintenance measures into consideration when growing traditional varieties. The requirements of a garden and its use have changed in recent years, and so the 29th edition included many new vegetable and ornamental plant varieties in addition to those which were well known in Böhmig's day.

Meanwhile, a greater emphasis has been given on how a contribution to maintaining the diversity of our native fauna and flora can be made in even the smallest gardens. Today, most gardening enthusiasts are aware of their responsibilities in this regard. They have recognized that our native animals and plants need to be protected, and that establishing a near-natural garden can offer an ideal habitat in which these organisms can thrive. They know, too, that implementing biological pest control methods in the house and garden is wiser in the long run than immediately resorting to chemical means. Accordingly, it has also been important to give advice on how plant pests and diseases can be combated using natural methods. Similarly, tips have been added on how to plan a near-natural garden without having to forego the pleasures of double-flowering rose cultivars or splendid lilies.

To continue to be able to enjoy the diversity and beauty of nature in our gardens in the future, it is helpful to prune died-off plant stalks and seed heads not in the fall, but only later, in the spring—these will then provide a home for many useful insects during the winter. Meanwhile, hedgehogs can overwinter in small piles of leaves or brushwood in a shady, sheltered corner, while a piece of deadwood can help wild bees and beetles (and their larvae) to survive.

Greenhouses or glasshouses, meanwhile, have a different significance now than they did many years ago, when issues of supply from the garden were much more important. Today, greenhouses are primarily used to grow healthy vegetables without the use of pesticides or artificial fertilizers.

Balconies, terraces, and winter gardens enable us to relax and take pleasure from our plants, regardless of whether they are winter hardy or need to overwinter in a frost-free environment. All the associated problems have been sufficiently noted and appropriate advice given. Other tips, such as those regarding soil cultivation, for example, have been brought in line with the current state of knowledge. This also applies to the issue of peat: it has long been known that further unchecked peat extraction may lead to the downfall of our wetlands. Accordingly, the book contains tips on how peat can be used effectively and alternatives to consider.

By employing the right measures at the right time, plant growth and flowering can be fully optimized and fruiting enhanced, yielding a richer harvest and greatly enhancing the enjoyment of our plants and gardens. Accordingly, attaining a beautiful and bountiful garden and taking pleasure in our plants remains the central focus of this book. It shows how the necessary work can be made easier to manage, and that this represents just a minor outlay for considerable pleasure and enjoyment, which is enhanced still further by outstanding yields.

A note on plant names: in the tips and tables, the botanical (Latin) names of the plants are given in addition to the English plant names, because the English designations can vary greatly from region to region, which can lead to confusion. Every now and then, the botanical name of a species needs to be changed. This is often necessary because of genetic studies and the concomitant new findings. As a rule, the older name that is no longer valid, but represents a synonym, is also given in parentheses. Since taxonomists are not always in agreement when it comes to renaming, it is necessary to determine which publication should be used as a basis for the botanical names. For this book, we have largely followed the "new Zander": Erhardt, W., E. Götz, N. Bödeker, and S. Seybold; 2014: *Zander: Dictionary of Plant Names*, 19th edition, Verlag Eugen Ulmer, Stuttgart, Germany.

—Bärbel Röth, Flarchheim, Spring 2018

ABOUT THIS BOOK

First of all, readers should be aware that this book is divided into two main parts. The first part comprises the tips themselves, which contribute to good plant growth, flowering, and rich yields in the garden. For better orientation, these are subdivided into the following sections:

- Winter
- Spring
- Summer
- Fall

The second part comprises special tables and lists of vegetable and ornamental plant varieties, with indications of their soil requirements, planting times, planting widths, and more. Additionally, the tips for the gardening year from January to December are subdivided according to the following headings:

- General
- Vegetables
- Ornamental Plants
  - Ornamental Gardens
  - Terraces and Balconies
  - Winter Gardens, Flower
    Windows, and Rooms

Since the topic of ornamental plants is extensive, ranging from flowerbeds in the garden to plants in the house, in windows, on the terrace and balcony, and in winter gardens, the tips in this section have been further subdivided accordingly. This means that important tasks relating to ornamental plants in all areas can be carried out at the optimal time.

Within the individual tips themselves, readers will find specific techniques, advice, and recommendations for successful gardening and plant cultivation.

The illustrations associated with the individual tips explain the tasks, working methods, and work sequences in more detail. Cross-references (for example ▶ **TIP 728**) refer to tips elsewhere that contain information on the same subject, and that should be noted as well. Sometimes, references are also made to a table in the second part of the book.

The second part of the book consists of tables that provide detailed information on the individual topic areas, with specific plant species and varieties. Here you will find listings of ornamental plants such as trees and shrubs, winter-hardy perennials, creepers, and climbers, as well as aquatic plants, grasses, and ferns, and, not least, indoor plants. Many vegetable varieties are listed too, along with their specific soil and climate requirements. Among other things, you can find information in the individual tables on site and environmental conditions, maintenance measures, growth forms, fruit sizes, development times, and harvesting tips, as well as on pests that attack our vegetable and ornamental plants. This second part, too, follows the same General – Vegetables – Ornamental Plants sequence. These tables will provide gardening enthusiasts with a wealth of knowledge to enable them to enjoy a rich harvest through the lively and healthy growth of their plants.

With these introductory guidelines, we hope that users of this book will be able to find the right section quickly and easily, while also enabling them to delve deeper into the extensive and fascinating world of horticulture.

We wish all gardening enthusiasts every pleasure and success with caring for their plants, resplendent flowering, outstanding yields, and, not least, enjoyment and relaxation in their gardening activities.

JANUARY

Winter

All the plants are still lying dormant beneath a dense layer of snow and are quietly awaiting beautiful sunny days. Similarly, the birds that have not migrated south are dreaming of summer and bountiful food sources. They are our helpers in combating vermin and other pests. Specially built feeding sites are the meeting places for our feathered friends, who will soon be delighting us again with their chirruping and song.

During the cold time of year, it is important not to neglect the birds' care and feeding. Their feeding sites should be kept clear of snow, and their feed supply should be replenished continually as required.

GENERAL

1 **The garden should serve primarily as a place to relax after a day's work and during the weekend.**

This is something that we need to remember when we acquire a garden, since building on and looking after even the smallest plot of land requires a considerable work input. Accordingly, it is important for us to know how much effort we are prepared to put into a garden as a place for relaxation without it becoming too much of a burden.

2 **Water and soil conditions, together with the overall situation, are the most important factors to consider when taking on a garden.**

Pure sandy and loamy soils always require considerable improvement measures. Habitable microclimates can be established on cold and windy sites through appropriate planting.

3 **Water and electrical connections make gardening work easier.**

Ideally, water and electrical connections should already be present, or should be planned for in new construction, taking local factors into consideration. A water supply is of prime importance for gardening success. NB: Connections to an electrical supply should be made only by a registered electrician!

4 **An excessively high or low water table will reduce the value of the gardening land.**

Expensive drainage measures will not be practicable in most cases. If the water table is too low, it will be necessary to plan for a high water demand. Ornamental gardens can be adapted to the conditions by a suitable choice of plant species.

5 **If a vegetable garden is to be established outdoors, the total area should not exceed 240 square yards.**

For intensive vegetable growing, such an area will require considerable work, especially in spring and in the fall; the success of the entire year is dependent on the timely completion of the necessary tasks in spring. Combining a vegetable garden with an ornamental garden is very common—the latter is more expensive to plant at the beginning, but requires less work than a vegetable garden later on. ▶ **TIP 6**

6 **To supply enough vegetables to feed a family, an area of at least 60 square yards per person will be required.**

This assumes intensive use of the available land; most of the work will need to be done during the five months from March to July, involving a total of nearly 200 working hours. If a neglected garden is taken on, the required work in the first year will be considerably greater.

A good supply of compost is essential for healthy plant growth and high yields in the vegetable garden.

7 **If the soil requires considerable improvement, an ornamental garden should preferably be established over a period of two or more years.**

To avoid land lying fallow, it should be planted in the meantime with simple crops that do not need a great financial or work outlay, such as potatoes—these will also greatly contribute to soil improvement. The same applies if new fruit or vegetable gardens are being established.

8 Humus improves the soil.

Humus-rich soils have a good structure and promote healthy plant growth. Humus is formed at the end of the decomposition process (composting). Accordingly, all garden waste and a goodly proportion of kitchen waste should be composted. However, unlike plant waste, animal or cooked kitchen waste does not break down without unpleasant odors, and can attract rats, martens, or foxes—for this reason, it is best not to compost such materials. Kitchen waste should be cut up as finely as possible to speed the decomposition process. Weeds with considerable seed production, or diseased plants (with clubroot, for example), do not belong in the compost. The mature compost is suitable for soil improvement and as manure. One- or two-year-old compost can be incorporated into outdoor beds; for pot plants, a three-year decomposition process is required. Commercial, ready-made compost should not be used for planting directly, or used for sowing seed, without the addition of earth. Combining compost with earth yields compost earth—it should be remembered that it is not possible to make a complete distinction between the two in the garden, because it is always possible for earth to end up on the compost heap as well.

9 Coarse organic waste—such as small branches and twigs, which can be ground up with a chipper or shredder—facilitates good aeration in the compost.

There are many different chippers with a range of performance levels, and these determine the thickness of the branches that can be ground up. Stones, plastics, and metal do not belong in either the chipper or the compost.

10 This is the best time for working and turning the soil heap.

Compost soil is valuable only if the compost heap has been properly maintained. This includes turning over the compost. Everything that has been on the outside should now end up on the inside and vice versa, ensuring that both wet and dry materials are mixed. Compost heaps should be turned at least once a year. Like other soil heaps, a compost heap should not be higher than 3 ¼ ft. If, when it comes to turning, the outside layer is already frozen, use a mattock to break it into coarse chunks, and then stack these loosely, covering them with the material that had originally been inside. This ensures excellent aeration of the compost heap, and greatly aids the decomposition process.

11 The compost bin can be placed over a 4 in. thick layer of peat or, preferably, bark humus.

To minimize peat extraction and to protect wetland areas, the use of peat in the garden should be avoided wherever possible. Bark humus is a suitable alternative to peat and has similar properties. ▶ TIP 18 Such a layer is especially important where the compost will be sprinkled with plant fertilizer tea or nutrient solutions over the course of the year. This layer takes up the substances that could otherwise be washed out by precipitation, ensuring that the nutrients are not lost. When the compost heap is turned, the soil layer of bark humus is mixed between the compost soil, and the new place is again given a layer of bark humus. This is followed by chopped-up kitchen or garden waste, which is covered by a thin layer of garden earth. This, in turn, is followed by chopped-up waste and a loose covering of leaves, earth, or grass cuttings. Good aeration is important here. If too much moist material has accumulated, it should always be interspersed with material that is rather coarse, such as chopped-up wood waste, to avoid putrefaction and rotting. Despite this, the compost must always be uniformly moist, since otherwise no decomposition will take place.

12 Compost heaps or thermocomposters do not take up much space, and garden waste decomposes faster.

The double-walled, and therefore heat-insulating, construction of the thermocomposter aids faster composting. Since birds are unable to peck or scratch at the compost, the surrounding area can also be kept cleaner. A range of sizes are commercially available: 60 gal. is suitable for smaller gardens, while 125 gal. is required for larger gardens. Decomposition continues into the winter, provided temperatures do not fall below 32°F for a longer time.

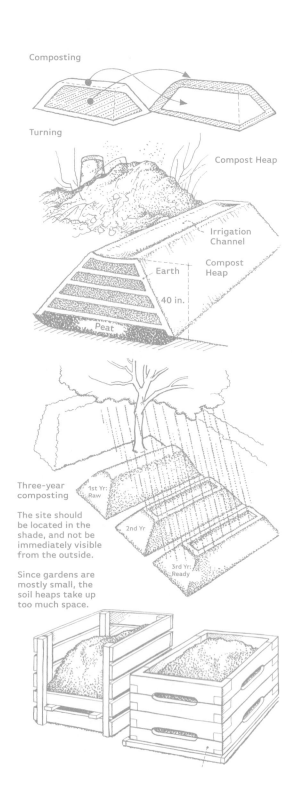

Composting

Turning

Compost Heap

Irrigation Channel

Compost Heap

Earth

40 in.

Peat

Three-year composting

1st Yr: Raw

2nd Yr

3rd Yr: Ready

The site should be located in the shade, and not be immediately visible from the outside.

Since gardens are mostly small, the soil heaps take up too much space.

13 Acidified soil is unsuitable for growing plants.

If house and garden waste is piled too high onto the compost, or if there are too many grass clippings or leaves, the soil will become acidified. Turning the compost and occasionally scattering agricultural lime (in the form of limestone dust, dolomitic lime, or algae lime, with different brand names) will help counteract this. The lime binds excess acids that are present in the humus and mobilizes particular nutrients. Lime should not be applied if stable manure has been used in the composting.

14 So-called quick composters will reduce the time required for complete decomposition.

Bacterial and fungal growth will lead to a significant acceleration of the composting process. The compost will warm up to 122 to 140°F within a few days, and the compost heap will gradually shrink in size, since the rapid decomposition process will cause it to fall in on itself. Additionally, the high internal temperature will kill off many weed seeds.

15 In frosty weather, ready compost earth can be spread over land that has been tilled in the fall. Use a coarsely meshed upright sieve to deal with large clumps of material.

Compost is a nutrient-rich alternative to stable manure. Rather than being mixed into the soil in the fall, it is spread over the tilled land and worked into the surface in the spring. Compost earth should not be sieved too coarsely or too finely. The sieve should be set up flat enough so that only very large lumps and stones remain behind.

16 Soot and wood ash contain important nutrients and should be added to the compost heap.

Soot contains mainly nitrogen, while wood ash is especially rich in potassium and phosphorous. A small proportion of coal ash will not diminish the value of the wood ash. It is best to add these ashes and soot to the compost heap while decomposition is still taking place. That way, the nutrients will be more effective than they would be if they were added to the soil directly.

17 Avoid using peat for soil improvement whenever possible.

Peat extraction destroys wetlands, which are also valuable habitats for unique plant and animal species. Accordingly, peat is gradually being superseded as a soil improvement material. Meanwhile, as well as having good characteristics, such as water retention and structural stability, peat also has less-desirable characteristics for soil improvement. For example, peat has a low nutrient content, as well as a low pH—in other words, it is acidic. In the garden, these characteristics are useful for acid-loving plants only, such as rhododendrons, garden azaleas, hydrangeas, and astilbes. By contrast, most garden plants prefer a weakly acidic, neutral, or weakly alkaline soil. For pot plants, substrates with good structure and water retention are most important, but here, too, there are drawbacks. If the peat becomes too dry, it will no longer take up water. If this is not remedied immediately, the plant will dry out. The soils of commercially available pot plants usually still contain a very high peat content.

18 In the specialist trade, bark humus and wood fibers, among others, are offered as alternatives to peat.

These materials have similar properties to those of peat. Bark humus is made from chopped-up, fermented, or composted conifer bark, is structurally stable, weakly acidic, has soil-aerating properties, and is nutrient-poor. Bark humus is also available with additional nutrients. Wood fibers have a peat-like structure, similar soil-aerating properties, a somewhat higher pH value than peat, and a low nutrient content. Wood fibers, too, are available with additional nutrients. They are extracted from wood fragments (primarily conifer wood) without bark, and from wood chips through heating, mostly through the application of steam and pressure.

19 Commercially available potting compost often contains a high proportion of peat.

Peat-free potting compost generally consists of bark humus, compost, and wood and coconut fibers. When buying potting compost, ensure that it has a low peat content, or, better still, that it is peat-free.

20 Bark mulch is used to cover the soil.

Bark mulch should not be confused with bark humus. Bark mulch consists solely of chopped-up bark, and often contains growth-inhibiting substances to suppress weeds. Bark mulch is good for covering the soil as a protection against drying out, or to protect sensitive herbaceous perennials against black frost. In the case of newly planted trees and shrubs, it should be used to cover the tree pit.

21 Snow is the natural protective cover for all plants that are growing outdoors.

Snow lying on paths and open ground can be put to good use if it is spread over cultivated land. It is especially useful as a protective layer for wintergreen perennials, woody plants, and other low-growing plants that are susceptible to black frost. If spread over tilled land, snow will also increase the all-important soil moisture level.

22 Snow-covered land should not be tilled; the snow must be removed first.

The ground beneath a thick snow covering is often frost-free, which means that it can also be tilled in January. However, the snow should not be mixed in with the soil because this will impede the warming up of the soil in spring. Since snow that is present in the soil only thaws slowly, the soil will stay wet for a long time, and sowing or planting will be delayed. Accordingly, it is important to remove the snow before tilling. This task can be made much easier by freeing up only a strip of land to begin with. This strip is tilled first, and then covered with the snow from the next strip to be tilled. Today, there is often a different perspective on tilling land. More and more, it is being realized that intensive digging sometimes does more harm than good. ▶ TIP 1213 to ▶ TIP 1219

23 When planting trees, shrubs, or perennials, trenches should be dug—two spade cuts deep in medium-heavy soils ("double digging"), and at least three spade cuts deep in very heavy soils ("triple digging").

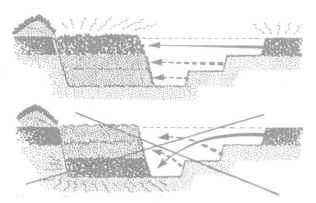

Both techniques are described in ▶ TIP 1217 and ▶ TIP 1218. Deeper trenches are dug at least three spade cuts deep to loosen up the soil. While "triple digging" is rarely used anymore, this procedure is still sometimes employed, particularly in heavy soils, or in those which have been completely taken over by couch grass; follow the technique described in ▶ TIP 1217, ensuring the upper topsoil does not end up further down. Frost in the soil makes triple digging

more difficult; accordingly, frost clumps should not end up in the lower soil layers, where they will thaw only slowly, and will also hinder the warming of the upper soil layer. If the work is delayed until the soil is frost-free, spring will often arrive first. However, there are so many gardening tasks to be done during the spring that there is usually no time left for triple-digging the trenches. In any case, it is better if the soil where trenches are to be triple-dug is still exposed to frost for a period of time.

24 Mineral fertilizers will already be required in early spring.

For most perennial plants, regardless of whether they are aromatic herbs or flowering plants, an initial fertilizer application is often necessary in late February if it is to be fully effective. Since most mineral fertilizers take up moisture from the atmosphere, they should be purchased only when they are required, since otherwise they will become watery or hard, making them more difficult to spread. Fertilizers in sealed plastic sacks can be stored for longer.

25 Complete fertilizers with trace elements contain all the important nutrients required for plant growth.

With a complete fertilizer, it is possible to provide plants with everything that they need for good growth. In addition to a range of mineral substances, these mainly include nitrogen (N), phosphorous (P), and potassium (K). Nitrogen-rich complete fertilizers are applied mainly in the spring or during the main growth period. However, as a general principle, only nitrogen-poor fertilizers should be applied from early August.

26 Apply mineral fertilizers to the uppermost layer of the soil before tilling. As the plants grow, apply as surface fertilizer or dissolve in water.

For trees, shrubs, perennials, and other long-term crops, scatter mineral fertilizers over the plants dry and lightly rake them in afterward. For annual crops, apply them dry or as a nutrient solution as soon as the plants exhibit good growth. To avoid damage to the plants, spray with water after applying fertilizer. Granulated fertilizers are easier to apply and roll off the plants by themselves. Light but frequent fertilizer application is better than too much all at once.

27 Excessive fertilizer application damages the plants and places stress on the environment.

Components that are not taken up by the plants can end up in the groundwater and cause considerable harm. Organic fertilizers are more suitable, because they contain all the required nutrients. These fertilizers are not effective immediately, but they ensure a continuous supply. The risk of overfertilizing is much smaller when using organic fertilizers.

28 Fertilizer application with organic substances has many benefits.

Organic fertilizers can be of animal origin, such as manure or hoof and horn meal, or purely plant material, such as compost. Unlike mineral fertilizers, organic fertilizers have a better long-term effect, and they are also not so readily leached from the soil.

29 Compost and manure are naturally occurring materials. They improve the soil, while also acting as fertilizers.

The fact that compost is essential as a fertilizer and for improving the soil characteristics should be well known. ▸ TIP 8 to ▸ TIP 16 Stable manure or manure from the hardware store in the form of pellets helps optimize yields in in high-demand ("heavy-feeder") vegetable species and makes the leaves of rose plants shine. Fresh manure is either composted or spread over the beds in the fall, and then mixed into the uppermost soil only. Fresh horse manure in particular generates a lot of heat during decomposition and is therefore ideal for use in cold frames.

30 Fertilizer tea made from manure, compost, or plants generally stimulates immediate strong growth.

These act both as fertilizers and to invigorate the plants, and are often applied to protect against pests. You can also make them yourself with plants such as nettle or field horsetail. Fertilizer teas should be strongly diluted for use with sensitive plants. Specialist dealers also offer dried herbs or powder for making the tea. To combat pests, fill a spray bottle with undiluted tea and spray the affected plant areas on three consecutive days—exercise caution, however, since some plants will not tolerate such high concentrations.

31 You can also make your own nettle fertilizer tea.

Loosely fill a plastic (not metal) container with freshly gathered nettle leaves. These plants should be cut closely above the ground; larger plants can be chopped up as required. Add water at a ratio of about 1:10, in other words 1 lb. of nettles to 10 pints of water. Cover the mixture with an airtight lid and stir daily. With the onset of fermentation, bubbles will form on the surface. The odor is very unpleasant, but can be alleviated somewhat by scattering rock dust into the mixture. After 8 to 14 days, when no more bubbles form, the fermentation is complete. Next, dilute the manure at a ratio of 1:10 (for young plants 1:20, and for lawns 1:50) and apply with a watering can. If the manure is applied or sprayed in the evening, the odor will have largely dissipated by the following day.

32 Green manuring loosens the soil, protects it from evaporation, and suppresses weed growth.

It also protects against muddiness and leaching of nutrients during heavy rain. Legumes such as lupines and some clover species will also enrich the soil with the aid of the bacteria in their root nodules, which fix nitrogen. Plants for green manuring can be sown either several weeks before tilling the soil (at least five weeks, depending on the plant species) or after the beds have been harvested. They can be mown before the seed ripens and can then be used as a mulch layer. In spring, they are worked into the uppermost soil.

33 Hoof and horn meal is a fertilizer that remains long active.

Hoof and horn meal is won from the hoofs and horns of slaughtered animals. Depending on grain size, the fertilizing effect will be faster (1/16 to 1/8 in.) or slower (1/8 to 1/5 in.). Hoof and horn meal contains plenty of nitrogen.

34 Sugar beet extract is used as an organic liquid fertilizer.

Such fertilizers are offered with a range of nutrient (NPK) ratios, for example, NPK = 4:3:6. This means 4 percent nitrogen, 3 percent phosphorous, and 6 percent potassium. ▸ TIP 25 Special organic liquid fertilizers are commercially available for a wide range of plants. It is important to note which original substances the fertilizers contain, so follow the application instructions exactly, and seek advice if necessary. The nutrient ratio and trace element content are important here.

Winter should be used for repairing and sharpening garden tools. That way, you will have more time for the plants in spring and summer.

35 Use the winter off-season to repair damage to cold frames.

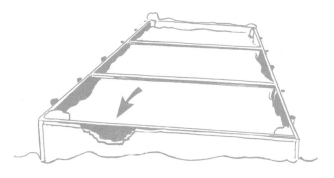

Cold frames are often used as early as February, when they are warm and heated, packed with horse manure. In older wooden boxes, check the posts and replace them with new ones if necessary. The side wall edges will often be damaged, which means that the glass panes will no longer sit tightly in place.

36 Repair fences in winter rather than waiting until spring, and deal with any holes that are used by wild rabbits.

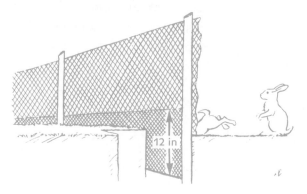

12 in

A fence that separates two gardens always belongs to the garden on which the posts or beams are standing. The outermost side of the pickets (palings) or the wire mesh delineates the exact boundary. Since it is possible to nail the pickets to a wooden fence from the neighboring side only, neighbors must allow access to their land for any improvements to be made. However, the fence owner must compensate the landowner for any damage. To ward off wild rabbits and hares, it is best to secure the garden boundary with wire mesh. This must penetrate at least 12 in. deep into the soil or else the animals will burrow underneath the mesh. Only well-galvanized wire mesh will last for several years.

37 Don't wait until garden tools are needed before repairing them.

From February, garden tools will need to be ready for use at any time. Broken handles should be replaced, since otherwise they can lead to nasty injuries. Missing rake teeth should be replaced with new ones, preferably made of hardwood. Spade blades whose edges are slightly damaged can generally be made usable again after a few file strokes. In the case of pressure spray tools, it is mostly important to clean the spray nozzles, or replace them with new ones.

Invest in quality garden tools. They will make the work easier.

38 When buying new garden tools, consider their suitability for the task at hand.

Garden tools should be made so that the particular task can be performed without using excessive force. Accordingly, they should be well made; in the long run, cheap tools will turn out to be the most expensive. For spades, hoes, rakes, and wire brooms, the handle should be long enough for you to work without bending over. One-piece hand spades last the longest, while ash-wood handles are the best for shovels. Painted watering cans will rust quickly—accordingly, it is best to use plastic or galvanized cans.

39 Working with a spade or gardening fork is made easier if the handle length matches your body height.

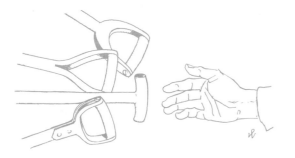

Digging is still the most strenuous gardening task. It can be made easier by selecting the right handle length, which is 33 in. on average. Shorter people should use a 30 in. long handle, and taller people a 35 in. long handle. The shape of the handle is also important—a D-shaped handle takes some getting used to, while a knob handle is suitable for lighter soils only. For the most part, spades and forks with a T-shaped handle are used.

40 The spade blade and gardening fork prongs should be made of high-quality steel.

When buying spades and gardening forks, ensure that the blade and prongs will meet the highest requirements. A blade size of around 11 in. long and 7 in. wide is suitable. The lower edge can be slightly curved, but it should not be pointed in the middle. Whether the upper edge should be widened for stepping on is debatable; this makes the spade heavier. The prongs

of the gardening fork should be very stable for working in heavy soils and be made of the highest-quality steel. Prongs that are triangular in cross-section are the best—others will bend in heavy soil. Penetrating the soil with a gardening fork requires only half of the force that is required for a spade.

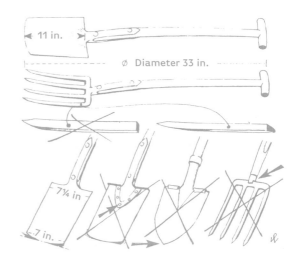

41 For light soil types, a wooden rake is sufficient. For heavy soils, use an iron rake.

A rake belongs in every garden. Wooden rakes are suitable for light and humic soils. The prongs of rakes made of light metal will wear down over time. Accordingly, iron rakes are the most suitable, and can also be used for heavy soils.

> *Only loosen the uppermost layer of soil in the vegetable garden. This ensures that the moisture remains in the soil.*

42 A grubber, cutlivator, mattock, garden claw, or "pig's tooth" are the most useful tools for preparing the planting beds in the spring.

The land already tilled in the fall may not be turned again in the spring. Only the uppermost layer of the soil should be loosened using a grubber, cultivator, or, best of all, a mattock. A garden claw is also suitable for light soils. A "pig's tooth" has only one sickle-shaped prong and does not require much application of force.

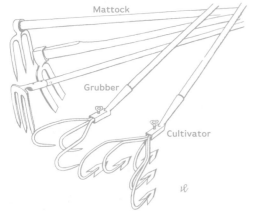

43 Double-edged pruning shears can be used for perfect cutting.

Pruning shears, also known as secateurs, are required for roses, as well as in fruit and vegetable, herbal, and ornamental gardens. The blades must be made of the highest-quality steel so that the sharpness is retained. A cut with the shears must not result in a pressure wound to the plant; accordingly, double-edged shears are preferable, even if they are expensive to buy. The size depends on the primary tasks involved. For working with fruit trees and other trees and shrubs, the shears should be 8 in. long. For roses, perennials, and herbs, smaller shears around 7 in. long will suffice. The shears should also have a nut lock to prevent loosening. As well as the usual gardening shears, special shears are also available for picking strawberries, grapes, and for cutting flowers. They hold the fruit or the flower firmly after cutting, so that it is possible to work with one hand.

44 Gardening knives are needed for a wide range of tasks. Typical pocketknives are generally unsuitable.

Gardening knives come in different shapes and sizes. The most important point is that the blade is made of special steel that will hold its sharpness for a long time. A grafting knife is important for grafting trees and shrubs, and for many other tasks. Budding knives are used for grafting, especially for roses.

Those with a release on the back of the blade are the handiest to use. A budding knife with the release on the handle needs to be turned around every time to release it after a T-cut. The release on the handle is made of horn or brass. Pruning knives have a strongly curved blade, for making a long cut—the handle should be 4 ½ in. long. For gardening knives with a slightly curved blade, a handle length of 4 in. is sufficient. Multi-blade gardening knives with two to four blades are somewhat heavy and generally awkward to use.

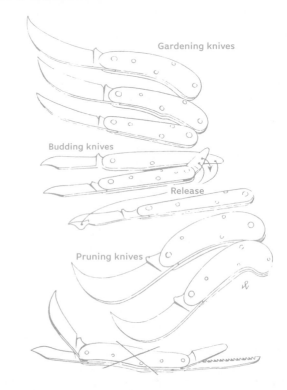

45 Pruning saws are useful only if the saw blade is adjustable for both sides.

The saw blades must be easily adjustable, and they must be easily loosened and the next blade inserted with a lever lock. They should be at least 12 in. long, but not longer than 16 in. So-called branch saws do not have a frame that holds the blade. Accordingly, they are wider and stronger, and more coarsely toothed. The blade length is 12 in. There are also branch saws with a handle into which a pole can be inserted, making it possible to work in higher tree crowns.

46 A transportation device belongs in every garden.

A small two-wheeled cart with pneumatic tires is generally sufficient for transporting soil, sand, manure, waste, etc. A wheelbarrow with pneumatic tires and a capacity of 2 to 3 cubic feet is also suitable; combination designs are also available. In a good cart, the weight will be centered mostly over the wheel, which makes the work much easier.

47 A leaf rake is better than an ordinary rake for clearing garden paths.

A leaf rake is also highly suitable for keeping garden paths free of weeds. If it is drawn over the paths often, weeds will not have a chance to establish. A leaf rake consists of narrow, galvanized metal strips in a fan-like arrangement. The strips are lightly curved at the ends.

48 Watering cans should have a capacity of 1 ½ to 2 or 2 ½ gal.; coarse rose (spray) attachments are the most suitable.

Since 1 quart of water weighs over 2 lbs, two filled 2-gallon watering cans mean a load of 35 lbs. to carry. For a healthy person, this is not too much, provided they do not need to be carried far. Plastic watering cans are lighter than zinc ones. The nature of the rose attachment is important—in particular, it must not drip.

49 When it comes to watering hoses, the longer the hoses, the greater the wear and tear. Storage is also important.

The most common hose length is 50 ft., but if the water taps are close enough to the garden, a 25 ft.

long hose is very handy. With practical fittings installed at the corners of the plant beds, it is possible to protect both the hoses and the plants. After use, wind the hose onto a reel and store in a shady place. Long-wearing rubber hoses have two or three inner canvas linings. Expandable hoses are easy to use. They are connected to a tap and will extend to around three times their original length through water pressure. Once emptied out, they contract again and can be stored without taking up much space.

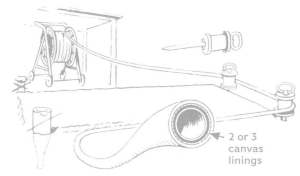

2 or 3 canvas linings

50 Quick-release connectors save time and make work easier.

These can be attached to the tap and hose, making it easy to attach and extend the hose.

51 Sprinklers make watering easy.

There are spray, rain gun, and rocker arm sprinklers. With a spray sprinkler, it is possible to reach every corner of the garden, whether lawns, shrubs, or flowerbeds. A fine spray can be set for sensitive plants. Rain gun and rocker arm sprinklers are economical choices for large gardens and lawn areas.

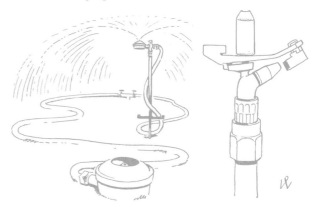

52 A small garden seeder makes sowing easy and helps save on seed usage.

Before sowing, the machine needs to be set to the right seed size. Garden seeders with a device to mark the next row are best. In this way, it is necessary to mark out one row with the cord. For simple sowing with a seed interval of 1 to 4 in., there are seeders with a replaceable magazine (roller) for different seed sizes, and with seed storage.

53 Cords and lines of the same thickness should be tied together and fastened so that they hold well, but also so that the knots can easily be undone.

See the sketches below for examples.

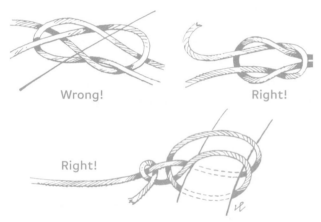

Wrong!

Right!

Right!

54 A furrow opener and a good garden line or row marker are essential gardening aids.

On heavy soils, a furrow opener is preferable to a usual garden line for marking out planting rows. It is possible to make your own adjustable furrow openers. Holes with a diameter of ⅖ in. are drilled in a 2 × 1¼ × 48 in. beam and fitted with pegs of the same thickness and length. To be able to mark out different intervals, pegs are attached to both sides. On one side they are 4 in. apart, and on the other side 6 in. This makes it possible to mark out row intervals of 4, 6, 8, 10, 12, and 18 in. Ordinary twine is not suitable for use as a garden line, which should be around ⅛ in. thick, so that a good furrow results when the line is tied off.

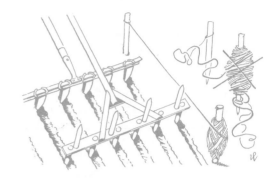

55 Hand spades and a dibber make planting easier, while small grubbers can be used to clear up the ground between closely spaced plants.

A hand spade is used not just to prepare a place for balcony plants, but also to lift out plants of all kinds, or even divide some plants into portions. A broken-off spade handle with a T-shaped grip will also serve very well as a dibber. It should have a blunt tip, so that the planting hole will also be wide enough underneath and take up the plant's roots. A small grubber, also known as a hand grubber or "hen's claw," can be used to loosen the soil as preparation for planting. It can also be used to remove wild herbs with shallow root systems.

56 The correct choice of lawnmower depends on the size of the lawn and the grass type.

Lawns are attractive only if they are mown regularly at short intervals. The most useful and suitable lawnmowers are those fitted with horizontally rotating blades (sickle mowers). These are robust in the presence of unevenness and foreign objects such as small branches. Spindle mowers cut the grasses cleanly, like scissors, but are much more sensitive. There are gasoline-powered lawnmowers and electrically powered ones. Electric mowers are lighter and quieter, and are almost maintenance-free; gasoline-powered mowers, on the other hand, need regular oil changes. The spark plugs and air filters should also be checked occasionally and changed if needed. Gasoline mowers are very loud and emit exhaust gases when in use. Accordingly, an electric mower is more suitable for smaller lawns. A battery-powered or hand mower will also suffice for very small areas.

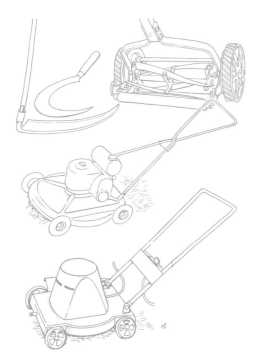

57 Grass clippers, sickles, and electric grass trimmers are needed for lawn edges and the smallest areas.

When mowing a lawn, the edges should not be forgotten. Meanwhile, a lawn dethatcher (scarifier) can be used to remove moss from the lawn and ensure good soil aeration.

58 A rain gage, thermometer, and weathervane are important for monitoring the weather.

The rain gage must be freestanding, but also protected from the wind, so that the rain (or snow) is not blown away. It should be mounted on a post 3 to 5 ft. above the ground. Meanwhile, the thermometer should hang about 4 ft. above the soil. The exact air temperature is measured in the shade. Maximum-minimum thermometers make it possible to read off the daily maximum and nightly minimum temperatures.

59 A bed measuring stick can be made in January.

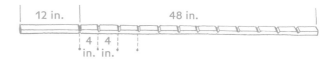

All vegetable beds should be laid out in one width—this makes it much easier to prepare and work the soil. A normal vegetable bed, including the path, is 5 ft. wide; since the path is 1 ft. wide, this leaves 4 ft. of usable area. With this width, it is possible to reach the middle of the bed from both sides without any difficulty. Wider planting beds make the work more difficult, while narrower ones are a waste of land, since the ratio between the usable land area and the path is less favorable. A straight, planed stick with dimensions of around 1 × 2 × 60 in. can be used as a measuring stick. At one end, the path width can be marked with a notch encircling the entire stick. The rest of the stick (48 in.) is then marked at intervals of 4 in. Here, too, a notch serves as the most durable marking. Using such a prepared measuring stick, it is easy to mark out the intended row intervals.

> *Attracting birds to your garden is a form of biological pest control.*

60 Nesting boxes for birds are important—birds devour pests in the garden.

Birds devour large numbers of harmful insects and their larvae—for this reason, too, we should provide suitable nesting opportunities for native birds. Existing nesting opportunities should already be cleaned and repaired in January, including any cracks in the nesting boxes, since the resulting wind drafts would be harmful for the chicks. As part of the maintenance, it is also important to check whether the nesting boxes are protected against rain and storms. Replace boxes that have become rotten with new ones.

61 This is the time to build nesting opportunities for our helpers in biological pest control.

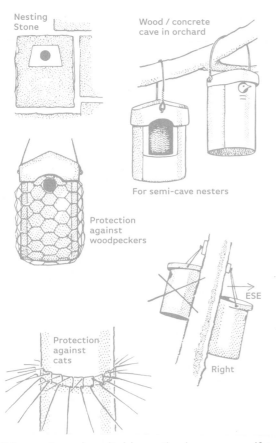

It is easy to make suitable nesting boxes yourself, taking the requirements of the individual bird species into account. This means not just the size of the box, but especially that of the entrance hole. In general, the diameter of the entrance hole should be 1½ to 2 in. However, blue tits and other small birds do not occupy such boxes; for these, the opening should have a diameter of only 1¼ in. Additionally, not all bird species want round entrance holes. Garden redstarts, for example, prefer a slit-like opening that is not too narrow; they do not belong to the primarily hole- or cave-nesting species. Establishing breeding sites for owls is another option. To make the nesting boxes easier to clean, they should be built so that the front or back sides can be easily removed; boards that are 1 to 1½ in. wide are the most suitable. An overhanging, watertight roof protects the entrance hole against rain. When hung up, the front of the nesting box should face southeast so that the sun does not shine directly into the entrance hole. The boxes should not wobble, and they must remain secure in a storm. The height at which the box is to be hung up is also important. Blue tits prefer to nest not higher than 13 ft.; for starlings, however, the height is unimportant. All nesting boxes should be hung up in such a way that cats cannot reach them. This is especially important for semi-cave nesters (garden redstart, white wagtail), whose entrance slit is fairly wide. All trees fitted with a nesting box should have a fixture on the stem that cats cannot climb over.

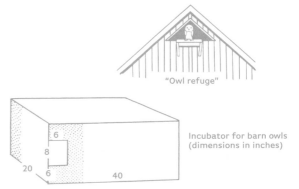

62 Feeding sites for non-migratory birds in winter are also easy to make.

To assist our helpers against pests during the worst times of the winter, feeding sites can be set up. Although birdhouses are commercially available in all sizes, it can be satisfying to build your own. A roof with a wide overhang is important to protect the feed from moisture, since wet feed can harm our feathered friends. The roof should protrude far enough at the front so that no rain or snow can get in, even at the open entrance side. The birdhouse must also be safe from cat predation. Accordingly, an open site should be chosen that makes it impossible for cats to creep up unnoticed.

63 These days, feeding birds is once again regarded as acceptable, even all year round.

For decades, leading ornithologists recommended feeding birds only when there was complete snow cover and constant frost with temperatures below 23°F. It was considered unwise to begin feeding them as early as September, and the indications on many

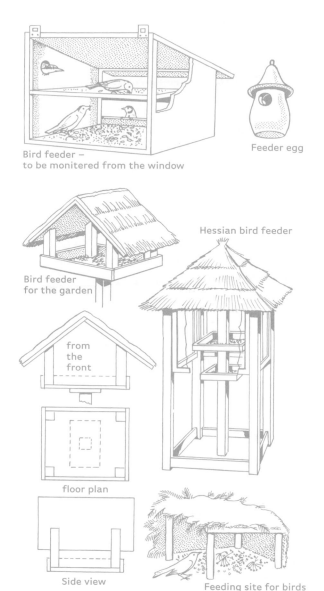

Bird feeder –
to be monitered from the window

Feeder egg

Hessian bird feeder

Bird feeder
for the garden

from
the
front

floor plan

Side view

Feeding site for birds
that eat soft food

should not be fed even in the wintertime, since this would mean that animals with a poor gene pool—that would not normally survive the winter—would be able to reproduce, hindering normal natural selection. It was also claimed that birds that visited our birdhouses were mostly just species that were common, and not threatened with extinction. Rare bird species that would never or only very seldom be seen in birdhouses, however, would have to survive the winter on their own in any case.

Despite all this, days of hard frost with snow and hoar frost are the worst time for birds, and many of them would soon starve if we did not help look after them. For all these reasons, feeding birds is now a highly controversial topic. The most recent studies have shown that birds do not eat food that is unsuitable for them unless they are facing imminent starvation. One thing is clear: owing to human intervention in nature, their food sources are becoming more and more limited. Accordingly, it is once again being advised to feed birds in the winter, and even all year round. However, only quality feed should be used, and the feeding sites should always be kept clean. Further recommendations are available from organizations such as the National Audubon Society (audubon.org), Birds Canada (birdscanada.org), and the British Trust for Ornithology (bto.org).

64 It is important that birds' natural food sources are retained.

If, for example, perennials are cut back only in spring, grain-eating birds such as finches, buntings, and siskins can pick the seed heads empty. These plants offer a refuge for overwintering insects, and therefore a food source for birds. It is most important to retain existing habitats for birds, or to establish new ones. This can be achieved by planting berry shrubs or sowing plants that will still bear seed in the fall.

65 Leftover food scraps, potatoes, and bread are unsuitable as bird feed.

These contain spices and salt that can be lethal for the animals, even in small quantities. Salted bacon rinds, carrots, or other vegetable scraps are also unsuitable. Large pieces of bacon rind may stick to the flight feathers of small birds so that they are then unable to fly. If, in dire need, birds eat frozen food scraps, they can easily develop digestive disorders

feed packages were considered to serve only the feed manufacturers themselves, and not actual bird protection. Feeding after winter was regarded as out of the question, and as especially harmful during the breeding season, since it was claimed that the chicks, with their digestive systems adapted solely to easily digestible soft animal nutrition, might have had difficulty with sunflower seeds or other hard-to-digest seeds, often leading to the young birds' deaths. In some circles, it was also suggested that the birds that may result in their death. Blackbirds love soft foods, such as apples, but these should not be left lying around for too long. Any food residues should be removed quickly. Sunflower seeds, millet, grain, oats, feed rings and feed "dumplings," and coconut shells with beef fat or beef tallow (suet) are all suitable. The feeding site should always be kept scrupulously clean, since feed spoiled with droppings can harbor disease agents.

66 A cheap feed that is suitable for nearly all bird species is a mixture of wheat bran and beef tallow (suet).

A little vegetable oil should be added so that the beef tallow does not become hard and brittle. The tallow should be melted first before adding the wheat bran. A roughly equal mixture of beef tallow and wheat bran will yield a loose mass that robins will eat. The less bran that is added to the tallow, the more liquid the mixture; this can be spread over tree bark, where it will be eaten by tree creepers, long-tailed bush tits, and woodpeckers. For blue tits and nuthatches, add sunflower seeds to the tallow-bran mixture and pour it into small flower-pots. These can then be hung on trees, taking care to provide protection against cats.

67 When selecting bird feed, take special note of blue tits' requirements.

As well as leaving out typical commercially available bird feed with a large proportion of sunflower seeds, we should also hang up the familiar blue tit rings and "dumplings." These are difficult for sparrows to reach, which otherwise often consume most of the bird feed.

> *Knowledge is power, and in the garden knowledge is crucial for a successful gardening year.*

68 If there is a raging snowstorm outside, this is an ideal opportunity to catch up on the specialist literature and expand your knowledge.

Good gardening books and specialist journals often pay for themselves with tips on how to improve yields or maintain plant health. When it comes to pest control, prevention is better than cure—accordingly, in addition to learning about possible pests and diseases and how to combat them, it is important to find out how to prevent them from occurring in the first place.

69 It is necessary to know and recognize the causes of damage.

To prevent plant damage, it is necessary to know the cause. We distinguish between parasitic (living) and non-parasitic (non-living) causes. Parasitic causes are due to organisms (parasites). Here, we also distinguish between different pests such as snails, mice, or worms, and diseases such as bacteria, fungi, or viruses. Non-parasitic causes are maintenance errors such as under- or oversupply with water and nutrients, unfavorable soil characteristics, and unfavorable site conditions such as frost, heat, hail, or storms.

70 Prevention is better than cure.

There is more to organic gardening more than just gardening without chemicals—it is also about gardening so that plant damage does not occur in the first place. Nearly all garden pests have natural enemies. To drive parasites away, it is important to establish habitats (e.g., heaps of leaves, brushwood, or deadwood, and dry stone walls or stone heaps) for useful animals such as toads, hedgehogs, salamanders, tadpoles, and blind-worms. Useful insects also overwinter in the died-off inflorescences and seed heads of summer flowers and perennials. Accordingly, these should be cut back only in the spring. Ground-covering layers, including leaves, will provide overwintering sites for many useful animals. It is not strictly necessary to mow the lawn every week; it too is a habitat for useful insects. In a near-natural garden, it is most important to plant more single-flowering varieties of annual flowers, perennials, and ornamental plants instead of double-flowering varieties that often have neither pollen nor nectar. Many wild herbs, but also marigolds, foxgloves, and oxeye daisies, will attract useful animals.

71 If the plants are set too close together, they will inhibit each other's growth.

Many failures in useful gardens, but also ornamental ones, result from growing plants too close together. It is true that every place in the garden should be utilized to the fullest. However, high yields and healthy growth are possible not through growing many plants on a small plot of land, but through maintaining optimal planting widths. Here again, it is important to consult the specialist literature. Take brief notes, and you'll be sure to do the right thing when the time comes for sowing and planting.

72 A cottage or cloister garden, even as part of an overall garden, is an oasis of calm.

If you're still planning a garden, you can also consider establishing a cottage garden, full of colorful summer flowers that alternate with vegetable or herb beds. Possibilities for planting include hollyhocks, oxeye daisies, lavender, bellflowers, vetches, lupines, lilies, peonies, tulips, and carnations—seemingly a mishmash, yet mostly well planned. The beds are enclosed within low box hedges, and the narrow paths are often scattered with gravel. In former times, there was a fountain or a round planter bed in the middle with a small tree, a standard rose, or a round flowerbed. The inspirations for such gardens with symmetrically laid out paths are in fact medieval cloister gardens. Typical of these gardens are crossing paths that divide the garden into several smaller beds.

VEGETABLES

73 To attain good yields of individual vegetable species, be sure to take soil exhaustion into account when drawing up a planting plan in January.

If one vegetable species is planted in the same area several times in succession, the yields may become smaller and smaller. This is known as soil exhaustion. The nature of its cause is complex and has not yet been fully explained. In general, it is assumed that every plant species exhausts the soil in a specific way. Owing to root activity, certain substances are released into the soil and root remnants are left behind, which can then inhibit subsequent growth of the same plant species. Meanwhile, repeated cropping of the same vegetable species can result in an increased frequency of certain pests and diseases, through an increased presence of their agents in the soil. This problem will be less frequent if the vegetable species and organic fertilization are changed every year; in other words, if a particular crop rotation is maintained. Meanwhile, there are also certain incompatibilities between vegetable species that should be considered when drawing up a planting plan.

74 In a vegetable garden, remember that different species have different soil humus requirements.

The humus requirements and humus utilization properties of the individual vegetable species are very different. A distinction is made between high-demand ("heavy-feeder") species that need a fresh humus supply (stable manure, compost, etc.) and low-demand ("light-feeder") species that do not. Accordingly, land for growing vegetables is divided into two halves. One half is supplied with a large amount of humus, while the other half is given lime. An area supplied with fresh humus is said to be in the first position in a crop rotation, and the other area in the second crop rotation position. Vegetable species that should definitely be in the first position include cauliflower, Brussels sprouts, headed cabbage, cucumbers, chard (seakale beet), stalk celery and celeriac (root celery), melons, and zucchinis. Crops for planting beds in the second position include root crops, peas, beans, onions, and leeks; to these can be added tomatoes, eggplant, peppers, spinach, Chinese cabbage, curly kale, and annual kitchen herbs.

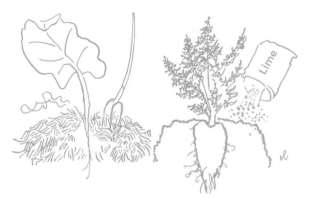

75 Garden owners who do not have a large area available for cultivation, but have a high requirement for vegetables, should plant the area intensively.

Where it is possible to do so, plant the beds with a main crop and an aftercrop. The main crop is the dominant crop for the year that occupies the land for the greater time, such as tomatoes or cucumbers.

As an example of such a land use, in late March, plant early lettuce as a first crop, followed by tomatoes as the main crop from 15 May; in September, lamb's lettuce is then sown as an aftercrop. In regions with a less favorable climate, it may be possible to plant only two crops in succession. In order that the land does not lie fallow in such cases, application of organic fertilizer then follows the second crop. This prevents the spread of weeds and leaching of nutrients from the topsoil into the deeper soil layers.

A brief period of cultivation between two main crops is known as a catch crop. After cauliflower as the main crop, for example, spinach can follow as a winter crop, while in the following year bush beans can be planted as the main crop. Another form of intensive use is mixed culture. This has the advantage over monocultures in that the individual species are less likely to fall victim to pests and diseases. A well-known example is the mixed growing of onions and carrots. Other possibilities include kohlrabi and lettuce, cucumbers and celery, carrots and red radishes, bush beans and cucumbers, fennel and basil, black salsify (viper's grass) and beets, cabbage and marigolds (*Tagetes*), cucumbers and dill, beans and summer savory, and so on.

Meanwhile, there is also the option of planting the spaces between planted or sown vegetables at wide intervals with a short-lived vegetable species, for example red radishes between lettuce, or lettuce between staked tomatoes.

In mixed cultures, it is particularly important to take account of the growth forms of the individual species, so that one cropped species does not suppress another. This can be achieved by increasing the intervals between the plant rows.

76 Vegetables and herbs need the sunniest place in the garden.

When planning the garden, it is important to reserve the sunniest spots for vegetable growing. With just a few exceptions, vegetables are annual species. They need 8 to 12 weeks to grow, flower, and ripen the fruit, and during this brief development period they need the best conditions for growth. Accordingly, soil, light, and water are important factors for growing vegetables in home gardens.

77 For perennial aromatic herbs and new plantings of rhubarb and asparagus, a place should be reserved in the cultivation plan where they can remain over a period of several years.

Here, it should be remembered that rhubarb can also thrive on semi-shaded sites, although in this case the shoots will appear somewhat later. For asparagus and perennial aromatic herbs, a sunny site that is somewhat sheltered from the wind is all but essential. Since the height of the herbs varies greatly, this should also be taken into account in the planning.

78 When preparing a cultivation plan, annual aromatic herbs are best planted in the crop rotation of the vegetable species.

For some herbs, no special site is necessary. Dill, for example, is best sown extensively with carrots or in a cucumber bed. Parsley and garden cress can be used to provide a border between other beds; the site can also be semi-shaded. Nasturtiums, from which the leaves, buds, flowers, and also the young fruits can be used as spices—a little-known fact—are also suitable for growing as climbers on fences, so that they, too, do not need a special site.

79 One of the most important tasks in January is to order or obtain the seed so that it will be available in time for the scheduled planting date.

The required seed quantity for every vegetable species can be easily calculated on the basis of the cultivation plan, and with the aid of ▸ **TABLE 5**. For especially weather-sensitive vegetable species, such as cucumbers or beans, reserve seed should be taken into account in the planning in case further seed needs to be sown later on.

80 The seeds of some vegetable and aromatic herb species are viable for a brief time only.

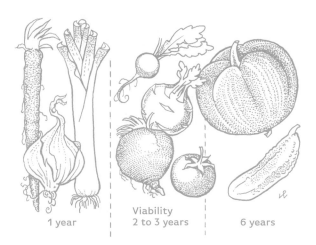

1 year   Viability 2 to 3 years   6 years

This especially applies to lamb's lettuce, parsnips, leeks, black salsify (viper's grass), onions, summer savory, dill, and other aromatic herbs as well. In general, the viability of their seed drops significantly in the second year following the harvest. For these species, it is therefore necessary to buy new seed every year.

81 Before ordering new seed, inspect the remaining stock from the previous year.

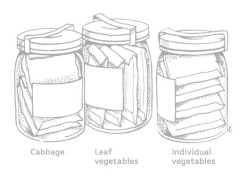

Cabbage   Leaf vegetables   Individual vegetables

In many vegetable species, the seeds will remain fully viable over a period of several years, which means that seed from the previous year can be used again, provided it has been stored properly. Seed must not be stored warm, and it will also not withstand high humidity. It is a good idea to store the seed packets in sealed, airtight preserving jars. The room temperature should not be warmer than 54°F. This will ensure relatively stable storage conditions. However, to avoid failures it is advisable to check seed from the previous year for its viability.

82 To check seed viability, you will need a germination bowl or shallow dish and blotting paper or paper towels, as well as a location where the germination samples can be kept at a temperature of around 68°F.

For all small seeds, count out 100 seeds for the germination test. For beans, peas, and similar seeds, 50 seeds will generally be sufficient. A smaller quantity is inadvisable, since the statistical error will be increased. Distribute the seeds in the germination bowl or shallow dish on cut-to-size and moistened blotting paper so that they are not in contact with one another. Then cover them with another layer of blotting paper. It is important to keep the blotting paper moist at all times, and to ensure that the temperature reaches the correct levels. For this, it is also advisable to cover the germination vessel with a glass plate or a similar item. By continually counting out and removing the germinated seeds, it is easy to calculate the percentage germination rate. The mean germination rate in vegetable and aromatic herb seeds varies between 80 and 90 percent. If the result of the germination test is lower, it will be necessary to sow proportionally more seed per square foot of land. Seed with a germination rate of less than 50 percent should no longer be used, since, even in the seeds that do germinate, the growth will seldom be vigorous enough for the shoots to break through the soil.

83 The duration of the viability test varies greatly depending on the vegetable species.

For celery, parsley, and carrots, it is around 20 to 21 days, for cucumbers, leeks, beets, tomatoes, and onions, around 14 days will be required, and for other vegetable species, 10 days.

84 Be sure to take note of the varieties involved when ordering new seed.

In addition to following all cultivation measures exactly, selecting the correct variety is crucial for growing success. This is even more important because varieties that have been bred especially for different growing conditions, harvest times, and uses are now increasingly available. For example, for lettuces, red radishes, and many other vegetable species, there are special varieties available for planting in small greenhouses or cold frames, for early planting outdoors, and for growing in the summer and fall. This means that there are always several varieties available for planting from early spring until fall. Beginners should first check the best varieties that have thrived in the immediate vicinity. Meanwhile, as a rule, new varieties should be carefully tested first before replacing those which have proven to be successful.

85 Community or allotment gardeners and home gardeners should preferably grow vegetable varieties that require only a short development period.

This means that the areas available for cultivation can be used much more efficiently. The additional time gained can be used to grow suitable initial crops or aftercrops, something which is not possible with varieties that have a longer development period. If certain varietal characteristics such as frost hardiness or good storage characteristics in the winter months are not a priority, early varieties may be grown at a late stage with the same success as the time-consuming late varieties. This applies to cauliflower, headed cabbage, and kohlrabi, for example.

86 Seeds from vegetable species whose seedlings must be raised in greenhouses or cold frames need special conditions for growth.

This applies especially to tomatoes, peppers, and eggplants. On the one hand, it is rewarding for gardeners to grow these plants; however, they must be sufficiently vigorous at the time of planting to yield good results. To raise the above plants, in addition to a germination temperature of 64°F, or, for a time, at least 68°F, plenty of light is also required. Gardeners who do not have a greenhouse will need a warm window ledge with additional lighting. However, only a few plants can be grown there, which means that, as a rule, the outlay involved is hardly worthwhile.

87 If you have enough chicory roots, you should heel in a suitable number of them for sprouting in January.

Suitable containers include buckets, stoneware pots, and crates. These are set up in rooms with a temperature of 59 to 64°F. Additionally, the advice in ▶ **TIP 1229** should be followed.

Roots heeled in from late November to mid-December will yield shoots that can be harvested in January.

88 Curly kale can also be harvested in a heavy frost if care is taken with the cut-off parts.

It is well known that curly kale tastes best when it has been exposed to a heavy frost. When frozen, the leaves are brittle, so they must not be subject to any pressure. Avoid damage by placing them loosely in a basket or a similar container, and leaving them somewhere where they can thaw gradually. When harvesting, only heads with healthy leaves should be cut if a second harvest is expected in spring. The stalks then sprout again very early, and the tender shoots will make a tasty early vegetable. Although curly kale is winter hardy, the leaves are sensitive to the winter sun if there has been a hard frost and no snow has fallen. During such times, cover the plants with spruce brushwood or a protective winter fleece.

89 **Especially in January, winter-cress should be newly sown on a weekly basis.**

At a kitchen window or in another light, frost-free location, sow cress in shallow bowls, or other suitable containers on blotting paper, or in a shallow sand or soil layer, and keep constantly moist. After 14 days, the cress is ready for cutting, and serves as a valuable nutritional supplement at this vitamin-poor time of the year.

90 **Freshly harvested leeks are tastier than those which have been heeled-in in the cellar. However, they must be grown on a site with good frost protection.**

Leeks are a delicious vegetable throughout the winter. To be able to harvest them outdoors at any time, make sure that the soil does not freeze over too quickly or too severely. This can be achieved with a covering of leaves or straw, which will duly prevent any losses. If covering material is in short supply, the leeks can also be dug up and heeled-in as closely together as possible at a sheltered site.

91 **In order for rhubarb to sprout as early as possible in the spring, provide a thick protective covering for it no later than early January.**

Leaves

Rhubarb is one of the earliest vegetables to appear and produces shoots as soon as the soil is frost-free. Accordingly, ensure from the outset that the land does not freeze over to a great depth. A thick layer of leaves, further secured by a sheet of foil and spruce branches, will keep frost at bay. However, the protective layer must be prepared before the upper soil layer is frozen solid. Early January is therefore the latest date that such a layer will be completely effective.

92 **From early January, rhubarb can be set up in the cellar or a similar room to sprout shoots.**

Place the rootstocks close to one another, and fill the spaces between them with sand or earth. They should be kept constantly moist. The darker and warmer the room, the longer and tenderer the leaf stalks will be.

93 **The cover over the vegetable storage clamps (mounds) must not be allowed to freeze up. Depending on the weather conditions, it can be further reinforced with leaves, straw, and earth.**

If you do not have a compost (clamp) thermometer, it will be necessary to check the surrounding area from time to time to determine how deeply the frost has penetrated the soil, and then add protective material on this basis. Here, it is important not to be too anxious, and not add a thick protective layer. If the clamp contents are packed too tightly, they may begin to rot. For this reason, remove the additional protective layer when milder weather sets in, and replace it again only if required. ▶ TIP 1322

94 **From January, vegetables heeled-in in the cellar should be inspected weekly, and the heeling-in substrate checked for its moisture content.**

If this is not done, patches of rot can easily set in. This can spread very rapidly and jeopardize the entire heeled-in content. Even small patches of rot found in any inspection should be removed. Remove even moderately affected vegetables and use them as soon as possible. If mice have become established in the vegetable cellar, take measures to combat them immediately. As in the past, the safest method is still typical snap traps, since poison should not be laid anywhere near foodstuffs. A dry heeling-in substrate (sand or earth) is better than a moist one. If the heeling-in site has dried out completely, sand especially will need to be moistened slightly. However, the water must not be allowed to come into direct contact with the vegetables.

95 **As soon as weather conditions permit, late-harvested vegetable beds can be tilled once again.**

Here, it is important that the soil is free of snow and not too wet. ▸ **TIP 22** A thin frost layer that can be penetrated with a spade should not prevent this important task from being completed. The results of a soil test will show whether sufficient phosphorus and potassium are present as nutrients in the soil.

ORNAMENTAL PLANTS

Ornamental Gardens

96 **A distinction is made between deciduous (summer-green), wintergreen, and evergreen plants.**

Deciduous plants are all plants that lose their leaves in the fall, together with herbaceous perennials that enter dormancy at this time. Wintergreen plants lose their leaves not in the fall, but only in the spring. Evergreen plants retain their leaves (including needles) over a period of several years. A typical example of these are our conifer trees. However, the larch, for example, is deciduous.

Prune ornamental shrubs at the right time for future bloom.

97 **Winter pruning of deciduous trees, shrubs, and hedges should be done on frost-free days.**

Pruning during heavy frost generally leads to damage, because the shoots will then be thin and brittle. Hedges of flowering shrubs that bloom as early as March, for example forsythia (*Forsythia*), flowering quince (*Chaenomeles*), and others, should not be pruned in winter if you want to enjoy their flowering to the fullest. They are best pruned to the right shape as soon as flowering has ended. Hedges such as privet (*Ligustrum*) or common hornbeam (*Carpinus betulus*) may be pruned in winter without any concerns.

98 **If broad-leaved hedges have become too open at the base, radical pruning back is the only solution.**

The hedge must be pruned back well into the old wood so that the hedge can build itself up again from scratch. How deep the pruning can go will depend on the height of the hedge and the broad-leaved species that it consists of. At least the upper two thirds will need to be cut back, so that a 6 ft. hedge will be only 2 ft. high after pruning. All lateral shoots should be pruned back to one or two buds. Hedges with gaps should be dealt with in the same manner. In spring (March and April), the gaps should be filled with new plantings of vigorous specimens. In hedges of evergreen species, radical pruning back should take place in late March/early April, and replanting in April/May.

99 Silver lace vine or Russian vine (*Fallopia baldschuanica*, syn. *Polygonum aubertii*) growing on a trellis or pergola should be thinned out in frost-free weather.

Silver lace vine can be severely cut back without a reduction in flowering abundance. If it has become bare at the base, cut it back to 16 to 20 in. above the ground. In an early spring, and well supplied with nutrients, it will soon reach its former height again.

100 Flowering shrubs that have developed their buds during the previous summer should not be cut back in winter.

These mainly include lilac (*Syringa*), forsythia (*Forsythia*), wisteria (*Wisteria*), golden chain tree (*Laburnum*), daphne (*Daphne*), and cherry tree and flowering almond (*Prunus*). In winter, restrict any work on these plants to thinning; remove excessively aged shoots entirely. If the shrubs have grown too high, they should be cut back right after flowering.

101 Flowering shrubs whose flowers develop on short shoots from the previous year should be cut back only slightly.

This group of flowering shrubs includes nearly all bridewort (*Spiraea*), deutzia (*Deutzia*), weigela (*Weigela*), and viburnum (*Viburnum*). If the annual shoots are cut back slightly, they will produce fewer, but vigorous, flowering stems. However, in general they should be cut back only if the shrub form needs correcting. Otherwise, older shrubs should be thinned only, and excessively aged shoots cut back almost to ground level.

102 In winter, cut back only flowering shrubs that develop their flowers on vigorous annual shoots.

The best known of these are California lilac (*Ceanothus*), Japanese spirea, (*Spiraea japonica* 'Anthony Waterer'), and panicle hydrangea (*Hydrangea paniculata*). Depending on the thickness of the shrub, these should be cut back in much the same way as bush roses. Always cut back weaker shoots more than thick ones; remove very weak shoots entirely. Panicle hydrangea will develop best if just one or two buds are left on each annual shoot. However, fat, round, terminal buds are flowering stems.

103 Shred any cut wood.

The shredded wood can be used to cover the soil between woody plants and perennials to ensure uniform soil moisture. It can also be composted.

Good winter protection guards against losses and is essential for good plant growth in the spring and summer.

104 In rock and perennial herb gardens, and on dry stone walls, continually check whether the winter protection is still in order.

This is especially important in weather with heavy frosts where there is no snow lying. In such cases, protective coverings consisting only of conifer brushwood should be reinforced accordingly. Small or chopped-up branches or bark are suitable for this; unlike wet leaves, for example, they will not prevent air from reaching the plants. Where brushwood and twigs have been hung on dry stone walls, check to ensure that the wind has not blown the protective materials away.

105 During heavy frosts in early January, apply light brushwood protection to forget-me-nots, and also pansies if need be.

The biennial forget-me-not is essentially winter hardy. In harsh situations in winters with little snow, however, it may freeze back to such an extent that the plants then look unsightly in spring. In some years, pansies may suffer this fate as well, if they have grown too high going into winter. This problem can be largely avoided by applying a light conifer brushwood covering layer.

106 In the case of covered, packed rhododendrons on exposed sites, check to see whether the protection has been damaged by winds.

From January, harsh east winds in combination with the winter sun can cause damage even to winter-hardy rhododendrons. This can be avoided if the protection is in good order. The ground covering should be checked often as well.

107 If heavy frost is expected, roses should be provided with an additional covering of leaves or conifer brushwood if there is not enough snow lying.

In winters with little snow, bush roses may freeze right back to the piled-up earth, and often an inch or so deeper still. In such years, a covering of leaves 4 to 8 in. thick should be added in early January. In spring, the leaves are then worked into the earth between the roses. This, in turn, ensures the required annual humus enrichment of the soil.

108 A very thick snow layer on conifer trees and shrubs can be carefully removed to avoid any snow breakage.

This should be done immediately following a snowfall—in the case of wet snow, while it is still snowing if possible. It is best to use a wooden rake, knocking gently against the snow-covered stems from underneath. Since other evergreen trees and shrubs may also be affected by snow breakage (*Rhododendron*, for example), these should be treated in the same way.

109 In heavy frosts, swamp pools that are occupied by sensitive plants should be provided with additional protection in early January.

The best material for this is dry brushwood. Leaves are less suitable, because they are usually too wet, and lie too densely. Aeration suffers as a result, which some swamp plants tolerate poorly.

110 Dahlia, gladiolus, and begonia bulbs should be checked in January to ensure that no losses occur.

Dahlia bulbs must never be left to lie too moist to avoid damage to the root collar, which produces shoots in the spring. If any mold is observed on the remnant stems, this should be removed and the bulbs thoroughly aired straightaway, since otherwise the mold may spread to the root collar very quickly. Bulbs lying on top of one another should be laid out separately. Gladiolus bulbs that have been stored under too moist or cold conditions often suffer from storage rot; rotting bulbs should be removed immediately, and the healthy bulbs transferred to a warm and dry place. This may also be necessary for cool-stored tuber begonias.

111 **Water lilies that are overwintering in the cellar should be inspected from time to time to ensure that they do not dry out or rot.**

Died-off plant parts should be removed carefully. If the plant substrate has become too dry, it should be moistened so that the rootstocks will not suffer. In frost-free weather, the overwintering site should be aired so that the plant heads remain healthy.

112 **Carnations (*Dianthus*), candytufts (*Iberis*), and winter heath (*Erica carnea*) overwintering outdoors are often targeted by rabbits, and may be devoured entirely.**

If the garden fencing is not rabbit-proof, the endangered plants should be protected against rabbit browsing. One sure solution is to cover them with wire netting—this should preferably be stretched over the individual plants in the form of an arch. It is only at the sides that the protection will not be complete,

since here the netting is an easy obstacle for rabbits to overcome.

113 **Arranged in a vase, flowering twigs from attractive garden trees and shrubs can elicit spring feelings even in January.**

Budding twigs of witch hazel (*Hamamelis*), winter jasmine (*Jasminum nudiflorum*), forsythia (*Forsythia*), flowering almond and cherry tree (*Prunus*), viburnum (*Viburnum*), and hazelnut (*Corylus*) can be brought indoors to flower. The selected twigs should be densely covered with buds. The warmer the room, the more quickly flowers will develop. In a somewhat cooler place, the flowers will develop more slowly, but they will then be more beautiful and last longer. The twigs should be freshly cut before placing them in water. Wherever possible, the water should be changed daily, and be at room temperature. If dissolvable tablets are added to keep the water fresh, it can be changed at longer intervals.

Flowering branches from the garden bring spring into the home.

114 **In January, the flowers of the Christmas rose (*Helleborus niger*) will make a splendid floral arrangement for a vase.**

Christmas roses will not suffer in winter if they are protected against strong frosts and wind. This is often necessary only from early January. The simplest protection is an appropriately large box without a lid. This is placed over the budding or already-flowering plant and filled with dry leaves so that the frost cannot penetrate. Once the frost has subsided, remove the frost protection right away so that the Christmas roses do not become etiolated or fall victim to fungal attack. There are different species, breeds, and varieties. *Helleborus niger* 'Praecox' often flowers as early as November. Colored Christmas roses are of hybrid origin and flower at different times, mostly from late March.

Terraces and Balconies

115 **At this time of year, only winter-hardy plants will still be left on the terrace and balcony—all others should overwinter in frost-free rooms.**

On frost-free days, check whether the evergreen plants in particular need watering. In containers, they will dry out faster than if planted outdoors. Moisture is also lost during frost through transpiration. Replace any frost protection that the wind has blown away.

> *Proper care of container plants in winter is essential for healthy growth and abundant flowering in the summer.*

116 **Tub plants that are overwintering in frost-free conditions must also be watered in winter.**

Evergreen plants, such as *Agave*, *Citrus*, oleander, myrtle, *Schefflera*, bay tree (*Laurus nobilis*), angel's trumpet (*Brugmansia*), and palms, among others, constantly lose water from their leaves through transpiration, even in cool rooms. This water must be replaced to avoid the plants drying out. Each time, however, always wait until the soil is almost dry before watering. In frost-free weather, the overwintering room should always be aired. In overly dark, damp rooms, mildew can easily occur on some plants, and this can often be avoided by providing fresh air. Plants that lose their leaves in winter can be left to stand a little drier.

117 **Geraniums, hanging carnations, and fuchsias in a cool overwintering room should be cleaned constantly, and they should always be provided with fresh air.**

These plants always lose some of their leaves in winter. Remove these leaves before they rot or go moldy and endanger the healthy leaves and shoots. Trim the shoots only if they exhibit patches of rot.

Winter Gardens, Flower Windows, and Rooms

118 **Airing the overwintering rooms is important for healthy plants.**

To prevent the spread of bacteria or fungi, the overwintering rooms should be sufficiently aired in mild weather.

119 **Little-heated corridors and stairwells are also suitable places for overwintering plants.**

These spaces are often not especially light, but they are very cool. Here, the plants need even less water than they would in cool and light rooms.

120 **The climate in the winter garden is dependent on the respective use.**

If the room is used for looking after flowers, the plants will determine the temperature, humidity, etc. that needs to be maintained. If it is used as an expanded living room space, the user will need to feel comfortable in it as well. This is the case at 68°F and above; accordingly, plants should be selected to suit these conditions. Except for some larger decorative specimens, these will predominantly be flowering plants. Naturally, the temperature should not fall below a certain minimum, even on ice-cold winter days. Particular attention should be paid to the nightly drop in temperature, especially in cool or unheated winter gardens. If necessary, the plants should be put in a frost-free place on very cold nights.

121 **Plants on extended flower windows are greatly endangered on nights with heavy frost.**

This is especially true if the window does not have its own heating. If need be, newspapers can be spread out between the windowpane and the plants, and these will protect the plants from much of the cold. If the flower window has windowpanes facing into the living room, these should be opened, at least on very cold nights, so that the warm room temperature will prevent any plants from freezing.

122 In winter, some indoor plants will suffer more from large temperature fluctuations than from somewhat lower temperatures.

Rooms that are at a temperature of 72°F or more during the day, but only 50 to 54°F at night, are unsuitable for many plants. This especially applies to plants that need a temperature in winter of at least 60°F, such as dumb canes (*Dieffenbachia*), aglaonemas (*Aglaonema*), saffron spikes (*Aphelandra*), *Philodendron* species, *Monstera*, and others. These will thrive better at a constant temperature of 60 to 64°F than when they are subject to large temperature fluctuations.

123 Water indoor plants according to the room temperature.

Owing to the poorer light conditions, most indoor plants grow only a little during winter. This applies especially to plants that are kept at a temperature of 54 to 59°F. These should be watered only if the soil surface is dry. If the soil is kept too wet, there may be root damage that can lead to the plants' death. In particular, the well-known large- and small-leaved rubber plants (*Ficus*) are sensitive to excess water. Only those plants that are kept in rooms with very warm and dry air will need much water during the winter, and this should be supplied at room temperature.

124 In the case of tank bromeliads such as *Neoregelia*, *Aechmea*, and others, ensure that there is always water in the plant's leaf-tanks.

At high room temperatures, water evaporates from the bromeliad leaf-tanks quickly, and it should therefore be topped up regularly. The substrate, too, should not be allowed to dry out completely; it needs to be only moderately moist. Hard water should be avoided; rainwater is more suitable. However, at temperatures below 54°F, the water must be removed from the leaf-tanks, since otherwise the plant will rot.

125 Avoid applying fertilizer to or transplanting most indoor plants in January.

Owing to the low growth in winter, the nutrient requirements are small, and so fertilizer should not be applied in January or February. Transplanting in January may lead to losses; for plants, transplantation is always a major intervention that they can overcome without damage only under the most optimal conditions (plenty of light, moist air, and corresponding warmth). It is better to wait until March or April for these tasks, transplanting only if absolutely necessary, for example if the plant's roots are diseased.

126 Popular indoor plants include large- and small-leaved rubber plants (*Ficus*).

Rubber plants are also often known as indoor figs. The fruit of *Ficus carica* (which is winter hardy only in some conditions) is the well-known edible fig. However, this *Ficus* is more suitable as a winter house or tub plant. The large-leaved rubber plant (*F. elastica*), which has been fashionable since the mid-20th century, is still popular today. The leaves of the fiddle-leaf fig (*F. lyrata*) are even larger. For many years, small-leaved rubber plants have also been cultivated, such as the Benjamin fig (*F. benjamina*), which is also available in white-and-colored forms. The creeping or climbing fig (*F. pumila*) grows decoratively as a hanging plant or on a moss pole at temperatures of 50 to 79°F, or also at cooler temperatures for a short time. All the other abovenamed rubber plants love a site with plenty of light, but not full sun, and where the air is not too dry, at temperatures of 60 to 72°F. Except during very great heat in summer, they should be watered only sparingly; in other words, only when the plant substrate has dried out properly again. However, completely dry soil is just as dangerous as constantly wet soil.

Young palms make beautiful indoor plants, while older ones make decorative outdoor container plants.

127 Most palms are decorative tub plants; when they are young, they are also suitable as indoor plants.

Even if most palms grow to be quite large with age, they are still suitable as indoor plants when they are young. The two date palms, *Phoenix canariensis* and *P. dactylifera*, are well known; only the former is suitable for growing indoors. Both should spend the winter in a cooler room. The European fan palm (*Chamaerops*), Chinese windmill palm (*Trachycarpus*), and fan palm (*Livistona*) should also be overwintered at cool temperatures. The decorative fishtail palm (*Caryota*), Weddel palm (*Lytocaryum*, syn. *Microcoelum*), *Chamaedorea*, and the miniature date palm (*Phoenix roebelenii*) are suitable for warm winter sites. Madagascar palm (*Pachypodium lamerei*) is not actually a palm. It comes from southern Madagascar and needs to be handled in accordance with the climate there; in other words, watered moderately in summer and sparingly in winter. It will tolerate full sun, while the young plants need light shade.

128 With the right handling, the German primrose (*Primula obconica*) will flower more abundantly, and for longer.

The inflorescences of the German primrose generally develop several flower levels; however, the uppermost ones are usually fairly meager. Accordingly, the entire inflorescence should be removed before the upper flower levels open. This will encourage new flowering stems to develop rapidly, with larger flowers. German primroses should also be given fertilizer in the winter, since they consume plenty of nutrients. Weekly fertilizer applications contribute greatly to abundant flowering. Today, there are also primin-free primroses available that do not cause skin irritations.

129 Baby primroses (*Primula malacoides*) can be kept only in light and cool rooms.

This attractive primrose is a winter houseplant that thrives at temperatures of only 43 to 50°F, or also up to 59°F. In warm rooms, the leaves will become long, the flowers will lose their color, and the plant will become unsightly. A light, cool place is highly suitable, even if the temperature drops to freezing for a brief time.

130 Primroses (*Primula vulgaris*) and oxlips (*P. elatior*) flower richly and colorfully.

They develop their flowers well at lower temperatures and at a light site. After flowering, they can be transferred to the garden in the spring. ▶ TIP 1201

131 In January, amaryllis (*Hippeastrum*) plants that are capable of flowering need to be kept in a warm place.

Despite this, they should be given hardly any water. They should be watered more only when the flowering stem becomes visible. Otherwise, growth may be inhibited, and only leaves will develop. Provided no flowering stem is present, an amaryllis plant will also need hardly any light. However, once the new flowering shoot is visible, the plant should be kept in a light place and at a temperature of around 64°F. At 59 to 60°F, the flowers will take longer to develop, but will be much more beautiful. If the bud or flowering stem is visible, this is also the best time for replanting. ▶ TIP 600

132 During the winter resting period, don't allow the fire lily (*Cyrtanthus*, syn. *Vallota*) to become completely dry.

The fire lily is related to the amaryllis, but all the plant parts are smaller. Its beautifully vivid salmon-pink flowers develop in summer. In winter, at 41 to 50°F, only moderately moist soil, but not dry, is sufficient for the fire lily. It also retains its leaves in winter, and therefore requires a well-lit place in the window. In summer, however, it should be well watered. Transplanting is generally required only after three to five years. The bulbs may be embedded only about halfway into the soil, and in pots that are not too large.

133 Place hyacinths that have been suitably prepared in jars or pots in the window of a warm room in early January.

A paper funnel, which serves as light protection, should initially remain over the bulb. Special hyacinth jars have proven to be the most effective; they are filled with water until just beneath the base of the bulb. To avoid rotting, the bulb base itself should never be immersed in water. The hyacinth jars are initially kept cool, and are then put in a slightly warmer place only when the roots have reached the bottom of the jars. If the paper funnel is removed before the inflorescence has grown 4 to 5 in. out of the bulb, the inflorescence will remain very short, and the leaves will be long. If the hyacinth bulbs have been transferred to pots or jars very late, they should not be kept in a warmer place until the flowering stem is about 2 to 2 ½ in. long. The above applies only to bulbs that were planted by early October. Here, too, however, it is necessary to wait for this flowering development stage. Hyacinths in soil must always be moist, since otherwise their growth will be inhibited. Following flowering in late spring, the bulbs can be planted in the garden, and will often delight us again with flowers in the following year.

Keep Norfolk Island pines, camellias, azaleas, and alpine violets in a cool and dry place.

134 The Norfolk Island pine (*Araucaria heterophylla*) needs to grow in a cool place.

The plant is most comfortable at temperatures of 41 to 54°F, and then needs only a little water. It should be watered only if the soil has dried out. If it is too wet, the plant's roots will suffer, and it will lose its lower branches. If its winter site is too warm, it will develop long shoots because of the poor light conditions, and will soon become unsightly. In warm, dry room air, it will often be attacked by red spider mites, which will be evident by the yellowish branches. Temporary relief may be achieved at a winter site that is cool, light, and without excessively dry air, along with frequent spraying with water; in cases of severe infestation, acaricides (miticides) can be used to combat the infestation. However, care should be taken as these are strong poisons—be sure to read the instructions on the package! In summer, place the plant on the balcony or terrace, sheltered from the wind.

135 Camellias with buds develop their flowers best at a cool site.

For flower development, keep camellias with flower buds at temperatures no higher than 59°F. In this way, the flowers will develop slowly but surely, and the flowering period will be longer. After flowering, temperatures of 37 to 46°F will be sufficient. The plants should then be watered very sparingly. If camellias lose their buds, this can be due to a variety of causes, for example root ball and air dryness, variable light levels from turning the plant around, excessively high temperatures, and also waterlogging. If a camellia is brought from the cold into a very warm room, it should be no surprise if the buds then begin to drop off. If the root ball has dried out, watering will no longer help—instead, immerse the pot in a container of water, over the edge of the pot, until no more air bubbles rise to the surface.

136 The root balls of azaleas that are grown indoors must never be allowed to dry out. They will flower for much longer on cool sites.

Azalea potting soil consists of conifer needle soil or a peat culture substrate. The plants often suffer from dryness when the plant substrate still appears to be moist. The peat retains a proportion of the moisture, which means that this is no longer accessible for the roots. For this reason, azaleas grown in plant substrates rich in peat should be kept constantly moist. The same applies to conifer needle soil; once these two substrates have dried out completely, it is very difficult for them to take up water again. Here, as with camellias, the only solution is to immerse the pot completely in a water-filled container, with the water over the edge of the pot, until no more air bubbles rise to the surface. Azaleas will soon lose their flowers in a warm room; they will last longer if they are kept cool. The temperature can fall almost as low as 32°F without damage to the azaleas.

137 The staghorn fern (*Platycerium*) makes an interesting indoor plant.

This attractive fern is an epiphyte; for this reason, it is also grown in orchid baskets or on cork bark. At around 57°F, its temperature requirements in winter are not especially great. However, it will also tolerate higher temperatures and drier room air if the substrate is kept moist. Similarly, temperature fluctuations are not a problem for most of the species. Staghorn ferns can also be hung a little away from the window, since in nature it grows only under the leaf canopies of large trees. Accordingly, it does not require an especially light site, and does not like harsh sun at all.

Indoor plants grow better with supplemental lighting.

138 Low-growing plants that need high air humidity should be grown under glass.

Attractive and decorative leafy plants tend to suffer the most when the air humidity is low. Under glass, they are protected from dry, heating air, as well as from dust. Glass containers are commercially available in many different sizes. The bottom of the containers should ideally be covered with humic earth that is kept constantly moist. In order that the high humidity is maintained, aquarium containers and similar vessels are covered with glass panes. Position the glass containers in a warm, light place, but not in full sun. Suitable small plants include selaginella (*Selaginella*), nerve plants (*Fittonia*), small-leaved ivy (*Hedera*), creeping or climbing fig (*Ficus pumila*), baby's tears (*Soleirolia*), maidenhair fern (*Adiantum*), miniature African violets (*Saintpaulia*), radiator plants (*Peperomia* species), bromeliads such as earth star (*Cryptanthus*) or neoregelias (*Neoregelia ampullacea, N. pygmaea*), and also small-growing orchids such as *Pleurothallis*.

139 A enclosed bottle garden has its own microclimate.

A carboy or demijohn often makes a decorative container for small plants in an indoor setting. For drainage, first pour in an approximately 1 in. deep gravel layer, followed by a layer of charcoal, and finally potting mixture. This is done using a rolled-up piece of cardboard, a funnel, or a cardboard tube. Two long wooden sticks are best for planting. The root balls of the young plants are shaken out sufficiently so that they will pass through the bottle's neck, and they are then pushed and manipulated with the sticks into a prepared hollow with soil, and pressed into place. Lower plants are positioned at the front, and the larger ones in the background. Water by using a narrow hose along the inner wall of the container; then seal the top with a perforated foil. The evaporated water then precipitates on the bottle wall and runs back down into the earth, creating a cycle. On suitable plants ▸ **TIP 138**.

140 Display cabinets for growing plants in living spaces are containers that are glass-faced on all sides with nearly optimal environmental conditions.

Display cabinets can be set up at any time of the year, since optimal environmental conditions can be created artificially. The size of the cabinet depends on the extent of the plants. Even when set up in front of a window, the light levels will mostly be inadequate. Accordingly, additional lighting with fluorescent (LED) tubes is necessary. There should be ventilation holes above and below for aeration; additionally, a small fan should circulate the air. This should be set up so the circulation is both horizontal and vertical. In a living space, additional heating will hardly be necessary. It is important that the windowpanes on one broad side at least are installed as sliding doors, so that planting and maintenance tasks can be carried out easily.

141 Cacti will not dry out in winter, but they may rot if watered too often.

Waterlogging in the root zone is the cause of most losses. In winter, the plants enter a resting period during which their life functions shut down. They will then need a place that is as dry, light, and cool as possible. For most species, temperatures of 46 to 50°F are sufficient. They should be watered only in exceptional cases, when the temperature in dry air has risen and there is a danger that the plants will shrivel up.

Ventilation holes

Moisture-proof lamps

Window-panes on the long sides

Heating

142 Orchid cacti are grown without a distinct winter resting period.

True orchid cacti with their large, attractive leaves have been achieved by hybridization and selection (varieties) of different species of several genera (for example, *Epiphyllum*) that in nature grow mostly as epiphytes in rainforests. They must therefore be kept uniformly moist, and not too cold in winter, although brief dry periods will do no harm. Orchid cacti include the Christmas cactus (*Schlumbergera*), Easter cactus (*Rhipsalidopsis*), and also *Rhipsalis*.

143 In winter, many succulents prefer similar care to that of cacti.

Succulent plants can store water and nutrients in their tissue; they include representatives of many plant families. They especially include species of the genus *Sedum*, for example burro's tail or donkey's tail (*S. morganianum*), *Aeonium*, *Agave*, *Aloe*, *Crassula*, *Echeveria*, tiger jaws (*Faucaria*), *Gasteria*, *Haworthia*, *Fenestraria*, *Lithops*, and many others. In winter, they need a light, cool place, and only very little water.

144 Succulent plants for warm winter sites will often flower splendidly.

Succulents that tolerate warmth in winter include flaming Katy (*Kalanchoe blossfeldiana*), cathedral bells (especially *Kalanchoe pinnata*), crown of thorns (*Euphorbia milii*), carrion flower (*Stapelia*), desert rose (*Adenium obesum*—poisonous!), and others. These succulents, too, should be placed in a very light place; their water requirements will depend on the respective site temperature.

145 Snake plant or bowstring hemp (*Sansevieria*) does not tolerate low temperatures.

The saying associated with the snake plant, "none has ever dried out, but many have rotted," is well justified, at least for cool winter sites. Snake plant is an ideal indoor plant, because it tolerates warmth of around 68°F or more, as well as dry air. However, even in warm rooms it may rot quickly if exposed to cold outside air coming through the windows when the room is being aired in winter.

146 African hemp (*Sparmannia africana*) makes a splendid indoor plant and flowers in winter.

This plant is a member of the mallow family. It comes from South Africa and is also known as Capeland African hemp. Its radiant white flowers with reddish yellow stamens appear above its large, lime-green, velvety leaves, making a wonderful contrast. In large, light rooms that are not too warm, African hemp contributes greatly to improving the room climate, but it will also thrive in cool stairwells. The warmer the site, the more watering is required. ▸ TIP 1383

147 The genus *Aechmea* is an undemanding indoor plant.

It tolerates dry heating air, and will tolerate not being watered occasionally. However, its leaf-tanks should always be filled with water; rainwater is best for this. After flowering, bulbils form that will flower again when they reach the right size. They can be removed from the parent plant and replanted.

148 The genera *Guzmania*, *Vriesea*, and *Billbergia* are also bromeliads.

Like *Aechmea*, they also tolerate dry heating air, provided their leaf-tanks are always filled with water (rainwater). Even when not flowering, they are highly attractive. The actual blooms are mostly inconspicuous, unlike the conspicuous bracts, which are mostly red- or blue-colored.

149 Flowering gardenias (*Gardenia*) are especially elegant.

Gardenias are not the easiest indoor plants to grow. They do not like dry heating air, and do not survive best in warm rooms with somewhat higher humidity. The plant substrate should always be uniformly moist, and direct sunlight should be avoided. If these requirements are met, the plant will reward us with wonderfully fragrant, beautiful, large white flowers.

150 Some orchids are genuine and low-maintenance indoor plants.

In most cases, these are hybrids, or crossbreeds that are not found in nature in this form. Natural species are often somewhat more difficult to care after. In January, these orchid hybrids (*Phalaenopsis*, for example) do not need much looking after. They need only a little water on dark, sunless January days, provided they are not kept too warm. Instead of watering, it is often better to spray them with water that has a low lime content. Wipe the leaves occasionally with a damp sponge, while keeping a lookout for pests or diseases.

FEBRUARY

WINTER

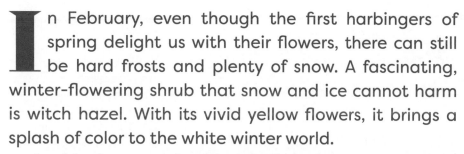

In February, even though the first harbingers of spring delight us with their flowers, there can still be hard frosts and plenty of snow. A fascinating, winter-flowering shrub that snow and ice cannot harm is witch hazel. With its vivid yellow flowers, it brings a splash of color to the white winter world.

At this time, we should already be preparing for the upcoming gardening tasks that will need to be done. At the end of the month, for example, new garden paths can be laid, older ones improved, or work begun on building cold frames. Meanwhile, bulbs and tubers put into storage in the fall should be examined for pests and diseases.

GENERAL

151 Garden paths should be laid so that they can still easily be walked on even after prolonged rainfall.

It is not enough simply to mark out a path and then spread gravel over it. Instead, the path needs to be constructed properly from the outset. In this way, it will be possible to push a cart over it even after rain. The following tips describe how best to lay a path.

> *Properly laid paths make it possible to walk around the garden at any time of the year.*

152 In permeable sandy soils, the path bed should be about 4 in. deep, and in heavy soils at least 6 in. deep.

The path bed is covered with the foundation or substructure, so that the path is easily water permeable and can be walked on in any weather. The above depths are intended as a guide only, since the depth of the foundation will also be dependent on the intended use. If vehicles will be driven on the path, the path bed should be 2 to 4 in. deeper, or even more. The extra work involved will prevent any problems from arising later.

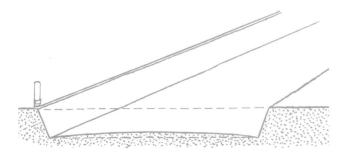

153 The path width is determined by the type of use.

A sealed path should not be less than 2 ½ ft. wide. If, in addition to a main path, subsidiary paths are to be laid as well, the former should be 3 ¼ to 5 ft. wide, so that two people can walk alongside one another, and the other paths 2 ½ ft. wide. In ornamental gardens, subsidiary paths are often laid with flagstones.

154 When excavating the path bed, the lateral slope should be taken into account so that the foundation (substructure) will be the same depth overall.

Before excavating the path bed, its course should be determined exactly. On straight paths, this should be done with two parallel cords, stretched taut, that mark the path edges. Along these edges, first make a spade cut so that the cords can be removed before the earth is excavated. The predetermined depth of the path bed ▸ **TIP 152** should be adhered to exactly, and the earth underneath it should not be loosened. Since the final path surface needs to be higher in the middle than at the edges, the edges should be excavated about 1 in. deeper than the middle. The lateral slope will be dependent on the path width; generally, 2 percent will be sufficient. Once the path bed has been properly excavated, any uneven places should be smoothed out and the foundation tamped firm, without losing the path's convex form. For this reason, the path should be tamped firm from the edges toward the middle.

155 To avoid earth transports, distribute the excavated earth over the surrounding land.

This is possible only with normal paths that have been excavated to a depth up to around 10 in. Alternatively, it is possible to dig up the native topsoil first and carry away the soil layer below. However, if it is only an inch or so thick, this, too, can be distributed over the surrounding land.

156 Suitable materials for the foundation (substructure, base course) include brick fragments, concrete waste, loose stones, or gravel.

Gravel is suitable only for narrow paths with a shallow path bed; generally, the material applied will be that which is cheapest and available locally. A mixture of two or three of the abovenamed materials is also feasible. Since two different grain sizes will then be required, fine gravel can be mixed with coarse loose stones, for example.

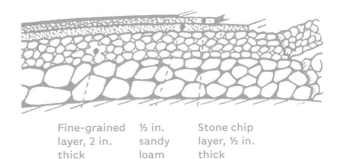

Fine-grained layer, 2 in. thick   ½ in. sandy loam   Stone chip layer, ½ in. thick

157 If only one kind of material is available for the foundation, it will need to be sieved to yield two different grain sizes.

A coarse-meshed sieve is best for this. It should be set up on two supports, and not set upright as is usually the case. In this way, the sieved material obtained will not be too fine-grained. Loose stones for the foundation do not need to be sieved, but two different grain sizes, around 2 in. and 1 in. in size, respectively, are the most suitable.

158 Every layer of the foundation should be rammed or rolled so firmly that its form will remain intact later.

The coarsest material is always laid on the bottom of the path bed: with an overall depth of 6 in., this layer should be about 3 in. thick. If the grain size is variable, distribute the coarser components at the edges. This will give the raised middle of the path extra firmness and stability. Distribute the 2 in. thick second layer, which consists of the sieved, finer grain size, in the same way. However, it should be distributed only when the mixture below has been tamped firm. ▶ TIP 154 An intermediate layer that now follows must firmly bind the cover layer with the foundation. A loam-sand mixture is best for this, or a sandy loam or loamy sandy soil mixture in a pinch. Distribute the binder course, which is only ½ in. thick, evenly with a rake. After this, it, too, must be watered down well and tamped firm. Here, the material must be allowed to dry first before tamping, since otherwise it will remain stuck to the tamp itself. The uppermost layer is the wearing course. It, too, is ½ in. thick and consists of stone chips or binding gravel. The wearing course is similarly tamped firm so that it is pressed partly into the binding layer. The wearing course is preferably applied in two working steps, with a little over ¼ in. tamped firmly and the rest (a little less than ¼ in.) merely raked.

159 If a garden path is to have firm edges, the edge stones will need to be reset before the path seal material is put in place.

As a general rule, firm path borders are not recommended for ornamental gardens; strips of grass are better. Path edges help prevent the path from being muddied by soil from hoeing and digging. To keep border stones or flagstones (slabs) firmly in place, they must be set 6 to 8 in. deep in the ground. They will be even more robust if the edge stone on the planter bed side is provided with a cement mortar base beneath the soil surface. The thickness of the edge stones determines how many inches the path base needs to be widened by. They should be set so deep in the ground that they protrude only 1 ½ to 2 in. above the earth that borders the path. The stones or slabs must be so tightly set against one another that not even dry earth can penetrate any gaps. Only once the borders have been firmly laid can work on the path foundation begin.

160 Clinker bricks, natural stone, or cement slabs are suitable as edge stones.

Hot-fired clinker bricks are very weather-resistant, which means that the path edge will hold up for many years. Natural stone slabs are suitable only if they have three smooth sides. They must consist of weather-resistant stone. Sandstone slabs are not recommended for path edges. Cement slabs need to be only 1¼ in. thick, but should be 10 in. wide and at least 24 in. long.

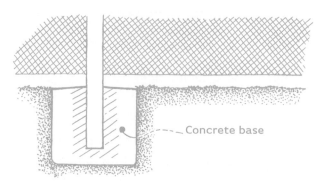

Concrete base

Planter bed borders and edging with corresponding plants are the most attractive.

Wood rounds or ceramic elements installed vertically.

Roof tiles are less attractive.

Wood rounds are optically attractive, but are not long lasting.

Boards are reminiscent of partitioned areas.

In the past, grass edges were often bordered with metal strips.

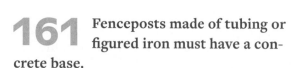

Stones used for borders should be cut to the appropriate size and shape.

162 When erecting a wire fence, the first and last posts, and also the corner posts, should be further secured with supporting elements (struts).

This is also necessary when tubular posts have a concrete base. It is only by using struts that the posts will be secure enough that they will not give way when the wire netting is stretched in place. Tension wires should be tightened using appropriate tensioners.

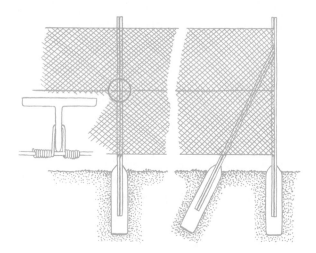

161 Fenceposts made of tubing or figured iron must have a concrete base.

This will give them greater stability. Additionally, the iron will last longer if the bases are so long that they end about 4 in. above the ground surface. Their upper edge should not be level, but instead slightly tilted so that water will run off easily.

163 A wooden garden gate will not warp if it has been properly secured with diagonal supporting beams.

Otherwise, the gate will soon become crooked. If, from the point of view of the observer, the hinges are on the left and the latch on the right, the supporting beams must form a "Z."

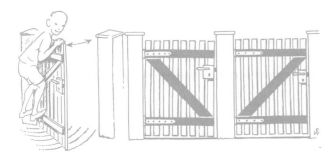

cold frames are involved, the side boards are set only 2 to 3 in. into the ground. This is sufficient to prevent wind drafts from coming in the sides. With 1 ¼ in. thick boards, a post will be required every 5 ft. If the boards are thinner, the interval between posts should be only 3 ¼ ft.

164 Cold frames may be constructed in frost-free weather using the boards and posts that have been prepared in January.

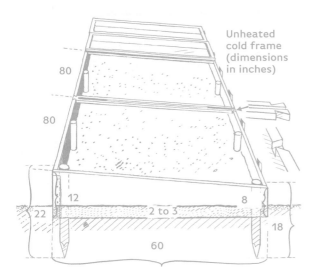

Unheated cold frame (dimensions in inches)

80
80
12
8
22
2 to 3
18
60

However, there must be no frost left in the ground or it will be impossible to hammer in the posts. A tightly tensioned cord will indicate not only the exact orientation of the posts, but also their height. In single cold frames, the posts at the lower side are about 4 in. shorter than those at the upper side, while in double cold frames, all the posts must be of the same length, except for the saddle posts, which are 4 in. longer than the others. This means that the cold frame windows will be tilted in the same way as they are in simple cold frames. The boards are nailed to the upper edge of the posts, and the posts of the higher side are angled slightly. This will ensure that the window lies properly on top of the frame. Every second window joint should be fitted with a slat, so that the side walls of the cold frame cannot be pushed inward or outward. Since mostly unheated

165 The length of the cold frame is dependent on the width of the windows.

Normal cold frame windows are 5 ft. long and 3 ¼ ft. wide; so-called Dutch windows are only 2 ⅗ ft. wide, while having the same length. Accordingly, four normal windows or five Dutch windows can be laid over a cold frame with a length of 13 ft. If intermediate sizes are used, the window will protrude over the edge and can easily be caught by the wind, or there will be an open gap where cold air can get in. The advantage of Dutch windows is that they are more easily moved around by one person than normal windows.

166 Significantly less material is required to build a double cold frame as compared with that required for a single cold frame.

Apart from the boards required for the two gable sides, for a single 33 ft. long cold frame, 33 ft. boards with a width of 8 in. and 33 ft. boards with a width of 12 in. are required. Together, this makes a total of 54 sq. ft. For a 33 ft. long double cold frame, 66 ft. of boards with a width of 8 in. are required, in other words, 43 sq. ft. of wood. If the saddle board is taken into account as well (10 × 1 ft. = 10 sq. ft.), the same number of boards are required, but the area covered by a double cold frame is twice as large.

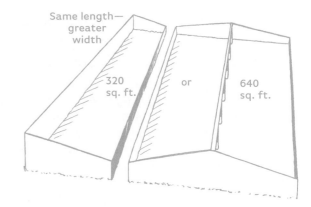

Same length— greater width

320 sq. ft.   or   640 sq. ft.

167 Build simple cold frames in an east-west direction, so that the windows are tilted toward the south, but build double cold frames in a north-south direction.

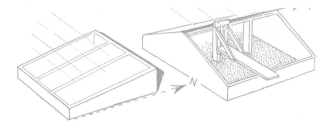

These orientations should be maintained as far as possible, although the terrain or situation will sometimes require a small deviation. Single cold frames will warm up more quickly. However, owing to the smaller air space, they will also tend to overheat more quickly, since the sun's rays strike the glass almost perpendicularly. Many plants will thrive better in double cold frames than in single ones because they are not so strongly affected by the intense midday sun. Only during the middle of the day can the sun's rays strike the windows almost perpendicularly. Working in a cold frame is just as easy as working in a single box if a fixture is built as shown in the diagram.

168 The seed requirements for spring sowing should be determined in good time.

As a rule, garden centers only offer a basic selection of seeds. A better selection is available from specialist seed dealers, or from the seed company itself, from which catalogs can be ordered, making it easy to make your selection at home. All good seed companies have a website.

169 Transportable cold frames can be quickly transferred to other planter beds, without disturbing the plants.

So-called transportable cold frames can set up even in a frost, because there are no posts to be hammered in. The posts joining the boards are short, and only their pointed ends are pushed into the soil. They are set up so that the lowest board is also pressed a little into the soil, which prevents cold air from getting in. Transportable cold frames are particularly important when the growth of young plants needs to be promoted, and they are also suitable for quick installation in the fall. To make them easily transportable, they are often built for only two to four cold frame windows.

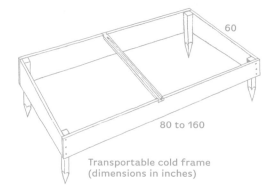

Transportable cold frame
(dimensions in inches)

170 Light soils in a sunny, frost-free location can be prepared for sowing as early as late February.

To retain the winter moisture in the soil, work the land that was already dug up in the fall using only a grubber. After this, stake out the planter beds, and trample the paths firm.

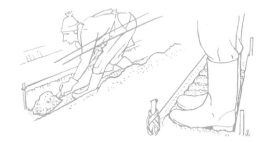

VEGETABLES

171 The vegetable beds should all be of the same width, and in such a way that the work can be carried out conveniently (TIP 59).

The bed width of 4 ft. mentioned earlier should be used, even if the land plot in question cannot be divided up evenly as a result. In such cases, a residual border strip should be left over for vegetables for planting in small quantities only. For annual herbs, such a narrow strip is often desirable.

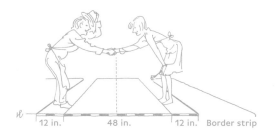

12 in.   48 in.   12 in.   Border strip

172 **Chicory shoots that have been heeled-in in the cellar or cold frame, or grown in containers, can be harvested as soon as they have reached a length of 4 to 5 in.**

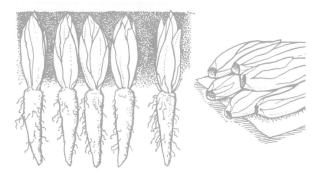

Chicory is tasty only if the leaf shoots have developed with the complete exclusion of light. In a completely darkened room or with an opaque cover over the growth container, time can be taken with the harvest. When the growth is forced using a cover layer or substrate, the chicory should be harvested when the shoots penetrate the substrate; alternatively, it is possible to make the cover layer thicker.

173 **If seed is to be sown in unheated cold frames in late February, the windows should be laid in place about three weeks beforehand and covered with straw mats.**

In December, the soil in the cold frame was covered with a layer of leaves. These leaves can now be removed and packed up against the side walls of the cold frame. This provides effective insulation and protects the subsequently sown seed against large temperature fluctuations. The straw mats are rolled from top to bottom over the cold frame windows in such a way that they also cover the cold frame walls. When

the sun is out, they are removed so that the sun shining on the windows can warm up the soil. Air bubble foil can also be laid underneath the straw mats, greatly improving the heat insulation.

> *Fine-meshed wire netting will protect the cold frame against moles and mice.*

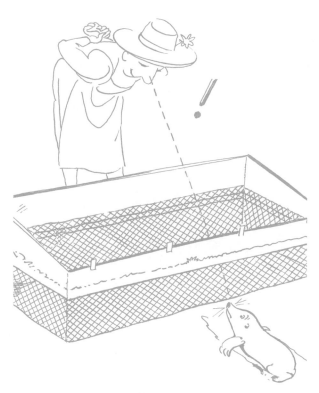

174 **For packing heated cold frames, obtain the necessary material (fresh horse manure, dry leaves, or straw) in good time for packing the frames in mid-February.**

The most suitable material is horse manure with short straw if possible, straight from the stable. For added insulation, line the inner sides of the frames with 1 in. thick polystyrene slabs, followed by a flat layer of leaves on the ground, and then a 10 to 12 in. high layer of manure, packed as evenly as possible. Very dry manure should be well moistened. If no horse manure is available, use straw instead; however, this will need to be well trampled in place and thoroughly wetted with lukewarm water. The windows can then be laid in place and covered with straw mats, although these should be removed in sunny weather.

175 As soon as the manure or straw layer has warmed up, cover with an earth layer.

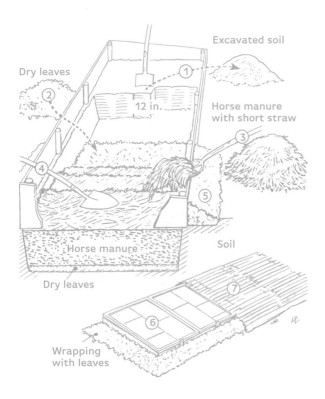

Dry leaves

Excavated soil

12 in.

Horse manure with short straw

Horse manure

Soil

Dry leaves

Wrapping with leaves

First, cover the manure with a 2 in. thick layer of leaves, followed by 4 to 6 in. of good compost earth. Once the earth has been added, the cold frame will be protected against cold outside temperatures, and uncovered only in sunshine.

176 The air and ground temperatures in the cold frame can be raised significantly and regulated with electric heating cables or mats.

These are fitted professionally to the interior walls or laid in the ground. If the windows are additionally covered with the usual frost protection mats, the heating will be sufficient to maintain the temperature in the frame above freezing point, even in heavy frosts. The electrical connections should be made by a professional electrician only.

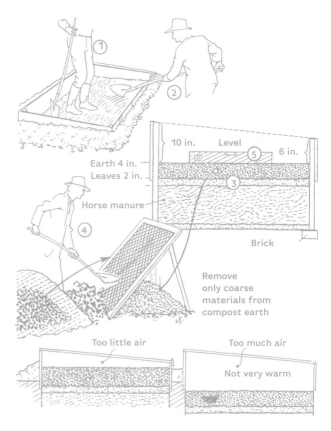

10 in.   Level   6 in.

Earth 4 in.
Leaves 2 in.

Horse manure

Brick

Remove only coarse materials from compost earth

Too little air

Too much air

Not very warm

177 From mid-February, cold frames and small greenhouses are very suitable for raising young plants for early growing outdoors.

This especially applies to growing lettuce and kohlrabi. The seeds for these plants are sown in rows 4 in. apart. The seeds should be sown as thinly and evenly as possible, with a seed depth of ¼ in., to ensure vigorous, uniformly developed plants. Ideally, the cold frame should not be ventilated before the seedlings emerge. If vegetable growing is combined with raising the seedlings in a cold frame, it will be necessary to divide the areas up with boards or similar, in view of the different ventilation conditions. If the cold frames are ventilated, the young plants will be hardened off and acclimatized.

178

Small greenhouses can be used to bring the growth of the vegetable species forward.

Compared with cold frames and foil/plastic tents, an advantage of a small greenhouse is that smaller temperature variations can be expected, thanks to the greater air volume and better options for ventilation, which will benefit the plants' growth and development. A further advantage is that small greenhouses are highly suitable for tall-growing vegetable species such as cucumbers, tomatoes, peppers, eggplants, and Peruvian ground cherries. It is most important that these greenhouses be utilized as rationally and intensively as possible. Accordingly, at least in spring, a mixed culture of kohlrabi, lettuce, red radishes, and kitchen herbs, such as parsley, chives, and basil, should have priority. Climbing beans, too, are well worth growing in a greenhouse.

179

Use of the small greenhouse begins in late February, with vegetable species that have low warmth requirements.

Since, as a rule, greenhouses cannot be heated, they are effectively available for use from late February to at least late October. From late February, they can be used to grow lettuce, radishes, red radishes, and kohlrabi. Three to four days before planting, thoroughly water the envisaged area to fully utilize the soil water storage capacity. This means that watering during the initial growth phase will not need to be greater than absolutely necessary, which will also protect against disease. The soil preparation, and the planting or sowing, are done as described for growing in cold frames. Before planting or sowing, it is wise to apply a low-phosphate complete fertilizer in the form of a basic fertilizer application. Protect the

greenhouse against heavier frosts with straw mats, air bubble foil, or other suitable materials.

180

When harvesting curly kale, only the leafy heads should be cut off, so that the stalks will be able to sprout new shoots.

For delicious vegetables in the spring, the stalks should be left standing as high as possible. These will mean that numerous shoots can already be harvested when there are still no fresh vegetables available for harvesting in the garden.

181

In late February, plant the warm-packed cold frame with pregrown lettuce plants, sowing red radishes between the rows.

The cold frame is ready for planting as soon as the applied earth layer has warmed up. Carefully level the earth surface with a wooden rake, and mark out the rows with a furrow opener. The planting width should be at least 8 × 8 in.; however, 10 × 10 in. is preferable. This will ensure better-quality heads and reduce the risk of rotting. For the early planting date, young plants grown in pots are recommended. They should be well hardened off in order to withstand any frosts that might still be expected, without any damage. As a precautionary measure against the frequent problem of lettuce rot, ensure that the root balls extend about ¾ in. above the soil surface. The spaces between the plants can be used to plant red radishes. In the middle, between the lettuce rows, plant one seed grain every 1 to 1 ½ in., pushing each seed about ½ in. into the soil using finger pressure. After planting, leave the cold frame closed for several days. In strong sunlight, however, it should be ventilated to avoid buildup of excessive temperatures.

182 In favorable years, lettuce can also be planted in unheated cold frames if the soil is completely frost-free.

The cold frame must be prepared accordingly. ▸ **TIP 173** As soon as the soil surface can be worked, it should be turned over. This also provides an opportunity to add humus in the form of compost or half-rotted stable manure if this has not already been done in the fall. Lettuce will respond to this with vigorous growth. Planting and mixed culture should follow the description in ▸ **TIP 181**. If another heavy frost follows planting, which cannot be ruled out entirely, the lettuce plants will be undamaged, provided they have been well hardened off first.

183 To be able to harvest carrots in good time, use special early varieties for early sowing.

Sowing in late February is advisable only on humic sandy soils in a sunny location. Otherwise, the seeds will stay too long in the soil, which could lead to losses when they sprout. The row interval should be 8 in., and early-sprouting varieties should be planted between the rows to indicate the location of the slow-sprouting ones. Here, see also ▸ **TIP 255** and ▸ **TIP 256**.

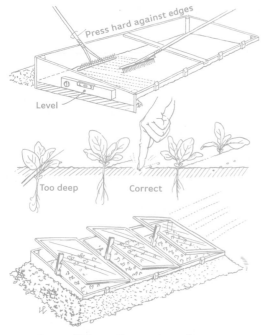

For ventilation, a flower pot can also be used instead of a notched peg.

After sowing seeds in the garden, covering with them with floating row covers protects them from birds.

184 You can raise pepper plants yourself if a warm room with a light window is available.

Sowing should begin in late February if the plants are to be ready for planting by mid-May. Raising the plants yourself is worthwhile only if not too many plants are required and a heated cold frame is available for the potted plants. The seeds are best sown in small plastic pots with a special seeding compost. If this is homemade, it needs to be low in nutrients and free of pathogens. This can be achieved by steam treatment and mixing in sand. Leave a ½ in. gap between the soil surface and the pot rim. Plant three seeds per pot and cover with ¼ in. of soil. Then carefully sprinkle with water and cover with a glass pane. For germination, the seeds require a temperature of 68 to 75°F. As soon as the seedlings emerge, remove the glass pane. Constant moisture should be ensured at all times, and the seedlings should be thinned carefully after two days.

185 Broad (fava) beans tolerate a degree of cold, so they can be planted in late February if soil conditions allow.

Broad beans prefer medium to heavy soils and are grown in the second position in a crop rotation. On light soils, they will give good yields only with a high humus content and a sufficient water supply. Broad beans have no special requirements when it comes to crop rotation; however, they will thrive only in open locations with full sun. The earlier they are planted, the better the yield will be. Provide a row interval of 20 in. and plant not in beds, but instead as shelter for wind-sensitive vegetable species; for example, one row at the edge of a planter bed intended for cucumbers is sufficient. Plant one seed grain every 3 to 4 in. within the row at a sowing depth of 2 to 2 ½ in.

186 Radishes and red radishes are sown in unheated cold frames, transportable cold frames, or foil tents as soon as the soil is frost-free and can be tilled.

The cold frames and transportable cold frames should be prepared for sowing as described in ▸ **TIP 173** and ▸ **TIP 182**. Radishes and red radishes are best dibbled, in other words laid individually. ▸ **TIP 187** For this cultivation, it is essential to use special forcing varieties.

187 For sowing red radishes, construct a dibble board—a fast-working way to ensure the best use of the sown area.

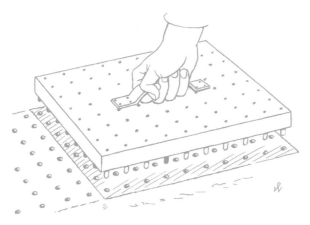

A dibble board is a large, smooth board, about 12 × 16 in. in size. Holes (⅖ in. in diameter) are bored at 2 × 2 in. intervals and fit with wooden dowels or pegs that protrude ¾ in. from the board. Attach a handle to the upper side of the board.

When sowing, press the dibble board onto the ground so that all the pegs penetrate the soil to the same depth. Then insert a red radish seed into each hole that has formed in this way. The soil must be sufficiently moist or the holes will fall in on themselves. Once the entire area has been sown, rake over the holes so that the seeds are covered with soil.

188 In a growing year, black salsify must be sown very early to yield long and thick roots.

Good black salsify otherwise develops only on deep, nutrient-rich soil that has been loosened in the fall to a depth of at least 8 in., and also in regions with a warm spring and long fall. Black salsify belongs in the second position in a crop rotation, but should not be grown following highly demanding crops such as cabbages. Sowing should take place in late February, weather conditions permitting, with a row interval of 12 in. Sow one seed grain about every inch, at a depth of about ½ in. Since black salsify seed retains its full germination capacity for one year only, new seed needs to be purchased every year. A germination test is also advisable.

189 From early February, Spanish onions can be sown in small pots.

The Spanish onion is a mild-tasting subspecies of the normal (yellow) onion and can attain a weight of 1 to 3 lb. (or more) under favorable conditions. It needs a longer development period, and, in accordance with its Spanish origins, has greater warmth requirements. Place three or four seeds in each pot, later leaving only the most vigorous plant standing. The site for raising the plants should have plenty of light, with temperatures around 59°F. The plants remain there until the two-leafed stage, after which temperatures of 50 to 54°F will be sufficient. Additional lighting is helpful. Naturally, sowing later is also possible, but the onions will then be correspondingly smaller.

190 For onions, too, the principle of "the sooner, the better" holds, so that sowing may already begin in late February, in favorable weather conditions.

Onions germinate at soil temperatures as low as 35 to 37°F. A requirement for success is a carefully prepared, finely crumbed seedbed. Only annual seed germinates well, so a germination test is advisable even in the case of newly bought seed. The sowing depth is important; set the onion seeds about ¼ in. deep in the soil. The row interval is 8 in. Using red radishes as an indicator crop facilitates or eases the task of hoeing the soil before the seedlings appear, in order to combat weeds. Lightly press in the soil after sowing so the seeds are adequately covered.

191 In February, too, check earth clamps regularly to ensure that they have not been affected by frost, or that there has been no rotting during milder weather.

The simplest way of checking this is to use a compost thermometer; otherwise, spot checks of the clamp temperature will be necessary. It is especially important to use less frost-protective covering during mild weather.

192 Mild weather means that it is necessary to ventilate the vegetable cellar constantly. Most importantly, cleaning the vegetables must not be forgotten.

Both these measures will improve the storage characteristics of the cellared vegetables and protect against losses. Restack vegetables stacked in heaps at short intervals. Vegetables that are no longer completely fault-free should be cooked as soon as possible.

193 Marjoram can be sown in bowls or pots in late February.

The fine seeds should not be planted too densely, and should be laid only ¼ in. deep in the soil. The containers for sowing need a place with plenty of light and temperatures of 59 to 68°F. Later, three or four plants can be pricked out into 2 ¾ in. pots and placed in a heated cold frame.

194 All about onions. . .

For gardening enthusiasts who are looking for new crops to plant in the wintertime, onions are a welcome option. In addition to regular (yellow) onions, growers who need onions for cooking all year round can also turn to shallots and leeks.

195 For onions, too, connoisseur selections are available. They can grow in the herb garden and have many uses.

Small bulblets can be harvested in summer from crow garlic, rocambole (sand leek), and tree onions. They grow on 20 to 28 in. long stalks. Leaves and flowers can be harvested from curly onions and garlic chives (Chinese chives or Oriental garlic; white and pink flowering). The leaves of spring onions/scallions can be harvested in March, even before chives appear. They do not form any bulbs, but can be easily divided for planting.

196 Leeks with a garlicky taste are especially welcome for summer cuisine.

The sulfur-containing compounds that are responsible for the smell of garlic, and that ultimately escape through the lungs and skin pores, can be only partially neutralized with the aid of household remedies. Ramsons, garlic chives, rocamboles (sand leeks), and Chinese leeks have only small proportions of these compounds.

ORNAMENTAL PLANTS

Ornamental Gardens

197 If a greenhouse is available, summer flowers and perennials can be sown already in early February.

Many summer flowers and perennials require advance planting. Some of them have a very long growing season before flowering, or it may be the case that they should flower from May on, if possible. If so, they must already be sown in February: for example, sages (*Salvia*), plants for the terrace and balcony, such as geraniums (*Pelargonium*), petunias (*Petunia*), and busy Lizzie (*Impatiens walleriana*) need to be considered in February or they will not flower in May. These also include annual climbing plants, ▸ **TIP 376**, where they are required for visual screening as early as possible, for example, black-eyed Susan (*Thunbergia alata*) or cup-and-saucer vine (*Cobaea scandens*). Advance planting in a cold frame from March/April is normal for many summer flowers. However, if a heated greenhouse is available, it is possible to sow these plants in early February; a well-lit windowsill is also an option. If the seeds are sown from mid-February, they will germinate about 7 to 14 days later, in which case there will be enough light to raise the seedlings on the windowsill as well.

198 By using your own seed material, you can also propagate rare summer flowers and perennials.

Many typical summer flowers can also be bought from May as young plants or plants already in bloom. However, the diversity and selection of seed material is much larger, especially when it comes to perennials. Meanwhile, there is no substitute for the joy of watching a plant grow from a small seed grain, not to mention the lower costs involved. You can also collect seed yourself from certain summer flowers and perennials. The seed should be stored in a dry, cool place, and the containers, small screw-cap jars, or paper bags should be well labeled. Seeds of summer flowers from winter-cold climatic zones have a natural germination inhibitor so that they do not germinate before the end of the winter. These seeds must be overwintered in a cool, dark place.

199 Containers and soil for sowing.

Sowing is done using bowls or pots with the appropriate soil. Seed soil and other aids are available from dealers, for example small turf pots, or preferably wood fibers, and other decomposing material. After pricking out or thinning, the seedlings are later planted in their own pots, and hence the roots are protected. They can then continue to grow undisturbed. Indoor greenhouses are also suitable, which also means that it is no longer necessary to cover the bowls or pots with foil to achieve a higher air humidity. Another option for sowing is to use the lower sections of egg cartons made of recyclable material. Following germination, the seedlings with their small root balls, together with the protective carton, can be transplanted to larger containers without disturbing root growth.

200 Seedlings need warmth, light, and air humidity, as well as room to grow.

For the success of all early planting, the provision of light and warmth in the right balance is crucial. High warmth and low light levels lead to long, thin shoots (leggy growth). Adequate light but cold in the root zone, combined with waterlogging, can cause mold. In March, the incoming sunlight, especially behind or under glass, may already be enough to burn the young plants. In such cases, it may be necessary to provide sun protection; cover the seeds with a thin sand or earth layer and gently press them in. The larger the seeds, the thicker the covering layer needs to be. Some plants, such as lupines (*Lupinus*) or pansies (*Viola ×wittrockiana*), are specifically dark-germinating plants, and must be sufficiently covered with earth. Others, such as foxglove (*Digitalis*), are light-germinating plants and need only a thin covering. Very fine seed material is best sown in bowls, so that it will later be possible to select the most vigorous specimens from the many seedlings. The seeds may be mixed with dry, fine-grained sand, or sown with the aid of a folded paper strip. If the seedlings become too large, they must be pricked out or thinned to ensure continued healthy growth. In a heated room, the air humidity is usually not very high. Here, the seed bowls and pots should be covered with perforated foil so that they do not dry out. It is best to use a spray bottle for adding moisture.

201 Every frost-free winter's day should be utilized for ventilation, and to check the storeroom for gladioli, dahlias, and others.

Dahlia bulbs are subject to the greatest risk if the air in a storage room is too moist. If they have been stored too closely together, they should be restacked or separated. Check gladiolus bulbs continually to ensure that storage rot does not spread. ▸ TIP 110

Appropriate pruning of ornamental tree and shrub species is crucial for a natural growth form and rich flowering.

202 Thinning out and possible cutting back of ornamental trees and shrubs should be completed during February.

Here, all the information given in ▸ TIP 100 to ▸TIP 102 should be followed. Shred the cut-off parts for mulching or composting. Twigs and branches with pests or diseases should be burned (taking proper account of local regulations and dates). When it comes to thinning out, don't forget climbers and creepers. ▸ TIP 99.

203 Remove all coppicing from grafted trees and shrubs.

From grafted lilac trees, all ground shoots, or stocks, should be removed right back to the point of insertion. They cannot be used for vegetative propagation, because they develop from the base, onto which the varieties have been grafted. The same applies to other ornamental trees and shrubs that are not supported by their own roots.

204 Ornamental trees and shrubs that were planted in the fall without cutting back must be cut back during February, or by the end of March at the latest.

For this cutting back, the differences outlined in ▸ TIP 100 to ▸ TIP 102 are not relevant. Here, the aim is to achieve a dense framework of branches. In genera or species that do not produce many shoots, two-thirds of the growth is cut back, while in those that produce many shoots about half the growth is left. Additionally, all weak shoots should be removed entirely; see the drawing associated with the next tip for how this should be done. On no account, however, should a hedge cut with shoots of the same length be carried out. This cutting back does not apply to dwarf and conifer trees and shrubs that have been planted from containers without damage to the root ball.

205 Wild roses that do not require winter protection should be pruned in late February in frost-free weather.

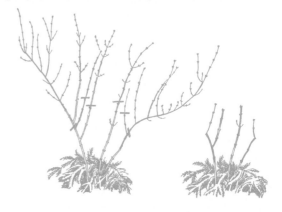

In the case of wild roses, pruning can mostly be limited to thinning measures. At most, old, excessively large bushes can be strongly cut back. In doing so, the oldest shoots at ground level should be cut off so that the shrubs with the young shoots can assume their natural growth form again. If, every year from the outset, as in the case of gooseberries or currants, an older shoot is removed here and there and a younger shoot is left to grow in its place, a radical cutback to encourage regeneration will seldom be necessary.

206 The planting sites for orna-mental trees and shrubs should be prepared in February, on frost-free ground.

Here, it is sufficient if the soil is loosened to a depth of two spade cuts (double digging). If a group of shrubs is to be planted, it is best to dig up the entire area in this manner. ▶ **TIP 1217**. For individual plantings, an area of about 10 sq. ft. should be prepared. Mix in compost soil, including rotting stable manure, with the soil to ensure good growth.

207 The selection of ornamental trees and shrubs for planting in March is best made at this time.

The application is the most important here; for high-lighting individual specimen plants, particularly lush and conspicuously flowering trees and shrubs should be used. Examples include flowering currant (*Ribes sanguineum*), deutzia (*Deutzia*), mock orange (*Phil-adelphus*), lilac (*Syringa*), forsythia (*Forsythia*), golden chain tree (*Laburnum*), hibiscus (*Hibiscus syriacus*), flowering quince (*Chaenomeles japonica*), viburnum (*Viburnum*), daphne (*Daphne*), bridewort (*Spiraea*), Japanese dogwood (*Cornus kousa*), tamarisk (*Tam-arix*), weigela (*Weigela*), flowering almond (*Prunus tri-loba*), cherry apple (*Malus* hybrids), saucer magnolia (*Magnolia ×soulangeana*), star magnolia (*Magnolia stellata*), and others. To cover up unsightly areas such as compost, hazel shrubs such as purple giant filbert (*Corylus maxima* 'Purpurea') or golden leaf hazel (*Corylus avellana* 'Aurea') can be planted. Details such as sizes and flowering times are listed in **TABLE 9**; for climbers and creepers, see **TABLE 14**.

208 During hard frosts in February, protect evergreen trees and shrubs against the effects of the often very intense sunlight.

If, in February, the soil is still frozen solid, the plants will be unable to take up any water. This means they may dry out, since transpiration from their leaves increases markedly in the sunshine. For protection, hang shade coverings in front of the plants—old cur-tains or towels will also do, if need be.

209 As soon as frost-free, dry weather sets in, water ever-green trees and shrubs.

This is especially important in years with low-precipitation winters. Before watering, the soil beneath the plants should be vigorously loosened up with a grubber so that the water can easily penetrate downward. Water the plants thoroughly so that the root balls are well moistened. After watering, apply a soil covering of compost, if this has not already been done in the fall.

210 Once the soil has thawed out completely, check to see that perennials that have been planted in the fall have not been pushed up out of the ground by frost.

If this is not done, there may be considerable losses caused by the plants drying out. The degree of loosening will determine whether the plants need to be uprooted entirely and replanted, or whether it will be sufficient to press them firmly back nto the ground. If the soil is only moderately moist, it is advisable to water it afterward.

211 If hedges are to produce vigorous shoots in spring, they will need to be pruned by late February.

This applies to all hedges comprising privet (*Ligustrum*) or common hornbeam (*Carpinus betulus*). Forsythia (*Forsythia*), flowering quince (*Chaenomeles*), and other spring-flowering species should be pruned after the flowering period, provided the hedge is free of defects. These, too, should be pruned right back by late February at the latest, regardless of the flowering stems. ▶ **TIP 97**.

When building a dry stone wall, proper preparation reduces the work outlay required.

212 If the construction of a dry stone wall is envisaged, preparations can begin in February.

Many garden tasks need to be done in the spring, and so it is better to begin tackling them now. This includes excavating the soil for a dry stone wall foundation, a step which is almost always required. With a solid substrate (loam), excavating to a depth of 6 to 8 in. is sufficient; in looser soils, a depth of at least 12 in. will be required. The depth is also dependent on the height of the wall in question. However, the above indications are only for dry stone walls that are no more than 32 in. high.

When excavating the foundation, do not loosen the soil layer beneath since the foundation requires a firm base. If the base is loose, it should be tamped firm. For overcoming differences in levels in dry stone walls, cut back the earth behind the wall as far as necessary to ensure there won't be any difficulties in layering the

stones. A dry stone wall needs an open, sunny site. If the direction is determined by non-sloping terrain, the wall should run from northwest to southeast. The front side should face southwest.

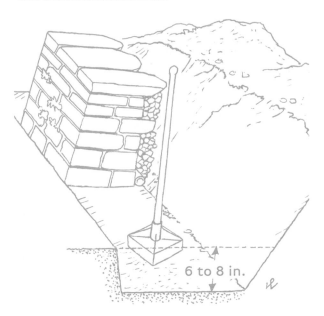

6 to 8 in.

213 The most important aspect to consider when building a dry stone wall is the stones to be worked.

Stone types that can be easily worked are the best. These include limestone, sandstone, and graywacke; slate can also be used. In areas where it is present, granite can also be used. Flat stones are easy to work with, and so they should be purchased already hewn to size. They do not need to be all the same size, also given that stones of different sizes in a wall look better. The most important point is that largely continuous layers can be laid with one size, since horizontal layers should run in a straight line. Stones that have already been exposed to the effects of weathering for a longer time are preferable to those which have been freshly cut.

214 The first flowers will appear in rock and perennial herb gardens in late February.

Sometimes, snowdrops (*Galanthus nivalis* and other species), winter aconite (*Eranthis hyemalis*), amur pheasant's eye (*Adonis amurensis*), some wild crocus species, donkey's ears (*Narcissus cyclamineus*), and others may already flower in early February. Accordingly, conifer brushwood and leaves lying too densely should be loosened or partially removed so that the flowers can develop unhindered.

> *Freshly fallen snow will not harm spring-flowering plants or their blooms.*

215 Snow falling in February or March will not harm flowering shrubs.

These include witch hazel (*Hamamelis*), daphne (*Daphne*), winter jasmine (*Jasmimum nudiflorum*), and early-flowering rhododendron (*Rhododendron* 'Praecox'), which are used to snow and cold in their home territories. In these cases, snow may also lie on their flowers without doing any damage. However, brushing the snow off may damage the flowers; lightly shaking the shrub is acceptable, but not essential.

216 If the soil is frost-free, any forgotten tulip bulbs may be planted in February.

The bulbs will need to have been stored properly. ▶ **TIP 922** and ▶ **TIP 923**. Take care not to damage the bulb base, which in most cases will already be swollen, or any shoots that may be already present. The bulbs should not be pressed into the ground, but instead planted properly. ▶ **TIP 1168**

Terraces and Balconies

217 In February, too, winter protection for miniature gardens and stone troughs should be checked regularly.

Owing to storms, conifer brushwood coverings on open terraces may have been blown away. These should be laid back in place to protect the plants from both frost and sunlight. In particular, frost that has penetrated from the sides will push freshly planted herbs right out of the earth, which means

they may dry out. Here, too, a check should be made; the plants should be pushed back into the soil or replaced. Winter protection will still be required until no further hard frosts are expected.

218 Carnations, such as *Dianthus caryophyllus*, that are overwintering in frost-free conditions should be cut back in late February.

The long, old shoots should be cut well back. This will cause the plant to produce shoots vigorously and develop well, supported by regular fertilizer application. A light, well-ventilated, and cool place at a temperature of around 41°F is important so that the growth of the new shoots does not become leggy. Keep the soil only moderately moist until vigorous shoot growth necessitates a greater water uptake. Replant if necessary.

219 Overwintering geraniums should be cut back in late February.

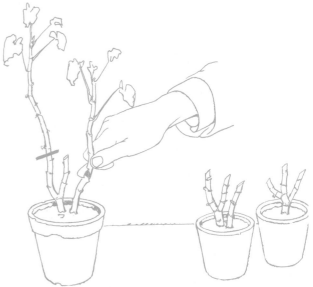

To attain bushy plants, cut back every shoot to two or three leaf attachments in which buds (eyelets) are present. Remove the old soil, and cut back the roots by about half. Then transfer the plants to small pots with potting mixture. Keep the soil only moderately moist until shoots appear. Lantanas are treated in the same way.

220 In late February, fuchsias should be cut back by a little more than half.

This will ensure that they produce shoots vigorously and develop a bushy form. If perennial fuchsias have become too tall, they can also be cut back to the biennial wood. In order that the new shoots will be short and vigorous, a cool and light place at temperatures of around 54 to 59°F is required. Keep the soil only slightly moist until the new shoot develops. After this, the plants can be again watered more generously.

Winter Gardens, Flower Windows, and Rooms

221 Give amaryllis (*Hippeastrum*) plants with buds fertilizer in February if they do not need to be transplanted.

They will generally flower better in smaller pots rather than overly large ones. Accordingly, amaryllis plants should be left in the same pot for two to three years, provided they can get enough nutrients and do not acidify the soil. Adding sufficient nutrients during the growing period is important for healthy development and plentiful flowering in the coming year.

222 Once the kaffir lily (*Clivia*) develops its buds, apply fertilizer.

As soon as the plants develop the first buds between the leaves, give them water and fertilizer in the normal way. If the inflorescence develops beneath the leaves, it will extend outward if it is sprayed with water at a temperature of 104°F. The plant should be transplanted after flowering.

223 Died-off hyacinths and tulips should continue to be watered if they are to be planted in the garden later.

The flowers will have drawn many reserve nutrients from the bulbs that will need to be replaced. Accordingly, proper care and regular fertilizer applications are necessary. Remove any flowers that have become unsightly, with as little damage to the leaves as possible.

224 Bellflowers (*Campanula isophylla* and *C. fragilis*) whose shoots have become too long should be cut back in late February.

Older, longer shoots are often bare at the base. To make the plants attractive again, cut back these shoots to just above the ground. The shoot tips that will then appear can be used to raise young plants. Take cuttings by using a sharp knife just under one leaf. In order that they develop roots, they should be inserted about ½ in. deep into pure sand in correspondingly large pots, and so close together that their leaves are just touching. They will develop roots best at temperatures of 54 to 57°F. Transplant the pruned old plants into sandy potting mixture and put them in a light, airy place, where they will soon develop into splendidly flowering hanging plants.

225 Gloxinia tubers that have been in dry storage can be planted in pots in late February.

This can also be done up until early April. A mixture of bark, potting mixture, compost, and sand is sufficient as soil, or also just sandy compost with bark. The substrate should be lumpy. To ensure good water uptake and soil aeration, provide each pot with about 1 in. of small stones or polystyrene granules at the base. The diameter of the pots should be no more than three times greater than that of the tubers. Press the tubers only shallowly into the soil, and do not cover them with plant substrate. Keep the soil only moderately moist until the roots form and the shoots are visible. It is important that the plants are kept in a place that is warm and light, but not sunny.

MARCH

SPRING

With the coming of the month of March, spring has truly begun, and young shoots are appearing everywhere. In particular, tuber or bulb plants, such as snowdrops, spring snowflakes, and crocuses, but also early daffodils or narcissi, will delight us with their beautiful flowers.

Plants that have been protected against hard frosts can now be gradually freed of their coverings and become accustomed to the sunlight. On windless days, we can begin to sow parsley, peas, and carrots. In late March, the planting time for perennials can also begin. Window and balcony planters, along with containers for the terrace, can be occupied by spring-flowering plants from mid-March. If the ground is still frozen, evergreen trees and shrubs will still need to be protected from direct sunlight.

GENERAL

226 Fixed or anchored water containers must be cleaned and checked to ensure that they are still watertight, while portable ones need to be set up again and checked to make sure that they are in good working order.

Walled containers and those with mortar often suffer from the effects of frost. If cracks have appeared in the mortar, these and the surrounding areas should be cut away and the cut surface then moistened, so that good bonding for new mortar will be achieved. If the uppermost layer (roll layer) has been affected by freezing, it is best to replace it completely. A water-repellant substance should be added to the mortar.

227 Inspect the water supply, which has been switched off during the winter, for pipe damage, and remove frost protection materials from the taps.

The water supply will often need to be available from late March; accordingly, any repairs should be completed in good time. Often, the washers in the taps will have suffered damage during the winter.

228 If the garden does not have a water connection, watering from a rain barrel with an electric immersion pump can make work easier.

Immersion pumps are very efficient, and permit many garden areas to be watered easily.

229 Water is best distributed with a perforated hose or a small sprinkler.

A perforated hose is used for watering between the plants; just lay the hose in place and turn on the water tap. This facilitates sparse watering with droplets or a spray mist, mostly within the width of a plant bed, while also protecting the soil. A small sprinkler, too, can make watering much easier. ▶ TIP 51

Good quality sprinklers make watering the garden easy.

230 In early March, hang new nesting boxes for birds, and clean or repair old boxes.

Check nesting boxes in good time to see whether they need to be repaired, so that there will be no need to disturb the brood. At the same time, they will need to be cleaned, since the birds will build a new nest before they breed. Make sure the boxes are firmly attached to their support so that they will not swing back and forth in the wind. They should also be tilted slightly, since rainwater must not be allowed to penetrate inside through the entrance hole. In small gardens, only one nesting box for blue tits should be hung up.

231 Nesting boxes on trees and shrubs, as well as bird's nests in hedges, should be made safe from cat predation.

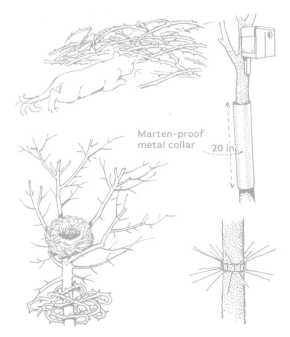

Marten-proof metal collar — 20 in

A spiny ring on tree stems will protect bird's nests against predation by cats; in the case of shrubs and hedges, only spiny or thorny branches will provide protection. These must be laid so densely that cats will not be able to crawl through them.

232 In March, the planting time for (deciduous) trees and shrubs begins. Be sure to observe legally prescribed distances from neighboring properties.

Tall-growing trees can rob neighboring gardens of light and sun. Accordingly, it is best to stay somewhat further back from the boundary than the law demands. At this stage, it is still too early to plant conifers.

VEGETABLES

233 In small gardens, early March is the best time to plant kohlrabi and cauliflower.

Remember that early cauliflower will occupy the plot for at least 50 to 55 days, which means that the main crop, such as tomatoes or cucumbers, can be planted only at a relatively late stage. The planting width for kohlrabi is 10 × 10 in., and for cauliflower 12 × 16 or 16 × 16 in., depending on the variety. A catch crop with an early red radish variety can yield an additional harvest in mid-April. For soil preparation and carrying out the planting, the tips given for growing in cold frames apply.

234 Broccoli has much the same soil, climate, and previous-crop-related requirements as cauliflower.

Broccoli is a vegetable species that is similar to cauliflower. However, the flowers are more loosely arranged on long, thick, fleshy stalks, and are predominantly green or violet in color. The excellent flavor of broccoli should be emphasized, along with its relatively high nutrient content. It grows well in every garden, and, unlike cauliflower, it also grows under less favorable conditions.

235 From mid- to late March, broccoli can be sown in a heated cold frame.

Since, owing to its growth characteristics, broccoli can be harvested over a longer period, generally only a few plants are required. To attain vigorous young plants, plant single seed grains at 1 in. intervals. The sowing date as given above facilitates planting from late April to early May.

236 Vegetable peas, but also vetches, beans, clovers, lupines, and sweet peas, are members of the legume plant family, and have a symbiotic relationship with nitrogen-fixing bacteria.

If the roots of legumes encounter free-living, one-celled bacteria of the genus *Rhizobium* in the soil, the bacteria find their way into the plant via the root hairs. The plant then develops spherical root nodules. With the aid of enzymes, the plants convert, or "fix," nitrogen from the atmosphere into a form that can be taken up by the plant. Legumes alone have this capacity.

237 Vegetable peas do not tolerate organic fertilizers well.

Vegetable peas do not thrive on arable land that has been freshly covered with stable manure; accordingly, they should be planted in the second position in a crop rotation. They have no special requirements as regards the previous crop, but they are nevertheless incompatible with themselves in this regard and should be planted again on the same area only after a break of three or four years.

238 Vegetable peas include split peas, wrinkled peas, and sugar peas.

Wrinkled peas, as the name implies, have a wrinkled kernel and a better flavor than split peas. However, they are more sensitive than split peas when it comes to seedling emergence and are therefore unsuitable for sowing in March. The dry kernel is unsuitable for gastronomic purposes, because it remains hard even when cooked. Split peas have a round and smooth kernel, are relatively undemanding in terms of temperature requirements, and are therefore of special importance when it comes to sowing in March. Sweet peas, meanwhile, have no parchment layer on the insides of the pods, which means that both the green kernel and the pods can be utilized.

239 Peas are not especially demanding when it comes to the soil, provided that it has been well tilled and is rich in humus.

For early sowing, lighter soils are more suitable than heavy ones, because they warm up more quickly and therefore promote seedling emergence and the plants' ongoing development. In addition to normal phosphorus and potassium fertilizers, nitrogen fertilizer should be added at a rate of 2 oz. per 100 sq. ft. Avoid further nitrogen applications since these promote only the leaf growth and delay the harvest. The soil pH should not be allowed to fall below 6. Accordingly, timely soil tests are always valuable.

240 Four rows of peas can be grown in a normal vegetable bed. This corresponds to an interval of 12 in. between rows, and an interval of 6 in. to the edge of the bed.

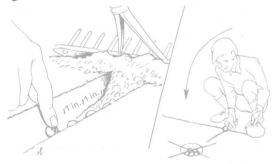

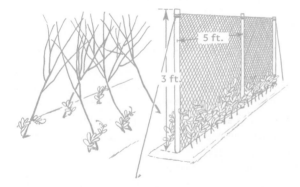

Peas are sown individually as a continuous row, and not in bunches, as is often done with bush beans. The area seed requirement, depending on the grain size, is about 1 oz. per square yard. Make the furrows for sowing deep enough so that the pea seeds can be covered with 2 in. of earth. Then lay one pea seed about every inch and push the seeds into the soil a little. When the rows have been covered over again, they are then gently pressed in.

To make harvesting easier, it is useful to sow peas in double rows. After sowing two rows, separated from one another by 8 in., leave an intermediate space of 20 in., and then sow a second double row. Depending on the variety, the peas will reach a height of 24 to 32 in. Erect a sheet of wire netting between each double row on which the peas can climb.

241 In the first days of March, foil houses, foil tents, and cold frames can also be planted.

Give preference to lettuce, kohlrabi, and cauliflower; sowing of radishes, red radishes, and carrots is also possible. See the notes given in ▸ **TIP 181** and ▸ **TIP 179**.

242 In frost-free weather, sown seed in cold frames should be ventilated daily.

The main task is to remove the covering material every day, and to put it back again in the evening, even if there is no danger of frost. Light and air are the main requirements for achieving healthy, vigorous plants. However, do take care with watering. Only water the plants if the upper soil layer has dried out, but in that case so thoroughly that watering will not be required again straight afterward. Water on sunny days only, so that the plants dry out quickly with the ventilation, and do not begin to rot.

243 In early March, place early potatoes in shallow boxes for initial germination and leave them in a light, airy place at 54 to 59°F.

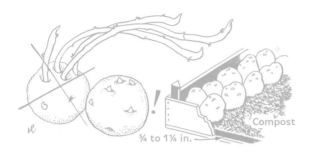

By germinating the potatoes in boxes, the harvest can be brought forward by at least 10 to 14 days, and the yields will also be greater. This should be started around five weeks before laying the tubers, which, based on experience, should be done in the second week of April. Accordingly, in early March, place the seed potatoes in a single layer in the boxes so that most of the eyes are facing upward. Sufficient light is crucial for short, vigorous shoots to develop.

244 From early March, outdoor planting of kohlrabi can begin on light, humic soils, weather conditions permitting.

Kohlrabi needs a standing room of 10 × 10 in. Although it will withstand light frosts, using frost protection hoods is recommended. To bring the harvest time forward, cover the bed with slit foil or fleece. ▸ **TIP 249**

245 From late March, cauliflower, lettuce, Brussels sprouts, and kohlrabi can be sown on outdoor seedbeds.

Sowing is done in rows at intervals of 6 in. Sow seeds as sparsely and uniformly as possible to obtain vigorous plants.

After sowing, it is helpful to cover the rows with a ½ in.

thick layer of compost. This will result in better seedling emergence.

246 Turnips can be sown as early as mid- to late March.

Turnips are a special kind of vegetable beet. They develop into small, globose beets, usually with a white coat and white tender flesh that has a pleasantly sweet flavor. Eaten raw as a salad, they are a special delicacy. They are often erroneously traded as radishes, although they lack the sharp radish taste. Sow in well-prepared, humic soil, which should be as light as possible, with a row interval of 8 in. and 4 in. within the row, and a seed depth of ½ in. If the seedlings emerge too close together, thinning will be essential. Cover early-sown seed with foil or fleece, and later with netting for protection against insects.

247 Chard prefers deep, humic, and sufficiently moist soils.

Extremely light or heavy soils are unsuitable if they are not made usable through the addition of large amounts of compost or stable manure. Chard roots penetrate deep into the soil, which, accordingly, should be loosened to a great depth. Chard can be grown in the first or second position in a crop rotation.

248 When growing chard, the final use should be taken into account.

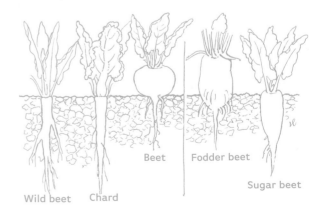

Wild beet   Chard   Beet   Fodder beet   Sugar beet

To begin with, chard can be used in much the same way as spinach. In this case, row intervals of 10 to 12 in. will be sufficient. The second option concerns the exclusive use of the leaf ribs ("stalk chard"); in this case, a row interval of 14 to 16 in. is required. Sowing can take place from mid-March. The seed depth should be about 1 in. For stalk chard, following emergence, the plants are thinned to 14 to 16 in. in the row so that they have sufficient room and develop the widest possible leaf stalks. The new, highly decorative varieties with a range of leaf stalk colors from red and orange to yellow and white similarly require plenty of room. They make an interesting focal point in the garden, and should be situated accordingly.

249 In March, lettuce planted outdoors can be harvested 10 to 12 days earlier if the beds are (completely) covered with foil or fleece.

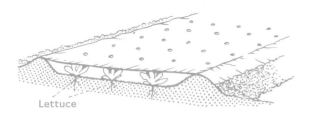

Lettuce

For this, use perforated or slit foil; it is also worth making a small earth wall at the edges of the bed to lift the foil a little off the ground. To avoid the foil being caught by the wind, cover the foil edges with earth. As a rule, leave the foil on the plants for about three weeks; however, the exact date for removing it is dependent on the weather and plant development. It is helpful if dull weather is predominant at this time, since strong sunlight can burn the leaves. If the beds to be covered are not too large, it may be helpful to use a wooden frame with the foil stretched over it. This method of bringing the harvest forward can also be used for kohlrabi and red radishes, for example. If a fleece is used, it can remain on the plants until shortly before the harvest. However, it must be loosened as required to give the plants sufficient room to develop. In the case of taller species such as kohlrabi and radishes, it is useful to stretch the foil over a metal or wire frame.

250 Lettuces planted in a small greenhouse in late February should be watered only sparingly until the heads begin to form.

Otherwise, the plants' root systems will be too shallow, while the wetting of the aboveground plant parts will promote disease. If the sun is strong, ventilate the plants liberally. During the last days of March, when the heads begin to form, give nitrogen fertilizer as a surface application, at a rate of 2 oz. per 100 sq. ft.

251 Sow lettuce plants for summer harvesting no later than the end of March.

Use special summer varieties. Sowing can be done on outdoor seedbeds; a row interval of 4 in. is sufficient. Sow the seeds sparsely, with a seed depth of about ¼ in. If only a few plants are required, it is preferable to sow in 2 in. pots; these are then placed in a cold frame. To ensure a continuous outdoor lettuce harvest until the fall, subsequent sowing will be required at intervals of two to three weeks until late July.

252 Iceberg lettuce is a special kind of lettuce.

Iceberg lettuce differs from ordinary lettuce, thanks to its hard, crunchy leaves with strongly wavy or curly leaf edges. The head is much larger, and, depending on the variety, can attain a weight of 1 to 1 ¾ lb. Iceberg lettuce requires 14 days more development time than ordinary lettuce. However, it is also very robust and heat-tolerant. There are red-leaved varieties as well.

253 Carrots come in a range of different sizes, including short and semi-long varieties.

There are round, short, semi-long, and long carrots; depending on the color, a distinction is also made between white, yellow, and red varieties. Pigments, sugars, and natural flavor substances determine the quality and enjoyment. Differently colored carrots are the result of a natural genetic diversity that has originated from breeding and can make a visually attractive change.

254 Carrots grow best on warm, light, and deeply loosened soils with a high humus content. These will also yield the earliest harvests.

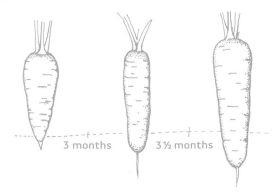

3 months   3 ½ months

Early carrots in particular grow more slowly on heavy soils and can be harvested only after a longer time. Soils that are prone to strong encrustation are unsuitable. Like all root vegetables, carrots do not tolerate fresh organic fertilizer, and should be grown in the second position in a crop rotation. They are also sensitive when it comes to fresh lime application. Any lime application (below pH 6.5) is best reserved for the previous crop.

Carrots place no great demands on the previous crop, but they should not be planted following celery or a previous carrot crop. For an early harvest, the right variety is also required. Short and semi-long varieties with short development times are preferable. Both types can be harvested around three months after sowing.

> Mix carrot seeds with double the quantity of dry, fine sand, which will allow for correct sowing density.

255 March is the main time for sowing early and medium-early carrot varieties.

The row interval should be generally 8 in. Carrot seeds are relatively small. Carrots are mostly sown too densely, so don't go overboard. Using seed belts or encapsulated seed makes it easier to keep to the prescribed intervals. The seed depth should be ¼ to ½ in. After the rows have been sown, press in the seeds.

Dry sand!

256 For carrots, the time from sowing to seedling emergence can often take four weeks, so an indicator crop is strongly recommended.

Red radishes are the most suitable indicator crop. Before covering the seed furrows, lay a seed grain every 3 to 4 in. The radishes will appear after several days and indicate where the rows are, so that hoeing can take place accordingly. They will also yield an additional harvest.

257 Like carrots, parsnips are members of the carrot family.

Parsnips look like large, white carrots, with a broad root head. They are a tasty and nutritious root vegetable; their nutritional value exceeds that of carrots and kohlrabi. Parsnips prefer a medium to heavy, humus-rich soil that is as deep as possible. As root vegetables, they do not need any fresh organic fertilizer, and are best grown in the second position in a crop rotation. They have much the same nitrogen and phosphorous requirements as late carrots, but their potassium requirements are significantly greater.

258 Parsnips need around seven months to develop fully, and therefore should already be sown in March.

Sow at row intervals of 12 in. and a seed depth up to ½ in. Since parsnips emerge late, an indicator crop (red radishes) is required. Following emergence, thin out plants to about 4 in. within the row. Sowing later in April to early May is possible, but will result in smaller roots.

259 There is a big difference between common (curly) and root parsley, which should be taken into account when buying seed.

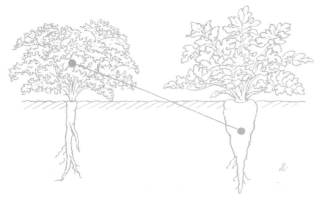

Because parsley is used not just as a spice for dishes, but also as a garnish, generally only common, curly-leaved parsley is planted. In the case of root parsley, it is mainly the roots that are used in the fall and winter. Root parsley has smooth leaves.

260 For common parsley, a place in the garden is required where the plants are particularly well protected against wintry north and east winds.

They can also grow in semi-shaded sites, and, since they will grow there to a maximum height of 8 in., they can also be planted as edging. Parsley grows best on sandy loam soils with a high humus content, but it does not tolerate any fresh organic fertilizer. For root parsley, the soil needs to be tilled to a considerable depth.

261 Because parsley germinates more quickly and reliably when the earth has already warmed up a little and is no longer as wet, sowing should not take place before 15 March.

Germination normally takes place after about three weeks (indicator crop required!). For common parsley, a row interval of about 5 to 6 in. is sufficient when sowing; for root parsley, 10 in. is required. Plant parsley seeds very shallowly in the soil; for earlier sowing, this is particularly important to note for heavy soils.

262 Leeks should be sown in a cold frame in about mid-March, if especially thick leek stalks are to be harvested.

Plant the seeds in rows, but very sparsely. The row interval should be 4 in. Until the seedlings emerge, the sown area should be covered with straw or reed mats. During the germination period, the seedbed should always be kept uniformly moist, and it must also be ventilated on sunny days.

263 The best sowing time for broad beans is early to mid-March, since they will tolerate some cold during their early growth.

Broad beans are very suitable as a protective shelter crop for cucumbers, melons, and other wind-sensitive plants. Since they grow well when freestanding, they may be planted a row at a time at the edges of plant beds that are intended for cucumbers or other wind-sensitive vegetable species. They will develop well if given sufficient fertilizer. Of course, broad beans may also be planted in beds of their own—sowing is done as described in ▶ **TIP 185**.

264 Red radishes grow best on sunny sites and on light to medium, humus-rich soils that are not prone to encrustation.

Red radishes do not tolerate fresh organic fertilizer, since this affects the tuber formation and promotes pests. When applying fertilizer, remember that red radishes are among the especially chlorine-sensitive vegetable species; select the fertilizer accordingly.

265 Favorable soil and climate conditions will allow red radishes to be sown from early March.

From this time on, subsequent sowing is possible until early September. Red radishes are generally sown too densely; in fact, the tubers will develop properly only with uniform sowing at sufficiently large intervals. The seeds should be sown in rows laid at intervals of 3 to 4 in. Within the rows, sow the seeds individually at intervals of 1¼ in. This effort is worthwhile for the results obtained. Overly dense stands may need to be thinned. The seed depth is also important; red radishes should be sown only around ½ in. deep. Sowing the seed too deep will affect the tuber form and delay the harvest. It is helpful to cover the early outdoor sown areas with foil or fleece.

266 Depending on the variety and sowing time, red radishes need 22 to 55 days from sowing to harvest.

In addition to development time, as dependent on the variety, the sowing time has a considerable impact on the time required from sowing to the fully developed tubers. Compared with sowing in May, seeds sown in March need almost double the development time. In selecting the variety, note that varieties for growing under glass and plastic foil are only partially suitable for growing outdoors, since, under these conditions, the tuber quality will suffer.

267 Under favorable soil and weather conditions, early radishes may be sown in mid-March.

This early sowing is worthwhile only on humic, light soils that warm up quickly. Varieties with a short development time are suitable, for example, 'Runder Weisser.' The row interval should be 6 to 8 in., while the seeds are planted at intervals of 4 in.

268 Rhubarb places no special demands on the soil, provided sufficient nutrients are available.

Rhubarb can be harvested earlier on light soils in sunny sites than on heavy, dense soils. However, it will also thrive on semi-shaded sites. It is important that the soil be loosened to as great a depth as possible.

269 Rhubarb needs to be planted in the first days of March if a small harvest is still to be expected in the first year.

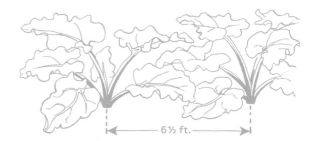

The main planting time is in the fall, but rhubarb can also be planted in early March. The most important point is that vigorous plant sections with at least one dense head are present. Since rhubarb needs plenty of space, the planting width should be 6 ½ × 6 ½ ft. When planting, it is important that the plant sections do not end up deeper in the soil than they were before. Plant very securely in place and water generously.

270 **Perennial rhubarb plantings should already be given fertilizer during March.**

Rhubarb needs plenty of nitrogen. Accordingly, preferably before the shoots develop, apply a complete fertilizer along with the same quantity of nitrogen fertilizer. The fertilizer mixture should be sprinkled dry over the planted area, and then worked into the soil. Then thoroughly water the area so that the fertilizer reaches the root zone as quickly as possible.

> *Covering rhubarb plants in early spring will bring the harvest forward by 8 to 10 days. Boxes, high baskets, or foil tents are suitable.*

271 **Those who love butterhead lettuce and leaf lettuce can begin with direct sowing in March—this will enable delicious lettuce leaves to be harvested in late April.**

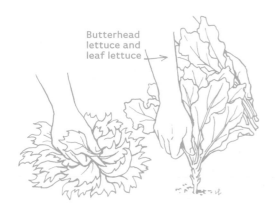

Butterhead lettuce and leaf lettuce

Butterhead lettuce needs a row interval of 6 in., and leaf lettuce 10 to 12 in. In shallow furrows, sow the seeds sparsely. Following seedling emergence, thin out leaf lettuce in the row to 10 in. Both kinds of lettuce, which do not form heads, have no special soil requirements, and will grow wherever there are sufficient nutrients.

272 **Interesting variants of leaf lettuce include oak-leaf lettuce and curly lettuce.**

Oak-leaf lettuce has leaves that resemble those of an oak and are reddish brown or yellowish green in color, depending on the variety. Curly lettuces, meanwhile, are compact plants that develop strongly wrinkled red leaves (Lollo Rossa) or green leaves (Lollo Bionda). Both types can be planted or sown several times consecutively from March to August. The planting width is 12 × 12 in. They are grown in the same way as ordinary lettuce. If planted in March, it is worth covering the bed with foil or fleece to bring the harvest forward.

273 **Black salsify has demanding soil requirements if it is to be grown successfully.**

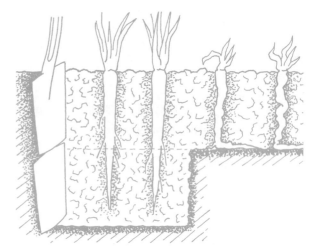

Light to medium-heavy, stone-free, humus soils are the most suitable for growing this plant. Although the soil must have a high humus content, black salsify does not tolerate organic fertilizer, and should be planted in the second position in a crop rotation. Improve humus-poor soils by adding large quantities of good compost. The soil for black salsify must be loosened thoroughly to a depth of more than 8 in. if perfect roots are to be obtained.

274 **Black salsify needs to be sown as early as possible.**

In spring, use a grubber to work over the soil that has been deeply loosened in the fall and then rake smooth. The best time for sowing is from early to mid-March; sowing any later will mostly result in poorly developed roots.

Select a row interval of 12 in., and lay a seed grain every inch at a depth of around ½ in. Since it takes up to three weeks for the seeds to emerge, an indicator crop (red radishes) is useful. Following emergence, thin out the seedlings to 2 to 2 ½ in.

275 Although chives have no special soil requirements, they grow best in sandy loam soils with a high humus content.

Any soil can be improved for growing chives by adding large quantities of humus. Owing to their growth form, they are also suitable as edging plants. Chives will also tolerate semi-shade, which means that it is always possible to find a place for them to grow. Since they are also fully winter hardy, they can be grown in all climactic zones.

276 Chives are propagated either by sowing, or by dividing old stands. The seeds remain fully viable for one year only.

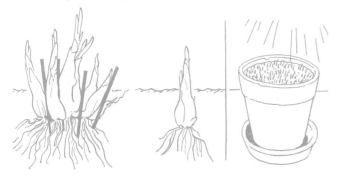

Sowing is done in mid-March in an unheated cold frame, or from late March outdoors. Chives are sown relatively densely because they are not planted individually, but in small tufts. Separate old stands as soon as their heads are visible. Be sure not to place the separated plants deeper in the soil than they were before. A row interval of 8 in. is sufficient, with an interval of 8 in. within the row as well.

277 Celery and celeriac (root celery) need temperatures of 64 to 68°F.

Celery is sensitive to low temperatures during cultivation. Sow from early to mid-March in seed bowls, with the seeds barely covered with earth. After sowing, carefully moisten, lay a glass pane over the top, and place in a warm room. It will often take three weeks before the seedlings emerge. As soon as the first vegetative leaf appears, prick out the plants at an interval of 2 × 2 in. into a heated cold frame, or straight into small pots. At first, they should be ventilated only a little, but later they are hardened off in good time. Celery can be sown in subsequent crops every 14 days from mid-March to May.

278 Growing white asparagus is advisable only in humic, warm, sandy soil.

These soils warm up more quickly, can be harvested earlier, and, as such, make harvesting easier. The deep soil excavation and turning required (digging three spade cuts deep, or triple digging) should already be done in the fall or winter. An asparagus plot will yield good harvests for at least 15 years if it is well looked after.

279 On the prepared land (triple digging) on which asparagus is to be grown, dig out the ditches in late March. A north-south orientation is the most suitable for the dams to be built later to warm up.

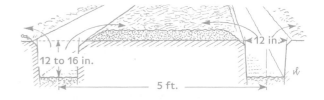

The interval from the middle of one ditch to the next is 5 ft. Each ditch is 12 in. wide and 12 to 16 in. deep (deeper on light soils than on heavy ones). Spread the excavated material over the space between the ditches.

280
After digging the ditches, cover them with a 6 in. thick layer of coarse compost.

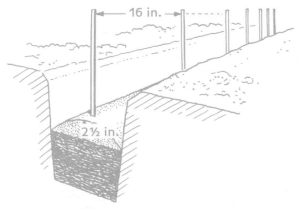

Finally, a 2 to 2 ½ in. layer of good compost earth is added in the form of a dam. The compost earth can also be used to create a small hillock for every plant at 16 in. intervals. The plants can now be brought in.

281
Asparagus is planted from late March to mid-April. The roots of one-year-old plants are spread evenly across the plant hillock or dam.

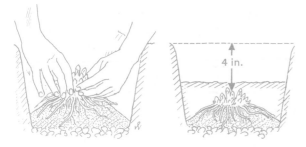

It is best to use one-year-old plants, since they tend to grow better. They should be planted so that the asparagus plant heads are around 4 in. below the original soil surface. Note that the asparagus root-stock always grows strictly in one direction. At the point where the died-off shoot is situated, there is a gap between the roots growing on all sides. This gap must always point in the same direction, toward the ditch, since, otherwise, over the years the asparagus stalks will grow toward the dam sides. After planting, cover the plants with a 2 in. layer of the same earth that makes up the plant dams or hillocks, then water thoroughly.

282
Green asparagus is easier to grow than white asparagus, and the soil requirements are also not as critical.

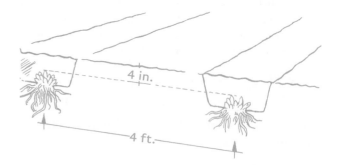

Green asparagus stalks do not need to work their way through the earth walls, but develop above the ground instead. Accordingly, green asparagus can also be grown in heavy soils (sandy loam or loamy sand). Laying out the ditches, ▸ TIP 279, is done in the same way as for white asparagus, but here a depth of 12 in. and a row interval of 4 ft. are sufficient. Plant green asparagus so that the heads of the young plants are covered by about 4 in. of earth. Growing green asparagus in areas where frequent night frosts can occur in spring (April/May) is not advisable; there may be considerable losses through freezing of the asparagus stalks, which are very frost sensitive.

283
For harvesting asparagus as green asparagus, it is not necessary to erect dams, but the soil to be planted must be loosened carefully during March.

It is best to wait until the soil surface has dried out somewhat before undertaking this work, and then proceed carefully with a grubber. The soil should be loosened sufficiently shallowly so that neither the roots, nor the heads of the asparagus suffer any damage.

284 During the last third of March, erect dams on the white asparagus beds to be harvested.

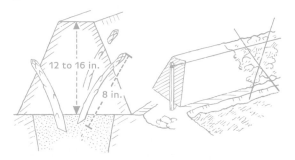

The dams must be high enough so that the asparagus stalks growing out of the sides can attain a length of 8 to 8 ½ in. Accordingly, the height of the dams should be around 12 to 16 in. Stretch a line or cord over the length of the plant row to ensure that the dams are all the same height.

Next, remove the earth between the plant rows; there must also be no lumps in the dams. Rake the finished dams smooth and lightly tap them firm with a flat shovel. This will give them a flat surface, which will make the asparagus stalks easy to recognize when they emerge.

> *Covering emerging asparagus with black foil or floating row covers will bring the harvest forward and prevent the asparagus tips from discoloring.*

285 During March (before the shoots sprout), give two-year-old asparagus beds a nitrogen-rich fertilizer application.

Complete fertilizers usually do not contain enough nitrogen. Accordingly, a pure nitrogen fertilizer should be added, such as sodium nitrate (soda niter) or calcium nitrate. Since this will be only the first annual fertilizer application, ½ oz. of complete fertilizer per square yard is sufficient, along with the same amount of one of the above nitrogen fertilizers, after which light hoeing is advisable. Here, be careful not to damage the shoot tips beneath the surface.

286 Spinach will thrive in all humus-rich gardens and places no special demands on climate.

However, growing spinach on heavy soils is not recommended. Cultivation following black salsify, beets, chard, lamb's lettuce, and spinach itself should also be avoided. Plant spinach only as a previous crop or an aftercrop. Sow spring spinach in early March if possible. Sow at a depth of ½ in., with a row interval of 8 in.

287 New Zealand spinach is a member of the carpetweed family, and delivers high yields in the summer months.

The plant forms much-branched, long shoots lying on the ground with leaves that are spinach-like but very fleshy. New Zealand spinach has a similar health value to regular spinach. It thrives best on light to medium, humus-rich soils, and delivers good yields even on semi-shaded sites.

288 New Zealand spinach is frost sensitive and therefore requires advance planting.

The seeds are sown in small pots. In each pot, plant three seeds in sandy compost soil, and place the pots in a cold frame or on the windowsill of a light, frost-free room. Six to eight plants can meet the needs of a four-person household.

289 Early varieties of savoy cabbage and white cabbage can be planted in March.

Very-early-ripening varieties, which have pointed heads, are especially suitable. They need to be grown in warm, sandy loam or loamy sand soils, with plenty of humus. Only soils of the first position in the crop rotation should be considered. A planting width of 16 × 16 in. is sufficient.

290 Onions have special soil requirements and should be sown as early as possible.

These grow best on medium loam and loess soils that have a high humus content and dry out early in the spring. Sandy or heavy and wet soils are unsuitable. Additionally, onions do not respond well to fresh organic fertilizer. The area for planting should not be dug up, but merely worked with a grubber and raked carefully. The best time for sowing is early to mid-March; a row interval of 8 in. is sufficient. Sow the seeds as sparsely as possible and not deeper than ½ in. An indicator crop is advisable. Once the shoots appear, thin out any onions growing too closely together.

291 Seed (planting) onions, too, need to be planted in March if large onions are to be harvested in good time.

In climatically less favorable situations, growing cooking (yellow) onions from seed onions is more reliable than growing them from sown onions. The success is dependent on the size of the seed onion. It should be only about the size of a hazelnut, since the larger the seed onion, the greater the loss through unwanted shoots. The row interval should be 10 in, with an interval of 3 in. within a row. Set the onions only about ½ in. deep in the soil; in other words, the neck of the onion must be visible.

The space between onion rows can be utilized by planting a row of red radishes.

292 A slightly later date can be selected for growing seed onions themselves.

The best time for seeding is between late March and early April. Only special seed onion varieties should be used for this purpose. The row interval should be 8 in. The resulting dense stand ensures that the onions remain small and the leaves die off earlier.

293 Sandy loam or loamy sand soils with plenty of humus are the best for growing tarragon.

The plants, which grow to a height of up to 5 ft., need a sunny, sheltered site. A distinction is made between Russian and fragrant or French tarragon. Russian tarragon is more robust, but less spicy, and can be propagated from seed; French tarragon, meanwhile, is more aromatic and can be propagated only through division.

294 Since one or two tarragon plants are generally sufficient for a household, it is best to obtain plants through separating them, or through advance planting.

These are planted in late March or early April at intervals of 16 × 16 in. and watered well. If using seed, sow directly on site, and thin out the stand later to the above planting width. The plant will later require a standing area of 10 sq. ft. French and Russian tarragon are different in flavor.

295 Chervil is not very cold sensitive and can be planted outdoors from as early as mid- to late March.

The soil should be loose and moderately moist. If sowing is to be done in March, select a sunny site. Sow the seeds very sparsely, ¼ to ½ in. deep, with a row interval of 6 to 8 in., and always keep the soil uniformly moist. To ensure a continuous harvest, subsequent sowing is necessary every two to three weeks until mid-August. From May, semi-shaded sites are preferable to ensure early flower development.

296 In mid- to late March, sow garlic in situations with full sun.

For planting, parts of the bulb, the cloves, are used. Accordingly, the bulbs should not be divided until just before planting. Note that large cloves also tend to develop larger bulbs. The row interval is 8 to 10 in. Within a row, plant the cloves at intervals of 4 to 6 in., and about 2 to 2 ½ in. deep. If using brood bulbs, a planting depth of around 1 ½ in. will be sufficient.

297 Garlic prefers nutrient-rich, deep soils that are not too light.

It belongs in the second position in a crop rotation and has much the same nutrient requirements as yellow onions. It needs relatively little water. While in the spring it is helpful to maintain the soil moisture as constant as possible, in the fall the soil should be dry

and warm to enable the bulbs to ripen better. Garlic does not tolerate waterlogging.

298 True lavender thrives on deep, humic, slightly calciferous soils with good drainage.

The site should receive full sun and be sheltered from the wind. Lavender does not tolerate fresh organic fertilizer. To raise the plants yourself, sow seeds in March in a heated cold frame or in seed bowls on the windowsill. The seedlings will emerge in two to three weeks. It is better to buy ready young plants and plant them from late March to early April at an interval of 12 in.

299 Thick horseradish stems can be grown only in deep, humic sandy soils that warm up quickly in spring.

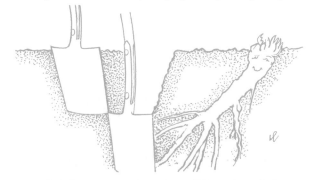

Here, it is important that the soil has already been worked to a considerable depth in the fall, and that plenty of humus in the form of peat or good compost and hoof and horn meal has been mixed in. Horseradish needs uniform moisture levels and plenty of space, which means that it is best planted at the edge of the garden where it cannot be crowded out by other plants.

300 For planting horseradish, which should be done during March, root cuttings are needed that appear in the fall when harvesting the thick stems.

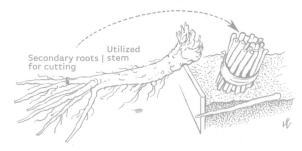

The root cuttings are about ½ in. thick secondary roots that are too thin to be used for eating. These are overwintered in sand, in the cellar, but are also available from specialist dealers.

301 Prepare the root cuttings for planting horseradish by removing all the lateral roots and rootlets.

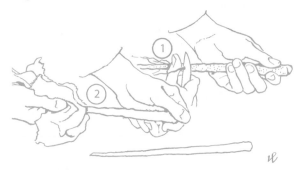

All the lateral shoots should be cut off cleanly without damaging the root cuttings themselves. In order to remove even the smallest rootlets, thoroughly rub the cuttings clean using a rag.

302 Horseradish root cuttings are always planted in the soil at an angle of about 30°, rather than vertically.

The angled planting makes the work to be done on the horseradish stems in the summer much easier, ▸ **TIP 851** while also greatly promoting growth. Plant the root cuttings in a row at an interval of 12 in.; the heads of the cuttings should be flush with the soil surface.

303 Sage prefers calciferous, highly permeable, and humic soil.

Waterlogging and fresh organic fertilizer are not tolerated. If the soil is too heavy, loosen it by adding sand and plenty of compost. Select a sunny, sheltered site. Since only a few plants are needed for domestic use, and growing seed always results in a mixture of different sage forms, it is better to obtain pregrown or divided plants. A planting width of 16 × 16 in. is required; do not plant the plants any deeper than they were before.

304 A dry, sunny place is best for growing thyme.

A rock garden or a dry slope, for example, makes a good site. Calciferous, loamy-sandy soils with a normal humus content are desirable. Thyme grows poorly on moist, heavy soils, and the plant also loses its spicy flavor.

Sow thyme in small pots in late March and cover with only a thin layer of soil, since it needs light for germination. Put the pots in a cold frame or on the windowsill and keep only moderately moist. Since not many plants are required, in this case, too, it is easier to obtain young or divided-up plants. They need a planting width of 8 × 8 in.

305 All perennial aromatic herbs that have been growing for at least one year need fertilizer in March before they produce new shoots, and should be cut back.

Here, it is best to use complete fertilizer, which is simply applied dry between the herbs. Around 1 oz. is needed per square yard of cultivated land. Hoe in the fertilizer, and water the prepared land thoroughly.

ORNAMENTAL PLANTS

Ornamental Gardens

306 As soon as the ground in March is frost-free, remove (or at least loosen) winter protection from perennials.

Take care not to damage any new shoots that are already present; meanwhile, remove diseased and died-off plant parts. Leave the covering material itself nearby in case heavier frosts are still to come.

307 For rose bushes, the heaped-up earth that was used as frost protection should be removed during the final third of March. On exposed sites, it is best to wait longer.

When removing the earth heaps, the soil must be completely frost-free, since otherwise shoots may be damaged.

308 Bent-over stem roses should be removed from the earth in late March, but they should remain bent over.

If this task is carried out too late, the buds will have produced shoots, and will break off easily.

> *Roses must be pruned correctly to ensure plentiful flowering and long flower stalks.*

309 Annual pruning back of roses should be done after following the advice given in TIP 307 and TIP 308.

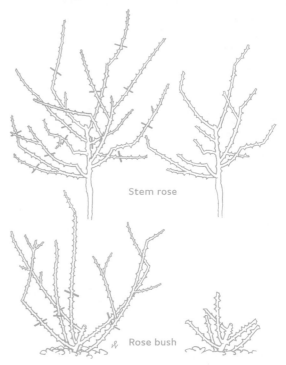

Stem rose

Rose bush

Roses bloom predominantly from shoots that develop on shoots of the previous year. To attain vigorous young shoots with beautiful flowers, prune back the plants quite severely. Weakly growing shoots should be pruned back to three, and vigorously growing shoots to five or six vigorous buds. Remove all weak shoots. The plant interior must not be allowed to become too dense. For climbing roses, see ▶ TIP 552.

310 If planting new roses, preparations should be made in March.

Deep loosening of the soil to a depth of two spade cuts is helpful. Since roses will grow for many years, improve the soil with humus substances such as rotted stable manure or compost earth. Work these into the upper parts of the loosened soil only, since humus will acidify if too little oxygen is present. In mild situations, roses can already be planted in March.

311 Roses are classified according to their use in the garden.

Gardeners distinguish between roses based primarily on their use. There are noble roses, climbing roses, bed roses, dwarf roses, shrub roses, and wild roses. Noble, climbing, bed, and dwarf roses can be trained as stem or standard roses. Cascade roses (around 55 in. high) are climbing roses grafted onto a stem; half-standard roses (around 24 in. high) are dwarf roses grafted onto a stem; and standard roses (around 35 in. high) are bed or noble roses grafted onto a stem.

312 Before buying roses, it is important to consider how they will be used.

Noble roses, also known as hybrid tea roses, generally bear single, "nobly" formed, often wonderfully fragrant blossoms on mostly long stalks. These are highly suitable for use in vases, bouquets, or as single flowers. Climbing roses are vigorously growing varieties that need a stable climbing support. Bed roses flower both long and frequently, and mostly in flower heads. They are robust and long lived, compact, low, bushy in form, and highly suitable for group plantings. Dwarf roses grow about 12 in. high and are often planted in containers. Shrub roses reach a height of up to 6 ½ ft., are very robust, and, as a rule, are not trimmed. These days, lower-growing varieties are also bred. Shrub roses have flowers with the character of noble roses (these are often nostalgic varieties), and they will flower again repeatedly throughout the summer. By contrast, wild roses have simple, single flowers that appear only once in the early summer. They are suitable for both large gardens and hedge planting and offer a veritable paradise for birds and wild bees. Their fruits, rose hips, have many uses in cooking.

313 The right variety is crucial.

In the rosary or tree nursery, and in the pages of catalogs, all roses tend to look beautiful. However, for those wanting to plant roses in their own gardens, feelings of joy over the anticipated flowers can quickly turn to annoyance. Either the plant does not bloom at all, or the flowers are not as appealing as they appear in the photographs, and the leaves seem to be diseased. In such cases, this is because the wrong variety has been selected. When buying roses, it is essential to buy only those varieties that are resistant to diseases, especially black spot and mildew, as well as pests. A list of healthy roses is given in **TABLE 13**.

314 In rose beds, it is important match colors and plant heights appropriately.

Roses come in many different colors, with multicolored, red, pink, orange, salmon, yellow, and white varieties. Red- and pink-flowering varieties go together well, as do white roses with salmon- or orange-flowering varieties. Take care, however, since the orange or salmon colors generally do not mix well with pink- and red-flowering varieties.

315 In mild weather, winter jasmine (*Jasminum nudiflorum*) may flower as early as February.

In very mild winters, it may even flower occasionally in late December. It is best planted at the south side of a wall, so that it is protected from harsh winter winds, and somewhere where its vivid yellow flowers can be admired from a warm living room. These appear before the leaf shoots. It is unsuitable for heavy loam or calciferous soils. Here, it is necessary to improve the soil, for example with a mixture of humic garden earth, or compost and sand.

316 The climbing hydrangea (*Hydrangea anomala*) can be used to plant up walls and building faces even in the shade.

This attractive, slow-growing climbing shrub is seen all too seldom. It can also climb tree trunks, or be used as a ground cover in the shade. It is important for the plant that the soil is damp to moist. The distinctive white flower heads appear in June/July. The leaves turn an attractive yellow in the fall, while the reddish brown shoots are decorative in winter. Spring pruning promotes branching development. On damaged walls (cracks and crevices), hydrangeas can cause damage with their holdfasts (rhizoids).

> *Hedges not only make good screens, they also are important homes for birds and small animals.*

317 Hedges (except for conifer trees and shrubs) can also be planted in the spring as soon as the soil is frost-free.

The best time is between mid-March and early April. Water freshly planted hedges generously and often. On establishing hedges, see ▶ **TIP 1267** to ▶ **TIP 1276**. A distinction is made between freestanding and trimmed hedges. For the former, there is a large selection of beautifully flowering shrubs and low trees, while for trimmed hedges, privet (*Ligustrum*) or common hornbeam (*Carpinus betulus*) is generally used. A list of suitable trees and shrubs is given in **TABLE 11**.

318 Deciduous ornamental shrubs can be planted on frost-free soils in March.

Deciduous trees and shrubs are generally planted in October, but those planted in March will generally also grow well. Sensitive shrubs such as butterfly bush (*Buddleja*), Warminster broom (*Cytisus ×praecox*), and St. John's wort (*Hypericum*), or the climbing and creeping clematis (*Clematis*), birthwort (*Aristolochia*), silver lace vine or Russian vine (*Fallopia baldschuanica*, syn. *Polygonum aubertii*), and wisteria (*Wisteria*) are best planted in March, or, in unfavorable weather or on exposed sites, also from April. Particular points to be noted are given in ▶ **TIP 1279** to ▶ **TIP 1282**.

319 Attractive ornamental trees and shrubs are listed in **TABLE 9**; here are just a few general suggestions.

Already in the early spring, we can admire the vivid golden-yellow flowers of the forsythia (*Forsythia*)—this plant belongs in every garden. Garland flower (*Daphne cneorum*), witch hazel (*Hamamelis*), and winter jasmine (*Jasmimum nudiflorum*) flower even earlier. Lilac (*Syringa*) is a must in the garden, as is the summer-flowering mock orange (*Philadelphus*), with its delightful fragrance, or fruiting barberries (*Berberis*). Plants that are attractive in larger gardens include golden chain or golden rain tree (*Laburnum*), magnolia (*Magnolia*), and tamarisk (*Tamarix*). Climbing and twining woody plants should also not be forgotten. Ivy (*Hedera*) and climbing hydrangea (*Hydrangea anomala* subsp. *petiolaris*) are also options for shady sites, while wisteria (*Wisteria*) and Virginia creeper (*Parthenocissus*) love sun. The roots of clematis (*Clematis*), meanwhile, need shade. Silver lace vine or Russian vine (*Fallopia baldschuanica*, syn. *Polygonum aubertii*) will cover large areas very quickly.

320 Following winters with low precipitation, rhododendrons and other evergreen broad-leaved trees and shrubs should be watered strongly.

For all rhododendrons, the soil in the root zone and beyond should always be moist right through. This also applies to other evergreen broad-leaved species such as holly (*Ilex*), cherry laurel (*Prunus laurocerasus*), and mountain laurel (*Kalmia latifolia*). Give the soil as much water as it can take; repeat the watering four or five times at intervals of around one hour. This can also be combined with fertilizer application. For the final watering, a complete fertilizer solution can be added to the water. The fertilizer can also be scattered dry on the ground and hoed in. For rhododendrons, the fertilizer must not contain any lime. Commercially available special fertilizers are best.

321 Old mahonias should be cut back occasionally, preferably in March.

For mahonia bushes to be well shaped, they should be heavily cut back from time to time, with all shoots cut to around 8 in. However, they will not develop flowers or fruit in the first subsequent year. Mahonias are highly suitable for shady sites, as underplanting for freestanding hedges, for example. With their evergreen, glossy leaves, they make dense "living fences" all year round. They also delight us with their splendid golden-yellow flowers and blue-striped fruits. These slow-growing shrubs can also be used as tub plants. ▶ TIP 1188

322
In late March, planting perennials for flowering in summer or later can begin. At this time, they can also be divided and transplanted.

Spring-flowering plants should be left undisturbed or their flowering will be jeopardized. Perennials that have grown too large should be dug up without damaging their roots. When dividing the plants, each resulting partial plant should have a healthy head with several shoots. Trim the roots a little and immediately return the plant sections to the soil so that they are not exposed to drying air for any length of time. When planting, it should be noted that perennials, too, are prone to the effects of soil exhaustion. ▶ TIP 73 Accordingly, no plants of the same genus should be planted again in the same spot.

323
It is crucial that dense, large perennials that have occupied a site for a long time be divided when transplanting.

The resulting partial plants will grow well and produce many flowers. Large, undivided perennials will generally struggle, and produce fewer and smaller flowers.

324
Divided-up parts of the plant should not be combined with the rhizomes of perennial weeds.

Otherwise, the new planting site will quickly become infested with weeds. In particular, it is important to watch out for the rhizomes of couch grass and bindweed. Young plants of these species will develop very quickly from every piece of rhizome. Accordingly, every divided-up part of the perennial should be examined carefully first.

325
Columbine (*Aquilegia*), sea holly (*Eryngium*), lupine (*Lupinus*), and pincushion flower (*Scabiosa*) are difficult to propagate by division.

The taproots have hardly any fibrous roots on their heads, which makes the divided-up plants more difficult to grow. Only planting securely in place and providing constant moisture will lead to root development. It is best not to divide columbine, but to raise young plants from seed instead. Sea holly can be propagated through root cuttings, which are nevertheless best bought from specialists.

326
In rock gardens, check all plants for frost damage and replant affected areas.

Weak plants should also be removed. Divide or cut back vigorously growing plants that are crowding out their neighbors. If the plants are removed with their root balls, they can be grouped together. For this, the soil should be moist. Be sure to water the plants afterward.

327
Dry stone walls should be built by the end of March so that they will not be planted up too late.

If preparations for building dry stone walls have already been taken care of in February, ▶ TIP 212, it should not take long to put them up.

Dry stone walls with richly flowering alpine plants brighten up every garden.

328
The thickness of a dry stone wall is primarily dependent on the wall's height.

The thickness should be around one third of the height, but not less than 10 in., so that the roots of plants can also penetrate backward into the joints. This thickness refers to the base of the wall; however,

it should not taper off too much from bottom to top.
▶ TIP 212 and ▶ TIP 213

329 Dry stone walls can also be built where there are no changes in levels.

Here, the wall must generally remain low, but it will still always be appealing. Use it to define the boundary of a garden or to provide a seating corner. Alongside a path, it should be possible to plant up both sides, and it should be very low.

330 Water should not be allowed to collect behind a dry stone wall.

The space behind the foundation, ▶ TIP 212, and the lowest stone layer should be filled with coarse gravel or broken stones. Otherwise, freezing water could push the wall in.

331 In dry stone walls, only the soil in the joints is available for the plants to utilize.

The stones are laid without mortar in nutrient-rich sandy loam soil. The soil must be moist, but not too wet, since otherwise it will lie too closely. The joints should be about 1 in. thick, or a little wider in low dry

stone walls, so that the plants have sufficient earth. The horizontal layers are best laid stone on stone, and the hollow spaces filled with earth.

332 Dry stone walls are built with a slight backward lean.

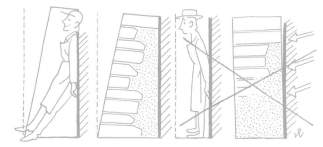

For a 24 in. high dry stone wall, a backward lean from the vertical of 2 ½ in. is sufficient. This means that the pressure of the earth on the wall will be withstood better, while rainwater will also be able to penetrate the joints and reach the plant roots.

333 The transverse joints in a dry stone wall run in parallel, while longitudinal joints are staggered.

Use stones of around the same thickness for each layer. ▶ TIP 213 The stones of the individual layers can be of different thicknesses, but uniformly thick layers look better. Stone slabs about 4 to 5 in. thick are the most suitable for use in low walls.

334 The dry stone wall must be properly in contact with the earth behind it.

To achieve this, lay a long stone with its narrow side facing forward. This means it will penetrate deep into the earth, ensuring good contact with the earth and stability. Fill in the free cavity behind the wall with the excavated soil from the foundation, and tamp firm so that the soil will not settle further afterward.

335 Ideally, the dry stone wall should be planted up as soon as it has been erected.

Accordingly, the plants will need to be available in good time, and it must already be clear where they will be planted. For this, a plan will need to be drawn up first, showing where each genus and species will be planted. Perennials that are planted when the wall is constructed will grow better than those planted later.

336 Plants with small root balls are the most suitable for planting for dry stone walls during construction.

The small earth balls should be pressed as flat as the gap width in the wall will allow, while protecting the roots. The place where a vertical gap meets with a horizontal one is usually the most suitable place for planting. Press the plants as deep into the gap as they had been before in the pot. Then press moist earth into the root balls so that the plants will be firmly in place. Careful watering is required. It should be noted that many plants develop very large cushions. In order that the stones make a proper impact as well, no more than six plants should be planted per square yard of wall area.

337 Greater changes in level make it necessary to build steps.

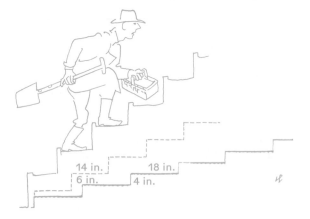

These should be comfortable to walk on. Accordingly, the step height should not be more than 6 in.; 4 to 5 in. is better. Their height also determines their width (stair run). With a step height of 6 in., a width of around 14 in. is sufficient, while for a height of 4 to 5 in., a width of 18 or 16 in., respectively, is usual.

338 The stringers can be designed as dry stone walls or banks.

If there are only a few steps, a bank will be necessary, which is best sown with grass. A small rock garden can also be planted. ▶ TIP 346 and ▶ TIP 347

339 When laying the steps, set the bottom one especially firmly in place.

Well-developed loam soils usually do not require a foundation; tamping in broken stone is generally sufficient for other soil types. Insert the remaining steps in the same way, and ensure they are set firmly in place with no wobbling.

340 Steps should not be set exactly horizontally.

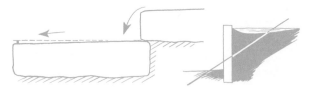

There must be a gradient toward the front of about 4 percent. It must not be possible for rainwater to pool.

341 Steps, dry stone walls, and paved paths should always be built using the same stone type.

This is especially the case if the above construction types are all adjacent to one another—they should form a coherent unit.

342 All stone types are suitable for paving stones.

Sandstone or limestone slabs that are about 2 in. thick are the best of all, but paving stones should always be of one stone type only, 16 to 24 in. in size. The average stride of 24 in. also indicates the optimal distance from center to center. Pathways are laid particularly in grassed areas and beds planted with perennials. In grassed areas such as lawns, lay the slabs slightly below the ground surface so that they will not impede mowing. In perennial beds, however, they should be slightly raised above the surface so that they will always remain clean. Always set the slabs themselves firmly in place.

A pathway set in the grass invites you to take a walk into a world of green.

The slabs are aligned to match a stride of about 24 in.

24 in.   24 in.   24 in.

Right

Wrong

Incorporation of the lawn in the path—paved pathway with the path borders running in parallel.

Typical mistakes:
More than three corners meet one another.
The smallest pieces are smaller than a hand.

Paved pathway without grass joints (firmly laid).

Using bricks, clinker bricks, and artificial stones, attractive patterning can be introduced for the pathway.

Be careful when using combinations—ensure that the stones match one another in terms of their form and color.

343 When laying paving slabs, a hammer or mallet and a spirit level are required.

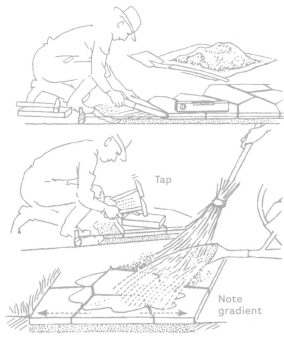

Tap

Note gradient

Paths with a closed paving structure should have a sand bed 4 in. deep.

All the slabs must be laid flat; only wide, closed paths made from regular paving slabs are tipped slightly so that rainwater will run off. If need be, a lining of sand can be added underneath, but in any case the slabs should not be hammered too hard in case they break. To avoid breakage, place a short piece of board on the slab to be hammered.

344 For regular paving, use slabs of concrete, brick, or artificial stones.

In the garden, these are best laid dry. In order that they lie firmly, they should have a lining or base layer of about 1 to 2 in. of sand; with closed paving and a loose substrate, the base can be up to 4 in. thick and the elements laid right up against one another with narrow joints. If using different stones or colors, the combinations need to be considered very carefully. After laying, sweep and wash away the sand between the joints. On edging see ▸ **TIP 160**.

345 Where terrain in the garden is to be raised or soil removed, any trees that are already present should be dealt with accordingly.

If earth is to be filled in, the tree trunks should not be covered up, since otherwise the trees will die from a lack of air. If earth is to be removed, the earth beneath the crown in the tree's drip zone should remain at the existing level and be enclosed by a wall. The earth can be transported away beforehand.

346 A rock garden can be used to overcome differences in levels.

A rock garden can also be designed on level ground, and even on the smallest scale. It needs only to blend in harmoniously with the overall design; for example, it should not be situated under trees, and it should not end up as a heap of rocks with just a few weakly growing plants. As a transition to a heath garden, ▸ TIP 355, or a swamp pool as a wetland biotope, ▸ TIP 353, a rock garden can provide an accent in the garden in much the same way as a staircase or a paved pathway.

347 In addition to rocks, suitable earth is needed for the rock garden plants.

As a rule, only one rock type is used. ▸ TIP 213 and ▸ TIP 331 If only different types of rock are available, they should not be mixed, but instead arranged in groups. Add humus to the existing soil; in loam soils, mix in sand to improve the soil structure. Compost earth is very suitable for this. If there are places to be occupied by heath plants, an acidic, humic substrate is required. Since many rock garden plants thrive on lime, limestone rocks should also be present.

348 The substrate for a rock garden must be thoroughly prepared.

If a grassed area is available, and if earth is to be filled in, it is crucial to remove the grass cover, since otherwise it will act as an insulating layer. Loosen the soil to a considerable depth (if possible, two spade cuts deep) to promote good rainwater seepage.

Rock gardens are a paradise for plant collectors and flower enthusiasts.

349 A rock garden should not be designed to look like a molehill or plant hillock.

A rock garden should imitate nature. In addition to steep walls, similar to a dry stone wall, plan shallow depressions, miniature gorges, and spreading mats. In this way, a diverse range of sites for special plants will be created, which will ensure that they grow and flower particularly well. ▸ TIP 352 See the sketch for building such a plant hillock with good drainage (page 88).

350 Basic rock garden construction should begin as soon as the soil is frost-free.

Stones for dry stone walls, ▸ TIP 213, are also suitable for rock gardens. They should be incorporated with their flat side facing down. Only larger stones should occasionally be laid individually. Grouping the rocks together is effective. Slightly flattened-off stones stacked one on top of the other in homogeneous layers correspond to layers of stones in nature. Arrange them horizontally, or, even better, slightly tilted. This will provide many opportunities for planting. ▸ TIP 352 "Found" and rounded stones can also be used to great effect. However, they must never stand upright, but instead always lie on their broadest side, and slightly embedded in the ground.

351 A properly drained soil and substrate is necessary for good plant growth in rock gardens.

Many rock garden species grow wild in rock crevices or on rock fell-field ground; only a few species will tolerate waterlogging or constantly wet soils. Accordingly, lay a layer of water-permeable material, such as coarse gravel, beneath the plant substrate.

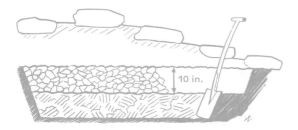

352 **Rock gardens can be planted up in late March, or also later if the plants have root balls.**

The smaller the rock garden, the lower growing the perennials should be. Plants should preferably be flowering in several different places at all times of the year. Plants with root balls will continue to grow undisturbed, but divided-up plants—excluding those with taproots—will generally grow well after frequent watering. Leopard's bane (*Doronicum*) and asters (*Aster alpinus* and *A. dumosus*) can be replanted at this time, for example, without affecting their later flowering. Cushion herbs especially should be used extensively, but bulb and tuber plants should not be forgotten. Particularly for larger areas, low and creeping trees and shrubs, such as Alison or madwort (*Alyssum*), bearberry cotoneaster (*Cotoneaster dammeri*), or hedge veronica (*Hebe*), but also wintergreen false cypresses, such as *Chamaecyparis obtusa* 'Nana Gracilis', have a special appeal. These plants are listed together with their soil requirements in **TABLE 12** and **TABLE 17**. (See illustration on page 88.)

353 **A wetland biotope (swamp pool) can also be established in small gardens.**

In frost-free weather, construction can already begin in March. A commercially available plastic pool is highly suitable for this purpose. However, it is also possible, in the envisaged size, to excavate a hollow around 20 in. deep with shallow, tapering edges. So the water does not drain into the substrate too quickly, place a 2 ½ in. (or, better still, 3 to 4 in.) loam layer over the bed and tamp it in firm. Pond foil sheeting can also be used as an impervious layer. Humic earth should be used as a substrate, and filled flush with the level of the garden, perhaps with the center slightly depressed. Planting can begin in late March.

> *There are flowering rhododendrons for every temperate garden, but be sure to take note of their need for acidic soils.*

354 **Rhododendrons and some other trees and shrubs need acidic soils.**

Rhododendrons, hydrangeas, astilbes, many heather species, and other base-intolerant plants do not grow in limestone areas. They need specially prepared acidic soils, and can be set in a planting ditch, corresponding to the size of the plant, not less than 20 to 24 in. long or wide, or 12 to 14 in. deep. A container with perforated walls, with an acidic substrate in which the plant grows, set into the earth, is also suitable. In dry periods, the soil moisture level will then be more constant as a result. Commercially available rhododendron potting soil is suitable as a substrate.

355 **A well-designed heath garden is something special.**

The design will be dependent on the soil type and situation. Heath plants do not tolerate calciferous soils, and they demand a sunny site. Sandy humus soils or humic sandy soils are ideal, as is heath soil from the garden center. On frost-free soils, this work can already begin in February. Balled transplants can be incorporated in late March. Improve the design by using stepping-stones, and, depending on the size of the feature, groups of different grasses and columnar junipers. A heath garden combined with a wetland biotope or swamp pool, ▸ **TIP 353**, or with a group of rhododendrons, ▸ **TIP 354**, or a rock garden is especially attractive.

THE ROCK GARDEN

A heap of rocks does not (yet) constitute a "rock garden."

Take particular note of "undesirable rocks". . .

. . . or natural groupings!

Angled stones placed on their ends look unnatural.

Rocks that are too small will soon be overgrown, and will have no impact.

Unimaginative.

Angular rocks are suitable for architectural rock gardens (such as dry stone walls).

"Jagged alpine look" in rank and file.

Naturalness.

We use round stones for "natural" rock gardens.

The rocks lie "naturally" on the massif, and generally lie one on top of the other.

Establishing a rock garden

If laid correctly, none of the stones can fall down.

This will ensure that the rock garden receives full sun.

Sunny and shady sides.

This will ensure that more shade-loving plants will grow in the rock garden.

In general, larger blocks are set at the foot of the rock garden.

A large rock on top of a hillock can either grace a rock garden or spoil the effect entirely.

Earth consisting of one part each of loam, river sand, and fine scoria.

Building rubble, river gravel, or road gravel.

River sand with a grain size of $\frac{1}{16}$ to $\frac{1}{8}$ in. to prevent washing out.

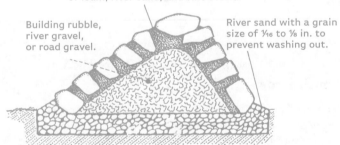

Steps to the Hanging Gardens of Babylon?

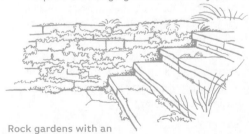

Rock gardens with an architectural character can be enchanting.

> *The sundial—a garden highlight, an ornament, and a timepiece in one.*

356 A sundial in the garden will indicate the correct time only in full sun.

It must not be shaded from any side, and is most effective when erected on a lawn, accessible by paving stones. It can also be a focal point in a rock garden.

357 If a sundial is to show the correct time, it needs to be set up by a professional.

Since the indicator (gnomon) needs to be parallel to the earth's axis, an exact calculation is required for the location in question. The dial may be set up horizontally, vertically, or tilted.

> *Pools and waterfalls are attractive features in the garden.*

358 For aquatic plant pools or a garden pond, any earthworks should be completed in good time.

To look after aquatic plants, a pool with a water depth of 12 to 16 in. is sufficient. Fish will also thrive in such a pool during the warmer time of the year. If fish are to remain in the pool during winter, the water depth must be at least 32 in., and reeds or other material should be used to ensure adequate aeration or ice-free places.

359 First of all, the site, shape, and size of the pool need to be considered.

The site should be selected so that the pool gets five to six hours of sun during the day. Additionally, it should not be situated near any large trees, because leaves falling in the water could affect the water

WATER POOL FOR PLANTS, WITH FLAT BANKS

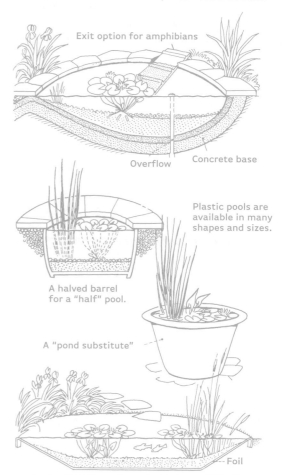

Exit option for amphibians

Overflow   Concrete base

Plastic pools are available in many shapes and sizes.

A halved barrel for a "half" pool.

A "pond substitute"

An "artificial" small pond with "natural" banks.

Foil

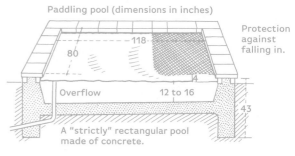

Paddling pool (dimensions in inches)

118

80

Overflow   12 to 16

4

43

Protection against falling in.

A "strictly" rectangular pool made of concrete.

A paddling pool is often much easier to construct than a pond.

Such an "artificial puddle" is a delight for children.

quality. The choice between a rectangular form or that of a natural pool will depend on the character of the garden. A rectangular pool is suitable for a strictly architecturally designed garden, while a naturally shaped pool might be best for a large natural garden. Garden ponds should not be too small. As a basic rule, the larger the pond, the more easily a natural equilibrium will be established, and maintenance requirements will be minimized.

360 A near-natural garden pond is a refuge for native flora and fauna.

A garden pond is an important habitat for native plants and animals; native plants can also establish on the pond's banks. Swamp plants are often commercially available as well. In many garden ponds, however, the pond banks are just as dry or moist as the surroundings. Swamp plants need a constantly moist substrate. It is also possible to design the pond so that it includes swamp-like zones. Commercially available plastic pools often have several zones of different depths. At one place at least, the water should be more than 32 in. deep so that fish or other small animals will be able to overwinter in frost-free conditions.

361 Aquatic plants will supply the pond with the necessary oxygen.

Without enough aquatic plants, there will not be a natural equilibrium in the garden pond. Native aquatic plants such as common water moss (*Fontinalis antipyretica*), mare's tail (*Hippuris vulgaris*), soft hornwort or tropical hornwort (*Ceratophyllum submersum*), round-leaved water crowfoot (*Ranunculus circinatus*), yellow water lily, yellow pond lily, or brandy bottle (*Nuphar lutea*), and of course pondweeds (*Potamogeton*), **TABLE 19**, are important oxygen producers. Use dense and fast-growing aquatic plants sparingly. Otherwise, it's preferable to use a few select aquatic plants, rather than too many different ones.

362 Fish, amphibians, aquatic insects, and other animals are at home in the garden pond.

Without the presence of fish, too many mosquito larvae in the garden pond will develop to adulthood. The selected fish should not be too large, and should be native species such as the bitterling (*Rhodeus amarus*),

belica (*Leucaspius delineatus*), or nine-spined stickleback (*Pungitius pungitius*). They do not need to be fed constantly, and a pond filter and pump are also unnecessary. Newts, frogs, or toads do not need to be introduced; as a rule, they will become established themselves if the conditions are right. Some of these animals take part in combating pests in the garden; for example, newts devour snails and insect larvae. Dragonflies are not poisonous, nor do they sting or bite humans; they are very useful and help eradicate mosquitoes and aphids. Their larvae develop in the water.

363 Paddling pools for children.

The most suitable paddling pools for children are commercially available inflatable pools made of plastic. These are easy to clean and can be emptied or filled with water as required. Children should not use planted-up pools or near-natural ponds for play, so as not to disturb the ponds' biological equilibrium.

364 Digging a hole for the pond with a spade or shovel requires a considerable physical effort that should not be underestimated.

For larger pools, the basic earthworks are best done with the aid of a small dredger. Use the excavated earth for a protective wall on the weather-exposed side (north, northwest), or for establishing a rock garden. If necessary, it may need to be transported away.

365 Although many now choose to install prefabricated plastic pools, you can also build your own pool.

Foil, roofing felt, or loam or clay can be used for a waterproof lining. Calculate the material requirements from the area to be covered. If roofing felt is used, at least two layers will be required; additionally, the individual layers must overlap one another by at least 4 in. When installing the lining, glue the overlapping edges together, and glue the second layer crosswise over the first. Foil is welded together. Clinker brick stones laid lengthwise or natural stones can be used for the bank edges. For lining with clay, the layer must be 6 in. thick. Water pools can also be made of concrete, and potentially also lined with tiles, if so desired. If natural soil is to be spread over the bottom of the pool, this will need to be done before the pool is filled with water. Allow the water to flow gently over a board so the earth will not be stirred up.

366 Garden pond with a foil lining.

After digging the hole for the pond, smooth off the base and clear it of any stones, roots, or other objects. Then cover with a 2 in. thick layer of fine sand, followed by the sheet of special foil, spread out smoothly. The lengths of sheeting are welded together and the seams sealed. Securely fasten the foil at the edges, dig it in, and cover with stones.

THE HOMEMADE GARDEN POND

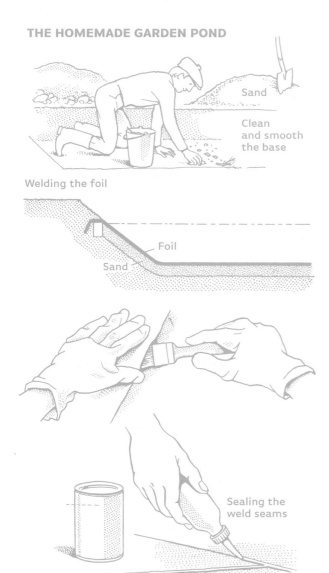

Sand

Clean and smooth the base

Welding the foil

Foil

Sand

Sealing the weld seams

367 Depending on the circumstances, the water pool can be lined with clay.

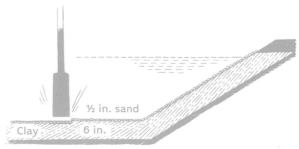

½ in. sand

Clay   6 in.

This procedure is suitable only if there is a clay source nearby. The clay must be uniformly moistened so that it can be tamped firmly without sticking to the tamp itself. The clay layer must be 6 in. thick. Form the bank edges in the same way as when using foil. ▶ **TIP 366** The clay layer is covered with a ½ in. thick layer of coarse sand, which is hammered into the upper clay layer. This may need to be premoistened.

368 If required, a water outlet can also be provided.

If the water needs to be replenished from time to time, or perhaps drained in the fall, a water outlet can be installed at the deepest place in the pond. A submersible pump can perform the same function. In larger ponds, a biological equilibrium is generally established, so that emptying the pond is unnecessary, and water is added only if required.

369 Stepped ponds can be designed in accordance with nature.

In the middle, there is a deep-water zone for fish. This is followed by a shallow zone for plants and small water lilies, as well as a swamp zone for plants that tolerate waterlogging. In very small pools, it is sufficient when the edge zones taper off flat. For aquatic plant pools with a vertical edge, consider an exit option for small animals.

370 Aquatic plants can also be placed in the pool in containers.

Shallow baskets made of wire or plastic can serve as a plant container. Fill these up to 2 in. from the rim with earth with sand mixed in. After planting (see **TABLE 19** and **TABLE 20**) cover the earth with sand. However, it will also be completely adequate if the aquatic plants are set only in (non-calciferous) gravel without earth. Over time, sediment will fill the interstitial spaces, and mud will form, containing sufficient nutrients.

2 in.

371 Clean existing ponds in late March and check whether they are still watertight.

Remove the frost protection materials that have been applied to emptied ponds in the fall and use as mulch for trees and shrubs or compost them. Only after thorough cleaning are the ponds carefully refilled with water, which should be allowed to run over a board.

372 In late March, the newly constructed wetland biotope (swamp pool) is ready for planting up.

The selection of swamp plants, **TABLE 19**, is dependent on the size of the biotope. For very small pools, use low-growing plants only (no tall ones) such as the yellow-flowering marsh marigold (*Caltha palustris*). For swamp pools with an area of around 10 sq. ft. or greater, flag iris or yellow flag (*Iris pseudacorus*) is suitable.

373 Remove frost protection materials from wetland biotopes (swamp pools).

If the wetland biotope has been protected against frost in the fall, the materials can be removed in late March.

Songbirds, attracted by bird-baths, bring joy into the garden and help eradicate pests.

374 Birdbaths should be cleaned and filled with water in March.

Bowls, flat natural stones with a hollow, a small pool with stones, or a custom-made birdbath of variable depth can all be used. Position the birdbaths so the birds will notice any approaching cats in good time. Suitable places include the corners or ends of terraces and dry stone walls.

375 Summer flowers that require advance planting should be sown in an unheated cold frame from mid-March.

In particular, these include snapdragons (*Antirrhinum*), China asters (*Callistephus*), marigolds (*Tagetes*), zinnias (*Zinnia*), and straw daisies (*Xerochrysum*). Avoid sowing the seeds too closely together so that the plants can develop well. Each plant needs a planting width of about ¾ × ¾ in. If they are any closer together than this, they should be thinned out. Cover the seeds with a layer of sand or earth as thick as a seed and lightly press them in. Keep the seedbed moist until the seeds germinate. Afterward, water carefully or the seedlings may suffer from root fungi. Watering should take place only if the soil surface can quickly dry out again on sunny days if the cold frame is ventilated.

376 Annual climbing plants, such as cup-and-saucer vine (*Cobaea scandens*) and morning glory (*Ipomoea*) are sown in pots in mid-March.

Lay three or four seeds slightly covered in sandy compost earth in 3 ½ to 4 in. pots, which are best placed in a light window in a warm room. In heated cold frames, ▸ **TIP 174** and ▸ **TIP 175**, the pots are embedded in the soil. Keep the pot soil constantly moist until the seeds germinate. Other attractive annual climbing plants

BIRDBATHS

Establish birdbaths out in the open, and not behind hedges.

Birdbath hollowed out of sandstone.

Recessed pool with stones for birds to perch on.

Through a diagonally designed base, the feathered bathing guests can choose their own water depth.

A bathing pool made out of concrete, and not round or rectangular.

Homemade birdbath

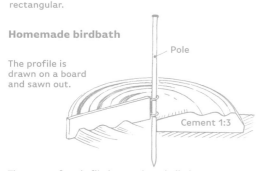

The profile is drawn on a board and sawn out.

Pole

Cement 1:3

The cut surface is filed smooth and oiled well prior to use. The template is turned around a central pole.

that should be treated in the same way include gloxinias or creeping snapdragons (*Asarina*), with crimson to purple-red flowers, lighter on the inside, and also white, pink, or blue-violet; black-eyed Susan (*Thunbergia alata*) with its typical vivid orange petals and dark "eye," and new breeds with white, light yellow, and orange-brown petals, with or without an eye; and glory flowers (*Eccremocarpus scaber*) with vivid orange or golden-yellow flowers.

377 **The sweet pea (*Lathyrus odoratus*) is not frost-sensitive— its seeds can be planted outdoors from mid-March.**

Small-flowering varieties bloom more abundantly than large-flowering ones. Sweet peas thrive on well-tilled, humus-rich soils, and do not tolerate fresh stable manure. For lasting success, change the site annually. If they are to flower every year on the same site, it may be necessary to replace the soil.

378 **Sweet peas (*Lathyrus odoratus*) can be sown in single or double rows.**

Along fences, only a single row is sown. To form a partition on a planter bed, sow in two rows about 8 in. apart, with a climbing frame between them. A Christmas tree from the previous year with all of its needles removed can be used as a climbing frame; the result is a highly attractive sweet pea pyramid. Place seed grains about 2 in. apart in the row and set ½ to 1 in. deep. The seeds remain viable for two years.

Starting annual seeds indoors will ensure brilliant displays of flowers in the summer.

379 **Bring gladiolus flowering forward through advance planting of the bulbs.**

Only use large, healthy bulbs. After treating the bulbs against fungi, press them into a roughly 1 ½ in. thick moist layer of garden earth, with sand mixed in, in shallow boxes. Separate the bulbs from one another by about 1 in. The boxes can be kept dark and at a temperature of around 59°F until the shoots appear. Then plant the bulbs in a sheltered site in mid-May.

380 Advance planting of canna lily (*Canna*) should take place from late March.

Cut

Canna lilies can be planted in pots as early as late March. Divide rootstocks that have grown too large. Each divided piece must have at least one vegetative bud. Select the pots so that a divided piece will just fit in and no more. Cover the pieces with only a shallow layer of sandy compost or potting mixture. They can be left to stand at 59 to 64°F, initially in the dark, but in the light after the shoots appear.

381 Prepare tuberous begonias for planting in May for borders and window boxes.

In late March, lay the tubers, which should have been overwintered in dry, not-too-cold conditions, in shallow boxes in a roughly 2 in. thick layer of compost earth with bark humus. Position the tubers so their rounded-off side with root remnants comes below, and the shoot-forming side is not covered up. At 60 to 68°F, keep the substrate only moderately moist until the shoots appear.

382 Tall grasses must be cut back in March.

Before new culms develop, the dried-up ones should be trimmed just above the ground. Evergreen grasses such as blue oat grass (*Helictotrichon sempervirens*) or pampas grass (*Cortaderia selloana*) should not be cut; only the dried-up leaves and culms are removed.

Terraces and Balconies

383 If there are frosts, winter protection will still be required for plant containers standing outside.

In March, the level of sunlight is already quite intense. This stimulates the sap flow in the plants, which begin to grow shoots and lose a lot of water through transpiration, but without being able to replace the water from frozen soil. Without sufficient protection, they may be at risk of dehydration.

In frost-free weather, remove the frost protection materials to avoid leggy shoot growth. However, leave the materials close by as they will be needed again on clear frosty nights.

384 In miniature gardens and tubs, return plants that have been forced up by frost to the soil.

Frost often lifts perennials freshly planted in the fall clear out of the ground so that they can dry out. The plants should be pushed back into the ground or replanted altogether and carefully watered.

> *Plant up window and balcony boxes with early spring-flowering plants and bulbs. They can be switched out with summer-flowering annuals.*

385 Window and balcony boxes, dishes, troughs, and tubs for summer flowers on the terrace can be planted with spring-flowering plants from mid-March.

These will provide an attractive display until it is time for planting summer flowers in mid- to late May. As a substrate, use potting mixture or compost earth, which should be kept uniformly moist, but not wet. Suitable plants include pansies (*Viola ×wittrockiana*), primroses (*Primula*), daisies (*Bellis*), forget-me-nots (*Myosotis*), and wallflowers (*Erysimum cheiri*, syn. *Cheiranthus cheiri*).

386 Overwintered tub plants may be watered regularly again from March on.

Nearly all tub plants have a cool resting period up until March during which they use only a little water and no nutrients. From now on, they may be watered more thoroughly again. First, loosen the upper soil layer or replace it with a nutrient-rich potting mixture; then apply fertilizers from late March. This is also the best time for replanting, should it be necessary.

387 Examine tub plants frequently for pests and diseases.

Once growth resumes in March, clean tub plants thoroughly. (If need be, wash the leaves, and remove dried-up branches and leaves.) Especially on unfavorable sites during winter, they may be subject to pests, such as scale insects, mealybugs, and aphids, and also red spider mites. These should initially be combated with a nettle fertilizer tea, ▶ **TIP 31** resorting to chemical means only when all else fails. Special remedies for individual pests are commercially available. Many are poisonous; follow their instructions for use very strictly. Biological control is ultimately less harmful, **TABLE 31** and **TABLE 32**.

Winter Gardens, Flower Windows, and Rooms

388 Too much sun in March may damage plants growing behind glass.

In winter, only a little light was available to the plants; consequently, their tissues became soft. On sunny days, without protection, plants may begin to show signs of "burns." Sun protection measures are therefore crucial for south-facing sites.

389 Cleanliness and hygiene, together with optimal environmental conditions, are essential for healthy growth in the winter garden.

In March, regular care of plants in the winter garden can resume. However, active care involves not just applying fertilizer and watering, but also cleaning out, removing dust, loosening the substrate, cutting and pruning, tying up, and, especially, replanting. Early detection of pests or diseases through regular checks is also important. This makes treatment easier and leads more quickly to the desired success. Optimal light and temperature conditions are especially important—accordingly, provide shade if the sun is strong.

390 From March, give indoor plants fertilizer again.

With the onset of growth, indoor plants can be given fertilizer every two weeks, and later every week. The number of applications and dosages are dependent on the age, size, and condition of the plants, and on the fertilizer itself. Plants growing in peat substrate will need to be given fertilizer more often than those in compost-rich soil. In addition to plant substances, apply organic materials such as bone meal or hoof and horn meal. Storage and long-acting fertilizers, such as fertilizer sticks, save on frequent applications. Azaleas, camellias, heather plants, and others do not tolerate lime-containing fertilizers; special fertilizers for these plants are commercially available. The same applies to orchids and bromeliads.

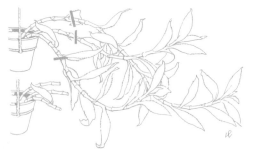

When cutting back indoor plants, shoot tips may be used for propagation.

391 Camellias and azaleas that have finished flowering should continue to be maintained correctly.

They should still be left in a light, cool place, with moderate watering and a special fertilizer application. These plants must not be allowed to suffer from water or nutrient deficiency.

392 Cyclamens (*Cyclamen*) often lose their leaves after flowering.

Cyclamens can lose their leaves after flowering. In such cases, keep them drier, and no longer apply fertilizer. Mostly, they will develop new shoots in June/July. ▸ **TIP 935**

393 Indoor plants should be cut back in March.

In dark and warm sites, indoor plants will grow too high. To attain more compact specimens, cut them back 10 to 14 days before replanting. This applies to African hemp (*Sparmannia*), Indian mallow (*Abutilon*), and Chinese hibiscus (*Hibiscus rosa-sinensis*), for example. The cut-off tips can be used as cuttings for raising young plants.

394 Many indoor plants can be grown from cuttings.

The cuttings develop wound (callus) tissue at the cut surface, from which roots may grow. As a rule, the cut should be made closely under a leaf attachment point; in some cases, it can also be further away, as in coleus (*Plectranthus scutellarioides*, syn. *Coleus blumei*). Many cuttings can also be made to produce roots by placing them in warm water (where possible, over 64 to 68°F), which should reach·above the leaf attachment. Once 1 ¼ to 1 ½ in. long roots have formed, depending on the species, plant the cuttings individually or several together in soil or in a hydroponic vessel. However, most cuttings will produce roots more reliably in a peat-sand mixture with slightly warm soil. Following root production, plant them first in small pots, and then transfer to larger ones after root penetration of the soil.

395 Umbrella grass or galingale (*Cyperus*) is propagated in water.

Only the tuft can be used. Shorten the radiating leaves, and ensure that the point where they attach to the culm is always under water.

396 Cuttings can be taken from shoots, stems, and leaves.

Shoot cuttings are taken from the tip of the shoot, and, as a rule, should have two or three leaves. To reduce transpiration, shorten very large leaves, from African hemp (*Sparmannia*), for example. Plants with long shoots, such as philodendron (*Philodendron*) and devil's ivy (*Epipremnum*), can also be propagated with partial cuttings. These, too, should have at least two or three leaves.

In the case of stem cuttings, such as in dumb cane, either the whole stem or stem sections with one bud each can be laid horizontally in a mixture of compost earth and bark humus. New shoots will develop from the buds.

Leaf cuttings, including partial leaf cuttings, will quickly produce young plants when the slightly shortened leaf stalk is placed in a mixture of compost earth and bark humus. New shoots will grow at the base and can be raised individually, for example in African violets (*Saintpaulia*) and leafy begonias.

Stem cutting from a dragon tree

Partial stem cutting from a dumb cane or mother-in-law's tongue

Yucca stem cutting

397 Cuttings grow better in high air humidity.

Cuttings need warmth (especially soil warmth) and high air humidity to grow. In a small greenhouse, flower window, or display cabinet, the air humidity will be sufficient; only heating needs to be supplied. In a living room, a commercially available "room greenhouse" that can also be heated can be used, or a transparent foil can be placed over the container.

SMALL CONTAINERS FOR RAISING YOUNG PLANTS

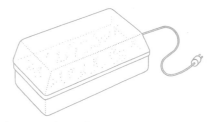

Window greenhouse for propagation, with ground tray and transparent lid, also with heating.

Grow only a few cuttings in bowls! Fill with propagation substrate shallowly and cover with a glass pane, or fill with propagation substrate to the rim and cover with a foil bag.

398 Propagate some plants using bulbils.

Spider plants or spider ivy (*Chlorophytum*) develop young plants in the inflorescence, and some *Kalanchoe* species at the leaf edge—small plantlets with roots that can be planted straight into the soil.

399 Cacti, too, resume their growth in March.

Following a long dry period over winter, new growth is stimulated in March. Water them only a little to begin with. A light place at a window is important.

With the right selection, orchids, will bloom splendidly in the home.

400 To grow orchids indoors, it is best to seek proper advice.

Young plants

Phalaenopsis grows best in warm rooms, while *Miltonia*, *Vuylstekeara*, and many *Oncidium* species and their hybrids grow better in cooler rooms. Young plants are less suitable for looking after indoors; only flowering specimens or those that will bloom prodigiously are likely to be successful. However, flower windows, display cabinets, and winter gardens are all suitable.

401 Orchids need a crumbly, well-aerated planting substrate, and do not tolerate cold water.

Rainwater is the most suitable for watering. If the tap water contains too much lime or salts (have it analyzed), it must be suitably prepared first (refer to the specialist literature). The planting substrate should consist primarily of granulated bark. Ready-made orchid earth is available from dealers. A general rule of thumb is that the plant container should be immersed in water or thoroughly watered once a week, so that the substrate can absorb the water. Water collecting in the saucer underneath should be poured away. In dry room air, spray the plants often. Many orchids have a quiet period with only moderately moist planting substrate, which is barely watered as such, but almost only ever sprayed instead.

402 In March, many orchids begin to sprout shoots and grow new roots.

They do not need to be replanted every year, but only if the plant substrate has rotted, or if the container has become too small. Baskets or pots are suitable as containers. Transplant the plants as soon as new shoots and roots develop. In a new container, begin at the bottom with a drainage layer using bark pieces or polystyrene granules. Some plants, for example *Cattleya*, should be set in the substrate at the edge of the container so that there is sufficient room for the next shoots; place *Phalaenopsis* and Venus' slipper or slipper orchid (*Paphiopedilum*) in the center of the pot. Water newly replanted orchids very sparingly until the roots have become properly anchored in the plant substrate. They should not be placed in full sun.

Remove old plant substrate

Cut back died-off roots

403 Growing orchids on wooden blocks is primarily suitable for small-growing orchids.

This growth method for small-growing plants, to create conditions that largely correspond to the growth conditions at the plant's natural site, necessitates a rather higher air humidity, such as in a winter garden, closed flower window, or glass display cabinet. Cork, pine and oak bark, elder branch fragments with bark, pieces of old grapevines, and, for larger blocks, oak and robinia branches with raw bark are suitable substrates. First cover the substrate with a thin layer of moss, into which the roots are embedded. Then tie the components together firmly with a synthetic thread, and attach a hook to the substrate for hanging up. Spray the blocks often with water, or immerse in water every two to three days (or more often if it is very hot). It is also possible to tie up the orchids without a substrate, in which case they will need regular spraying and fertilizer applications.

404 Bromeliads must be protected from intense sunshine as early as March.

Following the dull winter days, soft-leaved bromeliads such as *Guzmania* and *Nidularium* are light-sensitive. In particular, air plants, *Vriesea*, *Neoregelia*, and *Aechmea* are suitable for living rooms. These are flowering plants that can be kept for a long time, and include some splendid leafy plants. Remove dry leaves by pulling them away from the sides. In all species, there must always be water in the plants' leaf-tanks. These should be cleaned in March and filled with fresh rainwater.

APRIL

Spring

At this time, the flowers of our native fruit trees are among the most beautiful of the year. Vivid in radiant white, the apple tree flower's delicate pink tone is always a surprise; its beauty is quite equal to that of roses. It's no wonder, because apples and roses are both members of the rose family. Just a few days later, and the splendid display is already over.

Now is the time to think about tasks in the garden, since April is one of the busiest months of the year in this respect. Seed must be sown in good time, and many perennials are ready for planting out. But beware—night frosts can still do a lot of damage!

GENERAL

405
We can ignore the damage that our chickens cause in our own gardens—but we must ensure that they do not visit our neighbors' properties.

For the damage that chickens cause in other people's gardens, it is the chickens' owners who are responsible. This is also the case when the fence is not chicken-proof and belongs to the owner of the affected garden. Chicken-keepers must ensure that their animals cannot find their way into neighboring gardens. However, this does not release neighbors from an obligation to keep their fences in good order. Accordingly, picket fences should be sufficiently impervious at the base so that not even small chickens or bantams can slip through. Wire netting is the best solution here.

406
Poultry, rabbit, and goat manure (without bedding material) that is to be used for manure tea application later should be left to ferment in April.

For this, watertight containers are required that can be set up so that they receive full sun. To avoid overly large containers, the above substances are used at a ratio of 1:2, in other words with double the water quantity. Dilute the manure when it is ready to be applied.

> *Compost heaps break down more quickly in the shade.*

407
Protect earth or compost heaps from the sun.

Earth heaps standing in the shade do not dry out as quickly, and they also break down more rapidly. Sunflowers are useful for shading the compost. For planting these, dig a trench 12 in. wide and just as deep at the south side. Mix the excavated earth with a large quantity of compost earth and then backfill it. Sunflowers can be grown on this strip, or, alternatively, corn and pumpkins, which for the most part will grow vigorously.

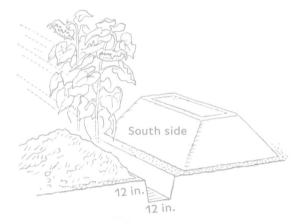

408
Jerusalem artichoke, or topinambur, is a sunflower species that serves as excellent feed for small animals, thanks to its nutrient-rich rootstocks.

Since this perennial spreads rapidly and will often grow more than 6 ½ ft. high, it should be grown as a visual barrier. Plant the winter-hardy rhizome tubers in April at a minimum interval of about 14 in., and around 4 in. deep in the ground. The herb can be used as feed for small animals, and the tubers may even be eaten as vegetables. Jerusalem artichoke contains inulin, and is used as a substitute for starch. Because eating the tubers does not raise the blood sugar level, they are also good for diabetic patients.

409
Beer can be used to combat slugs and snails (here, note that only slugs are harmful to our plants).

Beer is a biological control agent that can be used against slugs and snails. Plastic cups or similar containers, embedded in the soil right up to the rim, are filled with beer, the aroma of which will be sure to attract the slugs. The animals are numbed, and then drown. Commercially available slug traps have a roof cover to prevent dilution of the beer by rainwater; they are easy to use and clean. Be sure to replace the beer after several days. Slug fences made of stable wire netting are also effective—they should be 12 in. high and half embedded in the ground with the edge bent outward. However, the slug fence must not be in contact with the plants or it will be easy for the animals to crawl over it. Providing shelter and overwintering opportunities for hedgehogs, toads, lizards, blind-worms, and newts will help reduce future slug infestation. ▶ **TIP 643**

> *The use of the planted area determines whether fleece or a vegetable net should be used.*

410 Consider fleeces for earlier and later planting.

In addition to foil tunnels and cold frames, fleeces can be used for earlier or later planting. Their high water permeability, low weight, and also their high stability and water storage capacity make their use in the garden universal. However, remember that it is easy for the ground beneath a fleece to get too hot in summer. Accordingly, fine-meshed nets have also been developed for vegetable growing.

411 Lay out nets to protect against vegetable pests and birds.

Lay vegetable nets loosely over the beds immediately after sowing or planting. When plant growth begins, it must be possible to loosen them further at a later stage. To prevent vegetable flies from getting in, bury the net edges in the ground or weigh them down with sandbags. Some vegetable flies reproduce two or three additional times during the year following the initial generation in April. If vegetable nets with a mesh width of $\frac{1}{32}$ in. are left to remain over the beds until the harvest, they will keep vegetable flies away.

412 Combat weeds on paths.

Even in winter, many annual weeds will germinate and grow, while perennial weeds will grow new leaves. They are best dealt with by hoeing so that they do not spread further.

413 Many garden tasks need to be completed in April.

There will be sunny days, to be sure, but the weather can change quickly and turn cool and frosty. Rain and sun alternate with one another constantly. To get through all the jobs that need to be done at this time, every sunny day needs to be utilized, if possible. The beds for sowing and planting need to be prepared, and for many perennials this is the best time for planting; summer flowers can be sown directly on site. Good soil loosening is important, and germinating weeds should be removed. If there is no rain, it is necessary to ensure that the newly sown seed and new plantings are kept uniformly moist, while ventilating cold frames should also not be forgotten. Except for the newly planted beds, an initial fertilizer application should be given to all perennials in April.

414 If there is danger of frost, protect newly sown seed and new plants accordingly.

Custom-made garden fleeces are available from specialist dealers for this purpose. These are both light and moisture permeable. Lay these lightweight fleeces over the plants and weigh down the corners with stones. Plant stakes can also be driven in the corners of the beds and covered with foil. These, too, are weighted down at the corners with stones. Many perennials and woody plants will already be growing, and may suffer considerable damage from frost. Cover them with frost protection hoods made of fleece (light and moisture permeable) or plastic (with a small hole at the top).

VEGETABLES

415 Cauliflower is demanding and can be grown successfully only on the best soils.

The best soil is a deep sandy loam or loamy sand with a high humus content. The land intended for growing cauliflower must have been given considerable amounts of stable manure in the fall; in other words, cauliflower must be in the first position in a crop rotation.

416 Cauliflower grown outdoors can be harvested in the first half of June if vigorous plants with root balls are available in early April.

Buy the plants, which should be early varieties, from a specialist dealer. A planting width of 20 × 20 in. is required. Once the plants have been well hardened off, they will tolerate light frosts. However, in any case, obtain frost protection hoods or cover the plant beds with foil or fleece. To harvest cauliflower over a longer period, until the fall, for example, subsequent plantings at intervals of two to three weeks are possible, and recommended, until mid-July. Growing Romanesco broccoli, a special form of cauliflower, is also recommended. Its green flowers appear to be comprised of many small conical flowers, and are very attractive. Romanesco broccoli has the same growing requirements as normal cauliflower, is very tasty, and has a higher vitamin C content. Since specialist dealers offer hardly any young plants, you can raise the plants yourself. Sowing them in early April allows planting to be done around mid-May. Subsequent sowing of Romanesco broccoli is possible until early July.

417 Cabbage root fly and swede midge can cause considerable damage to cauliflower.

These pests lay their eggs from mid-April to mid-May. The larvae of the cabbage root fly devour the roots of the young cauliflower plants, affecting the plants' growth, while the swede midge larvae cause such sucking damage to the heart leaves that they become twisted and crippled, so that the head does not form. After planting, lay a fine-meshed vegetable net over the young plants in such a way that they can grow properly. Bury the sides of the nets in the ground or weigh them down with sandbags.

> *Cover cabbage plants with insect nets or fleece immediately after planting to protect against cabbage root fly.*

418 Broccoli can be sown in an unheated cold frame in early April or in an outdoor bed from mid-April.

These dates enable planting out to be done in the last days of May or in the first half of June. Sow single seed grains only at an interval of 1 to 1½ in. to obtain vigorous plants.

419 Eggplants are best grown in a small greenhouse, foil house, or cold frame.

Eggplants should be grown as a second crop for summer use. Plant in a small greenhouse or heated cold frame in late April. The planting width is 20 × 20 to 30 × 16 in. Fertilizer application and watering is the same as for tomatoes. Eggplants have a greater warmth requirement than tomatoes, and, accordingly, sufficient covering material should be provided as protection against night frosts. They may be planted in beds or large tubs. Small-fruiting varieties can even be grown together with herbs in balcony boxes.

420 From early to mid-April, wrinkled peas may be grown in favorable areas that are largely unaffected by late frosts.

In unfavorable areas, it is better to wait until mid-April, noting what has already been advised for peas in ▶ TIP 239 and ▶ TIP 240.

421 For plants in cold frames, remember to ventilate and water the plants in April.

As soon as the sun shines or the outdoor temperatures exceed 50°F, all the windows of the cold frames should be opened. Do this in such a way that the wind will blow across the windows, and not into the plants themselves. Water on sunny days only, so that the plants will quickly dry off again.

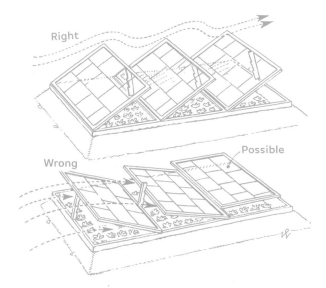

> *Careful ventilation of the cold frames will contribute to plant development and not allow them to be stunted by cold or heat buildup.*

422 Spanish onions that have been pregrown in pots can be planted out in late April.

It is important that the plants are hardened off in good time. In unfavorable or cold weather conditions, it is better to postpone planting out until early May. Spanish onions need a planting width of 12 × 8 in. It is helpful to cover the plants with frost protection hoods until the danger of late frosts has passed. If advance planting is not an option, sow the seeds directly outdoors from April on. In this case, too, covering or building over the plants with foil is recommended. Once the seedlings emerge, thin them out to 6 in. within a row. With direct seeding, the onions will not be as heavy as they might be otherwise, but they will still be larger than normal (yellow) onions.

423 In the last 10 days of April, cucumbers and tomatoes for summer use can be planted in small greenhouses and foil houses.

Harvesting of the advance planting, such as lettuce, will already be freeing up the area, which means that, from 20 to 25 April, cucumbers or tomatoes can be planted directly into the partially harvested stands. However, this planting date necessitates additional protective measures against the impacts of frost. Accordingly, straw mats, air bubble foil, or other material should be kept on hand. As a rule, only special house cucumber or house tomato varieties should be used for this cultivation.

424 Growing house cucumbers necessitates the optimal configuration of all growth factors.

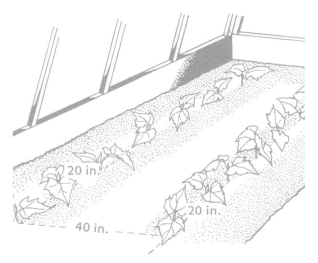

This also includes careful soil preparation. House cucumbers are sensitive to waterlogging, and thrive in warm, highly permeable soils. This can be achieved by bringing in stable manure, compost, or straw. Add at least one bucket of compost at every plant site. Provide a row interval of 40 in., and 20 in. for the interval within a row. The basic fertilizer to be applied per square yard should be around 1 oz. of a low-phosphate complete fertilizer. After planting, water the plants thoroughly. The young plants are best bought from a specialist dealer.

425 As a general rule, house cucumbers are grown from only one shoot.

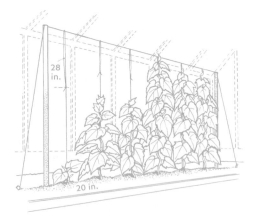

This necessitates the construction of a simple support structure. Drive thick stakes in the ground at each end of a cucumber row and anchor them in firmly. Their length is dependent on the height of the greenhouse; there should be a gap of about 6 in. between the top of the stake and the greenhouse roof. Stretch a wire as tightly as possible over the stake ends, and anchor it well in the ground on both sides. Then, loosely attach a line to the root collar of the plant, draw it over the tensioned wire, and attach the end of the line at least 28 in. below the wire so that the attachment point remains movable. With increasing length as a result of growth, the main shoot will grow in a spiral around the line. This will cause the line to tighten, and so it must then be possible to lengthen it. With the aid of the 28 in. long reserve section, the lines must then be "slackened" in good time to prevent the roots from being pulled out of the ground.

426 Another option for growing house cucumbers is to grow them on straw bales.

Compressed bales with a weight of 25 to 35 lb. are the most suitable. Set the bales in trenches 4 to 6 in. deep in the lengthwise direction of the plant rows, with the excavated earth piled up against the sides. After this, water the structure thoroughly, add 9 oz. of a low-phosphate fertilizer per linear yard, and pour about one-and-a-half bucket loads of good compost earth on top of each planting site. Planting can then take place after five to six days.

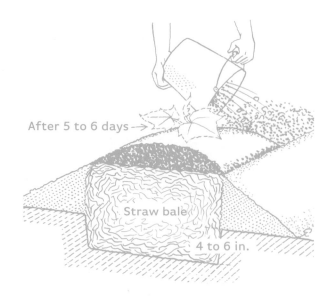

427 Growing cucumbers in a cold frame should be done primarily as a second planting for summer use.

Cucumbers may be sown or planted in heated cold frames from mid-April, and in unheated cold frames from late April to early May. If cucumber plants from advance planting are available, two are grown under each cold frame window (5 × 2 ⅗ ft.). Normally, three plants will also be sufficient for two windows. The same planting density applies as for sowing. Here, lay three cucumber seed grains per seed site and cover with around ½ in. of earth. Later, after the germinated seedlings have developed their first normal leaf, allow only the most vigorous plant to remain at the seed site. Do not pull the remaining plants out of the earth, but cut them back instead, so as not to disturb the remaining plant's development. In a cold frame, as a minimum, supply every plant or seed site with good compost earth. However, a base layer of fresh stable manure or straw is even better.

Cucumbers may already be planted between the first partially harvested crops. This will facilitate earlier harvests.

428 **Cucumbers prefer very warm conditions; accordingly, provide sufficient covering materials.**

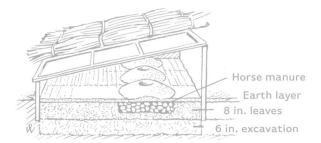

Horse manure
Earth layer
8 in. leaves
6 in. excavation

Cover the cold frames with straw mats or similar covering materials every night, even if no night frosts are expected. This will reduce the temperature fluctuations between day and night. Retain the coverings until June. In the initial period after planting or sowing, the cold frames should not be ventilated if possible, or only if the temperatures climb above 77°F. In such cases, always ventilate the cold frame windows on the lee side of the wind.

429 **From mid-April, transfer preregerminated early potatoes (TIP 243) to warm humus- and nutrient-rich soil.**

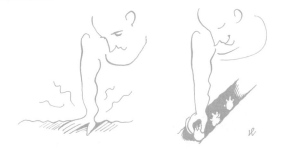

If the soil has not yet warmed up, it is better to wait until late April. Only land that has had plenty of humus added to it in the fall is suitable. For early potatoes, an open, sunny site is essential. Potatoes grow fastest in humic sandy soils.

430 **Good harvests of early potatoes are possible only if the rows are 2 ft. apart.**

This means that only two rows can be laid in a normal bed (4 ft.) if the early potatoes are grown in beds. If more than two rows are to be planted, omit the bed paths to save space. On the marked-out rows, open a 4 in. deep furrow with a hoe or plowing device, lay the potatoes in the furrow at 12 in. intervals, and cover with earth.

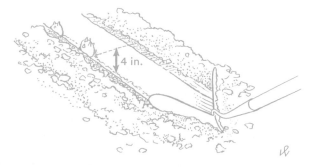

4 in.

431 **Growing Florence fennel can begin in early April.**

Originally a typical Italian specialty, Florence fennel has also become popular in other countries, and connoisseurs value this tasty and highly versatile vegetable. The right variety is crucial for the growing period in question. While certain varieties such as 'Zefa Fino' can be grown several times consecutively from spring to fall, other varieties may not be sown until early July or else they will flower without forming tubers. Florence fennel is frost-sensitive, and needs warm advance planting. Sow it straight into small pots (three or four seed grains per pot), ensuring that an optimal germination temperature of around 68°F is maintained. Thin out the seedlings to one plant per pot, after which temperatures of 59°F are sufficient. Depending on requirements, further seed can be sown at intervals of two to four weeks until around 20 July.

432 **Growing common fennel for seed is worthwhile in warmer situations.**

Plant this perennial herb individually at the edge of a vegetable bed, or in a herb or perennial bed. It will grow up to 6½ ft. high and needs a planting width of about 20 × 20 in. If it ripens in September or October, harvest the brown seeds for fennel tea or for use as a cooking spice. The aroma is like that of anise. The seeds of brown or green Roman fennel have smaller grains and a spicier flavor.

433 In early April, give kohlrabi and cauliflower grown in small greenhouses or foil houses their first surface fertilizer application.

Apply the fertilizer at a rate of 2 oz. per 100 sq. ft. and work into the soil immediately, or alternatively give it as a 0.3 percent nutrient solution. With the onset of flower development, give cauliflower a second surface fertilizer application in the same quantities.

434 Light to medium soils that have a high humus content and warm up quickly are best for early outdoor cultivation of kohlrabi.

Application of fresh organic fertilizer is not required. Only potted plants should be used for planting in early April, because they grow faster and can be harvested sooner. Kohlrabi needs sufficient room if the tubers are to develop quickly and well. Accordingly, the planting width should be at least 10 × 10 in., or better still 10 × 12 in.

435 The planting depth, too, is critical for tuber development.

Planting should be only so deep that the upper roots are just covered with earth. Planting too deep will delay development and lead to excessively long, extended tubers or even unwanted shoots.

436 Early kohlrabi will develop much faster if it is covered with plant protection hoods, or if foil or fleece is built over it.

On their supports, the hoods have an edge that should be covered with earth to keep out the wind.

Even better for the plants is an area-wide covering of perforated foil or fleece. This will enable the kohlrabi to be harvested 5 to 10 days earlier.

437 In some years, kohlrabi suffers severe infestation from the larvae of the cabbage root fly and cabbage gall weevil.

Combat cabbage root fly in the same way as for cauliflower ▸ **TIP 417**. The larvae of the cabbage gall weevil cause tuberous growths on the kohlrabi roots, which, unlike clubroot, contain small larvae inside. Preventive measures are the same as for cabbage root fly.

438 If kohlrabi is to be grown for use in summer and the fall, sow it in April.

Sow summer varieties in early April, and again at the end of the month, if kohlrabi is to be harvested over a longer period (July, August). Varieties for the fall must be sown in the last 10 days of April. Sow seeds either in an outdoor seedbed, or, if the demand for plants is not too high, in 2 in. pots or pot palettes that are set up in a cold frame.

439 Headed cabbage has the same high soil, water, and nutrient supply requirements as cauliflower.

Early varieties prefer light to medium soils that will warm up quickly, while late varieties deliver the highest yields in medium to heavy, deep soils. A good humus supply is essential for headed cabbage; accordingly, it belongs in the first position in a crop rotation. However, early varieties will also do well after a previous crop that has had a humus application. In the crop rotation, all cabbage species should be avoided as a previous crop.

440 Early red cabbage requires a planting width of 20 × 20 in. to develop firm heads. It can be planted from early to mid-April.

Planting is the same as for cauliflower ▸ **TIP 416**. In small gardens, planting in beds will hardly be necessary, in view of the small requirement for the plants. Accordingly, it is especially suitable for growing in mixed cultures. It is important that the young plants are not set deeper into the soil than they were before. The use of plant protection hoods is recommended. Only use varieties with a short development time for early cultivation.

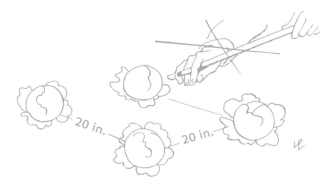

441 Early white cabbage can be planted out in early April if soils that are warm and not too heavy and well-hardened-off plants are available.

Early white cabbage is not quite as demanding as red cabbage or cauliflower; nevertheless, the soil must be rich in humus and nutrients. For varieties with pointed heads, a planting width of 16 × 16 in. is sufficient; other early white cabbage varieties should have a planting width of 20 × 16 in.

Early varieties of headed cabbage with the shortest possible development times allow the space to be used twice.

442 Early savoy cabbage can also be planted in early April, if this has not already been done in the second half of March (TIP 289).

Varieties with pointed heads will make do with a planting width of 16 × 16 in. All other varieties should have the same planting widths as for early white cabbage.

443 Late headed cabbage and Brussels sprouts can be grown in an outdoor seedbed.

Sow the seeds in early April. After the seedlings emerge, thin them out to an interval of ¾ in. within the row. Keep the seedbed constantly moist and monitor for flea beetles so they can be combated in good time. Growing late headed cabbage in small gardens is not actually recommended. Those who still wish to try should select only varieties with optimal storage characteristics and avoid mid- to late varieties altogether.

444 All cabbage species that have been planted in early April or earlier, including kohlrabi, should be given their first nutrient application in the final third of April.

Since the rows will have not yet grown together, spreading dry mineral fertilizer is the quickest method. Apply 1 oz. of complete fertilizer per square yard and lightly hoe it in. Water the ground thoroughly afterward so that the nutrients reach the root zone.

445 In warmer weather, sufficiently ventilate greenhouses and foil houses.

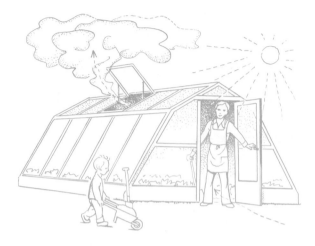

This applies especially to lettuce and kohlrabi; additionally, as the plants develop further, the water demand increases greatly. Depending on the weather conditions, lettuce needs to be watered once or twice a week; kohlrabi, and especially cauliflower, should generally be watered every other day.

446 Firm lettuce heads can be attained outdoors on warm, humus-rich soils.

Lettuce grows best on humic, loamy sand soils, and belongs in the second position in a crop rotation. Soils that tend toward encrustation or have a pH of less than 6.5 are unsuitable. Do not plant lettuce twice in succession on the same plot, or following endives or chicory. On light soils, cabbage and cauliflower should also be avoided as previous crops.

447 The earlier the planting date, the more important the use of potted plants when planting lettuce.

If weather conditions permit, planting can take place from early April. If a continuous supply of lettuce is required, it is best not to plant too much at once, but instead to undertake new plantings at intervals of 14 to 18 days, while also utilizing all the options for mixed culture. Selecting the appropriate variety is always crucial for growing success.

448 Lettuce that has been planted too deep in the soil will develop abnormal or only poor-quality heads.

Under no circumstances should the lettuce be planted deeper in the soil than it had been before. It is also essential that the still-recognizable cotyledons remain above the soil. In the case of potted plants, only around two thirds of the root ball should go into the ground. If the plant tips over after planting, there will be no harm done.

449 Lettuce in early cultivation requires a planting width of at least 8 × 8 in.

However, a planting width of 10 × 10 in. is even better. This will yield better-quality and larger heads, and the danger of rotting is less than in a dense stand. Iceberg lettuce and Batavia lettuce need a standing room of 12 × 12 in. Following planting, cover the ground with frost protection hoods, foil, or fleece.

450 In early April, sowing of iceberg and regular lettuce for the summer harvest can begin.

Only use special summer varieties. The time from sowing to planting out is approximately four weeks, followed by another eight to ten weeks from planting to harvest. Calculate the approximate date for sowing using these times as a guide.

> *Red-leaved lettuce varieties are especially tender and less susceptible to attack by aphids.*

451 To obtain a good chard harvest, sowing must take place by about mid-April.

Sowing should be done by dibbling, with an interval between seeding sites in a row of 6 to 8 in. for Swiss chard, and 16 in. for Sicilian broad-rib chard. Place the seeds about 1 in. deep. After the seedlings emerge, thin them out so that the plants can develop well.

452 In our climatic conditions, melons have only a limited potential for cultivation.

While muskmelons (sugar melons) can be grown successfully in small greenhouses and in cold frames, watermelons only seldom yield a satisfactory result, even in the most favorable situations. Fully ripened muskmelons can be very flavorful. A distinction is made between cantaloupe melons, netted melons, and smooth melons. For our conditions, the Charentais types, a form of cantaloupe melon, have proven to be the best. The fruits are globose, partially flattened, and ribbed. They have orange-colored flesh and reach an individual weight of about 2 lb. The skin of netted melons has a cork-like, netted structure. They remain somewhat smaller, and are less flavorful. Smooth melons develop more oblong fruit without ribs or a net structure. Their flesh is mostly greenish white to cream-colored, and they, too, are less flavorful, but often very sweet.

453 Melons place high demands on the soil and climate.

In particular, melons require plenty of warmth and strong sunshine; accordingly, cultivation is possible only in climatically favorable situations, and even then not before late May/early June. Cold, wet, and changeable weather does considerable damage to the plants. Gardeners who nevertheless decide to grow the plants outdoors need to select a sheltered, south-facing site in front of walls, house walls, pergolas, etc. A light to medium, highly water-permeable soil that can warm up quickly is the most suitable.

454 To avoid disappointments when growing melons, it's preferable to grow them under glass or foil.

Growing melons in heated or unheated cold frames for summer use has proven its worth. Growing under foil tents is also possible, but is less recommended. Cultivation in a small greenhouse is relatively reliable.

455 Melons have lower nutrient requirements than cucumbers.

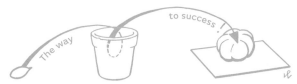

However, it is essential that the soil be improved through generous applications of organic fertilizer. Apply organic fertilizers as preparation for the plants, with due regard for melons' chloride sensitivity. Fresh lime application is also not tolerated, which means that the required pH of more than 6 must be attained in good time. Melons are not sown directly on site, but pregrown in pots instead. Raising the plants takes about six weeks. For growing the plants in cold frames, the planting date will be around mid-May, which means sowing the seed from early to mid-April. Plant the melon seeds 2 × 2 in. apart in seed bowls filled with sandy compost earth, cover with a maximum of ½ in. of earth, and place in a suitable room at 68 to 72°F. As soon as the first vegetative leaf begins to develop, prick out the plants into 3 ½ in. pots.

456 April is the best time to sow late carrots for harvesting in the fall and for storage.

Short and semi-long varieties for harvesting in August and September can also be sown in April. Here, too, an indicator crop should be used. Meanwhile, the guidelines for sowing given in ▸ **TIP 255** and ▸ **TIP 256** should also be followed.

457 To speed up the emergence and youthful development of carrots, covering with foil can be beneficial.

In April, quite unfavorable weather can greatly delay the emergence of carrots. Here, it is recommendable to cover at least part of the carrot planting bed with perforated foil. Stretch the foil over a wooden frame with stones underneath the corners to achieve the necessary ground clearance. In this way, the foil can remain on the beds until the carrots have grown to a height of around 4 in. This can speed up development by 14 days or more.

> *Use floating row covers stretched over metal or wire loops to protect plants from the harmful carrot fly and bring the harvest date even further forward.*

458 Leeks sown outdoors in April can still yield usable stalks as late as the fall.

Leek seeds are fully viable only in the first year following the harvest. To plant in mid-June, sow the seed in early to mid-April.

459 Broad beans (TIP 263) and peas (TIP 240) sown in March should be given their first fertilizer application as soon as they are 2 to 3 in. high, followed by a second application about three weeks later.

For the first application, use 0.7 oz./yd.² of nitrogen fertilizer, and for the second 1 oz./yd.² of complete fertilizer between the rows, and lightly work the fertilizer into the soil. This should be followed by watering. The

complete fertilizers, especially, can also be given as a 0.3 percent nutrient solution (2 to 3 gal./yd.²).

460 In dry, warm weather, water radishes and red radishes regularly so that the tubers will stay tender.

Tubers of good quality can be achieved only if the plants are always kept uniformly moist. Then they willl also be able to be harvested for longer and will not turn furry so quickly. Subsequent sowing can also take place in April, following the instructions in ▸ **TIP 264** and ▸ **TIP 266**.

461 When sowing summer radishes beginning in mid-April, ensure sufficiently large row intervals.

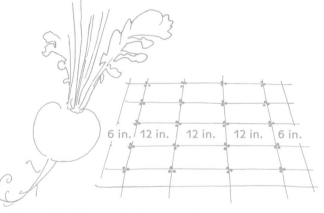

These should never be less than 12 in. In a row, lay two or three seed grains every 4 to 6 in. When the seedlings emerge, thin out to leave only one plant per seed site. Radishes must not be given any stable manure.

462 Beets do not make any great demands on soil or climate and belong in the second position in a crop rotation.

They do not tolerate fresh or organic manure, and will deliver optimal yields only on soils with a neutral pH. If necessary, lime can still be applied in the spring. Beets are also chloride-tolerant, but are sensitive to boron deficiency. They should not be planted following a previous beet crop, or following spinach or chard.

463 To harvest beets in summer, sow in late April.

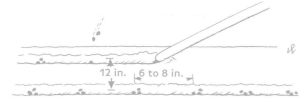

12 in.   6 to 8 in.

The row interval should be 12 in. In the row, lay three seeds at 6 to 8 in. intervals. When the young plants reach a height of around 2 in., thin them out to one plant per seed site.

464 Butterhead lettuce and leaf lettuce, which grow in every soil, can be sown repeatedly.

Butterhead lettuce and leaf lettuce do not produce any heads, but they yield lettuce leaves very quickly. More details on sowing are given in ▶ **TIP 271**.

465 Oak-leaf lettuce and curly lettuce, planted early and covered with foil, will yield the first harvests from late April.

As a rule, the harvest begins with plant weights of 7 oz. (oak-leaf lettuce) to 9 oz. (curly lettuce). It is not just the individual leaves, as with leaf lettuce, but the whole plant that is harvested. Both types of lettuce are very tasty, and the red-leaved types are extremely decorative, particularly when combined with green-leaved types. The excellent storage properties of curly lettuce following the harvest should also be emphasized.

466 Romaine lettuce, also known as cos lettuce, is closely related to lettuce.

This is probably the oldest form of garden lettuce and forms a dense rosette with an elongated head that is more or less closed at the top. Romaine lettuce has the same soil and nutrient requirements as lettuce, but tolerates higher temperatures and does not sprout unwanted shoots as readily. It also keeps for longer following the harvest. Additionally, there are also miniature types of romaine lettuce with a pronounced head, tender and crunchy inner leaves, and excellent flavor. These are especially appealing for home gardeners. Begin sowing in early April, preferably straight into 2 in. pots, or from mid-April in seedbeds outdoors. Subsequent sowing is possible until late July.

467 Asian lettuces are especially suitable for spring growing.

These include vegetable species and varieties that are mostly from different plant families and are well known from Asian cuisine. These include varieties from the cabbage plant family, for example, 'Red Giant' and 'Green Snow', which are particularly hot and spicy. For growing, note that they tend to produce unwanted shoots. Accordingly, select shoot-free varieties for summer growing.

468 The stalks of white asparagus need to be harvested as soon as their penetration of the dam walls is recognizable.

The dams erected in March ▶ **TIP 284** should be checked in the early morning and late afternoon. The most valuable stalks are those with white heads; these will begin to change color as soon as they are exposed to the light. This means they should be harvested before they have fully penetrated the dam surface.

469 **In order not to jeopardize the subsequent asparagus stalk growth, every stalk needs to be exposed completely.**

To do this, run your fingers down the asparagus stalk to its base. It should be cut off as closely as possible to the base with a sharp knife (asparagus knife).

470 **After the stalks have been cut off, repair and reshape the asparagus dams immediately.**

The earth that has been dislodged to expose the stalks is best piled back into place and gently knocked back into shape with a handy wooden board. At the same time, remove any weeds so the dams can always be monitored easily.

471 **Take steps to control asparagus fly as soon as the asparagus begins to sprout.**

The most endangered plantings are those which are not yet ready for harvesting and three-year plantings that are harvested only until 1 June. The asparagus fly lays its eggs on the asparagus heads breaking through the soil. The emerging larvae devour the shoots, which can then develop no further. The best protection is to spray the asparagus row heads with a systemic insecticide from 10 April to mid-June, repeating the procedure weekly.

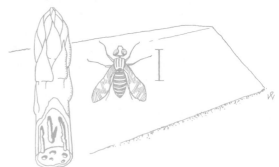

472 **The second fertilizer application for two-year-old asparagus can generally be combined with the filling of the ditches.**

Filling in is possible as soon as the asparagus shoots are near the normal soil surface. Distribute the fertilizer accordingly, and backfill the earth so the shoot tips are just visible.

473 **Mid-April is the latest planting date for new asparagus plantings.**

Asparagus plants sprout very early, so good growth is endangered from this time on. For everything that needs to be considered for planting, see ▶ TIP 278 to ▶ TIP 283.

474 **In the first days of April, give spinach and lamb's lettuce planted in the fall another application of nutrient solution containing a fast-acting nitrogen fertilizer.**

The nutrient solution is prepared with a concentration of 0.2 to 0.3 percent, and poured so that each square yard of cultivated land receives 2 to 3 gallons. This can also be done to delay the appearance of the flowering stems. Meanwhile, for winter and spring spinach, regular weed clearance and continual soil loosening are extremely important.

475 Small greenhouses can also be used for growing climbing beans.

This should be a second crop following lettuce, kohl-rabi, or other vegetable species that can be cleared in time. Sow the seeds from mid-April between the still-unharvested or only partially harvested previous crop with a planting width of 32 × 16 to 20 in., with four to six seed grains at each site. Advance planting in pots with subsequent planting out can be beneficial. Undertake the sowing (five seed grains in each 4 ½ in. pot) about 14 days before the planned planting date. Train the plants when the first tendrils appear by using poles or lines, as with cucumbers and tomatoes. If the temperatures rise above 68°F, ventilate the greenhouse thoroughly.

476 A suitable method for growing tomatoes in small greenhouses and foil houses is to use dwarf tomatoes.

This growing method facilitates an intensive use of the greenhouses with advance and subsequent planting, higher planting densities, and an earlier start to harvesting. Tomatoes have similar soil requirements to cucumbers. A sufficiently high humus content is important, and can be achieved by working in stable manure or other organic material. Loosen the soil to as great a depth as possible, and work in the basic fertilizer at the same time. The planting width is dependent on the envisaged cultivation period and the number of inflorescences that are to be left on the plant. It is useful to finish harvesting house tomatoes at the same time that the outdoor harvest begins. In this case, the interval from row to row should be 20 in., and a maximum of 16 in. within a row. Immediately after planting, water the tomatoes thoroughly. As a support for the tomatoes, a simple 4 ft. long stake driven 10 to 12 in. into the ground is sufficient.

477 Of course, tomatoes can also be grown in the greenhouse as a long-term crop.

In this case, the interval within a row should be 18 in., and between rows 32 to 40 in. Train the plants in the same way as for cucumbers. ▶ **TIP 425**

478 To bring the harvest forward a little, sow zucchinis in pots in late April.

Lay three seed grains each in 3 in. pots filled with compost earth, and place in a heated cold frame. Since two or three plants are normally sufficient to supply one family, the pots can also be placed on the windowsill in a suitably warm room.

479 As soon as the rows of onions and carrots sown in the beds in March (**TIP 256** and **TIP 290**) are easily recognizable, the indicator crop should be removed.

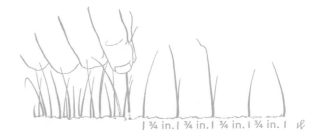

| ¾ in. | ¾ in. | ¾ in. | ¾ in. |

It has now fulfilled its purpose, and if left in place would otherwise only hinder the development of the vegetable species. Once it has been removed, it is crucial to thin out the young onion or carrot plants, as soon as it is possible to grasp hold of them. For both species, leave only one plant standing about every inch. After thinning, give 0.7 oz./yd.^{2} of nitrogen fertilizer or 1 oz./yd.^{2} of complete fertilizer as an initial fertilizer application, followed by thorough watering.

> *Careful thinning of vegetable seedlings improves quality and yield.*

480 **Garlic must be planted by 10 April at the latest if good yields are to be obtained.**

The recommendations in ▶ **TIP 296** should be followed.

481 **Lemon balm needs humic, permeable soil, and a sheltered sunny site.**

Loosen the soil to a considerable depth and supply plenty of compost, since lemon balm can grow for years in the same place. One or two plants should be enough to meet the needs of a household and can be obtained from a specialist dealer or as plant sections from a gardening enthusiast. The plant interval must be 12 in.

482 **In the garden, peppermint prefers a moist, semi-shaded, but airy place, and likes a nutrient-rich, humic soil.**

Mint forms stolons and needs a place where this will not become a problem, for example between scattered fruit trees or in a corner of the garden delineated by edging pavers. It's easy to obtain young plants in nurseries, but it is also possible to separate the stolons from old plants to use instead. Lay these shallowly in furrows at an interval of 12 in. and cover with only a little earth. When selecting the varieties, note the content of essential oils, since these are largely responsible for the mint's fine taste. Whereas 'Multimentha' mint has a high menthol content, apple mint and strawberry mint have a milder taste. Pineapple mint sets colorful accents in the garden with its whitish green foliage.

483 **April is the final date for pruning back perennial spice herbs that sprout aboveground shoots.**

These mainly include lavender and sage, hyssop, common rue, winter savory, and oregano. Depending on the growth vigor of the genera, cut back vigorously growing herbs to about half their height; cut back weaker ones to about a third. Plants that have suffered badly from frost should be cut back to about an inch above the ground.

484 **Perennial spice herbs that have been raised from seed can be planted during the final third of April.**

The recommendations in ▶ **TIP 293** to ▶ **TIP 304** should be followed. Covering the herbs with a plant protection hood is recommended in any case.

485 Chives sown in cold frames in March (TIP 276) can be planted out in the open in late April, provided the plants are strong enough.

Small plant bunches are taken in every case and planted at 8 × 8 in. intervals. Chives will also still grow very well in semi-shaded situations.

486 Borage prefers calciferous, medium, and humic soils with sufficient moisture in a sunny situation.

Borage grows 16 to 24 in. high, needs plenty of room for healthy development, and therefore does not belong in a herb bed, but is best left standing alone, for example along a garden fence. Sow directly on site from mid-April by dibbling, with a 12 in. interval between the seed sites. The seed depth should be about ¾ in., and the seedlings should be thinned out once they emerge. Subsequent sowing every four weeks up to July will ensure a continuous harvest into the fall. The edible blue flowers are suitable on cold platters or in a cucumber salad.

487 Annual savory places no special demands on the soil.

It thrives best on humus-rich, loose, and nutrient-rich soils. A site in full sun should also be ensured so that a strong flavor can develop.

488 Annual savory can also be sown in favorable situations from the last days in April.

The row interval is 8 to 10 in. Sow the seeds very sparsely and merely push them in place. Savory is frost-sensitive and should be covered with fleece or similar materials if there are late frosts.

489 Nasturtiums are versatile spice plants, and therefore deserve more attention.

Nasturtiums are mostly planted just as ornamental plants, but in this case decorative characteristics can be combined with useful ones. As balcony decorations or as a cover for garden fences, they can also yield enough spice for the household. It is not just the leaves and flowers that are suitable, but also the buds and the still-green fruits.

490 Nasturtiums grow best on nutrient-rich, medium soils with plenty of humus.

They are very frost-sensitive and may be planted outdoors only from mid-May. To attain vigorous plants by then, in early to mid-April sow three seeds per 3 ½ in. pot filled with sandy compost earth, and leave these on a light-filled windowsill or in a cold frame.

491 All vegetables that have been overwintered in clamps in the cellar should be used by late April if possible.

They should not be allowed to grow new shoots, since otherwise they will use up reserve substances that will then no longer be available to the vegetables. This is particularly likely if it is a warm spring.

> *Shaded, often unused places in the garden are suitable for growing edible mushrooms.*

492 From mid- to late April, fungal culture can begin on blocks of wood.

Of our native deciduous trees, the most suitable include beech, poplar, horse chestnut, plane, and apple and pear trees. The wood should have a moisture content of at least 50 percent and should not yet have been colonized by other fungi. Very dry wood should be wetted several times. Stems of 6 to 12 in. in diameter can be used, which are cut into approximately 12 to 20 in. long rolls. In selecting the wood type, note that softwoods (birch, poplar, willow, alder), will deliver a harvest more quickly, but will already be exhausted after three years, while hardwoods (beech, oak, plane, apple, pear) will be colonized more slowly by the mycelium, but will deliver a harvest for five to seven years. For the wood culture, mushroom spawn is available from dealers, particularly for oyster mushrooms, changeable agaric, conifer tuft, smoky-gilled woodlover, and velvet foot. As a rule, the spawn is supplied in the form of granules, which are easy to work with.

493 Several methods have proven to be effective for inoculating the wood.

The disk method is especially suitable for thicker stems. Cut a 2 to 3 in. thick disk out of the end of the stem, place the stem upright, cover the cut surface with a ½ in. thick layer of culture granules, and then lay the disk on top and fix it in place with a nail. To protect the culture from drying out and to prevent pests, attach a wide strip of foil over the saw cut (with staples or thumbtacks). It should lie as close to the stem as possible. In the cut method, make two cuts in the stem, as deep as possible and about 1 in. wide, that reach at least as far as the middle of the stem. The cuts must be around one quarter of the stem length from the respective stem end, and be opposite one another. Push the culture granules into the cut with a stick, and, once again, tightly cover with foil. For the borehole method, drill boreholes that are as deep as possible and ¾ in. in diameter in rows at intervals of 4 in. and opposite one another. After pushing in the spawn, cover the boreholes with a thick layer of foil.

494 Transfer the inoculated stems to their final site as quickly as possible.

A shady place in the garden is best. There, place the stems up against one another; for especially weak stems, position them around 4 in. deep in the soil for greater stability. To grow throughout the wood, the mycelium needs high air humidity and sufficient oxygen. Accordingly, cover the stems with perforated foil (five holes per square yard). In dry weather, moisten the stems regularly. If only a few blocks of wood have been inoculated, they can also be packed into large, perforated plastic sacks and stored in a suitable room. In this case, place them at their final site only in summer. The mycelium will begin to grow at temperatures of above 46°F and is frost-sensitive during the first weeks; accordingly, provide frost protection. Depending on temperature, wood type, and stem thickness, the time required for growing the fungi through the wood is two to six months.

495 When planting window boxes in April, try planting herbs as well so you will have spices readily available right next to the house.

Provided that a few critical factors are taken into account, herbs from a window-box herb garden can be harvested into the fall.

496 During planting time, specialist dealers will offer a wide range of soils for window-box and tub plants.

Soils to prevent waterlogging and rot (those with an especially loose structure) and those to aid water storage (with particular structural stability, owing to volcanic rock aeration particles) are suitable for window boxes and tubs, depending on the needs of the plant.

497 When applying fertilizer to window boxes planted with herbs, be sure to follow the product information and listed quantities on the packaging.

Excess nutrients will lead to excessive growth and encourage pests. A typical commercially available long-acting fertilizer that will be effective for up to six months will meet the additional nutrient requirements satisfactorily. Mix the fertilizer into the soil before planting.

498 Those who love color on their balcony can use these enchanting flowers right into the fall to create a flowerbed in the herb box, while the flowers themselves can be eaten as snacks.

Borage, nasturtiums, and marigolds are annuals, and can be germinated first or sown directly in the box.

ORNAMENTAL PLANTS

Ornamental Gardens

499 For establishing new lawn areas, prepare the ground carefully and apply nutrients and humus.

In April, the soil that was dug up in the fall, without containing any perennial wild herbs, should be covered with sieved compost earth that has been mixed with 2 to 4 lbs. of grass manure per cubic yard. The compost earth should be as free as possible from weed seeds. Lightly work it into the soil with a grubber. Afterward, trample firm the loosened surface again, with the aid of a wooden board if need be, and rake clean.

> *A properly maintained lawn sets off beds and borders beautifully.*

500 It is best to mark out flowerbeds in a lawn in advance.

Round and oval flowerbeds can only be marked out exactly if a garden cord or line is used. If the beds are to be rectangular, a ruler will be sufficient instead.

501 Flowerbeds in the garden may not be hilly in form, but only slightly raised.

If the beds are piled up too high, it will not be possible to keep them sufficiently moist in the middle of summer, because the water will run down the sides. It's best to cut out the edges of the beds with a spade. Then distribute the excavated earth over the middle and rake so that only a flat raised patch remains.

502 For a long-lasting lawn, use a suitable seed mixture.

Seed dealers or garden centers offer ready seed mixtures, prepared according to the soil conditions or intended use. There are also mixtures that contain clover, which are gratefully used by keepers of small animals. It is important that the seed mixture is properly viable. Some grass seed types are no longer fully viable as early as the second year following the harvest.

503 Only a dry and windless day is suitable for sowing grass seed.

The seed cannot be distributed effectively in the wind and rain. The seed is very light, especially the finer seed. Accordingly, there should be as little wind as possible, since otherwise some of the seed will be blown away and lost.

504 For a dense lawn, about 1 to 1.5 oz. of a properly viable grass seed mixture is needed per square yard.

To gain an idea of the required quantity, an area of one square yard is marked out and the weighed quantity distributed over it evenly. The density of the seed mixture will then be easy to recognize. The appearance of the lawn area will ultimately be dependent on how evenly the seed has been sown.

505 The best time for sowing grass seed is during the second half of April.

The more the soil has warmed up, the faster the seedlings will emerge. This applies especially to the finer grass species. Their seeds will often rot in wet, cold soils, and only the more robust species will emerge, along with wild herbs. If the weather is unfavorable, postpone the sowing.

506 Mark lawn edges by denser seed distribution in shallow furrows.

Over small areas, the furrows are best made using a hoe.

507 In addition to sowing the seed evenly, raking the grass seed and tapping the sown area firm are the most important tasks when laying a new lawn.

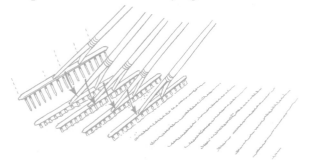

A normal rake is used; for light soils, a wooden rake will be adequate. Use the rake like a hoe—strike the tines shallowly into the soil at short intervals so the seeds are covered with a little earth or mixed in. After this, the grass seeds should no longer be visible. Finally, tap the soil firm with a shovel, or, for larger areas, press firm with a roller.

508 Keep the sown area uniformly moist until the grass seed germinates.

If the sown area dries out during the germination, the small seedlings will die off and the soil surface will become encrusted. The result will be a lawn that is full of gaps. Take care when watering to ensure that the seeds are not washed away.

509 Grass paths have a very natural appearance.

A lawn does not have to be just one large coherent area. The rich green of well-maintained grass paths makes a pleasing contrast to the colorful diversity of perennials, summer flowers, or ornamental shrubs. In such cases, the grass should not be any lower than the adjoining planted areas. The edges can be sharply cut out with a spade to obtain a well-defined lawn edge. A border between the lawn and earth with stones, pavers, or concrete will prevent soiling of the paths with earth or grass growth spreading into the plant beds, but it will also diminish the desired natural appeal. If a delineation must be made, then it is better to select suitable plants for the edging. For grass paths, robust species for sports grounds and playing fields are commercially available. Use pavers for the main paths that must be negotiated several times a day.

510 Rolled or ready-made lawns will quickly produce a dense grass cover.

There are different sizes of grass turfs that are about 1 in. thick and weigh 30 to 40 lbs. per square yard, depending on the moisture content. These should be laid straightaway. Prepare the soil base in the same way as for grass seed. The ready-made lawn is laid or rolled out, pressed or rolled flat, and then watered. It can then be walked on immediately.

511 Lay paving slabs on lawn areas before sowing the grass seed.

Paving slabs are laid before the area is ultimately prepared for sowing with a rake. The surface of the slabs should be a little below the soil surface, and should also be level. This means that the slabs will not impede mowing. Place each slab over a base course layer of sand around 1 in. thick. They will then lie more securely than they would if they were laid directly in the earth. ▶ **TIP 342** and ▶ **TIP 343**

512 Lawns with bare patches should be cut very short before improving them.

Loosen the areas to be improved to a shallow depth with a metal rake and cover with a thick layer of grass seed. Then spread a thin layer of sieved compost earth on top, rake it in, and tap firm with a shovel. Water the areas regularly until the grass emerges.

513 The presence of moss in a lawn is a sign that water, air, and nutrients are in the wrong balance.

This means that too little air is reaching the soil, which, in most such cases, is acidified. Here, only thorough aeration of the soil will help. For this, work the lawn with a sharp metal rake, once lengthwise and once crosswise. If there is a great deal of moss growth, repeat this procedure after several weeks. The removed matted grass and moss can be composted. However, if a forest-like garden corner has been established, the moss should be left to grow, forming a pleasing moss carpet. In most cases, this will be in shady places where a lawn would never establish successfully in any case.

514 In late April or in May, depending on the course of the spring, cut the lawn for the first time.

This will greatly promote grass growth, so that even sparsely growing areas will become dense again.

▶ **TIP 56** and ▶ **TIP 57** Raking the area clean is particularly important following the first annual cut. After cutting, water the lawn thoroughly and supply with nutrients. If the corresponding fertilizer solution (lawn fertilizer) is applied together with the water, the fertilizer will be distributed evenly over the lawn. For more heavily trodden lawn areas, repeat the fertilizer application during the summer. In dry periods, it is sufficient to use a sprinkler, or to water the lawn more frequently.

> *Alternative lawn plants can fill in dry, shady spots where grass won't grow.*

515 A beautiful lawn will not develop in shady places. To avoid bare patches, alternative plants can be used.

Low, shade-loving perennials, such as bishop's hat (*Epimedium*), yellow archangel (*Lamium galeobdolon*), wild ginger (*Asarum*), waldsteinia (*Waldsteinia*), and woody ground covers such as ivy (*Hedera*) and spurge (*Pachysandra*), will cover the ground more effectively than a poor lawn. For light areas under trees, some grasses that spread autonomously, such as wood sedge (*Carex sylvatica*), are highly suitable. Additional ground cover species are listed in **TABLE 18**.

516 A flower meadow instead of a lawn?

A species-rich flower meadow, something that is found only rarely in nature these days, is not just a beautiful sight, but also provides a habitat for small animals and many useful insects, such as butterflies, beetles, wild bees, and bumblebees. If it is feasible, it is well worth converting even part of a lawn into a flower meadow. The simplest method is to remove the lawn, backfill with earth, and sow a special seed mixture. This is done in the same way as for establishing a new lawn (as described in the previous tips). Seed mixtures for flower meadows are available from specialist dealers, and contain many different flowers, herbs, and grasses. It is also possible to prepare your own mixture. However, a requirement for a meadow with native flowering plants is a nutrient-poor soil. If the lawn has previously been fertilized often, the upper layer of soil should be removed together with the grass cover. An even simpler solution is to remove the grass cover only in certain places, loosen up the soil, and sow some of the seed mixture. Pregrown plants can also be used; these should be of a certain size, however, so that they will not be overwhelmed by the spreading grass growth. A newly established flower meadow will need to be mown at least three times during the first year, so that the slower-growing species will be able to survive during the next two to three years. In subsequent years, mowing twice will be sufficient, in late spring and in September/October, but not always at the same times, so that plants that flower either earlier or later will also be able to develop. There are also ready-made flower-meadow mats available from dealers that can be laid on top of old lawns.

517 As soon as the soil is frost-free, examine all the perennials that were planted in the fall to see whether the frost has pushed them up out of the ground.

In most cases, it will be enough to push any loose plants back into the soil firmly by hand. However, if the plants have been raised up very high through freezing they will need to be removed altogether and replanted. They should then be watered thoroughly.

518 Inspect dry stone walls in early April to ensure that all the joints are well filled with earth.

A mixture of sandy loam soil with rotted stable manure, or also compost earth and bark humus, is suitable for filling in the joints. At the same time, cushion plants that have grown too large, often overwhelming other plants, should be cut back, along with any plant parts that have been frozen off.

519 Ornamental shrubs with late shoot development can still be planted in April, as can all others in harsh, exposed situations.

After planting, presss the earth firm and then water thoroughly, so that the roots will develop a connection to the soil immediately. Excessive muddiness is not helpful; it is better to water more frequently, spraying the whole plant. Cover the planting site with an approximately 3 in. thick layer of mulch, which will keep the soil moist for a long time. ▶ **TIP 1279** to ▶ **TIP 1282**

520 Summer flowers for planting directly outdoors need a well-prepared soil.

Most summer flowers need a nutrient-rich, but not freshly manured soil. These should be thoroughly worked with a mattock or grubber ▶ **TIP 42**. The soil should then be raked to yield a finely friable soil, which is crucial for a seedbed.

521 Most summer flowers will need to be thinned out. Planting in bunches is better than rows and will also save on seed at the same time.

In the seeding furrows, plant three to ten seed grains per bunch, depending on the grain size. Once the seedlings have emerged, only the most vigorous should be left to remain. This will also make the plant stands more uniform than if they had been planted in rows.

522 Mignonette (*Reseda*) is suitable as an edging plant, and for fragrant cut flowers.

This tireless perennial flowering plant with its large flowering spikes can be sown from as early as mid-April. Since the seeds are tiny, sow them at a very shallow depth. Space young plants about 8 in. from one another. If mignonettes are grown in beds, the row interval should be 10 in. Vigorously growing varieties will grow to a height of about 16 in.

523 Annual candytufts (*Iberis*) make good edging plants and flower carpets.

These beloved ornamental plants for rock gardens or underplanting for roses can be sown in early April and thrive in every garden soil, although they thrive best in sandy loam. If planted in beds, a row interval of 8 in. is sufficient. Within a row, sow three to six seed grains in shallow furrows, 4 ½ to 6 in. apart. Candytufts grow 8 in. high on average.

> **Plant the edges of beds and paths with low-growing annuals for a colorful display.**

524 **Annual sweet alyssum (*Lobularia maritima*) will grow to a height of 4 ½ to 12 in., depending on the variety, and is especially suitable for beautiful edge planting.**

The plant thrives in full sun, and in soils that tend to be dry without excess nutrients. It blooms from June to December, and is also used as a ground cover, for rock gardens, and as cut flowers, including for window boxes and troughs on the terrace. Sowing begins in mid-April with a row interval of 6 to 8 in., depending on the variety. Thin the plants within a row so that there is one plant only every 4 to 6 in. If it is not too cold, the plants often germinate after eight days. Any flea beetles should be dealt with immediately.

525 **Creeping zinnia (*Sanvitalia procumbens*) blooms on sunny, dry sites.**

It is suitable for low borders and edging, and blooms from late June until the time of frost, with small yellow flowers reminiscent of sunflowers. Sowing is better done over a wide area than in rows; the plants will then develop well at an interval of 6 to 8 in. Creeping zinnia can also quickly fill gaps in a rock garden.

526 **Pot marigolds (*Calendula*) must be sown in April so they do not bloom too late.**

With their yellow- to orange-colored flowers, pot marigolds will do well in any soil, provided that sufficient nutrients are available. Sow the rather large seeds so that there are three to five grains every 8 to 10 in. Once the seedlings emerge, leave only one plant to remain at each interval. The dried and crushed flower heads have pharmaceutical uses, for brewing herbal tea, for example. A versatile, anti-inflammatory ointment can be made from marigold flowers, beeswax, and olive oil. Pot marigolds are somewhat prone to powdery mildew during long periods of wet weather, and if they are planted together too densely.

527 **Sunflowers (*Helianthus*) are often grown along fences—but they also protect compost heaps from too much sun.**

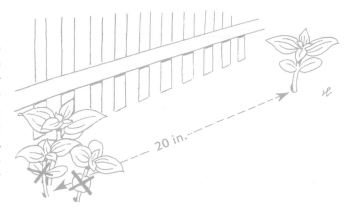

Depending on the variety, they grow to a height of 3 to 6 ½ ft. From mid-April, depending on the site, sow two or three grains each at intervals of about 20 in. Once the seedlings emerge, leave only the most vigorous plant at each interval to remain. The nature of the soil will determine the growth vigor of the sunflowers.

528 **Annual larkspurs (*Consolida*) deserve far greater attention. Some varieties grow to a height of 20 in., and others exceed 3 ft.**

They love deeply loosened, calciferous, and somewhat moist soils, but do not tolerate fresh stable manure. The row interval should be 8 in. for low-growing varieties, and 10 to 12 in. for taller ones. Following emergence, thin out the plantlets within the row to an interval of 4 or 8 in., respectively.

529 The paper daisy (*Rhodanthe manglesii*) yields delightful dried flowers.

This summer flower thrives on humic, slightly acidic sandy soils. The row interval is 8 in. Thin out the plantlets to an interval of 6 or 8 in. after they emerge. Sowing should be done in mid-April. For dried flowers, cut the flowers when the first blooms on the torus open, then bundle them together and hang upside down in a shady and airy place.

530 Dwarf morning glory (*Convolvulus tricolor*), which grows only 12 in. high, is a beautiful border plant that deserves far greater attention.

Calciferous soils that are not too rich in nutrients are best here. If dwarf morning glory is to flower well, it needs to be in the sun. Sow seeds in April/May, with a row interval of 10 in. Following emergence, thin out the plantlets to an interval of 8 in. in the row.

531 The opulently flowering African daisy (*Osteospermum*) grows to a height of around 12 in., depending on the variety.

The colorful, daisy-like plant is winter hardy only if grown in climatically favorable situations down to around 23°F; although perennial, it is grown and sold as an annual. However, it is possible to overwinter the plants that are not winter hardy in cool rooms as well. It is best to buy them as young plants or already flowering, in which case it is also possible to be certain that they are not specimens of the annual sun marigold (*Dimorphotheca*). Especially when buying seeds, these are in fact usually varieties of sun marigold. If genuine African daisy (*Osteospermum*) seeds can be obtained, these are best sown on a warm, somewhat loamy sand soil in a sunny situation. Wet soils are unsuitable. The best time for sowing is late April to May; a planting width of 8 × 8 in. is sufficient.

532 With its radiantly colored flowers, the rose mallow (*Lavatera trimestris*) belongs in every garden.

There are carmine-pink and white-flowering varieties that grow 24 to 35 in. high. Any garden soil that is not too wet will suffice; a sunny site is important. The rose mallow can be sown directly on site with a planting width of 20 × 16 in. Sow around 10 to 15 seeds in a bunch, which will then germinate after 14 days. Leave only the most vigorous plant left standing. The rose mallow is also suitable as a cut flower that will last for around one week. It blooms from July to September.

533 All gardeners should try their hand with the easy-to-grow yellow ageratum, also known as African daisy (*Lonas annua*).

The plant grows only 12 to 20 in. high and produces numerous vivid yellow umbels. It is a valuable plant for cut and dried flowers alike. Sowing takes place in April with a row interval of 10 in.; thin out the seedlings to an interval of 8 in. within the row. It is important that the site is sunny and not too moist. Flowering depends on the time of sowing; it begins in late July and lasts until the onset of frosts.

534 Vivid blue hound's tongue (*Cynoglossum*) resembles a tall forget-me-not.

This summer flower grows around 16 in. high. It can be planted directly on site in late March or early April. The planting width should be 10 × 8 in. Hound's tongue flowers from late June, and again in the fall after it has been cut back.

535 The flowers of the California poppy (*Eschscholzia*) have wonderfully vivid colors.

California poppy flowers open only in the sunshine. The plant reaches a height of 16 in. on average and loves warm, dry, somewhat loamy sandy soils. However, it will also grow in any other soil. It can be sown directly on site in early April. The row interval should be 12 in., with an 8 in. interval within a row. Seeds scattered in empty patches of a rock garden will later yield decorative tufts.

536 *Ursinia*, a genus of the chamomile family, is a highly attractive composite flower that is also suitable as a cut flower.

In particular, the species *Ursinia anethoides*, with its gold-orange blooms, yields beautiful cut flowers. It grows to a height of around 16 in. *U. anthemoides* grows only 12 in. high, and is also suitable for window boxes. This plant, which is only seldom seen today, grows best on warm, sandy soils. A sunny situation is required. Sow seeds from late April with a row interval of 10 in., and an interval within the row of 8 in. Advance culture under glass in February/March is preferable, so that the plants will flower in June/July.

537 Burning bush (*Bassia scoparia*) is an annual and can be sown directly on site in late April.

The plants will then be not quite as large as those which have been pregrown in cold frames, but they will still grow 20 to 24 in. tall. The filigree, delicate leaves of 'Trichophylla' turn red in the fall. Sow five or six seeds at intervals of 10 in., shallowly in the earth; once the seedlings emerge, leave only the most vigorous plant. If sown in a row, the result is a small, delicate hedge that can also be trimmed. Burning bush will grow in every garden soil that is not too dry, and is a good host plant for many insect species. In China and Japan, the cooked seeds are served as a delicacy (tonburi).

538 Quaking grass (*Briza*), foxtail barley (*Hordeum jubatum*), and hare's tail grass (*Lagurus ovatus*) are annuals.

With their beautiful spikes, they make an appealing vase decoration that will keep well. All three grasses place no special demands on the soil, which should not be too moist in summer. Sow the seeds in mid-April with a row interval of 10 in., and thin out within the row so that there is a small bunch left standing every 8 in. The seeds should be only barely covered with earth; afterward, pat the earth flat with a shovel. Keep the seedbed moist until the seedlings emerge.

Perennials that flower in the summer and fall can be planted well into spring.

539 Summer- and fall-flowering perennials, and perennial ornamental grasses, can still be planted in April.

However, they should have good root balls or they must be replanted as soon as they are divided. Special emphasis should be given here to ornamental grasses; they make an appealing focus in the garden, and in a vase as well. **TABLE 16**, **TABLE 17**, and **TABLE 21**. The roots of grasses dry out very quickly; accordingly, look for plants with good, moist root balls when buying them.

540 Ferns for shady and semi-shaded garden sites can still be planted at this time.

Balled plants should mainly be used. Some species will also grow well between light stands of trees and shrubs with generous watering. Others are more demanding when it comes to soil moisture and humus content. Almost all ferns love shady sites and air that is not too dry, **TABLE 22**.

541 Lay gladiolus bulbs in late April. They must be healthy and be planted in a different place each year.

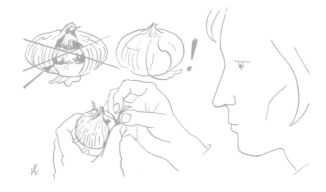

When buying gladiolus bulbs, look underneath the bracts for discolored or sunken spots. Diseased bulbs will infest the entire garden. If gladioli are planted in the same place for several years running, they will lose their resistance and become more prone to disease. Accordingly, it is best to change the site every year. Gladioli need a deep soil, not too dry, but still permeable; it should not have had a fresh fertilizer application.

> *Site rotation when growing gladioli is a plant health preventive measure, while planting them up to 4 in. deep in the soil protects them from falling over!*

542 If you have noticed disease in gladioli during the previous summer, disinfect the bulbs before they are returned to the soil.

A range of disinfectants are commercially available; be sure to strictly follow their instructions. Before disinfection, remove all the outer layers and leave the naked bulbs to soak in the disinfectant solution for 30 to 60 minutes. Following this treatment, they should ideally be put in the soil immediately.

543 Do not set gladiolus bulbs too shallowly in the ground or the inflorescences will fall over.

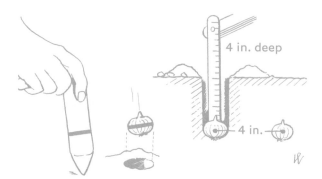

Lay the bulbs at an interval of 4 x 8 in. For this, either make correspondingly deep furrows, or make a hole with a dibber with a diameter that is appropriate for that of the bulbs. Depending on their size, they should be set 2 ½ to 4 in. deep in the ground. Fifty bulbs are required per square yard. To attain beautiful, large flowers, give them an application of complete fertilizer about 10 days later, followed by another application 6 weeks after that.

544 Montbretia (*Crocosmia*) bulbs are set in the ground in early April.

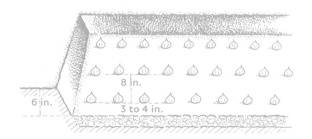

The longer montbretia bulbs are left undisturbed in one place, the better they will flower. When planting them for the first time, set them 2 to 4 in. deep in the soil. A row interval of 8 in. is sufficient, with an interval of 3 to 4 in. within the row. If this is done, you won't need to remove the bulbs in the fall; instead just cover with a thick, dry, protective layer of leaves or bark mulch, then cover with foil. Here, too, the bulbs should be checked for good health at the time of purchase.

545 The bulbs of the harlequin flower (*Sparaxis*) are laid in the ground in April.

Set the bulbs about 2 ½ in. apart nearly 4 in. deep in the soil, and treat the same way as gladiolus bulbs. In mild climates, they can also be overwintered in the open under a thick layer of bark substrate. This popular summer flower brings color into the garden, and is also suitable for cut flowers.

> *Roses can be planted in late spring and still flower that year.*

546   The month of April is still a suitable time for planting roses.

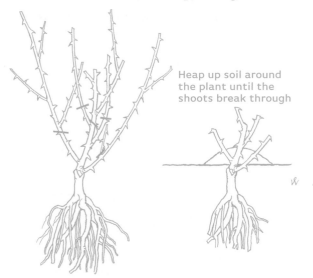

Heap up soil around the plant until the shoots break through

Preparations should be made as outlined in ▶ **TIP 310**. Before planting, shorten the roots somewhat, and prune back the aboveground parts. Leave only three to five eyes to remain on each shoot from the previous year; remove weak shoots entirely. In the case of climbing roses, cut the shoots back to eight to ten eyes. The planting interval for bush roses should be about 12 to 16 in. For planting roses in beds, maintain a row interval of about 24 in. Standard roses need a planting interval of 30 to 40 in., and climbing roses 3 ¼ to 6 ½ ft., depending on their use. The grafting location must always be 1 to 2 in. below the soil surface.

547   Firm and secure planting and liberal watering ensures that the roses grow well.

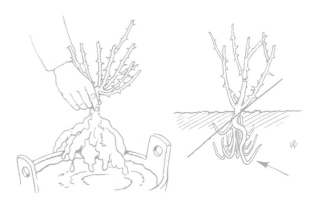

Injured roots can be cut back somewhat with a sharp knife before planting. Subsequently dipping them in a clay slurry will promote root development.

548   Plant standard roses at an angle, and not upright.

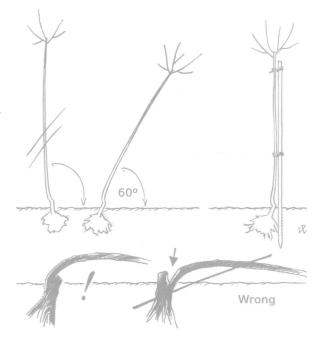

60°

Wrong

Since, for overwintering, standard roses are bent over by 90° and covered with earth, the stem is planted at an angle of about 60° to the soil surface and tied to a stake, so that it then stands upright. Only in this way is it possible to bend the stem over in the fall, because only an angle of 60° will still need to be overcome. It is important that standard roses are planted so that they can be bent over the grafting location near the root collar.

549   Climbing roses need a secure support for their long shoots.

Since climbing roses do not actually climb or twine by themselves, and they have no holdfasts, they need a support to which they can be tied. The best solution is to attach a suitable structure to firm standing walls of all kinds. Climbing roses on a wooden trellis or pergola are always eye-catching in the garden.

550 Frequent-flowering varieties of climbing roses should be preferred for new plantings.

Their floral splendor during the main flowering period is hardly less impressive than that of once-flowering varieties; meanwhile, they will produce flowers continuously throughout the summer. Varieties that are healthy, opulent, and flower frequently during the year include 'Amadeus' (red), 'Golden Gate' (yellow), 'Compassion' (pink), and 'Sympathie' (red).

551 Consider underplanting rose beds.

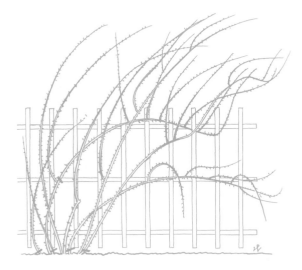

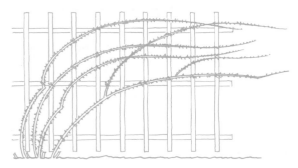

Rose beds or larger rose stands can be made to appear even more attractive in combination with other plants, and, by selecting an optimal color combination, an interesting long-distance optical effect can also be attained. Take care with noble roses, however, since they do not always tolerate underplanting. For underplanting shrub, climbing, or bed roses, low-growing species are suitable, such as candytuft (*Iberis*), catmint (*Nepeta*), white or blue lavender varieties, flossflower (*Ageratum*), and others. Ensure that the roses are not crowded out by the underplanting. Also note that these new plants, too, will consume water and nutrients, which will then no longer be available to the roses themselves. Accordingly, when underplanting is used, give the plants sufficient water and fertilizer.

552 The shoots of older climbing roses should be spread out well and newly tied up.

Remove very old and weak shoots. Arrange long annual shoots almost horizontally on the trellises; in this way, the most buds will be produced. Annual shoots are not pruned.

553 An aphid infestation on roses can be dealt with easily if there are enough ladybugs (ladybirds) in the garden.

The ladybugs will make quick work of the aphids, and their offspring soon afterward will provide reinforcements to combat future infestation.

> *Conifers and evergreen broadleaved trees and shrubs with root balls or taken from containers will grow willingly when planted out.*

554 Conifers and evergreen broadleaved trees and shrubs should not be planted out before late April.

The main time for planting these trees and shrubs is generally in late summer, but planting them in April can also be successful. It is important that the plants have a firm root ball; this is generally the case for container plants nowadays. There is no point, however, if the root ball covering in which the plants are delivered by the nursery contains only loose earth.

555 When planting evergreen species, the root ball covering should not be removed if it is made of burlap (sacking) or jute.

Excavate the hole for planting with a sufficient diameter, corresponding to that of the root ball, but not much deeper than necessary; plant the tree or shrub only as deep as it had been before. Beneath the plant, trample firm the backfilled earth so that it will not subside later and cause cavities to form beneath the roots. The free space around the root ball is initially filled to only half the ball height, and trampled firm only lightly. Only now is the ball covering opened and spread out on all sides. Afterward, fill the planting hole completely, and water the plant vigorously. If the planting site is covered with a layer of bark mulch, this will contribute greatly to rapid growth.

556 If evergreen trees and shrubs have been bought in plastic containers, they will need to be carefully removed from the containers before planting.

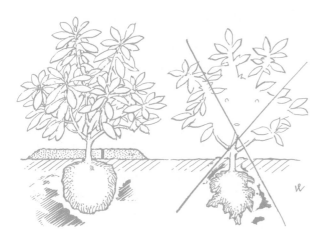

Soft plastic containers should be cut only once the root ball has been placed in the prepared planting hole, and then removed carefully. Meanwhile, plants in hard plastic or clay containers are removed carefully and then placed in the planting hole, as far as possible with their complete earth ball. The plants must not be set any deeper in the ground than they had been at the nursery.

557 Rare evergreen trees and shrubs are also suitable for the garden.

In addition to different forms of pine, spruce, and fir, evergreen trees and shrubs that are suitable for the garden include Japanese yew (*Taxus cuspidata* var. *nana*), plum yew (*Cephalotaxus*) or Japanese plum yew (*Cephalotaxus harringtonia* 'Fastigiata'), mountain laurel (*Kalmia latifolia*), microbiota (*Microbiota decussata*), and hiba (*Thujopsis*), along with the monkey puzzle tree or Chile pine (*Araucaria araucana*), which is closely related to the Norfolk Island pine (*Araucaria heterophylla*). However, the monkey puzzle tree is winter hardy only in warmer, sheltered situations (winegrowing climate), and is more suitable for larger gardens. The Japanese euonymus (*Euonymus japonicus* 'Marieke') is smaller, growing only around 5 ft. tall.

558 Juniper berries can be used in a variety of different ways.

The common juniper (*Juniperus communis*), like *J. sabina*, is native to central Europe, the latter primarily in the Alps. For the garden, especially heath gardens ▶ TIP 355, dwarf and columnar varieties of the common juniper are suitable. The evergreen varieties grow very slowly, and need plenty of sun, and dry, nutrient-poor soil that is as sandy as possible. They tolerate pruning and can also be used for protective hedges, for which two plants per yard are sufficient. The blue star juniper (*J. squamata* 'Blue Star') reaches a height of only 3 ft. and a width of 5 ft., even when mature. Some species, particularly the Chinese juniper (*J. chinensis*) and *J. sabina*, can be attacked by pear rust, which can especially damage young pear trees. Juniper berries (from *J. communis*) can be used to make gin, prepared together with grated apple make an excellent jam, and are also used as a kitchen spice, for example for sauerkraut or sauerbraten (marinated pot roast), and for medicinal purposes (tea).

559 April is a good time to plant evergreen hedges.

Beautiful hedges can be established using evergreen species such as Magellan barberry (*Berberis buxifolia*) and cherry laurel and its varieties (*Prunus laurocerasus*). Two species of privet, *Ligustrum vulgare* 'Atrovirens' and *L. ovalifolium*, ▸ **TABLE 11**, are in fact wintergreen, but have rapidly growing new shoots. For high, narrow, and columnar hedges, but also dense hedges, red cedar (*Thuja*) and false cypress (*Chamaecyparis*) are suitable. They are cut back somewhat only every two years.

560 Rhododendrons love shade and high air humidity.

Rhododendrons grow and flower best in the light shade of larger trees and shrubs, while at the same time they also love a high air humidity. If they are planted in sunny places, it is necessary to ensure a high air humidity during summer, and often as early as April, by frequent spraying. The soil beneath the plants, too, should always be kept moist. Most rhododendrons do not tolerate strongly calciferous soils.

561 Ivy (*Hedera*) is the best climbing plant for shady sites.

Ivy also tolerates deep shade and is therefore highly suitable for planting up unsightly places in the garden. Ivy does not need any maintenance because it grows firmly attached to walls; it can also make a good ground cover. Ivy on building façades is valuable for city ecosystems; here, many insects and bird species will find places to live and breed. However, the façade itself should be intact and free of any cracks or other damage.

562 In early April, false indigo (*Amorpha*), California lilac (*Ceanothus*), and butterfly bush (*Buddleja*) should be cut back to 6 to 12 in.

Generally, these species freeze back in winter; accordingly, cutting back should not be left until the fall. They will then produce flowering stems that are always vigorous. Cut back weaker plants more strongly than vigorous ones.

563 The sea buckthorn (*Hippophae*) has both male and female plants.

The sea buckthorn produces fruit only when there are also male plants growing near female ones. This should be taken into account in new plantings; around 3 to 6, or even up to 10, female plants should be allowed for each male plant. However, the gender can be determined only once the plants are three to four years old. In the male plants, the buds are closer together, and are markedly larger than those of the female plants. The fruits contain much vitamin C, and are often processed to make jelly and juice.

564 In clematis (*Clematis*), only from April on is it possible to determine what has been frozen in winter, and what can be cut back.

In harsh winters with little snow, clematis plants sometimes freeze right back to the ground if they do not have enough winter protection. However, they then generally produce new growth again from underneath. In early-flowering varieties, only cut off dried-up shoots. Long, healthy shoots should be tied up horizontally as far as is possible so that they develop new shoots along their entire length. **TABLE 15**

565 Clematis (*Clematis*) must be planted from late April, with firm root balls.

Clematis plants should be planted about 2 in. deeper than they were before. Take care not to damage the root balls in the process or subsequent growth will be impeded. There are a wide variety of species, hybrids, and varieties in many colors, **TABLE 15**. Many clematis plants, especially species that occur in nature (together with their varieties), develop attractive fruiting bodies in the fall.

> *Clematis are often native to forested areas; accordingly, the lower parts should be protected from direct sun.*

566 Protect the lower parts of clematis (*Clematis*) plants from direct sun.

Cover the soil with about 2 in. of compost earth and humus, or leaves, or also rotted (never fresh) stable manure. The lower parts of the plants are best protected by prior planting of 16 to 28 in. high perennials, to block direct sunlight.

567 Nearly all perennials, except for newly planted ones, will need nutrient applications in April.

A complete fertilizer can be used for this purpose; it makes no difference whether it is spread dry or otherwise applied as a nutrient solution when watering. Following the application of dry fertilizers, spray the plants thoroughly with water. Organic manure is especially suitable, in the form of compost, stable manure (also available as pellets from dealers), or manure tea. This ensures that the nutrients will not be washed out as quickly, and reduces the danger of overfertilizing. As a rule, fertilize weakly growing herbs less, and vigorously growing ones more. Diseased, ailing specimens should not be given any fertilizer at all. Before fertilizer application, remove any winter protection materials and died-off plant remains.

568 For planting boxwood edging, the soil needs to be well prepared.

Loosen the soil thoroughly and mix with plenty of compost earth. Set the young boxwood plants into the ground along a cord or line, so that they stand around 2 ½ to 3 in. above the soil. They must be planted firmly in place before being watered generously. Then trim the plants to the same height.

569 Boxwood edging that has become uneven can still be cut back in April.

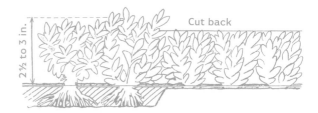

Here, the principle is to use the lowest plants for orientation, since boxwood plants will withstand severe cutting back. The plants will always develop vigorous new shoots. Boxwood edging with gaps is best replanted; remove all the plants and prepare the soil again.

570 Plant daisies (*Bellis*), pansies (*Viola ×wittrockiana*), and forget-me-nots (*Myosotis*) on their final site from early April.

If planted too closely together or on shady sites, the plants will grow too tall. They should be spaced at around 8 × 8 in.

571 Young snapdragons (*Antirrhinum*) will not be frost-sensitive if they have been properly hardened off prior to planting.

The planting interval depends on the variety and height. In a normal bed, five rows are planted with an interval of 10 in., or in the case of lower-growing varieties, 8 in.

> *Cool-season annuals can be planted out in early to spring to bloom with the bulbs.*

572 Stocks (*Matthiola*) can be planted from mid-April, since they can withstand light frosts without damage.

Plants that have been pricked out will grow more reliably than those from a seedbed. There are several varieties or classes with specific characteristics. Singly flowering seedlings can be recognized by their dark green cotyledons. Remove these from the other seedlings so that only double flowers are raised. Climbing forms will do well with a planting width of 4 × 6 in.; for all others, use a planting width of 8 × 10 in.

573 Carnations (*Dianthus caryophyllus*) tolerate light night frosts and can already be planted out in mid-April.

Since the young plants are raised under glass, they must be well hardened off at the time of planting. The splendid, tightly double carnations should not be planted closer together than 10 × 10 in. They flower around six months after sowing. Particularly large flowers can be obtained if the lateral shoots are removed.

574 Newly established ponds, or those that have been emptied or drained in the fall, can be planted up with aquatic plants in April.

If the plants are to be planted out freely in the pond, the earth must be low in both lime content and nutrients. A mixture of two parts sand or fine gravel and one part loam is best. Specific pond and aquatic plants are available from specialist dealers. The soil surface should be covered with a layer of sand about 1 in. thick; large gravel stones serve as anchors for the plants. The same applies to water lilies. It is sufficient, however, to set aquatic plants in (lime-free) gravel only, without any earth. Died-off plant parts and fish excrement will then accumulate between the stones, and the resulting mud will contain enough nutrients. Many aquatic plants are set in containers. ▶ **TIP 370** Before setting the plants in containers, clean both the plants and containers thoroughly. The covering layer of sand should also be replaced.

575 Algae in ponds are best combated with organic means.

Excess algal growth is mostly caused by excessive nutrient levels in the water, and often an excessively high pH value or an oxygen deficiency. To counteract this, keep fish numbers low, and continually remove leaves that have fallen into the pond and rotting plant remains. The banks should be designed so that no garden soil will be washed into the pond during heavy rainfall. The pH value, which should be measured often, should be between 7 and 8. If it is higher than 8, scatter wet peat in the water, preferably before expected rain. The peat will settle on the base, and will not make the water murky, but instead turn it a somewhat darker color. An even better solution is commercially available peat granules in fabric sacks. Use enough aquatic plants such as common water moss (*Fontinalis antipyretica*), since these are important oxygen providers. Do not employ chemical agents as these will also harm the plants and animals in the pond.

576 Ponds are more attractive when appropriate perennials grow at their edges.

The height of these perennials, which can be planted in April, is determined by the size of the pond. Here, select species that also have a connection to water in nature. Actual swamp plants are unsuitable if the soil adjacent to the pond is no moister than it is elsewhere in the garden. The site for the perennials should nevertheless be rich in nutrients and humus. Rather than surrounding the entire pond, the planting should be present on no more than three sides—this makes a better visual impression.

577 Winter losses in swamp pools or wetland biotopes can be replaced at this time.

By April, it is possible to recognize which plants have fallen victim to frost. These are then replaced with new plants. This is also an opportunity to divide plants that have run wild and are threatening to crowd out other plants. Remove young water plantain (*Alisma plantago-aquatica*) plants, since these are mostly vigorous self-seeders.

578 If the dry stone walls that were erected in March have not yet been planted up, this is a good time to do so.

Losses in older walls can be replaced. The procedure for planting up a dry stone wall is described in ▸ TIP 336.

Dahlia bulbs can already be planted out once the soil has warmed.

579 Dahlia bulbs can often be set in the ground as early as the end of April.

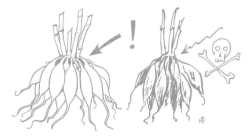

Tubers that have been overwintered will grow only if the tuber collar is healthy; this is the only place where they produce shoots. Inspect newly purchased bulbs accordingly. Tall-growing varieties need stakes, which should be set in the ground before planting. If this is done the other way around, the bulbs and roots will be damaged. Set dahlia bulbs so deep that they are covered with at least 4 in. of earth. The planting interval depends on the variety.

580 The splendid tiger flower (*Tigridia*) is greatly underappreciated.

The bulbs should be laid in a sunny situation 3 to 4 in. deep at an interval of 4 to 5 in. The tiger flower grows to around 20 in. high. Groups of around 10 are especially appealing in a perennial herb garden.

581 Freesia (*Freesia*) bulbs can be planted out in the open in late April; they flower from late July.

So-called paradise freesias deserve a lot more attention than they currently receive. They will tolerate a slightly shady site better than harsh sun. Set the bulbs 2 in. deep at an interval of 4 × 2 in. Accordingly, around 200 bulbs are needed per square yard. Freesias also need supports; these can be short slips, for example, although a finely meshed grid stretched over the plants is better. The freesias will grow through this and find their support accordingly. They should be watered sufficiently as they grow.

582 Shamrock (*Oxalis tetraphylla*) is too often neglected as a decorative edging plant.

To achieve a dense row at the edge of a plant bed, set the tubers about 1 in. deep in the ground from mid-April. The planting interval should be around 3 in. It is important that the tubers are overwintered in frost-free conditions. Shamrock plants are available as pot plants in December. They should be left to grow in a light, cool place.

583 For use as cut flowers in a vase, tulip plants should be left with at least two leaves when they are cut.

Otherwise, the newly developing bulb will be damaged, and it will not flower in the following year.

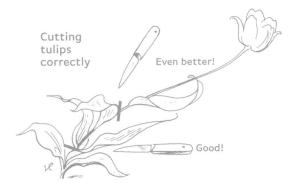

Cutting tulips correctly   Even better!   Good!

584 Gentians (*Gentiana*) include both calcicolous and calciphobous species.

Examples include the trumpet gentian (*Gentiana acaulis*, mostly available from dealers as hybrids) and *G. sino-ornata*, which flowers in the fall. The trumpet gentian is calcicolous; its site should be sunny, and the soil loamy and fresh. In contrast, *G. sino-ornata* demands humic, acidic soils that may not be subject to lime application. Both gentians are among the most beautiful of their genus, and so an effort should be made to improve the soil in accordance with their natural requirements. *G. septemfida* var. *lagodechiana*, which flowers from July to September, is less demanding.

585 The well-known bleeding heart (*Dicentra spectabilis*) will sometimes flower in April.

This winter-hardy perennial, with its mostly deep pink-colored, heart-shaped petals and white "tears," grows best on semi-shaded sites in the garden. On harsh sites, it should be covered with foil if exposed to hard night frosts. It is possible to sow them yourself. However, the seeds will germinate only if they have been exposed to cool temperatures for around two months, or brief frost. Climbing bleeding hearts, which are occasionally commercially available and produce yellow to orange blooms from June to August, can reach a height of 6 ½ to 10 ft., and are winter hardy only in sheltered situations or in a winegrowing climate. They can be raised from seed each year.

586 Perennials that flower in the late fall, such as asters or Michaelmas daisies and chrysanthemums, are planted in early April.

The same applies to sensitive varieties, such as *Anemone hupehensis*, rock or sun roses (*Helianthemum*), red hot pokers or torch lilies (*Kniphofia*), and tickseed (*Coreopsis*). Unlike most perennials in the garden, they should not be divided and replanted, because they are prone to die off in winter. ▶ **TIP 1171** and ▶ **TIP 1172** Frequent watering and a ground covering of compost soil will stimulate root development.

587 Native perennials, trees, and shrubs will also thrive in a near-natural garden.

A near-natural garden does not mean leaving a beautifully maintained garden to run wild. You can still plant noble roses with a clear conscience, or take pleasure from splendid hydrangeas or a fine Caucasian fir. That said, why not establish some native plants in the garden as well? They, too, produce beautiful flowers, while also providing insects and other animals with a habitat. Blooms from wildflowers, such as lily of the valley (*Convallaria majalis*), pasque flower (*Pulsatilla pratensis*), and harebells (*Campanula rotundifolia*), serve as a source of nutrition for honeybees and bumblebees. The same is true for single-flowering varieties of many garden flowers. They are no less attractive than showier double flowers, which mostly have little or no nectar. Accordingly, instead of large-flowering pansies with their stunted nectaries, it is better to plant sweet violets (*Viola odorata*) or dog violets (*V. canina*). Insects should always be well provided for in a near-natural garden: in spring with forget-me-not, columbine, globe flower, and broom; in early summer with carnations, larkspur, vetches, and oxeye daisies; in summer with marigolds, phlox, mallows, and lilies; and in the fall with mullein, dahlias, and autumn crocuses.

Terraces and Balconies

588 Hardened-off tub plants that can withstand short cold snaps down to 23°F can already be grown out in the open.

Provided they have not suffered from overwintering in excessively dark or warm conditions, spotted laurel (*Aucuba japonica*), strawberry tree (*Arbutus*), loquat (*Eriobotrya*), pomegranate (*Punica granatum*), Chinese windmill or fan palm (*Trachycarpus*), crape myrtle (*Lagerstroemia indica*), olive (*Olea*), laurel (*Laurus*), and others can be planted out in the open in April, away from exposed sites, and if possible near the house. In a cold spell, bring them inside again if need be, or cover with mats or bubble wrap. If, however, these plants have begun to produce shoots, they will need to remain in their winter quarters or the new shoots will fall victim to frost.

> *In April, container plants that have been overwintered can be moved outdoors to a shady spot to acclimatize before being put on display.*

589 Tub plants that have grown too large will need to be repotted.

In the case of very large tub plants that are difficult to repot, the uppermost earth layer at least should be renewed. Carefully remove as much earth as possible from the surface and replace with new soil. If replanting is necessary, however, and the root ball is badly matted, as is particularly common with palms, first cut off the lower part of the root ball in the form of a disk. Also remove a ¾ in. thick layer from the sides of the root ball.

590 Tub plants are suitable not just for terraces and balconies, but for house entrances as well.

Here, they are largely protected from harsh or drying winds. Depending on the situation, whether sunny, shaded, or semi-shaded, there are many trees, shrubs, and perennials that are suitable, as well as bulb plants and annual flowers.

591 Roses in pots are a trendy choice for south-facing house entrances.

There are beautiful potted roses in many colors and forms that are commercially available. However, only varieties that are not overly susceptible to pests and diseases, and that flower several times during the year, should be selected. If space is limited, because of stair stringers, for example, then miniature roses in pots are highly suitable (such as robust, disease-resistant, and frequent-flowering 'Charmant', with its nostalgic pink blooms). If plenty of room is available to the right and left of the door, bed roses or small shrub roses in tubs are also very decorative.

592 Rose stems make a romantic impact.

Rose bushes can grow outside the house, planted out or in containers. Wooden tubs make especially suitable containers, for example, whether left as natural wood or painted white, or rectangular or round. In the case of standard roses, too, there are remontant and disease-resistant varieties, for example 'Super Dorothy' with pompon-like pink flowers, or 'Super Excelsa' with densely filled, light carmine-red flowers. With these "portable" roses, even suitable underplanting, in terms of color and form, with small summer flowers or early-flowering, low perennials is possible. For overwintering, it's best to bring the roses into a cool, frost-free room. If this is not possible, they can be sunk into the earth, with or without a pot, and the crown protected as described in ▶ TIP 548.

593 For south-facing house entrances, and also for terraces and balconies, other plants that do not take up too much room and tolerate plenty of sun are suitable.

These include pussy willow (*Salix caprea* 'Pendula'), marguerite (*Argyranthemum frutescens*), limequat (×*Citrofortunella microcarpa*) and other *Citrus* species, angel's trumpet (*Brugmansia*), loquat or Japanese medlar (*Eriobotrya japonica*), Chinese hibiscus (*Hibiscus rosa-sinensis*), pomegranate (*Punica granatum*), *Schefflera*, rosemary, and *Solanum* species, such as Jerusalem cherry and eggplant.

594 For north-facing house entrances, too, there are suitable plants.

These include, for example, mahonia ▶ TIP 321 and ▶ TIP 1188, Japanese yew (*Taxus cuspidata* var. *nana*), cast-iron plant (*Aspidistra elatior*), spotted laurel (*Aucuba japonica*), and, if space is limited, gloriously flowering azaleas and tuberous begonias.

595 In April, replanting of overwintering summer-flowering species for the terrace and balcony can begin.

Geraniums, fuchsias, yellow sage, and others are cut back in late February/early March. They need to be replanted in April because the nutrients will have been exhausted and the soil structure will have changed. Remove the plants, shake out the root balls, trim the roots somewhat, and set the plants into fresh soil. All died-off plant parts should be removed cleanly. Press the plants gently into the soil and remember to water them.

596 In April, bowls planted with herbs and window boxes for the balcony or terrace can be prepared.

These can already remain outside in fine weather. If there are still frosts at night, the plants will need some protection, or, alternatively, they can be brought into the house overnight. Plant tubs for deep-rooting herbs such as dill are also suitable. Many herbs are available as young plants, and some as flowering plants in pots. In many cases, it is worth sowing herbs. The containers need a place in full sun and to be watered only moderately. A mixture of garden earth mixed with sand is suitable as a substrate.

Winter Gardens, Flower Windows, and Rooms

597 Plants in south-facing windows are endangered by strong incoming sunlight.

Following the long winter with its poor light levels, many plants are extremely sensitive to direct sunlight, especially during the middle of the day. Providing shade is essential.

598 April is an especially good time for repotting indoor plants.

For this, use potting mixture and well-rotted sandy compost earth. Thoroughly clean used pots both inside and out. Chemical agents should not be used for this. For drainage, place a layer of coarse sand or gravel (or small pot shards or polystyrene flakes) in the bottom of the pot. When replanting, press the new soil between the root ball and pot wall so that there is no free space or cavity. Fill each pot with earth so that a space of about ½ in. remains for watering. While the plants should be watered thoroughly immediately after repotting, they should be watered only moderately during the next two to three weeks. They will not need extra fertilizer as the new soil will already contain enough nutrients.

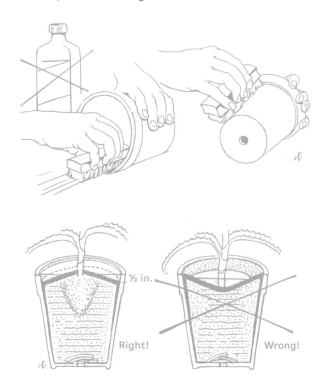

599 Give indoor plants with diseased roots more sandy soil when they are repotted.

While the normal proportion of sand in the soil is around one fifth, for plants with diseased roots, an earth to sand ratio of 3:1 is better. Such a mixture contains more air and dries out more quickly after watering. The drainage layer at the bottom of the pot should also be fairly thick. If necessary, repot the plants in smaller pots and cut them back. A rubber plant, for example, that has lost a lot of leaves during the winter and has diseased roots should be treated in such a manner.

600 Amaryllis (*Hippeastrum*), kaffir lily (*Clivia*), and fire lily (*Cyrtanthus*, syn. *Vallota*) can now be repotted.

Here, remove the upper soil layer without disturbing the root ball. A mixture of compost earth, loam, and sand in a ratio of 3:1:1 or commercial potting mixture should be used. Keep the earth only moderately moist until new roots form. The plants are more likely to flower in smaller pots than in large ones. Older specimens need to be repotted only every two to three years. In the case of the fire lily, the bulb should be embedded only about halfway in the soil, in a relatively small pot.

601 The red-flowering blood flower (*Scadoxus* 'König Albert' [King Albert], syn. *Haemanthus* 'König Albert') is only occasionally repotted.

This is a cross between *Scadoxus multiflorus* subsp. *katharinae* and *S. puniceus*. This plant is most likely to flower if its root ball is undisturbed. Only the upper soil layer should be renewed each year. If, from September, it is kept drier and at a cool site, it will retract its leaves in the winter. Another beautiful plant is elephant's tongue (*Haemanthus albiflos*), with white umbelliferous flowers and yellow to orange stamens. In summer, both plants can be placed in a shady spot in the garden or on the balcony. These exotic beauties are seldom seen nowadays, but it is worth propagating them from bulbs or seeds.

Emerald fern or foxtail fern is useful as cut foliage for small flowers in a vase.

602 The root balls of emerald fern or foxtail fern (*Asparagus densiflorus* 'Sprengeri') should be loosened when repotting.

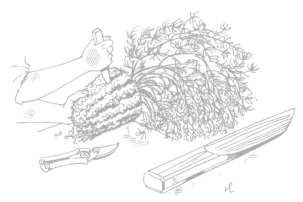

When they are healthy, the roots of old plants can often cram a pot so densely that it breaks. Such a thoroughly matted ball should be cut from top to bottom with a piece of wood that has been carved in the shape of a knife. The lower part of the root ball that is loosened up in this way can be cut off without any problem. When replanting into a larger pot, set the plant about ¾ in. deeper in the soil. There is also the variety 'Meyerei' with its foxtail-like fronds, and asparagus fern (*Asparagus setaceus*, syn. *A. plumosus*), with delicate fronds that are sometimes used as cut foliage in carnation or rose bouquets.

603 Flowering hydrangeas need plenty of water; their leaves must not be allowed to wilt.

If placed, over the pot rim, into a container filled with water, the leaves will soon recover, but their tips will often remain wilted. Accordingly, always water the plants generously, but be sure to remove water collecting in the saucer afterward; the roots do not tolerate standing water. Today, hydrangeas (*Hydrangea macrophylla*), with their large white, pink, or blue flower balls, are once again popular as indoor or tub plants. They do not tolerate calciferous soils, and thrive best on semi-shaded sites that are not too dry. Fertilizers for azaleas and rhododendrons are the most suitable for hydrangeas.

> *With hydroponics, you'll have hardly anything to worry about while you're away on vacation.*

604 Growing indoor plants with hydroponics is simple, clean, and saves time.

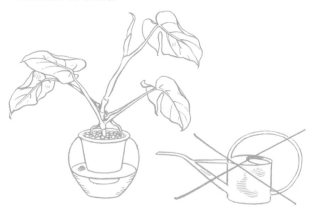

Hydroponics vessels consist of two parts: the outer vessel, or storage reservoir, and the insert or culture vessel, in which the plant stands, and with its roots grows through holes or slits into the nutrient solution. In addition to the hydroponics vessel, a substrate is required whose constitution will not change in the water, and that will also not release any substances that will damage the roots. Expanded clay is typically used, but pumice gravel or quartz gravel that is not too fine (with a grain size of around ⅛ in.) is also suitable. The outer watertight storage reservoir contains the nutrient solution and the water level indicator. The benefits of hydroponics are a better oxygen supply for the roots, and a constant, uniform source of water and nutrients.

605 Supplement the nutrient solution as required, and renew from time to time.

The water level indicator helps keep the nutrient solution at an optimal level. In addition to the main nutrients of potassium, phosphorus, and nitrogen, the nutrient salts used must also include all the essential trace elements. Special nutrient salts are available in the form of tablets or liquid fertilizer. Slow-release fertilizers that work on an ion-exchange basis will provide a nutrient reserve for about three months or longer, depending on the species, development stage, and size of the plant. Fertilizer tubes through which water is subsequently flushed are also useful. They, too, allow the water level to be controlled; the fertilizer itself is contained in a fleece bag. For all plants in hydroponics vessels, it is important that the nutrient solution temperature does not fall below 64 to 68°F for a longer period.

606 The transition from soil to hydroponics culture represents a major intervention in the life of the plant.

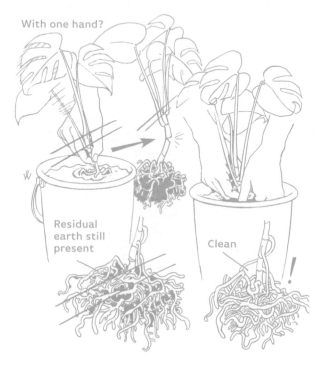

With one hand?

Residual earth still present

Clean

The roots are washed out thoroughly, since they need to be free of residual earth. In the case of heavily rooted balls, this is difficult to do without causing damage. Accordingly, young plants are more suitable because they can withstand this intervention better.

Growing hanging plants in hydroponic containers saves laborious watering.

607 Many green plants are suitable for hydroponics culture.

In the case of hanging plants such as devil's ivy (*Epipremnum*), grape ivy (*Cissus*), bellflowers (*Campanula isophylla* and *C. fragilis*), wax flowers (*Hoya*), tradescantias, and some philodendron (*Philodendron*) species, it is possible to save on laborious watering. Other suitable plants include dieffenbachias, screw pines (*Pandanus*), spider ivy or spider plant (*Chlorophytum*), umbrella grass (*Cyperus*), snake plant or bowstring hemp (*Sansevieria*), coleus (*Plectranthus scutellarioides*, syn. *Coleus blumei*), and many others. Owing to the constant water supply, they often grow better than they would in soil.

608 Growing using wicks or cast mold mats to ensure a lasting water and nutrient supply make work easier.

These are other systems that are available for the plants' long-term water and nutrient supply. In a modified form, in contrast to hydroponics, the plants grow in a normal plant substrate. The vessels have a water reservoir and an intermediate floor that separates the soil from the water beneath it, together with an overflow tube, a filling tube, and a water level indicator. Absorbent wick or fleece mats serve as the connection between the water reserve and the plant substrate.

609 In closed rooms, too, pests can also be combated using biological control.

If pests occur in the greenhouse, winter garden, on verandas, or in flower windows, these can be combated with corresponding useful animals. ▸ TIP 629 and ▸ TIP 639 If an infestation of aphids is discovered in the greenhouse, for example, these can be dealt with by deploying lacewings. These small greenish insects act in the background and are quite inconspicuous.

610 With the exception of freshly repotted plants, nearly all tub and indoor plants need sufficient nutrients in April.

Before applying fertilizer, water the plants. Liquid fertilizers have proven effective for tub and indoor plants. These can be easily measured out and added to the irrigation water. It is a good idea to use organic fertilizers, but note that it will take some time before the nutrients are taken up by the plant. If tub and indoor plants are given organic fertilizer in April, the nutrients will not be available to them during this important growth period. The principle here is that it is always better to apply fertilizer often and in small amounts than to do so occasionally but excessively.

611 In April, strong sunlight can already cause considerable damage to plants.

The plants are not yet used to full sunlight at this time. In particular, plants growing directly behind glass will need protection from the midday sun. Otherwise, leaf burns can result in the form of brown or black spots.

612 With its dark green, shiny leaves, the bay or laurel tree (*Laurus nobilis*) makes a splendid tub plant.

If you keep a bay tree as a tub plant, you will always have fresh bay leaves available for cooking—and these are far more effective than dried leaves. Prune the regularly so that it does not grow too large. A bay tree needs only a little water, especially if it is grown in a cool place. Additionally, the tough leaves will be almost completely unaffected by pests.

MAY

SPRING

The merry month of May brings many mild days with sunshine. Numerous bulb plants, such as tulips and daffodils, bloom in a great variety of colors. Tulips were already highly prized by the Ottomans, who developed many breeds and gave them poetic names. They first came to Vienna and Western Europe in the late Middle Ages, via Constantinople (now Istanbul).

In contrast to the winter-hardy tulips, many plants are still endangered by frost in early May. Accordingly, it is only after mid-May that tomatoes, cucumbers, peppers, and many summer flowers can be planted out, and tub plants and most indoor plants can finally be placed out into the open.

GENERAL

613 Use the first fine days in May for painting pergolas, arbors, fences, etc.

The paint will not only improve the appearance of these structures, but also protect the wood against rot. It is best to use an appropriate wood protection agent or varnish. Linseed oil is also suitable for this purpose. Warm, dry weather not only makes painting easier, but also promotes deep penetration of the agent into the wood and subsequent drying.

614 Owing to the soil tillage that has taken place in April, the surface layer of the paths will have suffered and will need to be renewed.

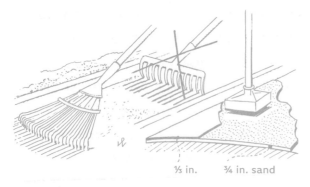

⅓ in.   ¾ in. sand

Before adding a new sand layer, rake the path clean with a wire broom. This will also destroy any weeds that may be present. The sand is then added in two layers: the first, around ¾ in. thick, is trampled or rolled firm, while the second, around ⅓ in. thick, is merely raked.

615 Garden boundaries can be delineated according to different criteria.

Generally this means building a fence or planting a hedge. Consider the nature of the delimitation to neighboring gardens or properties so the result is aesthetically pleasing.

616 Fences serve different purposes.

Should they be fences between home garden or community/allotment garden areas, they serve merely to mark the boundary, and can be low. If, on the other hand, they mark a property boundary, they should be built higher to make them more difficult to climb over.

617 Unwelcome weeds will already be growing everywhere in the garden at this time.

These not only spoil the garden's appearance, but also take water and nutrients from the soil that are then no longer available to the cultivated plants. Accordingly, weeds must not be allowed to flower and develop seeds. This can happen very quickly in the case of the common chickweed (*Stellaria media*), for example.

618 As early as the first days of May, soil maintenance is one of the most important garden tasks.

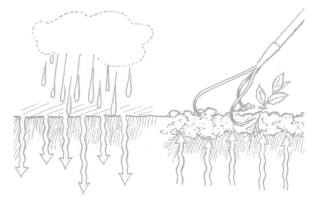

Hoeing has top priority. This ensures not only good soil aeration, but also maintains the soil moisture level. In this way, water from below rises through capillary action only as far as the loosened upper layer and will not evaporate. Accordingly, it is important to hoe the soil frequently, at least after every rainfall or after watering, as soon as the soil surface has dried off. As a result, watering will also not need to be as frequent, and weed growth will be inhibited at the same time.

GARDEN BOUNDARIES CAN BE DELINEATED ACCORDING TO DIFFERENT CRITERIA.

You can build picket or paling fences yourself (dimensions in inches).

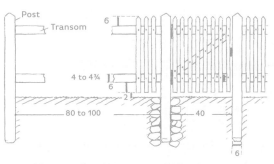

Delineating the boundaries with a low hedge provides a connection to neighbors.

Those who wish to move around uninhibited will prefer a higher "wall."

The round rod, round, half-round, and pointed.

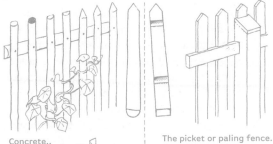

Concrete..

The picket or paling fence.

Wire netting is both cheap and long lasting. Climbing plants will help integrate it into the garden.

All kinds of wooden fences can be built with a little skill. Unfortunately, wood has only a limited life.

If need be, barbed wire must be extended across the garden side of the post.

These simple, "open" fences are found in the countryside.

A railing fence is expensive (tradespeople required!).

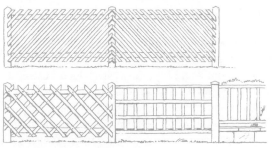

Ever-new variants using wood, tubes, or bamboo can be incorporated, as shown here.

Fences with diagonals do not look as rigid as vertical pickets or palings. Alternating the diagonal directions, crossings, etc. can be designed in an ornamental context.

> *An adequate water supply is a prerequisite for good plant growth, especially in dry periods.*

619 In May, water must always be available to the plants' roots.

The greatest attention should be given to plants that have only recently been set in the ground. This applies not only to vegetable plants, but also to perennials, roses, trees, shrubs, and newly laid lawns. Lightly spraying over the plants is pointless, since the water will not reach the roots. Proper watering means applying a total of 1 to 3 gallons of water per square yard of earth. Apply the larger quantities over light soils, and, likewise, on dry, hot days. On the other hand, greater care should be taken when watering heavy soils so that they do not become muddy.

620 Watering and spraying are two quite different cultivation measures.

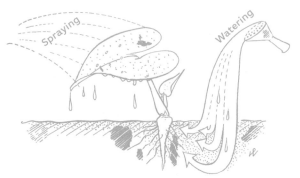

Watering in dry periods gives plants the possibility to meet their water requirements, while at the same time taking up nutrients from the soil. Spraying is generally done on warm summer days; in this case, only the aboveground plant parts will become wet. The resulting higher air humidity will reduce transpiration from the leaves, so that the plants will not wilt if the roots cannot meet the water requirement. However, it is best not to water or spray during the heat of the day in summer, but preferably in the mornings or evenings instead.

621 Beware that cold tap water is a shock for plants.

It is sufficient if the water used for watering is almost at room temperature. This can be achieved by immediately filling up another container following every watering.

622 Protect nesting boxes for birds against cats, as well as curious children.

Our feline friends are the avian brood's greatest enemies; accordingly, keep cats away from breeding sites. ▶ TIP 231 Children, too, should not play near birds' breeding sites. The birds will often stop feeding their young whenever humans are nearby.

623 Frequently replenish birdbaths with fresh water.

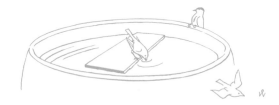

If a wooden board is laid across the water in a basin, it will not be long before the birds utilize this opportunity to drink. A stone can also be placed in birdbaths, for example in large, shallow basins; this aid is gladly used by the birds. The area surrounding the birdbath should be clearly visible to the birds so that cats cannot creep up undetected.

624 Moles are not pests as such—however, they can become an annoyance in the garden.

Unsightly molehills aside, even a large number of moles will not lead to plant damage. You can loosen the molehills by way of the tunnels so that they cave in. Moles themselves may not be trapped or killed. Chopped garlic (placed in the tunnels) or other strong-smelling materials can be used to drive moles away.

625 When it comes to voles, nothing should be left untried to eradicate these dangerous plant pests.

The most reliable method is to catch them with carefully set traps. Gas cylinders are effective only if all the tunnels are treated at once. If this measure is repeated several times, it is at least possible to drive the voles away from the area that has been gassed. Laying elderberry and walnut leaves in the tunnels, or also fish heads and chopped garlic, will often repel voles. They also avoid crown imperial (*Fritillaria imperialis*), lily leek or moly (*Allium moly*), daffodils, and spurge. Sometimes, a "vole frightener"—a device used to drive the voles away—can also be helpful. It releases vibrations or shock waves that signal danger to the animals. There are both battery- and solar-powered devices available. The effective range can be as great as 3000 sq. ft..

626 Butterflies are very welcome guests in the garden.

Many butterfly species are not only beautiful to look at, but are useful flower pollinators as well. If monarchs, peacock butterflies, admirals, or small tortoiseshells are to have a home in the garden, they will need to find appropriate plants there. Suitable nectar producers include the flowers of phlox, lavender, asters, golden alyssum (*Aurinia saxatilis*, syn. *Alyssum saxatile*), columbine (*Aquilegia*), heather (*Calluna vulgaris*), butterfly bush (*Buddleja*), spirea (*Spiraea*), flowering currant (*Ribes sanguineum*), coneflower (*Echinacea*), leopard's bane (*Doronicum*), pasque flower (*Pulsatilla vulgaris*), fleabane (*Erigeron*), tickseed (*Coreopsis*), bluebeard (*Caryopteris*), leopard plant (*Ligularia*), bugbane (*Actaea*, syn. *Cimicifuga*), and many others. However, the caterpillars, too, need food. They will find it in uncleared corners of the garden, where not only wild herbs such as nettles, wild carrots, and yarrow can grow, but also fennel, chervil, and dill. The caterpillars of the rare black apollo,

which is threatened with extinction, feed largely on the leaves of the bulbous corydalis or hollowroot (*Corydalis cava*).

627 Nectar-producing plants for honeybees, wild bees, bumblebees, beetles, and more should be present in every garden.

A veritable nectar source for bees, and also for bumblebees, butterflies, hoverflies, and beetles, is the meadow cranesbill (*Geranium pratense*). Its graceful, blue-violet, and blue-and-white flowers are on display all summer long. The plant is a perennial, and it is possible to buy it already flowering in May, or to sow it yourself. A beautiful variety is 'Rozanne.' Many mallows are also good nectar sources—whether the common mallow (*Malva neglecta*), musk mallow (*M. moschata*), blue or high mallow (*M. sylvestris*), or the cut-leaved mallow (*M. alcea*), all have enchanting flowers in violet to blue, pink, and white. Also belonging to the mallow family are the marsh mallow or white mallow (*Althaea officinalis*) and the hollyhock (*Alcea rosea*), both of which are also good nectar sources with attractive flowers. One plant that is important for wild bees and bumblebees that are already active in March, in view of its early flowering time (January to April), is the winter heath (*Erica carnea*), with varieties in red, pink, and white. The winter aconite (*Eranthis hyemalis*), too, already produces nectar and pollen during this time. The lacy phacelia or blue tansy (*Phacelia tanacetifolia*) is also an excellent nectar source.

628 Useful animals in the garden need suitable habitat conditions and must be protected accordingly.

Most plants are dependent on insect pollination to develop fruit. In order to continue to harvest apples, cherries, and plums, we also need to provide habitats for insects such as wild bees, bumblebees, and hoverflies. Other insects help us to eradicate plant pests, so that we can largely avoid resorting to chemical pesticides. Such useful animals in the garden include parasitic wasps, lacewings and hoverflies, ladybugs, ground beetles, assassin bugs and mites, and a range of wasps and spiders. Beyond insects, these animals also include toads, lizards, blind- or slow-worms, hedgehogs, bats, and of course birds.

629 Parasitic wasps can be used in a highly specific manner for combating certain pests.

There are many species of predatory wasps, which mostly act selectively on certain pests. Most of them have an ovipositor on their abdomen with which they lay one or more eggs in or on other insects (eggs, larvae, or pupae). The larvae hatching from their eggs then feed on the body matter of the host animals or on their eggs, larvae, or pupae. Some predatory wasps feed on aphids, others feed on caterpillars that cause damage to cabbage species, and still others on scale insects, greenhouse whitefly, food moths, or even the codling moth.

630 Use lacewings to combat insect pests.

These delicate, greenish insects with their filigree, net-like wings like to overwinter in dry leaves, but also in attic spaces. They do not tolerate winter cold well. Accordingly, lacewing boxes ▸ TIP 640 are useful overwintering aids. Lacewing larvae are effective against red spider mites, scale insects, aphids, wooly aphids, and mealybugs. They suck their prey dry with the aid of their powerful mouthparts. Their pupae are contained within small, white, felt or wooly cocoons.

631 Hoverflies are important pollinators and are effective against aphids.

Hoverflies have mostly a wasp-, bumblebee, or bee-like form and patterning. However, they are completely harmless, because they do not have a stinger. They can be distinguished by their flight behavior; as the name suggests, they hover during flight. Owing to their rapid wing movements, they remain suspended in one place in the air for a brief time, and then move very quickly to a new place. Adult hoverflies feed on nectar and pollen, and are important pollinators for a range of flowering plants. Their larvae also devour large numbers of aphids.

632 Ladybugs (ladybirds) are all-round useful animals.

They are perhaps the best known of useful insects in the garden; in most cases, they are the red seven-spotted lady beetle. The ladybugs and their larvae are specialized for devouring aphids, but they will also eat scale insects and red spider mites. Commercially bred, the Australian lady beetle is deployed in horticulture, mostly in greenhouses. The Asian lady beetle has greatly increased its numbers, and it is feared that it may eventually supplant the native species.

633 Ground beetles, too, are useful in the garden.

The ground beetles are a species-rich beetle family. In some years, golden (gilt) ground beetles may become plentiful in gardens. Ground beetles live under fallen leaves or under wood splinters and pieces of bark on the ground. The animals and their larvae eat insects that live in or on the ground, such as caterpillars, small snails, wireworms, cranefly larvae, and even Colorado beetles.

634 Use predatory ("assassin") bugs to combat greenhouse whitefly.

The light green bugs and their larvae feed predominantly on the eggs and larvae of greenhouse whitefly, but also on red spider mites, aphids, and thrips larvae. The bugs and their larvae penetrate their prey with their powerful snouts and suck them dry.

635 Combat aphids with gall midges.

Attracted by the fragrance of the aphids' honeydew secretion, the gall midges lay their eggs near their prey. More eggs are laid if the air humidity is higher. The orange-colored, worm-like larvae of the midges inject a poison into the aphids, which are then numbed and die, and are ultimately sucked dry. Gall midges will also feed on red spider mites.

636 Predatory mites attack both-ersome red spider mites and suck them dry.

The predatory mites of the genus *Phytoseiulus*, which are arachnids, suck red spider mites and their eggs dry. If the red spiders have already spun a web structure, they will be difficult and laborious to control. Accordingly, for commercially available predatory mites, it is necessary to stick exactly to the dates specified for their use. These predatory mites are dependent on warmth and high air humidity. Red spiders reproduce best in dry air. Accordingly, before deploying predatory mites, frequent water spraying should be carried out to boost the air humidity, so that the red spiders will not spread further, and to create better conditions for the predatory mites. Other prey species of predatory mites include scale insect larvae, thrips, and sciarid flies.

637   Nematodes are effective against a wide range of different pests.

Nematodes are threadworms, some of which are harmful to humans, animals, and plants, while others are used in biological control. The latter are used to combat strawberry weevils, slugs, fruit worm and codling moth, craneflies, mole crickets, and cutworms. Sciarid fly larvae cause considerable damage to sown cultures and can be combated with special nematodes.

638   Spiders, earwigs, and soldier beetles are indispensable in the garden.

They tend to be unwelcome in the house, and spiderwebs are considered unclean. Despite this, you should never kill spiders or even hunt them down with a vacuum cleaner. Placing a glass over the animal and slipping a piece of paper or card under the rim is the simplest method for catching spiders and liberating them outdoors. Without spiders, there would be infinitely more pests in the garden. The same holds for earwigs and soldier beetles. They are all inconspicuous little helpers that help protect our plants.

639   Useful insects are also commercially available.

Useful insects have long been bred commercially and can largely replace chemically produced insecticides. They are offered under a range of trade names and are particularly helpful in dealing with aphids or red spider mites in the garden. They are even deployed against mildew. For example, different ladybug species and hoverflies eat the moldy layer, even if this will grow again if we do nothing to prevent it. For the most part, it is lacewings, predatory nematodes, predatory mites against red spiders, and predatory wasps

against greenhouse whitefly that are offered commercially. The breeder or specialist dealer (garden center or website) will provide information regarding when and under what conditions they should be used. They must either be used immediately, or they can be stored for a brief time in the original packaging, protected from direct sunlight and warmth.

640   Insect hotels are nesting and overwintering aids for useful insects in the garden.

Insect hotels are mostly made out of wood. They can be bought ready-made, either designed for specific useful insects, such as lacewings or butterflies, or also for different species that are kept together such as wild bees, ladybugs, and earwigs. It is also possible to construct insect nesting boxes yourself. Tree trunk slices or thick blocks of wood in which small and large holes have been drilled to different depths are suitable for wild bees. Set up the boxes sheltered from the wind and in rainproof places under roof eaves or overhangs. Lacewing boxes for overwintering are filled with straw and set up in a rainproof location away from full sun, but facing south or southeast.

641   It is easy to build a hotel for hedgehogs and beetles yourself.

Underneath a roof overhang (such as a woodshed or garden shed), gather some small branches or twigs, as if for a small bonfire. Filled with wood chips, straw, or dry leaves, hedgehogs will soon move in and remain throughout the winter.

642   All helpers in the fight against pests should be able to feel safe and reproduce in the garden.

These include shrews, toads, moles, lizards, blind-worms, hedgehogs, bats, and, of course, birds. Unlike mice, shrews are not rodents, but insectivores that are related to hedgehogs and moles; they can even devour small snails. Owing to their strong smell, they are not eaten by cats. Toads and moles eat the eggs of slugs; lizards eat grasshoppers, cicadas, beetles and their larvae, bugs, ants, and slugs; blind-worms eat the eggs of the European red slug; hedgehogs consume slugs and the larvae of insect pests; and bats, too, eat small snails. That birds are useful devourers of pests is well known. You will find advice on setting up nesting boxes and on their food in several tips in this book.

643 Protecting useful animals makes an important contribution to environmental and plant protection.

In a well-cleared garden, in which brushwood, all fallen leaves, all old inflorescences, wilted summer flowers, and the cut-off remains of perennials have been cleared away, insects and other useful animals will search in vain for somewhere to spend the winter. If we want to help them get through the winter, such clearance should wait until the spring. Hedgehogs, blind-worms, and toads are happy to overwinter in piles of brushwood or in between twigs and small branches that are piled on top of one another and mixed with some leaves and straw. Seed capsules left on summer flowers or perennials serve as food for birds. A small heap of stones or a dry stone wall will provide shelter for toads and lizards. Instead of mortared walls and wire mesh fences, it is better to plant a hedge as a garden border—if possible, a freestanding one that comprises native flowering trees or shrubs. In smaller gardens, a trimmed hedge of hornbeam, privet, hawthorn, boxwood, or field maple will provide shelter for many useful animals. It is not necessary to mow lawns every week; occasionally, the odd wild herb or weed can also be ignored. One nettle left growing in a dahlia bed can serve as somewhere for butterflies to lay their eggs, for example. Instead of trees, perennials, and summer flowers with double blooms, more plants with single blooms and native wildflowers should be planted to offer insects and other useful animals protection and food.

VEGETABLES

644 From stalk celery, only the fleshy, tender leaf stalks are used. It does not develop any tubers.

Celery, or stalk celery, is a spicy vegetable that is not known nearly well enough. Refreshing peppery salads can be made using the leaf stalks, whether raw or cooked; they also go together well with asparagus.

645 Stalk celery makes similar demands on the soil to those of celeriac (root celery).

Nutrient-rich, deep soils are the most suitable. To avoid unwanted shoots, avoid planting before mid-May. Use potted or strongly pricked out plants with good root balls, planted at 16 × 16 to 20 × 16 in.; set them no deeper in the soil than they were standing before. The development time for stalk celery is about four weeks shorter than for celeriac, and it can be planted in several successions. The latest possible planting time is mid-July.

646 Cauliflower planted in early April (TIP 416) will need a generous fertilizer application in early May.

A nitrogen-rich complete fertilizer is the most suitable; 1 oz. can be applied per square yard. Water generously after applying fertilizer.

647 From early May, plant broccoli raised in heated cold frames in outdoor beds.

Broccoli belongs in the first position in a crop rotation and has the same high fertilizer requirements as cauliflower. The planting width should be 20 × 20 to 24 × 20 in. Otherwise, plant in the same way as for cauliflower. Subsequent sowing can take place until late May.

648 Bush beans make no great demands on the soil.

Medium, calciferous, and humus-rich loam soils are the most suitable. Extreme sandy or clay soils, or those which are highly acidic, are unsuitable. Bush beans prefer sunny situations with minimal rain. However, they also thrive in semi-shade, although the harvests will be later, and with smaller yields. Bush beans have no special requirements when it comes to the previous crop, although legumes of all kinds should be avoided.

649 **Bush beans are sensitive to chloride, which means that low-chloride or chloride-free mineral fertilizers must be used.**

Also remember that the beans have a high magnesium requirement, and so mineral fertilizers containing magnesium should be used wherever possible.

650 **Bush beans should not be sown before 15 May.**

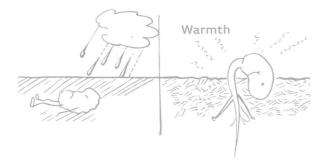

For germination, soil temperatures of 48 to 50°F are required. If sowing on heavy, wet soils, it is best to wait until late May. The beans can be dibbled or sown in bunches. If dibbled, lay the seeds singly at an interval of 1½ to 2½ in.; when sowing in bunches, sow five or six seeds every 12 in. The row interval is 12 in., and 1 in. is sufficient as a seed depth. Late sowing should be preferred in regions where root aphids are prevalent. The beans can be sown until mid-July.

> *Do not sow beans too early. Seed sown later in warm soil will quickly catch up to early plantings.*

651 **Chicory is regarded as a particularly valuable and tasty winter vegetable.**

Chicory contains a characteristic bitter substance that is highly prized by connoisseurs. This and many other valuable active substances act positively on the digestive system, and also on blood production and circulation. By crossing with radicchio, plants with attractive red coloration are commercially available, in addition to the well-known white chicory shoots. Chicory thrives best on deep, medium soils that are well supplied with humus. Too light or too heavy soils can be made usable with the addition of compost earth or peat substrate. Chicory does not tolerate fresh stable manure, and therefore belongs in the second position in a crop rotation. Deep loosening of the soil is especially important, since chicory develops a long taproot.

652 **Chicory is best sown in the first days of the second half of May.**

Sow chicory as sparsely as possible, with a row interval of 12 in. After the seedlings emerge, thin to 2½ to 3 in. The warmer the soil, the faster and more reliably the seedlings will emerge. Sowing chicory is still possible in early June; however, the roots will not be as thick as those in plants sown in May. Success in sprouting shoots in winter depends greatly on the thickness of the roots.

653 **Eggplants (aubergines) have even higher temperature requirements than tomatoes and peppers.**

Accordingly, even in milder regions, they should be grown under glass or a foil covering if possible, to provide rain protection from the outset, and to ensure the required temperatures. A high humus content and deep soil tillage are also important, along with good water permeability. Waterlogging is catastrophic for eggplants.

654 **Planting eggplants out in the open will be successful only if a completely sunny and sheltered site is available.**

Accordingly, they should be planted there only if they can be given a place up against a south-facing wall. Follow the advice relating to tomatoes given in ▸ **TIP 724**.

655 Eggplants can be planted in unheated cold frames and foil houses as soon as the previous crop has been harvested.

The planting width should be 20 × 20 in. Eggplants do not grow as vigorously as tomatoes, mostly reaching a height of only 24 to 32 in., but needing a support. They should be given fertilizer and watered as for tomatoes. Protect the cold frames at night until at least the end of May.

656 Even in the most favorable years, plant eggplants out in the open from late May only.

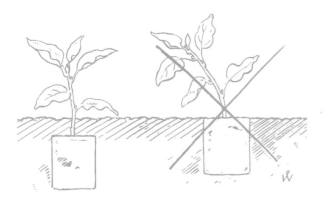

The planting interval should be selected as for cold frames. Set the eggplants in the ground about ½ in. deeper than they had been in the pot. The use of black mulch fleece is recommended without reservation, noting the information in ▸ **TIP 676**. Water the plants using water that has been prewarmed, and cover with cold frame windows or foil as soon as they have been planted. A simple frame that has been covered with windows or with foil stretched across it will be quite adequate. A frame height of 24 in. suffices.

657 When the peas have reached a height of 6 in., they should be heaped up.

This will anchor them better in the soil, while also suppressing weed growth in the rows. In double rows, heap up each row at the outer side only, which will result in the two plant rows being pushed together somewhat and growing more vigorously.

658 As an aftercrop for cultures that can be harvested in mid- to late June, sow turnips, rutabagas (swedes), curly kale, and Brussels sprouts in May.

For these vegetables, too, the plants are raised in an outdoor seedbed; for more details, see ▸ **TIP 443**. Turnips, rutabagas, and curly kale can still be sown in the second half of May, but Brussels sprouts should be sown in early May.

659 Pruning is an important step to be taken when growing house cucumbers.

About three to four weeks after it begins to grow, the main shoot of the cucumbers that have been planted in late April will reach the upper tensioned wire. Here, lay the shoot in a gentle arc over the wire, prune it back, and tie it firmly. As a rule, the plant will develop a larger number of so-called stem fruits. In the interests of better plant growth, remove the lower stem fruits in good time up to a height of at least 28 in. Following the first harvest of stem fruits, primary lateral shoots will develop on the main stem. However, in some cases, vigorous lateral shoots will already begin to develop close to the ground soon after the plant begins to grow. These must be removed up to a height of 12 in. or they will inhibit the growth of the main stem. From 12 in. upward, the lateral shoots are left, and are generally pruned back after fruiting twice or producing two sets of female flowers. If many lateral shoots develop, cut them back following the first signs of fruiting so that they do not exhaust the plant prematurely. Make all cuts about ¾ in. above the leaf in question, using the sharpest knife possible.

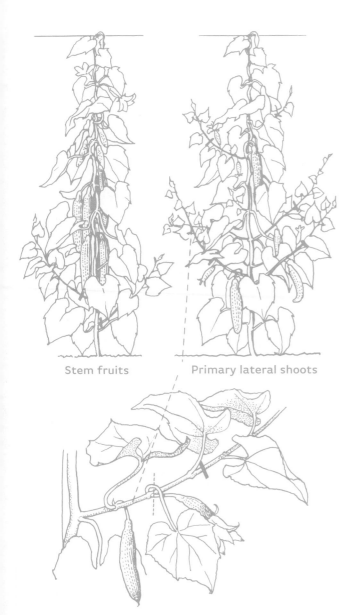

Stem fruits   Primary lateral shoots

661 **House cucumbers have very high soil and air humidity requirements.**

This also means that the water requirement is dependent on the developmental state of the plants as well as on the light and temperature conditions. This tends to be highest from May to July. Accordingly, in warmer weather, each plant requires about ½ to ¾ gal. of water. It is best to water in the morning, to ensure that the plant parts dry off by evening. Meanwhile, in high temperatures, as well as watering, the plants should also be sprayed with water to attain the required air humidity. In all watering measures, ensure that the root collar and leaves are wetted as little as possible, or that they dry off very quickly, to prevent harmful stem rot or other fungal diseases.

662 **Give house cucumbers their first surface fertilizer application no later than four weeks after planting.**

In selecting a fertilizer, note that cucumbers have a high potassium requirement and are also chloride-sensitive. Once the fruits begin to develop, fertilizer the plants weekly. A 0.3 percent nutrient solution should be prepared, and each plant given ¼ to ½ gal.

663 **To make it easier to walk on the paths between rows of cucumbers or tomatoes in the greenhouse or foil house, cover with a layer of straw or overlay with duckboards.**

660 **When growing house cucumbers, keep ventilation to a minimum.**

Ventilation is required only at temperatures above 82°F. Remember that any ventilation will reduce the air humidity, and, in turn, low air humidity will encourage the occurrence of red spider mites. If ventilation is necessary, compensate for the loss of moisture in the air by spraying.

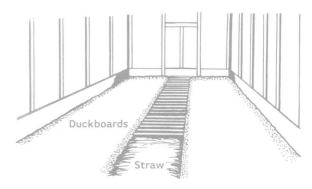

Duckboards

Straw

When plants are watered and sprayed daily, the paths between them can often become very muddy or softened, making it more difficult to move around in the greenhouse. An appropriately wide set of duckboards or a thick layer of straw can solve this problem and make maintenance and harvesting easier.

664 An unheated cold frame can be planted with cucumbers from early May.

Only pot-ball plants can be considered, with at least one normal leaf in addition to the cotyledons. Prepare the cold frame in the same way as an outdoor plot. ▶ TIP 669 In addition to the plants, covering material is essential to ameliorate the temperature differences between day and night. For cold frames, special cucumber varieties are suitable, as well as those for planting out in the open. Miniature cucumbers or varieties with short fruits just 6 to 7 in. long are especially recommended.

665 The weather is crucial when covering or ventilating cold frames in which cucumbers are growing.

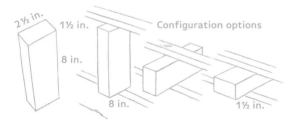

Ventilation should take place in sunny weather only. Place the wooden ventilation beams (slats 8 × 2 ½ × 1½ in.) under the windows in such a way that the wind cannot reach the plants. The cold frame should be covered every evening. Remove the covering early, as soon as it is light, so that the cucumbers do not miss out on any sunlight.

666 Expect good yields from cucumber cold frames if their water and nutrient requirements are met.

Prevent rapid drying out of the soil by covering the ground with straw, which should be kept constantly moist to ensure the high air humidity that cucumbers require. Apply a 0.3 percent nutrient solution of complete fertilizer once a week as soon as the cucumbers show through their healthy growth that they are properly rooted in the soil.

667 Opinions differ as to the effectiveness of pruning cucumbers grown in cold frames.

Pruned plants produce fruit that can be harvested earlier, and also deliver better yields. Pruning methods vary widely; the following methods have proven to be effective. As soon as the plant has developed four or five normal leaves, pinch off enough so that only two or three leaves remain. Cut the resulting primary lateral shoots above the fourth leaf. It is possible to stop at this point. Otherwise, the secondary lateral shoot can also be cut above the fourth or fifth leaf. Fruit tendrils can be pinched off two leaves above the first signs of fruiting. In the case of hybrid varieties, pruning can be omitted. For cutting, a sharp knife is required to cut the shoots in the middle between two leaves.

668 The local climate and soil are crucial to successful cucumber growing out in the open.

Cucumbers are among the most weather-sensitive vegetables; in particular, they are sensitive to cold and wind. In most cases, however, it is possible to create the necessary microclimate. For growing cucumbers, humus-rich, sandy loams and loam soils are the most suitable. Waterlogging, soil compaction, or soils tending to encrustation lead to failures. As a previous crop, all plants that improve the soil structure are suitable, especially leeks, celery, onions, and potatoes. Green manuring plants, too, make good previous crops. Do not immediately replant cucumbers in a place where they have just been grown.

669 When growing cucumbers out in the open, well-prepared soil is half the battle.

Cucumbers react very well to generous application of stable manure. If the necessary quantities of stable manure or other humus fertilizers are not available, a strip in the middle of the planting bed with a humus layer should be provided as a minimum requirement. Worked into the soil, the humus helps ensure better aeration and easier soil warming, considerably aiding the cucumbers' growth.

670 Sowing cucumbers out in the open should begin only when soil temperatures have reached 50 to 54°F.

As a rule, this point is reached only in mid-May. The seeds will not germinate in cold ground and will rot easily. Accordingly, it is also better to wait until late May or early June if necessary. The time delay will generally be made up for by the rapid emergence and better growth of the young plants.

671 Cucumbers can be planted in successive rows (dibbled) or in bunches.

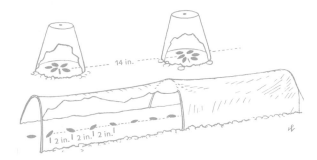

A normal bed generally contains only one row of cucumbers. Planting in bunches is preferable, since it is then also possible to work with protective hoods. The bunches are established at intervals of 12 to 14 in. For each bunch, lay five or six seeds shallowly in the soil (about ½ in. deep). When dibbling, the interval between the individual grains should be 2 to 2 ½ in. Water carefully after sowing, and then cover the seeds planted in bunches with protective hoods. The hoods provide protection from low temperatures at night and speed up the germination of the seeds. The bed can also be covered with a foil tent, which will be even more effective and bring the harvesting date forward.

672 A wide range of cucumber varieties are available for planting out in the open.

The planned use will determine the selection of the variety. If pickled cucumbers are specifically required, select a very high-yield hybrid variety that produces almost exclusively female flowers, and begin harvesting early. Here, however, note that these varieties must be harvested at intervals of at least two to three days, because their fruits become thick relatively quickly. If you are able to harvest only during the weekend, you should avoid these varieties, because the overly large fruits will then be unsuitable for either salad or pickled cucumbers. In such cases, it is better to select a "dual-use cucumber," the fruits of which are suitable for both purposes.

673 For those who greatly value "mustard pickles," special varieties are available for this purpose.

This group of varieties develop very large, cylindrical fruits with especially dense fruit flesh. They are harvested at the "yellow ripeness" stage, which, at the earliest, can be done three months after sowing. When harvested at an earlier stage, they will also yield good salad cucumbers.

674 If, following seedling emergence, the first normal leaf is ready to develop, thin out the cucumbers.

In the case of dibble-sown seed, leave only four or five plants standing per linear yard, and one or two plants per bunch. The weak plants should be removed as a priority; any gaps can be filled by the surplus plants. When removing the plants, however, take care to protect the roots in order not to jeopardize the growth following replanting. As a precaution, cover the freshly planted seedlings with a plant pot (not too small) immediately after watering, until they have bedded in.

675 **If cold frames or other options for raising the plants are available, advance planting of cucumbers for planting outdoors is crucial.**

This facilitates much earlier harvests. In late April/early May, lay three seed grains per each 2 ¾ in. pot filled with compost earth. Following emergence, thin out the plants to two plants per pot. It is important to keep the pots uniformly moist. From 25 May at the latest, vigorous cucumber plants will then be available that can be planted at an interval of 12 in. in the row.

676 **Another possibility to positively influence the start of harvesting and the yield is to use black mulch fleece.**

About one week before planting or sowing, lay black mulch fleece over the cucumber bed, and cover the sides with earth so that the fleece does not blow away with the wind. By the time of planting or sowing, the soil under the fleece cover will have already warmed up, providing good starting conditions for the young plants. At the envisaged planting or sowing site, make a crosscut with a sharp knife (cutting length 2 ½ to 3 in.) in which the plants or seeds are to be placed. Harvesting cucumbers that have been grown in this way can begin 10 to 14 days earlier, and deliver considerably greater yields.

677 **Because both the sown and planted cucumbers do not need all the space they have been allotted in the initial growth period, both sides of the bed can be planted with lettuce or kohlrabi.**

Plant the lettuce or kohlrabi in the prepared cucumber beds as early as April. Including these vegetable species means that the cucumber beds will be better utilized. They will also provide the cucumbers

with some shelter from the wind in the early stages of development.

678 **Corn has proven to be an effective protection for cucumbers in windy situations.**

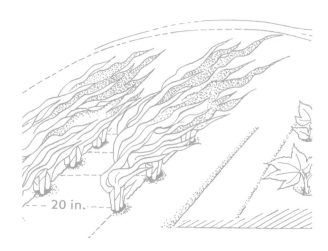

20 in.

Whether ornamental corn or sweet corn, which can be used as a vegetable, is involved, makes no difference here. Gardeners needing feed for their small domestic animals will prefer the former. The corn is not cultivated on the cucumber bed itself, but on the bed immediately adjacent to the west. As a rule, a strip of two planted rows is sufficient. Sowing is done at the same time as the sowing or planting of the cucumbers, with an interval of 20 in. between the two rows. The interval from the middle of one bunch to the next should be 14 to 16 in., to provide effective shelter from the wind. Cover the bunches with protective hoods, as done for cucumbers. This is especially necessary if sowing takes place before mid-May. Following emergence of the corn, only the two strongest plants per bunch are left to remain. ▸ **TIP 734**

Cucumbers with wind protection will thrive better and reward the gardener with greater yields.

679 **Instead of kohlrabi or lettuce, the edges of the beds can also be planted with celery.**

Since celery may be planted only after 15 May, the border strips can be planted with red radishes in early April. Each side of the bed is planted with just one row of celery 8 in. from the edges of the bed. Within the row, the planting interval is 16 in. More information on planting celeriac (root celery) is given in ▶ **TIP 683**.

680 **As soon as potato plant shoots have reached 3 to 4 in. high, heap up the earth.**

The earth is heaped up from both sides so that only the tips of the plant shoots remain visible. If there is a danger of night frosts, completely cover the plants with earth. The earth is then heaped up a second time when the plant height reaches 6 to 8 in. Before the earth is heaped up each time, give the potatoes a surface application of nitrogen-rich complete fertilizer.

681 **Precultivated Florence fennel (TIP 431) should be planted on outdoor plant beds from mid-May.**

Owing to the danger of late frosts, planting before 15 May is not recommended. The planting width should be 16 × 12 in. Florence fennel should not be planted too deep, since this will affect the tuber formation. Covering with hoods or foil is recommended until late May to protect against late frosts. With suitable varieties, sowing directly outdoors can begin in early May; the row interval is 16 in., and the plants are thinned out to 10 to 12 in. within a row. Here, too, frost protection should be employed.

682 **Celeriac (root celery) prefers moist, humic soils, and responds very well to fresh organic fertilizer.**

It should therefore be planted in the first position in a crop rotation, if possible. Celeriac makes no special demands on the previous crop, although it's best to avoid planting immediately after root vegetables. When applying mineral fertilizer, remember that celeriac prefers physiologically acid-acting fertilizers, and that heart-rot disease and dry rot will be more problematic if there is a boron deficiency.

683 **Expect celeriac (root celery) to produce large, smooth tubers only if planted as shallowly in the soil as possible.**

To avoid unwanted shoots, plant only after mid-May. Defect-free tubers can develop only if the base of the leaf stalks is still visible above the soil surface after planting. As a result, the tubers will develop in such a way that they are roughly halfway above the soil. The roots will then develop only from the part of the tuber that is embedded in the soil, while the upper part will remain smooth. The planting width should be at least 16 × 16 in.

684 **In May, early kohlrabi planted outdoors needs plenty of water and nutrients for good development.**

Once the tubers have begun to develop, there must be no impediments to growth—this means keeping the soil uniformly moist, especially during dry spells, to prevent the tubers from bursting. Meanwhile, give the plants a nitrogen surface fertilizer application of 0.1 oz. per 100 sq. ft., preferably as a 0.3 percent fertilizer solution.

685 **To ensure a constant supply during summer, sow kohlrabi during the first and last days of May.**

Prepare the seedbed and sow as described in ▶ **TIP 443**. Keep the sown areas constantly moist once the seedlings emerge.

686 The late cabbage varieties sown in April (TIP 443) to obtain young plants are planted out in the second half of May.

All late varieties need four to five months from planting to harvest. Late white and red cabbage varieties need the longest time. Depending on the variety, the planting width is 24 × 20 to 24 × 24 in.

687 Early cabbage varieties can be sown in an outdoor seedbed from early to mid-May for use in the fall and early winter.

This will allow planting out from late June to early July. Follow the advice given in ▸ TIP 443 when planting out.

688 In recent years, interest in edible pumpkins and squash has grown enormously. This is partly due to their dual use for both culinary and decorative purposes.

The range of available plants has expanded greatly in terms of shape, color, and size, and has become almost impossible to keep track of. In particular, varieties that can be used both for eating and decoration have gained in importance. In great demand are so-called microwave pumpkins, which, after the seeds have been removed, can be cooked in the microwave without removing their skins; these pumpkins are considered very tasty. In addition, there are special connoisseur varieties, such as spaghetti pumpkins.

All these species and varieties prefer humus- and nutrient-rich medium soils, but will also thrive on light soils if there is sufficient humus. In particular, the large-fruiting edible pumpkins tolerate semi-shaded sites very well, and can also be used to shade heaps of earth at composting sites, for example. In this case, they may be planted next to the heaps, but not actually on them. In contrast, varieties that are distinguished by their decorative colors need the sunniest site possible.

689 Since edible pumpkins and squash are very frost-sensitive, they should not be sown before 15 May or planted out before 20 May.

3 ¼ ft.

To be sure of success, lay three seed kernels at every sowing site; cover the seeds with only ½ to ¾ in. of earth. Once the seedlings emerge, leave only the most vigorous plant. Edible pumpkins and squash require a planting width of 6 ½ × 3 ¼ ft. If plant protection hoods are available, the hardened-off plants can be planted out after 15 May.

690 Muskmelons can be planted out under glass from early to mid-May, but should not be planted outdoors before late May/early June.

Melons that have been pricked out in pots in April can be planted out following the formation of the fourth or fifth vegetative leaf. In cold frames, plant one or two plants under each window. At the planting site, excavate the earth to one spade cut deep, fill the pit with organic material (stable manure or straw), and heap up the excavated earth in hillock form. Then plant the melons on top, no deeper than they had been in the pot. In a small greenhouse, prepare the planting sites in the same way, with an interval within a row of 20 in. Here, the plants are grown either on a level surface, or on lines or wires, as with house cucumbers. Outdoors, excavate an 8 in. deep furrow in the middle of the bed, fill with organic material, and form a flat dam on top. Plant the melons on this at 20 in. intervals. It is advisable to cover the plants with a protective hood or fleece immediately after planting.

691 Melons need sufficiently moist soil, but do not tolerate high air humidity.

The air humidity in cold frames and small greenhouses can be well regulated by ventilation, but foil tents are more problematic. After planting, the plants should be ventilated as little as possible at first; it is important that the temperatures do not fall below 59°F. At night, they should also be covered with mats or similar, often until as late as June. As the outside temperatures rise, ventilate the plants more often, and more thoroughly.

692 Melons first develop female flowers and fruits on the secondary lateral shoots.

It is only with careful pruning that a satisfactory harvest can be ensured. Pinch off the main shoot when the sixth leaf has developed normally. The pruning cut is made above the fifth leaf. Cut back the resulting primary lateral shoot after the third leaf. Secondary shoots develop on these lateral shoots, with the female flowers. Once the first fruits have reached walnut size, prune the shoots two leaves above the first signs of fruiting. In some circumstances, it may be necessary to leave a greater number of leaves on the plant so that there is sufficient leaf area available to enable the fruits to develop. When training along lines or trellises in a small greenhouse, cut the main shoot once it has reached the upper tensioned wire. The primary lateral shoots should be pruned back after the second leaf, while the secondary lateral shoots should be pruned back one leaf after the first fruit.

693 Late carrot varieties for harvesting in the fall and for storage can be sown from early to mid-May.

On humic sandy soils, seed sown until late May will also result in good yields; their development time is six months. On sowing, see ▶ TIP 255 and ▶ TIP 256. However, the row interval should be increased to 10 to 12 in.

694 Peppers need a warm place with full sun, and place greater demands than tomatoes on the climate, while placing similar demands on the soil.

Accordingly, they should preferably be grown under glass or foil. For planting outdoors, sheltered sites with full sun are crucial. Soils should preferably be well permeable, humus rich, and not too heavy, with a neutral or weakly acid pH. Peppers should be grown in the second position in a crop rotation. Their nutrient requirements, especially potassium and nitrogen, but also magnesium, are higher than those for tomatoes. They are also chloride-sensitive.

695 Depending on the type, peppers need a planting width of 16 × 16 to 24 × 16 in.

In a small greenhouse, the greater planting width and more vigorously growing varieties are preferred; plant these from mid-May. Experience has shown that it is best to train the plants using two shoots on lines or stakes. In foil tents, cold frames, and outdoors, too, the plants need a support to prevent the shoots from being broken off easily. Outdoors, plant peppers using black mulch foil or black mulch fleece, and no earlier than late May. Spicy peppers (chilis) are less sensitive and are therefore generally grown outdoors. A planting width of 16 × 12 in. is sufficient. After planting, an important maintenance task is to pinch off the terminal flowers in the branching of the lateral shoots.

Using black plastic mulch ensures a reliable pepper harvest.

696 Leeks have no special requirements when it comes to climate, but they need deep, humus-rich, medium soils.

Heavy soils will not yield satisfactory results. For leeks, organic fertilizer is essential—this should have been already applied in the fall, however. The pH value should be between 6 and 8. Apply lime just before planting if need be.

697 Especially thick stalks can be attained if leeks are grown in the second half of May—in other words, as a main crop.

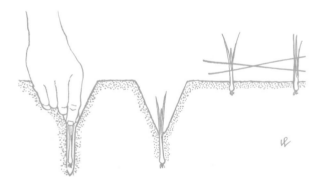

Furrows should be opened at intervals of 12 in. and should be around 4 to 6 in. deep. Before planting, cut back the roots and leaves back by a third. An interval of 5 to 6 in. within the row is sufficient. The furrows remain open at first. Thoroughly water the leeks immediately after planting.

Deep-planted leeks will develop a longer, white stalk.

698 Broad beans will deliver a good yield only if they have sufficient moisture.

Even during a relatively short dry spell, there may be a considerable infestation of black bean aphids. Accordingly, a uniform soil moisture level must always be maintained. From mid-May to late June, three or four applications of water of 5 to 6 gal./yd.² are recommended. Additionally, in May, a nitrogen-rich complete fertilizer should be applied at a rate of 1 oz. per square yard.

When the first fava bean pods appear, remove the shoot tips. This minimizes the danger of aphid infestation and promotes the development of the beans.

699 Radicchio is a cultivated form of salad chicory that develops heads, and originally comes from Italy.

The plants develop tightly closed, firm heads with a weight of 5 to 9 oz. The intensely colored wine-red head leaves with their white leaf ribs are highly attractive. Radicchio needs two to three weeks more development time than lettuce. Although it is also possible to do so earlier, it is safer to begin sowing in early May. Radicchio is quite sensitive when it comes to the development of unwanted shoots and must therefore be raised under warm conditions. Sow the seeds very sparsely in large pots or bowls and later prick them out into small 2 in. pots. The temperature during germination should be 77°F, and 68°F thereafter. The time from sowing to planting out is around five weeks. If it is not possible to maintain these temperatures, you will need to wait until late May. Subsequent sowing is possible until late June.

700 Subsequent sowing of red radishes and summer radishes is also done in May.

In this case, it is especially important to ensure that the beds in which red radishes or radishes have been sown never dry out. This will also help to keep flea beetles at bay. On sowing and thinning out, see ▶ TIP 264 to ▶ TIP 266, and also ▶ TIP 461.

> *When sowing radishes and carrots, remember to always use floating row covers. This will prevent radish fly and carrot fly infestation.*

701 Tender radish and red radish tubers can be achieved with diligent watering and fertilizer application.

Once they have emerged, do not give red radishes any pure water at all. A weak nutrient solution (0.1 percent) of a fast-acting nitrogen fertilizer is far better. Radishes should be given a once-weekly application of a 0.3 percent solution of a nitrogen-rich complete fertilizer.

702 In May, too, give rhubarb a generous fertilizer application and plenty of water.

In May, give the plants two surface applications of nitrogen fertilizer each. Then give them nitrogen-rich complete fertilizer every four weeks until August (1 oz./yd.²). Water the plants thoroughly after every fertilizer application.

703 To keep rhubarb plants from becoming exhausted, do not pluck them completely clean when harvesting.

Harvest

Each time they are harvested, leave around two thirds of the leaves on the plant. The leaf stalks should not be cut with a knife, but instead pinched off at the base. Pinch off developing inflorescences regularly.

704 Brussels sprouts are highly adaptable when it comes to climate. Their soil requirements are similar to those of headed cabbage.

Optimal yields can be obtained on medium, nutrient-rich, and deep soils. Brussels sprouts have a relatively high water requirement. All cabbage species should be avoided as a previous crop. Brussels sprouts belong in first position soils of a crop rotation. For mineral fertilizer application, take note of the high potassium and phosphate requirements, and ensure a good supply of trace elements. If the soil pH is less than 6.5, applying lime is advisable, preferably in the fall before planting.

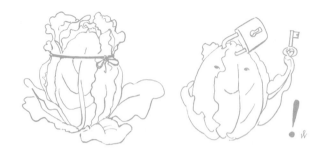

705 When Brussels sprouts are planted as the main crop or as protective planting for cucumbers, mid- to late May is the best time for planting.

When planted this early as the main crop, Brussels sprouts need planting widths of 24 × 24 in., because they will develop very vigorously when cultivated properly. When planted as protective planting for cucumbers, intervals of 20 in. will be sufficient.

706 During May, only heat-tolerant summer varieties of iceberg lettuce and regular lettuce should be planted.

The planting width for these varieties must be at least 12 × 12 in. The same interval applies to Batavia lettuce and curled lettuce, which are especially suitable for growing in summer.

707 Timely weeding and maintaining a constant soil moisture level are crucial for growing black salsify successfully.

These plants develop slowly to begin with and can be easily crowded out by weeds if they latter are not removed regularly. Prevent soil encrustation by regular hoeing. In early May, give black salsify an initial surface application of nitrogen fertilizer.

708 Romaine lettuce sown in April is ready for planting out from mid-May.

To attain well-developed heads, allow for a planting width of 12 × 12 in. Do not plant the plants any deeper than they already were in the seedbed or pot.

709 In May, the asparagus harvest is in full swing, and the stalks will need to be cut daily.

Not only must the vigorous stalks be cut, but all the weak ones as well. When harvesting asparagus, note, too, the advice given in ▶ TIP 468 to ▶ TIP 470.

710 In asparagus plants that are being harvested for the first time, finish cutting in the last days of May.

If cutting continues after this time, it may not be possible to achieve a full harvest the following year. The comparatively young plants will be excessively weakened from the long harvesting periods in the first year. Always remember that every asparagus stalk has developed at the expense of the rootstock.

711 Newly planted asparagus in particular should be kept weed-free, and can be given a nutrient application in the last week of May.

As with the planted ditches, do not allow weeds to establish on the land in between. A nitrogen-rich complete fertilizer can be applied, at a maximum rate of 0.7 oz. per square yard. In dry weather, water generously after applying fertilizer.

712 Broad beans are a suitable catch crop for newly planted asparagus.

The area between the rows can be sown in the second half of May. Broad beans will also yield a good harvest on asparagus soils. However, their primary value is that they shade the ground, which is particularly beneficial for asparagus growth. Dibble sowing with a row interval of 12 in. is recommended.

713 Planting out New Zealand spinach should wait until mid-May at the earliest.

In situations that are particularly at risk of late frosts, it is better to wait until late May; the plants should be thoroughly hardened off first. They need plenty of space so allow for a planting width of 40 × 20 in. Note that New Zealand spinach should not be planted any deeper than it had already been in the pots. As soon as the shoots have reached a length of around 5 in., remove the tips to stimulate branching. This should be repeated two or three times during June.

714 Climbing beans need sheltered sites and warm, humus-rich soils.

Soils that have been deeply worked in the fall and supplied with lime and are in the second position in a crop rotation are the most suitable for climbing beans. Heavy and wet soils, or waterlogged soils, are completely unsuitable.

715 To grow climbing beans successfully, roughly 10 ft. long poles or stakes are required, which should be erected before sowing.

To ensure these are safe in the wind, drive them about 16 in. deep into the ground. Two rows of poles are brought together at a height of 6 to 6 ½ ft. and are tied to poles or slats running horizontally on top. Such a support arrangement is better protected from the wind than individual vertical poles, which must also be longer because they need to be driven deeper into the ground. However, an advantage of freestanding individual poles is better aeration during periods of prolonged rainfall. Climbing beans are highly suitable as wind shelter for cucumber beds.

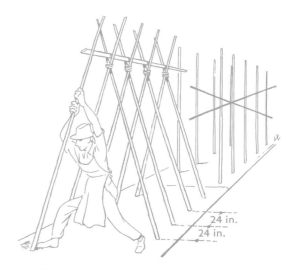

24 in.
24 in.

716 Poles made of corrugated and galvanized wire (minimum diameter ¼ in.), glass fiber, or similar stable materials are also suitable for growing climbing beans.

After they have been driven about 16 in. deep into the ground, three or four of these poles are brought into a pyramid shape at the top and tied together, yielding a suitably stable structure.

717 To attain optimal yields, sow climbing beans in the second half of May only.

Sowing later (early to mid-June) is recommended only in especially favorable situations. Climbing beans need a development period up until the harvest of at least 10 to 12 days longer than that of broad beans. However, the yields will be significantly higher and the beans can be harvested over a longer period.

718 Since climbing beans need a row interval of 2 ½ ft., plant only two rows in a normal bed (4 ft.).

For climbing beans, only bunched sowing is suitable. Lay the individual bunches at an interval of 2 ft. within the row. The above intervals should already be taken into account when setting up the poles. When laying the seeds, form a shallow channel with one hand in a semicircle around each pole. The distance from the pole must be around 3 in. Each bunch should consist of six or seven planted beans. See the sketch below for more details.

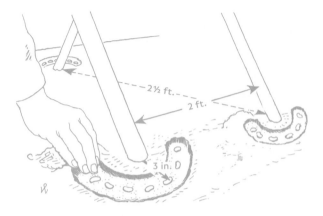

719 To make better use of climbing bean beds, plant kohlrabi or lettuce as a catch crop.

So both species can be harvested when the climbing beans have made greater progress in their development, it is best to plant the catch crop about two weeks before laying out the beans. Two rows about 10 in. apart can be planted in the middle of the bed.

720 Give house tomatoes planted in late April an initial surface fertilizer application in the last 10 days of May.

Here, it is important to note the correct nitrogen-potassium ratio. Too much nitrogen at the beginning of growth leads to vigorous leaf development, which then negatively impacts initial ripening. Accordingly, for the initial surface fertilizer application, select a complete fertilizer with a high potassium content and apply around 1.5 oz./yd.² in liquid form (0.3 percent). Remember, too, that tomatoes are chloride-sensitive.

721 When it comes to temperature, house tomatoes are less demanding than house cucumbers.

Despite this, temperatures that are suitably matched to the tomatoes' requirements are crucial for achieving greater and earlier yields. If the temperatures fall below 50°F over a period of several days, this will interrupt growth and inhibit fertilization (from

pollination). At the same time, temperatures above 90°F should be avoided during flowering and when the fruit ripens, since these will reduce the fruit formation and lead to yellow-flecked fruits. Accordingly, ventilate greenhouses and foil houses generously should the outside temperatures climb this high.

722 For house tomatoes, a good water supply is crucial for good plant development and fruit formation.

Tomatoes need a very generous, and, above all, regular water supply, but not high air humidity. Accordingly, it is important to provide the soil with plenty of water while at the same time keeping evaporation to a minimum. This can be achieved by covering the ground with organic material (straw or similar). Be careful, too, to wet the plants as little as possible when watering them. The average daily water requirement is 1 gal./yd.². Larger fluctuations in the water supply will cause the fruits to burst.

723 Maintenance of house tomatoes includes timely tying up and pinching off.

The lateral shoots appearing in the leaf axes should be pinched off as soon as it is possible to grasp hold of them properly. If the lateral shoots are left to grow too large, this will affect the growth of the main shoot and fruit development. The plants should not be tied up too tightly to avoid hindering the growth in the plant's thickness. When growing as dwarf tomatoes ▸ TIP 476, prune back the main shoot after the development of three, or, at most, four inflorescences, leaving one leaf above the final inflorescence. When growing over a long period, pruning back is done only when the main shoot has reached the upper tensioned wire.

Shaking the inflorescences two or three times each week helps fruit formation on greenhouse tomatoes. When the tomatoes are grown outdoors, bees and bumblebees will ensure pollination.

724 Tomatoes need an open site with full sun and warm, humus-rich soil.

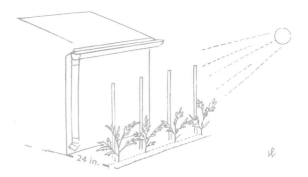

Heavy loam and lowland boggy soils seldom yield good results. Especially favorable sites include the south sides of walls, hedges, and fences. However, tomatoes should not be sheltered from the wind, since this makes them more prone to disease.

Although tomatoes tolerate fresh organic fertilizer well, they are better suited to planting in the second position in a crop rotation. In selecting fertilizers, remember that tomatoes are chloride-sensitive and have a high magnesium requirement. They like a neutral to weakly acid soil pH and react very sensitively to fresh lime application.

725 Even in favorable weather conditions, do not plant tomatoes before 20 May.

The soil must already be well warmed up so that there will be no interruptions to growth. Tomato plants should generally be bought from specialist dealers; be sure to check for vigorous, dense growth. Before planting, loosen the soil in the tomato bed to a depth of at least 8 in. This promotes soil warming and facilitates rapid growth.

726 Before planting staked tomatoes, drive in the stakes for stabilizing the tomato plants.

The stakes must be around 60 in. long, and are driven 16 in. deep into the ground. Previously used wooden stakes should be disinfected first to kill off any disease agents that might be present. Corrugated wire or glass fiber poles are preferable to wooden stakes. They are very durable and are easier to handle. Tie four of these poles together at the upper end to form a stable pyramid. Stake tomatoes need a row interval of 28 in., while an interval of 20 to 24 in. within a row is sufficient. Plants that have become too long can be set diagonally in the soil.

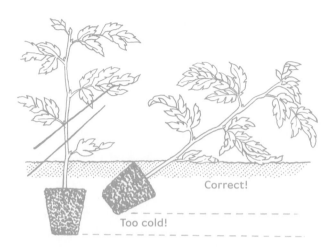

Correct!

Too cold!

727 Staked tomatoes should be trained using one shoot only.

It is possible to grow the plants with two or more shoots, but this is at the expense of a timely harvest and fruit size. Additionally, plants with one shoot will be better aerated, and will dry more quickly following rainfall, reducing the risk of disease.

728 It is generally necessary to pinch off tomato plants at the time of planting, or shortly afterward.

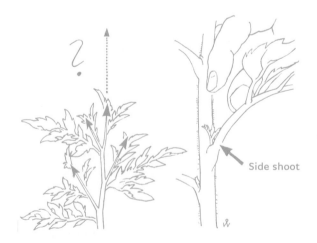

Side shoot

Here, "pinching off" means removing the lateral shoots. This must be done as soon as it is possible to get a firm hold of them. Larger lateral shoots will weaken the main shoot growth considerably.

Regular pruning of staked tomatoes results in earlier harvests and greater overall yields.

729 The maintenance requirements for bush tomatoes are considerably less, although there are certain drawbacks.

Since, in view of their growth characteristics, bush tomatoes do not need to be staked, there is no tying up to be done, and pinching off the lateral shoots is also not required. However, a disadvantage is that the fruits will become dirty in rainy weather and will also rot more easily if the weather stays moist. Generally, the fruit quality does not match that of staked tomatoes.

730 The planting width for bush tomatoes depends mainly on the growth vigor of the varieties involved.

Soil characteristics also play a role. Generally, the planting width for bush tomatoes should be 20 x 16 to 20 x 20 in.

731 Zucchinis have a wide diversity of uses in the kitchen and are becoming more and more popular.

6 to 8 in.

This squash species is generally a non-climbing vegetable squash with a compact, bushy growth. The fruits are more or less slim and cylindrical or club-shaped. Depending on the variety, they can be dark, medium, or light green in color. There are also varieties available that have white or golden-yellow fruits. A closely related species, button or pattypan squash, also belongs to the vegetable squash group. Its white- to ivory-colored or yellow fruits are disk-shaped and strongly notched at the edges to a greater or lesser extent. Additionally, the rondini types, with their globular, dark green fruits, also belong to this group. Sow all three species directly outdoors from 15 May. Zucchinis need a planting width of 40 × 40 in. Button squash grows much more vigorously, and needs a planting width of 48 × 40 to 60 × 40 in. To achieve earlier harvests, advance planting in pots in early May is recommended. Sowing or planting in mulch fleece is even better. Here, see also the advice given in ▸ TIP 676.

732 Sweet corn thrives only in full sun and on nutrient-rich, medium soils.

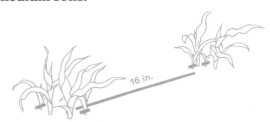

Extreme sandy soils and heavy soils that are prone to encrustation are unsuitable. Fresh, organic fertilizer application is crucial for good development. The nutrient requirements are considerable, especially for potassium.

733 Sweet corn is frost-sensitive, and should generally not be sown before 20 May.

Sowing is possible between 10 and 15 May on particularly sheltered sites only. Within a row, sow four seeds at an interval of 12 to 16 in. and thin out to two plants later on. The row interval is 24 in. With early varieties, subsequent sowing is possible until 20 July.

In early May, sow sweet corn seeds in pots in a cold frame

with three or four seeds per pot; leave the two strongest plants to remain and plant out in late May.

734 Sweet corn is highly suitable as a wind shelter for wind-sensitive vegetable species.

Typical examples include cucumbers, eggplants, and peppers. If using as a wind shelter, sow sweet corn in a double row, alternating the seed sites and gaps of the two rows to form a closed wind barrier.

735 If the month of May is especially hot and dry, all cabbage species, along with radishes and red radishes, will be endangered by flea beetles.

In cabbages, this especially affects young plants that are growing in the seedbeds. Accordingly, sprinkling with algae lime or rock dust should be carried out before serious damage occurs. This means checking the beds daily for the presence of flea beetles. Spraying the plants heavily with water helps combat these pests to only a limited degree.

736 All vegetable plants that are wilting for no apparent external reason should be examined immediately to determine the cause.

If you notice a wireworm infestation in the garden, you will need to carefully remove the wilting plants with the roots and surrounding earth. This is the only way to determine the cause or causes. Other than wireworms, cutworms may be responsible; they like to congregate right underneath the soil surface during the daytime. On protection against the cabbage root fly and cabbage gall weevil, see ▸ TIP 417 and ▸ TIP 437.

737 If the plants in carrot or onion beds turn yellow, this is usually due to damage caused by fly larvae.

At the first sign of such yellowing, remove the affected and neighboring plants, along with the surrounding earth. Additionally, ensure rapid growth and hoe the soil frequently. An even better solution is to cover the beds in good time with an insect protection netting or fleece.

738 To harvest garden cress and chervil continuously, subsequent sowing is required.

The intervals between sowing are two weeks for garden cress, and three weeks for chervil. Garden cress needs a row interval of 4 ¾ in. Sow these seeds in very shallow channels and do not cover with earth. On sowing chervil, see ▸ TIP 295.

739 Nasturtium plants pregrown in pots can be planted out from 20 May.

The pregrown plants are frost-sensitive; accordingly, cover with protective hoods after planting out. Plant non-climbing plants 12 × 12 in. apart, and climbing plants 16 × 24 in. apart. An interval of 8 in. along fences is sufficient (single row).

740 Nasturtium plants can be sown directly outdoors from mid-May.

In this case, plant the nasturtiums in bunches. Using the same interval described in ▸ TIP 739, plant three seeds per bunch. Once the seedlings have emerged, leave only the strongest plant to remain. Nasturtiums will flower only very sparsely in shady locations.

741 Garlic needs a surface fertilizer application in mid- to late May.

Use a complete fertilizer, scattered at a rate of around 1.75 oz./yd.^{2}. Immediately work it into the soil shallowly by hoeing. Using a pure nitrogen fertilizer is not recommended. Depending on the plant development, a second fertilizer application may be required three weeks after the first. One of the most important maintenance tasks is to constantly loosen the soil surface. During dry spells when the water requirement is at its highest (May/June), apply ¾ in. of water three or four times.

742 Marjoram grows best on light to medium, warm soils with a high humus content, and on sites with full sun.

Marjoram does not tolerate fresh stable manure and should therefore be grown in the second position in a crop rotation. Marjoram will generally not survive on loam soils in wet summers. In shady locations, its root development will leave a lot to be desired.

743 Marjoram is highly frost-sensitive, and therefore may not be planted out before 20 May.

Self-raised plants ▸ TIP 193 must be well hardened off before planting. The cold frame should be generously aerated every day, and should also remain open at night, if no night frosts are expected. When planting out marjoram, it should not be any deeper in the soil than it had been before. Two to four plants should be planted at each planting site. The row interval must be 8 in., while an interval within the row of 6 in. is sufficient.

744 **Basil needs a light, warm, and humus-rich soil, and a sheltered site in full sun to thrive.**

Basil is best planted on the south side of a wall or taller plants. Since it is not worth raising the plants yourself, they should be bought from a specialist dealer. They are planted in mid-May with a planting width of 10 × 10 in.

A warm, sunny site will greatly enhance the fragrance and flavor of spice herbs.

745 **Summer savory can be sown from early to mid-May.**

See ▶ **TIP 488** for more details. If pregrown plants are available, plant them after mid-May with a planting width of 10 × 10 in.

746 **Young borage herbs are more vigorous than old ones.** Accordingly, a second sowing can be carried out in late May.

See ▶ **TIP 486**.

747 **In the second half of May at the latest, buy and plant young plants of the perennial spice herbs lavender, sage, thyme, and lemon balm.**

However, as a rule, this is necessary only where no partial plants are available for reaching the objective earlier. The planting widths are 12 × 8 in. for lavender, 16 × 16 in. for sage, 8 × 8 in. for thyme, and 12 × 12 in. for lemon balm. On growing conditions, see ▶ **TIP 298**, ▶ **TIP 303**, ▶ **TIP 304**, and ▶ **TIP 481**.

748 **May is a particularly good month for establishing fungal cultures on hardwood lumps.**

The hardwood lumps are prepared as outlined in ▶ **TIP 492** to ▶ **TIP 494**. After inoculation, it is crucial to ensure that the woodpile does not dry out.

749 **Tree stumps can also be used for fungal cultures, provided that the tree was felled only during the previous winter.**

Oyster mushrooms, sheathed or two-tone woodtufts, conifer tufts, and velvet shanks or winter mushrooms are all highly suitable, for example. Inoculate tree stumps less than 12 in. in diameter according to the disk method. ▶ **TIP 493** In larger stumps, cut out two large wedges opposite one another (but not at the same height), cover the upper cut surface with spawn, and reinsert the wedges. Then cover the cuts with wide foil strips.

750 **May is the best time for planting champignons (mushrooms) in the garden.**

Hobby gardeners can prepare the necessary substrate for mushrooms themselves, but the outlay for the necessary raw materials, growing site, and time is considerable. Otherwise, the envisaged yields are generally too little to justify the time and effort involved for regular substrate generation. At least 1.5 to 2 yds.³ of quality horse manure is required, for example! For some time now, there have been specialized companies that offer both ready substrate and inoculated substrate, and even fully grown ready cultures, in sacks or polystyrene boxes. This makes it a lot easier to grow mushrooms in the garden.

751 In the garden or in a suitable room, either form planting beds, or fill boxes or sacks with the ready-made substrate.

The beds should be at least 20 in. wide and 8 to 10 in. high. If boxes are used, they should be at least 6 in. high. When using wooden boxes, it is important that the wood is untreated. If sacks made of synthetic materials are used, they must be large enough that a diameter of 12 to 16 in. with a height of 10 to 12 in. is attained when they are filled with substrate. Large plastic sacks can also be filled and then laid flat on the ground.

752 As soon as the planting beds or boxes are ready, inoculate the substrate with champignon (mushroom) spawn.

This is almost always delivered as grain spawn. For a bed or box area of one squareyard, 1 to 2 lbs. of grain spawn is required. The more spawn that is used, the faster the substrate will be occupied by the fungal mycelium. When growing in beds and boxes, work the grain spawn into the upper 2 in. of the substrate. For growing in sacks, evenly mix the spawn with the substrate before the sacks are filled. Around 1 lb. of spawn is required per 100 lbs. of substrate. Drill 10 to 15 holes in the filled sacks for aeration. Following inoculation, sufficient air humidity should be ensured; for beds and boxes, this can be achieved by covering them with perforated foil, sacks, or straw mats. The latter should be wetted regularly. It is also important to monitor the substrate temperature. If it exceeds 77°F, cooling will be essential—in other words, remove the foil covering, and, especially, open up any sacks of substrate. In any case, place the sacks where there is no direct sunlight. Also protect beds and boxes in the garden against heavy rainfalls.

Depending on the temperature, it takes two to four weeks for the mycelium to grow through and occupy the substrate completely. If already inoculated substrate has been purchased, it is also laid in beds or boxes, or filled into sacks, as described above.

753 A suitable place for growing wine-cap or burgundy mushrooms can be found in every garden.

The best time for establishing a wine-cap mushroom culture is in May and June. The straw of all grain species (other than corn) can serve as a nutrient substrate; all other materials are unsuitable. The straw should come from the previous year's harvest and still have a shiny gold to matte yellowish gray color. Do not use already decomposed, rotten, or dark-colored straw. For the actual culture, straw bales, preferably high-pressure bales are required, and can be obtained from farmers at a good price.

754 Wet the straw bales thoroughly before use.

Either put the bales in a large rainwater tank, for example, for two days, or water them several times each day for a week using a watering can or hose. The straw is wet enough if a handful of it releases a few water droplets when it is squeezed. After watering, bring the straw bales to their final site. It is important that they are in contact with the ground, as the mycelium will also need to spread into the soil.

755 Select a warm, sheltered site for growing roundhead mushrooms.

To ensure an optimal temperature for the mycelium growth (68 to 86°F), a sunny site is best, where an optimal microclimate can be achieved by partial shading. Semi-shaded sites can also be used successfully if the straw bales are protected from prolonged rainfall by using foil. In this case, however, the front side will need to remain open to ensure necessary aeration.

756 Inoculation with mushroom spawn is carried out one day after watering.

Using a robust dibber, drill 4 in. deep holes on both sides of the bale at an interval of 8 × 8 in. Then insert a walnut-sized lump of spawn and reseal the hole. Clean working procedures are important for successful growing; four cups of mushroom spawn are required for two straw bales. The bales should be covered with perforated foil, old sacks, or similar as a protection against drying out. In very dry weather, the bales must be sprayed occasionally (half a watering can per bale).

Community or allotment gardeners should take much greater notice of ready-made edible mushroom kits to make wise use of neglected places in the garden.

757 The shaggy inkcap or lawyer's wig is a high-yield, delicious mushroom that can be grown relatively easily in the garden.

Shaggy inkcap

In nature, it is found on grassland, compost sites, and in gardens. The fruiting bodies appear in bunches and grow very quickly. The scaly cap is initially cylindrical on the stem, and later becomes conical and rolls itself upward. The gills are first white, later they take on a pink to brown color, and then turn black. Then they disintegrate, yielding a dark inky liquid. The young mushrooms are extremely tasty and can be used to make fine mushroom dishes.

758 Shaggy inkcaps are grown in the same way as champignons (mushrooms) and can also be grown on the same substrate.

In fact, the shaggy inkcap is even more robust, and generally produces greater yields. However, it is a calcicolous mushroom, and, accordingly, an application of 1 lb. carbonic lime over 100 lbs. of substrate is recommended. In other respects, proceed with the readymade substrate in the same way as already described for champignons. This is also recommended for inoculation and the necessary maintenance of the beds and filled boxes or sacks. Shaggy inkcaps can be grown successfully on shady or semi-shaded sites in the garden, where a protective cover against rain and sun is also advisable. The best time for establishing a culture is from May to August.

759 Rat tail radishes are a rare vegetable for growing outdoors.

This easy-to-grow specialty is closely related to regular radishes and red radishes. The fruits can be enjoyed raw or steamed, baked, or boiled. Eaten raw, the pods taste like red radishes, while steamed they make a wonderfully spicy vegetable—this makes them ideal as a fresh, crunchy accompaniment to pan-fried, vegetable stir-fry, and wok dishes.

760 This annual culture is sown directly outdoors from May on.

Advance planting of rat tail radishes is not necessary. Since the plants have a bushy growth form and develop a great many pods, an interval of 16 × 16 in. between the individual plants is recommended. In view of the many pods, it may be necessary to support the plants with a stake. Regular watering and a loose, nutrient-rich soil at a sunny site will result in a high yield. The first pods appear after flowering and are best harvested when they are still young. Subsequent sowing can take place until July.

761 Inca cucumbers can be grown in large tubs and pots, and will also climb fences, trellises, and balconies. This rarity for community or allotment gardeners is a member of the cucurbit (gourd) plant family.

The seeds for greenhouse culture are raised from March, and for growing outdoors in late April, individually in small pots in the home. Following the "Three Saints' Days" (12–14 May), they can be planted out in the garden or in large planting troughs. With their powerful climbing tendrils, they can climb up anything within reach, and will attain a length of 2 to 4 in. on good humus soils. Every plant develops male flowers, with a racemose inflorescence, as well as female flowers, which grow individually. The plant is capable of self-fertilizing.

Large fruits can be stuffed like peppers, while the small ones can be eaten raw. They have a mild taste, like cucumbers, and the leaves and young shoots are edible as well. They can also be pureed in a blender and enjoyed as a juice or smoothie.

ORNAMENTAL PLANTS

Ornamental Gardens

762 **After mid-May, perennials should only ever be planted together with their root balls.**

This applies particularly to deep-rooted perennials. Plants that have been pregrown in pots can be planted out at any developmental stage.

763 **If, in peonies (*Paeonia*), some of the buds do not develop further, this is usually because they are suffering from gray mold.**

Owing to the disease agent concerned (*Botrytis paeoniae*), the outer layers of the buds are destroyed or become stuck together in such a way that the flowers cannot unfold. So the gray mold does not spread further, all the affected plant parts should be burned. Gray mold occurs especially in moist, warm weather.

764 **The silver ragwort or dusty miller (*Jacobaea maritima*, syn. *Senecio cineraria*) makes a beautiful edging plant.**

Although not winter hardy, it can be planted in pots in the fall, when it makes an attractive leafy plant for cool rooms. The plants can be raised from early March from seeds in a cold frame, or they can be bought as young plants from mid-May.

765 **All the summer flowers named in April (TIP 522 TO TIP 536) can be sown until mid-May.**

The late date is especially necessary in harsh locations. Delaying sowing any further will result in a flowering time that is too late for most summer flowers.

766 **In the first half of May, stocks (*Matthiola*), carnations (*Dianthus caryophyllus*), annual pinks (*Dianthus chinensis*), and snapdragons (*Antirrhinum*) can be planted.**

All of the abovenamed annual flowering species will not suffer from light late frosts if young plants are available that have been well hardened off. Accordingly, the above date also applies to higher-altitude locations ▸ TIP 571 to ▸ TIP 573.

> *Summer annuals can be used to fill gaps in perennial gardens.*

767 **Annual summer flowers can fill empty spaces in rock gardens and perennial borders.**

Gaps that have arisen through winter kills and cannot be filled by new plantings can be easily filled with summer flowers. The same applies to gaps that have arisen through the end of flowering of bulb plants (tulips, daffodils, etc.). The height of the summer flowers should be matched to that of the surrounding perennials.

768 **From mid-May, most pregrown summer flowers can be planted out.**

However, they must be well hardened off, since only then can they withstand occasional drops in nightly temperatures down to freezing. A more severe drop in temperature can be managed using light protection (hoods or foil). For planting marigolds (*Tagetes*) and zinnias (*Zinnia*), it is better to wait until late May; in many situations, the earliest possible date is 20 May. These annual flowers often fall victim to even the slightest cold spell and need a warm soil for fast and reliable growth. ▶ **TIP 375** The planting widths are given in **TABLE 25** and **TABLE 26**.

769 Cheddar pinks (*Dianthus gratianopolitanus*) and pinks (*D. plumarius*) form beautiful cushions, also in rock gardens, and along dry stone walls or stair stringers.

Cheddar pinks provide a habitat and nectar for useful insects, especially butterflies. In nature, they are in decline, and are endangered through trampling (hikers and climbers). Fast-growing, robust 'Eydangeri' forms dense cushions. Horticultural varieties are available in many colors, from purple to pink and white, as well as multicolored varieties. Both the above species prefer dry, sunny sites. They are also suitable for balcony boxes, troughs, and gravesite planting. In the greenhouse, they can already be sown in pots in February; they are then planted outdoors in May.

770 Russian statice (*Psylliostachys suworowii*) is an unusual dried flower for vase decorations in winter.

This plant is conspicuous with its pinkish red inflorescences with dense individual flowers on long, branched shoots. Since the inflorescences are cut only when they have finished flowering altogether, they are also very appealing on the site where they are growing. The pregrown and hardened-off plants from cold frames (sown in early May) can be planted out in mid-May. The planting width is 10 × 12 in.

771 As soon as tulips are finishing flowering, cut off their fruiting capsules.

Tulips often set seed, which strongly impedes the development of new bulbs.

772 Beds with flower bulbs that have finished flowering can be planted along with summer or annual flowers.

This especially applies to beds where tulip or daffodil bulbs have been left in the ground. Plant the summer flowers between the rows. The rows are mostly only 8 in. apart, so the interval within the rows should be somewhat greater, and in any case not less than 10 in.

773 Wild shoots often develop on the grafted bases of roses.

Cut off wildling here!

Since the base of the wild shoots is mostly below the soil surface, the soil needs to be carefully removed. It is important that the wild shoots are cut off at their base or shoots could sprout again from dormant buds. Also pay attention to wild shoots in standard and climbing roses.

774 Powdery mildew on roses should be treated immediately.

Do not wait until all the leaf uppersides are covered in a whitish gray dust before taking action. Before resorting to chemical means, try out proven domestic remedies. Spraying with strongly diluted milk or whey or a mixture of cooking oil and baking powder (with a few drops of dishwashing liquid as a wetting agent) can prevent further spread of the mildew. In dry and warm weather, repeat spraying after around eight days. You can also try using a tobacco extract. Mix the tobacco with water, leave the mixture to stand for two days, sieve the liquid, and spray it onto the leaves. Remove any affected plant parts. These can be added to the compost, since mildew fungi can exist only on living plants. If spraying plant protection agents (fungicides or insecticides), be sure to exercise extreme caution—follow the instructions on the packaging exactly. **TABLE 32**

775 Black spot on roses should be combated constantly until fall.

In this case, irregular, star-shaped, brownish black flecks develop on leaves that later turn yellow and drop off. This fungus likes to settle on the sticky excretions of aphids. Repeated spraying of the domestic agents named in ▸ **TIP 774** is called for; only when that does not help should you resort to fungicides. **TABLE 32**

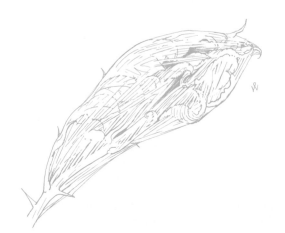

776 Cocooned leaves on rose shoot tips are indicative of the larvae of the garden rose tortrix (moth).

Close examination of these rolled-up leaves reveals greenish caterpillars around ½ in. long. Solve this problem by killing the caterpillars in the cocooned leaves. The shoot tips of the roses should be monitored continuously so that no serious damage arises. **TABLE 31**

777 Lengthwise-rolled rose leaves contain the larvae of the leaf-rolling wasp.

The larvae eat the leaf tissue and can cause considerable damage if they are present in large numbers. Remove and destroy the affected leaves, along with the ⅓ in. long caterpillars. **TABLE 31**

778 Rose sawfly infestation can be recognized by wilting shoots or shoot tips.

A distinction is made between rose shoot sawfly and rose tip-infesting sawfly. These are sawflies that feed on the rose shoot tissue. They are whitish in color and about ⅖ in. long. In the early stages, they can be dealt with by cutting off the wilted portion of the shoot back as far as the healthy section (destroy the cut-off shoots). Only if the pest spreads widely and affects a larger stand of roses should the use of approved insecticides follow, from late April or early May. **TABLE 31**

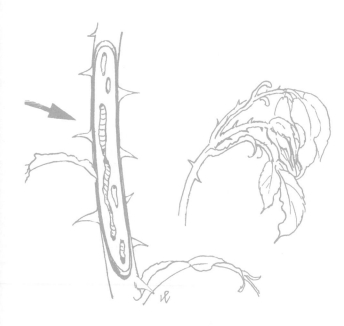

779 **Heather species (*Erica* and *Calluna*) should be cut back after flowering.**

In doing so, remove ⅓ to ⅔ of the length of the previous year's shoot. This will result in attractive bushes that are dense from the base up and will flower richly every year. If older wood is cut back too severely, however, it will often no longer produce new shoots.

780 **Conifers can be planted in spring until mid-May.**

The development of annual shoots in conifers planted after mid-May can be inhibited. If you have missed the planting deadline, it is better to wait until August. When planting, note ▶ **TIP 554** to ▶ **TIP 556**; see also **TABLE 10**.

Many ornamental shrubs, such as lilacs and rhododendrons, will flower better in the following year if spent flowers are removed and they are not allowed to set seed.

781 **Protect freshly planted conifers and evergreen broad-leaved trees from the sun and spray with water regularly.**

Sufficient watering, sun protection, and a higher air humidity are necessary for good growth. On how to achieve this, see ▶ **TIP 1099**.

782 **As soon as lilac has finished flowering, remove the dry inflorescences.**

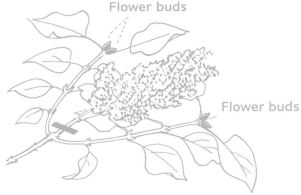

Flower buds

Flower buds

When doing so, be careful not to damage the new vegetative shoots, which develop the buds for the following year's flowering at their ends. Inflorescences that are not removed often set seed and require a lot of nutrients. The nutrients will then no longer be available to the new shoots, greatly weakening their development.

783 **Flowering almond (*Prunus triloba*) should be cut back severely after flowering.**

This will lead to the formation of long shoots with buds for the following year. Pruning should be done immediately after the end of flowering.

784 **The best time for planting pampas grass (*Cortaderia selloana*) is from mid-May.**

Pampas grass is one of the most beautiful solitary grasses, but generally needs winter protection ▸ TIP 1330. During the growing season, pampas grass needs plenty of moisture and nutrients; however, this steppe grass does not tolerate waterlogging. Accordingly, dig a deep planting ditch and fill it with a gravel layer about 8 to 12 in. thick. This should be followed by 12 to 16 in. of compost earth, mixed with rather coarse sand. The plant is set in this layer, along with its root ball. There are both richly and sparsely flowering varieties. The latter involve mainly the female-flowering forms of pampas grass, but also inexpensive seed plants that have not been adequately selected and verified. Huge bushes with more than 50 panicles are not uncommon if the plants have been well tended. The inflorescences, which are around 6 ½ ft. long, make a splendid dried decoration in floor vases. Even when the mostly creamy white, or, more seldom, pink-colored panicles appear only in September, the grass bunches will already be a splendid sight in the garden in the months beforehand. The plants usually need three years to develop fully.

785
Now is also the time to plant other solitary grasses and perennials, if they are growing in pots or containers.

Perennials with dried-up roots, and especially grasses, will now grow poorly. Only plants that have been divided in your own garden, whose roots have remained fresh, and which have been replanted immediately and well maintained, will grow well without difficulties.

786
Lay the tubers of the corn lily (*Ixia*) in a sunny place in early May.

Ixia species in many colorful varieties are rarities in the garden or in plant tubs. They are planted at 4 in. intervals, and 3 to 4 in. deep. In the fall, remove and overwinter the tubers in the same way as gladioli.
▸ TIP 1179, ▸ TIP 1181, ▸ TIP 1325 to ▸ TIP 1329

787
The sprouting tubers of tuberous begonias and the rhizomes of the canna lily (*Canna*) should not be planted out before 20 May.

These are both very frost-sensitive, and can also fall victim to light late frosts. For tuberous begonias, a planting width of 10 × 10 in. is usually sufficient. Depending on the thickness of the rootstock, canna lilies must be spaced 16 to 20 in. apart.

788
Most border and bed plants are frost-sensitive, and therefore should not be planted out on exposed sites before 20 May.

These include the well-known *Begonia* Semperflorens Cultorum Group, which flowers ceaselessly all summer long until the onset of frost, and which is highly suitable for semi-shaded to shady sites, as well as flossflower (*Ageratum*), lobelia, sages, and other summer flowers.

789 A ground covering on planting beds can save a lot of work.

If you cover the soil during the time between annual flowers and other plants with a mulch layer, you will hardly need to hoe the soil. The soil will also stay moist for longer, greatly promoting plant growth. In addition to bark substrate and compost earth, grass clippings and other weed-free organic waste, shredded if need be, are suitable as ground coverings.

790 Winter-hardy orchids are always a focal point in the garden.

Lady's slipper (*Cypripedium*) in several species and hybrids, Chinese ground orchid (*Bletilla striata*), as well as Indian crocus (*Pleione limprichtii*) and others need special treatment—be sure to consult the specialist literature! They love a sheltered site, and, mostly in unfavorable climates, a thick protective layer of needle (coniferous) litter in winter. In very wet periods in winter, they can also be covered with foil. NB: Orchids are subject to strict nature protection legislation and may not be removed from natural sites. Specialized nurseries offer these orchids from artificial raising as listed in **TABLE 30**.

791 In climatically favorable regions, some camellia varieties can also be planted out in the open.

Single, semi-double, and double-flowering varieties are available that are winter hardy in climatically favorable regions. Here too, however, sites that are as sheltered from the wind as possible should be selected. In less suitable regions, it is better to overwinter camellias under frost-free conditions. The best time for planting camellias in the garden is from mid-May to early July. After planting out, ensure that the root ball is sufficiently moist. The site should not be in full sun, but in light shade. The best place is somewhere where the camellia will receive afternoon sun. Without sunlight, only a very few buds (or none at all) will develop. The soil should be rich in humus and acidic (with a pH of around 5.5). When planting, excavate a ditch to a depth of around 20 in.; a drainage layer is also necessary, except on sandy soils. For backfilling, commercially available camellia potting soil is suitable.

Terraces and Balconies

792 In early May, tub plants that can withstand light night frosts can be left outdoors again.

Suitable plants include the European fan palm (*Chamaerops*), leadwort (*Plumbago*), oleander (*Nerium*), and myrtle (*Myrtus*). These should be allowed to stand next to the house for several days first for hardening off.

793 Tub plants that do not tolerate frost should be placed outdoors only from mid- to late May.

Following the "Three Saints' Days" (generally 12–14 May), frost-sensitive tub plants such as *Citrus*, *Bougainvillea*, camellias, bananas (*Musa*), coral tree (*Erythrina*), heliotrope, *Hibiscus rosa-sinensis*, *Tibouchina*, *Schefflera*, angel's trumpet (*Brugmansia*), and umbrella grass (*Cyperus*), and, after 20 May, all palms and young plants, can leave their overwintering rooms.

794 Not just lattice boxes covered in climbers, but planted peat walls, too, are suitable as wind or visual protection for seating areas.

These consist of two slatted frames 6 to 8 in. apart, covered with coarse wire netting. The structure is filled with well-moistened peat growing substrate that must never be allowed to dry out. Petunias, verbenas, hanging geraniums, sages, and *Tagetes* have all proven their worth as plantings. In shady places, hanging fuchsias, *Begonia* Semperflorens Cultorum Group, lobelias (*Lobelia*), or busy Lizzie (*Impatiens walleriana*) will grow better. These should be planted in May when there are no more late frosts, throughout the latticework—on both sides as well. Once the plants have grown into place, a constant nutrient supply must be ensured. It is best to water the structure with a highly diluted nutrient solution rather than with pure water. On ecological grounds, the peat growing substrate should ideally be replaced with compost earth with bark humus or wood fibers.

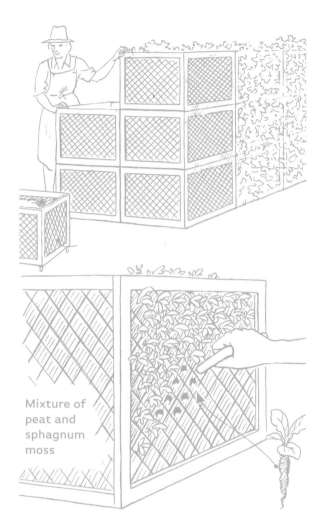

Mixture of peat and sphagnum moss

gravel along with their pots. Robust plants such as the genera *Opuntia*, *Disocactus*, *Heliocereus*, *Cereus*, and *Echinopsis* are suitable. The site will become particularly interesting once other succulent plants have been integrated as well. The genera *Aeonium* with section *Greenovia*, *Echeveria*, *Pachyphytum*, and others provide attractive species for this purpose. Plant the winter-hardy *Sempervivum* and opuntias in the early spring. It is worth using these as a framework for the succulents so they can spread undisturbed over the course of the year.

797 Lantanas (*Lantana*) make fine flowering plants for window boxes, winter gardens, and terraces.

They love plenty of sun and warmth, and will reward nutrient-rich soil and frequent fertilizer application with lush flowering. Young lantanas flower constantly in window boxes, while older tub plants can also be planted out in summer. Small, crowned trees are especially appealing on terraces and in winter gardens.

798 The gloriosa or climbing lily (*Gloriosa superba*) is a climbing plant that is around 5 ft. high, and develops its lily-like flowers from late June.

The splendid gloriosa lily, with its initially green, then yellow, and finally red flowers, grows best on sheltered and sunny sites along the house or on the terrace, or, better still, in the winter garden. Outdoors, place the rhizome in earth that is as humic and nutrient-rich as possible, but not before 20 May. It should be laid carefully and horizontally around 3 in. deep in the soil. Advance planting in a pot is even better. The tendrils of *Gloriosa* need a climbing structure around 5 ft. high. The plant is highly poisonous (colchicine).

795 In summer, cacti grow better on the terrace or balcony than in a room.

They should be brought outdoors only after the May frosts. Fresh air and sun promote healthy growth, firm tissues, and vivid colors, which will enable the plants to survive the dark wintertime better.

796 Cacti and succulents in tubs, or as a group on large terraces, are always attractive.

To achieve a near-natural design, gravel and rock chunks can be scattered on the ground to give the site a desert-like character. Sink the plants into the

799 Climbing nasturtiums (*Tropaeolum*) and cup-and-saucer vine (*Cobaea*) are suitable for planting trellises on the balcony or house.

Both these plants are annuals and are sown in nutrient-rich soil in flower boxes in early May. The young plants should be protected from late frosts. They need plenty of water and full sun in summer.

Achieve faster climbing with pregrown plants (sow in February ▸ **TIP 197** to ▸ **TIP 200**) with root balls that are planted out in the open only from mid-May. The shoots of the cup-and-saucer vine anchor themselves on the climbing structure, while the nasturtiums will need to be attached to it. Lay three or four seeds at an interval of 16 to 20 in. There are also bushy nasturtium varieties. In this case, sow seeds at an interval of 20 in. in boxes, or out in the open. ▸ **TIP 489** and ▸ **TIP 490**

800 The runner bean or scarlet runner (*Phaseolus coccineus*) is suitable for planting as a climber over larger areas.

Lay the red, white, or reddish white flowering beans directly in the soil in mid-May or in flower boxes at an interval of 4 × 3 in. Double rows are best for achieving a dense wall. Scarlet runners grow best on a framework or on cords that have not been pulled very tight, and they need plenty of water and nutrients. The young pods make a very tasty vegetable.

801 The spring planting of balcony and window boxes can be replaced with summer-flowering plants following the last night frosts.

The initial balcony box planting will generally be looking unsightly by this time. Now is the time to replace these plants with summer-flowering ones. Plant by the end of May to ensure they will give lasting pleasure. Compost earth or potting mixture is the best substrate. Long-acting fertilizers are also suitable, in the form of fertilizer sticks, for example.

802 Geraniums, petunias, and garden balsam (*Impatiens balsamina*) need medium-heavy soils, plenty of nutrients, and sun.

While petunias and balsam plants need plenty of water, geraniums should be watered more sparingly, and always allowed to dry off somewhat between watering. Geraniums and petunias in particular love plenty of sun.

803 Fuchsias, begonias, lobelias, pimpernel (*Anagallis*), sages, verbenas, and busy Lizzie (*Impatiens walleriana*) need humus-rich soil.

A combination of potting mixture and compost earth with sand is best. Frequent fertilizer application is important for these plants. Fuchsias, begonias, and busy Lizzie do not like full sun, but instead love moister places that are out of direct sun.

804 Splendidly flowering carnations (*Dianthus caryophyllus*) and slipper flowers (*Calceolaria*) do not like shade.

These thrive better on east- and west-facing sites than in the harsh midday sun. Uniform fertilizer and water application will ensure vigorous development. Carnations are available in white to deep-red flowering varieties with infinite intermediate shades, while slipper flowers usually bloom in yellow to golden-brown color tones.

805 In window boxes, too, every plant needs sufficient space.

Boxes with only a few plants tend to look sad, but if planted too densely the plants will all drive each other upward. The correct planting intervals are given in **TABLE 27**. Annual or biennial flowers whose growth largely remains low are the most suitable for window boxes. Tall-growing varieties may let too little light into the room. The species or varieties that are chosen will depend on the direction in which the window is facing. In south-facing windows, the edging or trailing lobelia (*Lobelia erinus*) will flower from mid-May, the Dahlberg daisy or golden fleece (*Thymophylla tenuiloba*) from June, and the moss rose (*Portulaca grandiflora*) from July. For west- and east-facing windows, select flossflowers (*Ageratum*), slipper flowers (*Calceolaria*), Mexican cigar plants (*Cuphea ignea*), or creeping zinnias (*Sanvitalia procumbens*), and for north-facing windows plants from the *Begonia* Semperflorens Cultorum Group.

Winter Gardens, Flower Windows, and Rooms

806 Plants in south-facing windows need additional shade.

With the exception of cacti and nearly all other succulents, only a few indoor plants will tolerate constant full sun. Especially behind glass, the temperatures can climb so high that the cell tissue of the leaves dies off, resulting in black spots. This not only looks unsightly, but can also affect the plant's development and a rich florescence. If it is not possible to change the plant's location in the winter garden or window, it is best to provide shade, especially during the middle of the day. Good shade can be provided by Venetian blinds or awnings. Indoor blinds reduce the available space for the plants; accordingly, outdoor blinds are more suitable. A portion of the light will then already be reflected by the glass pane, which means that the indoor temperature, too, will remain lower. By using blinds, it is also possible to save energy in winter, since radiation heat loss will be inhibited. Awnings, too, in front of the window will protect the indoor plants from too much sun. They will yield indirect light and can also be very decorative. In some cases, a drawn, translucent curtain will sufficiently protect the plants from intense sunlight.

> *Clean plants grow better and stay healthy.*

807 Indoor plants should be dusted regularly, and not only in winter.

Dust is constantly present in the air, and therefore on our indoor plants as well. Not only is it unsightly, but it can also be harmful, because it impedes photosynthesis, and therefore the plant's metabolism, and ultimately the buildup and retention of the associated products. Dust on leaves also allows harmful fungal spores to gain a foothold. Unfortunately, dust is unavoidable, but it can be kept within limits. The plants should be sprayed with water frequently, the best time being in spring, or outdoors in summer. The plants should be left outside only until there are no more drips. They should then not be placed in drafty places or in the hot midday sun. Frequent spraying with water is preferable to washing off the leaves. The bathtub can also be used effectively for smaller plants, and in the winter. The water should be lukewarm.

808   During gentle, warm rain, leave indoor plants outside for a while.

The rain will wash away the dust that has settled on the leaves over time. Fine rain will not damage the leaves of even sensitive plants. However, plants that are in flower should not be exposed to the rain. Many of our indoor plants can spend the entire summer outdoors. These include grape ivy (*Cissus alata*, syn. *C. rhombifolia*), kaffir lily (*Clivia miniata*), baby jade or jade plant (*Crassula ovata*), fire lily (*Cyrtanthus*, syn. *Vallota*), echeveria (*Echeveria* species), aralia ivy (×*Fatshedera lizei*), Japanese fatsia (*Fatsia japonica*), hydrangea (*Hydrangea macrophylla*), ivy (*Hedera helix*), *Kalanchoe blossfeldiana*, palms other than the Weddel palm (*Lytocaryum*, syn. *Microcoelum weddellianum*), passionflower (*Passiflora caerulea*), staghorn fern (*Platycerium* species), Easter cactus (*Rhipsalidopsis* ×*graeseri*), Indian azalea (*Rhododendron simsii*), ivy tree or umbrella tree (*Schefflera*), *Schlumbergera*, African hemp (*Sparmannia africana*), cape primrose (*Streptocarpus*), tradescantias, myrtles, citrus plants, and many others. They can be placed outdoors in late May. There, they should be given a suitable site, depending on whether they can tolerate the sun or prefer shade instead. However, not all of them can withstand the hot midday sun in summer—burns can be the result. ▸ **TIP 936**

JUNE

SUMMER

In June, many annual flowers, as well as herbaceous perennials, shrubs, and trees, delight us with their rich and splendid blooms. To ensure healthy growth, they also need to be supplied with water and nutrients. Further seed sowing is also possible. In addition to biennial cultivated plants for flowering in the following year—such as foxgloves, wallflowers, and Canterbury bells—these include numerous flowering herbs, as well as autumn cauliflower, winter endives, and bush beans. Additionally, many perennials, including dahlias, grow vigorously in June and will need to be staked.

GENERAL

809 Perennial weeds, such as field horsetails and bindweed, can quickly become a plague in the garden.

The best way to get rid of these is for every shoot tip above the ground to be hacked or cut off about an inch beneath the soil surface.

810 Wild herbs can be an indication of alkaline or acid soils.

A dense stand of field horsetails, for example, indicates a lime deficiency. Sheep sorrel (*Rumex acetosella*), teesdale violets (*Viola rupestris*), and field clover (*Trifolium arvense*) are a sign of very acidic soils. Meanwhile, corn buttercup (*Ranunculus arvensis*), common fumitory (*Fumaria officinalis*), sow thistle species (*Sonchus arvensis*, for example), and gallant soldier (*Galinsoga parviflora*) indicate weakly acidic or neutral soils. *Galium tricornutum*, fool's parsley (*Aethusa cynapium*), and dwarf spurge (*Euphorbia exigua*) indicate neutral to weakly alkaline soils. Finally, the common chickweed (*Stellaria media*) and dog nettle (*Urtica urens*) indicate humic and nutrient-rich soils, and the bothersome couch grass (*Elymus repens*) nitrogen-rich soils.

> *Pull weeds before they go to seed to reduce further infestation.*

811 Wild (weed) herbs should not be allowed to set seed in any garden.

Weeds that are setting seed will typically also grow in somewhat hidden places; the seed is mostly dispersed by the wind. Accordingly, these jeopardize not just your own garden, but those of your neighbors as well.

812 Remove the common chickweed (*Stellaria media*) early in the spring.

This weed, in particular, sets plentiful seed as a young plant, which is easily dispersed and can then infest the entire garden.

813 The gallant soldier (*Galinsoga parviflora*) should not be tolerated in the garden, because it is often infested with red spider mites.

If attention is not paid, cucumbers, beans, roses, and other ornamental plants will be affected by these pests. Regular monitoring will help, particularly in dry, warm weather. Red spider mites do not like moisture; accordingly, the affected ornamental plants or vegetables should be sprayed frequently with water. Only if there is a severe infestation should you resort to using commercially available special preparations (acaricides—note the instructions on the packaging!). **TABLE 31**

814 Grass clippings are good for ground covering (mulches), but are less suitable for composting.

If rotted stable manure or compost earth is insufficient for a ground covering, grass clippings from mowing the lawn can be used with similar success. This is better than composting them. Too many grass clippings in the compost will lead to the development of a slimy mass that is impermeable to the air, and also stinks. If, however, two parts grass clippings are mixed with one part chopped wood chips, bark mulch, or dry leaves, this will increase the air permeability. Before applying the ground covering, loosen the soil between the plants thoroughly.

815 Ladybug larvae are also known as antlions.

Wherever there are many ladybugs, their larvae will also be found on the plants in large numbers. Both are an unmistakable indication of aphids. Not just the larvae, but the ladybugs, too, devour a great many aphid pests. Accordingly, both the larvae and the ladybugs should be protected; avoid any spraying or dusting with insecticide.

Biological pest control should be the first plan of attack for weeds and insects.

816 Ladybug pupae should not be confused with the larvae of Colorado beetles.

These are very similar in color, but upon closer examination the differences are easy to see. Ladybug pupae are attached to the leaves in an immobile fashion and are legless. In contrast, the head and legs of Colorado beetle larvae are easily recognizable; the larvae also move about freely and feed on the leaves. In addition to potatoes, Colorado beetles afflict other members of the nightshade family, such as tomatoes.

817 The hedgehog is a valuable helper in the fight against garden pests.

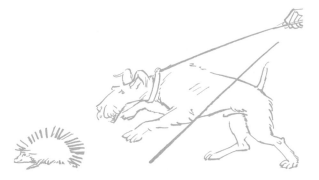

Hedgehogs hunt insects, slugs, and snails. Accordingly, hedgehogs should be looked after in the garden, and their resting places left undisturbed. Research their legal protection status in your local area. Regardless, they should not be removed from nature, or even from the garden, and brought into the house. If you see a young hedgehog in the garden in the late fall, set up a suitable feeding site. Injured or very weak animals should be brought to an appropriate veterinarian. There are also several websites, such as the British Hedgehog Preservation Society (british-hedgehogs.org.uk), which offer information about what you can do in your garden to protect hedgehogs from danger, how you can help them survive the winter, and which hedgehogs may be taken into human care.

818 Frogs and toads should be looked after the garden, because they eat slugs, snails, and other pests.

Children should be taught that they should touch useful toads only under supervision. These toads produce a secretion that can cause skin irritations in people who are allergic to it.

819 The first herbs can already be harvested in June.

Kitchen herbs and spices belong in every garden. They have appealing flowers, and generally nectar and pollen for useful insects as well, and they also have a wide diversity of uses in kitchen for spicing up and improving culinary dishes. Some are believed to have healing or relieving properties for a range of diseases. This has often not been scientifically proven as such, but many of them nevertheless promote and boost good health. They are used in "folk medicine," and in homeopathy as well. Most herbs love sunny sites. The soil should be sufficiently permeable so that it can dry out again quickly after rainfall. Raised beds provide good conditions for growth. ▶ TIP 1226 Chives, garlic, parsley, celery, dill, summer savory, marjoram, peppermint, sage, lavender, lemon balm, borage, thyme, lovage, and others are discussed in the tips for the vegetable garden.

VEGETABLES

820 In the case of celery, there must be no interruptions to growth during the main growing period.

The causes of these interruptions are mostly soil encrustation and dryness. Accordingly, ensure a constant soil moisture level and loosen the soil regularly. Celery planted in May should be given an initial surface application of nitrogen fertilizer in mid-June.

821 Plant cauliflower for harvesting in the fall by mid-June at the latest.

To achieve highly vigorous plants by the end of July, plant one individual seed grain every 1½ to 2 in. within the row. For this late cultivation, use medium-early varieties.

822 Cauliflower and broccoli that were planted in May will need plenty of water and nutrients in June.

They should be given surface applications of nitrogen fertilizer each at the beginning and end of June. For the second application, the use of a nutrient-rich complete fertilizer with trace elements is advisable. Additionally, be sure to keep the soil constantly moist.

823 To harvest beautiful white "flowers" from cauliflower, they must be protected from the sun and other weather influences early on.

The best method is to tie the longest leaf tips together as soon as the first sign of the flowers is visible. If the leaves are only bent over, it will be necessary to break the main leaf ribs completely or the leaves will simply grow upright again. The flowers need to be harvested before they open. Accordingly, daily monitoring is required, especially in periods of heat or dryness.

824 To harvest bush beans continuously, they should also be sown once or twice in June.

Varieties with a short development time are preferable.

825 Bush beans that were sown in May should be given another nitrogen fertilizer application before the stand becomes dense and closes up.

Apply around 1 oz./yd.^{2} of a fast-acting nitrogen fertilizer, but in the form of a nutrient solution between the rows to avoid leaf burns. Follow this application by sprinkling with clear water. A complete fertilizer solution can also be applied, while also remembering that bush beans are chloride-sensitive.

826 Although bush beans will survive with only a little water in soils that are not too light, dry periods should be bridged with generous watering.

Bush beans have their greatest water requirement during flowering, which means that beans sown in May will need plenty of moisture from late June to mid-July in particular. At the same time, this will help prevent infestation with red spider mites, whose presence is facilitated by dryness.

827 Careful working when harvesting rhubarb will prevent the leaf buds from breaking out and the stalks from breaking off.

Grip the stalks that are ready for harvesting right at the base with both hands, twist sideways, and pry out at the side with a small pull. Do not cut the stalks. Per plant, about five or six stalks can be harvested each time.

828 Rhubarb is often given rough handling, even though a foundation for successful harvests over the next few years can be laid at this time.

In June, give rhubarb an application of organic fertilizer from compost, hoof and horn meal, or stable manure. If no organic fertilizer is available, ½ oz. of complete fertilizer and ½ oz. of a pure nitrogen fertilizer can also be applied. Lightly hoe in the fertilizer. If there is no rain, transfer the fertilizers to the rhubarb's rooting zone through vigorous watering. The breaking out of the flower stalks should be done over this entire period. The harvest should be completed in mid-June to allow sufficient reserve nutrients to build up for the following year.

Stop harvesting rhubarb when the stems begin to toughen. Apply a layer of compost to ensure a good harvest the following year.

829 Eggplants can also still be planted in the first days of June.

They will generally be ready for harvesting hardly any later than those planted in May. However, vigorously growing pot plants are a prerequisite. ▸ TIP 654 to ▸ TIP 656

830 Curly kale for harvesting can still be sown until mid-June.

The plants are then planted out in the second half of July. This date will not deliver quite the same harvest yields as the June planting of curly kale, but it will allow beds that have been harvested by this time to be utilized fully. On sowing, see ▸ TIP 443.

831 In the second half of June, you can begin to plant up harvested beds with curly kale that was sown in May (TIP 658).

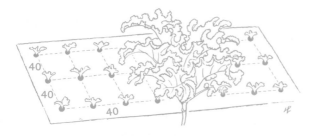

Since the curly kale that has been planted in June will develop very vigorously, only three rows will be possible in a normal bed (4 ft.). The interval between the plants must be 16 to 20 in. within a row.

832 To ensure good growth in house cucumbers, give special attention to regular watering and regulation of the air temperature.

On the water requirement, see the information given in ▸ **TIP 661**. The highest justifiable daily maximum temperature is around 90°F, while the minimum during the night should be 60 to 64°F. As soon as the temperature rises above 82°F, ventilation is essential. To avoid leaf damage, small greenhouses should also be shaded; linen sheets are highly suitable. Painting a lime brew onto the plants is also possible, but this may need to be repeated more often if the protective layer is partially washed off by the rain.

833 With the onset of fruit development, fertilize house cucumbers once per week.

Nutrient deficiency can be recognized by the younger leaves, especially, losing their healthy green color. In such cases, prepare a 0.3 percent nitrogen fertilizer solution and apply 1 to 2 quarts to each plant weekly. To ensure a sufficient supply of all nutrients and the most important trace elements, give a complete fertilizer application after one or two nitrogen fertilizer applications. Here, remember that cucumbers have an especially high potassium requirement and are also sensitive to chloride.

834 In June, too, pruning of cucumbers must continue carefully.

On the primary lateral shoots, secondary lateral shoots will also develop in addition to the flowers. Of these secondary shoots, only the one next to the main shoot is left to remain and is pruned again after the first one or two signs of fruiting. Thereafter, pruning is limited to the removal of the shoot tips and occasional thinning. When pruning the shoots, remove any diseased or yellow leaves at the same time. It is also important to cut off any fruits that exhibit deformities as early as possible in their development. Fruits that have grown too large or are already overripe will have a detrimental impact on the development of the normal fruit.

835 Cucumbers that have been planted out during the first days of June will often deliver greater yields than those planted directly on site in May.

This should be especially noted at higher altitudes, where the soil has often not warmed up enough in May. However, for June planting, vigorous, densely growing pot-ball plants are required. They are pre-grown in May, in cold frames. The use of mulch fleece is recommended to accelerate the growth.

836 Cold tap water is pure poison for cucumbers and other vegetable species that require warmth, such as peppers, melons, and eggplants.

Accordingly, these plants should not be watered using a garden hose. If you are growing them, ensure that you always have enough prewarmed container water available. Additionally, be sure to refill the container immediately after every evening watering.

> *Water warm-season vegetables such as cucumbers using water that has been left to stand for a while.*

837 Cucumbers growing outdoors should be given their first surface fertilizer application once the third normal leaf has unfolded fully.

The application should be given as a 0.3 percent nutrient solution. When selecting a fertilizer, remember that cucumbers are chloride-sensitive.

838 Early potatoes need plenty of watering to achieve high yields.

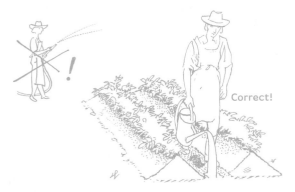

Correct!

Especially during dry periods, at least 3 to 4 gal./yd.² should be given so that the soil is thoroughly moist right through. In June, the potatoes should also be given a surface fertilizer application of calcium nitrate.

> *To prevent potato blight, always water between the rows, without wetting the leaves.*

839 Celery plots must be hoed regularly and given plenty of water.

Loosening the soil will result in better aeration and is especially important following rainfall or after watering. At the end of June, give celeriac (root celery) an initial surface application of nitrogen fertilizer.

840 In June, as a preventive measure, celery should be treated against leaf spot disease (*Septoria*) and celery scurf.

Leaf spot   Celery scurf

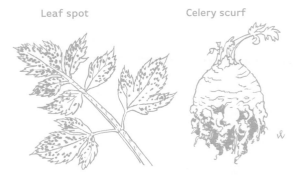

Both diseases affect tuber growth and quality, but can be combated effectively by spraying with special fungicides. Repeat the treatment at intervals of two to three weeks. Preventive measures include long intervals between cropping, using less-susceptible varieties, and mixed cultivation, for example with leeks, cucumbers, or bush beans.

841 Florence fennel has a high water supply requirement.

Especially when the tubers begin to form, soil moisture should be as constant as possible. Dry periods lead not only to tougher, fibrous tubers, but unwanted shoots as well. Nevertheless, waterlogging should be avoided when watering. Lightly heaping up the soil around the plants when the tubers begin to form will be beneficial for the tuber quality. At the same time, give a surface application of nitrogen fertilizer.

842 In the second half of June, begin planting late kohlrabi for winter use (storage).

This applies particularly to varieties with very large tubers, with their long development time of at least three months. By contrast, varieties such as 'Blauer Speck' can still be planted up until mid-July. Late kohlrabi needs a planting width of 12 × 12 to 16 × 16 in.; varieties with especially large tubers need as much as 24 × 20 in.

843 In kohlrabi, fluctuations between dryness and considerable moisture can cause the tubers to burst open.

Accordingly, it is most important that the kohlrabi beds remain uniformly moist so that there are no interruptions to growth.

> *A constant water supply and regular soil loosening will ensure good potato tuber quality.*

844 Kohlrabi is suitable as an aftercrop on harvested pea plant beds.

Cut off the aboveground parts of the pea plants flush with the soil surface. This means that the roots remain in the soil when the land is tilled for planting with kohlrabi. The nitrogen-fixing activity of the root bacteria is highly beneficial for the aftercrop, and, in this case, for the kohlrabi as well. To this end, use summer kohlrabi varieties. They will be ready to harvest in about two months.

> *Blue kohlrabi varieties are less prone to pest infestation and will remain tender for longer.*

845 Turnips and rutabagas can be planted in the first 10 days of June.

Sow the seed widely over an outdoor bed for raising seedlings. The time to planting out is five to six weeks. Regular watering during this time is crucial.

846 When planting iceberg and regular lettuce in June, select heat-resistant summer varieties.

The planting width is 12 × 12 in. Always remember to plant the regular lettuce as shallowly as possible, since only then will it be possible to harvest large, firm heads. There are red-leaved varieties for both lettuce types. Inside the heads, these are also yellow, very tender, and have the advantage of being less prone to aphid infestation.

847 Careful watering of iceberg lettuce is especially important.

Rot can set in, especially once the head begins to form, if the lettuce has been kept too moist. Plentiful watering (4 to 5 gal./yd.²) is recommended before the development of a closed stand, or until the heads begin to form. After this, there may often be no need to water the plants again before harvesting. However, if watering is still necessary, it should preferably be done in the early hours of the day, watering carefully between the plants so that the leaves will dry out again by evening. If the weather is wet over a longer period, it is advisable to erect a foil tent.

848 Pumpkins and squash deliver the greatest yields when they are continually sprayed with nutrient solutions.

They should not be given any pure water at all. The nutrient solutions should be weaker than normal, only about 0.05 to 0.1 percent. This corresponds to just 0.2 to 0.4 oz. of a nitrogen-rich complete fertilizer per 3 gallons of water. If such a fertilizer is not available, then alternate between a pure nitrogen fertilizer and a complete fertilizer.

849 In June, pruning melons is one of the most important maintenance tasks to carry out.

The pruning outlined in ▸ **TIP 692** should be continued as carefully as possible in June, since this is crucial for the expected yield. Allow only four or five fruits to develop per melon plant; this is the only way to ensure that attractive fruits can be achieved. Remove all other initial signs of fruiting as soon as it becomes clear that the initial fruits will develop further. Similarly, the lateral shoots without signs of initial fruit development should be removed directly at the base. In order that the melons do not rot, they should not lie on top of the earth; instead, place a protective layer underneath each melon, preferably a pane of glass. Wood is unsuitable for this purpose.

850 Melons grown under glass must be pollinated artificially.

Melons have dioecious (separate male and female) flowers. If the fruits are to develop, the pollen needs to be transferred from a male flower to a female one.

This task is generally performed by bees. To be sure that this actually takes place, rather than just relying on nature, you will need to perform this task yourself. The simplest way of doing so is to pluck a male flower and press its stamens carefully against the stigma of a female flower. To ensure success, repeat the procedure over several days. The best time is during the middle of the day, in sunshine.

Under no circumstances should tap water be used for watering the melons, since this will be highly detrimental to the plants' growth. Instead, take water from a container or pond. The same applies for applying nutrient solutions. Always ensure that the soil near the root collar stays dry.

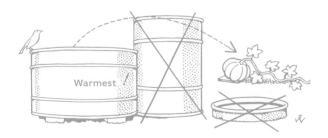

851 The secondary roots of horseradish that were planted in March (TIP 301 and TIP 302) are laid bare at the end of June, and all their lateral roots are removed.

This is essential to attain thick horseradish stalks by the fall. The secondary roots are laid bare down to the roots at their lower end. Roots on the upper part are cut off with a sharp knife, after which the secondary roots are rubbed with a coarse cloth to remove the fine roots. Only then is the earth heaped up over the stalks again. The thicker lateral roots can be heeling-in in sand and used to meet summer requirements.

852 Even when planted during the first half of June, medium-early carrot varieties will still result in satisfactory yields by the fall.

They will need three-and-a-half to four months from sowing to harvest. Accordingly, if they are sown in early June, they will be ready to harvest by early October at the latest.

853 During their growth, parsnips need a lot of hoeing work and an adequate water supply.

In particular, it is necessary to ensure that no soil encrustation occurs after precipitation. From late June, the water requirement climbs more sharply, so that, as a rule, the parsnips will need to be watered five times at about 2 qts./sq. ft. each by the end of August. In June, and again in July and August, give them a surface fertilizer application of 0.1 lb. N per 100 sq. ft.

854 Leeks planted in June will still develop thick stalks by the fall.

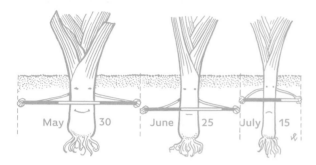

Leeks should be planted on beds that have already been harvested. They may be planted after all vegetable species, except bulb plants.

The latest possible date for planting is in late June—see ▸ **TIP 697** for more detailed information on planting. Give leeks planted in May a surface fertilizer application of 0.1 lb. N per 100 sq. ft. at the end of June.

855 When broad beans begin to develop capsules, break off the leafy shoot tips.

The capsules will then develop much more quickly. Meanwhile, infestation by black bean aphids will also be reduced, since they prefer the tender shoot tips.

856 To develop large capsules with tender kernels, broad beans need plenty of water and nutrients.

In June, watering two or three times during the month at 5 to 6 gal./yd.^{2} each is advisable, depending on the weather conditions. Additionally, broad beans should be given a second surface fertilizer application when the capsules begin to develop.

857 Harvest broad beans when their seeds are almost completely developed, but still very tender.

The right time for harvesting is important, because only soft kernels will yield a tasty vegetable. The kernels in the capsule must not yet have developed a black "beard." If harvested a little earlier, the kernels will be a little smaller, but all the tenderer for it.

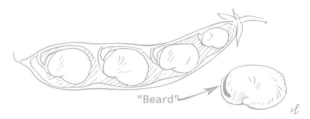

"Beard"

858 Radicchio needs at least the same planting width as lettuce.

Radicchio sown in May will be ready for planting out in June. For this, select a site that is as sunny as possible. Depending on the variety, the planting width should be 12 × 10 to 12 × 12 in. The most important tasks following planting are constant soil loosening and regular watering. Further seed can be sown throughout June. Although direct sowing is possible from mid-June, it is best to stick with advance planting followed by planting out.

859 In June, too, red radishes can be constantly sown and harvested.

On average, they will need 30 days at most from sowing to harvest. On seed requirements and sowing, see ▸ **TIP 265** and ▸ **TIP 266**. Uniform watering, along with covering with protective nets or insect protection fleeces to guard against summer cabbage fly, is crucial for good tuber quality.

860 To ensure that radish requirements for July and August will be met, it is necessary to sow them in June.

The most suitable are medium-early varieties with a development time of 50 to 60 days. A row interval of 8 in. is sufficient for these varieties; single them out to 3 to 4 in. within the row. Here, too, provide insect protection once the seedlings have emerged.

861 Sowing of fall and winter radishes can begin in mid-June.

Depending on the variety, these will need 12 to 17 weeks for their development, which means that harvesting can begin in September. The row interval is 12 in. Within a row, lay three seeds as a bunch every 6 in., about ½ in. deep. As soon as the cotyledons have developed fully, thin out the plants to one plant per bunch.

862 **For watering fall and winter radishes, the same applies as for red radishes.**

When applying fertilizer, avoid excess nitrogen, since this will affect the keeping characteristics of the winter radishes. Accordingly, it is best to use a potassium-rich complete fertilizer with a low nitrogen content.

863 **Brussels sprouts will deliver good yields only if they have been planted by mid-June.**

If they are planted any later than this, the yield will be very dependent on the course of the weather during the fall. See also ▸ **TIP 704** and ▸ **TIP 705**. For June plantings, a planting width of 20 × 24 in. is generally sufficient (in other words, 20 in. within the row).

864 **For use in winter, beets can be successfully sown directly on site until the end of June.**

On seed and spacing requirements, see ▸ **TIP 463**. Give beets that were sown in late April for harvesting in summer a surface fertilizer application in June. A potassium-rich, but nitrogen-poor complete fertilizer is recommended. Beets need relatively little water and should be watered only during dry periods.

865 **In early June, late red, white, and savoy cabbage varieties can still be planted for storage purposes.**

Here, see the information given in ▸ **TIP 686**. Late cabbage that was planted in May should now be given regular water applications, as well as an initial surface manure application in late June.

866 **From late June, powdery mildew can occur in black salsify.**

The mildew must be combated at the first sign, using a sulfur preparation or organic fungicide, if the treatment is to be successful. Regular watering as required has proven to be an effective preventive measure.

867 **Romaine lettuce planted in May (TIP 708) is given two or three surface fertilizer applications in June, and plenty of water.**

Since lush, tender leaves are what counts in romaine lettuce, it should be watered with a 0.3 percent nitrogen-rich complete fertilizer solution. Additionally, the soil must be hoed constantly and watered sufficiently as soil encrustation and dryness can lead to unwanted shoots in the plants.

868 **Following completion of the white asparagus harvest (22 June), level out the dams as soon as possible.**

To begin with, using a digging fork, loosen the soil of the paths between the dams that have been trampled firm during the harvest. Take great care when leveling off the dams themselves, since every asparagus shoot is important for the following year's harvest. After the leveling off, apply rotted stable manure or compost and worked it in well.

869 **White (and green) asparagus that is ready for harvest is given a primary fertilizer application (mineral fertilizer) after the dams have been leveled, or after the end of the harvest.**

Once the humus has been worked into the soil, distribute 1 oz./yd.^{2} of a nitrogen-rich complete fertilizer. The fertilizer is hoed in only superficially. If conditions are dry, water the ground watered so that the fertilizer will act as quickly as possible.

870 The one- and two-year asparagus beds, including those which were laid in the spring, are given a surface manure application in June.

The best choice is a nitrogen-rich complete fertilizer, applied at a rate of around 1 oz./yd.²

871 The most important animal pests affecting asparagus are the asparagus fly and asparagus beetle.

The asparagus fly jeopardizes the two-year asparagus beds in particular, and also the three-year beds that have been harvested until 1 June. Weekly spraying with systemic insecticides is the most helpful. In cases of severe infestation, the asparagus beetle, too, will need to be combated using suitable insecticides. Accordingly, regular monitoring of the beds is required.

872 Where asparagus is endangered by rust, preventive measures can limit the spread of the disease.

The first sprayings with typical commercial preparations must be done now, before the asparagus foliage has unfurled. Repeat the sprayings at two-week intervals, and follow the manufacturer's instructions exactly.

873 When the climbing beans are around 6 in. high, the leaf bunches should be heaped somewhat around each pole.

To do so, press the bean shoots far enough toward the poles so that the shoots can reach them. From time to time, it will be necessary to check whether all the beans have taken a hold. Before heaping up, apply a nitrogen-rich surface fertilizer at a rate of around 1 oz./yd.²

874 House tomatoes have a high nutrient requirement and should be given fertilizer once a week from early June.

Give the fertilizer in the same way as for house cucumbers. ▶ TIP 662 Additionally, carry out all other maintenance measures regularly. This includes tying up and pinching off, as described in ▶ TIP 721 and ▶ TIP 722.

875 In the case of staked tomatoes, it is important not to neglect pinching off the lateral shoots and tying the primary shoot securely.

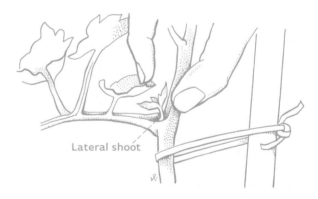

Lateral shoot

To protect the leaves, pinch off the lateral shoots using the fingers as soon as it is possible to grasp hold of them. Sometimes, shoots will form at the tips of the inflorescences, and these, too, should be pinched off. When tying the primary shoot securely, remember to take the growth in thickness into account. Accordingly, never tie up the shoots too tightly or their growth will be impeded.

876 Tomatoes are given their first surface fertilizer application in early June.

Apply a nitrogen-rich complete fertilizer at a rate of 1 oz./yd.². If the bed has been covered with a mulch fleece, this quantity should be given as a 0.3 percent nutrient solution.

877 For cultivation on open land, sow winter endives from mid-June so that vigorous plants will be available in late July.

Sowing early is associated with the risk of unwanted shoots. Around five weeks are required from sowing to planting out. It is important to sow the seeds very sparsely. The seeds will need around one week to germinate. Once the seedlings have emerged, thin them out to 1¼ in. to achieve vigorous young plants. Subsequent sowing in late June/early July is recommended. Keep the sown areas constantly moist.

Winter endives are an extremely healthy and nutritious raw vegetable for the fall, and should be planted far more often than they are.

878 The best time for sowing sugarloaf is from mid- to late June.

This vegetable is a special form of salad chicory. It develops firm, yellowish green heads that resemble a sugarloaf, and is considered a valuable and high-yield salad vegetable for the fall and winter months. It is highly suitable as an aftercrop following early vegetables and makes no special demands on the soil or climate. Sowing before 10 June is not recommended as this may lead to unwanted shoots. Sow the seeds directly on open land with a planting width of 16 × 12 in. on places that have been correspondingly marked out, laying three or four seed grains in each place. Once the seedlings have emerged, thin them out in good time.

Sugarloaf is a sweet, crunchy chickory that is easy to grow and is a versatile vegetable for salads and cooking—it is well worth trying out.

879 Sweet corn can be sown again for the last time in early June.

For this date, only early varieties with a short development time are suitable. For advice on sowing, see ▶ **TIP 733**. Sweet corn that has been sown in May is given a surface fertilizer application in mid-June. For this, use a nitrogen- and potassium-rich complete fertilizer and spread it at a rate of 1 oz./yd.².

880 Spanish onions have a higher nutrient requirement than regular (yellow) onions.

For this reason, they are given a surface application of nitrogen fertilizer in early and late June, preferably in liquid form. When the onions begin to form, the water requirement increases as well, so a regular water supply should be ensured from this point on.

881 Seed onions can be given another surface manure application in late June.

A complete fertilizer with a high potassium content is best. Apply at a rate of 1 oz./yd.² and work it shallowly into the soil.

882 Onion fly will also still need to be combated in the first half of June (TIP 737).

At higher altitudes and in unfavorable spring weather, onion flies of the first generation will often still be flying until mid-June.

883 Subsequent sowing of dill, garden cress, and chervil is still possible in June.

This will ensure a constant supply of these popular vegetables. See also ▸ TIP 738!

884 From late June, harvest fresh borage leaves constantly for use as a spice.

The spiciness of the leaves is little affected even during the flowering time. Further sowing is also possible in early June. ▸ TIP 486

885 In June, take only single leaves from newly planted spice herbs, such as lovage and lemon balm.

This also applies to lavender, sage, and thyme. In any case, these herbs are so flavorful that only a few leaves are ever required at any one time.

886 When sown early, nasturtiums will already yield spicy leaves in late June, and sometimes buds as well.

The spice potential of this plant is still far too little known, and it is certainly worth trying out. When pickled in good-quality vinegar, the buds make an excellent substitute for capers.

887 During June, give all perennial and annual spice herbs a surface fertilizer application.

The best method is to prepare a 0.2 percent nutrient solution of a low-nitrogen complete fertilizer. If the herbs receive too much nitrogen, their spice potential will decline markedly.

888 As soon as peppermint shows the first signs of rust, cut all shoots flush with the ground.

This disease occurs particularly in wet weather. The first signs are small brown flecks on the leaves. Once the shoots have been cut back, the peppermint will generally produce healthy shoots again. Dispose of the affected plant parts immediately. ▸ TIP 1087

889 Two to three weeks after inoculation, the substrate for growing champignons (**mushrooms**) or shaggy inkcaps will have been occupied completely by the mycelium.

The covering can be removed from the beds and garden boxes at this time. In the case of standing sacks, roll back the foil to the substrate surface, and for sacks lying flat, cut off and remove the entire upper side. The substrate surface must now be covered with a layer of moist earth 1½ to 2 in. thick. You can prepare the earth for covering yourself, using a mixture of sandy garden earth and peat in a ratio of 2:1. To achieve the necessary pH value of 6.5 to 7 for champignons, or 7 to 8 for shaggy inkcaps, the addition of about 3 to 5 percent lime is required. The covering earth should always be kept uniformly moist, which is made easier by covering it with sacks or straw mats. After around 14 days, the mycelium will be visible at the surface, and the first fruiting bodies will appear one to two weeks later, provided the temperatures are favorable.

ORNAMENTAL PLANTS

Ornamental Gardens

890 Wallflowers (*Erysimum cheiri*), Canterbury bells (*Campanula medium*), foxgloves (*Digitalis*), and hollyhocks (*Alcea*) are sown in June for flowering the following year.

Here, a sheltered, sunny bed out in the open is sufficient. ▸ TIP 520 and ▸ TIP 521. The seed should be sown sparsely enough that the young plants will have enough room to develop. Foxglove seeds are so small that 10,000 seed grains weigh less than 0.1 oz. Cover these seeds with a very thin layer of earth; the seeds will emerge evenly only if the seedbed is never allowed to dry out completely. Once foxgloves are present in the garden, they will generally disperse by self-seeding—it will then be possible to enjoy the splendid flowers each year, and bumblebees will delight in the nectar. As a rule, only a few plants are left to remain or are planted in suitable places. Remember that foxgloves are highly poisonous.

891 The Asiatic poppy (*Meconopsis*) needs a cool site with high air humidity.

The yellow-flowering Asiatic poppy (*M. cambrica*), with its large, vivid flower cups, is a feast for the eyes in the garden. This perennial is self-seeding on suitable sites. The blue poppy (*M. betonicifolia*) does not like dry heat. It grows better on moist, semi-shaded sites and on humic, weakly acidic soils. After advance planting, it is planted in April at intervals of around 12 in.

892 Standard roses should be secured against wind by tying them to stakes.

Here, not only should the place for tying on the stake be checked, but also the stake itself. Older stakes often snap off flush with the soil. Tie rose stems to the stake in such a way that no rubbing will occur, even in strong winds. The stake must reach into the crown.

Pruning roses in summer will promote a second flowering period.

893 In order that the roses will soon bloom again, the shoots should not be pruned too heavily when cutting the flowers.

In particular, the entire annual shoot should not be cut off, since otherwise the new shoot would then have to develop from the older, only weakly developed buds. As a rule, prune the flower stalks no further than the first strong eye of the shoot.

894 If rose flowers are left to wither on the plant, they should be removed soon afterward.

The longer they are left to remain on the plant, the more the new growth will be delayed, and with it the second flowering period.

895 The withered blooms of climbing roses, too, should be cut off.

This should be done without damaging the annual long stems. They should not be pruned back or only weak lateral shoots will develop. In late June, the shoots are often so long that they need to be secured.

896 To promote the second shoot growth, give all roses fertilizer in June.

Use a nitrogen-rich complete fertilizer, preferably a special rose fertilizer; either spread it over the plants dry and lightly hoe into the soil, or apply with the irrigation water. More environment-friendly solutions include organic fertilizers such as compost, hoof and horn meal, and stable manure, also available in the form of pellets from the garden center. If there is no rain, the nutrients can be transferred to the root zone by watering thoroughly afterward.

897 Aphids (greenfly) on roses and other ornamental plants should be combated using biological means.

When it comes to biological control of aphids on roses and other ornamental plants, we tend to think of ladybugs, lacewings, or their larvae. However, these will hardly be present if too many highly poisonous insecticides have been sprayed in neighboring gardens. It is also possible to utilize earwigs, which also devour copious quantities of aphids—provide resting places for earwigs in upturned clay pots. For this, the pots are filled with straw or wood wool, and placed over the tops of stakes or poles. Alternatively, treat the affected shoots with a nettle fertilizer tea.
▸ TIP 31

898 In hot weather, gladioli will often be affected by thrips.

As soon as black, roughly 1/32 in. long, dash-like insects can be seen on the gladioli, it is safe to assume that these are thrips. They will be accompanied by the yellowish larvae, which have a similar form. When they occur in large numbers, gladiolus thrips damage not just the leaves, but the flowers and buds as well. The latter will then no longer flower. Lacewings and predatory mites are suitable for combating the thrips. Savory (*Satureja*), rue (*Ruta graveolens*), and chamomile (*Matricaria chamomilla*) also serve as protective plants against thrips. The animals do not like

moisture; accordingly, spray the gladioli frequently in warm, dry weather. Only in very severe cases of infestation can insecticides be used, with spraying repeated at weekly intervals until no more thrips can be detected. Be careful, as insecticides are poisonous—note the instructions on the packaging!

899 Only when the flowering stems develop should gladioli be watered intensively and plentifully.

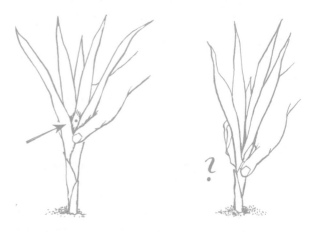

This development is easy to detect, by taking the flat side of the gladiolus shoot between the thumb and forefinger. Feeling from the ground up, it can be determined from a bulge how far the flowering stem has emerged out of the bulb. If no bulge can be determined, then it is still too deep in the plant.

900 In order for gladioli to flower in September, the bulbs can still be laid in early June.

In this case, it is best to use larger bulbs, because the smaller ones will generally need more time to develop. Plants from smaller bulbs will bloom only from October and be endangered by early frosts.
▸ TIP 541 to ▸ TIP 543

901 Tall dahlia varieties must be protected against wind breakage.

The dahlias are tied to poles. If the poles were not put in place at the time of planting, they must be hammered in such a way that the bulbs will not be damaged. Drive them in deeply so that the plants will be anchored properly. Later, they should not tower too high above the dahlia shoots, but they should also not be too short. Use string that is not too fine when tying up the plants.

902 Tall perennials often tend to fall apart, and so they should be tied to poles as a precaution.

Tie up the plants in such a way that the poles are not visible. The plants should be held only lightly together so that their natural growth form is not lost. In the trade, there are also supports or metal poles available in different lengths that are staked around the plant and hooked to one another, so that it is not necessary to tie up the plants.

903 Cushion plants that cease flowering in late June short be trimmed to limit their extent.

This is especially necessary for older plants. Shoots to be removed that are prostrate on the earth with roots are highly suitable for propagation. They should be replanted straightaway, but initially kept moist and in the shade.

904 By mid-June, divide and replant perennials for flowering in the spring.

Perennials that have been divided in early June will develop so vigorously by the fall that they can fill the place set aside for them in the coming spring. Ensure protection against the sun and a sufficient water supply until the partial plants have grown.

905 During the hot time of the year, regular hoeing can have a crucial impact on the water balance in perennial plantings.

This is especially important where water evaporation has not been reduced by soil coverings (mulches). Don't wait until the soil surface has already become encrusted—loosen the soil surface after every rainfall or watering.

906 Gardeners who are interested in irises (*Iris*) should not miss the main flowering time in specialist nurseries in early June.

Today, there are countless garden varieties and breeds of irises. The range is so large that it is always possible to find something new for the garden. Typically, the colors of the individual varieties are inadequately described in catalogs or on the internet—accordingly, a visit to the nursery can help avoid disappointments.

907 From time to time, all the new shoots of climbing plants need to be tied up.

This is necessary so that these shrubs retain their correct form. It is especially important for fast-growing plants such as silver lace vine or Russian vine (*Fallopia baldschuanica*, syn. *Polygonum aubertii*) and wisteria (*Wisteria*). Accordingly, train the shoots in such a way that the area that the plants occupy is filled out evenly, with no gaps.

Deadheading is the removal of withered flowers. It allows new buds to develop.

908 The sweet pea (*Lathyrus odoratus*) flowers very richly when the withered flowers are removed continually.

Since vetches are self-fertilizing, they set seed regularly. This seed formation requires plenty of nutrients that are otherwise lost to the plants, and to new flower formation as well.

909 In flowering shrubs that do not develop any decorative fruits, remove the remaining inflorescences after the end of flowering.

This needs to be done before the plants set seed, because the seeds require a great deal of nutrients, and this correspondingly weakens the annual shoot growth.

Severe cutting back of larkspurs and other spring-flowering perennials often promotes a second flowering in the fall.

910 Larkspurs (*Delphinium*) will flower again in the fall after cutting back.

Immediately after flowering, cut the plants back to around 4 in. above the ground—this will stimulate the new growth to produce flowers again in the fall. After cutting back, remember to water and apply fertilizer.

911 Winter-hardy perennials should be cut back before they develop seed.

There are many perennials for which seed formation should be prevented. This will enable them to gather strength for flowering in the following year; additionally, some will flower again in the fall. ▸ **TIP 910** These include fleabane (*Erigeron*), shasta daisy (*Leucanthemum maximum*), and Helen's flower or sneezeweed (*Helenium*). In tickseed (*Coreopsis*), cutting back the individually withered flowers will ensure that the flowering lasts for an unusually long time.

912 In particular, give evergreen trees and shrubs that have been planted in spring plenty of water in dry periods.

In June, they are generally not so well rooted that they can take up sufficient water from their surroundings. Watering is especially important for trees and shrubs with firm root balls. Once these have dried out completely, it is difficult for them to take up water again, and this can lead to the plants' death. Rhododendrons are particularly susceptible in this regard.

913 If newly planted hedges are to develop vigorous shoots, it is important to remember to water them.

This is particularly important for hedges that are standing in the root zones of older trees. These take up more water from the soil than might be expected. This should also be taken into account for older hedges.

914 Pruning the shoot growth of hedges can begin in late June.

Before pruning, check whether there are still any occupied birds' nests present. If so, the pruning will need to be postponed. Do not cut the old wood; instead, cut back the new shoots to their base. To ensure an orderly appearance, set up a cord (line) before pruning. Using an electric hedge trimmer makes the work easier.

915 Lawns that have been established in spring should be mown for the first time when the grass is just reaching a height of 4 in.

Only after this cut will the lawn maintain its density. Make the first cut with the mower cutting height set at 2 in. so that the grasses will have a sufficient leaf mass remaining to build up their new growth. With good maintenance, the grass can be cut back to a lower height for future mowing.

916 After every cut, give the lawn nutrients, and, in dry periods, water.

Newly established lawns are not given fertilizer after being mown for the first time. Later, this is important, however, because lawn grasses need plenty of nutrients. Gaps in the lawn and the presence of annual herbs are often the result of nutrient deficits in the grasses. Lawns that have been laid in late spring should be watered regularly.

917 To raise young perennials from seed, they need to be sown in June.

Here, however, only perennials that germinate immediately are suitable. If in doubt, seek advice from a professional. Sow the seed over a wide area, and keep the bed uniformly moist until the seedlings emerge.

Bulbs should be dug after the leaves turn yellow.

918 The bulbs of tulips, daffodils, and others should be removed from the earth once the aboveground plant parts have turned yellow.

Only then will the bulbs have developed fully. Removing them from the ground too early will be at the expense of the next year's flowering.

919 If the new site for the flower bulbs is already free, the bulbs can go straight back into the ground.

In this case, there is no need to dry the bulbs. Instead, they should be cleaned and sorted into two or more sizes. In this way, the smaller bulbs, which are not yet ready for flowering, can be planted separately. After one year, most of the bulbs will have grown to become capable of flowering.

920 To avoid damaging the flower bulbs, use a digging fork for clearing the flowerbeds, and not a spade.

Since most flower bulbs are deep in the soil, drive the digging fork somewhat deeper than necessary into the ground when clearing the beds. In this way, too, injuries to the bulbs can be avoided.

Disinfecting bulbs will protect them from the spread of fungal diseases.

921 Daffodils can usually remain in the soil for many years, while tulip bulbs should be cleared out every two years.

If diseases are observed in tulips during the flowering time, they must be cleared out of the planting beds in the same year. Set the bulbs that are still healthy in the ground at a site where no tulips or other flower bulbs have been before. Before laying them in place, they can be disinfected with a fungicidal plant protection agent. The instructions on the disinfectant packaging should be followed exactly. Dispose of any diseased bulbs.

922 Following clearance, flower bulbs must be dried out first.

If the new site is not yet available, avoid leaving the bulbs in the sun if possible. An airy, shady spot is suitable for drying. Spread out the bulbs in one layer only, over a dry base.

923 From the time of storage to the time for planting out, the flower bulbs must not be allowed to become moist.

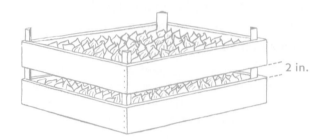
2 in.

The completely dry bulbs should preferably be placed in shallow boxes, in no more than two layers. If the boxes are to be stacked, ensure a 2 in. intermediate space between them. Rats and mice seem to have developed a particular taste for tulip bulbs. If this is not taken into account, major losses must be reckoned with. It is best to find a suitable storage place that is free from rodents. Traps and baits will be of little interest to the animals if they have tulip bulbs to feast on instead.

924 In early June, cuttings of winter-hardy chrysanthemums (*Chrysanthemum ×grandiflorum*) with well-developed roots can be planted.

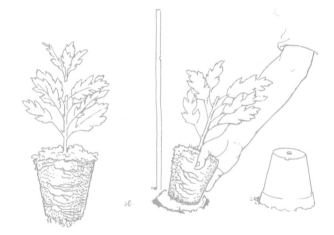

The shoot tip can be removed, so that they grow with more than one shoot right from the outset. In exposed areas, later-flowering varieties often fall victim to frost. These chrysanthemums need a planting width of 10 × 10 in., or, better still, 12 in.

925 **In June, fuchsias and geraniums, among others, can be planted in beds.**

Except for fuchsias, all the plants will prefer a sunny site. For geraniums, the ground should not be too moist or nutrient rich. Otherwise, they will develop too many leaves and will bloom poorly. The flowers of single-flowering varieties will tolerate rain better than those of double-flowering ones.

926 **Although there are disease-resistant varieties of China asters, even some of these will suffer from Verticillium wilt.**

Since this is a fungal disease that is difficult to combat, you should avoid anything that promotes its spread. It is important to remove affected plants immediately, even if they show only the slightest wilt symptoms. They should be burned or thrown in the garbage can. Very often, the wilt begins on individual plant parts only, but gradually the whole plant will become affected and die. If you have Verticillium wilt in your garden, you should not plant China asters on the same bed again for four to five years. The land should be given several lime applications during that time.

927 **In June, China asters are often so severely affected by aphids that all the leaves curl up.**

This inhibits the plants' growth. Accordingly, combat the aphids before greater damage occurs. The aphids tend to sit on growing shoot tips and under the leaves in particular. If there are no natural enemies present, such as ladybugs and lacewings and their larvae, or earwigs, spray the plants with a nettle fertilizer tea. ▸ TIP 31 A range of wild herbs, such as common groundsel (*Senecio vulgaris*), are highly susceptible to aphid infestation. If the animals are not eradicated in good time, they may spread to the cultivated plants as well.

928 **Some plants can help us protect against plant pests and diseases.**

Summer savory, for example, is said to be effective against aphids, flea beetles, thrips, and carrot fly; nettles help against fungal diseases; and dill helps protect against the cabbage white butterfly, carrot fly, and onion fly. Firm scientific evidence of these and other interrelationships is not yet available or is otherwise only inadequate. Nevertheless, it is possible to make one's own observations and test the results when planting or sowing.

Terraces and Balconies

929 **The final balcony and window boxes should be planted up in early June.**

What needs to be taken into account, and which plants are suitable, is described in ▸ TIP 801 to ▸ TIP 805.

> *Wait until the plants in balcony and window boxes develop buds before applying fertilizer.*

930 **In June, give the plants in balcony and window boxes their first additional nutrients.**

The time point depends on their development; it has come as soon as the plants are showing buds. As a rule, do not fertilize geraniums any earlier or they will develop too many leaves before they flower. Give all healthy and growing plants a nutrient solution of fully water-soluble complete fertilizer once a week. Then water them generously.

931 **All inflorescences that are finishing flowering should be removed.**

This will greatly improve the plant's overall appearance, and will otherwise stimulate it to flower richly. In geraniums, it is best not to remove the entire inflorescence, but first to attend to all the withered individual flowers, since there are many buds that will still open. In petunias, plucking off the withered flowers is particularly important. These summer flowers set seed very easily, which will affect the plant's ability to produce flowers.

Winter Gardens, Flower Windows, and Rooms

932 **In June, it is also possible to take cuttings from a range of hanging plants, such as devil's ivy (*Epipremnum*), philodendron (*Philodendron*), and indoor ivy (*Hedera*).**

On taking and planting the cuttings, see ▸ TIP 393 to ▸ TIP 397.

933 **Watering pot plants frequently will make the soil surface muddy, and then solid.**

As a result, the soil will be inadequately aerated, and the roots will suffer from oxygen deficiency. Accordingly, loosen the soil surface at intervals of around three weeks. The best tool for this is a flower stick or piece of wood that has been shaped and pointed like a spade. Make sure that no roots are damaged when loosening the soil.

934 **Watering indoor plants can be made easier by adding water to the saucer or cachepot.**

As soon as watering is necessary, add the water to the saucer or cachepot. After about an hour, check to see whether the plants have taken up the water. It is essential to remove any leftover water or the plants' roots will risk becoming diseased. Most indoor plants, except for umbrella grass (*Cyperus*), screw pine (*Pandanus*), and some others, will not tolerate waterlogging.

935 **Cyclamens must be transplanted between early June and July so that they will flower in winter.**

By June, they will be fairly dry, and the leaves will still be green. Often, the plants will also have no more leaves, but the tubers will begin to produce shoots. Since most of the roots will have died off, remove the tubers from the pot and plant in fresh, humic potting mixture. The plant should then be placed in a window with plenty of light. However, it can also be put in a sheltered, semi-shaded spot in the garden, or, alternatively, the whole pot can be embedded in the ground. Water it sparingly to begin; only when a number of leaves have developed should it be watered normally. Do not apply fertilizer until the potting mixture has been densely occupied with new roots.

936 **"Oversummering" indoor plants out in the open promotes their growth.**

From June, many indoor plants will do better in the garden or on the terrace or balcony, where they have plenty of light and fresh air, than they will in a darkened room. They will also benefit greatly from the nightly air humidity, and ultimately the dew as well. However, they need to be protected from the burning hot sun, and also from the wind. In the garden, the pots can be embedded in the soil, so that they will not dry out as quickly—while you are on vacation, for example.

937 For many indoor plants, spending the summer out in the open is beneficial, but at the same time they also run the risk of being exposed to all garden pests without protection.

From slugs and aphids to greenhouse white fly, all garden pests will potentially also attack indoor plants. There are a number of options for protecting the plants. Slugs are probably the hungriest pests. There are many ways to combat them, but none has any absolute certainty of success. Slug fences are the most effective solution. These are available from dealers and are set at least 4 in. deep in the ground. They must be completely freestanding; if there is any direct contact to the plants, the slugs can potentially climb over them. Snails, on the other hand, do not need to be controlled, since they cause hardly any damage.

938 Not all indoor plants can withstand a summer outdoors.

Indoor plants that grow in tropical zones, such as dumb canes (*Dieffenbachia*), ornamental-leaved begonias (*Begonia* Rex Cultorum Group), devil's ivy (*Epipremnum*), philodendron (*Philodendron*), and all rubber plants (*Ficus*), should remain inside all year round. They do not tolerate cool nights down to below 54 to 57°F well, as can occur in summer. On the other hand, all these plants benefit from a spell outside on warm, sunny days, or in a warm summer rain shower. However, if so, they should still be brought back indoors at night.

JULY

SUMMER

Sun, heat, and dryness are typical for the month of July, and impact gardening work accordingly. Plants should now be watered daily, and in many cases even twice daily. In July, many roses will still delight us with their splendid blooms, along with summer flowers and perennials. The rose has been adored and admired by people for more than 2000 years as the king of the flowers. Their fruits are the well-known rose hips.

In July, too, there are still gardening tasks to be carried out. This is the time for planting late cauliflower and curly kale varieties, for example, and for sowing lamb's lettuce and pansies. Meanwhile, most of the bulb plants that have flowered in the spring will have withdrawn their leaves, and the bulbs can now be removed from the ground.

GENERAL

939 **Before the hot summer weather arrives, ensure that there is sufficient available rainwater.**

A rainwater tank that collects water from the roof will seldom be sufficient. It is also possible to place two, three, or even more tanks next to one another and fill them with the aid of siphoning. For each subsequent tank, a piece of hose that is twice as long as the tank is high will suffice. Fill the hoses with water, while keeping the ends blocked with your thumbs. Place one hose end in the first full tank, and the other end in the empty tank. Thanks to the laws of physics, once this has been done, all the tanks will fill with water to the same level. Special rainwater tank connectors are also commercially available, as well as rainwater tanks with an oak barrel, tree trunk, fountain, column, rock-face, or even amphora look, with a filling and emptying set, and also an automatic fill-stop function that can be installed in the downpipe.

940 **Open-top water containers are often large breeding grounds for mosquitoes.**

The best protection against mosquitoes is a tightly fitting lid to cover up the container. If mosquito larvae are still present, or if covering is not possible, drain the container completely before it is refilled. If this is done, any larvae that are present will be unable to develop further. Otherwise, all that can be done is to skim off and destroy the larvae, which are mostly found at the edges, near the water surface. In suitable ponds, fish can take on this function. ▶ TIP 941

> *Fish in a pond devour mosquito larvae.*

941 **Fish in a pond will greatly reduce mosquito numbers.**

Mosquitoes prefer to lay their eggs in standing water. Fish, meanwhile, will decimate any larvae that are developing in the pond. However, this will also mean not using any insecticides. If the pond is not deep enough, the fish will need to be removed in winter and overwintered in suitable containers. ▶ TIP 358

942 **Commercially available sprays against flies and mosquitoes must not be used to combat pests in the garden.**

These nearly always contain substances that are harmful to plants, which means that the plants themselves may die, along with useful animals in the garden. When buying pesticides, be sure to tell the sales staff what you want to use it for.

> *Good soil management will yield many flowers and a bountiful harvest.*

943 **Stable manure should be handled so that it can be worked into the ground in a half-rotted state in the fall.**

Horse manure, from a farm or riding school, for example, keeps very well and can be regarded as long-lasting humus. Half-rotted (or more) stable manure can be worked well into the soil, and it can also be used where deep digging is not possible. This especially applies to roses and berry shrubs, for example.

944 **If possible, keep stable manure in a semi-shaded place so that it does not dry out too quickly.**

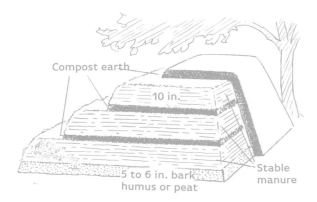

First cover the storage site with a 5 to 6 in. thick layer of bark humus (ideally) or peat. This layer will absorb any substances that have been washed out by the rain so that they will not be lost. The heap should be built up loosely, and in layers. A thinner layer of compost earth comes in between each manure layer, around 10 in. thick. At the end of the process, cover the entire heap with a layer of compost earth. If compost earth is unavailable, use garden earth instead. The height of the heap should not exceed about 3 ¼ ft., to ensure good aeration. The final layer of earth should never be allowed to dry out completely during the storage period.

945   A good, lasting humus source will develop from stable manure, compost earth, and bark humus.

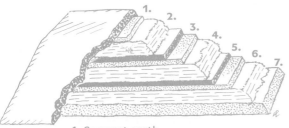

1. Compost earth
2. 2 to 3 in. bark humus or peat
3. 8 in. stable manure
4. 2 to 3 in. compost earth
5. 2 to 3 in. bark humus or peat
6. 8 in. stable manure
7. 5 to 6 in. bark humus or peat

For the most part, fresh stable manure breaks down rapidly in the soil, especially in sandy soils. A mixture of stable manure, compost, and bark humus is longer lasting, and is best made in July. In contrast to ▶ TIP 944, the manure layer should be only about 8 in. thick. In between are layers of compost earth and bark humus; each layer should be 2 to 3 in.

thick. The final layer on top is compost earth. Around mid-September, turn over the heap so that all the substances are well mixed. Ideally, bark humus should be used, instead of peat.

946   Manure from small ruminants can also be used to improve the soil.

In view of the significantly higher nutrient concentration, it is advisable to compost this manure. To boost the proportion of humus, alternate the manure with layers of compost, or wood shavings or cattle waste.

947   If compost is needed at short notice, older earth heaps should be turned once more in July, if possible.

Here, the inside of the heap ends up on the outside, and vice versa. In addition, each new storage site should first be covered with a layer of bark humus about 5 to 6 in. thick that will absorb all the nutrients that have been washed out in the rain.

948   In summer, loosening the soil surface is one of the most important cultivation measures.

This applies not just to vegetable beds, but to all other parts of the garden as well. The soil surface should be hoed after every rainfall or watering. It is best to wait until the soil surface has dried out and no longer sticks to the hoe. Hoeing will ensure that the soil moisture is retained for longer. If a soil covering is used, this will largely take up the soil moisture, so that hoeing is unnecessary.

VEGETABLES

949   For celery, in addition to watering and loosening the soil, do not forget about fertilizer applications.

Give celery a second fertilizer application around the middle of July. In order that the plants will develop thick but tender stalks, apply 1 oz./yd.^{2} of a nitrogen-rich fertilizer, with subsequent watering.

950 Mid-July is the last possible date for planting out late cauliflower.

This involves plants that were sown in June and hand raised ▸ **TIP 821**. One day before removing the plants, water the seedbed thoroughly so that the plants will retain a small earth ball. The planting width should be 20 × 20 in.

951 Broccoli planted in May will be ready for cutting in mid- to late July.

Cut

The broccoli is ready to harvest when the individual buds of the flower are already well developed, but still firmly closed. Especially in very warm weather, it is important not to miss this point in time, because the flowers, or also the individual buds, will then open up relatively quickly, with a corresponding decline in quality. When harvesting, in addition to the "flower," the thick, fleshy stalk should also be used ("sprouting broccoli"). Accordingly, cut off the stalk around 6 in. below the flower.

952 After the middle flower has been harvested, broccoli will also produce lateral shoots with smaller flowers.

With good plant development, this means that the harvest can continue until September. The plants must be watered and fertilized regularly until the end of August.

953 Full bush bean harvests from late planting can be expected only if the seeds are sown no later than 15 July.

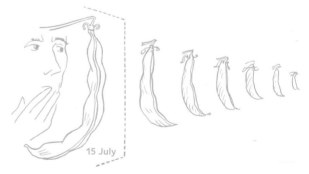

15 July

Bush beans that have been sown any later than this will barely still yield a harvest, because, in particular, the nights will already be too cold after 15 September. The fruits (capsules) of the beans will then no longer develop. On sowing, see ▸ **TIP 650**. For this late cultivation, only use varieties with a short development time.

954 The vegetative parts of the harvested bush beans should not be ripped out of the ground, but instead cut flush with the soil surface.

If this is done, the roots will remain in the soil, and so will the collected nitrogen that has been fixed by the nodule bacteria. This will benefit the subsequent crop. Additionally, the root system will enrich the soil with humus substances.

955 Chicory needs only occasional additional watering, but regular nutrient applications and soil loosening.

In July, an application of a nitrogen fertilizer with a high potassium content is required. Apply the fertilizer dry between the plants, and lightly hoe it in. In dry periods, thorough watering ensures that the nutrients are transferred to the root zone. Hoeing should be done at least once a week.

956 The best time for sowing Chinese cabbage is the second half of July.

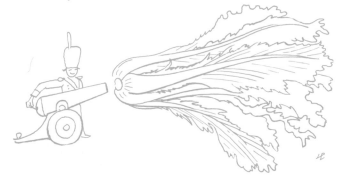

Sowing any earlier than this leads to unwanted shoots, while sowing after 1 August means that normal head development can no longer be expected. Chinese cabbage is also recommended as an after-crop, and, in view of the short development time, delivers a very high yield. Sow the seed in bunches (three or four seed grains per bunch) with a planting width of 16 × 16 in.; single out the seedlings following their emergence.

957 Chinese cabbage is relatively demanding when it comes to the climate, soil, and previous crop.

It does not tolerate wet and cold weather, to which it reacts with growth interruptions and rot. It is also a wind-sensitive vegetable species, which means that it should be grown in a moderately sheltered site. It can withstand short night frosts of 21°F, but not prolonged cold. Otherwise, it has the same soil requirements as cauliflower; a high humus content and a good water supply are necessary for successful growth. Chinese cabbage can be grown after all vegetable species that are harvested by July. However, avoid growing it after any cabbage species.

958 In eggplants, the flowers appear on the lateral shoots from late July.

Once they have appeared, cut off the upper part of the main shoot. Similarly, cut the lateral shoots two leaves above the first signs of fruiting, to promote the fruit development. Remove all redundant and non-fruiting shoots. In large-fruiting varieties, leave no more than three or four fruits per plant. In a foil tent or cold frame, cut the main shoot at this time, and later the fruit-bearing lateral shoots as well, two leaves above the first signs of fruiting. Pinch off all other lateral shoots continually. In the greenhouse or foil house, the eggplants are best trained to grow with two shoots and attached to stakes, or, similar to cucumbers, to lines that are suspended high up. Here, too, cut the fruiting lateral shoots two leaves above the first signs of fruiting, and remove all other shoots. Removing leaves near the ground and in the inner part of the plant improves plant aeration.

> *Pruning is the most important maintenance task when growing eggplants. Without pruning, the chances of growing success are slim.*

959 If you want to harvest large, juicy fruits, give eggplants two nutrient applications during July.

Applications are given at the beginning and end of July. A nitrogen-rich complete fertilizer is recommended.

960 Vegetable peas must be harvested as soon as the kernels are fully formed, but still fresh and juicy.

It is important not to miss this point in time, because the green kernels rapidly lose their quality. In very warm weather, the kernels can already be well past their best after just two to three days. Under normal temperature and humidity conditions, two or three harvests and a yield of 10 to 15 lbs. of green kernels per 100 ft.^{2} can be expected.

961 Sowing lamb's lettuce (corn lettuce) for consumption in the fall should begin in the last days of July.

It will be ripe for harvest in the second half of October. Since lamb's lettuce does not suffer from the frosts that often occur at this time, you can enjoy fresh, tasty salad vegetables right into December. Lamb's lettuce will thrive on every garden soil other than heavy loam soils. An open, sunny site is important. Sow the seed with a row width of 6 in. and a seed depth of ½ in.

Wholehearted!

962 Curly kale can still be planted up until late July.

Here, a planting width of 16 × 12 in. is sufficient.

963 House cucumbers will produce satisfactory yields only if all the necessary maintenance tasks have been carried out diligently.

In addition to regular watering and fertilizer applications, this also includes monitoring the air temperatures and carrying out the necessary pruning. Here, see the advice given in ▶ TIP 659 to ▶ TIP 661.

964 For cucumbers, watering and manuring are among the most important tasks to complete in July.

See the information given in ▶ TIP 837. Take care when hoeing the soil, since the cucumber roots are right underneath the surface. It is not necessary to hoe where ground coverings have been put in place.

965 The sooner the cucumber fruits are harvested, the quicker the subsequent fruits will develop.

If they are left on the plant for too long, some of the subsequent fruit may be rejected at a young stage. Accordingly, it is also a mistake to leave individual cucumbers on the plant for use as mustard pickles. Instead, it is best to use special varieties for this purpose.

Cucumbers should be harvested regularly every two to three days to boost both the yield and the quality.

966 **Cucumber fruits should not be torn roughly from the vines,** but carefully broken or cut off instead.

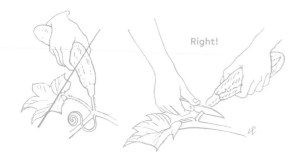

Right!

If the fruits are torn off, damage to the shoots will be inevitable, and can lead to the death of the entire vine.

967 **Early potatoes should be harvested only when the tubers are properly ripened.**

It is best to wait until the vegetative plant parts begin to turn yellow; the potatoes will then be much tastier. There will also be a considerable increase in yield during the final days.

Take care not to harvest early potatoes too early—this will only lead to a loss in both yield and quality!

968 **Florence fennel planted in mid-May will be ready to harvest in July.**

The harvest should begin when the tubers are about fist-sized. Pull the plant out of the ground, roots and all; then remove the roots, and cut off all the leaves around 1 in. above the tuber. Finely cut and marinated fennel makes a very tasty raw salad. Steamed or cooked, the tubers make a delicious vegetable side dish and can be paired with many other dishes. The tubers will keep in the refrigerator for up to four weeks, and, cut up finely and parboiled very briefly, are highly suitable for freezer storage.

Once it is ready to harvest, avoid leaving Florence or bulbing fennel in the garden for too long. It is better to store it in the refrigerator or freezer.

969 **Florence fennel for harvesting in the fall is sown from early to mid-July.**

The latest possible date is around 20 July. If sown later, adequate tuber development can no longer be expected. At this sowing time, too, the planting width should be 16 × 12 in.

970 **The main growth phase for celery begins in late July.**

Accordingly, water, nutrients, and regular soil loosening are especially important at this time. Apply 1 oz./yd.^{2} of a nitrogen-rich complete fertilizer in the final third of July.

971 **If a site for the late cultivation of kohlrabi becomes available only in late July, only plant varieties with a short development time.**

The latest planting date for varieties of the type "Blauer Speck" is around 10 July. The planting width is 12 × 12 in. From mid-July, early varieties only should still be used; for these, a planting width of 10 × 10 in. is sufficient.

972 **Rutabagas and turnips are not choosy when it comes to the soil conditions.**

Except for pure sand and clay, turnips will thrive on all soil types, provided the plants are given sufficient water and fertilizer. However, they do not tolerate fresh stable manure well, and so they belong in the second position in a crop rotation.

973 **July is the best time to plant rutabagas and turnips for eating.**

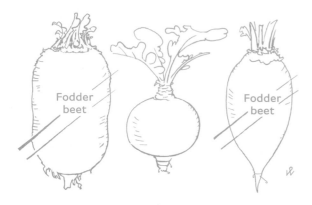

Fodder beet

Fodder beet

For rutabagas and turnips for eating, the size is not important, but tenderness and good taste are. These characteristics are often lacking in rutabagas and turnips that have been planted earlier. They must be planted firmly in the ground with a planting width of 16 × 12 in. After planting, water immediately.

974 **Early varieties of lettuce can be sown again from early July for harvesting in the fall.**

The main growth of the lettuce plant will then fall within a time with shorter days and fewer high temperatures, so that in early varieties, too, good head development can be expected. On sowing, see ▶ TIP 251.

975 **In July, too, melons must be grown with the attention they need.**

In particular, this includes any cutting and pruning, pollination, and careful watering and aeration. Unlike cucumbers, melons grown under glass are not shaded, even with the strongest incoming sunlight. In warm, dry weather, the windows can be removed from the cold frames. From the flowering to the first signs of fruiting, water only sparingly.

976 **Early July is the latest date for removing lateral roots in horseradish (TIP 851).**

Use the cut-off lateral roots for making cucumber pickles. They will keep for longer if they are heeled-in in wet sand.

977 **Thick horseradish stalks will be attained only if two fertilizer applications are given in July.**

Give the first application several days after removing the lateral roots, and the second in late July. For each application, 1 oz./yd.² of a nitrogen-rich complete fertilizer is required.

978 **Carrots may still be sown in early July, provided that early varieties are used.**

Short and medium-long varieties are suitable for sowing at this time. Depending on the variety, they need 75 to 95 days from emergence to harvest, with full harvests in October. Exact details on sowing are given in ▶ TIP 254 to ▶ TIP 256.

979 **Carrots that have been sown in May or earlier for use in the fall and winter are given a surface fertilizer application in July.**

Use a low-nitrogen complete fertilizer with a high potassium content at a rate of 1 oz./yd.². This should be followed by thorough watering.

980 **Bok choy, also known as pak choi, is a leaf-stalk vegetable that is related to Chinese cabbage.**

The plants do not develop a head, but thick, fleshy, generally white leaf stalks instead; when growing, they resemble Swiss chard.

They attain growth heights of 12 to 20 in, and harvest weights of 7 to 14 oz. Mini or baby bok choy varieties remain a lot shorter with weights of just 4 to 5 oz. Important from a nutritional physiology perspective, in addition to valuable substances such as vitamin C, carotin, potassium, and iron, are their excellent flavor characteristics—which are quite different from typical cabbage—and the many ways they can be prepared for eating.

Bok choy is grown as an aftercrop, and can be sown from mid-June to mid-August. If sown any earlier, unwanted shoots will be the result. Advance planting in small pots and direct sowing are both possible. With advance planting, the cultivation period will be reduced by 8 to 10 days, and there will be a lesser risk of unwanted shoots; in this case, the time from sowing to planting out will be around four weeks. The planting width is 12 × 12 in.

981 In terms of the nutrient supply, bok choy is less demanding than Chinese cabbage.

The basic fertilizer application is already taken into account at the time of advance planting. Additionally, around three weeks after planting, a surface application of nitrogen fertilizer is recommended. Following sowing or planting out, light watering of 3 to 4 gal./yd.² is advisable in dry conditions.

982 Appropriate watering and fertilizer application are crucial for growing peppers successfully.

Peppers are watered only at longer intervals, but at a rate of 5 gal./yd.². The main water requirement period is from mid-July to late August. For surface fertilizer application, use a complete fertilizer, with 0.2 oz. N/yd.² applied over two or three individual applications, and given as a 0.3 percent nutrient solution.

983 If peppers are grown in a small greenhouse, cold frame, or foil house, expect the first harvest as early as mid-July.

This especially applies to early-ripening varieties with less vigorous growth and mostly conical, yellow or yellowish green fruits. Harvest pepper fruits as soon as they are around 3 to 4 in. long and have a diameter of 1½ to 2 in.

984 In July, leeks planted in May and early June require plenty of nutrients, water, and continual hoeing.

In order that the deeply planted leeks will develop properly, the soil must be loosened continually. From mid- to late July, the soil can be additionally heaped up around the plants. The resulting furrows can be used for irrigation. From July, leeks need more water, with at least two applications of 3 to 4 gal./yd.² each. In late July, give the second surface fertilizer application of 0.2 oz. N/yd.². A mixture of a complete fertilizer and a pure nitrogen fertilizer at a ratio of 1:1 is recommended.

985 Early July is the latest possible date for sowing radicchio.

Only varieties with short development times are suitable, since radicchio that is sown at this time will not be ready for harvesting until early October. Head development of June plantings begins in early to mid-July, and they should be given a surface application of nitrogen fertilizer. To avoid any risk of rot, they should be watered only at greater intervals, but thoroughly, and in the early part of the day if possible.

986 Early to mid-July is the best time for sowing fall and winter radishes.

Sowing any later than this will result in failures. Fall and winter radishes make no special demands on soil and climate. However, extremely light and especially heavy soils are less suitable, and can have a detrimental impact on the outer and inner tuber quality.

987 Fall and winter radishes need a development time of at least 90 days until the harvest.

The tubers will only develop optimally with a row interval of 12 in. and a 6 in. interval within the row. For each bunch, sow two seed grains about ½ in. deep, and thin out later to one plant.

988 Rhubarb is given its final surface fertilizer application in late July.

For every square yard of cultivated land, spread a mixture of 0.7 oz. each of a nitrogen fertilizer and a potassium-rich complete fertilizer. Then work the fertilizer shallowly into the soil, followed by watering.

989 In July, Brussels sprouts need plenty of water and continual soil loosening.

Especially after watering or rainfall, regular hoeing is required for good loosening and aeration of the soil. Around mid-July, give Brussels sprouts a surface application of nitrogen fertilizer.

990 In the first 10 days of July, it is still possible to plant red cabbage for harvesting in the fall.

Only early varieties are suitable for this planting date. These can also be used for short-term storage until December. They need a planting width of 20 × 20 in.

991 When white butterflies are in flight, all cabbage species, including kohlrabi, are endangered by the butterflies' egg-laying.

In some years, the feeding caterpillars of the white butterfly can strip the leaves bare. This is easy to avoid if the eggs are eliminated instead of the caterpillars. The eggs are found as larger or smaller heaps on the undersides of the cabbage leaves. With their yellow coloring, they are almost impossible to miss, and can be easily squashed.

992 In July, too, there is still time to plant curly and leaf lettuce.

Give leaf lettuce a row interval of 8 × 10 in.; the curly types need a planting width of 10 × 10 in. Batavia lettuce and oak-leaf lettuce can also be sown in July, either directly or in pots. The planting width for both types of lettuce is 12 × 12 in.

993 In July, too, black salsify needs continual nutrient applications and plenty of hoeing.

For manuring, select a complete fertilizer with a high potassium and magnesium content, and spread it at a rate of 1 oz./yd.^{2} in mid-July. Regular soil loosening will make a crucial contribution to the root development.

994 Romaine lettuce planted in May will be ready for cutting from late July.

Older varieties that are not self-closing or plants that have grown too open should be tied up 8 to 10 days in advance. Tie together the tips of the outermost leaves so that the inner leaves will turn pale under the exclusion of light and take on a tender consistency.

995 Frequent hoeing promotes the development of the vegetative parts of asparagus and significantly boosts the following year's yield.

This applies to both white and green asparagus. It is important not to damage the asparagus shoots when hoeing.

996 In July, too, special attention should be paid to asparagus pests and diseases.

See ▸ **TIP 871** and ▸ **TIP 872** for more details.

997 In late July, sowing spinach for use in the fall can begin.

The row interval should be 8 in. Seeds should be sown ½ in. deep.

998 New Zealand spinach will deliver higher yields from early July.

Forced shoot growth

Both the shoot tips and individual young leaves are harvested. Regular harvesting of the shoot tips will lead to constantly appearing new shoots in the leaf axils. New Zealand spinach can be used in cooking just like regular spinach, and has a similar but somewhat stronger flavor. With good development, weekly harvesting is now possible until September/October. The requirements are generous watering and a good nutrient supply. Every 14 days, apply nitrogen as a 0.2 percent nutrient solution. Nitrogen-rich complete fertilizers should be alternated with a pure nitrogen fertilizer.

999 For tomatoes, applying fertilizer and pinching off the lateral shoots are the most important tasks in July.

These are discussed in ▸ **TIP 875** and ▸ **TIP 876**. As soon as the fruits of the lower bunches are fully developed, remove the leaves covering them up so that the tomatoes will receive more sun and dry off more quickly after rainfall.

1000 For planting white and savoy cabbage in July, only early varieties with a short development time are suitable.

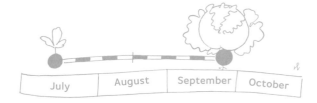

July   August   September   October

If you haven't raised the plants yourself, you should pay particular attention to this point when buying plants ▸ **TIP 443**.

They will need only a little more than two months from planting to harvesting, which means that, even in the event of unfavorable conditions in the fall, they will be ready to harvest by October. These varieties are unsuitable to store for winter use.

1001 Winter endives thrive best on medium-heavy to light soils with a high humus content.

They prefer a sheltered, sunny location and have a high water requirement. Winter endives are highly suitable for planting after peas, as well as after early carrots and other vegetable species that will have been cleared from the vegetable plot by this time. However, avoid growing them after lettuce. Winter endives grow best on neutral to weakly alkaline soils.

1002 Winter endives are already planted from mid-July.

Here, the plants that were raised on an open seedbed in June ▸ **TIP 877** are used. Winter endives need a planting width of 12 × 12 in. A total of 1 oz./yd.² of complete fertilizer should be worked into the soil before planting.

1003 Shallow planting is essential for the optimal development of winter endives.

They must not be planted any deeper than they were in the seedbed. Planting them too deep will impede their growth and may also lead to unwanted shoots.

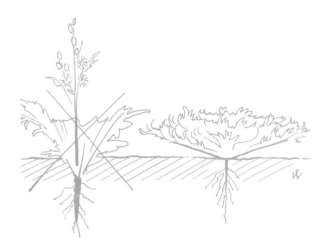

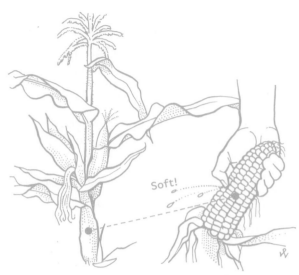

1004 If you wish to use your cold frame or small greenhouse for endives, you will need to sow on an outdoor seedbed in the first half of July.

The time from sowing to planting out is about four to six weeks, which means that the fully grown plants will be available from mid-August. On what needs to be considered when sowing, see ▶ **TIP 877**.

1005 For sweet corn to develop large, juicy cobs, it must also be given a surface fertilizer application in July, and the soil must be hoed regularly.

Give the surface manure application of 1 lb N per 1000 sq. ft. in the first third of July. Follow this immediately by watering, so that the nutrients will reach the root zone quickly. Hoeing should be done at weekly intervals if no ground covering has been used. Particularly in damp weather, lateral shoots may develop on the stalk base. These should be pinched off.

1006 Depending on the sowing date, the sweet corn harvest begins in the second half of July.

The harvest can start as soon as the kernels are fully developed, but still tender. This condition is known as milk ripeness. The kernels can still be pressed easily with the fingernail, but already have a yellow color. External signs are the drying out of the corn silk and the onset of husk discoloration.

1007 Spanish onions are given their last surface application of nitrogen fertilizer in late July.

Any later nitrogen applications will have a detrimental effect on storage characteristics. Depending on the soil nutrient supply, a further potassium application can be made at this time or in August, to promote ripeness and storage characteristics. A uniform water supply and continual loosening of the soil are otherwise important for the development of large onions.

1008 Basil for drying is harvested during July at the beginning of flowering.

Cut the herbs just above the soil and make them into small bunches. These are hung up in the shade in a well-ventilated place. If the leaves are stripped from the shoots, they will need to be dried on sieves. Leave two or three plants standing to ensure a constant supply of fresh leaves.

1009 In summer savory, the best spice characteristics are obtained just before the buds begin to form, and then again during full flowering.

For drying to use in winter, it is best to wait for full flowering. Aromatic dry herb material can be obtained from summer savory only if the instructions for basil ▶ **TIP 1008** are followed.

1010 Further sowing of chervil (garden chervil) can still take place in July.

A row interval of 6 in. is sufficient. Note that the seeds should be only barely covered with earth.

1011 In the case of marjoram, make the first cut for drying as soon as the flower buds have developed.

This is done in the same way as for basil. ▶ **TIP 1008** In marjoram, too, the leaves can be stripped from the shoots. However, it is best to do this only once the bundles are completely dry. The dry leaves must then be placed immediately in airtight containers so that no spice flavor is lost. The dried bundles keep very well in perforated foil bags.

1012 If peppermint is cut for drying in July, expect another good harvest by the fall.

Cut the peppermint plants about an inch above the soil in the budding stage. Only the leaves that have been stripped from the shoots are dried. For drying, use a wooden frame spanned with gauze, hung up in a shady, well-ventilated place.

1013 After every cut, chives need not just water, but nutrients as well.

Even if the chives are not required at a particular time, they should still be cut before the buds develop. This should be followed by watering. Additionally, they should be given a surface application of nitrogen fertilizer.

1014 In July, too, fertilize aromatic herbs to obtain a good harvest.

This especially applies to those herbs that are intended to supply cooking spices by the fall. These should be given fertilizer every three weeks with a 0.2 percent nutrient solution, using a low-nitrogen fertilizer, since nitrogen has a detrimental effect on the flavor.

1015 Around three or four weeks after applying the covering earth, expect the first harvests of champignons and shaggy inkcap.

As soon as the membrane on the underside of the cap tears, the champignons are ripe for harvesting and can be carefully twisted out of the substrate. The mushrooms will appear in several harvesting waves. After each harvest, remove the diseased and died-off mushrooms. Meanwhile, also ensure that the covering earth remains uniformly moist.

The shaggy inkcap mostly grows in large groups and must be harvested at the right time. The cap flesh should be firm and white, and still lie tightly against the stalk in the form of a cylinder. The edge of the cap must not yet be brown or black. If this is the case, however, the mushrooms should still be harvested, but they will no longer be suitable for further processing. The harvested mushrooms must be consumed within 24 hours, or 48 hours if they have been stored in the refrigerator. Harvest at 14-day intervals.

ORNAMENTAL PLANTS

Ornamental Gardens

1016 Roses are given their final fertilizer applications in July, so that the shoots will ripen well by the fall.

If the fertilizer is applied only later in the year, the shoots will be unable to ripen and will generally freeze back severely, even in relatively mild winters. When applying fertilizer in July, use a potassium-rich fertilizer with a low nitrogen content, or, alternatively, a special rose fertilizer. Spread the fertilizer between the roses in such a way that 1 oz./yd.^{2} can be hoed in. If no rain is expected, then water the ground thoroughly to bring the nutrients into the root zone. Stable manure is highly suitable for roses and is also available in the form of pellets from the garden center.

1017 In climbing roses that flower once a year, cut back shoots that have finished flowering.

This will make room for shoots in the current year that will develop the flowering stems in the following year. Following cutting back, the shoots are distributed over the trellis and attached to it with no gaps.

1018 Remove rose shoots that are overhanging above paths to avoid injury.

Young rose shoots, too, are covered with thorns, and can potentially cause serious injury. Children at play are especially at risk if they are running quickly along the paths.

1019 For grafting roses, you will need wild stock that is fully immersed in sap, and fully ripened scions.

Grafting (budding) roses is an interesting and rewarding task for many gardeners. It is relatively easy to do if you are properly acquainted with the steps involved. The grafting will be successful only if the bark can be removed from the wood properly, as is the case from July to early September. The scions are generally fully ripened as soon as the flower at their end is wilting. Only the current year's shoots are suitable as scions, which are cut off with a sharp knife just before budding. Cut away the shoot tip to the first well-developed buds ("eyes"). Then, remove all the leaves except for the remaining leaf stalk about ½ in. in length and the leaf-like structure on the stalk. The scions prepared in this way are then wrapped in a moist cloth.

1020 In nurseries, seedlings of special rose varieties serve as a basis for grafting.

Amateur gardeners can also avail themselves of another solution. Take vigorous wild shoots of the widely distributed dog rose (*Rosa canina*), or from your own rose bed. Grafting takes place as a bud graft on these wild shoots flush with the soil surface. The following spring, the wild stock is cut off above the "eye." From this, the newly grafted rose will develop over the summer, and can be planted at its final site in the fall.

1021 The activities associated with grafting or budding follow a prescribed sequence.

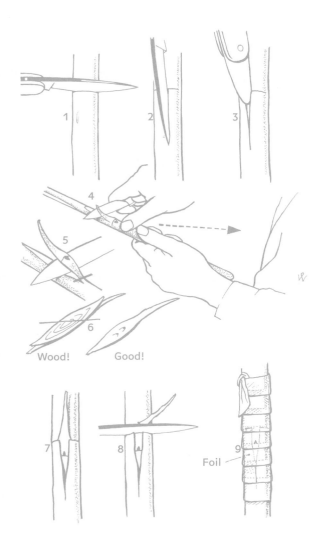

Wood!   Good!

Foil

First, a so-called T-cut is made in the wild stock. Next, an "eye" is cut out of the scion, and the grafting eye is inserted. Finally, the grafting site is bound up. The T-cut is made about ¾ in. long. With the aid of the trigger on the grafting knife, the bark edges of the T-cut are raised slightly. When cutting out the grafting eye, the scion is held in the left hand such that its upper end points toward the body. The right hand sets the knife about ½ in. beneath a well-developed "eye" and cuts this out. It must be wood-free; only at the connection point on the inner side is a thin strip left to remain attached to the bark. Now the grafting eye is inserted into the longitudinal cut and the bark section extending over the cross-section is cut off. Bast (phloem) is suitable for binding. Quick connectors and grafting strips are also commercially available. The binding must hold the wild stock and the

scion firmly together, and the T-cut must no longer be visible after binding. The "eye" must be freestanding and must be unaffected by the binding procedure. For roses, coating the binding with grafting wax is not required.

1022 When grafting, do not shorten the shoot above the grafting site of the wild stock.

This would otherwise result in a sap blockage, in which the grafting eye could suffocate.

1023 Rose stems are grafted in the same way as bush roses.

This requires especially vigorous wild stock shoots that have grown as straight as possible. The eye of the standard rose is grafted at the desired height. The shoot above this point remains until the spring. Remove any shoots below the grafting site before grafting.

1024 Cats love catnip.

Plant catnip (*Nepeta racemosa*) under or adjacent to roses, in rock gardens, or as an edging plant. There are tall- and low-growing varieties. For the garden, the dry-tolerant varieties with silver-gray leaves are especially suitable, such as 'Superba', which forms low, violet cushions, or the dark-violet-flowering 'Walkers Low', which is taller and more upright. Both varieties need plenty of sun and a permeable, low-nutrient soil. They flower from late April to early June. If they are severely cut back after flowering, almost to the ground, they will flower a second time. This also inhibits self-seeding. Most cats love catnip and will happily roll around in the plants. Sow the seeds out in the open in April and cover with a little earth. The planting width is around 12 × 12 in. If quick-flowering plants are required, purchase young plants or specimens that are already in flower.

Planting bearded irises with the top of the bulb above the soil promotes growth and rich flowering.

1025 For bearded irises, a group that is included in the sword irises, the second half of July is the best time for dividing and planting.

Unlike swamp and meadow irises, the bearded iris (*Iris barbata*) needs a dry, sunny site. Bearded irises flower in May and June, and dwarf-growing (so-called *nana* varieties), sometimes as early as mid-April. When the plants have spread widely, they often produce fewer blooms when flowering. Use a digging fork to remove old plants with branching rootstocks (rhizomes) and shake off the clinging earth. The rootstock is then divided. Cut back the leaves by around one third, and the roots to one hand width. For planting, spread the roots out in a fan and press into place. Plant the iris so that the upper half of the rhizome remains clearly visible. This is especially important in heavy soils. Thorough watering is essential for good growth.

1026 The Siberian iris (*Iris sibirica*) loves a greater level of moisture.

Accordingly, it is planted at the same depth as other perennials. If possible, select a site that corresponds to its natural requirements, preferably one that is somewhat moist at the water's edge. With its vivid blue flowers, it will be a garden highlight in May and June. Today, it is almost only cultivated varieties that are available, and their flower sizes and richness differ from the wild form. As well as white flowers, the available range includes violet, wine-red, and yellow flowers.

1027 Heathers, evergreen broad-leaved trees and shrubs, and astilbes need a great deal of water during dry periods.

Once their root balls have dried out completely, these plants will take up water only with difficulty. Accordingly, they should be watered regularly. Astilbes, as decorative shade perennials, will also tolerate a lot of sun if they are kept sufficiently and uniformly moist. However, if they are left to dry out in hot weather, they will soon become unsightly.

1028 Pond water should not be changed in summer, but only topped up.

Some aquatic plants do not tolerate changes of water well; meanwhile, the water itself may often become cloudy. Accordingly, only replace evaporated water, to maintain a constant water level.

> *When planted in groups, bulbs make a bigger statement in the garden.*

1029 In July, nearly all flowering bulb plants will have retracted their leaves and can be removed from the ground.

How this is done, and what needs to be taken into account, is described in ▶ **TIP 918** and ▶ **TIP 923**.

1030 Snowdrops, crocuses, grape hyacinths, spring snowflakes, and spring squills or bluebells should be allowed to spread out over the site over a period of several years.

Taboo!

These bulb and tuber plants are effective only in groups. After just several years, they will have propagated through their brood bulbs or tubers so much that dense, impressive tufts of flowers result. For this to occur, they must be left to grow undisturbed.

1031 Do not remove the seed heads of crocuses or other wild species of bulb and tuber plants.

In this way, they will be self-seeding and support vegetative propagation as mentioned in ▸ TIP 1030. It does not matter if they develop in different places. They do not need much space and are desirable because they are among the earliest plants in the garden to flower, enriching the garden with their blooms.

1032 The winter aconite (*Eranthis hyemalis*) should be transplanted only if local site conditions make this necessary.

This early-spring-flowering plant is best left to develop undisturbed and is self-seeding. It thrives on sunny and semi-shaded sites, for example in front of leafy trees or shrubs. Take care if digging up the tubers, as these are earth-gray in color. Winter aconites are effective only in groups of several plants. Plant the tubers around 2 in. deep, and at the same interval from one another. The soil must be rich in humus. Tubers that have been laid too late often dry out or exhibit poor shoot growth. With its fragrant, radiant yellow flower cups, it is one of the first plants in the year to produce nectar for wild bees and bumblebees.

1033 Early July is the best time to sow pansies (*Viola ×wittrockiana*), daisies (*Bellis*), and forget-me-nots (*Myosotis*).

A good seedbed is one in which bark humus (commercially available) has been worked into the topsoil. This promotes the root development of the young plants. These seeds are fairly small, and should therefore not be sown too densely. Otherwise, only spindly plants with long shoots will result. The space between the individual grains should be about ½ in. If the seedlings have still emerged too densely, thin them out as soon as it is possible to grab hold of the plants.

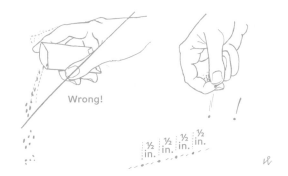

1034 The Iceland poppy (*Papaver nudicaule*) is a summer-flowering biennial and can be sown in the first half of July.

The seeds are very fine, and are therefore covered with only a very little earth. Until the plants germinate, cover the seedbed with conifer brushwood or sheets to shade against strong sun. Later, the seedlings must be thinned out. Iceland poppies are suitable as cut flowers and flower in red, white, and orange color shades from June to October. They should be cut as soon as the buds are showing color. Following mild winters, this poppy can even grow as a perennial, and is often self-seeding.

1035 Earwigs often cause damage to the flowers of dahlias and lantanas (*Lantana*). They are best caught using traps.

For traps, place flowerpots (with a diameter of about 4 in.) upside down on dahlia stakes. Block the hole in the base with clay or putty, and stuff the inside of the pot with fine wood wool. The traps should be checked each morning. In general, however, note that earwigs are otherwise numbered among the useful animals: they devour aphids, as well as other small insects and their larvae.

Terraces and Balconies

1036 Tub plants need especially plentiful watering during hot periods.

Since the plants are mostly exposed to the elements, they lose a great deal of water through transpiration on hot, windy days. If necessary, water them twice a day, but, wherever possible, not during the middle of the day, and not with water that is too cold.

1037 If petunias that have grown too long and straggly are cut back, they will soon flower vigorously again.

If the petunia shoots have grown long and straggly, they should be cut right back. They will then produce shoots from underneath and will bloom vigorously again. Always remove withered flowers immediately.

1038 Pests that attack tub plants can be controlled with the help of useful animals.

Mostly, lacewings, predatory nematodes, and predatory mites are deployed to combat red spider mites; parasitic wasps combat greenhouse whitefly, codling moth, and plum fruit moth. You can find out from breeders or specialist dealers when and under what conditions they should be deployed.

Winter Gardens, Flower Windows, and Rooms

1039 Avoid heat buildup in winter gardens by installing shade and ventilation fittings.

Winter gardens can quickly warm up during hot summer days, resulting in heat damage to the plants. Accordingly, do not neglect shade and ventilation fittings at this time.

1040 Leafy plants on moss poles hardly need to be tied up.

Devil's ivy, philodendrons (*Philodendron*), indoor ivy, and others can be hung easily with their shoots dangling. They grow better with a pole or perforated plastic tube wrapped in moss. With their roots on the shoot, they anchor themselves in the moist moss and then form an upright plant column. The moss needs to be sprayed frequently with water so that it does not die off. Do not use hard, lime-containing water for this; instead, rainwater is the most suitable.

1041 Gloxinias are among the most beautiful indoor flowering plants.

They do not tolerate any direct sun, although they will thrive in a light place. In the shade, the flowers will not develop properly, and they will lose their radiant color. The plants need plenty of water and nutrients while they are growing.

1042 Large-growing and large-leaved green plants need plenty of water and nutrients.

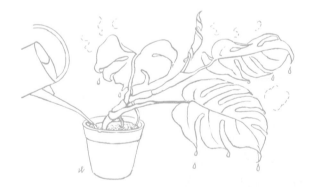

In particular, Swiss cheese plant (*Monstera*), palms, philodendrons (*Philodendron*), ivy tree or umbrella tree (*Schefflera*), *Citrus*, dieffenbachias, and others must not be allowed to dry out under any circumstances. Yellowing and loss of the lower leaves is a clear sign of substrate dryness. In July, the plants will tolerate weekly fertilizer applications, and will reward these with vigorous growth.

Methods for watering indoor plants while you are on vacation should be tested in advance.

1043

If you intend to leave indoor plants on their own while you are on vacation, you will need to ensure that they do not dry out.

Plants in a foil bag

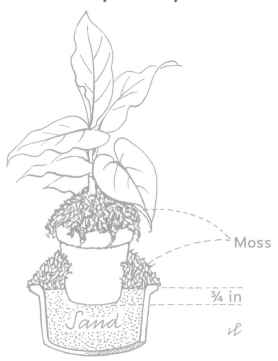

Moss

¾ in

Sand

The best aids here are deep saucers, bowls, or large planters or cachepots that are filled with moist sand or gravel. They must have a diameter that is around 1½ in. greater than the pot base, so that a ¾ in. wide gap remains. Set the pots about ¾ in. deep into the sand and surround the rest of the pot with moist moss. The pot surface should also be provided with a thick layer of moss. On the day of your departure, fill the saucer with water, and moisten the moss thoroughly. The moisture will then be retained for about two weeks if the plant is left in the shade. The pot with the moist material can also be placed in a transparent foil bag.

1044

If a watering or capillary mat is used, further watering will not be needed again for a longer time.

Using this method, the plants stand on a piece of felt or fleece that is constantly moist. While you are on vacation, you can also lay an absorbent cloth in the bathtub, on which the plants stand. If the tap is left to drip a little, the cloth will stay wet and the plants can take up water through the hole in the base of the flowerpot.

Watering mat: the tap drips onto a mat, ensuring that it stays uniformly moist.

1045 If used wisely, a wicking procedure can replace normal watering.

Wicking Procedure

Thick, prewetted strands of wool, glass fiber wicks, or fleece strips will lead water from a higher-standing container into the vessel containing the plant. The higher the supply container and the shorter the path, the moister the earth will become. Several plants can be watered from one supply container.

1046 To bring the Mediterranean to your garden, grow palms and oleander (*Nerium oleander*), rosemary (*Rosmarinus officinalis*), bay or laurel tree (*Laurus nobilis*), and lemon tree (*Citrus*).

Mediterranean plants are sunworshippers, and like dry and warm conditions in summer. Cool winter months are characteristic of the climate in their native territories. However, they would not withstand the cold, harsh winters in our latitudes. Accordingly, here, they are maintained in large plant containers as so-called tub plants. They spend the summer months on the balcony or terrace, or in the garden, and respond well to a sunny, sheltered place. Add a bench or a seating area with a rocking chair, and you will have the perfect setting for a Mediterranean holiday in your garden. In winter, place these plants in as light a room as possible; cool, but also frost-free. In summer, water the plants generously, but in winter only sparingly. The leaves of rosemary and the bay tree can be used as cooking spices.

1047 It is worth trying to grow Ceylon cinnamon (*Cinnamomum verum*, syn. *C. zeylanicum*).

Cinnamon is best grown in a winter garden that can be heated, but it will also thrive in large rooms with plenty of light. From mid-May to September, it can also be grown on the balcony or terrace, or in the garden. Young plants are rather more sensitive; they like to be constantly warm, not much below 64°F, and with a high air humidity. Not just the bark, but also the leathery, glossy, evergreen leaves (which are reddish as shoots) contain the essential oils that are responsible for the typical cinnamon flavor. As the name implies, Ceylon cinnamon comes from Sri Lanka, while another species of the same genus, *Cinnamomum aromaticum*, syn. *C. cassia*, comes mainly from China, and also from Vietnam, Sumatra, and Japan. Cassia cinnamon is drier and hotter in taste, is used mostly in the baking industry, and contains much more coumarin (which, in larger quantities, can be harmful to health) than the finely flavored Ceylon cinnamon.

AUGUST

SUMMER

In August, the weather stays very warm. This means plentiful watering, frequent spraying, and ventilation in greenhouses and winter gardens. Many vegetables, such as cucumbers, melons, and eggplants, but especially tomatoes, are now ripe for harvesting. Tomatoes originally came from the Andes in South and Central America; the Maya, and other peoples as well, grew tomatoes there. Initially, the tomatoes themselves were not much larger than cherries. Columbus brought tomatoes with him back to Europe, but it was only around 100 years later that they were first cultivated in Italy.

August is essentially a month for harvesting in the garden. Despite this, there are still other tasks to attend to. Tuber and bulb plants such as crocuses, crown imperial, Madonna lilies, and grape hyacinths all need to be transferred to their new sites.

GENERAL

1048 Any cold frame windows that are not required must be stacked so that their frames will not suffer moisture damage.

The best place for storage is a shed, but cold frame windows can also be stacked out in the open. Do not leave the bottom window to lie directly on the ground; instead, put bricks underneath to prop it up. So the frames do not lie one on top of the other and end up sticking to one another, place a piece of wood under each corner. Cover the uppermost window with roofing felt or foil that hangs down against the weather-facing side, and weigh it down against the wind using stones.

1049 Water hoses should not be left to lie in the sun or they will become brittle and porous.

Preferably wind them up on a hose reel after every use. It will nevertheless suffice if the hose is rolled up and left in a shady place. Hanging up the hose is not recommended, because it could then develop kinks very easily, which would soon render it unusable.

1050 Iron fenceposts often rust immediately above the soil surface.

The posts are affected by soil moisture at these points. Accordingly, the lower sections should be especially well protected and coated with a good rust protection agent, repeatedly if necessary (and always in good weather).

1051 As early as August, on pergola, arbor, and shed walls, and on wooden fences, it is often possible to find dead caterpillars covered in small, yellow cocoons.

Out of ignorance, these cocoons are often regarded as caterpillar eggs and destroyed. In fact, however, these are the pupae of predatory wasps, which lay their eggs inside living caterpillars. The wasp larvae that hatch from the eggs live and grow inside the caterpillars and kill them. In this way, predatory wasps help us combat garden pests. Accordingly, it is essential to protect the cocoons.

1052 Make sure that children understand that ladybugs are useful insects that should not be caught or killed.

It is not just the ladybugs themselves that are useful, but their larvae as well. Both feed largely on aphids (greenfly). Ladybugs are always found in large numbers wherever our cultivated plants are subject to severe aphid infestation.

VEGETABLES

1053 **Chinese cabbage that has been sown in July should be thinned out in early August.**

The optimal time for thinning out is when the first normal leaf has developed following the cotyledons. It is best to water the bed thoroughly before thinning out. Chinese cabbage should be given an initial surface fertilizer application around mid- to late August. Spread complete fertilizer at a rate of 0.7 oz./yd.² and water the plot afterward.

1054 **The eggplant harvest begins from around mid-August.**

Allow the fruits to grow as large as possible, but be sure to harvest them while they still have a glossy surface with a greasy feel to it. Fruits that have been left too long have a dull, mat surface with no gloss. Under glass or foil, well-developed plants will yield six to eight fruits, while outdoor plants will mostly yield only three or four fruits. The harvested fruits can be kept longer if they are stored in a cool and well-ventilated place. Outdoors, the fruits are also often eaten by slugs.

1055 **In August, the cucumber harvest needs special attention.**

The harvesting sequence follows the intended use of the fruits. For use as dill pickles or gherkins, they should be harvested at a size of 2 ½ to 3 ½ in., while fruits from 3 ½ to a maximum of 6 in. in length are suitable for preparing as pickled cucumbers. The use of smaller fruits necessitates relatively frequent harvesting. This especially applies to many hybrid varieties, which need to be harvested every two to three days because the fruits grow very quickly and become thick, with a considerable drop in quality.

1056 **The vegetative foliage of early potatoes should be disposed of following the harvest if the leaves show even the slightest signs of disease.**

Potato leaves are often affected by potato blight and brown rot (*Phytophthora*). The agents of this disease also cause considerable damage to the leaves and fruits of tomatoes during wet summers. Take careful note of the crop rotation, and do not grow the same crops one after the other on the same plot.

1057 **In August, all cabbage species that were planted in June or earlier (including turnips, rutabagas, and kohlrabi) must be well supplied with water and nutrients.**

On applying fertilizer, see ▸ **TIP 822**, ▸ **TIP 865**, and ▸ **TIP 989**. The information given there applies to August as well.

1058 If there is even the slightest sign of tuber-like growths on the roots when harvesting cabbage species (including kohlrabi), all the stalks should be destroyed.

This is mostly the result of the dreaded clubroot, or it can also be caused by the larvae of the cabbage gall weevil. In any case, the stalks along with all their roots should be carefully dug up and destroyed. Under no circumstances may they be put in the compost heap.

1059 Florence fennel for harvesting in the fall should be given a surface fertilizer application in mid- to late August.

In dry weather, the plants should then be watered immediately so that the fertilizer will be able to act as quickly as possible. Regular watering and loosening the soil surface are the most important maintenance tasks to undertake during the summer months.

1060 Lettuce that has been sown in July will be ready for planting out in the second half of August.

Water the seedbed thoroughly before the young plants are removed ▸ **TIP 974**, so that the earth will remain attached to their roots. This will promote the plants' growth enormously. A planting width of 10 × 10 in. is sufficient.

1061 In edible pumpkins and squash, be sure to note in good time that the plants do not develop more than the recommended number of fruits per plant.

This number can vary greatly, depending on the variety, and is generally mentioned on the seed packet or in the description of the variety in the seed catalog. Before removing excess fruit, wait until the others are about the size of a tennis ball. At the same time, all the shoots should be shortened so that two leaves are still present after the last fruit left hanging on a tendril.

> *For pumpkins and squash, the fewer fruits that remain on a plant, the better the quality.*

1062 Melons are harvested only once they are completely ripe.

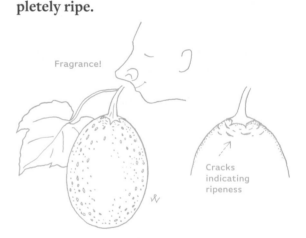

Fragrance!

Cracks indicating ripeness

The full and typical melon flavor is attained only if they are harvested at the right time. Full ripeness is recognizable by the fragrance, and by the fine cracks that appear just underneath the beginning of the stalk. Once harvested, the fruits can be left to lie in an airy place for two to three days. This will enhance the fragrance and flavor even further.

1063 Up to mid-August, subsequent sowing or planting of bok choy (pak choi) is possible.

Sowing any later than this will no longer guarantee success. Meanwhile, bok choy also needs uniform watering up until the harvest. In August, the individual watering applications should be 4 to 5 gal./yd.[2].

1064 Bok choy needs only around 42 to 50 days from planting to harvesting.

Accordingly, the earliest sown seed from July will be ready to harvest in the last 10 days of August. Do not leave the plants in the ground for any longer than 50 days or the fleshy leaf stalks will become fibrous. For cooking, the stalks can be steamed like asparagus, or cut into pieces and cooked as a side serving for fish dishes. When chopped finely and served with herbs and mayonnaise, bok choy can also make a tasty raw salad. The leaves can be used in the same way as spinach. Bok choy is easily digested and recommended as a diet food.

When growing bok choy, make a note of the planting date, since the stalk quality will begin to decline sharply 50 days after planting.

1065 Peppers can be harvested when they are green, as soon as they have reached their normal size.

At this stage of ripening, they are especially suitable for use as stuffed peppers; fully ripe red or yellow fruits are more suitable for salads.

1066 The measures to be carried out for attaining thick leek stalks are the same in August as those in July (TIP 984).

Give a surface fertilizer application in late August, using a complete fertilizer at a rate of 1 oz./yd.^{2}. Two water applications of 5 to 6 gal./yd.^{2} each are also necessary during this month.

1067 Radicchio planted in June will be ready to harvest from early August.

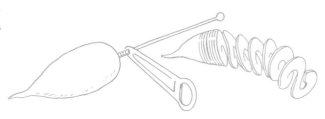

Radicchio is ready to harvest when the heads have attained a weight of at least 5 oz. It is harvested without the enveloping leaf. Radicchio can be used in the same way as lettuce or mixed with other leafy salads. Note that radicchio has an even higher bitter substance content than chicory. This bitter taste can be ameliorated by removing the thick leaf ribs and then washing with cold water.

Cut the leaves into fine strips or pluck into bite-size pieces. A radicchio-fruit salad is also highly recommended. If stored in perforated foil bags, radicchio heads will keep fresh in the refrigerator for five to seven days.

1068 Only fast-growing winter radishes will stay tender. Accordingly, in August, too, they must be given sufficient water and nutrients.

Winter radishes should be given a surface application of nitrogen fertilizer in late August; meanwhile, maintaining a uniform soil moisture level is vital.

1069 The first days of August are the right time for sowing Japanese radishes.

These are relatively mild-tasting radish varieties from East Asia. Depending on the variety, the tubers can reach lengths of more than 16 in. in deep soils. There are also varieties with round or wide conical tubers. Lay two or three seed grains about ½ in. deep in the ground every 6 in. The row interval should be 12 in. After the seedlings emerge, single them out. If sown before late July, there will be an increased risk of unwanted shoots.

> *Japanese radishes need soil that has been loosened to a considerable depth, since their tapering roots can grow very long.*

1070 Beets sown in June should be given another surface fertilizer application in early to mid-August.

To keep the nitrate content of the beets low, select a potassium-rich complete fertilizer with a low nitrogen content and apply at a rate of 1 oz./yd.² Further maintenance measures include constant loosening of the soil and timely weed removal.

1071 Stop applying fertilizer for black salsify by late August if the plants are to keep well during the winter.

Proceed as described for July under ▶ TIP 993.

1072 Early to mid-August is the best time for sowing spinach for the fall.

It is also possible to sow at the end of August, but this will lead to a late start to harvesting and a lower yield. Sowing is carried out as outlined in ▶ TIP 997. Keep spinach sown in late July constantly moist in August, and provide a surface application of nitrogen fertilizer at the end of the month.

1073 Remove the lower tomato leaves if they show signs of disease.

However, it's important to remove them as soon as they show the first flecks, so that the healthy leaves will not be infected. Removing the two or three lowest leaves will also improve ventilation within the stand and the ripening of the first fruits.

1074 In early August, cut off the tips of the main tomato shoots or the subsequent fruiting bodies will no longer ripen.

In doing so, only one leaf is left to remain above the last well-developed inflorescence. Additionally, in August, every lateral shoot that appears on the tomato plant should be removed in good time.

> *Cut back some of the tomato plants above the third or fourth bunch of fruits—this will speed up the beginning of the harvest.*

1075 The soil for winter endives planted in July should be properly hoed in August. They should also be given their first nutrient application.

The soil surface should be kept constantly open, since the roots of the endives are especially hungry for oxygen. Because they are watered often, the upper soil layer will tend to solidify over and over. During the last 10 days of August, give the plants a nitrogen fertilizer application. It is best to use a complete fertilizer with a high potassium content.

1076 Winter endives sown in early July for growing in a cold frame or small greenhouse can be planted out in the second half of August.

When planting, note the instructions given in ▶ TIP 1001 to ▶ TIP 1003.

1077 Sugarloaf has developed so much by late August that its water demand now increases markedly.

In dry periods, it should therefore be watered generously, with 4 to 5 gal./yd.² per watering. It is also important to loosen the soil constantly, since sugarloaf reacts sensitively to soil encrustation. Just before the heads begin to develop, give the plants a nitrogen fertilizer application.

1078 Yellow onions that have been raised from bulbs are harvested for winter only once the leaves have died off.

They are then properly ripened and will keep better in winter than those which have been harvested too early. The frequent practice of trampling the still-green shoots has no impact on the ripening of the onions and should be discouraged.

1079 Given good growth, yellow onion harvesting can begin in early August, even if the leaves are still green.

Yellow onions that were sown in February will attain the required size in early August; they can be harvested constantly from this point on. As a rule, the leaves will begin to die off in mid-August. If the onions are already ripe, the entire stand should be harvested, since leaving them in the ground for a longer period will affect their storage properties and increases the risk of rot. The harvest and subsequent cleaning should be done very carefully, because yellow onions are highly sensitive to physical pressure. They should be stored in the same way as other dry onions. Yellow onions can be stored for only a limited time, and therefore should all be used by about December.

> *Harvest yellow onions in dry weather and leave them in a warm place to ripen further.*

1080 It is a little-known fact that nasturtium flowers, as well as the leaves, are incredibly spicy.

Nasturtiums tend to flower so abundantly that some of their flowers can be picked continually without spoiling the plant's decorative character.

1081 To pickle nasturtium buds and fruits as capers, it is essential to harvest them at the right time.

The buds must be fully grown, but still completely firm. Harvest the fruits while they are still unripe and fully green.

Capers!

1082 Early August is the final date for sowing chervil outdoors.

It will then still be ready for harvesting by September. On the sowing procedure, see ▸ TIP 1010.

1083 Garlic may be harvested only once the vegetative parts have died off completely.

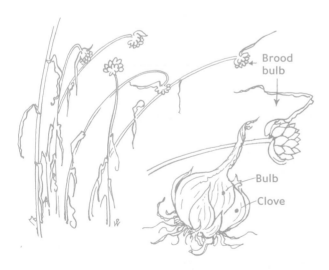

Brood bulb

Bulb

Clove

The bulbs must be properly ripened if they are to keep well during the winter. Use a digging fork to dig them out of the ground and store to dry in an airy place. After this, they are cleaned and sorted. Select the largest bulbs possible for growing in the following year. The brood bulbs that have developed in the inflorescences can also be used for this purpose.

1084 In regions with mild winters, peppermint can be divided and replanted in late August.

Peppermint will deliver good yields only if it is grown on a new site every three years. When buying new plants, select only varieties that have a high spice content. The best is the Mitcham peppermint with the variety 'Polymentha.' Make sure that the part plants come from healthy stands and do not suffer from peppermint rust. ▸ TIP 1087

1085 Peppermint develops underground rhizomatous suckers that are torn apart when separating the plants.

3 to 5 shoots

The partial plants must not be too small, and should include three to five shoots. On a normal bed, plant only three rows, each at an interval of 16 in. Within a row, a planting interval of 8 in. is sufficient. Shallow planting and subsequent watering are important.

1086 For peppermint, moist soils are better than dry. The earth must be rich in humus in any case.

Admittedly, peppermint will also thrive in full sun, but a warm, semi-shaded place is better. Accordingly, they may be planted between loose stands of berry shrubs or on beds that receive only morning or afternoon sun.

1087 In wet summers, peppermint rust infestation may be so severe that the leaves become unusable.

Frequent loosening of the stand and keeping the beds free from weeds are effective preventive measures. The rust appears as dark flecks and reddish brown sporangia on the leaves. At the slightest sign of infestation, cut all shoots flush with the soil surface and burn them. No leaf or shoot remnants may remain on the beds. The new shoots following this cutting back will generally be rust-free. ▸ **TIP 888**

Rust!

1088 During August, lavender needs to be cut back by about half for it to develop shoots again.

It will withstand the winter best if it is treated in this way. Cut back the plants when all the flowers have been harvested, but by mid-August at the latest.

1089 Chili pepper fruits must be allowed to ripen fully to be at their spiciest.

Accordingly, they should be allowed to turn properly red while still on the plant. For storage, they should be dried when they are completely hot; if this is done, they will retain their spiciness for at least two years.

1090 For winter requirements, do not cut sage any later than the end of August.

This will be the second harvest if the shoot tips have already been cut off in late June. It is best if only leaves from the shoot tips are dried. Dry sage leaves quickly in a shady place so that they will retain their spiciness.

1091 For thyme, the last harvesting date is at the end of August so that the new shoot growth will not be too young going into winter.

When harvesting, cut the thyme shoots to about 3 in. above the soil surface. Bundle and dry the harvested material in the same way as for marjoram ▸ **TIP 1011** and basil ▸ **TIP 1008**. If stored in well-sealed containers, the dry material will retain its spiciness for a considerable time. Cascading thyme is especially dense growing.

1092 Roundhead cultures planted in May will yield the first mushrooms from mid-August.

The fruiting bodies should not be cut, but instead carefully twisted off, while being careful not to disturb neighboring mushrooms that are still small, since these will otherwise wither and die. They should not be harvested continuously; instead, alternate harvesting waves with breaks in a rhythm of approximately 14 to 20 days. Roundcaps can grow very large indeed—cap diameters of 8 in. and individual weights of over a pound are not uncommon. They should be harvested at the latest when the mushroom caps are extended out horizontally. There is little waste from cleaning, since it is not necessary to remove the cap skin, and it is only the end of the stalk that needs to be cleaned. Roundcaps are very tasty and can be used in many different ways.

> *Leave mushrooms to grow as large as possible!*

1094 Large yew tree (*Taxus*) specimens can be transplanted if, in early August, preparations are made for the following year (August). First, it is necessary to become familiar with any relevant tree protection stipulations.

ORNAMENTAL PLANTS

ORNAMENTAL GARDENS

1093 Hedges that consist of conifer species are best trimmed in August.

In such hedges, the side walls should not be vertical, but instead taper off toward the top. Otherwise, it will not be long before they will become bare from below, owing to a lack of light. Occasionally, individual shoots will protrude at the sides and top of the hedge. Before trimming begins, cut these back about an inch more using garden shears. Only then should a hedge trimmer be used.

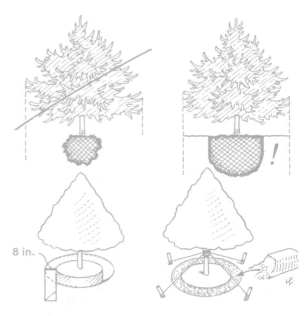

The diameter of the root ball must correspond to the size of the plant; as a rule, it should be a little over half the diameter of the crown. For example, a yew with a diameter of 6½ ft. should have a root ball about 3½ ft. in diameter. At a distance of 22 in. from the stem, for example, in this particular case, a ditch about 8 in. wider is dug out, for which all the roots should be cut off cleanly. The ditch is dug as deeply as required to contain all the roots that have grown downward. The ditch is then filled with moist peat and trampled firm. Give the yew plenty of water right into September. Shelter the plant prepared in this way from wind pressure, preferably by using three or four short posts. Attach these to the yew in such a way that it cannot sway back and forth.

1095 The yew prepared in the previous year (TIP 1094) is transplanted in August.

In addition to the ditch from the previous year that has been filled with peat, a wider ditch is now excavated. It must be so deep that it will ultimately be possible to excavate beneath the root ball. Since the plant will have developed many fibrous roots in the peat, the root ball will generally hold its shape without the need for further intervention. However, if this is not certain, it will be necessary to surround the root ball with a tightly fitting wooden framework or wire netting. The plant is now hauled out of its bed with the aid of wooden boards shoved underneath the ball. Depending on the local conditions, the plant is transported to its new site with the aid of a low vehicle, or by using wooden rollers that have been shoved underneath the boards. Meanwhile, a hole to take the tree must already have been dug at the new site. To fill up the intermediate space that remains once the tree has been set in place, a mixture of earth and peat is used in a 1:1 ratio, or a peat substrate. Thorough watering and trimming of the plant ▶ TIP 1094 are the most important tasks following transplantation.

1096 Conifers and evergreen broad-leaved trees and shrubs can be planted or transplanted from late August.

The procedure described in ▶ TIP 1094 and ▶ TIP 1095 is generally successful for yew trees. It can also be attempted for other conifers that are not too large, but only if this is absolutely necessary. (Again, consult the relevant tree protection stipulations.) Wherever possible, only young conifers with good root balls should be transplanted; they should not have been growing in the one place for more than two to three years. Very large specimens of spruce, fir, pine, etc. can also be obtained from tree nurseries. These are suitable for planting, because they will have been transplanted in the nursery every two years. In this way, a closed root ball develops that will hold together well even after transplanting.

1097 Conifers and evergreen broad-leaved trees and shrubs from tree nurseries should be transported and planted in such a way that their root balls are retained.

The root balls are generally wrapped in jute or burlap. This wrapping remains on the plant. The procedure for handling the plant is described in ▶ TIP 555 and ▶ TIP 556. Carefully remove trees and shrubs from any plastic containers before planting.

> *Newly planted trees and shrubs need special care for the first two years after planting.*

1098 All large, freshly planted conifers and evergreen broad-leaved trees and shrubs should be protected from wind pressure until they are securely rooted.

If a post were to be hammered in right next to the stem, the root ball would be destroyed and the plant's further growth endangered. Accordingly, hammer in the securing post at an angle, missing the root ball, or, in the case of wide-growing plants, hammer it in further away from the stem.

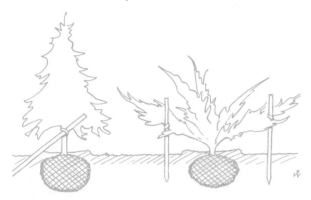

1099 Freshly planted conifers and evergreen broad-leaved trees and shrubs will establish better if they are protected against transpiration.

Diligent watering is not enough just on its own. To protect against excessive transpiration, the best solution is to build a light slat structure around the plant, covered in burlap that is kept constantly moist. If it is not possible to surround the plant completely, erect a light supporting structure on the sunny side of the plant. This is then covered in burlap or cloth, and similarly kept moist. The structures and burlap can later serve as winter protection and are removed only in spring.

1100 Nearly all perennials that have finished flowering can be divided and replanted from late August.

This means that they will have enough time to take root before the fall, and they will survive the winter well. Their growth will be greatly promoted if the soil between the freshly planted perennials is covered with compost earth or grass clippings. Once the soil covering is in place, water the plants as soon as possible. In this way, the soil underneath will remain uniformly moist for a long time.

Tiger lilies can be easily propagated using the bulbils that form along the stem.

1101 The brood bulbs of the tiger lily (*Lilium lancifolium*) can be planted in August.

As with other lilies, only a little space is required for laying the brood bulbs: a row interval of 5 to 6 in. and an interval of 2 in. within a row are sufficient. A planting depth of just under 2 in. will be enough. An easier option to lay the bulbs in 1½ in. deep furrows that are then covered up. Either way, the area should be covered with a mixture of sand and bark humus, along with some added compost.

1102 The Madonna lily or white lily (*Lilium candidum*) should be transplanted before the new shoot develops in late August.

This lily species, with its wonderful, pure white blooms, sends out a new shoot after the aboveground parts die off, and overwinters together with its leaves. Accordingly, it is important not to miss the right time for transplanting, which is roughly in the first half of August. Brood bulbs can be obtained from bulbs that have been in the same place for around three to four years. These will often already bloom in the following spring. Madonna lilies have the greatest impact when they are planted in tufts or groups. The site must be sunny, and the bulb tips covered with only 1¼ to 2 in. of earth.

1103 Many flower bulbs and tubers can be planted in the second half of August.

Squills (*Scilla*), flowering alliums (*Allium*), crocuses (*Crocus*), spring snowflakes (*Leucojum vernum*), puschkinias (*Puschkinia*), glory of the snow (*Chionodoxa*), snowdrops (*Galanthus*), grape hyacinths (*Muscari*), bulb irises (*Iris danfordiae*, *I. reticulata*, *I. histrioides*, and *I. bucharica*), and others are laid about 2 to 4 in. deep in the soil. In nearly all cases, the flowers will be at their most attractive when several bulbs or tubers are laid closely together in groups. More information about the different species and what you need to know is given in **TABLE 23**.

1104 The snake's head fritillary (*Fritillaria meleagris*) needs soil that is not too dry.

The plant is at home near water and swamp pools, and grows especially well at sites that are very moist, at least at the beginning of the growing season. It can even withstand flooding for a brief time. For the garden, there are varieties with deep red, pink, reddish violet, brownish, or crimson-colored flowers with variably distinct checkerboard patterns.

1105 If snowdrops, spring snowflakes, crocuses, daffodils, early low-growing tulips, and other flower bulbs are to bloom on lawns, plant them only at the edges or in the corners.

If flower bulbs are spread over the entire lawn, they will mostly be mown away along with the grass during the first cut in April/May. This is not good for species that have already passed their flowering. They need their leaves until these turn yellow to make up for the growth substances that have been used. Additionally, bulbs that are sown at the edges and corners should be planted only in tufts. This makes them easy to see when mowing the lawn, and it is easier to leave them to grow undisturbed.

Flowers in a lawn are not a problem when mowing if they are planted at the edges or in the corners.

1106 Camas or quamash (*Camassia*) bulbs should be set 6 to 8 in. deep in the ground in August.

These are sensitive to waterlogging, and therefore need water-permeable, well-drained soil. They are winter hardy in warmer regions. However, on harsh, exposed sites they need a protective layer of leaves or compost earth mixed with some sand, along with bark mulch. There are species with blue, violet, cream, and white flowers. The flower "candles" reach up to 3¼ ft. high and are most effective when several are growing together.

1107 The rhizomatous, fleshy roots of the foxtail lily or desert candle (*Eremurus*) are set 8 in. deep into the ground.

These decorative plants thrive best in sandy, dry soils in full sun. Loamy soils should be well drained. When planting, spread out the rootstock like a starfish on the sand and then cover with more sand. Loose winter protection is advisable in the year of planting. Reaching up to 6 ½ ft. high with candle-like inflorescences, the plants should be grown individually. Some species include pure white, salmon-pink, and orange-yellow flowering varieties. **TABLE 23**

1108 If bulbs of autumn crocuses or naked ladies (*Colchicum autumnale*) are planted in August, they will already bloom in late September or early October.

The foliage will appear only in the spring. The flowers will be most effective in tufts or groups. Accordingly, always plant three specimens in a group, 6 in. apart from one another and 4 to 8 in. deep in the soil. They grow best in somewhat loamy, heavy soils, even without much humus. Although the plants love full sun, they will also thrive on semi-shaded sites. They will flower best if left undisturbed for a longer time and should be transplanted only if absolutely necessary. When transplanting, single out the small bulbs and plant separately from the large ones. Note that all autumn crocus plant parts are poisonous!

1109 Crocuses that bloom in the fall, such as Bieberstein's crocus (*Crocus speciosus*), must be planted in early August so that they will bloom in October.

The crocus bulbs (corms) are best planted in groups of about 10 together, 2 to 4 in. deep, and about 2 ½ to 3 in. apart within a group. They bloom especially abundantly if they are left to grow undisturbed in the same place for a long time. Their flowers are similar to those of autumn crocuses, but have only three stamens, whereas the flowers of autumn crocuses have six.

1110 Only select richly flowering varieties of crown imperial (*Fritillaria imperialis*).

Crown imperial thrives best on a sunny site with a deep, fertile, and humus-rich soil. Lay the bulbs about 8 in. deep in the soil and at least 10 in. apart. In loose, light soils, the planting depth needs to be 12 in. Adequate moisture and additional fertilizer are helpful during shoot development.

1111 When planting or transplanting peonies, ensure that the root crown is covered with no more than 2 in. of earth.

Peonies should be transplanted and divided only when absolutely necessary. The best time for doing so is during the months of August and September. It generally takes two years before they will flower properly again. If they are planted too deep, they will not develop any flowers. Peonies love sunny sites.

1112 Biennials are planted in early August so that they will flower abundantly in the coming year.

If vigorous wallflowers (*Erysimum cheiri*), foxgloves (*Digitalis*), hollyhocks (*Alcea*), carnations (*Dianthus caryophyllus*), sweet Williams (*Dianthus barbatus*), and Canterbury bells (*Campanula medium*) are needed for the coming year, they will need to be planted in the first third of August. All of them require sunny sites. They make no special demands on the soil, provided it is rich in nutrients and humus. The planting width should be at least 10 × 10 in., or, in the case of hollyhocks, greater.

1113 Plant pansies (*Viola ×wittrockiana*), daisies (*Bellis perennis*), and forget-me-nots (*Myosotis*) in the second half of August or in early September.

Set the plants that were sown in early July ▶ **TIP 1033** at an interval of 6 to 7 × 8 in. They should be planted at their final site only in the spring, since not all the plants will survive the winter well, and any decorative planting would otherwise be uneven and full of gaps.

1114 Ivy (*Hedera helix*) and Boston ivy (*Parthenocissus tricuspidata*) will cover entire house walls within a few years.

Both of these climbers are falsely accused of destroying the plaster on house walls. They are held fast only by their rhizoids (ivy) or adhesive disks (Boston ivy), and do not penetrate the rendering or masonry, provided these have not already been damaged. The holdfasts may nevertheless penetrate existing gaps and cracks, and through their growth cause already damaged masonry to split open. Roof connections, wall openings, and downpipes must be constantly kept free of growth. Since the leaves lie on top of one another like roof tiles, they also protect intact masonry from excess moisture. A particularly beautiful form of Boston ivy is 'Veitchii'. The different forms of true ivy do not grow as quickly. Instead, they are undemanding, and will grow even in deep shade. Only the varieties with colored leaves are somewhat more particular and slower growing.

1115 **Dahlias flower more abundantly the more often the unsightly and died-off flowers are removed.**

This applies especially to single-flowering varieties. They set seed easily, which inhibits the development of more flowers.

1116 **The "eyes" (buds) of the roses that were grafted in May will have grown in place by mid-August.**

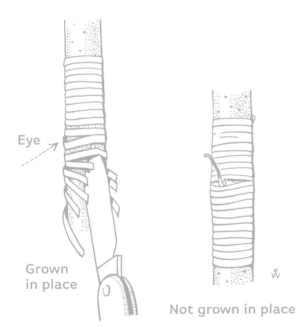

Eye

Grown in place

Not grown in place

This can be recognized by the died-off residual leaf stalk and the fresh-green eye of the inserted standard rose. The binding can now be removed. To do this, cut it at the side of the shoot opposite the eye. A sharp knife is needed; the bark of the shoot must not

be damaged in the process. Remove the shoots of the base only in spring. ▶ TIP 1019 to ▶ TIP 1022

1117 **Roses in which the inserted eyes have not grown in place in July can be re-grafted in August.**

This is done exactly as described in ▶ TIP 1019 to ▶ TIP 1022. The new grafting site can be located below or behind the old one. Additionally, grafting can be done throughout August.

Terraces and Balconies

1118 **Trees and shrubs in tubs are given fertilizer only until August, so that the wood will mature properly.**

This is necessary to prevent losses during overwintering. To promote the proper consolidation of the tissue, the final fertilizer applications should contain potassium and phosphorus in particular.

1119 **Tub plants that were not transplanted in the spring can still be dealt with in August.**

This should not be left any later so that the soil will still be well penetrated by the roots. In trees and shrubs, the new annual shoots should be almost completely mature.

Balcony plants will flower for longer if they always have sufficient water and nutrients.

1120 **Balcony plants need sufficient water and nutrients in August.**

If the soil has not been given a proper fertilizer application, give the plants a fast-acting complete fertilizer application or a fertilizer solution. Always water the plants thoroughly after each fertilizer application.

Winter Gardens, Flower Windows, and Rooms

1121 **If amaryllises (*Hippeastrum*) are to flower on time, the bulbs must mature properly.**

Plants with four leaves are mostly large enough to be able to flower. In order that their bulbs will now mature properly, they should be watered less and less from mid-August on, with no further watering at all after the end of the month. Meanwhile, the site must also be very sunny during this time. Spray the leaves on sunny days so that they will not turn yellow and die off too quickly.

> *Potted azaleas and camellias should be dipped in water occasionally so that the soil always remains uniformly moist.*

1122 **Azaleas and camellias, too, need plenty of water in August.**

These plants are no longer given fertilizer in August. However, they must not lack water, or the camellias will lose their buds and azaleas will never develop them in the first place.

1123 **In the fall, springtails will often be noticeable in the soil of indoor pot plants.**

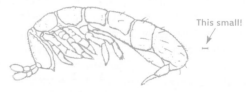

This small!

These will mostly appear if the soil has been kept too wet. Springtails reproduce in large numbers only on earth that is constantly wet, and will damage the plants by gnawing the roots. New infestations can be prevented if the soil surface is always allowed to dry out properly before the next watering. Adding some sand to the soil surface is also helpful. This will dry very quickly after watering, depriving the springtails of a suitable habitat.

1124 **From late August, even indoor plants that are sensitive to the sun will hardly need any further shade.**

It is mostly sufficient if shade-loving plants in the window and winter garden are provided with some shade only during the middle of the day. All other plants will be able to withstand full sun from late August on.

1125 ***Phalaenopsis* mostly flowers again on the old inflorescence.**

The inflorescences of the moth orchid (*Phalaenopsis*) should not be cut off after flowering; a new flowering stem will often develop at the node of the stalk from out of the axis of the scale-like bracts. Remove only withered or dried-up tips. If the inflorescences need to be shortened, leave at least three nodes remaining.

1126

Geranium cuttings for the coming year should be taken in August.

Short lateral shoots are the most suitable for use as cuttings. They should be carefully broken off at the base and will develop roots easily. Head cuttings from a shoot must be cut off cleanly with a sharp knife, directly beneath the beginning of the leaf stalk. Leave these cuttings to lie for one day to allow the cut surface to dry; that way, they will not begin to rot so easily. Remove any existing flower and bud shoots as these will inhibit root development. Compost earth containing around one quarter sand is filled loosely up to and over the rim into 2 ¾ to 3 in. pots, and the cuttings are then pressed firmly into the soil. Alternatively, several cuttings can also be planted at the edges of one large pot. The cuttings are then watered generously, but only a little from then on, until the roots develop.

½ in.

SEPTEMBER

The summer heat has now passed. During sunny days in the fall, many tasks can still be completed in the garden. In vegetable gardens, onions are harvested, and spinach and lamb's lettuce are sown at the beginning of the month. Many flowering perennials can be divided and replanted. Tub plants are prepared for their winter quarters, and conifers and evergreen broad-leaved trees and shrubs generously watered again to prevent any possible drying out.

GENERAL

1127 In September, make concerted efforts to combat mice and voles to minimize the damage they can cause in winter.

The best recourse is to set traps with appropriate baits, or also a "vole frightener." ▸ TIP 625

1128 In September, dry the fruits of elder and rowan trees to provide good winter feed for birds.

Hang up the fruit stands in an airy place, sheltered from the rain, until they are completely dry. In winter, they can be mixed in with the rest of the bird feed. However, if these berries are left to hang on the trees, the birds will eat them in September when sufficient other food is still available.

1129 In September, all bird baths should be thoroughly cleaned once more.

They should remain filled with water at all times. This is especially important in dry, warm weather.

1130 Compost should be checked for places where it is too moist or too dry.

This is best done now, in late summer; this also applies to thermocomposters. Dry and moist materials can be mixed with the aid of a digging fork. If there is too much moisture, some clay mineral flour (bentonite) can be added to soak up the excess water. This can also be done using slightly crumpled newspaper.

1131 Even the last birds will have left their nesting boxes, and all their young will have flown away.

Accordingly, this is the time to thoroughly clean the nesting boxes, since pests such as fleas, mites, or ticks may have become established in the meantime. If necessary, an overwintering site can also be prepared for queen bumblebees. By now, in September, their colony will have died out, and only the queens will be overwintering. In early spring, long before other bees, they begin to seek out pollen and nectar, and thus assist in pollination. Bees mostly take flight at temperatures from around 50°F, but queen bumblebees will do so from just 35°F. Fruit varieties that produce their flowers very early will benefit accordingly.

1132 The first hedgehogs will soon begin their search for suitable overwintering sites.

We should support these useful animals by making our gardens more welcoming for them. This means not clearing away leaves under bushes, while also leaving piles of brushwood undisturbed, cutting back hedges only in the spring, but also, above all, not using poisons in the garden. A bowl filled with water (not milk!) should also be available at all times. It is also possible to prepare your own hedgehog overwintering site. This means gathering up small twigs and dry leaves or straw in unused corners, under shrubs, or in other protected places, and putting a fruit box over them upside down—leave it open at one of the narrow sides to prevent it from being blown away by the wind. Heaped-up leaves can also be protected from being blown away with wire netting (press the ends into the earth). Natural stones or bricks, covered with attached roofing felt or a stone concrete slab, for example, can be used to build a small hedgehog house. Hedgehog houses are also commercially available, although they are not necessarily cheap. NB: Hedgehogs occasionally overwinter in compost heaps as well. Accordingly, before removing or turning over compost, check to see whether a hedgehog has made a home for itself inside.

VEGETABLES

1133 To prepare small greenhouses and foil houses to be ready in time for growing suitable vegetable species for use in the fall, harvesting of summer crops needs to be completed by early September at the latest.

Remove the harvested plants carefully, and loosen the soil thoroughly. In most cases, it will be helpful to replenish the soil water content by watering generously (8 to 10 gal./yd.^{2}) three to four days before introducing the crops for the fall. This helps the plants become established. The most suitable plants for the fall are lettuce, kohlrabi, winter endives, and red radishes. The required plants must be raised in good time through sowing on seedbeds out in the open. The latest date for planting out is 10 to 15 September. Needless to say, only varieties with a fast development time should be used for this cultivation.

1134 By the first half of September, celery is generally far enough advanced that it can be "bleached."

Although nearly all present-day varieties are "self-bleaching," which means that they have white to light yellow leaf stalks, the leaf stalks will be tenderer if the plants that are ready to harvest are tied together and wrapped with black foil from the ground to the base of the leaves. The bleaching process takes about 10 days.

1135 In early September, give late cauliflower another surface fertilizer application.

For this, use a 0.3 percent solution of a complete fertilizer and a fast-acting nitrogen fertilizer. These fertilizers are mixed in a 1:1 ratio.

1136 In late September, cauliflower that has not yet fully developed must be protected from early frosts.

If night frosts are expected, it is best to cover the ground with foil or fleece. For this, the transportable foil tunnels and tents that were used in the spring can also be deployed if the cauliflower stands are correspondingly large.

1137 In September, Chinese cabbage is undergoing its main development phase, and therefore needs plenty of water and nutrients.

Depending on the weather conditions, two or three water applications of 5 gal./yd.^{2} each are required in September. When the heads begin to develop, give the Chinese cabbage another surface application of a fast-acting nitrogen fertilizer.

1138 Lamb's lettuce that is intended for the spring harvest should be sown by mid-September at the latest.

If sown any later, the plants will mostly be too small going into the winter, which can considerably reduce the yield in spring. On sowing, see ▶ **TIP 961**.

For lamb's lettuce, too, cold frames that have become available should be used. These have the advantage that harvesting is also possible in frost and snow.

1139 In order that curly kale can develop plenty of leaf mass before the onset of frosts, it should be given a surface nitrogen fertilizer application.

Fertilizer solutions are better than dry spread fertilizers. With solutions, the curly kale also receives the water that is required to make the nutrients effective. Apply the solutions at a 0.2 percent dilution.

1140 Late kohlrabi that is intended for winter use (TIP 842) will also benefit from another surface fertilizer application in September.

So that the kohlrabi will keep well in the winter, in September use only low-nitrogen complete fertilizers with a high potassium content. Apply the nutrient solution at a 0.3 percent dilution in early September.

1141 Delicious turnips and rutabagas can be attained only if plenty of water and sufficient nutrients are provided.

In early September, give the rutabagas or turnips another nitrogen-rich complete fertilizer application at a rate of about 1 oz./yd.²

1142 Lettuce that is not yet ready for harvesting by late September should be covered up using cold frame windows or foil.

This will ensure that the heads will develop more quickly and reliably if early varieties have been planted. The support structure for placing the windows must be 10 to 12 in. high. Instead of cold frame windows, frames with foil stretched over them can be used, or alternatively the foil tents or tunnels from spring.

1143 Pumpkins and squash are very sensitive to the night frosts that can often already occur in the second half of September.

Accordingly, these vegetables must be harvested as soon as there is any danger of night frosts. Left in a frost-free, airy place, they will mature further and will keep there until about December. However, continual monitoring is necessary to ensure there is no rot.

1144 In September, available space in cold frames can be used to grow red radishes.

A fast-growing variety is the most suitable. Dibbled sowing is essential. ▸TIP 187

1145 In early September, red radishes sown outdoors, too, will eventually be ready to harvest in warm, sheltered situations and on light humus soils.

The advice given in ▸TIP 1144 should also be followed.

1146 As soon as the rhubarb leaves turn yellow, the plants can be divided and replanted.

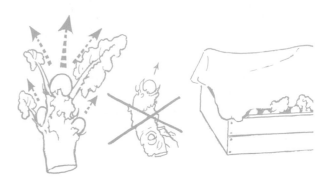

Rhubarb planted in late September will already yield a small harvest the following year. Ensure that the rootstocks that have been dug up are not exposed to the air for any length of time. Divide old rootstocks in such a way that each piece has at least one vigorous head.

1147 Before planting rhubarb, deeply work the land to a depth of two spade cuts if possible, and apply plenty of humus.

However, the humus should be worked into the upper soil layer only. Rhubarb thrives in all soil types. In light soils, the spring harvest can take place much earlier than in heavy soils.

1148 **When planting rhubarb, remember that the plants develop a very considerable leaf mass.**

Accordingly, provide a planting width of about 6 ½ × 6 ½ ft. Otherwise, they will develop only weak leaf stalks. For more information on rhubarb, see ▸ **TIP 268** to ▸ **TIP 270**. When buying rhubarb, be sure to ask about the variety. Make use of suppliers on the internet. Rhubarb can be left to grow in the same place for up to ten years; accordingly, select both the site and the variety with great care. 'Victoria', 'Goliath', 'The Sutton', and 'Sutton Seedless' have very high yields, but also need plenty of space.

In fall, cover the buds of rhubarb plants with 1 in. of soil and water generously.

1149 **For spinach for use in spring, sow seeds until around 15 September.**

If sown any later, the spinach will be too small going into the winter, and will often suffer as a result of winterkill. When sowing, note the advice given in ▸ **TIP 997**.

1150 **To harvest especially tender winter endives, begin "bleaching" in late September.**

For this, gather up the leaves lying flat on the ground as if they were a shock of hair, and tie up the uppermost tips with a string or rubber band. This may be done only when the plants are dry. Only the plants that are actually required in the coming days should be bleached. The bleaching process itself takes 12 to 16 days. Tying up the plants is not required if the plants are covered with black foil; this also reduces the time needed for bleaching by nearly half.

Since only a few plants are required at any one time, a frame made of wide boards or boxes, with black foil stretched over it, is particularly useful for bleaching purposes.

1151 **Corn cobs that have affected by boil (smut) must be removed in good time and destroyed.**

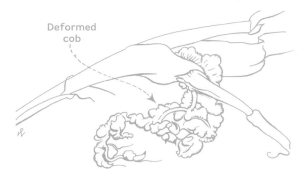

Deformed cob

This disease is characterized by boil-like growths that gradually turn brown. In this case, it is best to destroy the entire plant by burning it.

1152 Planted and sown onions should be harvested during September.

If the leaves are still green following a rainy summer, lift the onions a little using a digging fork. This will cause most of the roots to be torn, and the ripening process will be accelerated accordingly. The widespread practice of stamping on the leaves is not recommended under any circumstances.

1153 Late-sown crops of summer savory must be harvested and dried by around mid-September.

If the plants are left any longer, they can fall victim to early frosts. See ▸ TIP 1008 and ▸ TIP 1009 on harvesting and drying procedures.

1154 Chervil for winter use is sown in pots or bowls toward the end of September.

Leave the containers with the sown seed out in the open until the onset of early frosts. After that, place them in the window of a well-lit room. If you have access to a cold frame, dig the plants into the earth up to the rim of the container. Ten pots will be sufficient for the winter requirements of a household. Sow the seeds at intervals of 14 days in two pots. Once the seeds have produced shoots, bring the pots into a well-lit, warm room. Sandy compost earth is best for sowing; it should be kept constantly moist.

1155 If you want to dry lovage leaves for winter use, they will need to be harvested during September.

Do not dry the leaves in the sun or they will lose much of their spiciness. This will also happen if the dried leaves are not stored in sealed, airtight containers.

1156 The second marjoram cut takes place in late September.

On the drying procedure, see ▸ TIP 1008 and ▸ TIP 1011. Generally, buds will not form for the second cut. Accordingly, the harvest should not be delayed, but the recommended date observed instead.

1157 To harvest fresh parsley continuously during winter, it should be planted in pots in September.

Both garden parsley and parsley root can be used for this purpose. Parsley root does not have any curly leaves, however. For these, deeper—in other words, larger—pots must be used, because the roots are significantly longer than for garden parsley. Remove the plants from the earth, taking care to protect the roots, and plant in pots immediately. They will suffer from storage in the air. They should be planted only as deep as they have been before. For garden parsley, pots with a diameter of 4 ¾ in. will be sufficient; for parsley root, they should have a diameter of at least 5 ½ in. As many plants as possible should be put in each pot. It will be sufficient if the planting interval for garden parsley is 1 in., and 2 in. for root parsley. Use sandy compost earth for potting.

1158 The planted parsley then stays out in the open until the onset of frost, or it can be placed in a cold frame. The pots are sunk into the ground up to the pot rim.

After sinking the pots in the ground, thoroughly water the parsley so that the roots are in intimate contact with the soil. As long as the pots are outside, the soil must not be allowed to dry out.

1159 If chives are planted in pots during September, they can be harvested all winter long.

It is worth planting vigorous clumps only. Otherwise, proceed as outlined in ▸ **TIP 1158**.

1160 A range of cruciferous species are designated as rucola or hedge mustard. All are suitable for growing in home and community or allotment gardens, both outdoors and in greenhouses.

The two most important species differ from one another in terms of their leaf form and taste. At one time, oil used to be won from the seeds of arugula plants. Sand rocket or Lincoln's weed, meanwhile, is well known as a cooking herb and medicinal plant.

1161 The annual arugula is also known by the names of rocket, Italian cress, or by the botanical designation *Eruca sativa*.

It is an undemanding, but much-prized salad plant and spice herb. The leaves are not as strongly laciniate as those of the perennial species.

Arugula plants need a warm site, sun, and a permeable, humic soil. They are also well suited to growing in cold frames. The seed is sown in spring, from March, at two-week intervals until September. If the final sown seed is covered with a fleece, harvesting will be possible into the winter. Arugula is a good previous crop, aftercrop, and secondary crop. Sow seed in rows of 6 to 8 in. or broadcast sow, ⅕ to ⅖ in. deep. Later, thin out the plants to an interval of 6 in. Arugula can also be grown well in pots.

1162 The perennial sand rocket or Lincoln's weed is also known under the botanical designation *Diplotaxis tenuifolia*.

Sow seed from March to early September with a row interval of 6 to 8 in., and a seed depth of 2 to 4 in. Since the germination time is 14 to 25 days, the seed should be sown only when the soil is warm. Sand rocket can be bought in pots at weekly markets or from specialist dealers. If planted in beds, fresh green rocket salad can be harvested until the onset of frost. This species is winter hardy and will produce shoots again in the spring.

1163 Since both species are cruciferous plants, this should be taken into account in annual crop rotation planning.

A cultivation pause of at least three years should be maintained with other cabbage species and with green manuring plants, such as mustard.

ORNAMENTAL PLANTS

Ornamental Gardens

1164 For planting lilies, September is the best time.

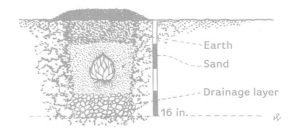

While the white or Madonna lily (*Lilium candidum*) is already planted in August, ▸ **TIP 1102**, September is more suitable for all other lilies. Nearly all lilies love a warm site and a soil that is not too heavy. Loam soils should be improved by adding sand and compost. In the planting ditch, add a layer of gravel first, then cover with sand. The bulbs are embedded in the sand; this will ensure good drainage, even in heavy soils. The soil above the tip of the bulb should be loose and rich in nutrients, since most lily species develop roots on the shaft. Earth that has been mixed with compost and sand is the most suitable. Lilies love sun, but directly above the soil surface they like shade, which, in a natural environment, is provided by the neighboring plants. If such natural shading of the soil is not possible in the garden, it can be accomplished by a covering layer of compost earth or bark mulch. However, select the site so that ground cover plants will later assume this function. The earth layer above the bulb tips should be twice as thick as the height of the bulb. Plant large, flat bulbs at a greater depth, so that the earth layer is three to four times as high as the height of the bulb. **TABLE 23**

> *If flower bulbs are planted at the right time and at an optimal depth, they will be sure to bloom splendidly in the following year.*

1165 The bulb and tuber plants described under TIP 1103 and TIP 1104 can also still be planted in September.

If possible, finish planting by 15 September so that the plants will be able to develop sufficient roots before the onset of frost.

1166 The Siberian or lavender mountain lily (*Ixiolirion*) needs especially plentiful sun and warmth.

Additionally, this still-little-known steppe plant with its lily-like flowers needs sufficient space—it will not tolerate being crowded out by vigorously growing perennials. The site should be warm, humic, and permeable. Lay the bulbs around 4 in. deep in the fall, and cover with compost earth or bark mulch.

1167 Daffodils thrive in sandy loam soils with a good humus content.

Lay the bulbs around 4 to 6 in. deep, preferably in September. On beds, the row interval is around 8 in.,

and the interval within a row 4 to 6 in. If planting daffodils in groups, an interval of 6 in. on all sides is sufficient. Humus soils can be improved with compost earth. The plants will fail in soils that are wet and lime-deficient (in other words, acidic).

1168 The main planting time for tulip bulbs is October, but they can already be put in the ground in the final third of September.

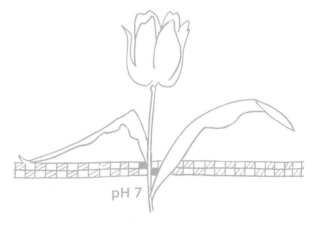

Tulips place no special demands on soil conditions and can thrive in every garden soil. A somewhat sandy soil with a neutral pH (pH 7) is especially suitable, but only if it is not too dry in the spring. The planting depth for tulip bulbs is 4 to 6 in.; in heavy soils, 3 in. will be sufficient. As a row interval, 8 in. is sufficient, with an interval of 4 in. within the row. If laid in groups, allow for an interval of 4 to 5 in. on all sides. Plant the bulbs by the end of October, so that they will still be able to develop roots and establish properly.

1169 When laying hyacinth bulbs, it is important not to damage the root crown at the base of the bulb.

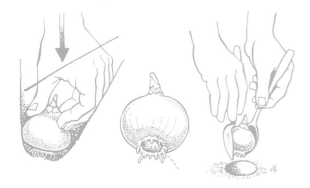

The planting depth for hyacinths depends on the soil conditions. In heavy soils, lay them only 3 to 4 in. deep, and in light soils around 5 in. deep. Hyacinths, too, make a better visual impact when they are grown together in groups.

1170 Once daffodil, tulip, and hyacinth bulbs have been laid, cover the soil with a compost layer.

This will ensure that the soil underneath remains uniformly moist for a long time, so that the bulbs will soon develop roots.

> *Flowering perennials can be divided and planted in early to mid-fall, so that they have time to settle in before winter.*

1171 Most flowering perennials can be divided and planted in September.

When dividing the plants, cut off all the aboveground parts a little above the ground. Once the plants have been dug up, cut back the roots somewhat. Shallow rootstocks can be divided by hand, while densely growing rootstocks may require a spade. If the plant parts are too small, they will flower only sparsely in the first year. The planting hole must always be somewhat larger than the plant part so that the roots will grow vertically into the ground and the root ball can be pressed in at the sides. Firmly setting the plants in the soil and watering are requirements for good growth. The required planting intervals are given in the perennials tables. **TABLE 16** and **TABLE 17**

1172 Perennials that are sensitive or bloom in the fall should be replanted only in the spring.

Winter chrysanthemums that bloom in late fall (*Chrysanthemum ×grandiflorum*) and late-flowering monkshood (*Aconitum*) are best replanted in the spring. Often, they will not develop roots properly before the onset of frosts and can suffer damage in winter. The same applies to perennials that are generally sensitive as young plants, such as the Japanese anemone or windflower (*Anemone hupehensis*), rock rose or sun rose (*Helianthemum*), red hot poker or torch lily (*Kniphofia*), and tickseed (*Coreopsis*). Even a good winter protective covering will not always sufficiently protect in such instances.

1173 In September, too, winter chrysanthemums need plenty of water.

If the weather during the fall is dry, the flowers of winter chrysanthemums that bloom in September and later will not develop properly. When watering, the leaves should remain as dry as possible, so that they will not become diseased and die off prematurely.

1174 Winter-hardy carnations should be protected against rabbit grazing in September.

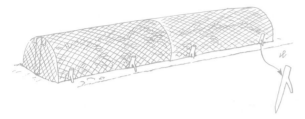

Rabbits graze especially keenly on carnations during the wintertime. Covering the plants with wire netting will provide effective protection.

1175 Purchase freesia bulbs in the spring, since it is not worth overwintering them.

Freesia bulbs are given special treatment in nurseries for perennials; they should not be used again for flowering in the garden. They are always purchased freshly in the spring.

1176 Remove the bulbs of early-flowering gladiolus varieties from the ground in September.

It is best not to wait until the aboveground parts have turned yellow or died off completely. It has been shown that disease agents in the bulbs in the ground can develop very quickly. This can be prevented, or at least ameliorated, by harvesting the bulbs early. However, this does not mean that the bulbs should be removed from the ground too soon. The earliest suitable time can be recognized by examining the roots. As soon as the first signs of dying off are apparent—brown roots on the inside—the bulbs can be dug up. Remove one bulb from the ground as a sample.

1177 A digging fork is better than a spade for digging up gladiolus bulbs.

Damage to the bulbs can be largely avoided in this way. Even the smallest scratch on a bulb can provide a point for disease agents to attack. Damaged bulbs will often die off in winter storage, and can also infect healthy bulbs. The earth sticking to the roots of the bulbs should also be shaken off.

1178 The aboveground shoot of the gladiolus bulb is cut off to leave about 4 in. above the bulb.

Wrong!   4 in.   Right!

Breaking the shoot off at the base will mostly lead to damage to the bulb. Dispose of the cut-off shoots immediately—they nearly always harbor disease agents or pests that overwinter in the soil or can affect the bulbs as well, especially gladiolus thrips. The thrips not only overwinter on the bulbs, but can also spread among the gladioli that are kept in winter storage.

Well-dried gladiolus bulbs that are stored in an airy place will survive the winter.

1179 Put the harvested gladiolus bulbs in a well-ventilated room to dry out.

So they can dry out freely, place them in shallow crates that still let plenty of air circulate even after they have been stacked. A maximum of two stacked layers is permissible per crate. If need be, turn the bulbs over regularly until they have all dried out.

1180 Harvest gladiolus bulblets according to variety if they are to be used for propagation purposes.

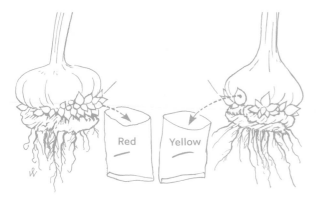

This is necessary to ensure that a bias is introduced to the existing assortment. If this is not taken into account, there will ultimately be too many bulbs of some varieties and hardly any of the others. This is especially true if only the larger bulbs are used for breeding. Some varieties produce many large bulblets, and others only a few small ones.

1181 Like the large gladiolus bulbs, the bulblets are first dried out in an airy place before they are put into winter storage.

However, they must not dry out so much that they become hard and produce only a few or irregular shoots in the spring. Bulblets can be stacked in a crate to a height of around 2 ½ in. but they must be turned over every day until they are dry.

1182 If cut at the right stage, dahlia flowers will keep for longer in the vase.

The best time to cut the flowers is in the early morning; only those flowers that have opened fully should be cut. Cut off all the lateral buds—they will not bloom themselves, and will only reduce the flowers' keeping properties. Leave only enough leaves on the flower stalks that might be required for a decorative effect. Put cut flowers in water immediately and ensure that they are not exposed to drafts. They must stand deep in the water, which should be changed daily.

1183 Dahlias will flower well into October if they are protected against night frosts.

September frosts are generally light, which means that light cloths hung over the plants will provide sufficient protection.

1184 When collecting sunflower seeds, they must be protected from being eaten by birds.

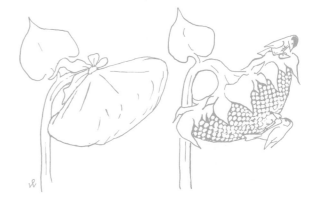

The easiest solution is to wrap the fruiting bodies with tulle or a similar air-pervious material. This needs to be done as soon as the first signs of seed formation are apparent.

1185 In order that they will retain their vivid colors, straw daisies (*Xerochrysum*) need to be cut in good time.

Cut straw daisies before the flowers have developed fully. This means waiting for dry weather. To dry the flowers, make a small bundle and hang it up in an airy, and, if possible, dark place. It is important that the flowers hang downward or they will end up having bent stalks.

> *Straw daisies should be hung up to dry with the flowers facing downward to keep the stalks straight.*

1186 Unlike straw daisies, African daisies or yellow ageratum (*Lonas annua*), paper daisies (*Rhodanthe manglesii*), and sea lavender (*Limonium*) need to have flowered fully for drying purposes.

These should be cut during the middle of the day when the sun is out. They are then dried according to the instructions given in ▶ **TIP 1185**.

1187 The fruit-bearing shoots of Japanese lanterns (*Physalis*) should be cut only after the orange-red involucres have developed a good color.

These make a lasting decoration for vases. When cutting them, remove the leaves so that only the fruits are left on the shoots. Then put them into vases filled with moist sand. Japanese lanterns can grow wildly and become a nuisance when they are situated between less vigorously growing plants. Since they tolerate semi-shade well, they can be planted between trees or shrubs. There, they form a dense stand in which neither chickweed nor groundsel can become established.

1188 It is a little-known fact that mahonia fruits can be used in the household.

The fruits are useful as an additive for jams, improving the flavor. Since people's tastes differ, it is better to make a test sample first. The berries lend the jam a beautiful dark color. Note, however, that the raw berries can be dangerous for children.

1189 Some ornamental shrubs bear vividly colored fruits in the fall. Since some of them are poisonous, children should be warned accordingly.

Poisonous to a greater or lesser degree are, especially, the fruits of the bladder senna (*Colutea*), daphne (*Daphne*), ivy (*Hedera*), pea shrub or pea tree (*Caragana*), honeysuckle (*Lonicera*), privet (*Ligustrum*), cherry laurel (*Prunus laurocerasus*), spindle (*Euonymus*), snowberry (*Symphoricarpos*), holly (*Ilex*), and cotoneaster (*Cotoneaster*).

1190 Conifers and wintergreen broad-leaved trees and shrubs should be watered vigorously in September so that they will survive the winter well.

When these plants are damaged during winter, it is mostly the result of dryness, rather than frost. In winter, too, the trees and shrubs transpire a great deal of water, which they need to replenish from the ground with the aid of their roots. However, this is possible only if there is enough moisture in the soil—if not, the plants will dry out.

1191 Damaged or withered terminal shoots of fir (*Abies*), spruce (*Picea*), and pine (*Pinus*) can be replaced with a lateral shoot.

The hitherto terminal shoot is used as a support, to which the lateral shoot is bound. However, if the tip has been broken off entirely, a pole can be used as a support instead.

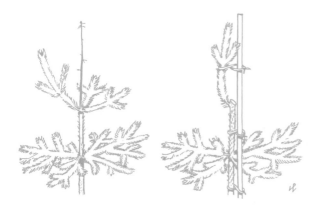

1192 A number of different bedding plants will continue to bloom for a long time if they are put in pots in late September.

In particular, geraniums, fuchsias, heliotropes, bulb and other begonias, and also marigolds (*Tagetes*) will tolerate this well. Using a hand spade, they are levered out of the earth, including their root ball, and pressed into appropriately sized pots. After watering, they can be left in a well-lit place in a cool room.

> *Annual larkspur, cornflower, pot marigolds, and other cool-season annuals can be sown now for early spring bloom.*

1193 Annual summer flowers sown outdoors in the second half of September will bloom significantly earlier in the following year than if they were sown in the spring.

Especially suitable are poppy (*Papaver*), larkspur (*Consolida*), pot marigolds (*Calendula*), cornflower (*Centaurea cyanus*), corncockle (*Agrostemma*), love-in-a-mist (*Nigella*), and others. The young plants of these summer flowers withstand the winter well, provided their sites are not very windy. In a normal bed (4 ft.), sow five rows, and within the row lay the seeds in bunches. The interval between bunches is around 8 in. After the seedlings have emerged, all the plants are left to stand; they are thinned only in spring. A loose cover of spruce brushwood is beneficial.

1194 Dittany (*Dictamnus*) should be transplanted only as a young plant.

This splendid plant, which grows to a height of 3 ft., has become rare in nature. It needs a drier, heavier soil, and is best transplanted in the fall. It is propagated using seeds, as soon as these are ripe.

Terraces and Balconies

1195 Heather (*Erica gracilis*) will bloom for a long time if it is standing in a well-lit, airy, and always moist site.

If the root balls dry out, and the leaves, flowers, and buds wilt, the beauty of the plants will soon be a thing of the past. The flowers will lose their color rapidly in a room. Heather blooms best when planted in balcony boxes or tubs out on the terrace. It is not worth trying to cultivate the plants further; instead, purchase them afresh each year.

> *If protected from the first frosts, flowering plants growing directly next to the house will continue to bloom into fall.*

1196 If the plants are protected from the first night frosts in a balcony box, they will generally continue to bloom for a long time.

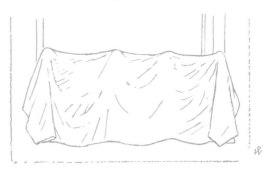

Spread-out newspapers or towels are sufficient protection against light night frosts. Poles placed underneath will prevent these materials from lying on the flowers themselves. Individual boxes can be brought indoors during very cold nights.

1197 Move sensitive tub plants to a safe place before the first night frosts.

The following tub and pot plants next to the house, or on the terrace and balcony should be put in a safe place in good time before the onset of light night frosts: *Bougainvillea*, citrus (*Citrus*), angel's trumpet (*Brugmansia*), *Lycianthes rantonnetii*, powder puff tree (*Calliandra*), heliotrope or turnsole (*Heliotropium*), Chinese hibiscus (*Hibiscus rosa-sinensis*), glory bush (*Tibouchina*), banana (*Musa*), camellia (*Camellia*), cockspur coral tree (*Erythrina christa-galli*), ivy tree or umbrella tree (*Schefflera*), and umbrella grass (*Cyperus*). Many sclerophyllous trees and shrubs can be left where they are.

1198 Cacti and other succulent pot plants will suffer even in light night frosts.

Accordingly, they should be brought inside before the first frost. If they are exposed to frost, rot will mostly be unavoidable. They should be given less water at their winter site.

Winter Gardens, Flower Windows, and Rooms

1199 *Crossandra*, a rediscovered beauty with improved varieties, flowers tirelessly from May to October.

This splendid plant with its vivid salmon-pink to orange-colored flowers needs plenty of light, but must be protected from the hot midday sun. It will tolerate temperatures of 60 to 64°F well. The soil should always be moderately moist. From August/September, the decorative green spikes are seen, from whose scale-like bracts the flowers appear. If the plants have become too large, they can easily be cut back (after flowering). Propagate using head cuttings, preferably in an indoor greenhouse, in April/May.

1200 Poppy anemones (*Anemone coronaria*) and Persian buttercup (*Ranunculus asiaticus*) for the winter garden should be potted in September.

In order that the tubers will sprout evenly, they are first left to soak in prewarmed water for about 12 hours. Plant at least 2 in. deep in containers with humic, loose earth. They are then left to stand in a cool place at 46 to 50°F. In a winegrowing climate, they can stand out in the open, planted about 3 in. deep, with a good winter covering. They will then bloom from March on.

1201 Primroses (*Primula vulgaris*) and oxlips (*P. elatior*) are highly suitable as winter-flowering plants for cool rooms.

To this end, plant in pots in September. However, it is only worth potting vigorous, healthy plants, since weak specimens will produce too few flowers. Before potting, water the primroses thoroughly so that the root balls will be well retained. Then use a hand spade for digging them out. The root ball should be large enough to fit into a 4 in. pot. Garden earth is sufficient for filling the pot to the rim.

1202 The kaffir lily (*Clivia*) needs a cool period to develop flower buds.

Without such a cool period, the plant will not bloom. Accordingly, from September to late November, it should be kept at a temperature of 50 to 59°F. During this time, water the plant only moderately until flowering in spring.

1203 Indoor and winter-garden plants can still be replanted in early September.

If replanted later, the earth will often not be properly penetrated by the roots. This can lead to winter losses, since such plants can easily develop diseased roots. ▸ TIP 598 and ▸ TIP 599

1204 Florist's gloxinia tubers should be overwintered.

Even in late-flowering florist's gloxinias (*Sinningia*), the leaves will have wilted in September. The tubers can be overwintered in a dark place at around 64°F in a pot or layered in dry earth.

> *Bulbs of hyacinths and tulips can be potted up now and placed in the cold frame for winter flowering.*

1205 In September, set hyacinth bulbs in special jars or vases for forcing bulbs or plant in pots.

Fill the hyacinth jars with water only to the point that it still does not touch the base of the bulb, since otherwise the bulbs will rot. The occupied jars must be left for two months in a cool place (43 to 46°F) in order for roots to develop. Provide each bulb with a light-tight bag immediately after it has been set in place. For planting in pots, use sandy, well-layered compost earth or potting mixture. The inner diameter of the pots may be only 1 in. larger than the bulbs. After planting, the upper half of the bulb must remain

above the earth. The plant is then watered, and sand spread over the substrate in order to be able to separate this earth from the earth in the pot when removing the bulb. Like for the hyacinths in jars, provide the plants with a light-tight bag, or, alternatively, bury the pots in the soil in the garden. A box with earth on the balcony can also serve the same purpose. The bulbs should be covered with about 4 in. of earth. If kept constantly moist, they will soon develop roots. ▸ TIP 1350 and ▸ TIP 1375

1206 Low-growing tulip varieties make beautiful pot plants from January on, if vigorous bulbs are planted in pots in September.

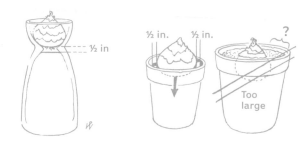

Early varieties are especially suitable. Use sandy compost earth or potting mixture for planting. In each pot, plant three bulbs about 1 in. apart. The pots should be sufficiently large so that a gap as wide as a finger is left between the bulbs and pot rim. Press the bulbs only up to about two thirds of their height into the earth. Once planted, water the bulbs so that earth in the pot is moistened right through. Leave the pots in a dark place at a temperature of 43 to 46°F. A hole in the earth outdoors is better still. In this case, dig out the earth to a depth of about 6 in. and place the pots closely together in this hole. Cover the surface of all the pots with a ½ in. thick layer of sand so that the soil that will be added on top can be easily removed. Water thoroughly, and then cover the pots with the excavated earth. For further treatment, see ▸ TIP 1350 and ▸ TIP 1375.

1207 Often, there are already cool nights toward the end of September.

For the most part, indoor rooms will not yet be heated on warm sunny days in September. The transitional period up until indoor heating begins is difficult for those indoor plants that need warmth. With falling night temperatures, indoor plants will suffer if they are given too much water so their watering quantities should be cut back. This applies especially to rubber plants (*Ficus*), snake plant or bowstring hemp (*Sansevieria*), radiator plant (*Peperomia*), philodendron (*Philodendron*), some orchids, bromeliads, and others.

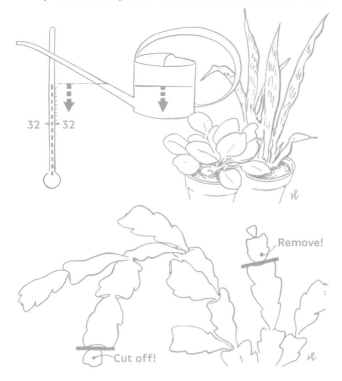

Remove!

Cut off!

1208 For the Christmas cactus (*Schlumbergera*) to develop buds, it needs a resting period from September on.

In September, gradually reduce the watering quantities, without letting the earth become totally dry. The site must be sunny, and, at least at night, as cool as possible (50 to 59°F). Remove incompletely developed cactus joints at the attachment points, because they will not develop any buds. If buds appear, mostly in November/December, give the plants a moderate amount of water.

1209 In the second half of September, bring indoor plants that have spent the summer in the garden back inside.

By the end of September, the nights can already be getting decidedly cold. From this time on, all indoor plants should be back inside the house again. Beforehand, clean them well and remove all wilted or yellowed plant parts. A thorough inspection for diseases and pest infestation is important, including an examination of the leaf undersides. It is best to use a magnifying glass to help identify very small pests, such as the red spider mite.

1210 Florist's cyclamens (*Cyclamen persicum*) bloom in colors from white to a deep dark red with all shades in between, including bicolored.

After having spent the summer as almost leafless tubers in the soil, florist's cyclamens will again produce leaves and flowers in the fall. At this point, put the plants in a place that is as light and cool as possible. They will not do well in rooms with dry heating air, where they will soon wilt. They do not need very much water. In particular, the tuber should not be constantly wet or it may rot. It is best to water the plants by adding water to the saucer. Remove old and wilted leaves continually since they may harbor fungal spores. Once the final flowers have wilted in the spring and the leaves have begun to wilt as well, the plants can be left in a darker place, and from then on, watered infrequently. After the last night frosts, they are best left in a sheltered, shady place in the garden. From early June to July, set the tubers in fresh earth—sandy, humic potting mixture is best—and water some more. Miniature varieties with clear colors are very popular. They take up much less space and are looked after in the same way as the larger varieties.

1211

African violets (*Saintpaulia*) will have finished their flowering period in September, although some varieties also bloom all year round.

These plants from the Usambara mountains in northeast Tanzania are among the best loved of all flowering plants. Their velvety dark green leaves form a rosette that beautifully contrast the flowers, whose color spectrum ranges from white and pink to blue and violet, and also bicolored. There are single- and double-flowering specimens, and also miniature varieties. African violets like a warm place that is light, but not sunny. The temperature should not fall below 60°F if possible, and the water used for watering should also not be too cold. The plants can be easily propagated by using cuttings.

1212

The bird of paradise (*Strelitzia reginae*) is suitable for large, well-lit rooms.

With its bizarrely shaped, splendid flowers, this plant is highly decorative and exotic. In the summer, it prefers warm and sunny conditions, and in the winter, cool, but still light conditions. The flowers will not develop as well without sun. Regular watering is required in summer, and the substrate must always be kept slightly moist. The plant requires less water in cooler winter weather. From mid-May, it can grow out in the open, on the terrace or a sunny balcony. The site must be sheltered, since the plant does not tolerate drafts. It is also a sun worshipper, but it must nevertheless still be acclimatized to the sun outdoors. If the plant container has become too clogged up with roots, it's possible to replant young plants in the spring. In the case of older specimens, only renew the upper substrate layer. For propagation, partial plants with roots and at least three leaves can be removed carefully.

OCTOBER

Beautiful, "golden" sunny days in October lure garden lovers outdoors—and for gardening work that needs to be carried out in the fall. Look forward to a rich harvest of headed cabbage, fat kohlrabi, carrots, and many other vegetable species. However, curly kale should be exposed to frost before it is consumed, since it will then taste better.

Beds that have become free can be dug up at this time. Dahlias, gladiolus bulbs, and canna lilies will need to overwinter under dry and frost-free conditions, as will tuberous begonias, which need to be covered with a little earth. Parsley and chives can now be potted for winter use.

GENERAL

1213 In October, garden plots that have become free can now be dug up.

For this task, use a spade rather than a digging fork. The land that has been dug up is left to lie as large unbroken clods of earth. This means that frost and winter precipitation can penetrate deep into the soil. With the help of the frozen rain and snow water, the frost will burst open the individual soil particles and make the soil friable. In order that the soil is loosened to a sufficient depth, the entire spade blade is driven into the earth. Digging is made easier if the spade is held slightly at an angle and not vertically. The soil should be partially dried out for digging.

1214 Overzealous digging will destroy the soil structure.

Digging up the soil was once considered the most important component of gardening work. However, excessive digging can harm soil organisms such as bacteria, fungi, algae, nematodes, mites, and worms. These organisms live in different layers of the soil. They are accustomed to certain habitat conditions that are found only at a corresponding soil depth. In traditional digging, these soil layers are mixed up, and the organisms that are important for the soil life are largely killed off as a result.

1215 When digging up the soil, avoid turning over the clods.

If done wisely, important soil loosening in the fall can also be achieved by digging. However, make sure that the different soil layers are not mixed up as a result. This means that the clods of earth should not be turned over—instead, the soil only should be loosened. Accordingly, the spade is driven one spade cut deep into the soil, and the soil itself is merely eased forward. In this way, the lower layer will remain largely at the bottom, and the upper layer will again end up on top. After this, the earth is covered with compost but it is not worked into the soil because it may contain components that have not yet decomposed. In this way, the decomposition process can continue with exposure to the air. If buried, these non-decomposing components may simply rot instead.

1216 In organic horticulture, the soil is dug up only in exceptional circumstances.

In organic horticulture, it has become established practice that the land is not dug up in the fall. To loosen the soil, the surface is tilled only with a cultivator or digging fork. The digging fork is stuck into the soil, moved lightly backward and forward, and the process repeated at intervals of about an inch. The cultivator is dragged through the earth. Digging with a spade is reserved for new cropping land and very heavy loam or clay soils. In the fall, the beds are covered with a mulch layer consisting of leaves, compost, and plant remains. This protects the soil from frost, muddiness, and weed growth.

1217 If the land is to be planted with deep-rooting plants in the following year, cutting two or even three spade cuts deep (double digging or triple digging) may be beneficial.

For double digging, the dug trench must be two spade cuts wide to be able to dig up the lower layer as well. To do this, stand at a right angle to the dug trench. At the start of the work, lay the contents of the first two upper spade cuts to one side. These will be returned to the trench at the end of the work. Organic materials may be dug into the upper layer only.

1218 Digging trenches three spade cuts deep ("triple digging") for loosening the soil to a considerable depth has already been discussed in TIP 23, and is suitable for new plantings in heavy soils, in order to promote root growth.

In this way, fall plantings will still be able to grow their roots in the soil before winter sets in. Before beginning with such deep digging, the plot of land is divided up. This means that the earth that has been excavated for the first trench will not need to be transported far away. With triple digging, each soil layer is returned to the place where it had been before. The native topsoil must not be allowed to end up in the lower soil layers.

Through triple digging, all weeds can be dealt with, including couch grass. In this particular case, the uppermost layer that is infiltrated with the couch grass ends up right at the bottom, so that the second layer becomes the first, and the third layer becomes the second. The thickness of the individual layers depends on how deep the digging is to be done. In most cases, 24 to 30 in. will be sufficient, which means that the individual layers will be 8 to 10 in. thick.

1219 With triple digging, the soil can be improved with organic materials at the same time.

These materials must not be worked in at an excessive depth. They belong in the uppermost layer only or they will simply turn to peat and become worthless. The best approach is to spread stable manure and compost earth over the land once the triple digging is finished, and work it into the soil in the following

spring. Lime, too, should be spread over the surface only after the digging is finished, and then lightly hoed in. However, do not apply lime together with stable manure, since otherwise the nitrogen contained in the manure will be lost.

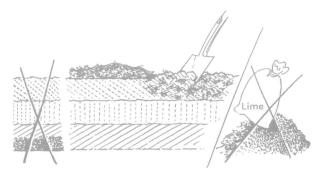

1220 Many plants do not tolerate fresh stable manure in the soil.

Stable manure may be applied or worked in only when it can be tolerated by the plants that have been planned for the area in the coming year. Plants that are sensitive to fresh stable manure include all root, tuber, and bulb plants. Examples include gladioli, tulips, lilies, and, among vegetables, horseradish, carrots, parsnips, red radishes and other radishes, and black salsify.

1221 Only wood ash is genuinely suitable for soil improvement.

The ashes of brown coal (briquettes) are unsuitable, because they grease the soil, which will affect soil fermentation. Wood ash mostly contains potassium and phosphorous, while soot contains nitrogen.

1222 Earthworms are exceptionally useful for maintaining the soil structure.

Earthworms live exclusively from humus substances that pass through their gut, which are then once again useful for the soil. They are unable to eat healthy roots or other plant parts. In their search for food, they pass through the soil countless times. In this way, they allow the oxygen in the air to reach the roots of the plants directly. Large numbers of earthworms are always a sign of humus-rich soil.

1223 **In late October, all compost heaps should be turned once more before heavier frosts set in.**

Of course, this job can also be done during the winter, but it is made far more difficult if the compost heaps are frozen. ▶ **TIP 10**

1224 **If you are able to obtain strips of sod, they should be stacked in heaps, since they make an excellent compost.**

For optimal aeration, the heaps should be at least 2 ½ ft. high and up to 3 ¼ ft. wide. The length is unimportant. When stacking the sod strips, note that the grass-covered sides should be underneath. If the heaps are turned once more in the spring and summer, and hoof and horn meal and/or bone meal are mixed in, you will have available usable compost by the fall. This is especially valuable for light soils. However, strips of sod that have been treated with salt solutions or road salt in the winter may no longer be used, owing to the high salt concentration.

1225 **From late October, watering hoses and sprinklers will no longer be required.**

Under no circumstances should the hoses be exposed to frost if they have not yet been emptied fully. Clean the sprinklers and place them in dry storage.

1226 **Now is also the time to establish a raised herb bed.**

A raised herb bed not only helps protect your back, but also offers herb such as marjoram, sage, lavender, and thyme ideal conditions for growth. These herbs do not like any waterlogging, and so the bed should be laid out in such a way that it will dry out again quickly following heavy rains. Raised beds can be constructed out of bricks or natural stone, or also wood. Stones necessitate a foundation, while a wooden construction can be purchased ready-made, or you can build one yourself. Set up the raised bed in a sunny place with a north-south orientation; with the required length it should not be more than 4 ft. wide, or, if accessible from one side only, 2 ft. The height can be between 20 and 32 in. To protect against voles and slugs, lay a close-meshed netting over the top initially. A base layer of natural or concrete stone (fragments) or coarse gravel, about 8 in. high, can be laid at the bottom for drainage, or you can also dig a trench 8 to 12 in. deep. For soil, select a permeable, low-nutrient mixture of garden earth and sand. The bed can also be filled with earth in the spring before planting begins.

VEGETABLES

1227 **Celery that has not been used by the onset of frosts is heeled-in in the cellar.**

For this, the plants along with their roots are removed from the soil and heeled-in in moist sand. The cellar must be well aerated.

1228 Harvesting of chicory roots can begin from mid-October.

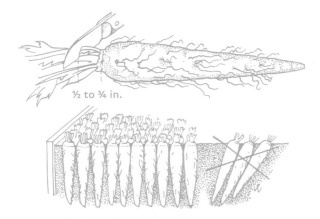

½ to ¾ in.

The roots must not be damaged when digging them out—see the advice for carrots under ▶ TIP 1244. Cut off the leaves ½ to ¾ in. above the root head. After being prepared in this way, the roots are initially heeled in for intermediate storage. A room that is as cool as possible, but frost-free, is the most practicable, so that the roots can be retrieved at any time. A cold frame is also suitable, provided the heeled-in roots are covered with a material to protect against frost. Only roots with a root head diameter of more than 1¼ in. should be used. Less vigorous roots are unsuitable for shoot production.

For intermediate storage, too, chicory roots should be heeled in as vertically as possible.

1229 For harvesting the first chicory shoots from December, start with shoot production in late October.

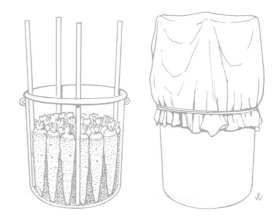

Before shoot production, the roots intended for this early harvesting must be exposed to low temperatures for a brief time. After cutting, they are best left to lie out in the open and covered only lightly with the cut-off leaves until they are ready to use. For the shoot production itself, large stoneware pots, buckets, and other such containers are highly suitable. After placing the roots side by side in the containers, fill them up to about 4 in. high with water. Then place them in a suitable room with temperatures from 59 to 64°F. The roots must always have sufficient available water. It is otherwise vital that the chicory shoots are able to grow in complete darkness. This can be attained by inserting four stakes in the container, covering them with black foil or similar material, and securing the material under the container rim, or simply placing a second container upside down on top of the first one.

1230 There is no need to hurry with the harvesting of Chinese cabbage, since it will tolerate frosts down to 21°F.

Anything that is not used immediately can be heeled in. However, Chinese cabbage may not be harvested in a frozen state. It should also only be harvested in dry weather.

1231   Eggplants grown under glass protection should be harvested before the onset of heavy frosts.

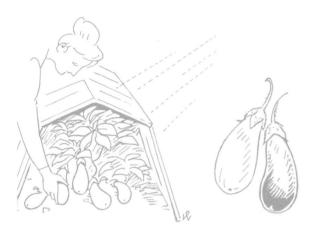

Fruits that are not yet fully ripened must be left to lie for at least eight days before they are used, so that the solanine that is present in unripe fruits has been broken down.

1232   If possible, harvest curly kale only after it has been exposed to frost.

It will then be much tastier. There is also no need for concern, because it will also withstand heavier frosts. Laying hawthorn branches or other thorny brushwood around the edges is the best deterrent against rabbit browsing.

1233   It is essential to protect Florence fennel against night frosts.

Plants that are not yet ready to harvest should be covered or built over with foil to protect against the effects of frost; they must nevertheless be harvested before the onset of heavier frosts at the latest. If kept in a cool cellar, with their roots heeled-in in moist sand, the plants can be stored until November.

1234   Celeriac (root celery) will continue to grow as late as October, but it must be harvested before the onset of heavier frosts.

Since the tubers are partly aboveground, they will suffer if the temperature falls below freezing. Do not harvest celeriac in a frozen state; it should be left to thaw out completely first.

1235   When harvesting celery, neither the tubers nor the heart leaves may be damaged.

A digging fork is the best tool for harvesting. It can be inserted in the soil well below the tubers, which can then be levered out of the ground. Gently knock or shake off any earth sticking to the tubers, while being careful not to harm them.

1236   Once celery is removed from the ground it must be prepared for heeling in immediately.

If it is left to lie with its leaves, these will draw moisture from the tubers, which will then begin to go soft. However, do not cut off the leaves, but instead remove them by hand (except for the heart leaves). The heart leaves should be left to remain on the tubers for heeling in. The remnants of the other leaves are scraped off with a blunt knife or a suitably fashioned piece of wood, and the roots cut off with a sharp knife to leave about an inch remaining.

Young celery leaves can be dried and used as cooking herbs.

1237 **A cool cellar or an earth clamp is suitable for storing celery tubers.**

In the cellar, moist sand is the most suitable heeling-in substrate. Plant the tubers into this side by side, so that the heart leaves and the heads of the tuber remain uncovered. The earth clamp is fashioned as described in ▶ **TIP 1240**.

1238 **Kohlrabi intended for winter use should be harvested before the onset of heavier frosts.**

For this, remove the leaves, except for the young heart leaves, and cut the stumps just underneath the tuber. Prepared in this way, the kohlrabi can be stored in earth clamps. ▶ **TIP 1240** For heeling-in in the cellar, the stumps along with the roots should remain on the tubers. The heeling in is done in moist earth or in sand.

1239 **Rutabagas and turnips should be left in the earth for as long as possible. However, they may not be exposed to heavier frosts.**

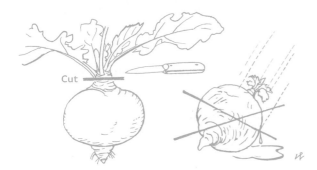

Cut

Rutabagas must not be damaged during harvesting because of the risk of them rotting in storage. Cut the leaves off cleanly about an inch above the rutabaga head. Harvest them during dry weather, since rutabagas that have been harvested when wet can easily rot. The best place for storage is an earth clamp. ▶ **TIP 1240** Smaller quantities can also be stored in the cellar. However, it must be cool there or the rutabagas will sprout shoots and become unusable.

Rutabagas are best harvested along with their roots and heeled-in in moist sand in the cellar.

1240 **Earth clamps may be dug only 4 to 6 in. deep and should be protected against mice.**

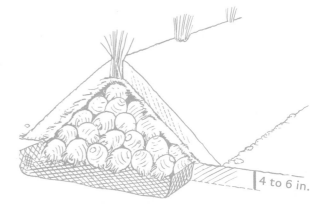

4 to 6 in.

Stack the harvested rutabagas, turnips, or other appropriate root vegetable in a pile that tapers off toward the top and cover with dry straw. Then pile the excavated earth evenly over the straw layer. Reinforce the earth layer further only if heavier frosts are expected. To aerate the clamp, a straw bundle approximately 4 in. thick is used, which must be in contact with the vegetables. A tightly meshed wire netting is the best protection against mice and should also be laid beneath the vegetables.

1241 White, red, and savoy cabbage will withstand certain degrees of cold, but they should still be harvested during the last days of October.

If cabbage is harvested in a frozen state, considerable bruising will result through handling and transportation, which will quickly turn to rot once the cabbage has thawed again. Wet harvested cabbage, too, can be stored for only a very limited time in clamps and in the cellar.

1242 Winter cabbage ▸ TIP 1241 is best stored in the cellar. Storage in earth clamps can often lead to considerable losses.

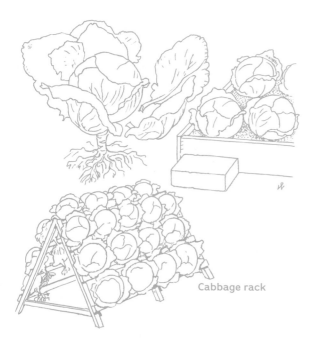

Cabbage rack

For heeling-in in the cellar, lift the cabbages out of the soil along with their roots. Then remove the outermost enveloping leaves so that only two or three leaves remain. The heads can be heeled-in in moist sand, stored on shelves, hung with the heads facing downward, or stored in a cabbage rack. Larger quantities are stored piled up in a pyramid with the stumps facing inward. Adequate aeration is important at all times. For overwintering in earth clamps, the stump is cut off. The clamps are prepared as described in ▸ TIP 1240.

Harvest cabbages for storage in dry weather to reduce losses from rot.

1243 During the last days in October, remove all horseradish roots from the earth and stack in moist sand in the cellar.

Horseradish is completely winter hardy, but it cannot be dug up when there are ground frosts. In the cellar, the plants are available at any time. The cellar must be cool, since otherwise the horseradish will sprout shoots and become worthless. When digging up the plants from the soil, even the smallest root fragments must be dug up as well. Otherwise, they will sprout shoots in the following year and become a very troublesome weed.

1244 Carrots that are intended for winter requirements should be removed from the ground on a dry day during the second half of October.

A digging fork is the most appropriate tool for this. Any carrots that have been damaged, despite taking all care, should be excluded from the harvest. The leaves should not be cut off, but twisted off instead, since otherwise the carrot heads will easily rot.

1245 Carrots are best overwintered in an earth clamp, and those for consumption in the short term stored in the cellar.

Prepare the earth clamp as described in ▸ TIP 1240. Effective protection against mice should be prioritized. Carrots are also at risk from mice in the cellar, where it is best to set mousetraps. In the cellar, the carrots should be heeled-in in moist sand.

1246 The fruits of vegetable peppers grown under glass should be harvested during the second half of October.

Despite the glass protection, the temperatures at this time will be so low that no further growth can be expected. However, even the half-developed fruits will still be usable as vegetables.

1247 Although parsnip roots will also withstand heavier frosts, it is better to harvest them in the fall and store them in clamps.

They should be harvested carefully using a digging fork, in order not to damage the roots, and the leaves should be twisted off. They will also make good fodder. Store parsnip roots in clamps in exactly the same way as carrots. If the roots are to be left in the ground over winter, they are best covered with a layer of leaves and brushwood so that they can be harvested at any time if need be.

1248 Leeks should be harvested in late October, and only in the quantities that are likely to be used in the foreseeable future.

The leeks are heeled-in in moist sand in the cellar after the roots and leaves have been shortened a little. The remaining leeks should be left out in the open, since leeks are relatively winter hardy, as long as the corresponding varieties have been selected.

Leek varieties with long stalks must be heeled-in in the cellar or a cold frame.

1249 Radicchio will withstand frosts of short duration only, down to 23°F.

If lower temperatures are expected, the vegetables must be harvested. Dig up plants with well-developed heads along with their roots, remove most of the outermost enveloping leaf, and heel in the plants in the cellar or a cold frame. In this way, the heads will stay fresh for longer.

1250 Winter radishes that have been harvested too early will not keep well. Accordingly, harvest them only when heavier frosts are imminent.

Radishes must be harvested in dry weather, and must not be damaged. Any earth sticking to them should be removed carefully and the leaves twisted off cleanly. Whether they should be stored in the cellar or in an earth clamp ▸ TIP 1240 over winter depends on the quantity involved. The cellar must be frost-free; a few degrees above freezing is best. If heeled-in in moderately moist sand, they will keep until the spring.

1251 When harvesting beets, avoid damage to prevent rotting in storage.

Twist off the leaves, rather than cutting them off. Depending on the harvested quantities, store the beets in earth clamps or in moist sand in the cellar.
▸ TIP 1239 and ▸ TIP 1240

1252 Although black salsify will not freeze in the ground even in severe frost, it should be harvested toward the end of October.

Harvesting according to requirements becomes very difficult once the earth has frozen solid. Frost penetration can be avoided only if the planted area and the immediate surroundings are covered with a thick protective covering layer. For this, use rotted stable manure, straw, or leaves. In severe winters, the layer must be 6 to 8 in. thick and sheltered from the wind.

1253 Careful harvesting is important if black salsify is to keep well when heeled in.

Use a spade when harvesting, and carefully twist off the leaves. Heel in the roots upright and in rows in moderately moist sand in a very cool cellar.

1254 The task of cutting off the asparagus foliage from the white asparagus that has been planted in the spring is combined with backfilling the earth.

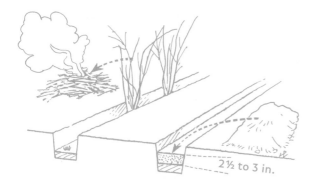

In these one-year-old plantings, the heads of the plants are only about an inch beneath the earth. To avoid damaging them, cut the foliage flush with the earth. Afterward, backfill the ditches with a layer of earth 2 ½ to 3 in. thick. For this, use some of the excavated earth lying next to the ditches.

1255 The yellowed asparagus foliage from cropped plots should be cut off around ¾ in. beneath the soil surface and burned.

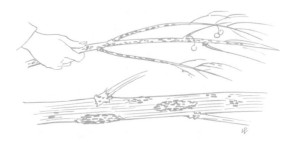

Asparagus foliage should not be placed in the compost. It may carry disease agents, such as harmful asparagus rust, which would then spread dramatically in the following year.

1256 Spinach and lamb's lettuce sowed in September (▸TIP 1149 and ▸TIP 1138, respectively) are given light winter protection during the last days of October.

Spruce twigs are the most suitable material for this. They prevent the danger of winter losses resulting from severe frost.

1257 Winter endives can be stored in a well-aerated cellar for winter use.

Before the onset of heavier frosts, remove the endives along with their roots from the soil and heel them in in moist sand in the cellar. Tie the plants together in bunches to save space. In a cold frame, endives will be protected from frost for a considerable time if the frame is covered with mats or similar material. The frames should be well ventilated in frost-free weather.

1258 The right time to harvest sugarloaf is from around mid-October.

Individual heads may also be harvested earlier. When determining the best time for the harvest, note that sugarloaf can withstand frosts down to 21°F well, which means that it is possible to harvest it as late as

November in favorable weather conditions. Even better is to harvest the plants along with their roots, and without the enveloping leaf, and to heel them in in sand in the cellar or another suitable room. They will then remain usable until January. The plants' use in the kitchen is comparable to that of chicory and winter endives. Cut into small strips, the leaves will make an extremely tasty salad, but they will also have an excellent flavor if cooked or steamed in butter.

> *If harvested along with the roots and planted in moist sand in the cellar, chicory and endive can be used until late January. Be sure to remove the enveloping leaf.*

1259 Store well-dried cooking onions in a dry, airy place at low temperatures.

If storing them on a house floor that is not always safe from frost, place them in a shallow layer. Do not touch frozen onions; then, once they have thawed out, they will then be just as usable as before.

1260 Lovers of garden cress and chervil can also sow these plants in pots, clay bowls, or shallow boxes.

Only very extensive sowing and a well-lit site will result in successful growth. Both these vitamin-rich spice herbs deserve a great deal more recognition than they currently receive.

1261 Lavender and sage that have been cut back in August (▸ TIP 1088 and ▸ TIP 1090, respectively) need winter protection in the last days of October.

Cover the soil between the plants 2 ½ in. high with rotted stable manure or with leaves. Afterward, distribute a layer of spruce twigs over the plants.

1262 In the last days of October, parsley and chives that have been planted in pots (▸ TIP 1157 and ▸ TIP 1159, respectively) are placed on a light windowsill.

15 Oct 30 Oct 15 Nov 30 Nov

At first, the soil should be kept just moderately moist. Unlike chives, parsley needs only a little water even after it has sprouted shoots. To harvest chives continually, place only one or two pots on the windowsill every two weeks or so. The remaining pots should be left in a frost-free place.

1263 Remove parsley roots from the ground before the harvest is hindered by frost.

Twist off the foliage rather than cutting it off. For using the roots as herbs for making soup, they should be heeled in or stored in clamps in the same way as carrots. Planted in pots ▸ TIP 1157, leaves can also be harvested in winter. However, the leaves will not be curly like those in normal cut parsley.

1264 All vegetable pepper fruits must be harvested by mid-October, even when they have been protected under glass in September.

All partially developed (green) peppers should also be plucked. They will continue to ripen and will then have good spice characteristics. Spicy peppers must be dried while they still have a hot taste.

1265 If heavier frosts are expected in late October, cover peppermint plants with spruce brushwood.

Leaves are unsuitable, while straw can be used in an emergency. Lay the spruce brushwood in two layers so that there will be no losses during winters with little snow.

1266 In October, the first oyster mushrooms can appear on wooden stumps that have been inoculated in April.

However, this applies only to cultures on softwood species. To develop fruiting bodies, oyster mushrooms need the effect of low temperatures that can be expected from October on. The mushrooms grow relatively slowly and need 10 to 14 days to attain a suitable size for harvesting. If grown on hardwoods, the harvest will need to wait until spring. This also applies to changeable agaric, velvet foot, and other species that grow on wood.

ORNAMENTAL PLANTS

Ornamental Gardens

1267 In windy regions, windbreaks are recommended for protecting larger gardens.

Hedges are not meant to block wind altogether, but merely to reduce the wind force. Accordingly, completely closed hedges are unsuitable for this purpose. These would deflect the wind upward, but not prevent it falling back into the garden uninterrupted. Light hedges, however, break up the wind in such a way that it blows through the garden with only half the force. For this reason, always establish windbreaks at right angles to the prevailing wind direction.

1268 Trees or shrubs with an erect growth habit are especially suitable for establishing a windbreak.

Since windbreaks occupy a strip of garden land, for smaller gardens, only species that do not spread out horizontally can be considered, such as a pyramidal form with nearly columnar growth.

1269 For demarcating garden boundaries, select a hedge rather than a fence, if possible.

Hedges are suitable for both visual and wind protection, but they should also occupy as little cultivated land as possible. They also provide a habitat for birds, beetles, and other useful animals. For this reason, the choice of tree or shrub species is very important. Common hornbeam (*Carpinus betulus*) is particularly suitable, since it will withstand severe cutting back. Accordingly, hornbeam hedges can be kept very narrow. For additional trees and shrubs, see **TABLE 11**.

Unsheared hedges are more natural and attractive than those that are closely trimmed. They are also more likely to serve as homes for birds and other wildlife.

1270 Hedges for larger gardens should ideally be free-standing.

Hedges consisting of flowering trees and shrubs are especially appealing. They separate spaces in the garden and delight us with their flowers, which, given a selection of different species and varieties, can also provide floral splendor over long periods during the year. Thanks to their individual growth form, but also their different foliage, leaf coloration, and maybe the bark as well, a varied design effect can be achieved. The spacing between the individual trees or shrubs is dependent on the species.

1271 Trimmed hedges have a very formal, severe appearance.

They must always be well maintained. Individual, long branches sticking out of the hedge are just as unsightly as bare patches. Trimming the hedges once or more annually incurs a high labor and cost outlay. However, for demarcating a boundary without a fence, they can be quite important, especially in small gardens.

1272 Hedges consisting of deciduous trees or shrubs are best planted in October or March, while those with evergreen broad-leaved or coniferous species are planted in April/May or August/September.

The strip where a hedge is to be planted should be dug and worked to a considerable depth. For this, a ditch is excavated—16 in. wide for a single-row hedge, and 24 in. wide for a double-row hedge. The earth, one spade cut deep, is deposited next to the ditch. The base of the ditch is loosened to a considerable depth, and the earth of the uppermost layer backfilled again. Since hedges must generally remain standing over a period of decades, the earth should be enriched with humus. Accordingly, mix in plenty of compost earth.

1273 The plant requirement per yard of hedge depends on the plant species and manner of planting.

For a single-row hedge, three to five plants are sufficient for one yard. Plant wider hedges in two rows with a row interval of 8 to 10 in.; for the interval within a row, 10 to 12 in. is sufficient. Before setting the

plants in place, slightly cut back their roots. Dipping the roots in a thick clay slurry will promote good initial growth. Hedge plants need to stand firmly and may not be planted any deeper than they have already been in the tree nursery. One exception is privet (*Ligustrum*), which can be planted as deep as the lowest branches. At the end, the surface is designed as a hollow (with a slightly raised edge) so that irrigation water will not run off. If the trees or shrubs are not planted immediately, their roots should be kept well and truly moist.

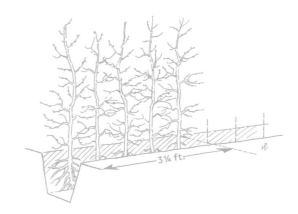

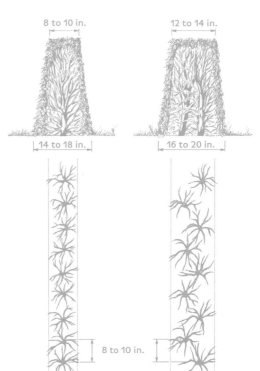

1274 Newly planted hedges should be cut well back so that they will become dense from below.

The plants will establish better if they are cut back immediately. This is especially important for hornbeam (*Carpinus*) and beech (*Fagus*), for which half of the length should be cut back. In the case of privet (*Ligustrum*), boxwood (*Buxus*), and other hedge plants, they should be cut back to around one third of their length.

1275 Old hedges with gaps in them can be closed up again through severe cutting back and intermediate planting.

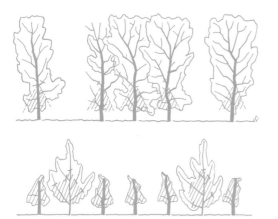

Only plants with dense roots are suitable for intermediate planting. As shown in the sketch, the old plants are cut back. Around two thirds of the length of the young, subsequently planted species are cut back. Their planting sites should be enriched with compost earth.

1276 As with all newly planted trees and shrubs, hedges, too, should be provided with a ground covering (mulch).

This will ensure that frost will not penetrate so quickly or so deeply. It will also ensure that the soil moisture will last longer, which is necessary for the hedge plants to become well established. Leaves can also be used as a mulch material, when they can be collected in the fall, or also bark.

1277 October is the best time for planting deciduous ornamental shrubs.

If the shrubs are planted by mid-October, they will still develop so many fibrous roots before the onset of heavier frosts that they will begin to grow as soon as the following spring. This especially applies to robust climbers and creepers such as ivy (*Hedera*), Virginia creeper (*Parthenocissus*), and honeysuckle (*Lonicera*).

1278 Sensitive ornamental shrubs such as butterfly bush (*Buddleja*), Warminster broom (*Cytisus ×praecox*), and St. John's wort (*Hypericum*) are best planted in the spring.

If planted in the fall, they will need special protection. Accordingly, creepers and climbers, too, such as clematis (*Clematis*), birthwort (*Aristolochia*), silver lace vine or Russian vine (*Fallopia baldschuanica*, syn. *Polygonum aubertii*), and wisteria (*Wisteria*) should be planted only in the spring.

1279 Every ornamental shrub needs as much space as necessary for it to develop unhindered, depending on the species.

Accordingly, it is crucial to know in advance how wide and how high the fully grown shrub will be. The growth height is particularly important, so that the lower shrubs will not be crowded out by the taller ones. **TABLE 9**, **TABLE 10**, and **TABLE 12**

1280 Soil preparation and fertilizer application are just as important for ornamental plants as they are for fruit trees and shrubs, for example.

For newly planted ornamental shrubs, rather than working stable manure into the soil, use the manure as a ground covering. It will still benefit the shrubs as soon as any digging takes place. The ground covering prevents any penetration by frost and retains soil moisture for longer.

1281 When planting ornamental shrubs, they should be cut back somewhat to achieve a balance between the branches and roots.

Depending on the growth vigor, all the shoots should be cut back to half or two thirds of their length. Cut back weakly growing shrubs more.

1282 Keeping the roots moist until planting, anchoring the plants firmly in the ground, and thorough watering are important when planting ornamental shrubs.

After digging a hole that matches the size of the root ball, set the shrub in place at the same height that it had already been at the nursery, and backfill with earth. Then press the earth firmly around the stem and water thoroughly, so that the roots will come into immediate contact with the soil. However, excessive muddiness will do more harm than good. Afterward, cover the planting site with a mulch layer 3 to 4 in. deep. Dipping the roots into a clay slurry first will stimulate initial growth.

1283 Roses planted in October will produce more vigorous shoots in the spring.

Roses that have been planted in October will still produce new roots before the ground freezes over. As a result, they will then produce more vigorous shoots than roses planted in March or April, and they will also flower around 10 days earlier. On planting bush, standard, and climbing roses, see ▸ TIP 546 to ▸ TIP 550.

1284 The shoots of roses planted in October should be cut back only in the spring.

After planting, the shoots should be shortened only a little, by around a quarter of their length. If they are cut back to their final extent, there is a danger that they will freeze back even further in winter.

In fall, mound the grafting site of roses with soil as protection.

1285 In late October, give all roses, including newly planted ones, winter protection.

The shoots of longer-established roses, too, should be cut back only a little, and not to their final extent. The earth surrounding bush roses should be heaped up in such a way that the grafting site is covered with earth, and, in this way, is protected. In heavy soils, it is best to use compost earth for this purpose, and not the soil in the immediate vicinity of the planting site. The hillock must be sufficiently high that the rose is covered up to about 6 in. above the normal soil level. Standard roses should be bent over, and their crowns covered with earth as described in ▸ TIP 548. So they remain bent over, hold them in place in the ground by a hook (forked branch). Earth should cover the plant so that the bases of all the branches are covered to a depth of around 4 in. The stems can also be covered with earth or with spruce twigs.

1286 The Japanese rose (*Rosa rugosa*) is suitable for covering up unsightly places in the garden.

It will grow into dense thickets and delight us with its many white, pink, or red flowers. Its large rose hips are especially valuable and are useful in the household.

1287 Brushwood is essential as a covering for sensitive plants.

Brushwood from conifer species is especially suitable as sun protection in winter, which all evergreen plants in rock gardens and dry stone walls particularly need. It will greatly reduce their transpiration, and the plants will be able to better withstand the winter.

1288 As soon as the leaves begin to fall, lawns should be raked more frequently.

A leaf rake can be used for this. If the leaves are left on the lawn, expect rot to set in.

1289 Grass should be mown in October for the last time.

Any long-term weeds that may be present can be dug up at the same time. ▸ TIP 514 Additionally, the mown grass can be carefully raked away. Lawn areas treated this way will make a good (optical) impression during the winter months.

1290 In October, too, sturdy perennials can still be divided and planted until the onset of frost.

These include astilbes, elephant ears (*Bergenia*), knapweed or star thistle (*Centaurea*), leopard's bane (*Doronicum*), phlox (*Phlox*), coneflower (*Rudbeckia*), globeflowers (*Trollius*), and others. Following thorough watering, provide the planting site with a ground covering.

1291 Wintergreen perennials, including those in rock gardens, should not be covered with wind-blown leaves.

Leaves are dangerous for these plants, especially if the leaves are lying on them wet. Rot is then often unavoidable.

1292 The seeds of some perennials need exposure to frost to germinate (frost/cold germinators).

This applies to many alpine plants, such as the Christmas rose (*Helleborus niger*), gentians (*Gentiana*), and others. The seeds are sown in the fall; the containers remain outside. Frost and snow water have a beneficial effect on germination. If the seed is sown before it is fully ripe, it will likewise germinate more readily in most cases.

> *Dig non-hardy tubers and bulbs and store them in a frost-free place.*

1293 Dahlia bulbs are removed from the earth following the first frost.

They must not be damaged when they are dug out or they will rot. A digging fork should be used for this. Remove the earth between and on the tubers or bulbs. Cut back the aboveground parts to a residual length of about 4 in., so that there are no more leaf remnants. Bring the bulbs into an airy, dry, and frost-free room for overwintering. Only properly dried-out dahlia bulbs can be overwintered without damage. They can be stored piled up in pyramids, in which case the bulb collars should remain free. However, it is better if they are covered in a layer of dry garden earth.

1294 Late-flowering gladiolus varieties, too, must be removed from the ground.

Under no circumstances should you wait until the ground is already frozen. On digging up and drying, see ▸ TIP 1177 to ▸ TIP 1181.

1295 In the case of the gloriosa or climbing lily (*Gloriosa*), dig up the rootstock as soon as the aboveground parts are dying off.

The fleshy rhizomes should be dug up carefully with a digging fork to ensure that they are not damaged. Once they are well dried off, they are heeled-in in dry garden earth and overwintered at a temperature of around 59°F.

1296 Remove the canna lily (*Canna*) from the ground following the first night frost.

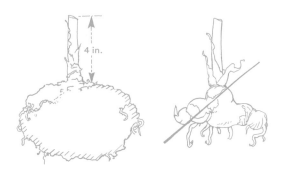

4 in.

The earth on the rhizomatous rootstock should not be shaken off. Cut back the aboveground parts to a residual length of 4 in. and remove all leaf remnants. The storage location must not be too cool; 50 to 54°F is best. Store the rootstocks in the winter storage just as they have been dug up. They are not dried beforehand.

1297 The bulbs or tubers of the Abyssinian or fragrant gladiolus (*Gladiolus murielae*, syn. *callianthus*), peacock flower or tiger flower (*Tigridia*), and Jacobean lily (*Sprekelia*) must be removed from the earth before the onset of frost.

They are treated and overwintered in the same way as for gladioli. Abyssinian or fragrant gladioli need overwintering temperatures of 59 to 64°F, and the Jacobean lily temperatures of around 54°F. The tubers of the peacock flower or tiger flower are overwintered under cool conditions, heeled-in in dry sand.

1298 The tubers of the montbretia (*Crocosmia*) can remain in the ground over winter.

However, these should be covered with a thick layer of leaves or compost earth. On exposed sites, the protective layer must be around 10 in. thick. Left in place where they are, montbretias will bloom the most abundantly. If they are removed from the earth, they should be treated in the same way as gladioli. ▸ TIP 1177 to ▸ TIP 1181

1299 Cyclamens (*Cyclamen*) should be carefully protected from severe frosts.

The species *Cyclamen coum*, *C. purpurescens*, and ivy-leaved cyclamen (*C. hederifolium*) are considered long lasting and winter hardy. Provide *C. coum* with some winter protection; if grown in a winter garden or cold flower window, it will bloom as early as January. On its native sites, such as in the high-altitude regions surrounding Lake Garda in northern Italy, it is wintergreen. In central Europe, it loses its leaves in winter. It produces new shoots again only after flowering in late summer. The ivy-leaved cyclamen, meanwhile, is a common sight in gardens. It blooms in late summer and enters dormancy in May. Pine needles make the best protective covering. For normal winters, a 2 in. thick layer over which spruce twigs can be laid is sufficient.

1300 Plant *Iris* ×*hollandica*, the Dutch iris, by late October.

This Dutch iris should be planted in late October, or in early November in warmer situations, at intervals of around 3 in., and approximately 4 in. deep. It blooms in May/June. There are varieties with violet-blue, yellow, and white flowers. A covering layer, about 4 in. thick, of compost earth or leaves is beneficial, and the plants can also be grown in a pot. The flowers will then develop earlier in the spring. They are mostly grown in greenhouses for cut flowers.

1301 Mulleins (*Verbascum*) are a special focal point in the garden.

Their vivid yellow flowers catch the eye from afar, with new ones produced each day until well into October. As a tea infusion, they bring relief from irritations of the upper airway (bronchitis and cough). The plant grows vertically upward to reach a height of around 6 ½ ft.; however, thanks to its slender growth habit, it does not overshadow any other plants. It is a biennial: the leaf rosettes appear in the first year after sowing, and the flowers in the second year. Once it is present in the garden, it is self-sowing, which means that you can look forward to flowering mulleins every year. Should a young plant appear somewhere where it is not wanted, it can be transplanted in summer. Generally, several plants will appear each year. The most vigorous are then selected and planted wherever they are desired the following year. They are most attractive when grown in groups of three. The site should be sunny, dry, and low in nutrients. Young plants are available from special nurseries in the spring, or they can also be grown from seed.

Terraces and Balconies

1302 In October, tub plants that can withstand night frosts down to 23°F for a brief time are moved to a suitable site.

In early October, there will often be night frosts down to 23°F already. When this happens, leadwort (*Plumbago*), manzanita or strawberry tree (*Arbutus*), spotted laurel (*Aucuba*), myrtle (*Myrtus*), oleander (*Nerium*), European fan palm (*Chamaerops*), bottlebrush bush (*Callistemon*), olive (*Olea*), and others should be moved to as sheltered a site as possible, until more severe or continuous frosts make it necessary to store them in frost-free winter quarters.

Bring container plants that you want to overwinter inside before the first frost. They will thrive best in cool and bright conditions.

1303 When hardened off, some tub plants will tolerate night frosts down to 14°F for a brief period, and can remain outdoors for a considerable time.

In particular, these include crape myrtle (*Lagerstroemia indica*), bay or laurel (*Laurus*), pomegranate (*Punica*), Chinese windmill palm or fan palm (*Trachycarpus*), laurustinus (*Viburnum tinus*), and others. These will grow better outdoors on a site that is as sheltered as possible than in rooms that are too warm and dark.

1304 In winter, tub plants make decorative leafy plants for light, unheated rooms.

In particular, windmill palms or fan palms, laurels, myrtles, loquats or Japanese medlars (*Eriobotrya japonica*), and others are suitable, even if the rooms such as stairwells, glazed verandas, or atria are not completely frost-free. If the plants are kept in a cool place, they will need only a little water, although the earth must not be allowed to dry out altogether.

1305 Tuber begonias can overwinter in dry garden earth.

Following the first night frosts, remove the tubers from the ground, and cut the shoot about ½ to ¾ in. above the tuber. When properly dried off, they are layered in dry garden earth and overwintered in a room at temperatures of 50 to 59°F.

1306 Move geraniums, fuchsias, and carnations to their winter site early.

They must not have suffered frost damage or they will rot. A frost-free, light, and airy room is best for over-wintering these plants, which should be left in boxes, keeping the earth almost dry, but providing ventilation as often as possible.

Winter Gardens, Flower Windows, and Rooms

1307 Persian violets (*Cyclamen*) can be kept in rooms only if they are left to stand in a light, cool place.

Otherwise, the buds will not develop further, the leaves will soon turn yellow, and the plants will die.

1308 If bromeliads are being kept in warm rooms, their leaf-tanks must always be filled with water in the winter as well.

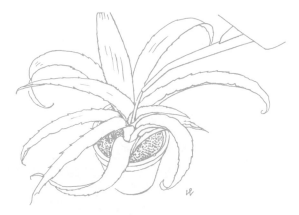

This is just as important as general watering, and also increases the air humidity in the room. Rainwater that is not too cold or prepared tap water is perfectly suitable. The green heads of pineapple fruits can be used for propagation. Before it is planted in a substrate of bark humus and sand, the cut surface must be allowed to dry properly. High levels of soil warmth and air humidity are required. The plants themselves will become quite large. A pineapple plant planted in the winter garden is particularly attractive.

1309 Crocus tubers and snow-drop bulbs can be planted in pots in early October and encouraged to flower indoors.

Several flower bulbs should always be planted in garden earth in pots that are not too large. After watering, they are left to stand in a cool place at 43 to 50°F. This way, the plants will be sure to bloom; if kept at warmer temperatures, they will develop only leaves.

1310 Persian buttercups (*Ranunculus asiaticus*) are planted in October.

Leave the tubers to soak in warm water and then plant them about 1½ in. deep, surrounded by a sand layer, in containers with humic, loose soil. They should stand in a frost-free and cool place, but this should be only moderately moist, since they can easily rot. Kept in an airy and increasingly moist place, they will develop a shoot with flowers early the following year, provided the temperatures do not exceed 59°F.

> *In fall, carefully inspect indoor plants for insects and diseases. Treat or discard any that are infected.*

1311 Since light conditions worsen steadily from late October on, the growth of most indoor plants will slow down significantly.

In rooms that are heated only a little or not at all, the water consumption will be low, and, accordingly, the plants should be watered less. In warm rooms, however, the plants will transpire a great deal of water, and should be watered plentifully. As a rule, however, the plants should be watered only if the soil surface is dry.

NOVEMBER

FALL

In November, the oncoming winter dormancy of the plants in the garden is already apparent. Many of them will need to be protected from frost and cold at this time, and so fallen leaves from trees and shrubs can serve as winter protection. Some deciduous trees will still delight us with their splendid fall coloring, such as maples with their leaves in various shades of orange and yellow, and oak and rowan trees in vivid red.

Before the first frost, ponds and containers need to be drained, and exposed water lines turned off. For birds that do not migrate to warmer climes in the south, food will begin to become scarce. We can make them familiar with feeding sites and help them through the winter by providing suitable feed.

GENERAL

1312 In November, it is high time to seal any gaps in fences.

Rabbits and hares will manage to seek out even the smallest gaps. When making repairs and sealing gaps, the potential snow height may also need to be considered.

1313 As long as the compost earth has not already frozen, it should be steamed in preparation for sowing in spring.

Frozen earth produces too much steam itself when it is subjected to steam treatment. This then condenses to water, and the soil becomes muddy and unsuitable for sowing seed, because it has lost its structure. Steam-sterilizing the earth not only kills disease agents and the eggs and larvae of animal pests and weed seeds, but also frees up nutrients that have been fixed in the soil. To ensure this, the steam must be left to act on the soil for about one hour. Steam-treating smaller quantities may also be done in an oven at temperatures of around 195°F.

1314 In November, water containers should be emptied out so that they do not suffer damage in hard frost and develop leaks.

Water containers that are not firmly anchored in the ground are best tipped over after having first been emptied out. Hard frost can cause considerable damage to concrete basins and those with brick walls.

Accordingly, they should be drained in November at the latest, and then sealed with a watertight covering. This work can already be done in October if water is otherwise no longer required for the garden. An exception is large fishponds (with a water depth of at least 32 in.) in which ice-free areas can be ensured with the aid of reeds or twigs that have been tied together.

1315 Water lines should be turned off and drained in November at the latest.

Frost can already be common in November. Accordingly, water lines that have not been made frost-safe should now be emptied out, and the taps opened so that no water can collect in the lines. In frost-safe lines, standpipes, and water taps especially, should be well protected!

1316 If there is already frost and snow in November, birds will have difficulty finding food.

When there is severe frost or snow on the ground, this is the time to begin feeding our feathered helpers in biological pest control. Blue tits especially should become accustomed to feeding sites through the use of bird-feeding rings. However, feeding should not be overdone at this time of year. ▶ TIP 63 On mild days, or when there is little frost, blue tits should still be eating plenty of insects—but they will neglect to do so if they are otherwise being overfed.

VEGETABLES

1317 Heel in the last Chinese cabbages in the cellar before the onset of severe frosts.

See ▸ TIP 1230 for more details on the procedure. Chinese cabbages will keep better heeled-in in the cellar than if left outdoors.

1318 In late November, a supply of leeks should also be heeled-in in the cellar or in a cold frame.

However, this will need to be done before the earth freezes solid. See also ▸ TIP 1248.

1319 With the exception of curly kale and Brussels sprouts, all stands of cabbage species that are still remaining outdoors should be harvested.

On handling the harvested products, see ▸ TIP 1238 to ▸ TIP 1239.

1320 If rhubarb shoots are to be grown in the cellar in January, the rootstocks should already be removed from the ground in the late fall.

Vigorous plants that are three to four years old are the most suitable. However, it is also possible to use older plants that will need to be replaced by younger ones in any case. As soon as the leaves have died off,

dig up the rootstocks along with their earth balls and initially lay them to one side in a cold shed or similar room. The frost will stimulate the rootstocks' shoot production. They will remain there until shoot production begins in January. It is necessary only to ensure that the root balls do not dry out.

1321 If black salsify is left in the ground, during November it must be covered with a protective layer 6 to 8 in. thick.

Rotted stable manure or leaves that are as dry as possible may be used for this. To keep the covering material dry, lay a sheet of foil on top and secure it against the wind. This will greatly increase the layer's insulation properties.

1322 With the onset of more severe frosts, protective coverings for the earth clamps ▸ TIP 1240 will need to be reinforced if no snow cover is present.

Straw and earth may be used for this. Two layers of bubble-wrap foil may also be used (in addition to wind protection), but it is essential to remove these again in mild weather.

1323 If asparagus or horseradish will be planted in the spring, preparations can already be made in November.

The land under consideration should be subjected to triple digging (white asparagus) or double digging (green asparagus and horseradish) as preparation. Enriching the soil with humus can be done using rotted stable manure or peat; see ▸ TIP 1217 to ▸ TIP 1219.

1324 Winter endives that have been heeled-in in the cellar ▸ TIP 1257 should be monitored continually to ensure that there are no losses.

These can rot very easily and can also infect neighboring plants. Moisten the sand repeatedly so the winter endives do not wilt.

ORNAMENTAL PLANTS

Ornamental Gardens

1325 Gladiolus bulbs should be stored in an overwintering room only once they are dry and have been cleaned.

The time for cleaning has come when the old bulb from the soil can be easily removed from the newly formed ones. Remove the remaining stalk section on the bulb when the cleaning is done. After cleaning, the bulbs can be treated against fungal attack.

> *Fall is a good time to feed the soil by applying a layer of compost to garden beds. If gladiolus bulbs are stored properly, they will produce beautiful blooms for many years to come.*

1326 Gladiolus bulbs should be sorted into diseased and damaged bulbs.

Diseased bulbs must not be stored along with healthy ones or there will be a risk of infection. Store slightly damaged bulbs separately from the others.

1327 Gladiolus bulbs need a dry, airy, overwintering place with temperatures of around 41 to 50°F.

The bulbs are best placed in shallow crates, in two layers. Store the crates one on top of the other, so that relatively little space is required. Gladiolus bulbs can also be stored in foil bags hung up in an airy place. These bags must be perforated so that condensation does not build up inside. During the winter, inspect the bulbs every four weeks or so for pests or diseases. If storing different varieties, remember to label them clearly.

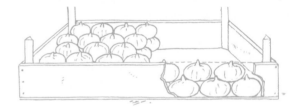

1328 Gladiolus bulbs can be affected by hard and dry rot.

These diseases can be recognized by brown, slightly sunken flecks with a partially raised edge. Severely affected bulbs will dry out, turn brown or black, and become mummified. To avoid damage, follow the instructions in ▶ TIP 1325 and ▶ TIP 1326.

1329 Storage rot or *Penicillium* bulb rot is usually the result of poor storage conditions.

These disease agents especially occur on damaged bulbs. Tissue damage resulting from other disease agents may also be an attack point for storage rot. Preventive treatment for all bulbs prior to storage will also help guard against storage rot. However, proper storage is still necessary.

> *A protective covering of leaves and brush can reduce the loss of marginally hardy plants in the garden.*

1330 Pampas grass (*Cortaderia selloana*) generally needs some winter protection.

It loves well-drained soils, and, in harsh climates, good winter protection. Accordingly, in November, heap up dried leaves around the plant, with a light topping of brushwood so that the wind cannot blow the leaves away. It is also helpful to tie the plant's leaves together at the top so that rainwater will not penetrate so easily into the interior of the plant, where it can cause rot. The plant's leaves are not trimmed, and dried-up leaves should be removed only in the spring. Young plants can also be overwintered in pots in a frost-free room.

1331 In exposed situations, wintergreen perennials in rock gardens can be provided with a loose protective layer of conifer brushwood.

In winters with little snow, the plants will suffer not from the cold, but rather from too much sun. This stimulates the sap flow, but if the ground is frozen the plants will be unable to take up any moisture and may dry out.

1332 In moist biotopes (swamp pools) on exposed sites, the plants should be provided with winter protection in early November.

Remove the dried-off shoots of the swamp plants. Then provide the plants with a protective covering of conifer branches.

1333 Water lilies and other aquatic plants in containers should be brought into suitable overwintering rooms after the pools have been emptied.

A light, frost-free room with temperatures of 34 to 41°F is the most suitable. In warmer temperatures, the plants will produce shoots prematurely. Before putting the plants into storage, clean them so that no rotting can occur. If necessary, water lilies can also be overwintered in empty ponds under a thick layer of leaves. Water lilies in very deep ponds can remain in the water, but the water must be so deep that it will not freeze to the bottom.

1334 If fish are to be overwintered in garden ponds, ensure that the entire water surface will not freeze over.

There are several possibilities for avoiding this. Polystyrene structures to keep the water from freezing over are available from specialist outlets. However, these structures must not be too small—they should have a diameter of at least 20 to 24 in. They are placed in the deepest part of the pond, and an air tube then ensures the necessary gas exchange. Floating pieces of wood, polystyrene plates, or bundled reeds (or also reed mats, straw bundles, or many thin bamboo sticks) can help to keep a place in the pond ice-free. A covering layer of small, transparent, polyethylene balls can also be useful. In long or particularly hard frosts, the pond will need to be monitored constantly. If there are many fish in the pond, an ice-free place may well be essential to their survival. In this case, it may be necessary to install a pond heating system with a thermostat.

1335 If the pond has already frozen over, it is vital not to hack a hole in the ice.

The noise would disturb the fish in their winter dormancy, and the resulting noise and shock waves could also injure them.

1336 If the pond is not deep enough, the fish will need to be overwintered in a pool in the house.

To be completely certain that all the fish will survive the winter, they should be removed from the pond and overwintered in a suitable pool in a cool, frost-free room. The fish should hardly be fed at all during the winter.

1337 Most grasses thrive best in well-aerated soils.

Well-aerated soils can be maintained by working in compost earth and bark humus mixed with sand. A soil sample can be taken to determine whether lime is needed. ▸ TIP 810

1338 In harsh climatic situations, provide biennial summer flowers, too, with a protective covering of conifer branches.

This is especially important for forget-me-nots (*Myosotis*), but is also recommended for Canterbury bells (*Campanula medium*), wallflowers (*Erysimum cheiri*), and pansies (*Viola ×wittrockiana*). Otherwise, losses in winters with little snow will be unavoidable.

1339 In harsh situations, butterfly bush (*Buddleja*), hibiscus (*Hibiscus syriacus*), salt cedar or tamarisk (*Tamarix*), and fringe tree (*Chionanthus virginicus*) will freeze back to the ground in winters with little snow.

Aim to prevent this by covering the ground underneath these shrubs with a layer of leaves up to 8 in. thick. Additionally, leaves should be heaped up high around every shrub.

Evergreen trees and shrubs should be protected from sun and strong winds during the winter.

1340 In harsh situations, protect rhododendron, holly (*Ilex*), and cherry laurel (*Prunus laurocerasus*) by building a light framework over them, covered with conifer branches.

This will reduce water loss through transpiration on sunny days. This framework will also protect against harsh east winds that likewise contribute to the plants drying out. Cover the soil underneath the plants with leaves too.

1341 Loosely piled conifer brushwood up to a height of around 4 ft. will provide sufficient winter protection for large-flowering clematis (*Clematis*) varieties.

Although most varieties are winter hardy, this is still advisable in harsh situations where the plants are exposed to east winds. As a result, they will not freeze back to the ground.

Terraces and Balconies

1342 Winter-hardy plants on balconies and terraces also need protection from frost.

The roots of winter-hardy plants in containers are especially endangered. The plants are exposed to frost not only from above, but also through the container walls from the sides and from below. The container walls provide no protection against severe frost. For this reason, in addition to a protective covering of conifer brushwood, protection at the sides is also required. The best solution is to surround containers—such as pots, bowls, and troughs—with polystyrene (also as a layer underneath) or to put them into larger containers that are filled with dry earth and crushed polystyrene flakes.

1343 Some tub plants need only a little light during winter.

Deciduous plants such as cockspur coral tree (*Erythrina crista-galli*), pomegranate (*Punica*), pink siris or silk tree (*Albizia julibrissin*), fig (*Ficus carica*), and others will tolerate dark winter sites. However, dwarf and Chinese windmill palms or fan palms will need rather more light. Important for all these plants is fresh air and soil that is moderately moist but never wet.

Winter Gardens, Flower Windows, and Rooms

1344 Many orchids enter a period of dormancy during the dark winter months.

Orchids on windowsills must still be sprayed frequently with water even during the dormant period because of the dry room air. In winter gardens, the relative air humidity is generally higher; here, a moderately moist plant substrate is nearly always sufficient. Plants that are growing new shoots must be watered a little more.

> *As the days grow shorter reduce the watering of indoor plants, letting the surface of the soil become dry to the touch between watering.*

1345 In November, take great care when it comes to maintaining indoor plants.

The light levels at the windows will also fall further and further at this time, and plant growth will decline. This means the plants will need less water. However, the water supply should be tailored to the room temperature.

1346 If the room is heated up more, the air humidity will fall.

Indoor fountains and air humidifiers can help to a certain extent. Bowls of water on the windowsill are more effective, with the plants placed above them on a framework; moist air will rise continuously in this way. However, the warm, dry air must not be allowed to affect the plants directly. If the windowsill is too small, it should be widened accordingly. A protective screen can also be helpful.

1347 In dry room air, thrips and red spider mites especially can spread.

These tiny pests can be recognized only by using a magnifying glass. Thrips are almost black, while their larvae are yellowish. The red spider mite may be a vivid red, orange, or yellowish color. As a precaution, spray all plants frequently with water, since these pests do not like moisture. If the plants have been affected despite this, if possible, wash the leaves, especially the undersides, with a mixture of dishwashing liquid and vinegar, and repeat the procedure at intervals of several days. An approved insecticide should be used only in cases of severe infestation. Often better than spraying is the application of systemically effective substances that will enter the plant sap. There are also prepared sticks with this effect that can be pressed into the soil. Take care when using insecticides; the instructions on the packaging must be followed exactly.

> *Persian violets (Cyclamen) must be left to stand in a light and cool place or they will die off quickly. Place potted cyclamen in a bright cool spot in the house to prolong their bloom.*

1348   Persian violets (*Cyclamen*) are unsuitable for warm rooms.

They like a light and cool place, since otherwise none of the flower buds will develop, the leaves will turn yellow, and the plants will become unsightly and die. In moderately warm rooms (up to 60°F), they will bloom in bright windows for months at a time. When watering, do not allow any water to get between the leaf and flower stalks or these will rot. It is best to add water to the saucer or a planter or cachepot, and to tip out any water that has not been taken up after about an hour. Persian violets love plant substrates that are not constantly wet.

1349   Camellias with buds must be left to stand in a cool place.

In strongly heated rooms, the air will become too dry. Camellias do not tolerate this well and will soon drop their buds. For the flowers to develop, temperatures of 37 to 46°F are already sufficient. The plants will then flower somewhat later, but they will be sure to do so, and for longer. At 59°F too, there will be no problems. It is important that the earth balls are always kept moist, but not wet.

1350   In late November, the first hyacinths and tulips can be put in a warmer place.

Here, however, the flowering stems must already be visible outside the bulb. For these plants to develop well, they must still be left in the dark. Accordingly, cover the jars or pots with light-tight cones. If the plants are watered too little during this time, the flowers will generally fail to grow. ▶ **TIP 1205** and ▶ **TIP 1206**

DECEMBER

WINTER

December is characterized by the holidays and the onset of winter; there are already cold frosty nights and the first days with plenty of snow. In frost-free weather, evergreen trees and shrubs should be watered, and vegetables and fruits in storage monitored constantly for signs of rot.

Hoar frost transforms the plant world into a winter wonderland. Especially attractive is the common or English holly, *Ilex aquifolium*. Its twigs with their decorative red fruits make splendid Christmas decorations. Take care, however, because the berries are poisonous. In the garden, the Christmas rose delights us with its white flowers, while in the winter garden we can enjoy beautiful flowering orchids and the splendid poinsettia.

GENERAL

1351 As soon as the gardening work in December is complete, thoroughly clean and grease all gardening tools.

This is especially important for spades, digging forks, and hoes, which should all be cleaned right back to the metal before being greased. Apply the grease or oil with a rag in a very thin layer only. Watering cans should be emptied and placed upside down, or, better still, hung up.

> *Well-maintained tools are easier to work with and last longer.*

1352 Cold frames that will be used again as early as February should be protected against severe freezing up.

Covering them with a layer of dry leaves about 12 in. thick is the best solution. Cover the area surrounding the cold frame as well or the frost will penetrate from the sides.

1353 If trellises are to be built, the necessary materials should be prepared.

All the slats need to be painted before the trellises are erected. Posts for freestanding trellises and wall hooks for wall-mounted ones should be protected against rust. Only galvanized wires should be used.

1354 Posts are required at the ends of freestanding trellises, and, in longer trellises, in between as well.

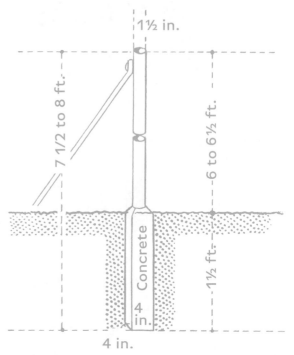

Iron pipes are better than wooden posts, which can quickly rot. The pipes should be at least 1 ½ in. in diameter. Since trellises are generally 6 to 6 ½ ft. high, pipes with a length of 7 ½ to 8 ft. are required, since about 1½ ft. of their length will be in a concrete base. About 4 to 8 in. of loose soil should then be added around the base. Concrete bases that are 1½ ft. long and 4 x 4 in. thick, in which the pipe ends are embedded ▸ **TIP 161**, will ensure stability. Seal the upper opening of the pipes against water ingress. The transition from the iron tube to the base should be at an angle, to enable rainwater to run off easily. The beginning and end posts are fitted with braces.

1355 The simplest trellis consists of horizontally stretched wires that are attached to wall hooks or secured firmly between posts.

Place the wires at intervals of 10 to 12 in. They will be sufficiently tight only if tension locks are used. The wall hooks must be long enough for the wires to be at least 6 in. from the wall.

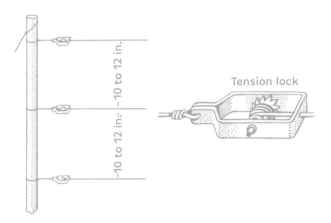

Tension lock

1356 In simple trellises, the vertical slats are attached to horizontal ones, which should have a thickness of ¾ × 1 ½ in. or 1 × 2 in.

As a rule, trellises are 6 ½ ft. high. The vertically standing slats are 5 ¾ to 6 ft. long and are attached 8 to 10 in. above the soil. A thickness of ½ × ¾ to ¾ × 1 in. (without knots in the wood) is sufficient. The interval from slat to slat is 10 to 12 in. In order that air can circulate freely between the trellis and the wall, intermediate spaces of 6 to 8 in. are required. Freestanding trellises with posts, between which three wires have been stretched, are suitable for raspberries and blackberries, for example, tied together in an arc, where they will produce an especially rich harvest.

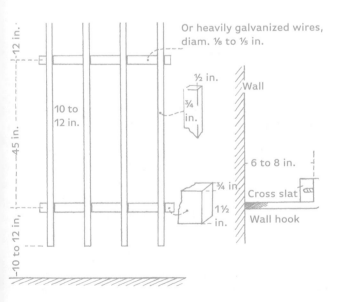

Or heavily galvanized wires, diam. ⅛ to ⅕ in.

Wall

½ in.
¾ in.

10 to 12 in.

12 in.

45 in.

10 to 12 in.

6 to 8 in.

¾ in.
1 ½ in.

Cross slat

Wall hook

1357 Trellises can consist of slats that are configured vertically and horizontally, or diagonally toward both sides.

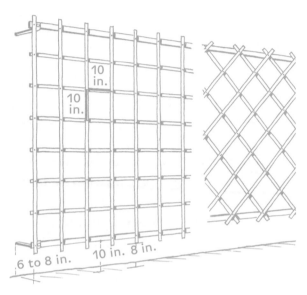

10 in.

10 in.

6 to 8 in.   10 in.   8 in.

The lengths of the sides of the squares should be at least 8 to 10 in. For these, knot-free slats that are ½ × ¾ in. thick are sufficient, held together at each intersecting point with a small finishing nail.

1358 Before the soil surface freezes over, measure the garden soil pH.

This can be done by conducting a soil test. For each area to be tested, a quantity of earth should be sampled at different points and mixed well before measuring the soil pH with a pH meter or litmus paper. The possible growth range of our cultivated plants is soil with pH values of between 4 and 8. The range between pH 6.5 and 7.4 is considered neutral; such neutral soil is suitable for growing most cultivated plants. Lower values indicate increasing soil acidity, which is suitable for rhododendrons and other acid-loving plants, for example. If the pH meter registers values of 7.5 and above, the soil is considered basic (alkaline), and only calcicolous plants can thrive there. ▶ TIP 810

1359 If it is possible to collect them, beech leaves should be used as a winter protection layer.

Beech leaves are highly suitable for this purpose because they rot only slowly. They can also be used in the garden as mulch, or to help warm the soil in cold frames in spring. When composted, they yield high-quality humus.

VEGETABLES

1360 Cold frames that are still occupied by winter endives and lamb's lettuce, for example, must be aerated thoroughly in frost-free weather.

This will prevent any risk of rot or mildew.

1361 Vegetables stored in the cellar should be monitored constantly to ensure that no rot patches develop.

Additionally, the cellar should be properly aired during every frost-free day. Use up any vegetables with rot patches immediately.

1362 Depending on the weather, the protective covering over earth clamps should be changed.

In severe frost, it should be built up further. ▶ TIP 1322 However, as soon as the weather is frost-free, remove the additional protection again. Otherwise, the clamps will become too warm, and rot will result.

1363 So curly kale will not turn brown in harsh east winds, provide a light, airy covering of spruce twigs, or cover with a winter protective fleece.

This is especially important in frosty weather when there is no snow. Harvesting, too, is made easier with such a protective covering. Meanwhile, hares and rabbits will not be able to get at the curly kale so easily.

1364 Enjoy Brussels sprouts at Christmas.

Brussels sprouts taste best after being exposed to the first light frost. When this happens, a proportion of the starch contained in the vegetables is transformed into sugar, lending the vegetables a slightly sweet taste. Harvest only as many Brussels sprouts as are required at any one time and leave the rest in the bed. Brussels sprouts are winter hardy; however, the plants should still be monitored regularly. If any have been affected by mold, it is best to harvest and use up the entire plant stand.

1365 In winter, it is worth experimenting again with the stores that have been built up during the summer.

Many dried herbs can be used for tea infusions. These include mint, marigold flowers, thyme, sage, fennel seeds, and many others. If they are stored separately in jars or tins, it is possible to constantly conjure up new flavor variations.

1366 Dried marigold flowers that you have gathered yourself can be processed to yield a useful ointment for skin care.

There are a number of formulations that can be used to make soothing ointments. When bottled in small quantities, the ointments will keep for several months.

1367 Hot peppers that you have grown and dried yourself should have a place in the kitchen.

When woven into a wreath with the dried stalks, they can make an attractive decoration for every kitchen, one that can be paired with garlic and onions.

1368 Go beyond sweet and sour beets.

If you're keen to try something new, why not follow the smoothie trend? Many vegetable species, such as beets, arugula, mint, cucumber, and basil, can be pureed in a blender. For a slightly sweeter taste, combine with avocado, banana, mango, or pineapple.

ORNAMENTAL PLANTS

Ornamental Gardens

1369 **In December, evergreen trees and shrubs should be watered once more.**

This is especially important if there has not been much precipitation in the fall. ▶ **TIP 1190** Trees and shrubs will still transpire water even on frosty days.

> *Water evergreen trees and shrubs well in late fall to help them survive the winter better.*

1370 **Christmas roses (*Helleborus niger*) should be protected from cold winds.**

The variety 'Praecox', with its particularly large white flowers, generally blooms in time for Christmas. In order that the blooms will not suffer, cover them with some conifer brushwood. ▶ **TIP 114** The Christmas rose is found in the Alps and elsewhere, and is protected under strict nature conservation legislation. All the plant parts are poisonous. The specific epithet *niger* means black, and refers to the black, rhizomatous roots. These were once used for making sneezing powder and snuff. They need exposure to frost to germinate. ▶ **TIP 1292**

Terraces and Balconies

1371 **Storms in the fall will often blow away winter protection on terraces and balconies.**

In order that the plants in bowls and troughs will not suffer from severe frost, ensure that the covering layers of conifer brushwood will not be blown away at any time.

Winter Gardens, Flower Windows, and Rooms

1372 **Higher humidity will benefit the plants' wellbeing.**

In winter, indoor plants suffer under poor light conditions, in overheated rooms, and in room air that is too dry. This especially applies to living rooms. However, in winter gardens and flower windows too, the air humidity can drop sharply through excessive heating when it has become very cold outside. This can be easily counteracted by misting or spraying plants.

> *Frequently misting houseplants will increase the air humidity at the same time.*

1373 **A stem covered in epiphytes is always a focal point in the winter garden.**

For this, either use a large branch of a stable wood species with as much secondary branching as possible, such as robinia, or fashion an epiphyte stem from plastic tubes, wire mesh, and cork. For anchoring, set the stem in concrete in a large clay pot, and then place some humic earth on top. Climbing plants can grow in this, such as the creeping or climbing fig (*Ficus pumila*) and many philodendron (*Philodendron*) species, which will then grow tendrils around the stem. Cork pieces and moss can be used to hide any unsightly areas. Plants that are suitable for growing in the branches include orchids, bromeliads (for example, tillandsias), ferns such as the attractive staghorn fern (*Platycerium*), and many other warmth- and moisture-loving flowering and leafy plants.

1374 Highlights in the winter garden include golden candle or lollipop plant (*Pachystachys lutea*) and shrimp plant (*Justicia brandegeeana*).

With their attractive spikes—golden-yellow in the golden candle or lollipop plant and reddish in the shrimp plant—both these plants are most effective when planted in groups. They can be heavily cut back in spring, after which they will readily sprout new shoots. The golden candle or lollipop plant comes from Peru and needs rather more warmth. It is propagated by tip cuttings, has a long flowering time, and loves high air humidity and plenty of light, but no direct sun. The shrimp plant grows under the same conditions, and it, too, can always be propagated further by using cuttings.

1375 If the bud shoots of hyacinths and tulips that have been kept in a warm place are as long as the leaves, you can remove their light-tight cones.
▸ TIP 1350

To enjoy the flowers of these plants over a long period, do not place them directly over the heater.

1376 The poinsettia (*Euphorbia pulcherrima*), also known as Christmas star or lobster plant, should be kept in a warm room.

Poinsettia bracts are mostly red and long lasting, but the plant can easily lose all its leaves if kept in a cool place. It also prefers somewhere that is not too dark, and the air humidity, too, should not be too low. It must be watered generously in rooms with dry air. Once it has flowered, it is generally discarded. However, it can also be cultivated further and produce flowers again the following year. For this, it is repotted in spring and the shoots cut back. In summer, it is best left out in the open in a well-lit site, but

without full sun. It will then flower around Christmas or shortly afterward. To be sure that it will already flower during Advent, it should be left in a completely dark place for at least 14 hours per day for about four weeks from late September.

1377 Some ornamental-leaved begonias, in particular the attractive *Begonia* Rex Cultorum Group, lose many of their leaves in poor light.

They should be given hardly any water when they are in a leafless state; otherwise, the roots will become diseased. However, the plants must still be kept warm so that they will grow attractive leaves again when there is better light in spring.

1378 Dust should occasionally be cleaned off leafy plants.

This is especially important in dry room air. The easiest way is to sprinkle the leaves with lukewarm water in the bathtub every two weeks. Washing off the leaves of large or large-leaved plants with a soft sponge and soapy water (rinse them with water afterward) is also a measure for preventive and active pest control.

Soapy water

1379   Cherry twigs in a vase will flower at Christmas time.

If, in keeping with tradition, cherry twigs are cut for a vase on 4 December (St. Barbara's Day) and kept in a warm place, they will bloom for about three weeks at Christmastime.

1380   From mid-December, you can also cut forsythia twigs and induce them to flower indoors.

The flowers will appear after around three weeks. Speed up the processs by laying the twigs in their entire length in warm water for around 12 hours after they have been cut. They can then be placed in a warm room in a vase of room-temperature water. The water must be changed frequently. Twigs of hazel and witch hazel are also suitable for producing shoots.

1381   Enjoy jasmine twigs on a festively laid Christmas table.

If cut before Christmas, twigs of winter jasmine (*Jasminum nudiflorum*) will open their flowers within several days at room temperature. However, this applies only during extended periods of mild weather. If there is already severe frost from mid-December, the twigs will need to be cut two to three weeks before Christmas instead.

1382   In December, most tub plants suffer from a lack of light.

In this final month of the year, there will be periods when it does not become properly light for days on end. Light-loving plants such as myrtle (*Myrtus communis*), oleander (*Nerium oleander*), rosemary (*Rosmarinus officinalis*), citrus (*Citrus*) plants, date palms (*Phoenix canariensis, P. dactylifera*), bougainvillea (*Bougainvillea glabra*), and many others will then suffer badly from a light deficit. During this time, they should be put in as light a place as possible and kept very cool and almost dry. A cool winter garden, well-lit veranda, or an unheated stairwell are ideal places for overwintering the plants. If it is not possible to provide these conditions for the above plants, it is better not to keep them at all, or instead store them somewhere else during the winter months, for example in a nursery that offers an overwintering service. Some tub plants that should similarly be kept cool in winter need only a little light; these are mostly deciduous plants such as the pomegranate (*Punica granatum*) or cockspur coral tree (*Erythrina crista-galli*), which can also be cut back heavily. Fuchsias, too, which will often bloom in their winter quarters into December, do not need to be kept in the lightest place.

Finally, there is a whole range of tub plants that need warmth and plenty of light in the winter as well, such as the Chinese hibiscus or rose of China (*Hibiscus rosa-sinensis*), which, if brought indoors early enough, will still open its splendid blooms over Christmas.

1383   One of the most beautiful indoor plants, which, owing to its size, can also be called a tub plant, is the African hemp (*Sparmannia africana*).

This is a tub plant that flowers during the winter months. Its splendid white blossoms can also be used to make an unusually fine Christmas decoration.

Sadly, this plant is seen all too seldom these days, although it is very easy to propagate. Cuttings with two or three leaves are cut off in late spring or in summer and develop roots readily in water. After this, they can be planted in humus-rich earth. In summer, they will thrive in a shady place outdoors. Here, they need plenty of water and regular fertilizer applications. They will also withstand the first cold nights in October, but must not be exposed to frost. In winter, they should be left to stand in a cool place and will thrive in both light and darker sites. In winter, too, their large, velvety, lime-green leaves transpire a great deal of water. Accordingly, remember to water them in winter as well—their root balls must always be moist!

1384   Ferns from warmer climatic zones make excellent indoor plants.

Ferns are leafy plants; they do not develop seeds, however, but instead reproduce by producing spores. In their native territories, many of them grow as epiphytes on trees, while many other species also grow as terrestrials in the moist atmosphere of the forest floor. With their diversity of forms and variable green colorations, they are among the most interesting and beautiful of all indoor plants. They need only a little light and will also grow in places where other plants would suffer from a light deficit. Most of them are grown all year round and constantly develop new fronds. Their substrates should be kept uniformly moist, but must never be wet. Many ferns like a warm place in winter as well, but some prefer a cooler place at this time of the year. All ferns will not tolerate dry heating air.

1385 The golden polypody (*Phlebodium aureum*), also known as the hare's foot fern, tolerates dry air better than other ferns.

This plant belongs to the polypod ferns (Polypodiaceae), and comes from subtropical and tropical America, where it grows epiphytically on trees. It is usually sold as a young plant; older specimens can grow very large and, individually, they are an impressive sight. It will grow very well in standard potting mixture, but clay granules or a loose substrate, such as that used for orchids, are better. The golden polypody also thrives at normal room temperature but will also tolerate lower temperatures of around 59°F.

1386 The Boston fern or sword fern (*Nephrolepis*), with its long, elegantly overhanging fronds, is very popular.

It is best grown in a flower stand, where its attractive, fresh-green fronds will make the greatest impact. Some varieties have wavy or curly, and also multi-branched fronds. Always keep the root balls uniformly moist. It is best to water them by adding water to the saucer or cachepot; after about one hour, discard the excess water.

1387 The ribbon fern (*Pteris*), with its silvery fronds, is extremely decorative.

There are several species of ribbon fern; it is usually the species *Pteris cretica*, the Cretan brake, which is available, of which there are also many varieties. As the name implies, it comes from the Mediterranean. Its fronds are about 6 in. long and ¾ in. wide. The varieties with colored or variegated leaves are highly suitable for indoors and need a warmer site than the green-leaved forms. *P. cretica* var. *albolineata*, with its lime-green leaves with dark green edges, is well known. *P. argyraea*, from India and Sri Lanka, is also very decorative with blue-green frond leaves that are silvery white at the base, so that the fronds appear to have silvery-white stripes.

1388 The maidenhair fern (*Adiantum*) is one of the smaller ferns.

This very delicate and finely branched fern must have warmth and a high humidity to survive. It also does not tolerate air drafts. This must be considered when ventilating, and with opened bottom-hung windows. If the root ball dries out, the fern will react by rolling up its fronds. Ideal sites for growing include window boxes and winter gardens, but with a little care it can also be grown indoors. Once the fern has become properly established, it will also tolerate less ideal conditions for brief periods.

TABLES

Gardens are endlessly diverse when it comes to their size, form, and design; the diversity of the plants grown in them is similarly endless, and it is simply not possible to describe every single vegetable variety, ornamental plant, flowering shrub, etc. in detail. Accordingly, in the following, specific information on "General" topics as well as "Vegetables" and "Ornamental Plants" has been summarized in tabular form.

This means that you can quickly familiarize yourself with the characteristics of arable soils, recommended fertilizer quantities in vegetable gardens, and species and varieties of ornamental plants with indications of their height, flowering time, and application, along with many other facts.

GENERAL

ABBREVIATIONS:

Roman numerals = month

E., M., L. = early, middle, late

Table 1. The Most Important Arable Soils and Their Characteristics

SOIL TYPE	GOOD CHARACTERISTICS	POOR CHARACTERISTICS	IMPROVEMENT MEASURES
Sandy soil	Warms up rapidly. Very good aeration. Rainfall is taken up well (up to saturation point). Can be tilled in any weather.	Cools off rapidly. Poor water retention capacity. Added organic fertilizers rot very quickly. Mineral fertilizers are washed out easily. Considerable irrigation measures necessary.	Preferentially use organic fertilizers; mineral fertilizers should be used in small quantities only, but frequently. Rotted stable manure or bark humus should not be worked into the soil, but applied as a ground covering instead.
Humic sandy soil	Heats up rapidly and stays warm. Easy to till. Good aeration and water retention capacity. Regarded as one of the best arable soils.	In dry conditions, the wind can blow the soil away if it is very fine-grained; the plants suffer accordingly. The soil surface can dry out very rapidly.	Organic fertilizers should be worked into the soil if possible; mineral fertilizers should be used in small amounts only, but frequently. Organic substances (such as bark humus or bark substrate, and stable manure) should not be worked into the soil, but applied as a ground covering instead.
Loamy sandy soil (medium soil)	Can be used for nearly all crops. Aeration is nearly always good. Mineral fertilizers are better retained than in sandy soils, and stable manure, too, is better utilized. Soil tillage is normal.	Warms up more slowly than humic sandy soil, but retains moisture for longer.	For this soil type, too, organic fertilizers are preferable. Additionally, a ground covering is most important to retain the soil moisture over a long period.
Sandy loam soil (medium soil)	Can be used for nearly all crops. Water retention and accumulation capacity are good. Aeration is satisfactory. Stable manure is well utilized. Soil tillage is normal.	Has no significant poor characteristics if regular addition of humus is ensured.	For this soil type, too, it is advisable to work with a ground covering, since this will save greatly on hoeing and watering activities. Calcium carbonate is better than caustic lime.
Loam soil	Water retention and accumulation capacity are very good. Mineral fertilizers are retained adequately. Utilization of stable manure is very good. If well supplied with humus, this is one of the best arable soils.	Aeration is less than optimal. Warms up relatively slowly in spring. Difficult to till. Needs plenty of hoeing work.	If ground coverings are used, the soil surface will not become muddy from rain and watering, and aeration will be improved. Work in compost and bark humus. Regular lime application will improve soil aeration.
Bog soil	Very good water retention capacity. Particularly suitable for bog and heather plants. Mineral fertilizers are very well retained. Addition of stable manure is superfluous.	Generally acidic, aeration is poor. Additionally, often very cold if no permeable substrate is present. Increased risk from frost.	If possible, establish a permeable substrate. If no bog plants are to be used, then supply generously with lime. Work coarse sand into the uppermost layer.

NOTE: "Good gardening soil" includes all soil types that have all but lost their original character through decades of intensive use, regular addition of humus and lime, and good crop rotation. As a rule, such soil only ever has good characteristics.

Table 2. Recommended Fertilizer Quantities for Vegetable Species Grown Outdoors

The recommended quantities indicate the requirements for pure nutrients. The necessary conversion to commercial fertilizer quantities can be taken from the table. In the case of nitrogen, individual applications may not exceed 2 oz./100 ft.². This quantity is best applied when the area for seeding or planting is being prepared. The plants are given the remaining nitrogen as required in several applications during the growing season. Here, too, the individual application quantity can remain under 2 oz./100 ft.², and fertilizer applied more frequently. In the case of potassium, individual applications may not exceed 7 oz./100 ft.². If greater quantities are required, the rest must be applied during the growing season, along with the nitrogen surface application.

	NITROGEN (N)		PHOSPHOROUS (P) AND POTASSIUM (K)						
VEGETABLE TYPE	REQUIREMENT	REC QTY (OZ./100 FT.²)	REQUIREMENT	REC. QTY ACCORDING TO THE CONTENT CLASSIFICATION OF THE SOIL (OZ./100 FT.²)					
				A P	K	B P	K	C P	K
Asparagus	very high	8 to 10	high	2.5	8.5	2	7	1.5	6
Batavia lettuce	medium	3.5 to 5	medium	2	7	1.5	6	1	4.5
Beets	medium	3.5 to 5	medium	2	7	1.5	6	1	4.5
Black salsify (viper's grass)	medium	3.5 to 5	high	2.5	8.5	2	7	1.5	6
Bok choy (pak choi)	medium	3.5 to 5	medium	2	7	1.5	6	1	4.5
Broad (fava) beans	medium	3.5 to 5	medium	2	7	1.5	6	1	4.5
Broccoli	very high	8 to 10	high	2.5	8.5	2	7	1.5	6
Brussels sprouts	very high	8 to 10	high	2.5	8.5	2	7	1.5	6
Bush (dwarf) beans	low	2 to 3	medium	2	7	1.5	6	1	4.5
Button squash	high	5 to 7	high	2.5	8.5	2	7	1.5	6
Carrots, early	medium	3.5 to 5	medium	2	7	1.5	6	1	4.5
Carrots, late	high	5 to 7	high	2.5	8.5	2	7	1.5	6
Cauliflower	very high	8 to 10	high	2.5	8.5	2	7	1.5	6
Celeriac (root celery)	high	5 to 7	medium	2	7	1.5	6	1	4.5
Chard	high	5 to 7	medium	2	7	1.5	6	1	4.5
Chicory	high	5 to 7	medium	2	7	1.5	6	1	4.5
Chinese cabbage	high	5 to 7	high	2.5	8.5	2	7	1.5	6
Chives	high	5 to 7	medium	2	7	1.5	6	1	4.5

1 SOIL SUPPLY LEVEL: A = LOW LEVEL, B = MEDIUM LEVEL, C = HIGH LEVEL.
2 THE RECOMMENDED VALUES APPLY FOR THE MAIN HARVEST PERIOD ON MEDIUM SOILS.

	NITROGEN (N)		PHOSPHOROUS (P) AND POTASSIUM (K)					
1 SOIL SUPPLY LEVEL: A = LOW LEVEL, B = MEDIUM LEVEL, C = HIGH LEVEL. **2 THE RECOMMENDED VALUES APPLY FOR THE MAIN HARVEST PERIOD ON MEDIUM SOILS.**								
VEGETABLE TYPE	REQUIREMENT	REC QTY (OZ./100 FT.^{2})	REQUIREMENT	REC. QTY ACCORDING TO THE CONTENT CLASSIFICATION OF THE SOIL (OZ./100 FT.^{2})				
				A P	K	B P	K	C P	K
Climbing beans	medium	3.5 to 5	medium	2	7	1.5	6	1	4.5
Cucumbers	medium	3.5 to 5	high	2.5	8.5	2	7	1.5	6
Curly kale	medium	3.5 to 5	medium	2	7	1.5	6	1	4.5
Eggplant (aubergine)	medium	3.5 to 5	medium	2	7	1.5	6	1	4.5
Florence fennel	medium	3.5 to 5	medium	2	7	1.5	6	1	4.5
Garden cress	low	2	low	2	6	1	4.5	0.5	3
Iceberg lettuce	medium	3.5 to 5	medium	2	7	1.5	6	1	4.5
Kohlrabi	medium	3.5 to 5	medium	2	7	1.5	6	1	4.5
Lamb's lettuce	low	2 to 3	low	1.5	6	1	4.5	0.5	3
Leeks	very high	8 to 10	medium	2	7	1.5	6	1	4.5
Lettuce	medium	3.5 to 5	medium	2	7	1.5	6	1	4.5
Melon	medium	3.5 to 5	medium	2	7	1.5	6	1	4.5
New Zealand spinach	high	5 to 7	medium	2	7	1.5	6	1	4.5
Oak-leaved lettuce	medium	3.5 to 5	medium	2	7	1.5	6	1	4.5
Onions, leek	low	2 to 3	low	1.5	6	1	4.5	0.5	3
Onions, seed	medium	3.5 to 5	medium	2	7	1.5	6	1	4.5
Parsley	medium	3.5 to 5	medium	2	7	1.5	6	1	4.5
Peas	low	2 to 3	medium	2	7	1.5	6	1	4.5
Peppers	high	5 to 7	high	2.5	8.5	2	7	1.5	6
Potatoes	high	5 to 7	high	2.5	8.5	2	7	1.5	6
Pumpkins/squash	very high	8 to 10	high	2.5	8.5	2	7	1.5	6
Radicchio	medium	3.5 to 5	medium	2	7	1.5	6	1	4.5
Radishes	medium	3.5 to 5	medium	2	7	1.5	6	1	4.5
Red cabbage	very high	8 to 10	high	2.5	8.5	2	7	1.5	6

1 SOIL SUPPLY LEVEL: A = LOW LEVEL, B = MEDIUM LEVEL, C = HIGH LEVEL.

2 THE RECOMMENDED VALUES APPLY FOR THE MAIN HARVEST PERIOD ON MEDIUM SOILS.

VEGETABLE TYPE	NITROGEN (N)		PHOSPHOROUS (P) AND POTASSIUM (K)						
	REQUIREMENT	REC QTY (OZ./100 FT.^{2})	REQUIREMENT	REC. QTY ACCORDING TO THE CONTENT CLASSIFICATION OF THE SOIL (OZ./100 FT.^{2})					
				A P	K	B P	K	C P	K
Red radishes	low	2 to 3	low	1.5	6	1	4.5	0.5	3
Rhubarb	very high	8 to 10	high	2.5	8.5	2	7	1.5	6
Romaine (cos) lettuce	medium	3.5 to 5	medium	2	7	1.5	6	1	4.5
Savoy cabbage	high	5 to 7	high	2.5	8.5	2	7	1.5	6
Scarlet runners	medium	3.5 to 5	high	2.5	8.5	2	7	1.5	6
Spanish onions	high	5 to 7	medium	2	7	1.5	6	1	4.5
Spinach	low	3	medium	2	7	1.5	6	1	4.5
Sugarloaf	medium	3.5 to 5	medium	2	7	1.5	6	1	4.5
Sweet corn	medium	3.5 to 5	high	2	8.5	1.5	7	1.5	6
Tomatoes	medium	3.5 to 5	medium	2	7	1.5	6	1	4.5
Turnips/rutabagas (swedes)	high	5 to 7	medium	2	7	1.5	6	1	4.5
White cabbage, early	high	5 to 7	high	2.5	8.5	2	7	1.5	6
White cabbage, late	very high	8 to 10	high	2.5	8.5	2	7	1.5	6
Winter endives	medium	3.5 to 5	medium	2	7	1.5	6	1	4.5
Zucchini	high	5 to 7	high	2.5	8.5	2	7	1.5	6

Table 3. Soil pH Values of Important Cultivated Plants

The pH value is the most important soil chemical characteristic. It influences the weathering of the mineral parent material, the soil water and air balance, the availability of plant nutrients, and microorganism activity.

The pH value indicates the acid content of the soil. The scale ranges from pH 1 (very acidic) to pH 7 (neutral) and pH 14 (alkaline). The ability of plants to take up nutrients from the soil is dependent on the soil pH value. This table lists the optimal pH values for growing the most important cultivated plants.

If the soil pH falls below a certain value, clay and humus particles may migrate to the soil horizon beneath, for example. If no compensatory measures are taken, the soils in our latitudes tend toward acidification. The reasons for this are the "breathing" of the plant roots and soil organism activity, along with external inputs, such as acid rain.

PLANT NAME	PH VALUE
VEGETABLES	
Asparagus	6.0 to 7.5
Beans	5.8 to 7.0
Beets	6.5 to 7.5
Black salsify (viper's grass)	6.0 to 7.5
Broad (fava) beans	6.0 to 8.0
Brussels sprouts	5.5 to 7.0
Carrots	6.0 to 8.0
Cauliflower	6.5 to 7.5
Celeriac (root celery)	6.2 to 7.5
Chard	6.0 to 8.0
Cucumbers	5.6 to 7.5
Curly kale	5.5 to 7.0
Horseradish	6.0 to 7.5
Kohlrabi	5.5 to 7.0
Lamb's lettuce	5.6 to 7.0
Leeks	6.0 to 8.0
Lettuce	5.6 to 7.5
Onions	6.5 to 7.5
Parsley	6.0 to 8.0
Peas	6.0 to 7.0
Potatoes	5.0 to 7.0
Pumpkins/ squash	5.6 to 7.5
Radishes	5.6 to 7.0
Red cabbage	6.0 to 7.5
Red radishes	5.6 to 7.0
Rhubarb	5.5 to 7.0
Savoy cabbage	6.0 to 7.5
Spinach	5.5 to 7.0

PLANT NAME	PH VALUE
Tomatoes	5.0 to 7.0
White cabbage	6.0 to 7.5
ORNAMENTAL PLANTS	
Alisons	6.0 to 8.0
Anemones	6.0 to 8.0
Asters	6.5 to 7.5
Bellflowers	6.0 to 8.0
Bleeding hearts	5.0 to 7.5
Brideworts	6.0 to 8.0
Candytufts	6.0 to 8.0
Carnations	6.5 to 8.0
China asters	6.0 to 8.0
Chrysanthemums	6.5 to 7.5
Columbines	6.0 to 7.0
Coral bells	5.0 to 6.0
Daffodils, narcissi	6.0 to 8.0
Dahlias	6.0 to 8.0
Daylilies	6.0 to 8.0
Deutzias	6.0 to 8.0
Forget-me-nots	6.0 to 8.0
Forsythias	6.0 to 8.0
Gladioli	6.0 to 8.0
Irises	6.0 to 8.0
Larkspurs	6.0 to 7.5
Lilacs	6.0 to 8.0
Lilies	6.0 to 8.0
Lupines	5.0 to 8.0
Marigolds	7.0 to 8.0
Peonies	6.0 to 8.0

PLANT NAME	PH VALUE
Phloxes	6.0 to 7.0
Poppies	6.0 to 8.0
Primroses	5.5 to 7.5
Rhododendrons	4.5 to 6.0
Rock roses	6.0 to 8.0
Roses	6.0 to 8.0
Snapdragons	6.0 to 8.0
Stocks	6.0 to 8.0
Tulips	6.0 to 8.0
Vetches	6.5 to 7.5
Violets	6.0 to 8.0
Wallflowers	6.0 to 8.0
Zinnias	6.0 to 8.0

VEGETABLES

Table 4. Crop Rotation

While nearly all gardening enthusiasts understand the importance of soil tillage, fertilizer use, and the most suitable varieties for successful cultivation, it needs to be stressed time and again that too little attention is still given to crop rotation. In fact, maintaining an appropriate crop rotation is at least as important for successful cultivation as the use of fertilizer, for example. Crop rotation errors can be more detrimental, and especially more lasting, than fertilizer errors, which can be corrected relatively quickly.

As a general principle, avoid growing the same vegetable species twice in succession on the same plot. However, vegetable species that are closely related in botanical terms, such as onions and leeks, radishes and red radishes, cauliflower and Brussels sprouts, or tomatoes and potatoes, for example, should also not be grown after one another.

All plants place specific demands on the soil, depending on the species. Through their root activity, they leave substances in the soil that are incompatible with subsequent plants of the same species, and therefore inhibit growth. The more distantly related two vegetable species are in botanical terms, the better they can be grown one after the other or also together. This finding is also important for mixed cultivation. Lettuce and radishes or red radishes, cucumbers and celeriac (root celery), or tomatoes and lettuce, for example, are highly compatible in mixed cultivation. The options for suitable crop rotation and combinations in mixed and catch crop cultivation are many, and increase with the number of vegetable species used.

Crop rotation errors are evident in an increased incidence of species-specific pests and diseases, and also in a drop in yield, which may be considerable. For example, the yield resulting from repeatedly planting the same vegetable species on the same plot as compared with an appropriate crop rotation may fall to 50 percent of the normal yield. If pests and diseases come into play as well, the losses may be even greater. It should otherwise be noted that different rotation break periods apply for the individual vegetable species to be sure of avoiding crop rotation losses. The necessary rotation breaks for the most important vegetable species are listed below.

Maintaining the rotation breaks is made much easier if vegetable cultivation is designed to be as diverse as possible, and if strawberries, early potatoes, and ornamental plants are also incorporated into the vegetable crop rotation. Precise annual crop planning with a simple sketch to show the crop allocation over the areas to be cultivated is crucial. Only in this way is it possible to keep track over the years of which vegetable species have been grown at a particular location, and when.

CROP	ROTATION BREAK
Asparagus	10 to 12 years
Beans	2 to 3 years
Beets	3 to 4 years
Black salsify (viper's grass)	4 years
Cabbage species	3 to 4 years
Carrots	3 to 4 years
Celeriac (root celery)	3 to 4 years
Chard	3 to 4 years
Cucumbers	3 to 5 years
Endives	2 years
Lamb's lettuce	1 to 2 years
Leeks	2 to 3 years
Lettuce	1 to 2 years
Onions	4 to 5 years
Peas	4 to 5 years
Peppers	3 to 4 years
Radishes/red radishes	2 to 3 years
Spinach	1 to 2 years
Tomatoes	3 to 4 years

Table 5. Sowing and Planting Table for Vegetables and Aromatic Herbs

VEGETABLE AND AROMATIC HERB SPECIES	VIABILITY (YEARS)	SOWING TIME (MONTH)	ROW INTERVAL (IN.)	PLANTING TIME (MONTH)	PLANTING INTERVAL (IN.)
Asparagus	-	-	-	L. III to M. IV	48 × 16
Basil	2	-	-	M. V	10 × 8
Batavia lettuce	3	E. III to E. VIII	-	IV to L. VIII	12 × 12
Beets	4 to 6	L. IV to L. VI	12	-	-
Black salsify (viper's grass)	1 to 2	III	10 to 12	-	-
Bok choy (pak choi)	3 to 5	E. VII to M. VIII	12	-	12 × 12
Borage	2 to 3	IV to V	10 to 12	-	-
Broad (fava) beans	3 to 4	III	20	-	-
Broccoli	3 to 4	L. II to E. VI	-	L. IV to E. VII	20 × 16 to 20 × 20
Brussels sprouts	4 to 5	IV	-	L. V to M. VI	24 × 20
Bush (dwarf) beans	3 to 4	M. V to M. VII	12	-	-
Butterhead/leaf lettuce	3 to 4	III to V	6 to 10	-	-
Caraway seeds	2	IV	12	-	-
Carrots	3 to 4	III to VI	8 to 12	-	-
Cauliflower	3 to 4	-	-	-	-
under glass and foil	-	-	-	III	16 × 16
Early cultivation	-	II to M. III	-	L. III to E. V	20 × 20
Summer cultivation	-	IV	-	L. V to E. VI	20 × 20
Fall cultivation	-	L. IV to M. V	-	M. VI to E. VII	20 × 20
Celeriac (root celery)	2 to 3	E. III	-	M. to L. V	20 × 12 to 20 × 16
Celery (stalk)	2 to 3	-	-	V	20 × 16
Chard	5 to 6	III to IV	12 to 16	-	-
Chervil	2	III to L. VII	8	-	-
Chicory	2 to 3	E. V to M. VI	12	-	-
Chinese cabbage	3 to 5	M. to L. VII	16	-	16 × 16
Chives	1 to 2	III to VI	-	V to VI	8 × 8
Climbing beans	3	M. to L. V	32	-	-
Cucumbers	6 to 8	-	-	-	-
under glass and foil	-	-	-	IV to E. V	40 × 16
outdoors	-	M. V to E. VI	32	-	-
Curly kale	3 to 4	M. V to M. VI	-	L. VI to L. VII	20 × 16
Dill	2 to 3	IV to VI	10	-	-
Eggplant (aubergine)	3 to 4	-	-	M. to L. V	20 × 20

VEGETABLE AND AROMATIC HERB SPECIES	VIABILITY (YEARS)	SOWING TIME (MONTH)	ROW INTERVAL (IN.)	PLANTING TIME (MONTH)	PLANTING INTERVAL (IN.)
Endives, winter	4 to 5	M. VI to E. VII	-	VII to E. VIII	12 × 12
Florence fennel	3 to 4	IV to M. VII	-	M. V to E. VIII	16 × 12
Garden cress	2 to 3	L. III to VI	5	-	-
Garlic	-	-	-	III to IV	8 to 6 × 6
Iceberg lettuce	3	L. III to L. VI	-	IV to E. VIII	12 × 12

Kohlrabi
  under glass and foil
  Early cultivation
  Summer cultivation
  Fall cultivation
	3 to 4
	-
	-
	-
	-
		-
		-
		M. to L. II
		E. IV to M. VI
		M. VI
			-
			-
			-
			-
			-
				-
				III
				III to E. VI
				M. V to E. VII
				E. to M. VII
					-
					8 × 8
					10 × 10
					10 × 10
					12 × 12
					to 16 × 12

Lamb's lettuce	3 to 5	VIII to IX	5 to 6	-	-
Leeks	2 to 3	III to M. IV	-	V to VI	12 × 6

Lettuce
  under glass and foil
  Early cultivation
 	
  Summer cultivation
  Fall cultivation
	3
	-
	-
	
	-
	-
		-
		-
		II
		
		L. III to M. VI
		VII
			-
			-
			-
			
			-
			-
				-
				L. II to III
				III to M. IV
				
				IV to E. VII
				M. to L. VIII
					-
					8 × 8
					8 × 8 to 10 × 10
					10 × 10
					10 × 10

Marjoram	2	-	-	L. V	8 × 6
Melon	5 to 6	E. III to M. IV	-	IV to L. V	40 × 20 to 48 × 20
New Zealand spinach	4 to 5	III to IV	-	M. V to E. VI	40 × 20
Oak-leaved lettuce	3	E. III to E. VIII	-	IV to L. VIII	12 × 12
Onions	1 to 2	E. III to M. IV	-	-	-
Parsley	2 to 3	III to IV	6 to 12	-	-
Parsnips	1	III to IV	12	-	-
Peas	2 to 3	M. III to L. V	12	-	-
Pepper, spice	3 to 4	-	-	M. to L. V	16 × 12 to 20 × 12
Pepper, vegetable	3 to 4	E. to M. III	-	M. to L. V	20 × 16 to 24 × 16
Pumpkin/squash	4 to 5	M. V	40	M. to L. V	40 × 40
Radicchio	3 to 4	E. V to E. VII	-	VI to E. VIII	12 × 12
Radishes	4 to 5	III to VIII	4 to 12	-	-

Red cabbage
  early varieties
 	
  medium-early
  and late varieties
	4 to 5
	-
	
	-
		-
		L. II
		
		IV
			-
			-
			
			-
				-
				IV
				
				L. V to E. VI
					-
					20 × 16
					to 20 × 20
					24 × 20
					to 24 × 24

Red radishes	4 to 5	III to VIII	3 to 6	-	-
Rhubarb	-	-	-	IX or III	40 × 40

VEGETABLE AND AROMATIC HERB SPECIES	VIABILITY (YEARS)	SOWING TIME (MONTH)	ROW INTERVAL (IN.)	PLANTING TIME (MONTH)	PLANTING INTERVAL (IN.)
Romaine (cos) lettuce	3 to 4	L. III to M. VII	–	E. V to M. VIII	12 × 12
Savoy cabbage early varieties	4 to 5 –	– L. II	– –	– IV	– 16 × 16 tto 20 × 20
medium-early and late varieties	–	IV	–	L. V to E. VI	24 × 20 to 24 × 24
Spanish onions	2	E. II to IV	10	L. IV to M. V	10 × 8
Spinach	1 to 2	II to III or VII to IX	8	–	–
Sugarloaf	3 to 4	M. to L. VI	16	–	–
Summer savory	1	IV	8	M. V	10 × 8
Tarragon	2	–	–	IV	16 × 12
Thyme	2	–	–	IV	8 × 8
Tomatoes under glass and foil	2 to 4 –	– –	– –	– IV to E. V	– 32 × 20 20 × 12
Tomatoes on open land outdoors	–	L. II to E. III	–	M. to L. V	32 × 20*)
Turnips/rutabagas (swedes)	3 to 4	IV to L. V	–	V to VII	16 × 12
White cabbage early varieties	4 to 5 –	– L. II	– –	– IV	– 20 × 16 to 20 × 20
medium-early and late varieties	–	IV	–	L. V to E. VI	24 × 20 to 24 × 24
Zucchini	4 to 5	M. V to E. VI	–	–	40 × 40

Table 6. Possible Sowing, Planting, and Harvesting Times for Vegetables Grown on Open Land Outdoors

• • • • • • • • • •   POSSIBLE SOWING PERIOD
———————   SOWING UNDER GLASS
– – – – – –   POSSIBLE PLANTING PERIOD
━━━━━━━   POSSIBLE HARVESTING PERIOD

EXAMPLE: When planting lettuce, beginning in late March with ongoing subsequent plantings, continual harvesting is possible from late May to late October.

VEGETABLE SPECIES		JAN	FEB	MAR	APR	MAY	JUN	JUL	AUG	SEP	OCT	NOV	DEC
BATAVIA LETTUCE				——••••	•••– ––	•– –•– –	•– –•– –	•– –•– –	•– –	━━━	━━━		
BEETS						••••	••••		━━━	━━━	━━━		
BLACK SALSIFY (VIPER'S GRASS)				••••	••					━━━	━━━	━━━
BOK CHOY (PAK CHOI)								•••	••••	━━━	━━━		
BROAD (FAVA) BEANS				••••	•••			━━━					
BROCCOLI			——••	•••••	– –– –	– –		━━━	━━━				
BRUSSELS SPROUTS	Early varieties				••••	– –– –				━━━	━━━		
	Medium-early and medium-late varieties				••••		– –– –				━━━	━━━	
	Late varieties				•••		– –					━━━	━━━
BUSH (DWARF) BEANS						••••	••••						
BUTTERHEAD/LEAF LETTUCE					•••••	••••••	••••••	••••	━━━━	━━━			
BUTTON SQUASH					——••	•••– –			━━━	━━━			
CARROTS	Early and medium-early varieties			••••	••••••	••••••	••••••	••• ━━	━━━	•••••	••••		
	Medium-late and late varieties			••••	••••••	••••••	••			━━━	━━━	━━━	
CAULIFLOWER	Early varieties	——••••	••		– –– –	– –							
	Summer varieties			——••	••••	•– –– –	– –– –	━━━	━━━	━━━	━━━		
	Late varieties				••••	•– –	–				━━━	━━━	

VEGETABLE SPECIES		JAN	FEB	MAR	APR	MAY	JUN	JUL	AUG	SEP	OCT	NOV	DEC
CELERY	Root celery		•••••			– –	– –				——		
	Stalk celery		••••••			– –	– –		——	——			
CHARD					••••	•• –	– –	——	——	——	——	——	
CHICORY	Root raising					•••	• –					——	
CHINESE CABBAGE								•••					
CHIVES													
CLIMBING BEANS						•••••	•		——	——			
CUCUMBERS	With raising				••	–	–	——	——	——			
	Direct sowing					••••		——	——	——			
CURLY KALE		——	——	——	••••••	•	– –	– –				——	——
CUT PARSLEY					••••	• ——	——	——	——				
ENDIVES	Summer				•••	••	– –	——	——				
	Winter					•••••		– –	– –	——	——		
FLORENCE FENNEL					•••••	•••	– –	– –	——	——	——		
ICEBERG LETTUCE					•••••	•••	——	——	——	——			
KOHLRABI	Early varieties	••••••			– –								
	Summer varieties				••••••	•••	– –	– –					
	Fall varieties				••••••	•	– –	– –		——	——		
LAMB'S LETTUCE		——	•••••	——	——				•••••	——	——	——	
LEEKS	Summer and fall		••••••		– –	– –		——	——	——	——	——	
	Winter			•••••	——	——							
LETTUCE	Early varieties	••••	– –	– –		•••	– –	——	——				
	Summer varieties				••••••••	– –	– –	– –	——				
NEW ZEALAND SPINACH					•••••	•	– –	——	——	——			
OAK-LEAVED LETTUCE				••••	•••••••	•••	– –	– –	——	——	——		
ONIONS	Spring onions			– –			——	——					
	Planting onions				••••		——	——					
	Seed onions			•••••					——	——			

VEGETABLE SPECIES		JAN	FEB	MAR	APR	MAY	JUN	JUL	AUG	SEP	OCT	NOV	DEC
PARSNIPS				•••	•••	••					━━	━━	
PEAS				•••	•••	•••	••	━━	━━	━━			
PUMPKIN/SQUASH	Pumpkin					••			━━	━━	━		
	Squash					•••	•					━	
RADICCHIO						── ••	•--	--━	━━	━	━━		
RADISHES	Early varieties				•••	•••	•	━━	━━				
	Medium-early varieties				•••	•••	••	━━	━━				
	Summer varieties				•••	•••	••	━━	━━	━			
	Fall and winter varieties						••	••			━━		
RED CABBAGE	Early varieties		•• ──		---	---	---	--			━━	━	
	Medium-late and late varieties			── ••	•••	---	--				━━	━	
RED RADISHES				•••	•••	•••	•••	━━	━━	━	━		
ROMAINE (COS) LETTUCE				── ••	•--	---	---	-- ━	━━	━━	━		
ROOT PARSLEY						••	••				━━	━	
SPINACH	Spring			•••	•••	••	━━						
	Fall							•••	•••	━━	━		
	Winter			━━	━━	━				••	••		
SUGARLOAF						••	••				━━		
TOMATOES				── ••		---	--		━━	━			
WHITE/SAVOY CABBAGE	Early varieties	•• ──	••	---	---	--	━━	━					
	Medium-early and medium-late varieties			── ••	•••	••	---	-- ━	━━	━━	━		
	Late varieties			── ••	•••	••	---	--				━━	
ZUCCHINI						── ••	•--	--━	━━	━	━		

Table 7. Important Pests in Vegetable Gardens

Repeated efforts should be made to combat pests using domestic remedies. Only when this proves ineffective, and in cases of heavy infestation, should approved insecticides be considered that are not otherwise harmful to useful animals.

The preparations are generally applied as a spray; some have a systemic action in that they are taken up via the roots and are transported with the sap flow to all parts of the plant. In this way, pests that cannot be reached directly by spraying are also targeted.

Useful animals for biological pest control, such as predatory mites, parasitic wasps, and lacewing larvae, can be used in winter gardens and greenhouses, while hoverfly larvae can also be used outdoors.

NAME OF PEST	SIGNS OF DAMAGE	PREVENTION AND CONTROL
Aphids (greenfly)	Aphid colonies present on and between the leaves. Leaves exhibit yellow patches, while heart leaves become deformed or curl up.	Repeated spraying or dusting with insecticides, change remedies, observe waiting period.
Asparagus beetle	Beetles and larvae eat the asparagus foliage. The beetles have a red, yellow, or reddish black patterning.	Collect the beetles.
Asparagus fly	Its larvae destroy the shoots even as they are developing; the shoot tips curl to one side, and the shoots wither and die. Maggots or brown pupae can be found in the shoots.	Remove affected shoots continually from VII (cut them off flush with the rootstock). Lay vegetable nets over green asparagus from IV on.
Bean/pea thrips	Adult insects and their larvae suck on all parts of the plant. Leaves and flowers become unsightly and wither.	Dry spells promote the pests' occurrence. Maintain long crop rotation breaks.
Bean seed fly	Poor seedling emergence, chewed chambers in cotyledons, heart of germinating plants destroyed; damage especially prevalent in unfavorable, cool weather conditions.	Maintain correct crop rotation; employ measures to promote seedling emergence (frost protection hoods, sowing only after 20 May); advance planting in pots.
Beet-leaf miner (especially on spinach)	Burrowing larvae present in the leaves.	Remove and destroy affected plants; ensure rapid growth.
Cabbage moth (diamondback moth)	The moth larvae eat the undersides of the cabbage leaves, leaving the upper skin intact ("window damage").	Combine with treatment for aphids. The same remedies can be used. Lay out vegetable nets immediately after planting.
Cabbage root fly	The flies lay their eggs on the roots collar of young cabbage plants (especially cauliflower). The larvae devour the underground plant parts.	Lay out vegetable nets immediately after planting.
Cabbage white butterfly	The caterpillars can devour the leaves of cabbage species (including kohlrabi) entirely.	Squash the conspicuous yellow egg clusters, remove the caterpillars. Lay out vegetable nets immediately after planting.
Carrot fly	The larvae create tunnels in the outer layers of the root vegetable body.	Mixed cropping, very early sowing, cover with vegetable nets, remove affected plants.
Cutworms (on cabbage, lettuce, carrots, and occasionally asparagus)	Naked gray caterpillars (larvae of owlet moths) devour the roots and root collar.	Deploy trap plants, lay bait, search for and destroy larvae underneath damaged plants, use approved preparations.
Flea beetles (on the young plants of all cabbage species, radishes, and red radishes)	Leaves initially perforated, later completely devoured. Jumping, shiny beetles around $1/10$ in. in size.	Keep soil constantly moist and loosened.

NAME OF PEST	SIGNS OF DAMAGE	PREVENTION AND CONTROL
Greenhouse whitefly (especially on cucumbers and tomatoes under glass and foil)	Leaves turn yellow and wither. White insects around ½0 in. in size can be found on the leaf undersides.	Following the initial occurrence, spray with approved preparations. Repeat the treatment after 5 or 6 days.
Mole cricket	Devours the underground plant parts of many vegetable species. Lives in channels directly beneath the earth.	Probe the channels with your fingers until you find the nesting sites, which lie somewhat deeper in the soil. The brood can be destroyed in this way. Special baits have also proven effective.
Onion fly	Its larvae eat into the heart of the young onion plants. The plants wither and die.	Mixed cropping, very early sowing, remove affected plants, water seed rows with recognized preparations. Deploy vegetable nets.
Pea moth	When harvesting the capsules, it is apparent that the heads have been eaten; yellow-green caterpillars up to ½ in. long and grains of excrement are present in the capsules.	Maintain correct crop rotation, sow very early and late varieties, preventive use of insecticides with short waiting periods.
Red spider mites	Bean and cucumber leaves turn prematurely yellow. On the leaf undersides, yellow and red animals can be found that are barely recognizable with the naked eye.	Ensure high air humidity by watering frequently; spray with recognized preparations.
Slugs	Causes damage through eating the young plants of many vegetable species.	Lay out special slug bait, slug fences, remove egg batches, deploy lettuce hoods.
Swede midge (particularly on cauliflower)	Midge larvae destroy the heart leaves, with no flower development as a result.	Spray the plants with systemic insecticides for several days after planting. Repeat the treatment multiple times. Lay out vegetable nets before the midges take flight.
Turnip root fly	Brown channels eaten into the outer layer of the tubers, in the case of red radishes also in the tuber interior.	Intensive watering helps prevent infestation; cover with vegetable nets.
Wireworm (click beetle larvae), predominantly on lettuce and potatoes	Lettuce plants wilt suddenly; hard, wiry yellow larvae with a dark head feeding on the roots.	Intensive soil tillage, no sowing on freshly dug-up lawn areas.

Table 8. Important Diseases in Vegetable Gardens

NAME OF DISEASE	SIGNS OF DAMAGE	PREVENTION AND CONTROL
Angular leaf spot (on cucumbers grown outdoors)	Initially transparent, blackish green, later brown, angularly defined leaf spots. Bacteria-containing slime droplets on the leaf undersides in damp weather. Fruits become deformed.	Long crop rotation breaks. Repeated spraying with copper preparations at intervals of 8 to 12 days. Destroy any affected plants.
Anthracnose (on beans and peas)	Irregular round brown spots with a more or less dark edge on leaves and capsules. The fungus also spreads to the seeds in the capsules, making them unusable.	Use healthy seed. Do not sow too densely. Use resistant varieties. Maintain the correct subsequent crop rotation.
Asparagus rust	The fungus damages the asparagus foliage so that it turns yellow and dies prematurely. Orange-colored pustules are initially seen on the lower part of the stem, and later dark brown rust spots on the stems.	If there is danger of rust, spray the plants with organic fungicides as soon as the foliage begins to grow. Repeat the spraying every 2 weeks. Dispose of affected foliage with the household waste.
Bacterial cancer of tomato	Begins with the wilting of individual pinnules, and later spreads to the entire plant. "Eye spots" may be present on the fruits.	Disinfect tomato stakes. Do not use a knife when pinching off. Apply copper preparations. Dispose of diseased plants with household waste.
Bean rust (predominantly on climbing beans)	The leaf undersides exhibit round, whitish pustules. Later, reddish brown pustules develop on the leaf uppersides and cause dark brown spots. In severe cases, the seed capsules, too, may be full of pustules.	Dispose of affected plants with the household waste, as well as prematurely fallen leaves. Disinfect the climbing beans, maintain the correct crop rotation.
Boron deficiency (especially in Brussels sprouts, cauliflower, headed cabbage, kohlrabi, and celeriac)	Poor head development in Brussels sprouts, premature opening of the heads, brown-discolored flowers in cauliflower; in celeriac, the youngest leaves turn black and die off, with brown flecks in the tuber interiors.	Avoid excessive lime and potassium/nitrogen application. Use boron-containing fertilizers. Conduct a soil analysis.
Bottom rot (on lettuce)	Soft, rotten, light brown spots on the leaf ribs that spread to the root collar, which turns brown and rots. The head can be easily lifted off. In late infestation, the entire lettuce head wilts.	Ensure sufficient ventilation, water sparingly. Remove diseased plants.
Celery mosaic virus	Low growth in later summer, young leaves exhibit lighter-colored veins. Diseased plants develop only small tubers.	Regular aphid control. Destroy affected plants.
Clubroot (on brassicas, including kohlrabi)	Tuberous growths on the roots. Leaves turn blue-gray and wilt.	On land that has been contaminated, do not plant any cabbage species for around 4 years. Apply plenty of lime in the meantime. Dig out cabbage stalks cleanly and dispose of them with the household waste. Treat the soil with antifungal substances before planting.
Cucumber mosaic virus	Mosaic-like patterning on the youngest leaves, impeded growth, plants develop only a few flowers, fruits remain small and show a yellow-green patterning, individual leaves, shoots, or entire plants can wither and die off.	Combat aphids regularly, remove suspicious or diseased plants.
Cucumber wilt (fusarium wilt under glass and foil)	Signs of leaf yellowing, starting from the bottom, with the leaves later turning brown. Gradual wilting and drying out of the entire plant.	Disinfect the soil. Use grafted plants. Remove diseased plants immediately.
Halo blight (on beans)	Light green, rapidly spreading spots on the leaves. The leaves turn yellow and dry out. On the seed capsules, the rounder spots look as if they are saturated with grease. The seeds, too, become diseased and unusable.	Do not sow diseased seed, and do not sow seed too densely. All diseased plant parts should be disposed of with the household waste. Select resistant varieties for growing.
Leaf spot (on celeriac)	Yellowish gray to brown spots appear on the leaves, resulting in leaf damage and small celery tubers.	When harvesting the tubers, dispose of all affected leaves with the household waste. Note the disease proneness of the different varieties.

NAME OF DISEASE	SIGNS OF DAMAGE	PREVENTION AND CONTROL
Mildew, downy (on spinach and lettuce)	Gray spots on the leaf undersides. In lettuce, young plants are already affected.	Do not sow spinach too densely. Plant lettuce very shallowly. Spray with recognized fungicides. Grow resistant varieties and maintain crop rotation.
Mildew, powdery (especially on black salsify and cucumbers)	Grayish white, floury spots on the leaves. Later, they merge and cover the entire leaf.	Preferentially plant resistant or robust varieties, avoid watering late at night, and let the plants dry out before nightfall. Do not plant too densely, ensure a sufficient nutrient supply, remove mulches, harvest remnants, and weeds. Follow the instructions for use of approved pesticides.
Molybdenum deficiency (particularly in cauliflower, Brussels sprouts, and headed cabbage)	Reduced leaf blades, heart leaves become twisted, wither away, or are entirely absent.	Conduct a soil analysis. Lime application required. Use ammonium or sodium molybdate.
Onion smut	The leaves turn blue-green, burst, and turn blackish. Most plants die; those which are left remain small and blackish discolored.	Following an outbreak of this disease, do not grow onions in the immediate vicinity for 6 to 10 years.
Potato and brown rot (on tomatoes, primarily those grown outdoors)	Attacks the leaves, petioles, stems, fruit peel, and fruit flesh. Grayish green, later brown to black spots, hard patches on affected fruit flesh. Transmitted by garden tools, plant remnants on stakes.	Employ drip irrigation, remove lower leaves, apply a mulch layer to the soil, maintain crop rotation breaks, train with one shoot, pinch off early. Follow the instructions for use of approved pesticides.
Root rot (on celeriac)	Scabby brown patches on the tubers that later turn to rot. The outermost leaves turn yellow.	Avoid predominantly nitrogen fertilizer applications. Do not use fresh stable manure. Do not plant too densely or shallowly.
Stem rot (on tomatoes)	Sudden wilting of the entire plant. The root collar is black, and no longer firm. Plants that have been affected early die off. On older plants, the lower leaves turn yellow and wilt.	Keep the root collar dry. Heap up the plants at the first sign of disease. They will then develop new roots above the affected area.
Take-all (on young plants of all cabbage species)	The plants topple over in the seedbed. The root collar is black immediately above the soil.	Avoid excessive soil moisture. Rotate the areas for raising seedlings. Disinfect the soil by steaming.

ORNAMENTAL PLANTS

Table 9. Attractive Broad-Leaved Trees and Shrubs for the Garden

There are numerous garden forms and varieties available for most of these species. For dwarf forms, see **TABLE 12**.

BOTANICAL NAME ENGLISH NAME SPECIES AND VARIETIES	GROWTH FORM, HEIGHT	SPECIFIC REMARKS, FLOWERING TIME, SUITABILITY
Abeliophyllum distichum White forsythia	Loose, upright, 5 to 6 ½ ft.	Humic garden soil, flowers white, almond fragrance; earlier than *Forsythia*, II to III.
Acer japonicum 'Aconitifolium' Japanese maple	Shrub-like, 6 ½ to 13 ft.	Permeable, humic soil, sheltered warm site, sunny, winter protection initially required for young plants; leaves deeply incised, vivid red in the fall.
Amelanchier Juneberry, serviceberry 1. *A. laevis*, Alleghany service berry 2. *A. lamarckii*	1. Large shrub, 13 ft. 2. Large shrub or standard tree, up to 16 ft.; important species for bird protection and nectar source for bees	Normal garden soil, also acid soils for *A. laevis*, cut off old wood at ground level, sunny to out of direct sun, flowers white, IV to V, fruits spherical, blue-black, edible, splendid red coloring in the fall (2. copper-colored leaf shoots).
Azalea Azalea		See *Rhododendron*
Berberis Barberry 1. *B. buxifolia* 'Nana' 2. *B. gagnepainii* var. *lanceifolia* 3. *B. julianae* 4. *B. ×stenophylla* 5. *B. thunbergii* 'Atropurpurea'	Bushy shrubs; nectar source for bees; 1. 14 to 20 in. 2. 4 to 5 ft. 3. 5 to 10 ft. 4. Up to 5 ft. 5. Up to 5 ft.	Evergreen, protect from strong winds and intense winter sun, tolerates semi-shade, flowers yellow, V/VI, decorative fruits, blue to blue-black, also red; 1. Dense, roundish growth, avoid overly harsh sites; 2. Picturesque growth, overhanging when old; 3. Upright growth, tough thorns; 4. Overhanging, loose growth, delicate leaves; 5. Coral-red fruits, crimson-red leaves.
Buddleja Butterfly bush 1. *B. alternifolia* 2. *B. davidii* 3. *B. ×weyeriana*	1. Overhanging shoots, 6 ½ ft. 2. Somewhat squarrose, long, slightly angled annual shoots, up to 8 ft.; attracts butterflies 3. Overhanging shoots, 10 to 13 ft.	No waterlogging, sunny; 1. Do not cut back, grows over walls and fences, light violet flowers; 2. Often freezes back in winter, produces shoots again in spring, will flower on thick shoots from VII to X after cutting back, young plants sensitive, accordingly plant in spring, winter protection required in first year, flowers in long panicles, pink, crimson to violet, also white; 3. Flowers golden-yellow, VII.
Calycanthus floridus Carolina allspice	Somewhat squarrose, 5 to 6 ½ ft.	Damp humic soil, sheltered place, sunny, also semi-shaded, flowers VI to VII, reddish brown with a spicy fragrance; attractive solitary plant.
Caryopteris ×*clandonensis* 'Grand Bleu' Bluebeard	Compact, much branched, up to 3 ¼ ft.; nectar source for bees	Humic garden soil, sunny to semi-shaded, flowers violet to dark blue, VIII to X, frost-sensitive (winter protection required), cut back in spring before new shoots grow.
Ceanothus California lilac 1. *C. ×delilianus* 'Gloire de Versailles' 2. *C. fendleri* 3. *C. impressus* 'Victoria'	1. Small shrub up to 5 ft. 2. Ground cover 3. Bushy branching, upright, 28 to 40 in.	Sandy humic soil, sheltered sunny place, plant in spring if possible, winter protection required, evergreen, cut back in late winter, flowering time VII to X; also suitable for rock gardens; 1. Flowers violet to blue; 2. Flowers white; 3. Flowers deep-blue, nectar source for bees.
Cephalanthus occidentalis Buttonbush	Shrub form, 3 ¼ to 5 ft.	Moist humic to moist soil, flowers whitish yellow, spherical, VII to VIII, yellow-orange coloring in the fall.

BOTANICAL NAME ENGLISH NAME SPECIES AND VARIETIES	GROWTH FORM, HEIGHT	SPECIFIC REMARKS, FLOWERING TIME, SUITABILITY
Chaenomeles Flowering quince 1. *C. japonica*, Japanese quince, Maule's quince 2. *C. japonica* 'Cido', Nordic lemon 3. *C. speciosa* 'Exima' 4. *C. speciosa* 'Nivalis' 5. *C. ×superba* 'Andenken an Karl Ramcke'	Wide bushy form, somewhat squarrose, forms runners; 1. Up to 3 ¼ ft. 2. 5 ft. 3. 5 ft. 4. 5 ft. 5. 4 ft.	Will also tolerate dryness on deep soils, suitable for cut flowers, sunny to semi-shaded; 1. Flowers red, IV; 2. Flowers orange-red, V/VI, orange-yellow quinces, edible; 3. Flowers pink, IV; 4. Flowers white, IV, often with subsequent flowering in summer; 5. Flowers vermilion, IV; *C. japonica* and *C. ×superba* are important nectar sources for bees.
Clethra alnifolia 'Rosea' Sweet pepper bush, white alder	Stiffly upright, 8 ft.	Damp humic to moist, slightly acidic soil, sunny to semi-shaded, pink flower candles, vanilla fragrance, VII to IX.
Cornus Dogwood, cornel 1. Cultivated forms of *C. alba* 2. *C. florida*, Eastern flowering dogwood, white dogwood 3. *C. kousa*, Japanese dogwood 4. *C. mas*, Cornelian cherry	1. to 3. Upright, bushy, 4. Shrub form; 1. 5 to 8 ft. 2. 10 to 13 ft. and higher 3. Up to 20 ft. 4. 10 to 13 ft. and higher	1., 2., and 4. Damp soil, semi-shade; 3. Dry soil, sunny; 1. Shoots red, glossy, 'Späthii' grows less vigorously with colorful decorative foliage, flowers yellowish white, V, fruits bluish white, VIII/IX; 2. Flowering V, bracts white, fruits scarlet, foliage turns scarlet to violet, 'Rubra' with pink to red bracts; 3. Flowering V/VI, bracts white/pink, fruits red; 4. Numerous flowers, golden-yellow, III/IV, before the leaves, fruits red, edible, nectar source for bees.
Corylopsis spicata Spike winter hazel	Shrub form, 6 ½ to 8 ft.	Undemanding as regards the soil, sunny, flowers light yellow, 2 to 2 ½ in. long spikes, fragrant, early spring flowering plant.
Corylus Hazelnut 1. *C. avellana* 'Aurea', Golden hazel 2. *C. avellana* 'Contorta', Corkscrew hazel 3. *C. maxima* 'Purpurea', Purple-leaved hazel	Shrub form; 1. Up to 10 ft. 2. Up to 6 ½ ft. 3. Up to 16 ft.	Soil not too dry, sunny to semi-shaded, also as undergrowth; 1. Leaves golden-yellow, later greenish yellow; 2. Shoots twisted in a corkscrew fashion; 3. Leaves large, dark crimson.
Cotoneaster Cotoneaster 1. *C. bullatus*, Hollyberry cotoneaster 2. *C. horizontalis*, Herringbone cotoneaster 3. *C. microphyllus*, Littleleaf cotoneaster	1. 6 ½ to 10 ft., loosely branched 2. 28 in., flat, up to 6 ½ ft. wide 3. Prostrate, dense, up to 20 in.	Undemanding as regards the soil, not too infertile and not too dry; 1. Summer-green, flowers reddish white V/VI, fruits red VIII/IX, sunny to semi-shaded; 2. Summer-green, herringbone-like branching, flowers white to reddish, scarlet fruits IX/XII, strongly reddish leaf coloration in the fall, nectar source for bees; 3. Evergreen, flowers whitish pink, VI, fruits red, IX/X.
Crataegus laevigata 'Paul's Scarlet' English hawthorn	Large shrub, mostly grafted as a tree form, up to 13 ft.	Undemanding as regards the soil, sunny, strongly double flowers, radiant carmine-red, long-flowering, V, nectar source for bees.
Cytisus Broom 1. *C. ×praecox*, Warminster broom 2. *C. scoparius*, Common broom, Scotch broom	1. Densely bushy, somewhat overhanging, 5 to 6 ½ ft. 2. Dense, ascendent, 5 to 6 ½ ft.	Permeable, light soil, warm, sheltered; 1. Flowers of the species light yellow, varieties also white ('Albus'), golden-yellow ('Allgold'), or crimson-red ('Hollandia'), IV/V; 2. Calciphobous, flowers vivid yellow, carmine-red, pink, carmine-red, red-brown, also bicolored.
Daphne mezereum Mezereum, February daphne	Upright, 28 to 47 in.	Calciferous, fertile soil, semi-shaded, flowers pink-red, 'Alba' white, before or together with frondescence, III/IV, berries vivid red, VI; highly poisonous.
Deutzia Deutzia 1. *D. ×hybrida* 'Mont Rose' 2. *D. ×magnifica*, Showy deutzia 3. *D. scabra* 'Candidissima'	Upright, shrub-like; 1. 6 ½ to 8 ft. 2. 6 ½ to 10 ft. 3. 6 ½ to 10 ft.	Undemanding as regards the soil, at its most attractive in full sun but will also tolerate some shade, in older bushes thinning out after florescence will stimulate flowering; 1. Flowers pink, conspicuous yellow stamens, VI; 2. and 3. Flowers white, double, VI/VII.

BOTANICAL NAME ENGLISH NAME SPECIES AND VARIETIES	GROWTH FORM, HEIGHT	SPECIFIC REMARKS, FLOWERING TIME, SUITABILITY
Enkianthus campanulatus Redvein enkianthus	Stiffly upright, 6 ½ to 8 ft.	Humic, slightly acidic, sufficiently moist soil, lily-of-the-valley-like flowers, pink-red, V to VII, attractive fall coloration.
Euonymus Spindle 1. *E. alatus*, Winged spindle 2. *E. europaeus*, Common spindle 3. *E. phellomanus*, Corky spindle	Upright shrubs; 1. Bushy, 5 to 6 ½ ft., occasionally higher 2. 10 to 13 ft. and higher 3. 6 ½ to 10 ft.	Undemanding, soil not too dry, vivid coloring in the fall; 1. Branches with wide, wing-like, suberized strands, fruits red, IX/X, fall coloration red or pink, long lasting, 'Compactus' up to 3 ¼ ft.; 2. Tolerates shade, abundantly fruiting, nectar source for bees; 3. Wintergreen, suberized strands more prominent than in *E. alatus*, fruits coral-red.
Exochorda racemosa Common pearl bush	Squarrose growth, 8 ½ to 10 ft. and higher	Damp, also sandy soil, sunny to semi-shaded, sheltered site, trim shoots after flowering for bushy growth, flowering V, pure white, in terminal racemes; solitary shrub.
Forsythia Forsythia 1. *F. ×intermedia* 2. *F. ovata*, Korean forsythia	Upright, slightly overhanging; 1. 5 to 6 ½ ft. 2. 3 ¼ to 6 ½ ft.	Undemanding, soil not too infertile or dry, warm, sunny place, tolerates some shade, flowers mostly appear before the leaves, yellow to golden-yellow, from L. IV (2. is earlier-flowering).
Fuchsia magellanica var. *gracilis* Hardy fuchsia	Upright, 4 ft. and higher	Humic garden soil, covering with leaves beneficial in winter, sunny to semi-shaded, flowers red/violet, VI to IX, nectar source for bees.
Genista tinctoria Dyer's broom	Loose-growing bush, up to 3 ¼ ft.	Infertile, dry garden soil, full sun, golden-yellow long panicles from VI to VIII; valuable nectar source for bees.
Halesia carolina Silver bell, snowdrop tree	Shrub-like, 10 to 13 ft.	Damp, slightly acidic garden soil, sunny, flowers white, pendent, IV to V.
Hamamelis Witch hazel 1. *H. japonica*, Japanese witch hazel 2. *H. mollis*, Chinese witch hazel 3. *H. ×intermedia* 'Ruby Glow'	1. 5 to 8 ft. 2. and 3. 6 ½ to 10 ft. 3. All species also higher, shrub or tree form	Damp, fertile, humic soil, not calciferous, sheltered site, sunny to semi-shaded, bizarre growth, long-lasting, vivid yellow colors in the fall, flowers tolerate frost down to 14°F, yellow to golden-yellow (in *×intermedia* 'Ruby Glow' bronze-red), will already flower from I in mild weather.
Hibiscus syriacus Hibiscus	Rigidly upright, up to 6 ½ ft. and higher	Permeable, nutrient-rich soil, warm, sheltered site, sunny, young plants particularly frost-sensitive (winter protection required), flowers white, pink, red, or blue-violet, single or double, VIII/IX, single-flowering varieties are frost-hardier than double flowering; 'Mathilda' with 8 to 12 in. large mauve flowers, 'Russian Violet' flowers pink-violet with white center.
Holodiscus discolor Cream bush, ocean spray	Wide bushy form, slightly overhanding, 6 ½ to 10 ft. and higher	Damp soil, sunny to semi-shaded, flowers in large panicles (up to 10 in.), overhanging, creamy white, VII/VIII; variety *ariaefolius* has deeply lobed leaves.
Hydrangea Hydrangea 1. *H. arborescens*, Tree hydrangea 2. *H. macrophylla*, Bigleaf hydrangea 3. *H. paniculata* 'Grandiflora', Panicle hydrangea	Densely bushy; 1. Up to 6 ½ ft. 2. 3 ¼ to 4 ft. 3. Up to 6 ½ ft.	1. Fertile, damp, humic soil, sheltered, semi-shaded, flowers greenish white, VII/IX, 'Grandiflora' has larger flowers, but is less susceptible to rain damage than 'Annabelle'; 2. Damp, humic soil, sheltered, warm, semi-shaded, if frost-damaged produces new shoots in spring, then flowers present only in the following year, pink, red, or blue, nectar source for bees; 3. Light, damp, humic soil, somewhat acidic, flowers in terminal panicles (up to 14 in. long), initially white, then pink, VIII/IX.
Hypericum patulum St. John's wort	Loosely bushy, 28 to 40 in.	Dry humic soil, light semi-shade, light winter protection, produces new shoots in spring following frost damage, richly flowering, flowers large, golden-yellow, VIII/X; 'Hidecote' more winter hardy than the species.

BOTANICAL NAME ENGLISH NAME SPECIES AND VARIETIES	GROWTH FORM, HEIGHT	SPECIFIC REMARKS, FLOWERING TIME, SUITABILITY
Ilex aquifolium Holly	Pyramidal, bushy, 4 to 6 ½ ft., higher still when old	Damp, humic, nutrient-rich soil, sheltered from harsh wind, protected from winter sun, fruits only when there are both female and male plants together (dioecious), evergreen, inconspicuous flowers, foliage glossy green, also yellow or whitely colored, vivid red decorative berries.
Jasminum nudiflorum Winter jasmine	Spreading, climbing plant, 6 ½ to 10 ft.	Permeable, humic, non-calciferous soil, sheltered, suitable for sunny walls and trellises, when freestanding branches loosely overhanging, yellow flowers appearing before the leaves, II/III.
Kalmia latifolia Calico bush, Mountain laurel	Wide and bushy, 5 to 6 ½ ft., occasionally higher	Humus-rich, damp, moist soil, semi-shaded, evergreen, laurel-like leaves up to 4 in. long, flowers white, pink, also carmine-red, V/VI.
Kerria Kerria, Japanese rose 1. *K. japonica* 2. *K. japonica* 'Pleniflora'	1. Densely and broadly bushy, 3 ¼ to 5 ft. 2. Upright, 5 to 6 ½ ft.	Permeable, nutrient-rich soil, sunny to semi-shaded; 1. Flowers yellow, V to VII, richly flowering, tolerates more shade than the double-flowering form, nectar source for bees; 2. Double-flowering golden-yellow flowers, not as richly flowering as the species.
Kolkwitzia amabilis Beauty bush, cold whisky plant	Upright, 6 ½ to 10 ft. high and wide	Permeable, nutrient-rich soil, warm, sunny, flowers delicate pink, V to VI, richly flowering solitary shrub; nectar source for bees.
Laburnum Golden chain tree, golden rain tree, bean tree 1. *L. anagyroides* 2. *L. ×watereri* 'Vossii'	Shrub- or tree-like, stiffly upright, 10 to 16 ft. and higher	Permeable soil, sunny or out of direct sun, flowers in pendulous racemes, yellow, V/VI; 1. Racemes 8 in. long, nectar source for bees; 2. Especially rich-flowering, racemes up to 20 in. long; all plant parts of 1. and 2. are poisonous!
Lonicera ledebourii Twinberry honeysuckle	Long shoots, wide, 5 to 6 ½ ft. high, occasionally higher	Soil not too dry, light semi-shade tolerated, flowers yellow or orange-yellow with red, V/VI, fruits blackish crimson, VII/IX.
Magnolia Magnolia 1. *M. kobus*, kobushi magnolia 2. *M. liliiflora* 'Nigra', Crimson magnolia 3. *M. ×soulangeana*, Lenne's magnolia, saucer magnolia 4. *M. stellata*, Star magnolia	1. and 3. tree-like or large shrub, 13 to 20 ft., occasionally higher 2. Shrub-like, 10 ft. 4. Wide and bushy, 6 ½ to 10 ft.	Damp, humic, acidic soil, sheltered, because late frost damages the flowers, especially in *M. stellata*, which flowers in III, flowering in all cases before or at the same time as shoot production; 1. Flowers white, IV/V, fruits cylindrical, red; 2. Flowers dark crimson-red, only slightly lighter on the inside, petals up to 4 ¾ in. long, V; 3. Flowers white or light crimson on the inside, pink to dark crimson outside, IV/V; 4. Flowers white, also pink or crimson, III/IV.
Mahonia aquifolium Mahonia	Densely bushy, 3 ¼ to 4 ft., occasionally higher	Soil not too dry, semi-shade well tolerated, evergreen, flowers in upright racemes, yellow, IV/V, fruits blue when ripe, leaves highly glossy; nectar source for bees.
Malus Decorative apple	Upright, bushy, height and width dependent on the species or grafting base	Also infertile, sandy soils, but then slower growing, flowers white to pink, red, or wine-red, single, semi-double, or double, V to VI, occasionally from L. IV, fruits yellow to red, decorative.
Paeonia ×suffruticosa Tree peony	Densely bushy, wide, up to 3 ¼ ft. and higher	Nutrient-rich, damp, deep soil, but also permeable, sensitive to waterlogging, sunny to semi-shaded, somewhat sheltered, slow growing, flowers yellow, white, pink to dark red, scarlet, or crimson, single or double, up to 6 in. wide, V to VI, frondescence endangered by late frost.

BOTANICAL NAME ENGLISH NAME SPECIES AND VARIETIES	GROWTH FORM, HEIGHT	SPECIFIC REMARKS, FLOWERING TIME, SUITABILITY
Philadelphus Mock orange 1. *P. coronarius*, Sweet mock orange 2. *P. ×lemoinei* 3. *P. ×purpureomaculatus* 'Belle Étoile' 4. *P. ×virginalis* 'Girandole', 'Schneesturm'	Upright, shrub-like; 1. Up to 10 ft. 2. 3 ¼ to 6 ½ ft. 3. 3 ¼ to 5 ft. 4. 5 to 6 ½ ft., already flowering as young plants	Soil not too dry, thin out older shoots every 2 years, remove excessively aged wood (darker, often split) near the ground, tolerates shade, more richly flowering on sunny sites, flowers white; 1. Growth somewhat overhanging, flowers single, V/VI, 'Aureus' 2 in. yellowish leaves, 'Zeyheri' 10 ft.; 2. Flowers semi-double, VI, 'Dame Blanche' up to 5 ft., 'Bouquet Blanc' 6 ½ ft., 'Manteau d'Hermine' up to 5 ft., 'Mont Blanc' 3 ¼ ft.; 3. Flowers single, crimson-red spot at the base, VI to VII; 4. Flowers tightly double, VI.
Pieris japonica Japanese pieris, lily-of-the-valley bush	Bushy, 5 to 6 ½ ft., occasionally higher	Damp to moist, humic, slightly acid garden soil, sheltered from the wind, semi-shaded, evergreen, panicles white, elegantly overhanging, IV/V; 'Valley Valentine' flowers red.
Potentilla fruticosa Golden hardhack, shrubby cinquefoil	Bushy, upright or broadly bushy, also nearly creeping; 28 to 40 in., also up to 5 ft.	Permeable garden soil, not overly nutrient-poor, sunny, flowers yellow to golden-yellow, also white, long-flowering, V to X; lower varieties for rock gardens, also for group planting; nectar source for bees.
Prunus 1. *P. laurocerasus*, Cherry laurel, laurel 2. *P. serrulata*, Oriental cherry 3. *P. triloba* 'Plena', Flowering almond	1. Bushy, wide, 3 ¼ to 5 ft. and higher, also low-growing and ground-cover varieties 2. Shrub- or tree-like, upright or overhanging, also columnar, 13 to 16 ft. and higher 3. Broadly bushy, 5 to 6 ½ ft.	1. Heavy, humic soil, semi-shade, also shaded, evergreen, leaves glossy green, flowers white, V, fruits blue-black, can freeze back somewhat in hard winters, will then produce new shoots, nectar source for bees; 2. Deep, damp soil, often grafted as a standard tree, flowers white, pink to dark pink, semi-double or double, also single, IV/V, attractive fall coloration in some varieties, *P. subhirtella* is similar, but lower growing and more graceful; 3. Permeable soil, sheltered, also semi-shaded, cut back long shoots after flowering, also grafted as a half-standard or standard tree, flowers pink, double, IV, before frondescence on the previous year's wood.
Pyracantha coccinea Burning bush, firethorn	Squarrose, thorny bushes, 5 to 8 ft., occasionally higher	Deep soil, sunny to semi-shaded, protection from winter sun, wintergreen, flowers white, V/VI, fruits red to yellow, IX/XI; can also be used as a hedge plant, fruiting branches can be used a vase decoration.
Rhododendron Rhododendron 1. *R.* 'Praecox' 2. Large-leaved hybrids and varieties, alpine rose 3. Small-leaved hybrids and varieties, azalea	1. Bushy, stubby, 3 ¼ to 5 ft. 2. Shrub-like, 3 ¼ to 10 ft. 3. Densely bushy, 12 to 24, also 32 in.	1. Mostly evergreen, flowers often endangered by late frost, flowers light carmine-red, III/IV; 2. and 3. Not too heavy, humic, slightly acidic, sufficiently moist soil, sheltered site, higher air humidity, light semi-shade, no waterlogging, varieties winter hardy to varying degrees, flowering V, protect from winter sun, ground covering with bark humus or bark mulch.
Rhus typhina Staghorn sumac	Squarrose, tree-like or large shrub, 10 to 13 ft. and higher	Permeable, also nutrient-poor soil, sunny, fast growing ('Laciniata' weakly growing), picturesque growth, large pinnate leaves ('Laciniata' with laciniate leaves), vivid red fall coloration, leaves green, also reddish tinged, red fruits in large spike-like fruit stands.
Ribes sanguineum Flowering currant	Upright, bushy, 4 to 6 ½ ft., occasionally higher	Undemanding as regards the soil, richly flowering in full sun, also tolerates semi-shade, can be cut back severely, flowers in pendulous racemes, dark red, IV/V, nectar source for bees.
Robinia hispida Bristly locust, rose acacia	Shrubby, 4 to 5 ft. and higher	Permeable, also sandy soil, sheltered from the wind because the wood is brittle, forms runners, grows wide, flowers pink to deep crimson, large, loose racemes, VI/VII; 'Macrophylla' flowers 10 days earlier, somewhat higher.

BOTANICAL NAME ENGLISH NAME SPECIES AND VARIETIES	GROWTH FORM, HEIGHT	SPECIFIC REMARKS, FLOWERING TIME, SUITABILITY
Salix caprea 'Pendula' Goat willow, pussy willow, sallow	Pendulous shoots, 5 to 6 ½ ft.	Damp, nutrient-rich soil, sunny to semi-shaded, flowers IV to V, cut back severely after flowering, nectar source for bees.
Sambucus nigra Common elder, elderberry	Shrub, also raised as tree, 13 ft.	Damp, nutrient-rich, also calciferous soil, sunny to semi-shaded, can be severely cut back, flowers white, V/VI; 'Laciniata' with laciniate leaves, 'Sörensens Glanzblatt' with highly glossy foliage.
Spiraea Bridewort 1. *S.* ×*arguta*, Garland wreath 2. *S. japonica* 'Anthony Waterer', Japanese meadowsweet, Japanese spirea 3. *S.* ×*vanhouttei*, Vanhoutte spirea	1. Shrub-like, overhanging, up to 6 ½ ft. 2. Shrub-like, 32 in. 3. Upright, overhanging, up to 10 ft.	Undemanding as regards the soil, will also tolerate some dryness, sunny; 1. Flowers white, richly flowering, IV/V; 2. 4 to 6 in. wide corymbs on shoot end, flowers vivid carmine-red, VII to IX, leaves in new shoot red, then dark green, narrow; 3. Flowers white, richly flowering, V/VI; all of the above can also be used for free-growing hedges.
Stephanandra Lace shrub 1. *S. incisa*, Cutleaf lace shrub 2. *S. tanakae*, Japanese stephanandra	Bushy, decorative; 1. 3 ¼ to 5 ft. 2. 5 to 6 ½ ft.	Damp, humic soil, flowers greenish white, brown-red, long-lasting fall coloration of the foliage; 1. Flowers VI; can also be used for free-growing hedges; 2. Flowers VI/VII.
Symphoricarpos Snowberry 1. *S. albus* var. *laevigatus* 2. *S.* ×*chenaultii*, Chenault coralberry	Upright, slightly overhanging, 3 ¼ to 5 ft., occasionally higher	1. No special demands for growth, flowers white to pink, VII/VIII, fruits white berries, long lasting on the shrubs, can also be used as a free-growing hedge; 2. Sheltered site, flowers pink, VI/VII, berries red with white dots.
Syringa Lilac 1. *S. meyeri* 'Pink Perfume', Meyer lilac, Korean lilac 2. *S.* ×*vulgaris*, Common lilac, French lilac	1. Densely bushy, 3 ¼ to 4 ft. 2. Rigidly upright, 8 ½ to 13 ft. depending on the variety	Damp, humic soil, sunny, also out of direct sun, flowers in terminal panicles; 1. Blue to purple-pink, very long flowering time, VI to IX, for borders and tubs on terraces; 2. 'Andenken an L. Späth' flowers dark crimson-red, single; 'Charles Joly' flowers crimson-red, double; 'Michel Buchner' flowers large, purple, double; 'Mme. Lemoine' flowers pure white, double (ungrafted).
Tamarix Salt cedar, tamarisk 1. *T. parviflora*, small flower tamarisk 2. *T. ramosissima*, salt cedar	Loose-growing, upright, 2. overhanging; 1. 10 to 13 ft. 2. 10 to 15 ft.	Light, permeable soil, also infertile or calciferous, warm, rather sheltered site, leaves scale-like on shoot; 1. Flowers light pink, V; 2. Flowers vivid pink in long panicles, VII/VIII.
Viburnum Viburnum, snowball bush 1. *V. carlesii*, Sweet viburnum 2. *V. opulus* 'Roseum', European cranberrybush, guelder rose 3. *V. plicatum* f. *tomentosum* 4. *V. rhytidophyllum*, Leatherleaf viburnum	1. Bushy, loose growing, 3 ¼ to 5 ft. 2. Wide, loose growing, up to 13 ft. 3. Broad, dense, up to 10 ft. 4. Rigidly branched, up to 13 ft.	1. Damp soil, warm, sheltered, not hot and dry, shaded, slow-growing, flowers white, pink on the outside, fragrant, semi-spheroid cymes, IV/V, fruits blue-black; 2. Damp soil, prone to aphid infestation in dry places, flowers white, delicate pink when wilting, fruits fiery red, fall coloration wine- to fiery red, nectar source for bees; 3. Damp soil, flowers white, V/VI, up to 4 in. wide corymbose cymes, wine-red fall coloration; 4. Damp to moist nutrient-rich soil, preferably shaded to sunny, evergreen, flowers up to 8 in. wide corymbose cymes, creamy white, V/VI, fruits red to black, VII to IX.
Weigela Weigela	Upright, densely bushy, up to 6 ½ ft., occasionally higher	Permeable, rather nutrient-rich soil, sunny to semi-shaded, thin out a little after flowering, 'Alexandra' flowers dark pink, up to 3 ¼ ft., V to VI, 'Eva Rathke' flowers ruby-red, also white and pink, 6 ½ ft., VI to VIII, *W. middendorffiana* flowers cream-yellow, up to 5 ft., V to VI.

Table 10. Recommended Conifers

Since most of the large conifer trees are unsuitable for growing in our gardens, some selected varieties and cultivated forms are also named here. For dwarf forms, see **TABLE 12**.

BOTANICAL NAME ENGLISH NAME #. SPECIES	GROWTH FORM, HEIGHT	SPECIFIC REMARKS
Abies Fir 1. *A. concolor*, Colorado fir, white fir 2. *A. lasiocarpa* var. *arizonica*, Arizona cork bark fir 3. *A. nordmanniana*, Caucasian fir 4. *A. procera* 'Glauca', Noble fir 5. *A. veitchii*, Veitch fir, Veitsch's silver fir	1. Pyramidal, over 80 ft. 2. Slender, 10 to 40 ft. 3. Slender and conical, up to 165 ft. 4. Broadly pyramidal, 26 to 50 ft., and higher 5. Slender, up to 66 ft.	Deep, nutrient-rich, moist soil, out of direct sun, somewhat calciphobous; 1. Vigorously growing, tolerates rather dry soil, loose growth form, needles up to 3 in. long, green to bluish green on both sides; 2. Slow growing, slender and columnar, needles soft, 1¼ in. long, 'Glauca' needles bluish, 'Compacta' 10 ft. high; 3. Branches arranged in regular levels, needles up to 1¾ in. long, tipped, not piercing, two white stripes on the underside; 4. Slow growing only initially, needles densely clustered, up to 1½ in., silvery dark blue; 5. Initially rapid, then slower growth, needles often somewhat twisted with two tips, two light stripes on the underside.
Araucaria araucana Chile pine, monkey puzzle	Pyramidal, crown conical, around 100 ft.	Very decorative, damp, somewhat moist soil, loves high air humidity, sunny, light protection required when young, unsuitable for harsh situations, needles narrow and triangular, stiff, dark green.
Calocedrus decurrens Incense cedar	Columnar to slender and conical, up to 130 ft., remaining low growing in cultivation	Damp soil, undemanding, somewhat sheltered, sunny, needles scale-like, contiguous, arranged in fours in false whorls, dark green; 'Columnaris' strictly conical, 'Glauca' needles blue-green.
Cedrus atlantica Atlantic cedar, Atlas cedar 1. *C. atlantica* 'Glauca', Blue atlas cedar 2. *C. atlantica* 'Glauca Pendula', Weeping blue atlas cedar	1. Loose, pyramidal, up to 66 ft. 2. Pendulous, 16 to 23 ft.	Permeable, calciferous soil, tolerates dryness better than waterlogging, needles can fall off in hard frost, protect young plants from winter sun; 1. Initially wide conical form, needles blue-gray; 2. Lateral branches of main branches hanging down like curtains, needles initially golden-yellow, later green.
Chamaecyparis False cypress 1. *C. lawsoniana*, Lawson's cypress, Oregon cedar 2. *C. nootkatensis* 'Pendula', Nootka cypress (syn. *Xanthocyparis nootkatensis*)	1. Growth and height from 6½ to 50 ft., depending on the variety, weakly growing 2. Slender and upright, 33 to 50 ft.	Permeable, humic soil, not too dry, sunny to out of direct sun; 1. 'Alumii' conical, 16 to 33 ft., needles blue with fan-like arrangement, 'Ellwoodii' conical to slender and columnar, up to 8 ft., needles dense, blue-green, 'Golden Wonder' columnar, needles yellow-green, 'Kelleriis Gold' 33 ft., needles greenish yellow to golden-yellow, 'Minima Glauca' initially almost spheroid, later upright 3¼ ft., needles bluish green; 2. Pendulous branches, widely spaced, needles fresh green, 'Aurea' needles yellow to yellow-green, 'Glauca' needles blue-green.
Cryptomeria japonica Japanese cedar	Slender and conical, up to 160 ft.	Soil not too dry, loves higher air humidity, sunny to out of direct sun, needles sickle-shaped, around 1 in. long, 'Compacta' up to 33 ft.
Cunninghamia lanceolata China fir	Crown conical, up to 66 ft., in cultivation lower, up to 13 ft.	No dry soil, semi-shaded, suitable for mild situations only, protect young trees from severe frost and winter sun, needles stiff, 1¼ to 2¾ in. long, dark green, 'Glauca' with bluish needles tolerates lower temperatures than the species.
×*Cuprocyparis leylandii* Leyland cypress	Slender and columnar, dense, up to 66 ft.	Nutrient-rich soil, also semi-shaded, up to 33 ft., 'Castlewellan Gold' needles golden-yellow, growth form wide and compact (6½ to 10 ft. wide).
Ginkgo biloba Ginkgo	Upright, up to 82 ft.	Light, moist soil, sunny, loose growth, loosely branched, leaves fan-shaped, often incised or lobed, rough and leathery, fresh green, golden-yellow in the fall; 'Pendula' branches long and hanging down.

BOTANICAL NAME ENGLISH NAME #. SPECIES	GROWTH FORM, HEIGHT	SPECIFIC REMARKS
Juniperus Juniper 1. *J. chinensis*, Chinese juniper 2. *J. communis*, Common juniper 3. *J. ×pfitzeriana* (*Juniperus chinensis ×J. sabina*), Pfitzer juniper 4. *J. sabina*, Savin juniper 5. *J. virginiana*, Eastern red cedar, pencil cedar, red juniper	1. Broadly projecting, up to 6 ½ ft., occasionally higher 2. 6 ½ to 10 ft. and higher 3. Broadly projecting, 10 ft. 4. Diffuse, 3 ¼ to 5 ft., 6 ½ to 10 ft. wide 5. Slender and upright, up to 13 ft., occasionally higher All of the above are at their most attractive when freestanding!	Permeable soil, undemanding, sunny; 1. 'Blue Alps' funnel-shaped, bushy and upright, up to 6 ½ ft., needles silvery blue-green, 'Keteleeri' upright, almost columnar, 'Monarch' slenderly spheroid, later upright and conical, needles piercing, 'Stricta' broadly upright, later conical, needles small, bluish; 2. 'Green Carpet' weakly growing, also suitable for plant tubs on the terrace, up to 12 in. high, up to 3 ¼ ft. wide, 'Hibernica', Irish juniper, short stem, slender, needles dense, blue-green, 'Suecica', Swedish juniper, rigidly upright, branch tips overhanging, needles bluish light green, 'Oblonga Pendula' broadly ascendent, picturesque pendulous branches, up to 16 ft. high; 3. Fast growing, up to 13 ft. wide, branches elegantly overhanging, needles fresh green, 'Pfitzeriana Aurea' weakly growing, up to 5 ft., young shoots golden-yellow, later yellowish green, 'Pfitzeriana Compacta' stubby, densely branched, up to 3 ¼ ft. high, up to 10 ft. wide, 'Mint Julep' slow growing, spread out flat, compact, up to around 3 ¼ ft. high, 8 ft. wide, needles pointed, fresh green, 'Old Gold' (similar to 'Gold Coast') slow growing, compact, broadly projecting, up to 3 ¼ ft. high, needles golden-yellow; 4. Needles bluish green, calciferous, 'Tamariscifolia' flat, loose, needles bluish green, 'Rockery Gem' needles blue-green, branches spreading horizontally, well branched, up to 20 in. high; 5. 'Skyrocket' slender, columnar, needles silvery green (similar to 'Blue Arrow'), 'Grey Owl' wide, densely bushy, branches directed diagonally upward to horizontally, tips overhanging, up to 10 ft. high, up to 16 ft. wide, needles with grayish blue frosting.
Larix Larch 1. *L. decidua*, European larch 2. *L. kaempferi*, Japanese larch	Broadly pyramidal, up to 100 ft. Does not tolerate crowding out by other trees and shrubs!	Damp to moist, deep, nutrient-rich soil, vivid yellow fall coloration; 1. Loosely pendulous branchlets, tolerates some dryness, 'Pendula' branchlets pendulous or lying on the ground; 2. Broadly growing, branchlets less pendulous, needles up to 1 ¼ in. long, soft, blue-green, 'Diana' up to 33 ft., up to 13 ft. wide, branches and branchlets twisted in a corkscrew fashion, 'Stiff Weeping' or 'Pendula' strongly pendulous branchlets.
Metasequoia glyptostroboides Dawn redwood	Broadly pyramidal, 100 ft. and higher	Damp, permeable soil, very fast growing, branches candelabra-like, needles fresh-green.
Picea Spruce 1. *P. abies*, common spruce, Norway spruce 2. *P. glauca* var. *albertiana* 'Conica', Alberta spruce, Alberta white spruce 3. *P. omorika*, Serbian spruce 4. *P. pungens*, Blue spruce, Colorado spruce	1. Broadly conical, up to 130 ft. 2. Very dense, conical, up to 6 ½ ft. 3. Pyramidal, slender, up to 115 ft. 4. Conical, up to 66 ft.	Medium-heavy, but no infertile dry soil, places fewer demands on the site than firs but more than pines, young plants need more sun than firs but less than pines; 1. 'Acrocona' marked cone formation already in young plants, needles glossy green, 'Inversa', strongly pendulous branches, 16 to 33 ft.; 2. Strictly conical, needles up to ½ in. long, fresh green, arranged on all sides, 'Blue Wonder' needles blue-gray; 3. Very slender, fast growing, needles dark green, tolerates summer dryness better than stagnant wetness, 'Nana' broadly conical, needles twisted, 10 ft. when fully grown, 'Pendula' weeping Serbian spruce, up to 33 ft., branches dense, overhanging, slightly twisted, 'Pimoko' flatly spheroid, 12 in.; 4. Needles silvery to greenish blue, 'Hoopsii' horizontally spreading branchlets, needles uniformly silver-blue.

BOTANICAL NAME ENGLISH NAME #. SPECIES	GROWTH FORM, HEIGHT	SPECIFIC REMARKS
Pinus Pine 1. *P. cembra*, Arolla pine, Swiss stone pine 2. *P. heldreichii* 'Compacta Gem', compact Bosnian pine, 'Smidtii', dwarf Bosnian pine 3. *P. nigra*, Austrian pine, black pine, Corsican pine 4. *P. parviflora*, South Japanese white pine 5. *P. strobus*, White pine	1. Initially slender and pw 2. Pyramidal, up to 6 ½ ft. 3. Broadly conical, spreading, up to 66 ft., occasionally higher 4. Loosely upright, up to 33 ft., up to 20 ft. wide 5. Upright, up to 66 ft. All pines will remain green right down to the ground, but only if they are freestanding.	Lighter, also sandy, infertile soil, sunny; 1. Slow growing, needles dark green in groups of five, 'Westerstede' up to 10 ft., very compact; 2. Slow and stubby growing, dense branching, closed structure, needles dark green, long, in groups of two; 3. Needles fresh to dark green, relatively long, 'Nana' dwarf black pine, shrub-like, young plants nearly spherical, older plants broadly upright, around 6 ½ ft., needles dark green, stiff, and piercing; 'Pyramidalis' ghost pine, slender and pyramidal, compact, needles dense, dark green, rigid, and piercing; 4. Moderately dry to damp, permeable soil, picturesque, needles up to 2 ½ in. long in groups of five, 'Negishii' growth weak, broadly conical, needles strongly twisted, uppersides blue-white, 'Tempelhof' growth strong, branches irregular, horizontal, needles somewhat twisted, blue-green; 5. Damp soil, fast growing, needles very long, arranged loosely in groups of five, 'Minima' up to 3 ¼ ft., weakly growing, flatly spheroid, needles grass-green, 'Radiata' up to 10 ft., needles shorter, blue-green.
Pseudotsuga menziesii var. *glauca* Douglas fir	Broad, loose growing, 66 to 100 ft.	Damp, light humic soil, fast growing, branches wider and looser than those of the spruce, almost horizontal, needles up to 1 ½ in. long, soft, fresh green, with two thin whitish stripes on the underside.
Sciadopitys verticillata Umbrella pine	Uniformly conical, in central Europe 33 ft. high at most.	Damp, sandy-humic, lime-deficient, permeable soil, semi-shaded, double needles 3 to 4 ¾ in. long, grouped together in umbrella-like whorls, deep green.
Taxus Yew 1. *T. baccata*, Common yew, English yew 2. *T. ×media*, Hybrid yew, Welleseley yew (hybrid between *T. baccata* and *T. cuspidata* var. *cuspidata*)	1. Upright or broad, up to 13 ft., depending on species and variety, older trees also taller 2. Irregular, broadly columnar, 6 ½ to 10 ft. All yews grow very slowly. All plant parts, except for red fruit flesh, are poisonous.	Damp, nutrient-rich soil, also calciferous, not suitable for dry, hot sites or waterlogging, tolerate shade well; 1. 'Nissens Corona' flat, up to 5 ft., 23 ft. wide, needles light green, 'Overeynderi', broad, pyramidal, up to 13 ft., 'Semperaurea', golden yew, broadly spreading, up to 6 ½ ft., needles golden-yellow, 'Fastigiata Robusta', column yew, slender and columnar, 13 to 20 ft., up to 3 ¼ ft. wide, needles wide and curved downward, fresh green, 'Fastigiata Aureomarginata', golden Irish yew, slender, columnar, rigidly upright, hardly over 10 ft., needles with yellow edges, later turning green; 2. 'Hicksii', Hicks yew, spreading branches, very dense growth, older trees somewhat looser, needles 1 in. long, in two rows, radiating on upright shoots, otherwise arranged in two rows, glossy dark green.
Thuja Red cedar 1. *T. occidentalis*, Red cedar 2. *T. plicata* 'Atrovirens', Western red cedar	1. Upright or broad, 33 to 50 ft. and higher, depending on the variety 2. Fast growing, conical with pointed tip, up to 40 ft., 10 ft. wide Plant and cones poisonous!	Needles scale-like, sufficiently moist soil, withstands cutting back; 1. 'Columna' vigorous growth, slender and conical, 20 to 50 ft., needles dark green, 'Holmstrup' slow growing, slender and conical, up to 10 ft., needles saturated green, 'Smaragd' upright, slender and conical, up to 16 ft. or higher, needles glossy fresh green, 'Yellow Ribbon' slender and columnar, up to 13 ft., 3 ¼ ft. wide, needles intensive golden-yellow; 2. 'Atrovirens' needles deep green and glossy, 'Aurescens' broadly conical, remains densely branched right down to the ground, shoot tips bronze-yellow.
Tsuga canadensis Canadian hemlock, eastern hemlock	Upright, broad, 50 ft. and higher	Somewhat sheltered site, sufficient moisture, fails on dry, hot sites, branches nearly horizontal with overhanging shoot tips and fine needles; weakly growing forms for rock gardens.

Table 11. Recommended Trees and Shrubs for Hedges

BOTANICAL NAME ENGLISH NAME SPECIES AND VARIETIES	BEST HEDGE HEIGHT, PLANT REQUIREMENT IN PLANTS/YARD, BEST PLANTING TIME (MONTH IN ROMAN NUMERALS)	SPECIFIC REMARKS, SUITABILITY
Acer campestre Field maple, hedge maple	6 ½ to 10 ft. and higher, 3 plants, III to IV and X	Broad-leaved, undemanding, can be grown in every garden soil that is not too cold and not too acidic, suitable for heavy trimming, also freestanding, only saplings with lateral shoots are good for planting.
Berberis Barberry 1. *B. buxifolia* 'Nana', Magellan barberry 2. *B. thunbergii*, Japanese barberry 3. *B. thunbergii* 'Atropurpurea', Purple leaf barberry 4. *B. verruculosa*, Warty barberry	1. 8 to 12 in., 6 plants, III to IV 2. 24 to 32 in., 3 or 4 plants, III to IV 3. 24 to 40 in., 3 or 4 plants, III to IV 4. 24 to 32 in., 4 plants, III to IV	Broad-leaved, places no special demands on the soil, thorny; 1. Evergreen, easily freezes out in excessively dry situations, also tolerates semi-shade; 2. and 3. Sun, will also tolerate sites out of direct sun, suitable for heavy trimming; 3. Deep crimson-red foliage; 4. Evergreen, glossy leaves, reliable, low, freestanding hedge.
Buxus sempervirens 'Blauer Heinz', 'Suffruticosa' Boxwood, common box	6 to 20 in., 6 to 15 plants, IV or IX	Broad-leaved, evergreen, alkaline soil, sunny to shaded, withstands heavy trimming, suitable for edging and low hedges, higher cultivated forms also available.
Carpinus betulus Common hornbeam, European hornbeam	3 ¼ to 13 ft., 3 or 4 plants, III to IV	Broad-leaved, nutrient-rich soil, sunny, light shade, withstands heavy trimming, young trees should have lateral shoots all the way down.
Chamaecyparis lawsoniana Lawson's cypress, Oregon cedar	3 ¼ to 6 ½ ft., 3 or 4 plants, IV or IX	Coniferous, humic, sandy loam soil, shade-tolerant, withstands heavy trimming, sunburn-affected plant parts in winter will grow out again.
Cornus mas Cornelian cherry	6 ½ to 8 ft., 2 or 3 plants, IV or IX/X	Broad-leaved, withstands trimming, calciferous, suitable for high, wide hedges, nectar source for bees.
Cotoneaster Cotoneaster 1. *C. acutifolius* 2. *C. dielsianus* var. *dielsianus* 3. *C. divaricatus*, Spreading cotoneaster	1. 3 ¼ to 8 ft., 3 or 4 plants, IV and IX 2. 3 ¼ to 6 ½ ft., 3 or 4 plants, IV and IX 3. 3 ¼ to 6 ½ ft., 3 or 4 plants, IV and IX	Broad-leaved, good garden soil at a site that is not too dry; sunny and semi-shaded; 1. For freestanding and trimmed hedges, very robust; 2. and 3. For freestanding hedges; both with decorative berry fruits in the fall.
×*Cuprocyparis leylandii* Leyland cypress	10 ft. (up to 20 to 23 ft.), 3 plants, IV or IX	Coniferous, evergreen, garden soil that is damp and not too dry, withstands heavy trimming, somewhat sensitive in harsh, windy situations, for high hedges.
Elaeagnus multiflora Cherry eleagnus	5 to 8 ft., 2 or 3 plants, IV or IX/X	Broad-leaved, not too dry humic soils, sunny, also produces fruits after not too heavy trimming, fruits edible, for dense hedges.
Fagus sylvatica Common beech, European beech	6 ½ to 13 ft., 3 or 4 plants, III to IV	Broad-leaved, damp, deep soil, withstands heavy trimming, young plants should have dense lateral shoots all the way down.
Forsythia ×*intermedia* 'Spectabilis', 'Weekend' Forsythia	5 to 6 ½ ft., 2 or 3 plants, IV or IX/X	Broad-leaved, undemanding as regards the soil, sunny, warm site, can be cut back or shaped following flowering, for freestanding hedges.
Gleditsia triacanthos Honey locust	6 ½ to 10 ft., and higher, 2 or 3 plants, IV and X	Broad-leaved, nutrient-rich soil that has been deeply worked, tolerates some dryness and heavy trimming, for thorny, narrow hedges.
Ilex Holly 1. *I. aquifolium*, Common holly, English holly 2. *I. crenata* 'Fastigiata', Boxleaf holly, Japanese holly	3 ¼ to 6 ½ ft., 2 or 3 plants, IV; both very slow growing	Broad-leaved, evergreen, damp, humic, nutrient-rich soil, protect from strong wind and intense winter sun, leaves glossy, decorative fruits only when both female and male plants are present, for freestanding and trimmed hedges, shade-tolerant.

BOTANICAL NAME ENGLISH NAME SPECIES AND VARIETIES	BEST HEDGE HEIGHT, PLANT REQUIREMENT IN PLANTS/YARD, BEST PLANTING TIME (MONTH IN ROMAN NUMERALS)	SPECIFIC REMARKS, SUITABILITY
Juniperus ×pfitzeriana Pfitzer juniper	5 to 6 ½ ft., 2 or 3 plants, IV or IX	Broad-leaved, evergreen, sunny, also semi-shaded, important bird protection species, for freestanding hedges.
Kerria japonica Japanese rose, Jew's mallow, kerria	32 to 48 in., 2 or 4 plants, IV or X	Broad-leaved, permeable, fertile soil, sunny, also semi-shaded, fewer flowers if heavily trimmed, flowers golden-yellow, V to VI; 'Pleniflora' with double flowers, grows higher.
Ligustrum Privet 1. *L. obtusifolium* var. *regelianum* 2. *L. ovalifolium*, Californian privet, 'Aureum', Golden privet 3. *L. vulgare* 'Atrovirens' 4. *L. vulgare* 'Lodense'	1. and 3. 24 to 48 in., 2. 4 or 5 plants, IV or X 3. to 10 ft., 3 or 4 plants, III to V 4. 12 to 16 in., 5 or 6 plants, IV or X	Broad-leaved, all sunny to semi-shaded; 1. Good soil, broadly growing, for freestanding hedges; 2. Wintergreen, leaves with golden-yellow edge; 3. and 4. Place fewer demands on the soil, foliage remains on the shrub in winter, for heavily trimmed hedges; 4. For low hedges.
Lonicera Honeysuckle 1. *L. nitida*, Box honeysuckle, 'Elegant' 2. *L. xylosteum*, Fly honeysuckle	1. 20 to 32 in., 3 or 4 plants, IV and IX/X 2. 4 to 6 ½ ft., 2 or 3 plants, III/IV and X	Broad-leaved; 1. Good soil, somewhat sheltered; grows back quickly after frost damage, evergreen, for heavy trimming, also for freestanding hedges; 2. Undemanding, for freestanding hedges only.
Mahonia aquifolium Holly grape, Oregon grape	20 to 32 in., 3 or 4 plants, IV/V	Broad-leaved, evergreen, damp soil, can be heavily trimmed, more attractive as freestanding hedge owing to its flowers and blue fruits, nectar source for bees.
Philadelphus ×lemoinei 'Erectus' Mock orange	32 to 100 in., 2 or 4 plants, IV or X	Broad-leaved, medium-heavy soil, sunny, richly flowering (white) when freestanding, for both freestanding and heavily trimmed hedges.
Potentilla fruticosa (syn. *Dasiphora fruticosa*) Golden hardhack, shrubby cinquefoil	28 to 40 in., 3 or 4 plants, III/IV and X	Broad-leaved, nutrient-rich, rather permeable soil, sunny, do not cut back too severely but trim to shape only, then also richly flowering.
Pyracantha coccinea Firethorn 1. *P.* 'Red Column' 2. *P.* 'Soleil d'Or'	1. 6 ½ to 10 ft., 1 or 2 plants, IV 2. 4 ¼ to 5 ½ ft., 2 or 3 plants, IV	Broad-leaved, deep soil, sunny or semi-shaded, wintergreen, withstands heavy trimming, attractive when freestanding, since it then produces many decorative berries; 1. Fruits red, already on young plants, resistant to scabs; 2. Fruits golden-yellow.
Ribes Currant, gooseberry 1. *R. alpinum* 'Schmidt', Alpine currant, mountain currant 2. *R. sanguineum*, Flowering currant	1. 32 to 48 in., 3 or 4 plants, IV and X 2. 5 to 6 ½ ft., 3 or 4 plants, IV and X	Broad-leaved; 1. Also sandy soil, also for semi-shaded situations, tolerates severe trimming, but more richly flowering when freestanding, flowers inconspicuous, greenish yellow, very early frondescence, including lower-growing varieties; 2. Undemanding, richly flowering in full sun, also semi-shaded, suitable for freestanding hedges only, light trimming to shape after flowering. vivid dark red racemes, for example 'Atrorubens' IV/V.
Salix purpurea Purple willow 'Nana', 'Gracilis', Dwarf purple willow	32 to 40 in., 2 or 3 plants, IV and X	Broad-leaved, undemanding, tolerates considerable dryness, delicate silver-gray foliage, red-brown wood, broadly growing, withstands heavy trimming.
Sambucus Elder 1. *S. nigra*, Common elder, elderberry 2. *S. racemosa*, Red-berried elder, red elderberry	6 ½ to 10 ft., 1 or 2 plants, IV to V and X	Broad-leaved, damp humus-rich, soil, for large, freestanding hedges, fruits edible (only when cooked); 1. Flowers white, V, Fruits black; 2. Flowers creamy-yellow, fruits red.

BOTANICAL NAME ENGLISH NAME SPECIES AND VARIETIES	BEST HEDGE HEIGHT, PLANT REQUIREMENT IN PLANTS/YARD, BEST PLANTING TIME (MONTH IN ROMAN NUMERALS)	SPECIFIC REMARKS, SUITABILITY
Spiraea Bridewort 1. *S. ×arguta*, Garland bridewort 2. *S. japonica* 'Anthony Waterer', Japanese spirea, Japanese meadowsweet 3. *S. ×vanhouttei*	1. 3 ¼. to 5 ft., 2 or 3 plants, IV or X 2. 24 to 32 in., 3 or 4 plants, IV or X 3. 5 to 6 ½ ft., 1 or 2 plants, IV or X	Broad-leaved, undemanding as regards the soil or site, richly flowering in a sunny situation, tolerates semi-shade and dryness, very richly flowering, for freestanding hedges; 1. Flowers white, IV/V; 2. Flowers vivid carmine-red, VII/IX, leaves of growing shoot red, then dark green, narrow; 3. Flowers white, V/VI.
Stephanandra incisa Cutleaf lace shrub	4 to 5 ft., 3 or 4 plants, IV or X	Broad-leaved, permeable, humic soil, sunny, be careful not to trim excessively, white panicles, VI, brown-red fall coloration, for freestanding hedges.
Taxus baccata Common yew, English yew	32 to 80 in. and higher, 3 or 4 plants, IV/V and IX	Coniferous, evergreen, humic, not acidic soil, also grows in shade, plant with firm root ball, water well at the time of planting, slow growing, suitable for heavy trimming.
Teucrium chamaedrys Wall germander	8 to 12 in., 8 to 10 plants, IV and IX	Broad-leaved, evergreen, permeable, humic soil suitable for heavy trimming, for evergreen edging.
Thuja occidentalis 'Ellwangeriana' Aborvitae, red cedar	3 ¼ to 6 ½ ft., 3 or 4 plants, IV/V or IX	Coniferous, evergreen, not too dry, humic soil, sunny or semi-shaded, plant with firm root ball, water well at the time of planting, tolerates heavy trimming, for narrow hedges; 'Brabant' vigorous growing, branches horizontal with dense branching, 'Holmstrob' with golden-yellow shoots, weakly growing, for small hedges, 'Rheingold' 5 ft., golden-yellow shoots.
Weigela Weigela	6 ½ to 8 ft., 1 or 2 plants, IV to V	Broad-leaved, permeable soil, sunny to semi-shaded, flowers large, ruby-red, V/VI, for freestanding floral hedges.

Table 12. Attractive Shrubs for Rock Gardens and Small Gardens

This table includes predominantly low- or dwarf-growing garden varieties of tall-growing broad-leaved and conifer trees and shrubs. NB: The growth forms and heights given in the second column refer specifically to these varieties.

BOTANICAL NAME ENGLISH NAME SPECIES	GROWTH FORM, HEIGHT	SPECIFIC REMARKS, FLOWERING TIME, SUITABILITY
Abies Fir 1. *A. balsamea* 'Nana', Dwarf balsam fir 2. *A. koreana*, Korean fir	1. Broad-growing, almost spheroid, 32 to 40 in. 2. Pyramidal, seldom higher than 6 ½ ft.	Damp, nutrient-rich soil; 1. Not suitable for warm, dry sites, 'Piccolo' up to 20 in.; 2. Humic soil, calciphobous, weakly growing, 'Molli' initially with cushion form, 24 in., 'Silberperle' 14 in., cones violet-crimson, already present on young trees, 'Verdener Dom' sugarloaf-like form.
Acer palmatum Japanese maple	Some varieties low and very stubby, 3 ¼ to 6 ½ ft. and higher	Permeable, humic soil, sheltered, warm, light shade, young plants need winter protection, cultivated forms decorative, thanks to foliage coloration, and also to fan-like leaf forms; 'Atropurpureum' with red foliage, 'Dissectum Ornatum' and 'Dissectum Garnet' leaves laciniate almost to the leaf base.
Berberis Barberry 1. *B. candidula*, Paleleaf barberry 2. *B. ×frikartii* 'Amstelveen', Amstelveen barberry 3. *B. thunbergii* 'Atropurpurea Nana', Japanese barberry, purple leaf barberry	Compact, up to 20 in., also somewhat higher	Damp, loam-containing soil, sunny, flowers yellow, V, fruits coral-red; 1. Evergreen, densely bushy, whitish branches, tolerates some shade, leaves elliptical, 1 in. long; 2. Evergreen, richly flowering, fast growing, individual branchlets slightly overhanging, leaves oblong, serrated, undersides blue-white; 3. Stubby growth, no thorns, leaves small, vivid red.
Calluna vulgaris Scotch heather	Prostrate, broad, 8 to 24 in.	Sandy humic soil (add bark humus and sand to loam soils), calciphobous, cut back older plants by one third in early spring.
Caryopteris ×clandonensis 'Heavenly Blue', Bluebeard, blue spiraea	Upright, loosely branched, bushy, 32 to 48 in.	Sub-shrub, permeable soil, tolerates dryness, sunny, light winter protection, cut back strongly in spring, flowers VIII to X, dark blue, in terminal, branched panicles on young wood, pointed leaves.
Chamaecyparis False cypress 1. *C. obtusa*, Hinoki cypress 2. *C. pisifera*, Sawara cypress	1. Broadly conical, up to 5 ft., occasionally higher 2. Densely bushy, 32 to 40 in. and higher	Soil not too dry, sunny to semi-shaded; 1. Weakly growing, dense branchlets twisted in a conchiform fashion, needles glossy moss-green, 'Nana Gracilis' and 'Pygmaea' both well-known dwarf forms; 2. 'Filifera', threadleaf Sawara cypress, slow growing, overhanging, needles fresh-green, very pointed, undersides whitish, 'Filifera Aurea', golden threadleaf Sawara cypress, golden-yellow needles, 'Plumosa' feathery curled branchlets, 'Plumosa Aurea' golden-yellow needles, spherical, 'Boulevard' silvery-blue needles, reaches a height of up to 10 ft. when fully grown.
Chamaecytisus purpureus Purple broom	Broad, 16 to 24 in.	Broad-leaved, damp, humic soil, flowers pinkish white to crimson-red, V/VI.
Cotoneaster Cotoneaster 1. *C. adpressus*, Creeping cotoneaster 2. *C. dammeri*, Bearberry cotoneaster 3. *C. horizontalis* 'Saxatilis', Herringbone cotoneaster 4. *C. salicifolius* 'Parkteppich', Willow leaf cotoneaster	1. Prostrate, up to 10 in. 2. Creeping, up to 12 in., 'Jürgl' up to 20 in. 3. Carpet-like, 8 in. 4. Broad, squarrose 20 in., up to 10 ft. wide	Soil not too dry and not wet, sunny or semi-shaded; 1. Densely covers ground, flowers reddish, VI, fruits bright red; 2. Evergreen, little branched, flowers white to reddish, V, fruits coral-red, 'Jürgl' also with overhanging shoots; 3. Evergreen, flowers white, VI, fruits bright red, IX to XII; 4. Flowers white, VII, fruits bright red, IX, frond-like branching, leaves small, ovate, glossy green.
Cryptomeria japonica Japanese cedar, dwarf varieties	Weak- to dwarf-growing, up to 20 in.	Damp soil, higher air humidity, sunny to out of direct sun, needles sickle-like; 'Cristata' shoots like a rooster crest, growth of 'Little Champion' broadly spheroid, 'Little Winmont' with broad, twisted branchlets and needles, needles yellowish green, 'Yokohama' broadly conical.

BOTANICAL NAME ENGLISH NAME SPECIES	GROWTH FORM, HEIGHT	SPECIFIC REMARKS, FLOWERING TIME, SUITABILITY
Cytisus Broom 1. *C. decumbens*, Carpet broom 2. *C. ×kewensis*, Kew broom 3. *C. nigricans* 'Cyni', Black broom	1. Prostrate, 4 to 8 in. 2. Creeping, 12 to 20 in. 3. Compact, 28 to 40 in.	Permeable, light soil, warm, sunny, for rock gardens, dry stone walls, also in perennial borders; 1. Flat, dense, vigorously growing, richly flowering, golden-yellow V/VI; 2. Branches up to 3 ¼ ft. long, thin, overhanging, flowers sulfur-yellow, V; 3. Flowers yellow, V to IX.
Daphne Daphne 1. *D. blagayana*, Balkan daphne 2. *D. ×burkwoodii*, Burkwood's daphne 3. *D. cneorum*, Garland flower, rose daphne	1. Ground cover, up to 12 in. 2. Bushy, up to 3 ¼ ft. 3. Prostrate, 8 to 12 in.	1. Soil not calciferous, humic, well drained, out of direct sun; flowers yellowish white, fragrant, IV/V; 2. Soil well drained, sunny, flowers pink, fragrant, V, subsequent flowering in the fall; 3. Permeable soil, well drained, sunny to semi-shaded, flowers light carmine-red; richly flowering and vigorously growing are 'Eximia' and 'Major', IV/VI.
Deutzia gracilis Slender deutzia, Japanese show flower	Densely bushy, 20 to 28 in., somewhat higher when older	Sufficiently damp soil, sunny, will also tolerate some shade, flowers white in upright panicles, V.
Erica Heath 1. *E. carnea* (syn. *herbacea*), winter heath 2. *E. tetralix*, Cross-leaved heath 3. *E. vagans*, Cornish heath	All upright as young plants, older branches later prostrate, forming bushy cushions, 8 to 20 in.	Soil light, acidic, not dry, do not plant too late in order that the heath can still establish roots, cover with bark humus, winter protection with brushwood during black frost, cut frozen-back branches only after new shoot growth; garden varieties in different colors, growth forms, and winter hardiness, selection of the best variety is important! 1. XII to IV, 2. VI to IX, 3. VII to IX; *E. gracilis* for balcony boxes.
Euonymus Spindle 1. *E. alatus* 'Compactus', Winged spindle 2. *E. fortunei*, Dwarf euonymus, 'Emerald Gaiety', Wintercreeper 3. *E. nanus* var. *turkestanicus*	1. Broadly upright, up to 3 ¼ ft. 2. Creeping to broadly bushy, up to 12 in. 3. 20 to 32 in.	Damp, humic soil, sunny or out of direct sun, evergreen broad-leaved shrub, ground cover, also cultivated forms with brightly colored leaves; 1. Branches densely branched, greenish with four cork-like wings, leaves ovate, 1 ¼ to 2 in. long, green, intense orange-red fall coloration; 2. Slow growing, leaves broadly oval, up to 2 in. long, narrow white edge, in winter somewhat reddish; 3. Flowers pink to red/orange.
Forsythia 'Melee d'Or' Dwarf forsythia	Compact, 3 ¼ ft.	Undemanding, flowers vivid bright yellow bells, III/IV, also as tub plant.
Genista Greenweed, woadwaxen 1. *G. lydia*, Lydia broom 2. *G. pilosa*, Hairy greenwood, prostrate broom	1. Prostrate, broad growing, up to 20 in. 2. Prostrate, up to 12 in.	1. Loose, deep, nutrient-poor soil, sunny, flowers large, golden-yellow, V/VI, arched gray-green shoots with bluish stripes, leaves sharply thorned; 2. Dry, warm, also infertile site, flowers golden-yellow, V/VI, 'Goldilocks' 16 to 24 in. and 'Vancouver Gold' 4 to 12 in., broadly bushy.
Hebe Hebe, hedge veronica 1. *H. armstrongii* 2. *H. buxifolia*, Boxwood hebe	1. Upright, up to 20 in. 2. Upright, up to 35 in.	Soil not too moist, sunny, evergreen shrub; 1. Densely branched, leaves scale-like, greenish bronze, flowers white, V/VI; 2. Leaves glossy green, decussate in four rows, flowers white in dense spikes, VI/VII.
Hedera helix 'Conglomerata' Common ivy, English ivy	Initially upright, later prostrate shoots, up to 12 in.	Damp soil, semi-shaded to shaded, leaves glossy deep green, curled, shoots stunted; 'Erecta' is similar, but grows upright.
Hypericum St. John's wort 1. *H. calycinum*, Aaron's beard, rose of Sharon 2. *H. ×moserianum*, Hybrid St. John's wort	1. Bushy, 12 to 16 in. 2. Semi-spheroid, tips over-hanging, 20 to 32 in.	Sub-shrub, evergreen in mild winters; 1. Damp, humic soil, semi-shaded, flowers golden-yellow, VII/VIII, covers the ground through runners, sprouts new shoots following frost damage; 2. Permeable soil, tolerates some dryness, flowers golden-yellow, VII to X, almost evergreen, carmine-red shoot tips, leaves ovate, mat green, 'Svenja' with orange-red stamens.
Ilex crenata 'Stokes' Boxleaf holly, Japanese holly, dwarf holly	Broadly upright, later dense, slow growing, 12 to 32 in.	Humic, damp to moist, acidic to neutral soil, semi-shaded to shaded, leaves evergreen, small, leathery, spoon-like (boxwood-like).

BOTANICAL NAME ENGLISH NAME SPECIES	GROWTH FORM, HEIGHT	SPECIFIC REMARKS, FLOWERING TIME, SUITABILITY
Juniperus Juniper 1. *J. communis* var. *saxatilis*, mountain juniper, Dwarf juniper 2. *J. horizontalis*, Creeping juniper 3. *J. squamata*, Blue star juniper, flaky juniper	1. Spread out flat, 6 to 12 in. 2. Creeping, 12 to 16 in., 6 ½ ft. wide 3. Flat, broad, densely branched, varieties up to 2 ft.	Permeable light soil, sunny, slow growing; 1. 'Hornibrookii' initially creeping, then ascendent, needles piercing, flat above, with silvery-white stripes, 'Depressa Aurea' compact, broad, and flat, needles golden-yellow, 'Repanda' needles bent inward, soft, silvery-striped above, dark gray-green; 2. 'Blue Chip', creeping juniper, densely closed dwarf shrub stand, needles silver-blue, 'Glauca' ground covering, needles steel-blue; 3. 'Blue Carpet' forms dense cushions, pointed needles, densely crowded, young shoots bluish, 'Blue Star' roundly compact, shoot tips pro-truding, needles silvery-gray, 'Meyeri', Meyer juniper, large shrub, branches ascending in a funnel-like arrangement.
Kalmia angustifolia Sheep laurel	Shrub-like, 3 ¼ ft.	Permeable garden soil, ground coverage through underground runners, also sunny, flowers 1 in. long racemes, crimson-red, VI/VII, 'Rubra' flowers dark red.
Larix kaempferi 'Wolterdingen' Japanese larch	Broadly cushion-like, up to 20 in.	Garden soil, sunny to semi-shaded, slow growing, after 10 years still only up to 20 in. high and 28 in. wide.
Lavandula angustifolia English lavender	Shrub-like, 16 to 24 in.	Sub-shrub, permeable garden soil, tolerates dryness, cut back after flowering, flowers violet-blue, 'Alba' flowers white, VII to VIII, also suitable for edging and low hedges; nectar source for bees.
Lonicera pileata Privet honeysuckle	Spread out, dense, 16 to 20 in.	Permeable, damp soil, sheltered from wind, produces new shoots after winter damage, flowers small, yellow, fragrant, V, elegantly overhanging branches, 'Lemon Beauty' yellow, 'Silver Beauty' white leaf edge.
Microbiota decussata Microbiota, Russian arborvitae	Broadly branched, up to 4 in., up to 6 ½ ft. wide	Permeable, light, humic soil, sunny to shaded, vigorously growing, evergreen, shoot tips somewhat overhanging, needles fresh-green, in winter coppery brown.
Philadelphus microphyllus Littleleaf mock orange	Bushy, up to 3 ¼ ft.	Medium-heavy soil, sunny to semi-shaded, flowers white, VI/VII.
Picea Spruce 1. *P. abies* 'Echiniformis', Hedge-hog Norway spruce, 'Pygmaea', Pygmy Norway spruce 2. *P. glauca* 'Conica', Dwarf Alberta spruce, dwarf white spruce 3. *P. pungens* 'Glauca Globosa', Dwarf blue spruce	1. Spheroid, up to 2 ft., spread out, up to 3 ¼ ft. 2. Conical with pointed tip, dense, up to 6 ½ ft., occa-sionally higher 3. More broad than high, up to 3 ¼ ft.	Permeable, fresh, humic soil, sunny; 1. 'Echiniformis' slow growing, around ¾ in. per year, round cushions, very dense, needles light green, 'Pygmaea' slow growing, stumpily conical, needles fresh green; 2. Slow growing, strictly conical, closed, light green needles, suffers in dry places; 3. Initially stubby growth, later broadly conical, needles silvery-blue, slightly sickle-shaped.
Pinus Pine 1. *P. mugo* subsp. *mugo*, Moun-tain pine 2. *P. pumila*, Dwarf Siberian pine, Japanese stone pine 3. *P. sylvestris* 'Watereri', Dwarf Scotch pine	1. Upright, prostrate branches, later ascendent, 3 ¼ to 13 ft. 2. Shrubby, older specimens 6 ½ to 10 ft. 3. Initially upright and bushy, later broad and round, adult specimens up to 6 ½ to 10 ft.	Light, also sandy, more infertile soils, not wet, sunny; 1. Weakly growing, withstands cutting back, needles up to 1 ½ in. long, dense, 'Gnom' up to 6 ½ ft., densely spheroid, later compact and upright, needles dark green, 'Laurin' up to 5 ft., broadly upright, needles dark green, leaf buds light yellowish green, 'Mops' up to 3 ¼ ft., flatly spheroid, densely branched, branchlets directed upward, needles short, dark green; 2. Slow growing without a main stem, broadly prostrate, needles blue-green, 'Glauca' up to 5 ft., needles bluish green; 3. Also suitable for poor, infertile soils, very slow growing, valuable form, almost as broad as high, needles blue-green.
Polygala chamaebuxus 'Purple Passion' Shrubby milkwort	Ground covering, 8 to 12 in.	Sub-shrub, infertile calciferous garden soil, dry and sunny, evergreen, flowers violet-red and yellow, IV to V (IX), violet fragrance.

BOTANICAL NAME ENGLISH NAME SPECIES	GROWTH FORM, HEIGHT	SPECIFIC REMARKS, FLOWERING TIME, SUITABILITY
Potentilla fruticosa (syn. *Dasiphora fruticosa*) Golden hardhack, shrubby cinquefoil	Broadly bushy, also ground-covering and almost creeping; 20 in., also up to 3 ¼ ft. Nectar source for bees!	Permeable nutrient-rich soil, sunny; numerous attractive and richly flowering varieties: 'Abbotswood' flowers white with yellow stamens, VI to X, leaves blue-green, 'Goldfinger' flowers lemon-yellow, VI to X, leaves silky-hirsute, 'Lovely Pink' tolerates dryness, flowers pink, V to IX, leaves silky-hirsute, 'Marian Red Robin' flowers vivid red, VII to IX, 'Pink Beauty' flowers vivid pink, VII to IX.
Prunus tenella Dwarf Russian almond	Shrubby, up to 3 ¼ ft. and higher	Permeable, light soil, dry, warm site, calcicolous, develops runners, flowers pink, up to 1 ¼ in. wide, IV/V, richly flowering.
Santolina chamaecyparissus Lavender cotton	Sub-shrub, up to 20 in.	Permeable soil, sunny, light winter protection, evergreen broad-leaved shrub, flowers golden-yellow, VII/VIII.
Skimmia japonica 'Rubella' Japanese skimmia	Broadly bushy, compact, 24 to 40 in.	Fresh, nutrient-rich soil, sunny to semi-shaded, evergreen broad-leaved shrub, flowers in yellowish white panicles, fragrant, V, fall/winter red berries, leaves long and narrow, leathery, dark green, glossy, similar to cherry laurel.
Spiraea japonica 'Little Princess' Japanese meadowsweet, Japanese spirea	Broadly growing, dense, 16 in.	Undemanding, sunny to semi-shaded, flowers delicate pink on 2 to 2 ¾ in. long corymbs, VII/VIII, richly flowering, leaves fresh green, oval.
Taxus Yew 1. *T. baccata* 'Adpressa Aurea', Adpressa aurea English yew 2. *T. baccata* 'Repandens', Creeping English yew 3. *T. baccata* 'Summergold', Golden English yew 4. *T. cuspidata* 'Nana', Dwarf golden Japanese yew	1. Shrubby to broadly bushy, 32 in., up to 3 ¼ ft. high and wide when older 2. and 3. Spread out, 20 in., up to 32 in. high and 10 ft. wide when older 4. Broad, dense, 3 ¼ ft. and higher, up to 10 ft. wide	Fresh, nutrient-rich soil, also calciferous, not suitable for dry, hot sites or waterlogging, tolerates shade well; all plant parts are poisonous, except for red fruit flesh! 1. Needles at the shoot apices golden-yellow, on growing shoots yellowish white, with green central stripe; 2. Branches horizontally spreading, tips slightly overhanging, needles dark blue-green; 3. Branches diagonally spreading, slightly overhanding, needles sickle-shaped, 1 in. long, with yellow edge, in summer also yellow only; 4. Branches spread out, needles dark green, very valuable.
Thuja occidentalis Arborvitae, red cedar 1. *T.* 'Danica', Danica arborvitae 2. *T.* 'Teddy', Dwarf cedar	1. Spheroid, compact, 20 to 24 in. 2. Spheroid, compact, 20 in., occasionally higher	1. and 2. Sufficiently moist soil, sunny, slow growing, evergreen conifer shrubs; 1. Growth spheroid, very densely bushy; 2. Needles short, soft, dark green (as sapling originated from *T. occidentalis* 'Kobold').
Tsuga canadensis Canadian hemlock, eastern hemlock 1. *T.* 'Nana', Dwarf Canadian hemlock 2. *T.* 'Pendula', Weeping Canadian hemlock	1. Compact, up to 3 ¼ ft. 2. Creeping or pendulous	Sufficiently moist soil, sheltered, high air humidity, evergreen coniferous shrub; 1. Branches almost horizontal, somewhat prostrate, nest-like depression in the middle, needles short, dark green, glossy; 2. Spreading unless tied up, then habit is pendulous.
Viburnum davidii Evergreen viburnum	Low, broadly projecting, densely branched, from 32 in. up to 5 ft. wide	Humus-containing, weakly acidic soil, semi-shaded, evergreen broad-leaved shrub, flowers pink-white in dense cymes up to 3 in. wide, VI, fruits dark violet, ovate, firm, leaves up to 5 ½ in. long, leathery, glossy dark green.

Table 13. Healthy Roses

Of the many available rose varieties, only a small selection of particularly beautiful roses can be listed here. However, regional suppliers (garden centers, tree nurseries) carry a wide range of roses in stock, often without varietal names. Accordingly, it is not possible to judge whether these are strongly susceptible to attack by pests and diseases, or whether they are remontant, in other words, flower often during the year.

• All the varieties named in this table are largely resistant to pests and diseases.
• All (except for *Rosa rubiginosa*) flower frequently during the year.

SPECIES ROSES: VARIETY	FLOWER COLOR, HEIGHT	SPECIFIC REMARKS
'Berolina'	Lemon-yellow with a rosy tinge, 3 ¼ ft.	Well branched, bud elongated and pointed, flower large, well double, strongly fragrant.
'Burgund 81'	Vivid, velvety blood-red, 3 ¼ ft.	Vigorously growing, much branched, bud large, almost black-red, flower very large, well double, weatherproof, finishes flowering all at once, robust, long, thick stalks, dark green foliage, slightly fragrant.
'Cherry Lady'	Cherry-pink, 32 in.	Bushy, grows very uniformly, flower well double, weak fragrance.
'Eliza'	Silvery-pink, 35 in.	Bushy, bud pink, flower well double, often in umbels, glossy foliage, light fragrance.
'Gloria Dei'	Light yellow with copper-red edge, 32 in.	Old, proven variety, vigorously growing, bushy, thick stalks, flower very large, tightly double, long lasting, weatherproof, glossy foliage, light fragrance.
'Louise Odier'	Pink, not fading, 5 ft.	Vigorously growing, flower strongly double, so-called historic rose (Bourbon rose), strongly fragrant.
'Polarstern'	Pure white, 3 ¼ ft.	Vigorously growing, bud pointed, greenish white, flower very large, strongly double, weatherproof, fragrant.
'Rebell'	Vivid red, 32 in.	Many shoots, flower well double, sometimes in umbels, weak fragrance, foliage very glossy; also as standard rose.
'Sterntaler'	Yellow, 35 in.	Well branched, flower strongly double, mostly in umbels, pleasing fragrance, foliage weakly glossy .
CLIMBING ROSES: VARIETY	**FLOWER COLOR**	**SPECIFIC REMARKS**
'Amadeus'	Blood-red	Bud dark red, flower well double, in umbels of 5 to 7 blooms, light fragrance, foliage strongly glossy.
'Golden Gate'	Golden-yellow, pure yellow when finishing flowering	Vigorously growing, bud large and broadly oval, flower well double, lemon fragrance.
'Ilse Krohn Superior'	Luminous pure white	Vigorously growing, flower large, strongly double, weatherproof, robust, strongly fragrant; also as standard rose.
'Jasmina'	Creamy light pink to light violet-pink	Bud round and medium-sized, flower strongly double, fruity fragrance.
'Laguna'	Powerful pink	Bud roundish, pink-red, flower well double, strongly fragrant.
'Rosanna'	Salmon-pink	Flower like that of a species rose, strongly double, mostly in umbels.
'Super Excels'	Light carmine-red, turning to light violet when finishing flowering	Shoots long, soft, and thin, therefore suitable for trellises and pergolas, flowers tightly double; also as standard rose cascade.
'Sympathie'	Velvety dark red	Vigorously growing, thick shoots, suitable for pergolas, walls, and rose arches, flower large, slightly double, in bunches, weatherproof, robust, wild rose fragrance.

SHRUB ROSES: VARIETY	FLOWER COLOR, HEIGHT	SPECIFIC REMARKS
'Burghausen'	Light red, approx. 6 ½ ft.	Vigorously growing, much branched, overhanging in arches, flower semi-double, bowl-shaped.
'Cinderella'	Delicate pink, 5 ft.	Bushy overhanging, well branched, flower large, well double, ball-shaped, 4 to 6 flowers per umbel, apple fragrance, strongly glossy foliage.
'Rugelda'	Lemon yellow with reddish edge, 6 ½ ft.	Upright, bushy, thick stalks, flower large, strongly double, in loose umbels, fragrant, foliage dark green and glossy.
'Schloss Eutin'	Creamy apricot with a dark center, 4 ft.	Upright, overhanging in arches, flower strongly double, camellia-like.
'Westerland'	Vivid copper-orange, 5 ft.	Bushy, slightly overhanging, flower large, well double, open center, long lasting, strongly fragrant, glossy foliage.

BED ROSES: VARIETY	FLOWER COLOR, HEIGHT	SPECIFIC REMARKS
'Bad Birnbach'	Vivid salmon-pink, 20 in.	Compact growth, flower well double.
'Diamant'	Pure white with yellow center, 24 in.	Compact to broadly upright, flower semi-double, strongly glossy foliage, robust.
'Kosmos'	Creamy white, 32 in.	Overhanging in arches, flower strongly double, nostalgic form, delicate fragrance.
'Rosenfee'	Flower pink, up to 28 in.	Bushy, bud salmon-red, flower well double, nostalgic form, very richly flowering.
'Sangerhäuser Jubiläumsrose'	Apricot, pink at end of flowering, 28 in.	Compact growth, flower strongly double, very richly flowering; also as standard rose.

DWARF ROSES: VARIETY	FLOWER COLOR, HEIGHT	SPECIFIC REMARKS
'Charmant'	Pink with yellowish white center and creamy-white reverse, 20 in.	Bushy, compact, bud small, pointed, flower small, double, nostalgic form, in umbels, robust, faint sweetish fragrance, strongly glossy foliage; also as half-standard rose (24 in. high).
'Coco'	Salmon-orange to salmon-pink, yellow center, 16 in.	Very compact, overhanging in arches, flower single.
'Pepita'	Strongly pinkish rose colored, 20 in.	Compact, well branched, flower strongly double, 6 to 8 flowers per umbel, strongly glossy foliage; also as half-standard rose (24 in.) and standard rose (35 in.).
'Sonnenröschen'	White with yellow center, 12 in.	Bushy, flower small, single, strongly glossy foliage.

WILD ROSES: SPECIES	FLOWER COLOR, HEIGHT	SPECIFIC REMARKS
Rosa rubiginosa (Sweet briar)	Light pink with yellow center, once-flowering, 8 ft.	Stiffly upright, overhanging in arches, flower large, single, rennet fragrance, foliage dark green, undersides with glands with wine and apple fragrance, scarlet-red rose hips.
Rosa rugosa (Japanese rose)	Crimson-pink with yellow center, flowers frequently, up to 5 ft.	Upright, overhanging in arches, little branched, forms runners, flower large, single, sweetish fragrance, foliage dark green, wrinkled, with gray-green undersides, golden-yellow in the fall, scarlet-red rose hips.

Table 14. Climbing and Creeping Woody Plants

BOTANICAL NAME ENGLISH NAME SPECIES	GROWTH FORM, HEIGHT	SPECIFIC REMARKS
Actinidia Kiwi fruit 1. *A. arguta*, hardy kiwi, tara vine 2. *A. kolomikta*, Kolomikta, miyamatatabi	1. Climber, 26 to 33 ft. 2. Climber, up to 10 ft.	Undemanding, sunny, fruits edible, gooseberry-like; 1. Leaves glossy dark green, flowers white, VI, fragrant; 2. Leaves white to pink in front, flowers white, large, fragrant; in most cases two plants are required, one male and one female, monoecious cultivars are now also available.
Akebia quinata Chocolate vine, five-leaf akebia	Climber, up to 33 ft.	Light soil, also out of direct sun, vigorously growing, for walls and pergolas, flowers brownish violet, fruits light violet, 4 in. long, VIII to X, foliage dark green, quinate (five-leaved), mostly wintergreen.
Aristolochia macrophylla Dutchman's pipe	Climber, twining, 16 to 20 ft. (also up to 33 ft.)	Deep, nutrient-rich, moist soil, sunny, also semi-shaded, for house walls (framework or wire), also for columns and tree stems, leaves 12 in. wide, heart-shaped, flowers yellow-green and crimson-brown, V/VI.
Campsis Trumpet creeper 1. *C. radicans* 2. *C. ×tagliabuana*	Creeping with holdfasts; 1. Up to 33 ft. 2. Up to 13 ft.	1. Soil not too dry, sunny, vigorously growing, holdfasts, flowers outwardly orange, trumpets yellow, seam scarlet-red, VI to IX, 'Indian Summer' flowers apricot-colored; 2. Deep, nutrient-rich soil, sunny, weakly growing, few holdfasts so plants need to be tied up, prune previous year's shoots in spring to leave three buds, flowers orange to scarlet-red, VIII.
Celastrus orbiculatus Oriental bittersweet, staff vine	Climber, twining, up to 40 ft.	Undemanding, sunny or semi-shaded, can cause other trees and shrubs to die off, needs a robust framework support on walls, flowers greenish yellow, VI, fruits only if both male and female plants are present, yellow, from IX, remain for a long time with red seeds.
Clematis Clematis (see TABLE 15)	Creeping with leaf tendrils, 6 ½ to 26 ft., depending on the species or variety	Permeable, nutrient-rich, damp soil, root zone cool and shaded, otherwise sunny or semi-shaded, suffers on hot, south-facing walls or in deep shade, loosen soil in planting hole to a considerable depth, root collar should be covered with 2 to 4 in. of earth.
Fallopia baldschuanica (syn. *Polygonum aubertii*) Silver lace vine, Russian vine	Climber, twining, up to 26 ft. or higher; nectar source for bees	Undemanding, sunny, vigorously growing, covers large areas very quickly, withstands severe cutting back, for pergolas, arbors, fences, with wire or supporting framework, flowers in white panicles, richly flowering, IX, fruits almost black.
Hedera helix Common ivy, English ivy	Creeping with holdfasts, up to 100 ft.	Moist and fertile soil, calcicolous, also shaded, evergreen scrambling ground cover, also climbing on walls and trees, flowers (older plants only) greenish yellow, IX/X, fruits in spring.
Humulus lupulus Hops	Climber, up to 50 ft.	Permeable soil, sunny, for large areas, variety aureus more delicate, up to 16 ft., leaves greenish yellow.
Hydrangea anomala subsp. *petiolaris* Climbing hydrangea	Self-climber through holdfasts, 16 ft. and higher	Damp to moist soil, for walls, tree stems, rockfaces, also as ground cover or freestanding (then only up to 6 ½ft., however), flowers white, 10 in. wide, VI/VII.

BOTANICAL NAME ENGLISH NAME SPECIES	GROWTH FORM, HEIGHT	SPECIFIC REMARKS
Lonicera Honeysuckle 1. *L.* ×*brownii* 'Dropmore Scarlet' 2. *L. caprifolium*, Italian honeysuckle 3. *L.* ×*heckrottii* 4. *L. japonica* 5. *L.* ×*tellmanniana*	Climber, twining: 1. Up to 10 ft. 2. Up to 16 ft. 3. Up to 10 ft. 4. Up to 16 ft. 5. Up to 16 ft.	Nutrient-rich, not-too-dry soil, sunny or semi-shaded, for walls, pergolas, and arbors (wire or trellis); 1. Vigorous growth, flowers outwardly red, yellow-orange inside, VI to X; 2. Flowers creamy yellow with reddish tinge, strongly fragrant, V/VI, fruits coral-red VIII to IX; 3. Weakly twining, richly flowering, flowers yellow inside, reddish outside, VI to IX, strongly fragrant; 4. Semi-evergreen to wintergreen on sheltered sites, flowers white; 'Purpurea' pink outside, creamy white inside, fragrant; 5. Strongly twining, flowers orange-yellow, V/VI, fruits light red, IX.
Parthenocissus 1. *P. quinquefolia*, Virginia creeper 2. *P. tricuspidata* 'Veitchii', Boston ivy, Japanese creeper, Japanese ivy	1. Climber, strongly twining, 26 to 33 ft. 2. Self-climbing with holdfasts	Not-too-dry site, sunny, covers large areas quickly, for walls, pergolas, or fences, flowers greenish, fruits IX/X, blue-black, leaves in the fall intense red; 1. Despite holdfasts grows better on a supporting structure (var. *engelmannii* with sufficient holdfasts); 2. Densely close growing, for sunny walls.
Wisteria Wisteria 1. *W. floribunda*, Japanese wisteria 2. *W. sinensis*, Chinese wisteria	Climber, twining; 1. 26 to 33 ft. 2. 40 to 60 ft. and even higher	Damp, nutrient-rich soil, sunny, sheltered site, for walls (with supporting structure), pergolas, and fences; 1. Flowers blue-violet, racemes up to 20 in. long, V/VI, 'Rosea' flowers pink; 2. Flowers blue-violet, racemes up to 12 in. long, 'Alba' flowers white.

Table 15. Recommended Clematis Plants

When trimming clematis plants, please note: The species and varieties designated with an asterisk (*) flower on the new shoot of the current year. Accordingly, before this shoot develops, all the weak shoots should be cut back severely early in the spring. Older plants can be strongly regenerated and cut back to about one third.

Other species and varieties that are not designated with an asterisk flower from the previous year's wood and are not cut back in spring. In these cases, trimming follows flowering. The natural forms mostly develop especially decorative fruiting bodies.

NATURAL FORMS: SPECIES	FLOWER COLOR	FLOWERING TIME	REMARKS, HEIGHT
alpina	Blue-violet to whitish blue or pure white	IV/V to VI and often VIII to IX	Not too wet soil, do not cut back; flowers bell-shaped, up to 10 ft.
montana	Vivid pink-red to white	V to VI	Richly flowering, very decorative fruiting bodies, no cutting back required; vigorously growing, shoots up to 33 ft.
serratifolia 'Golden Tiara'	Golden-yellow	VII to IX	Not too wet soil, 10 ft.; flowers broadly bell-shaped.
tangutica (Golden clematis)	Golden-yellow	VI (X)	* Flowers bell-shaped, often remontant, robust, 10 to 20 ft.
'Avant Garde'	Cherry-red	V to IX	* Flowers dish-shaped, with filamentous, pink-colored lamellae inside, yellow stamens, 10 ft.
'Dr. Ruppel'	Pink with carmine-red stripes	V to VI and VIII to IX	Large flowers, richly flowering, 10 ft.
'Ernest Markham'	Vivid dark red	VI to VII and IX	* Large flowers, richly flowering, vigorous growth up to 13 ft.
'Fujimusume'	Purple, lighter central stripe	VI to IX	Large flowers, richly flowering, up to 10 ft.
'Gipsy Queen'	Velvety dark crimson	VII to X	* Medium-large, vigorous growth up to 13 ft.
'Jackmanii'	Dark violet-crimson	VI/VII to X	* Richly flowering, robust, up to 13 ft.
'Josephine'	Mauve-pink to pink-red, purple-red when flowering finishes	V to IX	Flowers dish-shaped, with long, light-colored lamellae inside, 8 ft.
'Lady Betty Balfour'	Dark blue to deep velvety crimson, light-colored stamens	VIII to X	* Large flowers, vigorous growth up to 13 ft.
'Lasurstern'	Gentian-blue to pure blue, stamens white	V/VI and VIII/IX	Very large flowers, weaker growth, up to just under 10 ft.
'Mrs George Jackman'	White to ivory-colored	V to VI	Not disease-prone, flowers large, up to 11 ½ ft.
'Multi Blue'	Dark blue to violet	VI to IX	* Tightly double, 10 ft
'Nelly Moser'	Delicate purple-pink with dark stripes	VI to IX	Medium-large, up to 6 ½ ft.
'Niobe'	Vivid crimson-red to dark velvet-red, yellow stamens	VI to IX	* Slightly wavy edges, 10 ft.
'The President'	Dark blue to dark violet, undersides lighter, striped	V/VI and VIII/X	Occasionally remontant, 10 ft.
'Ville de Lyon'	Deep carmine-red, base lighter, seam darker	VI to IX	* Richly flowering, robust, up to 13 ft.

Table 16. Winter-Hardy Flowering Herbaceous Perennials

In the case of many genera, other species are also suitable, and varieties of many of the species listed here are also available from specialist dealers.

BOTANICAL NAME ENGLISH NAME SPECIES	FLOWER COLOR, FLOW-ERING TIME (MONTH), HEIGHT	PLANTING WIDTH	REQUIREMENTS AND SPECIFIC REMARKS
Achillea Common yarrow 1. *A. filipendulina* 2. *A. millefolium* 3. *A. ptarmica*	1. Golden-yellow, VI to IX, 24 to 48 in. 2. Pink to carmine-red, VI to X, 16 to 24 in. 3. White, VII to IX, 16 to 28 in.	10 to 14 in.	1. and 2. Undemanding, sunny, tolerate dryness, very vigorous growth through moisture in spring, good dried flower, nectar source for bees. 3. Loves more moisture and full sun, tolerates places out of direct sun; all suitable for cutting.
Actaea (syn. *Cimicif-uga*) species Bugbane	White, VII to X, depending on the species, 32 to 80 in.	16 to 28 in.	Humus-rich, rather moist soil, semi-shaded, in groups, also solitary.
Anemone Anemone, windflower 1. *A. hupehensis* var. *japonica*, Japanese anemone 2. *A. sylvestris* 3. *A. tomentosa*	1. White, pink to wine-red, VIII to X, 24 to 40 in. 2. White, V to VI, 12 to 16 in. 3. Delicate pink, VIII to X, 24 to 40 in.	1. 12 to 40 in. 2. 6 to 8 in. 3. 12 to 16 in.	Any soil that is not too moist, all tolerate sun to light semi-shade, suitable for cutting; 1. and 3. Plant in spring if possible, apply winter protective covering of leaves and brushwood in the first year of planting and in harsh places, solitary plant; varieties of 3. grow the most vigorously.
Aquilegia Columbine, granny's bonnet	White, yellow, red, blue, mostly bicolored, V to VI, 16 to 32 in.	8 to 12 in.	Any soil that is not too dry, sunny to semi-shaded, for groups and under light woody plants, easily propagated by seeding, richly flowering, attractive cut flower.
Aster Aster 1. *A. amellus*, Italian aster, Italian starwort 2. *A. dumosus*, Bushy aster, rice button aster 3. *A. novae-angliae*, New England aster 4. *A. novi-belgii*, Mich-aelmas daisy 5. *A. tongolensis*, East Indies aster	1. Light blue to dark violet, also pink to carmine-red, VIII to IX, 16 to 24 in. 2. White, pink, red, pur-ple-blue, VIII to X, 6 to 16 in. 3. Blue, pink, red, and salmon, IX to X, 3 ¼ to 5 ft. 4. White, pink to dark red, blue to violet, IX to X, 32 to 50 in. 5. Light blue to violet-blue, V to IV, 10 to 20 in.	1. 8 to 12 in. 2. 6 to 8 in. 3. 12 to 20 in. 4. 12 to 20 in. 5. 8 to 10 in.	1. Tolerates dry soil, full sun, suitable for heath gardens, can be divided in spring following shoot production, suitable for cutting; 2. Undemanding, full sun, very richly flowering, suitable for edging; 3. Nutrient-rich soil, full sun, also as solitary plant, suitable for cutting, more resilient than *A. novi-belgii*; 4. Undemanding as regards the site, full sun, divide and transplant old bushes in the spring, suitable for cutting; 5. Damp soil, sunny, good cut flower; all good nectar sources for bees. North American asters such as 2., 3., and 4. are now classified under the genera *Eurybia* and *Symphyotrichum*.
Astilbe Astilbe, false buck's beard 1. *A. ×arendsii* 2. *A. chinensis* var. *pumila*	1. White, pink to dark red, VII to VIII, 16 to 40 in. 2. Purple, VIII to IX, 12 to 16 in.	10 to 16 in.	Humus-rich, sufficiently moist soil, loves higher air humidity, effec-tive when growing next to trees and shrubs, also close to water; nectar source for bees.
Bergenia cordifolia Heart-leaf bergenia	Delicate pink to red, IV to V, 12 to 20 in.	10 to 16 in.	Undemanding, some varieties can suffer from late frosts in exposed sites, leaves decorative, evergreen, suitable for rock gardens and underplanting beneath trees and shrubs.
Campanula Bellflower 1. *C. latifolia*, Greater bellflower 2. *C. persicifolia*, Peach-leaved bell-flower, willow bell	1. Violet-blue, white, VI to VII, 32 to 48 in. 2. Blue, white, VI to VII, 24 to 32 in.	1. 12 to 16 in. 2. 10 to 12 in.	Undemanding as regards the soil, sunny to out of direct sun, suitable for groups, also in front of trees and shrubs, often heavily self-seeded, mostly good cut flowers; 1. Flowers with wide bells, hirsute on the inside, up to 2 in. long, var. *macrantha* flowers very large, dark violet, 'Alba' flowers very large, white; 2. Flowers with broad bells, 'Nitida' a very low-growing variety.

BOTANICAL NAME ENGLISH NAME SPECIES	FLOWER COLOR, FLOWERING TIME (MONTH), HEIGHT	PLANTING WIDTH	REQUIREMENTS AND SPECIFIC REMARKS
Centaurea Knapweed, star thistle 1. *C. dealbata* 2. *C. macrocephala* 3. *C. montana*	1. Crimson-pink, VI to VII, 24 to 28 in. 2. Yellow, VI to VIII, 32 to 50 in. 3. Blue, V to VII, 12 to 18 in.	1. 16 to 20 in. 2. 20 to 24 in. 3. 14 to 16 in.	Permeable, deep soil, sunny; 1. Leaf decoration plant, also for cut flowers; nectar source for bees. 2. Transplant only when young, solitary plant, nectar source for bees. 3. For colorful planted beds and wild perennial gardens.
Chrysanthemum ×grandiflorum Chrysanthemum	White to pink and red, yellow, bronze, copper, single and double, IX to X, 30 to 35 in.	12 in.	Full sun, winter-hardiness of the varieties is variable, winter protection may be required, transplant and divide only in spring, flowers rewardingly, popular vase decoration.
Coreopsis Tickseed 1. *C. grandiflora* 2. *verticillata*	1. Yellow to golden-yellow, also with eye 2. Yellow 1. and 2. VI to VIII, 10 to 32 in.	10 to 14 in.	Not too heavy soil, solitary, group plant, divide and replant in spring approximately every 3 years, varieties of 1. are suitable for cutting.
Delphinium Larkspur	White, cream, light to dark blue, violet, pink, VI to VII and IX, 28 to 64 in.	12 to 20 in.	Full sun, resilience varies depending on the variety, flowering in the fall through timely cutting back after the first flowering, for groups and solitary plants, decorative cut flower.
Dianthus plumarius Pink	Double, white, pink to red, V to VI, 8 to 12 in.	8 to 10 in.	Loves warm, permeable garden soil, well suited for edging, also for cut flowers.
Dicentra spectabilis Bleeding heart	Pink/white or white, V to VI, 24 to 32 in.	16 to 20 in.	Fertile, somewhat moist soil, sun to light shade, suitable for groups and solitary plants, also for cut flowers in large vases.
Dictamnus albus Burning bush, dittany	Pink or white, VI to VII, 24 to 32 in.	12 to 16 in.	Tolerates dryness, also light semi-shade, suitable for groups and solitary plants.
Doronicum orientale Leopard's bane	Yellow to golden-yellow, also double, IV to V, 12 to 28 in.	10 to 12 in.	Sunny to semi-shaded situations, lower varieties for rock gardens, higher varieties for borders and as cut flowers.
Echinacea purpurea Purple coneflower	Pinkish red to wine-red, VII to IX, 32 to 40 in.	12 to 20 in.	Loves moist and nutrient rich soils, fails on dry and infertile soils, solitary plant, also for cut flowers; nectar source for bees and butterflies.
Echinops ritro Globe thistle	Blue and violet, VII to IX, 32 to 48 in.	12 to 20 in.	For sunny, also rather dry sites, in groups and as solitary plants, suitable for dried bouquets; nectar source for bees.
Erigeron Fleabane	White to red, blue and violet, also double, VI to VII and VIII to IX, 20 to 24 in.	10 to 14 in.	Full sun, for groups and planted beds, remontant if cut back immediately after flowering, better to divide and transplant in spring than in the fall.
Eryngium bourgatii Mediterranean sea holly	Blue color shades, VI to IX, 16 to 28 in.	12 to 20 in.	Permeable, more dry soils, for groups and dried bouquets; nectar source for bees.
Filipendula Dropwort, meadowsweet 1. *F. rubra* 2. *F. vulgaris*	1. Pink, VI to VII, 4 ¼ to 6 ½ ft. 2. White, VI to VII, 24 to 32 in.	1. 16 to 20 in. 2. 14 to 18 in.	1. Moist soil, sunny to semi-shaded, 'Venusta' with vivid pinkish red flowers; 2. Tolerates dry soil, sunny, calcicolous; both suitable for perennial beds and natural gardens.
Gaillardia Blanket flower	Mostly multicolored (yellowish red), VII to IX, 10 to 24 in.	8 to 12 in.	Humic, permeable soil, for sunny, not too moist situations, often not long lived, suitable for cut flowers, lower varieties for rock gardens; nectar source for bees.

BOTANICAL NAME ENGLISH NAME SPECIES	FLOWER COLOR, FLOWERING TIME (MONTH), HEIGHT	PLANTING WIDTH	REQUIREMENTS AND SPECIFIC REMARKS
Geum ×cultorum Avens 1. *G.* 'Prinses Juliana' 2. *G.* 'Red Wings'	V to VIII, 20 to 24 in. 1. Orange-red 2. Deep scarlet-red	8 to 12 in.	Humic, permeable soil, sunny to semi-shaded, remontant, for groups and planted beds, also suitable for cut flowers, no self-seeding.
Gypsophila paniculata Baby's breath	White, pink, single and double, VI to VIII, 16 to 24 in.	16 to 32 in.	Full sun, tolerates dryness, older plants with taproots are difficult to transplant, suitable for dried bouquets.
Helenium Helen's flower, sneezeweed	Yellow, copper, brownish red to dark red, also bicolored, VII to IX, 16 to 24 in.	24 to 48 in.	Not too dry, sunny site, early varieties remontant if cut back early enough, for groups and solitary plants, also for cut flowers; nectar source for bees.
Helianthus decapetalus Thin-leaved sunflower	Yellow, also double, VIII to X, 48 to 60 in.	24 to 48 in.	Nutrient-rich soil in full sun, no excessive winter wetness if possible, for groups, and also for cut flowers.
Heliopsis helianthoides Oxeye	Yellow, single or semi-double, VII to IX, 28 to 50 in.	16 to 20 in.	Moist, not nitrogen-rich soil, sunny, does not tolerate winter wetness, good cut flower.
Helleborus niger Christmas rose, black hellebore	White, pink to crimson, X to III, depending on the species, 8 to 12 in.	10 to 14 in.	Calciferous, loamy, somewhat moist soil, semi-shaded, for underplanting of loose trees and shrubs, 'Praecox' white, for cut flowers in winter; nectar source for bees.
Hemerocallis Daylily	Cream to yellow, pink, orange, brown-red and black-red, also bicolored, VI to IX, 20 to 48 in.	16 to 20 in.	Any soil in a sunny or also semi-shaded situation, divide and transplant only when flowering vigor declines, decorative at the edges of ponds, also in front of trees and shrubs, valuable cut flower.
Inula orientalis Fleabane	Orange-yellow, VI to VII, 20 to 35 in.	12 to 16 in.	Permeable, not too moist soil, sunny, also suitable for cut flowers; nectar source for bees.
Iris Flag, sword lily 1. Hybrids and varieties of many sections and groups 2. *I. sibirica*, Siberian lily	1. All colors from white and yellow to dark blue, pink, and red-brown, V to VI, 14 to 40 in. 2. Blue to blue-violet, also white, VI, 24 to 40 in.	1. 14 to 20 in. 2. 12 to 16 in.	1. Not too wet soil, sunny, plant shallow, do not cover the upper half of the rhizome with earth, apply fertilizer to old plants or divide and replant in VII, effective in groups; 2. Moist, also heavy soils, for groups or as solitary plants, also at the edges of water and in front of trees and shrubs.
Kniphofia uvaria Red hot poker, torch lily	Yellow to orange and red, VI to IX, 24 to 40 in.	24 to 40 in.	Permeable, warm soil, sunny, variably winter hardy because they do not tolerate considerable winter waterlogging, winter protection, solitary plant.
Leucanthemum Oxeye daisy 1. *L. maximum* 'Dwarf Snow Lady', Shasta daisy 2. *L. ×superbum*, Shasta daisy	1. White, VI to VIII, 10 to 14 in. 2. White, also double, VII to VIII, 8 to 32 in.	1. 10 to 12 in. 2. 10 to 14 in.	Fertile soil, full sun, lower varieties for rock gardens, if possible divide and replant every 3 years in spring, suitable for cut flowers.
Liatris spicata Blazing star, button snakeroot	Crimson-red, also white, VII to IX, 20 to 30 in.	6 to 8 in.	Permeable soil, sunny flowers from above to below, suitable for cut flowers; nectar source for bees.

BOTANICAL NAME ENGLISH NAME SPECIES	FLOWER COLOR, FLOW-ERING TIME (MONTH), HEIGHT	PLANTING WIDTH	REQUIREMENTS AND SPECIFIC REMARKS
Ligularia Leopard plant 1. *L. ×hessei* 2. *L. przewalskii*	Yellow or orange-yellow, VII to VIII; 1. 35 to 60 in. 2. 32 to 60 in.	28 to 32 in.	Damp, fertile soil in a semi-shaded situation, leaves decorative, for larger borders only, solitary, also effective at water edges; nectar source for bees.
Lupinus polyphyllus Garden lupine	White, yellow, pink, red, blue and bicolored, VI to VII, 32 to 48 in.	12 to 16 in.	Not too dry and not too moist soil, sunny, cutting back immediately after flowering elicits second florescence, suitable for cut flowers.
Lychnis Campion, catchfly			See *Silene*
Lythrum Loosestrife 1. *L. salicaria*, Purple loosestrife, spiked loosestrife 2. *L. virgatum*, Loosestrife	Pink-red to carmine-red, VII to VIII, 24 to 48 in.	10 to 12 in.	Moist soil, sunny; 1. Can sometimes stand in water; 2. Tolerates rather more dryness; both nectar sources for bees.
Meconopsis betonicifolia Asiatic poppy, Himalayan blue poppy	Blue, stamens yellow, VI to VIII, 28 to 35 in.	24 to 32 in.	Non-calciferous, well-drained humic soil, light shade, cool, moist air, suitable for mountainous regions; also *M. cambrica*, flowers yellow.
Monarda Beebalm, wild bergamot	White, pink, red to dark liliac, VI to VIII, 32 to 48 in.	16 to 20 in.	Any not too dry soil, sunny or light semi-shade, low-maintenance, good for cut flowers; nectar source for bees.
Morina longifolia Whorlflower	White-pink, VI to VIII, 24 to 40 in.	12 to 16 in.	Calciferous, somewhat loamy, drier soil, sunny, as solitary plant.
Oenothera fruticosa Evening primrose	Yellow to bronze-yellow, VI to VIII, 18 to 24 in.	8 to 12 in.	Any soil in a warm, sunny situation, long flowering time, some varieties have glossy leaves, solitary plant; nectar source for bees.
Paeonia Peony 1. *P. lactiflora*, Common garden peony, white peony 2. *P. officinalis*, Common peony, cottage peony 3. *P. tenuifolia*, Fernleaf peony	1. White, pink, red, also yellowish, single and double, VI, 24 to 32 in. 2. White, pink, red, double, V, 20 to 24 in. 3. Red, pink, single, double, V/VI, 20 to 24 in.	24 to 35 in.	Nutrient-rich soil, sunny to semi-shaded, replant only occasionally, do not plant too deep, apply fertilizer often, flowering vigor dependent on variety, for groups, also solitary, valuable cut flower; 1. Loves rather loamy soil, countless varieties;2. Loves calciferous soil, many double garden varieties, mostly with pleasant fragrance; 3. Leaves tripartate and finely cut, therefore also attractive in non-flowering state.
Papaver orientale Oriental poppy	White, pink, red, also bicolored, single and double, VI to VII, 24 to 35 in.	16 to 20 in.	Permeable soil, sunny, tolerates dry periods, foliage retracts after flowering, for groups and solitary plants, also suitable for cut flowers (when the bud shows color).
Penstemon hartwegii 'Picotee Red' Galane	Red, with white throat, VI to VIII, 12 to 16 in.	12 in.	Humic, nutrient-rich, well-permeable soil, sunny to semi-shaded, flowers bell-shaped, foliage wintergreen, for small groups.
Phlomis samia Sage	Yellow, VI to VII, 32 to 48 in.	14 to 20 in.	Warm, dry soil, full sun, conspicuous solitary plant, also in groups, next to large rocks.
Phlox paniculata Garden phlox, summer phlox	White, pink, salmon and red to dark violet, VII to VIII, 28 to 48 in.	16 to 20 in.	Humic, somewhat moist soil, some varieties do not tolerate any lime, sunny, keep a lookout for eelworm infestation, destroy any affected plants; suitabld for groups, also solitary.

BOTANICAL NAME ENGLISH NAME SPECIES	FLOWER COLOR, FLOWERING TIME (MONTH), HEIGHT	PLANTING WIDTH	REQUIREMENTS AND SPECIFIC REMARKS
Physalis alkekengi var. *franchetii* Japanese lanterns	Inconspicuous, creamy white, VI, 16 to 28 in.	Approx. 14 in.	Damp to moist, nutrient-poor soil, sunny, spreading, with attractive fruits, fruits balloon-like, orange-red, cherry-like berries inside, unpalatable, slightly poisonous.
Physostegia virginiana Obedient plant	White, pink, wine-red, VIII to IX, 24 to 40 in.	10 to 14 in.	Moist soil, sunny, winter-hardiness dependent on the variety, winter protection for black frost in harsh situations, for cut flowers; nectar source for bees.
Platycodon grandiflorus Balloon flower	Blue, white, pink, VII to VIII, 8 to 24 in.	12 in.	Permeable, fertile soil, sunny to light shade, roots turnip-like, lower varieties also for rock gardens.
Polemonium caeruleum Jacob's ladder	Blue, white, V to VI, 24 to 32 in.	10 to 14 in.	Moist soil, sunny to semi-shaded, remontant following cutting back, for wild perennial gardens, also suitable for cut flowers.
Polygonatum ×*hybridum* Solomon's seal	White, V to VI, 20 to 35 in.	24 in.	Deep, not too dry, humus-rich soil, semi-shaded to shaded, can be grown for a long time in the same place, for smaller groups.
Primula Primrose, cowslip 1. *P. denticulata*, Drumstick primrose 2. *P. elatior*, Oxlip, paigles 3. *P. juliae*, Purple primrose 4. *P.* ×*pubescens*, Garden auricula 5. *P. vulgaris*, Primrose	1. White, pink, purple, crimson-red, IV to V, 8 to 14 in. 2. White, yellow, blue, red, IV to V, 10 in. 3. White, violet, red, IV to V, |]4 to 8 in. 4. Pink, red, also red-brown, yellow, and violet, IV to V, 8 to 10 in. 5. White, yellow, red, and blue to violet, IV to V, 4 to 6 in.	4 to 7 in.	Moist, humic soil, semi-shade, also light shade and sunny, for groups, also in front of trees and shrubs and for underplanting of light trees and shrubs, suitable for premature flowering, *Primula juliae* is mostly sold commercially as *P. pruhoniciana*, also suitable for rock gardens in somewhat shady and sufficiently moist sites, *P.* ×*pubescens*, garden auricula, tolerates more sun and somewhat loamier soil; leafless extended shoots should always be covered with earth again.
Pseudolysimachion Speedwell 1. *P. longifolium* 2. *P. spicatum*	1. Blue, white, VII to VII, 24 to 32 in. 2. Blue, pink to red, VII to VIII, 14 to 32 in.	1. 12 to 16 in. 2. 10 to 12 in.	1. Moist soil, sunny; 2. Permeable, rather more dry, calciferous soil, sunny; both suitable for cut flowers; nectar source for bees.
Rodgersia aesculifolia Fingerleaf rodgersia	White and light pink, VI to VIII, 3 ¼ to 5 ft.	28 to 40 in.	Nutrient-rich, damp to moist soil, shaded, somewhat endangered by late frost, large decorative leaves, valuable solitary plant.
Rudbeckia Coneflower 1. *R. fulgida* var. *sullivantii* 2. *R. nitida*	1. Golden-yellow with black stars, VII to IX, 20 to 24 in. 2. Yellow, VII to IX, 6 to 6 ½ ft.	1. 10 to 12 in. 2. 24 to 32 in.	Nutrient-rich soil; 1. Sunny to light semi-shade, cut flowers do not keep well; 2. Solitary plant, good cut flower; 1 and 2. nectar source for bees.
Salvia nemorosa Wild sage, woodland sage	Violet to dark violet, V to IX, 16 to 20 in.	10 to 12 in.	Permeable soil, full sun, remontant following timely cutting back; nectar source for bees.
Scabiosa caucasica Pincushion flower, scabious	Blue, also white, VI to IX, 24 to 32 in.	10 to 14 in.	Permeable fertile soil, sunny, remontant if seeding is inhibited until X, suitable for cut flowers.

BOTANICAL NAME ENGLISH NAME SPECIES	FLOWER COLOR, FLOWERING TIME (MONTH), HEIGHT	PLANTING WIDTH	REQUIREMENTS AND SPECIFIC REMARKS
Sedum Stonecrop 1. *S. hybridum*, Siberian stonecrop 2. *S. spectabile*, Ice plant 3. *S. telephium*, Orpine, livelong, harping Johnny, and other names	1. Yellow, VI to VIII, 4 to 6 in. 2. Pink-red to crimson-red, VIII to IX, 12 to 16 in. 3. Rust-red, VIII to IX, 12 to 16 in.	14 to 20 in.	Undemanding, sunny, for edging, wild perennial plantings, neighboring grasses, suitable for groups and rock gardens, attracts butterflies; nectar source for bees. 1. Also semi-shaded, the variety 'Immergrünchen' grows quickly, has the best ground-covering characteristics; 2. and 3. Numerous varieties, cut flowers keep well.
Sidalcea False mallow, prairie mallow	White, pink, pink-red, VII to IX, 32 to 48 in.	14 to 16 in.	Humic, neutral to lightly acidic, not too dry soil, sunny, winter protection, for colorful flower borders.
Silene Campion, catchfly 1. *S. chalcedonica*, Maltese cross 2. *S. viscaria* 'Plena', Sticky catchfly	1. Vermilion, VII, to 3 ¼ ft. 2. Carmine-red, also double, VI, 12 to 16 in.	1. 10 to 12 in. 2. 6 to 8 in.	Permeable, also somewhat dry soil, sunny, also as cut flowers; 1. Flowers in 4 in. flower heads, use in borders and cottage gardens; 2. Sticky secretions on the branching of the stalks.
Solidago Goldenrod	Light to golden-yellow, VII to IX, 16 to 40 in.	8 to 12 in.	Undemanding, sunny, cut off old inflorescences to prevent self-seeding, suitable for cut flowers; nectar source for bees.
Tanacetum coccineum Tansy	White and pink to dark red, single and double, V to VI, 16 to 32 in.	10 to 12 in.	Nutrient-rich soil, sunny, apply fertilizer or divide and replant if flowering vigor declines, do not transplant in the fall, cut flowers keep well.
Thalictrum aquilegiifolium Meadow rue	White to pink, VI to VII, 3 ¼ to 4 ft.	12 to 18 in.	Moist, humic soil, sunny, for shrub and tree borders and next to water, attracts butterflies; nectar source for bees.
Tradescantia ×andersoniana White spiderwort	White, blue, and violet to crimson-red, VI to VIII, 20 to 24 in.	12 to 16 in.	Undemanding, sunny and semi-shaded, self-seeds easily, decorative at water edges.
Trollius Globeflower 1. *T. chinensis* 2. *T. europaeus* 3. Varieties	Yellow to golden-yellow; 1. V to VI, 32 to 35 in. 2. and 3. V to VI, 24 to 32 in.	12 to 14 in.	Damp to moist, somewhat loamy, nutrient-rich soil, garden varieties also drier, sunny to light semi-shade; 1. Flowers bowl-shaped; 2. and 3. Flowers more spherical; suitable for cut flowers.
Veronicastrum virginicum Black root, Culver's root, physic	Blue, white, pink, VII to IX, 4 to 5 ¼ ft.	16 to 20 in.	Damp to moist, humic soil, sunny, also light shade, very richly flowering, leaves finely serrated, flowers in long spikes.
Yucca filamentosa Adam's needle, spoon-leaf yucca	Creamy white, VII to VIII, plant 20 to 24 in., inflorescence 4 ½ ft.	24 to 32 in.	Permeable, preferably dry, calciferous, not infertile soil, full sun winter protection in harsh situations, valuable solitary plant.

Table 17. Perennials for Rock Gardens

Varieties for many of the species named below are also available from specialist dealers.

BOTANICAL NAME ENGLISH NAME SPECIES	FLOWER COLOR, FLOWERING TIME (MONTH), HEIGHT	PLANTING INTERVAL	REQUIREMENTS AND SPECIAL REMARKS
Acaena magellanica and others New Zealand burr	Flowers inconspicuous, VI to VII, 2 in.	6 to 8 in.	Dry, light soil, forms runners, lawn-like growth, also for gaps in the rock, decorative foliage plant.
Achillea Common yarrow 1. *A. ageratifolia* 2. *A. chrysocoma* 3. *A. clypeolata* 4. *A. tomentosa* 5. *A. umbellata*	1. 3., and 5. White 2. and 4. Yellow; 2. VI to VII 3. and 5. VI to VIII 4. VI to VII 5. V to VII; All up to around 8 in.	6 to 8 in.	Permeable, not too humic soil, all tolerate dryness, also suitable for dry stone walls; 1. Creeping, leaves gray-white; 2. Cushion-forming, leaves green; 3. Creeping, leaves silver-gray; 4. Grows in a lawn-like fashion, leaves gray-green, villose-woolly; 5. Cushion-forming, leaves gray-white.
Adonis vernalis Spring adonis, yellow pheasant's eye	Golden-yellow, IV to V, 8 in.	8 to 10 in.	Permeable soil, sunny, tolerates dryness, difficult to divide, frost germinator, *A. amurensis* already flowers from L. II; nectar source for bees.
Aethionema Stone cress 1. *A. armenum* 2. *A. grandiflorum*	Pink, V to VIII, 8 to 10 in.	6 to 10 in.	Warm, fairly dry soil, sunny, does not tolerate wetness, hardly possible to divide, propagated best through seed, also for planting in gaps between stones or bricks, etc.
Ajuga Bugle 1. *A. genevensis* 2. *A. reptans*	Blue-violet, IV to V, 4 to 6 in.	6 to 8 in.	Damp, humic soil, sunny and semi-shaded, evergreen, rapidly forms dense carpets, divide in spring or in the fall; 2. Nectar source for bees.
Alyssum Alison, madwort 1. *A. moellendorfianum* 2. *A. montanum*	Light golden-yellow; 1. V to VI, 4 to 6 in. 2. IV to V, 6 to 8 in.	8 to 12 in.	Not too moist soil, tolerates dryness, also suitable for dry stone walls, plant between stones and in gaps between rocks or bricks; nectar source for bees.
Anaphalis triplinervis Pearly everlasting	White, VI to VIII, 6 to 8 in.	6 to 8 in.	Light, sandy soil, tolerates dryness, leaves silvery-haired, suitable for dried flowers.
Androsace Rock jasmine 1. *A. primuloides* 2. *A. sarmentosa*	1. Whitish pink, IV, to 6 in., VI to VII 2. Pink, V to VI, 4 in.	4 to 6 in.	Sandy-humic, not too dry soil; 1. Damp to moist, sandy-loamy soil, sunny to semi-shaded, forms runners; 2. No burning hot sun, also suitable for dry stone walls.
Antennaria dioica Cat's foot	Delicate pink, pink-red, V to VII, 4 to 6 in.	4 to 6 in.	Light, somewhat sandy and infertile soil, also in fine gravel, sunny, tolerates dryness, forms good ground cover, leaves silver-gray.
Anthemis marschalliana Chamomile, dog fennel	Golden-yellow, V to VII, 8 to 10 in.	6 to 8 in.	Light, not too nutrient-rich soil, does not tolerate waterlogging, sunny, tolerates dryness, also suitable for dry stone walls and edging.
Arabis Rockcress 1. *A.* ×*arendsii* 2. *A. caucasica* 3. *A. procurrens*	1. Pink 2. White, also double 3. White, all IV to V, to 8 in.	6 to 8 in.	Humic, permeable soil, full sun, the double form is valuable as a cut flower, old cushions can be rejuvenated through cutting back, also suitable for dry stone walls, edging, and ground cover; nectar source for bees.
Arctanthemum arcticum Arctic chrysanthemum	White, pink, light yellow, IX to X, 10 to 12 in.	8 to 10 in.	Undemanding as regards the soil, but not too dry, sunny and semi-shaded, grows in a low bushy form, valuable as late bloomer.

BOTANICAL NAME ENGLISH NAME SPECIES	FLOWER COLOR, FLOWERING TIME (MONTH), HEIGHT	PLANTING INTERVAL	REQUIREMENTS AND SPECIAL REMARKS
Armeria maritima Common thrift, thrift	White, pinkish red, V to VI, 6 to 8 in.	4 to 6 in.	Evergreen, undemanding, cushion plant for edging and dry stone walls.
Aster 1. *A. alpinus*, Alpine aster, blue alpine daisy 2. *A. dumosus*, Bushy aster, rice button aster	White, pink, blue, also double; 1. V/VI, up to 8 in. 2. VIII to X, up to 16 in.	6 to 8 in.	Sunny, divide and replant more frequently, suitable for groups, also for edging and cut flowers; nectar source for bees 1. Humic soil; 2. Undemanding.
Aubrieta deltoidea Aubretia	Blue, violet, pink, red, IV to V, 4 in.	6 to 8 in.	Permeable, humic soil, sunny, forms flat cushions, rejuvenate old plants by cutting back after flowering, also suitable for dry stone walls; nectar source for bees.
Aurinia saxatilis (syn. *Alyssum saxatile*) Golden alyssum, golden tuft	Golden-yellow, IV to V, 6 to 8 in.	12 in.	Well-permeable, loamy-humic soil, sunny to semi-shaded, plant individually or in groups, wintergreen, fragrant; nectar source for bees.
Bistorta affinis Himalayan bistort, fleece flower, knotweed	Pink to red; VII to IX, 6 to 10 in.	8 to 10 in.	Damp to moist soil, sunny to semi-shaded, for the crown or base of dry stone walls.
Campanula Bellflower 1. *C. carpatica* 2. *C. cochleariifolia* 3. *C. portenschlagiana* and *C. poscharskyana*	1. and 3. White, blue, violet 2. White, blue; 1. VI to VII, 8 in. 2. VI to VII, 4 in. 3. VI to VIII, 6 in.	6 to 8 in.	Humic, permeable, not too wet soil, sunny, also light semi-shade; 1. Forms small bushes; 2. and 3. Forms flat cushions by means of runners; all also suitable for planting up dry stone walls, gaps between bricks or stones, and cracks in the walls.
Carlina acaulis ssp. *caulescens* Carline thistle	Silvery-white, VII to VIII, 8 to 12 in.	8 to 10 in.	Dry, permeable soil, sunny, also suitable for heath gardens, the crowns of dry stone walls, and dried bouquets, attracts butterflies; nectar source for bees.
Cerastium Mouse ear 1. *C. grandiflorum* 2. *C. tomentosum*	White, V to VI, 4 to 6 in.	8 to 12 in.	Not too moist soil, do not apply fertilizer, sunny, creeping, runs wild easily, suitable for dry stone walls, cracks, banks, edging, variety columnae under 2. grows more stubbily, runs wild less.
Dianthus Carnation, pink 1. *D. deltoides*, Maiden pink 2. *D. gratianopolitanus*, Cheddar pink 3. *D. microlepis* 4. *D. petraeus*, Rock pink, fragrant snowflake garden pink	White to dark red; 1. V to VII, up to 8 in. 2. V to VI, 4 to 8 in. 3. VI to VII, 4 to 6 in. 4. VI to VIII, 6 to 8 in.	6 to 8 in.	Nutrient-rich soil, sunny, good water runoff, suitable for planting gaps between bricks/stones and cracks in dry stone walls, also in small rock debris; 1. Loves sandy, acidic soil, grows in a lawn-like fashion, leaves deep green; 2. Grows in a loose, cushion-like fashion, steel-blue cushions also decorative without flowers; 3. Forms dense cushions with silvery-gray leaflets; 4. Loves calciferous soils, grows in a lawn-like fashion, leaves bluish green.
Dicentra eximia Turkey corn	Pink, white, V to VII, 8 to 10 in.	10 to 12 in.	Moist, humic soil, light shade, in full sun only with sufficient moisture, suitable for underplanting of light trees and shrubs.
Dodecatheon meadia Shooting star	White, pink, red, V to VI, 10 to 14 in.	6 to 8 in.	Humic, somewhat moist soil, out of direct sun to semi-shaded, retracts growth in summer, flowers similar to alpine violets.
Draba Whitlow grass 1. *D. aizoides* 2. *D. bruniifolia* 3. *D. haynaldii*	Golden-yellow; 1. IV, 2 to 4 in. 2. IV to V, 2 to 4 in. 3. V to VI, 2 to 3 in.	4 to 6 in.	Not too infertile and not too light well-drained soil, also tolerates dryness, forms flat, richly flowering cushions with taproot, suitable for planting gaps between bricks and stones, and cracks, also suitable for dry stone walls.

BOTANICAL NAME ENGLISH NAME SPECIES	FLOWER COLOR, FLOWERING TIME (MONTH), HEIGHT	PLANTING INTERVAL	REQUIREMENTS AND SPECIAL REMARKS
Dryas Mountain avens 1. *D. octopetala* 2. *D. ×suendermannii*	Ivory-white, V to VI, 4 to 6 in.	6 to 8 in.	Calciferous, permeable, not too dry soil, sunny, feathery infructescences appear after flowering, protect from winter sun, valuable ground cover plant, also suitable for area plantings.
Euphorbia Spurge 1. *E. capitulata* 2. *E. epithymoides* (syn. *polychroma*) 3. Cushion spurge 4. *E. myrsinites*	1. Yellow, VI to VII, 4 in. 2. Yellow, IV to VI, 12 to 16 in. 3. Yellow, IV to VI, 4 to 6 in.	1. and 3. 6 to 8 in. 2. 12 in.	1. and 3. Permeable, also dry soil, freezes back in hard winters but recovers, sometimes self-seeding; 2. Good garden soil, sunny, fiery-red fall coloring, suitable for rock gardens, also for loose borders, as advance planting and adjacent to conifers growing down to the ground; all three species will also grow on dry stone walls.
Gentiana Gentian 1. *G. acaulis*, Trumpet gentian 2. *G. septemfida* var. *lago-dechiana*, Lagodekhi crested gentian 3. *G. sino-ornata*, Showy Chinese gentian	1. Blue, V to VII, to 4 in. 2. Blue, VII to IX, 6 to 10 in. 3. Blue, IX to X, 4 to 6 in.	1. 4 in. 2. and 3. 6 in.	Loamy-humic, somewhat moist and well-aerated soil, out of direct sun; 1. Calcicolous; 2. Prostrate, grows almost in rosette form, calcicolous; 3. Prostrate, calciphobous, needs a high proportion of humus (bark humus or forest floor).
Geranium Cranesbill 1. *G. cinereum* subsp. *subcaulescens* 2. *G. sanguineum*	Carmine-red; 1. VI to VII, 6 to 8 in. 2. V to IX, 8 to 10 in.	6 to 8 in.	Deep, not too moist soil, sunny, long-flowering, also suitable for planting in heath gardens and natural plant gardens, on banks and as edging.
Geum Avens 1. *G. coccineum*, Avens 2. *G. montanum*, Alpine avens	1. Yellow, orange, red, V to VII, 8 to 12 in. 2. Yellow, V to VII, 8 to 12 in.	8 to 12 in.	Humic, damp soil, sunny to semi-shaded; 1. 'Coppertone' flowers dark yellow, 'Feuermeer' flowers red; 2. 'Diana' flowers large, vivid lemon-yellow.
Globularia cordifolia Heart-leaved globe daisy	Light blue-violet, V to VII, up to 4 in.	4 to 6 in.	Permeable soil, calcicolous, sunny, wintergreen foliage, forms dense cushions.
Gypsophila Baby's breath 1. *G. cerastioides* 2. *G. repens*	1. White, V to VI, 4 in. 2. White, pink, also double; VI to VIII, 4 to 10 in.	6 to 10 in.	Permeable, medium-heavy soil, sunny, tolerates dryness, frequently remontant, also suitable for dry stone walls and banks, *G. repens* 'Rosea' is valuable, flowers delicate pink.
Helianthemum Rock rose, sun rose	White, yellow, pink, red, orange, also double, VI to VIII, 6 to 8 in.	6 to 8 in.	Permeable, light soil, sunny, rejuvenate older plants by cutting back after flowering, winter protection in the event of hard frost, also suitable for dry stone walls and edging.
Hepatica Liverleaf 1. *H. nobilis* 2. *H. transsylvanica*	1. Blue, white, red, also double 2. Blue, white 1. and 2. III to IV, 4 to 6 in.	4 to 6 in.	Humic, calciferous soil, shaded, plant in groups if possible, possible neighboring plants include *Cyclamen*, *Phyllitis*, *Asplenium*, and *Primula juliae*, suitable for growing in the light shade of trees and shrubs.
Heuchera Coral bell 1. *H. micrantha* 'Palace Purple' 2. *H. sanguinea* 'Splendens'	3. Delicate pink, VII to VIII, 8 to 24 in. 3. Scarlet, VI to VII, 16 to 20 in.	8 to 12 in.	Deep, humus-rich, damp to moist soil, sunny or semi-shaded, winter protection required for exposed sites, suitable for wild perennial gardens and edging, also as cut flowers; 1. Decorative red-brown leaves; 2. Leaves with lobed edges.
Hieracium ×rubrum	Orange-red, VI to VIII, 4 to 8 in.	6 in.	Undemanding as regards the soil, tolerates dryness, growth lawn-like, also suitable for dry stone walls, banks, and heath gardens.

BOTANICAL NAME ENGLISH NAME SPECIES	FLOWER COLOR, FLOWERING TIME (MONTH), HEIGHT	PLANTING INTERVAL	REQUIREMENTS AND SPECIAL REMARKS
Iberis Candytuft 1. *I. saxatilis* 2. *I. sempervirens*	White; 1. IV to VI, 4 to 6 in. 2. V to VI, 6 to 10 in.	1. 6 in. 2. 8 to 10 in.	Not too moist, deep, nutrient-rich soil, apply fertilizer every year after flowering, sunny, also light semi-shade, suitable for dry stone walls and edging.
Incarvillea Incarvillea 1. *I. compacta* 2. *I. mairei*	Pink-red; 1. V to VII, 8 in. 2. VI to VII, 8 to 12 in.	7 to 10 in.	Nutrient-rich, loamy, permeable soil, tolerates dryness, sunny to out of direct sun, turnip-like roots around 4 in. deep, plant in tufts, variety grandiflora of *I. mairei* with very large flowers.
Inula ensifolia Narrow-leaved inula	Golden-yellow, VII to VIII, 8 in.	10 to 14 in.	Undemanding, sunny, tolerates dryness, continuous flowering, suitable for dry stone walls, heath gardens; nectar source for bees.
Iris Barbata Nana Group (Miniature Dwarf Bearded) Dwarf irises of the Bartiris group	White, yellow, blue, violet, wine-red, IV to V, up to 8 in.	6 to 8 in.	Undemanding, sunny, tolerates dryness, no fresh stable manure, divide after flowering, plant shallowly, also suitable for banks and edging, also for borders, bowls, and balcony boxes.
Leontopodium Edelweiss 1. *L. alpinum* 2. *L. souliei*	White and felty; 1. VI to VIII, 4 to 8 in. 2. VI to VII, 4 to 6 in.	6 in.	Permeable soil without fresh humus, sunny, not too dry, no waterlogging, forms carpets, also suitable for dry stone walls.
Leptinella squalida New Zealand brass buttons	Yellow, inconspicuous, VII to VIII, 2 in.	2 to 4 in.	Damp to moist soil, tolerates semi-shade, evergreen, good ground cover, thanks to runners.
Lewisia cotyledon Cliff maids, imperial lewisia	White to yellow to pink and violet, V to VI, up to 10 in.	8 in.	Permeable, nutrient-poor soil, calciphobous, sunny to semi-shaded, wintergreen, also suitable for dry stone walls.
Linum flavum Golden flax, yellow flax	Yellow, VI to VII, 6 to 14 in.	6 to 8 in.	Somewhat dry, permeable, calciferous soil, sunny, also suitable for the crowns of dry stone walls and for heath gardens.
Nepeta Catmint 1. *N. ×faassenii* 2. *N. nervosa*	Lavender-blue, VI to VIII, 12 to 14 in.	8 to 10 in.	Permeable, preferably drier soil, sunny, warm site, remontant after cutting back, also suitable for dry stone walls and heath gardens.
Oenothera macrocarpa Missouri evening primrose, prairie evening primrose	Yellow, VI to IX, 6 to 8 in.	8 to 12 in.	Good, permeable, calciferous soil, sunny, stalks spread out and lying on the soil, also suitable for dry stone walls, and south-facing slopes; nectar source for bees.
Opuntia Prickly pear, tuna 1. *O. fragilis* 2. *O. phaeacantha*	1. Yellow, red, VII to VIII, 8 in. 2. Yellow, red, VII to VIII, up to 8 in.	8 to 12 in.	Permeable, rather drier soil, sheltered, sunny protect from winter wetness, also suitable for dry stone walls and south-facing slopes.
Phlox Phlox 1. *P. douglasii*, Alpine phlox, Douglas phlox 2. *P. stolonifera*, Creeping phlox 3. *P. subulata*, Moss phlox, moss pink	White, pink, red, with many intermediate shades, also lilac, V to VI, 4 to 6 in.	6 to 8 in.	Loose, deep, neutral to weakly acidic soil, sunny, in summer not too dry and not too hot, forms large cushion areas, also suitable for dry stone walls and edging.
Plantago nivalis Weegbree	Greenish, VII to VIII, 4 to 4 ¾ in.	4 to 6 in.	Permeable soil, sunny, protect from winter wetness, suitable for stones and rock cracks.

BOTANICAL NAME ENGLISH NAME SPECIES	FLOWER COLOR, FLOWERING TIME (MONTH), HEIGHT	PLANTING INTERVAL	REQUIREMENTS AND SPECIAL REMARKS
Potentilla Cinquefoil, five finger 1. *P. atrosanguinea* 2. *P. aurea* 3. *P. megalantha* 4. *P. nitida* 5. *P. ×tonguei*	1. Red, VI to IX, 12 to 18 in. 2. Yellow, VI to VII, up to 8 in. 3. Yellow, VII to VIII, up to 10 in. 4. Pink, VII to VIII, up to 3 in. 5. Orange-red, VII to VIII, 4 in.	1. and 5. 10 to 12 in. 2. to 4. 6 to 8 in.	Permeable, not nutrient-rich, preferably drier soil, sunny to light shade, for gravely, mat-like sites, also wide gaps between bricks and stones in steps and dry stone wall; 1., 3., and 5. Also suitable for planting of the base or crown of dry stone walls; all species also good for gravel patches and on rocks.
Primula Primrose, cowslip 1. *P. auricula*, Auricula, dusty miller, garden auricula 2. *P. beesiana*, Candelabra primrose 3. *P. cortusoides* 4. *P. japonica*, Japanese primrose, Japanese cowslip 5. *P. marginata*, Silver-edged primrose 6. *P. ×pubescens*, Garden auricula 7. *P. rosea*, Himalayan meadow primrose	1. Yellow, dark red, IV to VI, up to 8 in. 2. Variable, VI to VII, up to 20 in. 3. Pink, IV to V, up to 8 in. 4. Red, V to VI, up to 16 in. 5. Purple, III to IV, up to 6 in. 6. Yellow, pink, red, red-brown, violet, IV to V, 8 to 10 in. 7. Pink, III to IV, up to 7 in.	1., 3., 5., 7. 4 ¾ to 7 in. 2., 4. 7 to 10 in. 6. 6 to 8 in.	Loamy-humic soil with some sand, with no fresh fertilizer application, for spring flowerbeds, rock gardens, in light shade of trees, as edging, also suitable for dry stone walls provided the specific conditions are taken into account; 1., 3., 5. Moderately moist soil, which may also be dry for a brief time, light, almost sunny, but preferably shaded site; 2., 4., 7. More moisture in the soil, a small, moist gravel hollow in a rock garden and a semi-shaded situation are favorable; 6. Deep, moist soil, light shade, suffers under full sun and dryness in summer; also suitable for growing in pots.
Prunella Selfheal 1. *P. grandiflora* 2. *P. ×webbiana*	1. Pink, white, purple; 2. violet; 1. and 2. VII to VIII, 4 to 8 in.	6 to 8 in.	Sufficiently moist soil, sunny, also semi-shaded, forms large cushion areas, not spreading, also suitable for wide gaps between the stones or bricks in dry stone walls or between footpath slabs; nectar source for bees.
Pseudofumaria (syn. *Corydalis*) *lutea* Yellow fumitory	Yellow, V to X, 10 to 12 in.	8 to 10 in.	Undemanding, for gaps between stones or bricks in walls, also rock cracks, out of direct sun, self-seeding.
Pulsatilla Pasque flower 1. *P. halleri* 2. *P. vulgaris*	Violet to red, white, L. III to V, 8 to 10 in.	7 to 10 in.	Deep soil, sunny, no wetness, older plants have taproots and therefore can barely be transplanted, decorative seed heads, sow immediately after ripening or frost germinators, also suitable for dry stone wall; 2. 'Rödde Klokke' deep red, 'Weisser Schwan' white.
Sagina subulata Heath pearlwort, Irish moss	White, VI to VIII, 3 to 2 in.	2 in.	Damp to moist, humic soil, semi-shaded, forms evergreen cushions, can also be planted between paving slabs.
Saxifraga Saxifrage Mossy saxifrages: 1. *S. ×arendsii* 2. *S. trifurcata* Rosette saxifrages: 3. *S. callosa*, Limestone saxifrage 4. *S. cochlearis* 5. *S. longifolia* 6. *S. paniculata* Shade saxifrages: 7. *S. cuneifolia*, shield-leafed saxifrage 8. *S. umbrosa*, London pride	1. White, light yellow, pink to ruby-red, IV to V, 4 to 8 in. 2. White, V to VI, 4 to 6 in. 3. White, VI, 14 in. 4. Pure white, V/VI, inflorescence 10 in. 5. White, VI/VII, flower stalk up to 28 in. 6. White, VI/VII, flower stalk up to 18 in. 7. White, V to VIII, 6 in. 8. Pink, V to VI, 8 to 12 in.	1. and 2. 4 to 6 in. 3. to 6. 4 to 4 ¾ in. 7. and 8. 4 to 6 in.	1. and 2. Damp to moist, humic soil, semi-shaded, with sufficient moisture also sunny, apply fertilizer or compost in the fall, suitable for moister places at the foot of dry stone walls, and for edging; 3. to 6. Evergreen, permeable, calciferous soil, sunny to out of direct sun, forms rosettes, remove rosettes that have finished flowering, for gaps in walls and cracks, also suitable for dry stone walls and edging; 3. Leaves gray-blue, reddish at the base; 4. Leaves with crusty lime secretions; 5. Leaves up to 4 in. long, smooth and encrusted with lime; 6. Rosettes encrusted with lime; 7. and 8. Damp, humic soil, no heavy loam, light shade to semi-shaded, form dense carpets on suitable sites, for moist and shady places behind large rocks, at the foot of dry stone walls, and as edging.

BOTANICAL NAME ENGLISH NAME SPECIES	FLOWER COLOR, FLOWERING TIME (MONTH), HEIGHT	PLANTING INTERVAL	REQUIREMENTS AND SPECIAL REMARKS
Sedum Stonecrop 1. *S. acre*, Wallpepper 2. *S. album*, White stonecrop 3. *S. cauticola*, Cliff stonecrop 4. *S. selskianum*, Amur stonecrop 5. *S. spurium*, Two row stonecrop	1. Yellow, VI to VII, 2 in. 2. White, VI to VII, 2 in. 3. Carmine-red, VIII to IX, 8 in. 4. Yellow, VII to VIII, 6 in. 5. White, pink-red, VII to VIII, 4 in.	4 to 6 in.	Permeable soil, tolerates dryness; 1. Evergreen, forms dense carpets, bronze-green cushions and lawns, 'Aureum' leaves greenish yellow; 2. Forms carpets, bronze-red in the fall; 3. Grows as rosettes, leaves bluish green; 4. Short shoots, leaves spatulate, green; 5. Forms loose carpets, leaves green to dark crimson; all suitable for dry stone walls, as ground cover and for edging, attract butterflies; nectar source for bees.
Sempervivum House leek	Yellow, pink, red, VI to VII, 4 to 8 in.	4 to 6 in.	Permeable, somewhat humic soil, sunny, no waterlogging, tolerates dryness, suitable for dry stone walls, troughs, and bowls.
Silene Campion, catchfly 1. *S. acaulis*, cushion pink, moss campion 2. *S. schafta*, Caucasian campion, autumn catchfly	1. Pink, V to VIII, 4 in. 2. Deep pink, VIII to IX, 4 in.	4 to 6 in.	Permeable, somewhat calciferous, not too moist soil, sunny to slightly out of direct sun, suitable for troughs and dry stone walls; 1. Divide after 2 years.
Stachys byzantina Betony, hedge nettle, woundwort	Pink (small), VI to VII, up to 14 in.	10 to 12 in.	Permeable soil, sunny, no wetness, leaves white and felty, also suitable for dry stone walls; nectar source for bees.
Teucrium chamaedrys Wall germander	Crimson-pink, VII to IX, 12 in.	8 to 10 in.	Permeable calciferous soil, no wetness, for dry stone walls, heath gardens, edging; nectar source for bees.
Thymus Thyme 1. *T. pseudolanuginosus* 2. *T. serpyllum*	1. Pink, V to VII, 2 in. 2. White, pink-red, VII to IX, 2 in.	4 to 6 in.	Infertile, dry soil, sunny, avoid excess nutrients or moisture, forms flat cushions, suitable for dry stone walls, troughs, heath gardens, banks, attracts butterflies; nectar source for bees.
Veronica Bird's eye, speedwell 1. *V. armena* 2. *V. prostrata*	1. Dark blue, V to VI, 2 to 4 in. 2. Blue, pink to reddish, VII to VIII, 6 to 8 in.	6 to 8 in.	Permeable, infertile soil, sunny, no waterlogging, suitable for dry stone walls, troughs, and bowls, also heath gardens and borders.
Viola labradorica Labrador violet	Purple, IV to VI, 6 in.	6 to 8 in.	Permeable, humic garden soil, semi-shaded, leaves dark violet to red-brown, round.

Table 18. Low Perennials for Semi-Shaded and Shaded Places in the Garden and Plants as an Alternative to Lawns

BOTANICAL NAME ENGLISH NAME SPECIES	FLOWER COLOR, FLOWERING TIME (MONTH)	HEIGHT	REQUIREMENTS AND SPECIAL REMARKS
Ajuga reptans Bugle	Blue-violet, IV to VI	4 to 6 in.	Fresh humic soil, out of direct sun, evergreen, forms runners; nectar source for bees.
Asarum europaeum European wild ginger	Brown, III to IV	4 in.	Fresh humic soil, with creeping ground stem, leaves heart-shaped, wintergreen.
Brunnera macrophylla Siberian bugloss	Deep blue, IV to VI	16 to 20 in.	Fresh humic soil, semi-shaded, leaves roughly hirsute, self-seeding.
Carex sylvativa Wood sedge	V to VII	12 to 28 in.	Moist soil, light shade under trees, self-seeding.
Chiastophyllum oppositifolium Solar yellow	Golden-yellow, VI to VII	6 to 10 in.	Humic, not too wet soil, semi-shaded, evergreen, branched racemes, leaves rather fleshy, shoots creeping.
Convallaria majalis Lily of the valley	White, V	8 in.	Humic garden soil, spreads by way of runners.
Cortusa matthioli Alpine bells	Pink-violet, VII to VIII	10 to 12 in.	Humic, loose, calciferous, not too dry, always moderately moist soil, out of direct sun, creeping.
Cymbalaria (syn. *Linaria*) Toadflax 1. *C. muralis* 2. *C. pallida*	Blue-purple, VI to IX	2 in.	Light, humic soil, also suitable for gaps between bricks or stones in walls, out of direct sun to semi-shaded, forms runners, self-seeding.
Epimedium Bishop's hat, bishop's mitre 1. *E. pinnatum* subsp. *colchicum* 2. *E. pubigerum*	White, yellow, pink, red, IV to V 1. Yellow 2. Creamy white	8 to 12 in. 1. 10 to 14 in. 2. 8 in.	Humic garden soil, robust, older plants also dry-tolerant, leaves wintergreen; 1. Covers entire areas by way of runners; 2. Forms bunches.
Galium odoratum Sweet woodruff	White, V	6 in.	Damp, humic soil, spreads by way of runners.
Hedera helix Ivy	Greenish yellow, IX/X	12 in.	Damp moist soil, forms dense ground cover, flowers on older plants only, fruits appear in spring.
×*Heucherella tiarelloides* Alumroot	Light pink, V to VII	4 to 12 in.	Humic garden soil, not too dry, suitable as ground cover between shrubs and trees, also for shady sites in rock gardens.
Hosta tardiflora	Light-crimson-colored, VII to VIII	12 to 16 in.	Moist soil, decorative floral arrangements, blue-green, or green on lighter sites.
Lamium (syn. *Lamiastrum*) *galeobdolon* 'Florentinum' Yellow archangel	Yellow, V to VI	8 in.	Multicolored leaves, undemanding, for large areas, forms runners, vigorous growth; nectar source for bees.
Lithospermum (syn. *Buglossoides*) *purpurocaeruleum* Gromwell	Reddish blue, IV to VI	12 in.	Calcicolous, tolerates dryness, sunny or shaded, undemanding, for larger areas, forms runners.

BOTANICAL NAME ENGLISH NAME SPECIES	FLOWER COLOR, FLOWERING TIME (MONTH)	HEIGHT	REQUIREMENTS AND SPECIAL REMARKS
Lysimachia nummularia Creeping jenny	Yellow, V to VII	2 in.	Damp, also moist, humic soil, creeping shoots, also suitable for planting up walls and rocks.
Omphalodes verna Blue-eyed Mary	Blue, also white, IV to V	4 to 6 in.	Damp, humic soil, forms runners, blue or white carpets.
Pachysandra terminalis Japanese pachysandra, Japanese spurge	Greenish white, IV to V	8 to 10 in.	Damp, humic soil, forms runners, perennial, evergreen.
Polypodium vulgare Common polypody	8 to 16 in.	14 in.	Humic, moist, weakly acidic soil, native fern, creeping rhizomes, grows projectingly, somewhat dry-tolerant, also suitable for plant bowls and gaps between bricks or stones in walls.
Prunella grandiflora Selfheal	Violet to blue, VI to IX	6 to 10 in.	Undemanding, tolerates semi-shade and dryness, also grows on sunny sites with damp soil.
Pseudofumaria (syn. *Corydalis*) *lutea* Yellow fumitory	Yellow, V to X	8 to 10 in.	Undemanding, self-seeding, also grows in gaps in walls.
Pulmonaria angustifolia 'Azurea' Blue lungwort	Gentian-blue, IV to V	10 to 12 in.	Loose damp, humic soil, semi-shaded, forms blue-green carpets.
Sanicula europaea Butterwort, sanicle	White, V to VII	8 to 10 in.	Humic damp soil, tolerates deep shade.
Saxifraga Saxifrage 1. *S. cuneifolia*, Shield-leafed saxifrage 2. *S. umbrosa*, London pride	1. White, V to VIII 2. Pink, V to VI	1. 6 in. 2. 8 to 12 in.	Damp, humic soil, no heavy loam, light shade to semi-shaded, forms dense carpets on favorable sites, leaves wintergreen, leathery.
Tiarella cordifolia Foamflower	White, IV to V	8 to 12 in.	Humic soil, sensitive to dryness, leaves heart-shaped, slightly hirsute, forms runners.
Vinca minor Small periwinkle	White, blue, crimson, IV to V	4 to 8 in.	Humic soil, robust, also for large areas, creeping branching shoots.
Waldsteinia Waldsteinia 1. *W. geoides* 2. *W. ternata*	Yellow, IV to V	1. 8 in. 2. 4 to 8 in.	Both undemanding as regards the soil, robust; 1. Creeping rootstock, no runners; 2. Forms runners or carpets, leaves wintergreen.

Table 19. Aquatic and Swamp Plants

BOTANICAL NAME ENGLISH NAME SPECIES	FLOWER COLOR, FLOWERING TIME (MONTH), HEIGHT	PROPAGATION	USE AND SPECIAL REMARKS
Acorus calamus Calamus, flag root, sweet myrtle	Light green spadix, V to VII, 24 to 40 in.	Division in spring, shortly after shoots appear	Roots and leaves have medicinal properties, pond edge up to a depth of 8 in., swamp hollows, sunny, also semi-shaded, leaves iris-like, in 'Variegatus' with creamy-white edges.
Alisma plantago-aquatica Asiatic water plantain	White to pale pink, VI to IX, 16 to 28 in.	Division in spring or self-seeding	Swamp hollows, pond edge up to a depth of 12 in., sunny to semi-shaded, broad spoon-shaped aerial (emersed) leaves on long stalks.
Bistorta officinalis Adderwort, meadow bistort	Pink, V to VII, 12 to 28 in.	Division	Moist places, swamp hollows, water edges, sunny.
Butomus umbellatus Flowering rush, water gladiolus	Pale pink to reddish, VI to VIII, 32 to 40 in.	Division in spring or self-seeding	Pond banks, rootstock must stand in water, depth up to 16 in., loamy-swampy soil, sunny.
Calla palustris Bog arum, water arum	White bract, V to VIII, red berry spadix, IX, 6 to 10 in.	Careful division of larger plants	Swamp hollows and pond edges up to 4 in. deep, sunny to semi-shaded, rootstock creeping, leaves fresh-green, heart-shaped, putrefaction odor, berries poisonous.
Caltha palustris Kingcup, marsh marigold	Vivid yellow, also white and double, IV to VI, 8 to 16 in.	Division of the rootstock in summer after flowering	Swamps and pond edges, also suitable for moist, deep soil, sunny, 'Multiplex' golden-yellow, tightly double, often remontant; poisonous plant.
Ceratophyllum submersum Soft hornwort	Floats freely in water	By means of scions or winter buds	Underwater plant, good oxygen donor, takes nutrients from the water (thereby reducing algal growth), spawning plant for fish.
Cyperus longus Galingale, sweet galingale	Papyrus-like grass, VI to IX, to 40 in.	Easily done by seeding or division in spring	Swamps and pond edges, up to 12 in. deep, sunny or semi-shaded, forms runners, brownish spikes on long stalks.
Eichhornia crassipes Water hyacinth	Blue-violet, VI to IX, 6 to 8 in.	Division in summer	Floating (natant) plant with decorative flotation bladders, sunny, overwinter in dry and warm conditions.
Euphorbia palustris Marsh spurge	Yellow, V to VI, to 3 ¼ ft.	Sowing and division	Moist, wet swamp soil, with shallow water level, vivid yellow-orange fall coloration.
Fontinalis antipyretica var. *gigantea* Greater water-moss	Floats freely in water, can be weighed down with a stone (but do not plant)	Division in spring	Underwater plant, native, vigorous growth, broad leaves, easily suffers adaptation problems (leading to a golden-brown coloration), later good growth, good oxygen donor, not suitable for calciferous water, spawning plant for fish.
Hippuris vulgaris Mare's tail	Deep-water zone to banks	By means of runners	Underwater plant, reproduces vigorously, therefore suitable for larger ponds, shoots not branched, will also grow above the water level in shallow water.
Iris Flag, sword lily 1. *I. ensata*, Japanese water iris 2. *I. laevigata*, Japanese iris, rabbit-ear iris, shallow-flowered iris 3. *I. pseudoacrus*, Flag iris, yellow flag 4. *I. versicolor*, Blue flag, iris	1. Crimson, blue, white, VI to VII, 24 to 40 in. 2. Blue, pink, VII to VIII, 24 to 32 in. 3. Light to golden-yellow, V to VI, 24 to 32 in. and higher 4. Violet-blue, VI to VIII, 20 to 28 in.	Division after flowering, also IV/V	Moist swampy soil, sunny, calciphobous, best planted in containers, dry winter protection; 1. Formerly *Iris kaempferi*, in water only from early summer until after the flowering time, thereafter drier, in winter nearly dry; 2., 3. und 4. True swamp plants, tolerate constant wetness; 2. Numerous breeds; 3. A number of varieties, 'Berliner Tiger' yellow with brown patterning, 'Alba' white; 4. Variable species, flower velvet, pendulous leaves with yellow midrib and violet veins, hybrids and varieties.

BOTANICAL NAME ENGLISH NAME SPECIES	FLOWER COLOR, FLOWERING TIME (MONTH), HEIGHT	PROPAGATION	USE AND SPECIAL REMARKS
Juncus inflexus Hard rush	Brownish, fruiting bodies dark brown, 12 to 24 in.	Division in spring	Damp, also swampy soil, water depth up to 8 in., sunny to semi-shaded, calciphobous, culms ribbed, blue-green.
Lotus uliginosus Greater bird's foot trefoil	Yellow, VI to VII, 8 to 20 in.	By means of runners	Moist to swampy, lime-deficient soil, also water level up to 1 ¼ in., robust, sunny to semi-shaded.
Lysichiton Skunk cabbage 1. *L. americanus*, Yellow skunk cabbage 2. *L. camtschatcensis*, Skunk cabbage	Tepal; 1. Yellow 2. White 1. and 2. IV to VI, 12 to 20 in.	Division in summer after flowering	Swampy or shallow water level (4 in.), semi-shaded, light winter protection (leaves and brushwood), leaves up to 12 in. wide, bluish green.
Lythrum salicaria 'Robert' Purple loosestrife, spiked loosestrife	Salmon-carmine, VI to IX, 24 to 32 in.	Division in spring, also self-seeding	Damp to wet soil, sunny to semi-shaded, for moist to wet riparian zone, nectar source for bees, also attracts butterflies and bumblebees, good cut flower.
Menyanthes trifoliata Bog bean, water trefoil	White to pink, VI to VII, 8 to 12 in.	Basal shoots, in spring or early summer	Swamp hollows, pond edge, water level up to 6 in., calciphobous, sunny to semi-shaded, growth somewhat spreading, accordingly plant in containers.
Myosotis rehsteineri (syn. *palustris*) Lake Constance forget-me-not	Sky-blue, V to IX, 8 to 16 in.	Division in spring or after flowering	Swampy riparian zone, only partially in water, loamy humic soil, sunny to semi-shaded, creeping rootstock.
Nuphar lutea Brandy bottle, yellow pond lily, yellow water lily	Golden-yellow, VI to VIII, briefly flowering above the water	Division of rhizomes in late IV/V (plant parts with shoot)	Water depth not less than 16 in., sunny to semi-shaded, winter protection necessary for drained basins only, leaves initially underwater only, poisonous plant.
Nymphaea Water lily (see TABLE 20)	White, yellow, copper, pink, red, floating on water	Division shortly after shoots appear, end IV/V (plant parts with shoot)	Numerous varieties for every water depth (see separate list), sunny, winter protection with covering of leaves necessary for drained basins only, overwinter sensitive varieties in frost-free conditions in containers.
Nymphoides peltata Water fringe, yellow floating heart	Golden-yellow, VII to IX, flowering around 2 in. above the water	Division of rhizomes in spring	Water level not less than 6 in., nutrient-rich loamy soil, sunny, spreading growth, accordingly plant in containers.
Orontium aquaticum Golden club	Golden-yellow flower spadix, V to VI, 8 to 16 in.	Division in spring	Water depth up to 12 in., loamy humic soil, sunny, branched root system, provide winter protection or overwinter under frost-free conditions.
Pontederia cordata Pickerel weed	Blue flower spikes, VII to IX, 20 to 35 in.	Division in spring	Riparian zone, water depth up to 16 in., lime-deficient soil, sunny, if water has been drained overwinter under a thick layer of leaves or under frost-free conditions.
Primula Primrose 1. *P. florindae*, Himalayan cowslip 2. *P. vialii* (syn. *littoniana*), Vial's primrose	1. Golden-yellow, VII to IX 2. Purple, VI to VII, up to 16 in.	1. and 2. Division, also through seed	1. Moist sites, especially at water edges; 2. Moist sites, swamp zone, a small, moist pile of stones in a rock garden and a semi-shaded site are helpful.

BOTANICAL NAME ENGLISH NAME SPECIES	FLOWER COLOR, FLOWERING TIME (MONTH), HEIGHT	PROPAGATION	USE AND SPECIAL REMARKS
Ranunculus Buttercup, crowfoot 1. *R. aquatilis*, Water buttercup, water crowfoot 2. *R. circinatus*, Fan-leaved water crowfoot 3. *R. lingua*, Greater spearwort	1. and 2. White, V to IX, flowers above the water 3. Golden-yellow, VI to VIII, 20 to 60 in.	1. and 2. Sow in pots of under water or divide 3. Division in spring	1. and 2. Aquatic plants, water level 12 in. or more, humic sandy soil, calciphobous, sunny, good oxygen producers; 1. Soft, feathery submerged leaves; 2. Splayed, rigid submerged leaves, takes up considerable nutrients from the water (can be used to inhibit algal growth); 3. Swampy or water level up to 12 in., sunny to semi-shaded; poisonous plant.
Sagittaria Arrowhead 1. *S. latifolia*, Arrowhead, duck potato 2. *S. sagittifolia*, Common arrowhead	White (1. yellow, 2. brown-violet stamens), VI to VIII, 20 to 28 in.	Self-seeding	Swamp zone, water depth 4 to 20 in., sunny to semi-shaded, tubers like plover eggs, produces shoots in M. V, leaves die off in the fall (leave on the plant), *S. latifolia* 'Plena' with double flowers.
Schoenoplectus (syn. *Scirpus*) Club rush 1. *S. lacustris*, Bulrush 2. *S. tabernaemontani*, Zebra rush	Brownish flower spikes, VI to VIII; 1. 3 ¼ to 8 ft. 2. 24 to 48 in.	Division in spring	Swampy, deep soil; 1. Water level up to 40 in., vigorous spreading, culms grass-green, 'Albescens' with yellow-green longitudinal stripes; 2. Water level up to 16 in., also semi-shaded, culms gray-green, 'Zebrinus' zebra rush with white-green rings.
Stratiotes aloides Water aloe, water soldier	White, summer, 6 to 10 in.	Runners with rootlets in spring	Floating (natant) plant from a depth of 8 in., sunny, semi-shaded, forms runners, leaves heart-shaped, edges spiny.
Trapa natans Water chestnut, Jesuit's nut	Flowers white, inconspicuous, VI to IX	Sowing in the fall or spring directly on site	Floating, ornamental, green leaf rosettes, vivid red in summer, annual, self-seeding, seeds of the laciniate fruits edible.
Typha Bulrush, cattail, reedmace 1. *T. angustifolia*, Lesser bulrush 2. *T. latifolia*, Bulrush, cattail 3. *T. laxmannii*, Laxmann's bulrush 4. *T. minima*, Lesser bulrush	1. Spadix brown, VII, 5 to 6 ½ ft. 2. Spadix brown, VII, 5 to 6 ½ ft. 3. Spadix brown, VII, 4 ft. 4. Spadix brown, V to VI, 12 to 32 in.	Division in spring	Swampy conditions; 1., 2., and 3. Also water level up to 16 in.; 4. Only up to 4 in.; 1. Narrow-leaved; 2. Broad-leaved; 3. Spadix between foliage leaves; 4. Lesser bulrush, spadix almost spheroid.

Table 20. Water Lilies (*Nymphaea*)

FOR VERY SHALLOW WATER, SMALL ORNAMENTAL PONDS, AND CONTAINERS:			
WATER DEPTH	**SPECIES OR VARIETY**	**FLOWER COLOR**	**OTHER REMARKS**
4 to 12 in.	*tetragona* 'Alba'	White	Smallest water lily, young plants in a water depth of 4 to 8 in. only, otherwise up to 12 in.
4 to 12 in.	'Pygmaea Helvola'	Yellow	Dwarf water lily, richly flowering, also suitable for containers 10 in. in diameter
4 to 16 in.	'Pygmaea Rubra'	Pink-red	Dwarf water lily, richly flowering
4 to 16 in.	'Solfatare'	Initially yellow, later coppery-pink to orange-red	Dwarf water lily, richly and long flowering (up to X), propagation difficult, therefore rare
FOR SHALLOW WATER:			
WATER DEPTH	**SPECIES OR VARIETY**	**FLOWER COLOR**	**OTHER REMARKS**
6 to 20 in.	'Aurora'	Copper-pink	Copper-colored in full flower, then turning dark orange
8 to 16 in.	'Ellisiana'	Light to fiery red	Small blooms, richly flowering
8 to 16 in.	'Laydekeri Purpurata'	Light with dark carmine-red, shaded	Leaves with black-brown spots
8 to 28 in.	'James Brydon'	Cherry-red	Flowers tightly double, flowering very reliable, extent 18 to 22 sq. in.
10 to 20 in.	'Fröbeli'	Carmine-red	Flowers reliably only in cooler weather
12 to 24 in.	'Sioux'	Copper-pink	Initially flowers yellow, needs a sunny, sheltered site
16 to 32 in.	'Georgia Peach'	Peach-pink, lighter inside and at the tips	Flowers stellate, young leaves dark green with brown patterning, extent 15 to 30 sq. in.
16 to 32 in.	'Gloire du Temple-sur-Lot'	Pale pink	Leaves tightly double, extent 23 to 26 sq. in.
WATER DEPTH	**SPECIES OR VARIETY**	**FLOWER COLOR**	**OTHER REMARKS**
16 to 32 in.	'Lucida'	Red	Leaves with red-brown spots, extent 30 to 36 sq. in.
Around 20 in.	'Pink N Orange'	Pink-red with blue shimmer	Flowers bowl-shaped to stellate, extent 20 to 23 sq. in.

		FOR MEDIUM AND DEEP WATER:	
WATER DEPTH	**SPECIES OR VARIETY**	**FLOWER COLOR**	**OTHER REMARKS**
12 to 28 in.	*odorata* 'Rosennymphe'	Pink	Stellate flowers, richly flowering, extent 9 to 18 sq. in.
12 to 60 in.	*alba*	White	Native water lily, fragrant, robust
16 to 32 in.	'Marliacea Albida'	Pure white	Richly flowering, fragrant, extent 15 to 30 sq. in.
16 to 32 in.	'Rene Gerard'	Carmine-pink	Reliable flowering, extent 11 to 23 sq. in.
16 to 40 in.	'Darwin'	Pink	Tightly double, long flowering time; extent up to 30 sq. in.
16 to 40 in.	'Formosa'	Light red	Flowers medium-large, richly flowering, extent 18 to 22 sq. in.
16 to 48 in.	'Schwefelstern'	Sulfur-yellow	Large flowers
20 to 24 in.	'Gruss an Potsdam'	Light pink	Flowers open in stellate form, extent approximately 22 sq. in.
20 to 32 in.	'Masaniello'	Crimson-pink, carmine-red shading	Large flowers, extent 12 to 23 sq. in.
20 to 40 in.	'Escarboucle'	Vivid carmine-red	Flowers until the late fall, extent 31 to 47 sq. in.
20 to 40 in.	'Marliacea Rosea'	Delicate pink, later whitish	Large flowers, reliable flowering, also suitable for use as cut flowers
24 to 28 in.	'Rose Dawn'	Vivid pink, lighter toward the center	Flowers stellate, extent approximately 23 sq. in.
28 to 40 in.	'Marliacea Chromatella'	Light yellow	Large flowers, leaves darkly marbled, extent 15 to 26 sq. in.
35 to 48 in.	'Gold Medal'	Golden-yellow	Chrysanthemum-like flowers, fragrant

Table 21. Perennial Ornamental Grasses

BOTANICAL NAME ENGLISH NAME SPECIES	GROWTH CHARACTERISTICS, FLOWERING TIME (MONTH), HEIGHT	USES AND SPECIAL CHARACTERISTICS
Bouteloua gracilis Grama grass	Brown, horizontally separate spikes, VII to IX, 12 in.	Sunny site, not too wet, permeable soil, inflorescences stiffly upright, spikes nearly horizontal, directed to one side, for heath and rock gardens, also dry stone walls.
Calamagrostis ×acutiflora Feather reed grass	Upright yellow infructescences, VII to VIII, 48 to 55 in.	Sunny to semi-shaded site, produces shoots very early on, in VI human-height upright panicles, later yellow spikes, not spreading, often commercially available as 'Karl Foerster', solitary plant adjacent to trees and shrubs.
Carex Sedge 1. *C. grayi*, Mace sedge 2. *C. morrowii* 'Variegata', Japanese sedge 3. *C. pendula*, Drooping sedge, pendulous sedge	1. Inflorescences mace-like, VII to VIII, 20 to 28 in. 2. Deep green culms with a yellow edge, rigid spikes, IV to V, 12 to 16 in. 3. Leaves and brown spikes overhanging, VI to VII, 24 to 35 in.	1. Damp to moist, also swampy soil or shallow water level, sunny to semi-shaded, stays green for a long time in the fall, for rock or riparian gardens; 2. Sufficiently moist soil, evergreen, leaf edge yellowish green, forms glossy green, wide bunches when older, protect from winter sun, can also be used as a ground cover under tall trees and shrubs; 3. Humic, fresh, lime-deficient soil, shady to semi-shaded, evergreen, cut back lightly in spring, human-height inflorescences in VI, in groups or solitary.
Cortaderia selloana Pampas grass	Silvery-white fronds, also pink, IX to X, 1 to 6 ½ ft. and higher	Well-permeable soil in a sunny situation, no standing water, high water and nutrient requirements in summer, tie culms together in winter, plant in spring only, winter protection, plant singly.
Deschampsia cespitosa Tufted hairgrass	Yellowish, loose panicles, VI to VIII, 28 to 35 in.	Damp moist soil, but will also tolerate dryness, sunny to semi-shaded, also in tree shade; cut back yellowed culms in III.
Fargesia murieliae 'Simba' Muriel bamboo	Dense, compact, forms tufts, 3 ¼ to 6 ½ ft.	Humic garden soil or bamboo earth from the garden center, tolerates semi-shade.
Festuca Fescue 1. *F. gautieri* (scoparia), Bearskin fescue 2. *F. glauca*, Bue fescue 3. *F. valesiaca*, Volga fescue	1. Vivid green, dense cushions, 6 to 8 in. 2. Blue-gray culms, decorative as cushions, VI to VII, 6 to 10 in. 3. Blue-green culms, flat cushions, VI to VII, 4 to 6 in.	All evergreen, highly suitable for rock and heath gardens; 1. Tolerates dryness only in semi-shade, do not plant too densely, better as solitary plant, up to 10 sq. ft. in size when fully grown; 2. Sandy, humic, permeable soil, dry sunny site, then intensive coloration; 3. Tolerates dryness, also moist soil, sunny, remains very low-growing, also suitable for group planting.
Glyceria maxima 'Variegata' Reed sweet grass	Tube-like stalks, leaves white-striped, VII to VIII, 28 to 32 in.	Nutrient-rich, moist soil, tolerates brief periods of dryness, suitable for planting at pond edges.
Hakonechloa macra 'Aureola' Hakone grass, Japanese reed grass	Weakly growing, overhanging leaf culms, 10 to 16 in.	Damp to moist garden soil, sunny to semi-shaded, leaves longitudinally yellow-striped, for edging and rock gardens.
Helictotrichon sempervirens Oat grass	Blue-gray leaf culms, overhanging in arches, VI to VIII, 24 to 60 in.	Permeable soil, tolerates sun and dryness, evergreen, not spreading, highly decorative light yellow panicles, for planting alone.
Imperata cylindrica 'Red Baron' Cogon grass	Upright, 12 to 16 in.	Garden soil, sunny, leaves reddish colored, spring planting only, winter protection required, also for plant tubs.
Luzula Wood-rush 1. *L. nivea*, Snowy wood rush 2. *L. sylvatica*, Great wood-rush	1. White inflorescences, VI to VII, 12 to 20 in. 2. Broad spikes, fresh-green foliage, V to VI, 8 to 12 in.	Moist, somewhat humic soil, shady or semi-shaded, protect from intensive winter sun, evergreen, suitable for planting in groups as underplanting for trees and shrubs, generally at its most attractive only when established planting.

BOTANICAL NAME ENGLISH NAME SPECIES	GROWTH CHARACTERISTICS, FLOWERING TIME (MONTH), HEIGHT	USES AND SPECIAL CHARACTERISTICS
Miscanthus 1. *M. floridulus*, Pacific Island silver grass 2. *M. sacchariflorus*, Amur silver grass 3. *M. sinensis*, Chinese silver grass, tiger grass	1. Flowers only in favorable years in and optimal situation, IX to X, 8 to 11 ½ ft. 2. Silvery-white fronds, VIII to IX, 6 ½ ft. 3. Silvery inflorescences, VIII to X, to 6 ½ ft.	1. Damp, nutrient-rich soil, sunny, reed-like overhanging leaf canopy on high stalks, for riparian strips as solitary plant; 2. Medium soil, sunny, develops runners, divide in spring and replant, effective when planted in groups at ponds; 3. Medium soil, sunny, cut back only in spring, decorative foliage, yellow- and white-striped forms ("porcupine grass") suitable for bank edges.
Molinia Moor grass 1. *M. arundinacea*, Tall moor grass 2. *M. caerulea*, Purple moor grass	1. Decorative panicles, VIII to IX, 5 to 6 ft. 2. Slender panicles on wiry stalks, VIII to X, 16 to 32 in.	Undemanding as regards the soil, cut back in spring; 1. Sunny site, attractive fall coloration, infructescences decorative into the winter; 2. Sunny or semi-shaded, foliage highly decorative, fall coloration, white-colored forms such as 'Variegata', also suitable for rock, nature, and heath gardens, or in groups between shrubs and trees.
Panicum virgatum Switch grass	Brown spikes, VII to IX, 3 ¼ to 6 ft.	Not too moist soil, sunny or semi-shaded, elegant grasses for nature and heath gardens, in groups or as solitary plants.
Pennisetum alopecuroides Chinese fountain grass	Downy, brownish, often pink-tinged spikes, VIII to IX, 16 to 32 in.	Permeable, in summer moist soil, apply fertilizer occasionally, cut back in late spring, after about 5 years divide and replant, in groups or as solitary plants for heath gardens, suitable as dry grass.
Phalaris arundinacea 'Picta' Reed canary grass, ribbon grass	Upright panicles, VI to VII, 28 to 32 in.	Moist, nutrient-rich soil, sunny; leaves 12 in. long, glossy green, white-banded, for planting up pond edges.
Sesleria heufleriana Balkan blue grass, green moor grass	1 in. long, black panicle spikes, IV to V, 20 to 28 in.	Nutrient-rich, not-too-dry soil, lime-tolerant, suitable for planting up woodland edges or perennial beds.
Spartina pectinata 'Aureomarginata' Prairie cord grass	Spikes yellow-brown, overhanging, VIII to IX, 3 ¼ to 5 ft.	Undemanding as regards the soil, sunny, vigorously growing, for larger garden areas, also individually in ponds, can be used for dried bouquets.
Stipa Feather grass, needle grass, spear grass 1. *S. barbata*, Silver feather grass 2. *S. capillata*, Very slender feather grass 3. *S. pennata*, Feather grass	1. Overhanging feathery awns, VI to VIII, 20 to 32 in. 2. Upright bushy awns, VII to VIII, 24 to 32 in. 3. Upright panicles, overhanging, V to VI, 16 to 40 in.	Permeable, calciferous soil, sunny, for nature and heath gardens, for group plantings, also solitary plants; 1. Long, silvery glossy awns overhanging in arches, often appearing rather unkempt in unfavorable situations; 2. Hairless, light brownish awns, mostly upright, not unkempt, somewhat twisted together in low air humidity; 3. Dry, permeable, calciferous soil, sunny, awns 12 in. long, hairs splay out in a feather-like fashion.

Table 22. Ferns for the Garden

BOTANICAL NAME ENGLISH NAME SPECIES	GROWTH CHARACTERISTICS, HEIGHT	USE AND SPECIAL REMARKS
Adiantum pedatum American maidenhair, five finger fern	Palmate-pinnate, stalks dark, wiry, 20 to 24 in.	For moist, humic places in the rock garden, light semi-shade, produces shoots very early on, rhizome weakly creeping.
Asplenium (syn. *Phyllitis*) *scolopendrium* Hart's tongue fern	Fronds broadly lanceolate, leathery, 10 to 14 in.	Humic, not too acidic soil, in the rock garden or alpine garden on moist, shady sites, or for use in rock cracks; otherwise sheltered site, evergreen, varieties mostly undulate or twisted.
Asplenium trichomanes Maidenhair spleenwort	Fronds dark green, stalks glossy and black-brown, 4 to 6 in.	Damp humic soil, evergreen, older plants can be divided, for gaps in the rock and walls out of direct sun in rock gardens.
Athyrium Lady fern 1. *A. filix-femina*, Lady fern, southern lady fern 2. *A. niponicum* 'Metallicum', Japanese lady fern	1. Fronds doubly to triply pinnate, light green, 24 to 32 in. 2. Fronds green-silvery to metallic gray-blue, veins red-brown, 20 to 28 in.	Undemanding as regards the soil, not too dry, deep; shady or semi-shaded, summer-green, also suitable as underplanting or intermediate planting for trees and shrubs and in cottage gardens, fronds filigree, ordered in a funnel-shaped manner, garden forms mostly more finely pinnate or with pectinate fronds.
Blechnum Hard fern, deer fern 1. *B. penna-marina* 2. *B. spicant*	Fronds glossy, dark green, singly pennate, 8 to 16 in.	Moist, humic soil, shady or semi-shaded, calciphobous, infertile fronds evergreen, upright spore-bearing fronds summer-green; for larger areas and rock gardens.
Cystopteris bulbifera Berry bladder fern	Fronds vivid light green, doubly pinnate, up to 16 in.	Undemanding, fronds turn brownish on dry or overly sunny sites, green gemmae on the upper fronds, also suitable for underplanting.
Dryopteris Golden shield fern 1. *D. erythrosora*, 2. Japanese shield fern 1. *D. filix-mas*, Male fern	1. Stalks and young fronds red-brown, sporangia bright red before maturity, 32 in. 2. Fronds funnel-like, 32 to 40 in.	1. Moist, humus-rich soil, wintergreen, winter protection required against black frost; 2. Native species, will also tolerate sun given sufficient moisture, varieties mostly more strongly pinnate with the tips sometimes forked, solitary growing, also for planting in groups.
Matteuccia Ostrich fern 1. *M. pensylvanica* 2. *M. struthiopteris*	1. Fronds dark green, loose funnel 2. Fronds light green, forming a funnel; smaller sporangia-bearing fronds in the center of the funnel, 32 in., or up to 3 ¼ ft. in mature specimens	Moist, humus-rich soil, shady or semi-shaded, forms underground runners, sporangia-bearing fronds initially olive-green, later dark brown, suitable for area-wide underplanting under trees or groups of shrubs.
Onoclea sensibilis Sensitive fern	Fronds light green, double pinnate, 16 to 20 in.	Moist, humus-rich soil, also in shallow water, also sunny, better shaded, protect young fronds against late frost, spread by means of rhizomes, for area-wide planting.
Osmunda Royal fern 1. *O. cinnamomea* 2. *O. regalis*	Fronds light green, double pinnate, 3 ¼ to 4 ft.	Moist, humic, acidic soil, for banks, also suitable as solitary plant in a shaded bed, in swamp basins also sunny, dark brown fruit-bearing fronds.
Phegopteris connectilis Long beech fern	Fronds singly pennate, 6 to 8 in. long	Acidic soil, calciphobous, rhizomes creeping, for ground cover on humic, shaded garden places between light trees and shrubs.

BOTANICAL NAME ENGLISH NAME SPECIES	GROWTH CHARACTERISTICS, HEIGHT	USE AND SPECIAL REMARKS
Polypodium Polypody 1. *P. interjectum* 2. *P. vulgare*, Common polypody	Leaves somewhat leathery, dark green with lighter undersides, 8 to 12 in.	Moist, humic, weakly acid soil, shady, slow-growing; creeping rhizomes, fronds roll up in hard frost, also suitable as ground cover or in rock gardens, in moist situations will also grow epiphytically on moss-covered trees.
Polystichum 1. *P. aculeatum*, Hard shield fern, prickly shield fern 2. *P. setiferum*, Alaska fern, hedge fern, soft shield fern	1. Fronds leathery, glossy green, 24 to 32 in. 2. Fronds light green, not glossy, pinnate in a filagree fashion, 16 to 24 in.	Moist soil, shady, highly suitable as underplanting for broad-leaved trees and shrubs with a light crown or for wooded areas in the garden; 1. Evergreen; 2. Evergreen, slender ligulate fronds.

Table 23. Winter-Hardy Perennial Bulb and Tuber Plants

BOTANICAL NAME ENGLISH NAME SPECIES	FLOWER COLOR, FLOWERING TIME (MONTH), HEIGHT	PLANTING TIME (MONTH), PLANTING DEPTH	REQUIREMENTS AND SPECIAL REMARKS
Allium Allium 1. *A. aflatunense* 'Purple Sensation' 2. *A. christophii*, Star of Persia 3. *A. giganteum*, Giant allium 4. *A. karataviense*, Turkestan allium 5. *A. moly*, Lilyleek, moly 6. *A. oreophilum*, Pink lily leek 7. *A. schubertii*, Tumbleweed onion, Persian onion	1. Crimson-pink, V to VI, 28 to 35 in. 2. Light violet, VI to VII, 16 to 20 in. 3. Crimson-pink umbels, VI to VII, 55 in. 4. Light violet, V, 8 in. 5. Golden-yellow, VI, 8 to 10 in. 6. Carmine-pink, V to VI, 8 in. 7. Purple-pink, V to VI, 16 to 24 in.	1. VIII to IX, 2 to 4 in. 2. VIII to IX, 2 to 4 in. 3. VII to X, 4 in. 4. VI to X, 2 to 4 in. 5. VI to X, 2 to 4 in., in groups 6. VII to X, 2 to 4 in. 7. X to XI, 4 in.	1. Tolerates dryness, inflorescences up to 4 in. in diameter; 2. Tolerates dryness, infructescences up to 8 in. in size, for dry cut flowers, also for rock gardens; 3. Permeable soil, sunny, winter protection required on harsh sites, also suitable for dry cut flowers; 4. Permeable soil, sunny, leaves steel-blue, broad, rock garden plant; 5. Undemanding as regards the soil and site, sunny or out of direct sun, flowers stellate, self-seeding in favorable situations; 6. Permeable soil, warm, sheltered place; perennial for rock gardens; 7. Undemanding as regards the soil, in summer dry, sunny.
Alstroemeria Lily of the Incas, Peruvian lily 1. *A. aurea* 2. Ligtu hybrids (*A. ligtu* × *A. haemantha* with varieties)	1. Golden-yellow, orange-yellow to red, VII to VIII, up to 35 in. 2. Pink to orange and light violet, VI to VII, 24 in.	Divide in spring, 8 in.	Permeable soil, warm, sheltered place, sunny to out of direct sun, winter protection; suitable for cut flowers.
Anemone Anemone, windflower 1. *A. apennina*, Apennine windflower 2. *A. blanda*, Balkan windflower	1. Azure-blue, white, purple, pink, IV to V, 4 to 6 in. 2. Blue, white, pink, III to IV, 4 to 6 in.	Spring, divide after flowering, 2 to 3 in.	Both require damp, humic soil, not suitable for dry sites, out of direct sun to semi-shaded; 1. Leave undisturbed for as long as possible at the same place; 2. Numerous varieties, grows well in calciferous, not too cold soils; winter protection required.
Camassia Camass, quamash 1. *C. cusickii* 2. *C. quamash*, Quamash	1. Light blue, IV to V, 32 to 40 in. 2. Blue to dark blue, also white and violet, IV to V, 12 to 24 in.	VIII/IX, 6 to 8 in.	Fertile, in spring damp soil, in summer sunny and dry, should be left for a long time in the same place, also propagates by self-seeding, winter protection required in harsh situations; decorative cut flowers.
Chionodoxa Glory of the snow 1. *C. forbesii*, Glory of the snow 2. *C. sardensis*, Lesser glory of the snow	1. Blue, white, pink, III to IV, 4 to 6 in. 2. Gentian-blue, III to IV, 4 to 6 in.	III/IX, in groups, 2 to 4 in.	Permeable, in spring damp soil, warm, sheltered place, sunny or semi-shaded, occasionally self-seeding, suitable for the edges of groups of trees or shrubs, also for rock gardens.
Colchicum Autumn crocus, naked ladies	Light pink to violet, also white and double, VII to VIII, 6 to 8 in.	VIII, 4 to 8 in.	Damp, deep soil, sunny to semi-shaded; the tough foliage, around 12 in. high, first appears in spring.
Crocosmia ×*crocosmiiflora* Montbretia	Golden-yellow to orange and red, VII to VIII, 20 to 30 in.	III to IV, 2 to 4 in.	Sunny, winter protection, in extremely cold situations remove before the frost and treat in the same way as gladioli; popular cut flower.
Crocus Crocus	White, yellow, blue to violet, also striped, II to IV (*C. speciosus* VIII to X), 4 to 6 in.	VIII to X (*C. speciosus* VI to VIII), in groups, 2 to 4 in.	Permeable, humic soil, sunny to semi-shaded; only a few species prevail in lawns, which should be mown only after the crocus leaves have turned yellow; most of the species and varieties can be made to flower earlier in pots, *C. speciosus* flowers in the fall.

BOTANICAL NAME ENGLISH NAME SPECIES	FLOWER COLOR, FLOWERING TIME (MONTH), HEIGHT	PLANTING TIME (MONTH), PLANTING DEPTH	REQUIREMENTS AND SPECIAL REMARKS
Cyclamen Persian violet, sowbread 1. *C. coum* 2. *C. hederifolium* 3. *C. purpurascens*	1. White, pink, carmine, II to III, 4 in. 2. White, pink, carmine, VIII to IX, 4 to 6 in. 3. Pinkish red, VIII to IX, 4 in.	In groups, 2 in.; 2. 4 in.	Humus-rich, damp site, protected against the sun and drying winds, winter protection required against black frost and in exposed situations, all tolerate lime, but not waterlogging; for near-natural places in the garden, and for rock gardens.
Eranthis hyemalis Winter aconite	Yellow, II to III, 4 in.	In larger groups, 2 to 3 in.	Humic, fresh soil, sunny or shady, withdraws early in the summer, self-seeding on favorable sites.
Eremurus Desert candle, foxtail lady	White, yellow, orange, and pink, VI to VII, 32 to 80 in. (*E. himalaicus*, white flower candles)	VIII to IX, 6 to 8 in. deep on a sand bed	Permeable soil, sunny, plants suffer less from frost than from waterlogging, winter protection required only in the first year of planting, also for individual plants; suitable for cut flowers.
Erythronium Dog's tooth violet 1. *E. dens-canis,* 2. *E. tuolumnense*	1. Pink, white, light crimson, III to VI, 6 in. 2. Yellow, IV to V, 12 in.	In groups after flowering, 4 to 4 ¾ in.	Permeable, damp, humic soil, winter protection required only in the first year of planting; also for rock gardens; 1. Sunny or shady; 2. Light shade.
Fritillaria Fritillary 1. *F. imperialis,* Crown imperial 2. *F. meleagris,* Snake's head fritillary 3. *F. michailovskyi,* Michael's flower 4. *F. uva-vulpis,* Fox's grape fritillary	1. Orange, red, also yellow, IV to V, 28 to 40 in. 2. White and crimson, patterned, IV to V, 12 in. 3. Crimson-brown, edge golden-yellow, III to V, 6 to 10 in. 4. Chestnut-brown with yellow edge, IV, 10 to 12 in.	1. VII to IX, large bulbs 12 in., otherwise shallower 2. VII to IX in tufts, 4 in. 3. VIII to IX, 3 to 4 in. 4. VIII to IX, 4 in.	1. Deep, also clayey or loam soil, no waterlogging, sunny or semi-shaded, withdraws foliage after flowering; decorative for individual plants, herb borders or tree/shrub edges; 2. Damp to moist soil, sunny to semi-shaded; also suitable for rock gardens; often self-seeding; 3. Permeable, moist soil, sunny to out of direct sun; valuable, rare species; 4. Damp, permeable garden soil, sunny to out of direct sun, for near-natural gardens.
Galanthus Snowdrop 1. *G. elwesii* 2. *G. nivalis*	White, II to III, 6 to 8 in.	V to IX in groups, 4 in.	Undemanding as regards the soil, sunny or semi-shaded, self-propagating in favorable situations, *G. elwesii* sunny, for *G. nivalis* there is also a double form.
Galtonia candicans Summer hyacinth	Pure white, VII to VIII, 40 to 48 in.	IX to X, 6 to 8 in.	Damp soil, sunny, also out of direct sun, much water required during growth, light winter protection, also for individual plants; popular cut flower.
Hyacinthoides hispanica Spanish bluebell	Violet-blue, V, 8 to 16 in.	VII to X, 2 ½ to 4 in.	Undemanding, no heavy loam soil, calcicolous, warm, sunny to semi-shaded, varieties also white, pink, and double.
Hyacinthus orientalis Hyacinth	Pink, red, blue, white, delicate yellow, IV to V, 8 to 10 in.	VII to IX, in groups 4 to 5 in.	Permeable soil, sunny, winter protection in hard frost, good for sprouting shoots for winter flowering (also in hyacinth jars).
Ipheion uniflorum Spring starflower	Light violet-blue, blue, and white, III to V, 6 to 8 in.	Fall, 4 ¾ to 6 in.	Sandy loamy garden soil, not too moist, sunny to semi-shaded, new leaves appear in the fall, winter protection required, 'Rudolf Fiedler' gentian-blue, flowers for weeks at a time.

BOTANICAL NAME ENGLISH NAME SPECIES	FLOWER COLOR, FLOWERING TIME (MONTH), HEIGHT	PLANTING TIME (MONTH), PLANTING DEPTH	REQUIREMENTS AND SPECIAL REMARKS
Iris Flag, sword lily 1. *I. bucharica*, Bukhara iris, horned iris 2. *I. danfordiae* 3. *I. histrioides* var. *reticulata* 4. *I. ×hollandica*, Dutch iris	1. Yellowish white, IV to V, 8 to 12 in. 2. Yellow, III to IV, 4 to 8 in. 3. Light blue to dark blue and crimson-violet, III to IV, 4 to 8 in. 4. White, yellow, bronze-colored, blue, violet, V/VI, 24 to 32 in.	1. Fall, 4 in. 2. and 3. VI to IX, in tufts, about 4 in. 4. X, in small groups, 4 to 6 in.	1. Undemanding, soil not too moist, sunny, for rock gardens; 2. and 3. Sandy humic, fertile, slightly alkaline soil, sheltered, sunny, as dry as possible after foliage withdraws, winter protection required in harsh situations; rock garden plant, also suitable for dry stone walls; 4. Sandy, humic soil, sheltered, withdraws foliage after flowering, good winter protection required, or place in containers with earth in late fall and keep cool until flowering in spring.
Ixiolirion tataricum Ixiolirion	Violet-blue with pink, V to VI, 16 to 20 in.	VIII to X, in groups, 4 to 6 in.	Permeable, humic soil, sunny, leaves withdraw early in spring, often threatened by late frost; for rock gardens, or also as a tub plant in a cold or winter house.
Leucojum Snowflake 1. *L. aestivum* 2. *L. vernum*	1. White, V to VI, 14 to 18 in. 2. White with green tips, III to IV, 6 to 8 in.	1. IX to X, 4 in. 2. V to IX, 3 to 4 in.	1. Nutrient-rich, moist soil; sunny to out of direct sun, light winter protection; 2. Damp moist soil, semi-shaded, also out of direct sun, self-propagating in favorable situations.
Lilium candidum Madonna lily, white lily	White, VI to VII, 40 to 60 in.	VIII, bulbs may be covered with only just under 2 in. of earth	Nutrient-rich, permeable, somewhat calciferous soil if possible, sheltered from strong winds, sunny; suitable for cut flowers.
Lilium davidii var. *willmottiae* David's lily	Orange-red with brown speckles, VI to VII, 40 to 50 in.	IX to X, 4 to 8 in., depending on the soil and bulb size	Permeable sandy soil, in heavy soil embed bulbs in sand, shaded at ground level, otherwise sunny; decorative cut flowers.
Lilium lancifolium (syn. *tigrinum*) Tiger lily	Orange-red, spotted, yellow and red varieties, VII, 40 to 70 in.	IX to X, 2 to 8 in., depending on the soil and bulb size	Permeable, not calciferous soil, in heavy soil embed bulbs in sand, sunny, propagation by means of brood bulbs in the leaf axils; for cut flowers.
Lilium martagon Martagon lily, Turk's cap	Various wine-red shades, also white, VI, 32 to 60 in.	VIII to X, 4 to 6 in.	Permeable sandy, also somewhat calciferous soil, in heavy soils embed the bulbs in the sand, sunny to semi-shaded; the base of the plant should be in the shade; propagation from seed long and difficult.
Lilium regale Regal lily	White, varieties also yellow and reddish, VII, 4 to 6 ½ ft.	IX to X, 4 to 8 in., depending on the soil and bulb size	Permeable sandy, also calciferous soil, in heavy soils embed the bulbs in the sand, sunny, but shaded at ground level, flowers strongly fragrant.
Lilium speciosum Showy Japanese lily	Carmine-red on a white background, also red and white varieties, VIII to IX, 32 to 55 in.	IX to X, 4 to 8 in., depending on the soil and bulb size	Sandy, humic, somewhat acidic soil, sunny, somewhat shaded only at the base, no waterlogging, transplant after several years, winter protection required in harsh situations; valuable cut flower.
Muscari species Grape hyacinths	Light blue to dark violet, also white, IV to V, 4 to 8 in.	VIII to IX, in tufts, 2 to 4 in.	Undemanding as regards the soil, tolerates endosmotic root pressure, runs wild easily, accordingly plant in rock gardens with caution.
Narcissus Daffodil, narcissus	White, yellow, with white, yellow, pink, and red perianths, IV to V, 12 to 16 in.	VIII to IX, 4 to 6 in.	Undemanding as regards the soil, sunny or semi-shaded, plant wild species at a shallower depth, suitable for rock gardens; popular vase decoration.

BOTANICAL NAME ENGLISH NAME SPECIES	FLOWER COLOR, FLOWERING TIME (MONTH), HEIGHT	PLANTING TIME (MONTH), PLANTING DEPTH	REQUIREMENTS AND SPECIAL REMARKS
Narcissus 1. *N. bulbocodium*, Hoop petticoat daffodil, bulbocodium 2. *N. cyclamineus*, Donkey's ears	Yellow to golden-yellow; 1. III to IV, 4 to 8 in. 2. II to E. IV, 5 to 8 in.	IX to X, in tufts, 2 ½ to 4 in.	1. Permeable soil, sunny, dry in summer; 2. Somewhat humic, moist soil, out of direct sun; 1. and 2. Winter protection required in harsh situations; suitable for rock gardens.
Ornithogalum umbellatum Star of Bethlehem	White, stellate, IV to V, 6 to 8 in.	VIII to X, 4 in.	Not too heavy garden soil, sunny or semi-shaded, tends to run wild, do not place next to weakly growing plants.
Puschkinia scilloides Striped squill	Blue and creamy white, IV to V, 6 to 8 in.	VII to IX, 4 in.	Medium, rather moist soil, sunny or semi-shaded, for rock gardens, variety libanotica larger, both as plant and as flower.
Roscoea cautleoides	Sulfur-yellow, VI to VIII, 10 to 14 in.	IX to X (III), 3 to 4 in.	Humic, loamy, moist, well-drained soil, sunny, winter protection required; suitable for rock gardens.
Scilla Squill	Blue, occasionally pink or white, III to V, 4 to 12 in.	VII to IX, in tufts, 2 to 4 in.	Undemanding as regards the soil, tends to run wild, also withstands endosmotic root pressure from trees.
Tricyrtis hirta Japanese toad lily	Whitish with crimson stripes, VIII to X, 28 to 35 in.	IX to X (also III), 2 ½ to 3 in.	Damp, humic, somewhat acidic soil, semi-shaded, grows well under light trees and shrubs, valuable owing to late flowering time, cover with leaves in winter.
Trillium Trinity flower, wake robin, wood lily 1. *T. grandiflorum*, Great white trillium, large-flowered trillium 2. *T. sessile*, Toadshade, white trillium	1. White, turns pink as flowering ends, V to VI, 14 to 16 in. 2. Brownish crimson-red, IV, up to 12 in.	IX, 2 in.	Deep, damp to moist soil, out of direct sun to semi-shaded, suitable as underplanting beneath deep-rooting trees and shrubs; 1. Flower spread out, leaves light green; 2. Flower erect, leaves light green with dark green spots.
Triteleia 1. *T. ixioides*, Golden star, prettyface 2. *T. laxa*, Common triteleia, grassnut, Ithuriel's spear	1. Yellow to copper-colored, V to VI, 10 in. 2. Blue, V to VII, up to 20 in.	X to XI, 3 to 4 in.	Permeable, not too moist soil, sunny, flowers stellate, richly flowering, long flowering time, suitable for near-natural gardens, cut flowers.
Tulipa Tulip	From white, yellow, pink, and red to violet-red, also bicolored and double, III to V, 4 to 20 in.	VIII to X, in tufts, 4 to 6 in.	Garden soil with no added fresh manure, sunny, no waterlogging; wild species particularly suitable for rock gardens.

Table 24. Non-Winter-Hardy Bulb and Tuber Plants

BOTANICAL NAME ENGLISH NAME SPECIES	FLOWER COLOR, FLOWERING TIME (MONTH), HEIGHT	PLANTING TIME (MONTH), PLANTING DEPTH	REQUIREMENTS AND SPECIAL REMARKS
Anemone coronaria Poppy anemone, Spanish marigold, windflower	White, yellow, pink, red, blue, violet, also bicolored, single and double, VI to IX, 8 to 12 in.	IV to V, in groups, 2 to 3 in., soak bulbs in water for 24 hours beforehand	Humic soil, sunny, once the leaves die off overwinter at around 50°F in dry conditions, bulbs can also be laid from IX to X, in which case a winter protection layer at least 6 in. thick is required, also in containers; also suitable for rock gardens.
Babiana stricta Baboon flower	White, pink, purple, violet, VII to VIII, around 8 in.	V, in groups, 2 to 2 ½ in.	Nutrient-rich, humic soil, sunny or out of direct sun, overwinter under cool and dry conditions; for rock gardens and borders.
Begonia Tuberhybrida Group Tuberous begonia	Red, pink, orange, yellow, white, single and fringed, double and semi-double, VI to X, 6 to 10 in.	V, in groups, 2 in.	Humus-rich, warm soil, light semi-shade, remove tubers at the first sign of night frosts, overwinter at 50 to 59°F in dry conditions; also suitable for balcony boxes.
Calochortus Globe tulip, mariposa tulip	White, yellow, pink, red, also bicolored, VI to VII, 12 to 24 in.	L. X or V, in groups, 4 in.	Permeable, sandy soil, sheltered, warm, semi-shaded, protection against frost and wetness required in winter.
Canna indica Indianshot, Queensland arrowroot	Yellow, orange, pink, and red, also bicolored, VII to X, 20 to 55 in.	L. V, 4 in. deep, width of 16 to 20 in.	Humus-rich, fertile soil, sunny, not dry, remove from soil following the first frost, cut back shoot to 6 in., do not shake off earth, cover with sand, overwinter at 50 to 59°F in dry conditions.
Crinum ×powellii Crinum	Crimson-pink, VII to VIII, 40 to 48 in.	V, bulb collar should still be visible	Permeable, moist, nutrient-rich soil, sunny, flowers lily-like, fragrant, 6 in. long; overwinter bulbs in cool and nearly dry conditions.
Dahlia Dahlia	Many colors and forms, VII to frost, 8 to 32 and 32 to 60 in.	Bulbs L. IV, 2 to 4 in., (young plants from M. V, 2 in.)	Good garden soil, sunny, remove from ground after the first frost, cut back to around 4 in., overwinter at 39 to 50°F with not too low air humidity, provide aeration, cover with dry peat if necessary.
Eucomis Pineapple flower	Yellowish green, yellow and vivid pink, VII to IX, around 16 in.	M. V, in groups, 2 ½ to 3 in.	Nutrient-rich, humic, always moist soil, sheltered warm site, sunny, overwinter in cool conditions; conspicuous flowering plant.
Gladiolus Gladiolus 1. *G. murielae* (syn. *callianthus*), Acidanthera 2. Hybrids	1. White with star-shaped brownish red fleck, VII to VIII, 20 to 28 in. 2. Many colors, VII to X, 32 to 40 in.	1. L. IV, in groups, 4 in. 2. IV to M. V, 4 in.	1. Humic, warm soil, sunny, remove from the earth after the leaves have turned yellow and overwinter at 59 to 64°F in dry peat, strongly fragrant flowers; 2. Change site annually, sunny, remove from the earth after the leaves have turned yellow, trim leaves to 4 in., allow the bulbs to dry and overwinter cool at 41 to 45°F in an airy place.
Gloriosa superba Climbing lily, gloriosa lily	Red/yellow, L. VI, up to 63 in.	L. V, 3 in.	Nutrient-rich, humic soil, warm, sunny, advance planting in a pot is recommended; splendidly flowering climbing plant.
Ixia Corn lily	White, pink, red, yellowish, VII to VIII, up to 32 in.	E. V, in groups, up to 4 in.	Nutrient-rich, loose soil, sunny, overwinter as for gladioli; also suitable for cut flowers.
Mirabilis jalapa Four o'clock plant, marvel of Peru	Colorful, VII to X (flowers from the late afternoon, often in the morning as well, until about 11 a.m.), 24 to 32 in.	Tubers E. V, in group, 2 to 4 in. (spacing 12 in.) or in large plant tubs	Sandy garden soil, overwinter the tubers as for dahlias or leave in plant tubs and cut back the foliage above the tuber, sowing (III, under glass) and annual culture possible; hybrids with *M. longifolia* are strongly fragrant at night.

BOTANICAL NAME ENGLISH NAME SPECIES	FLOWER COLOR, FLOWERING TIME (MONTH), HEIGHT	PLANTING TIME (MONTH), PLANTING DEPTH	REQUIREMENTS AND SPECIAL REMARKS
Nerine bowdenii Nerine	Pink, IX to XI, 16 in.	V, Bulb collar should still be visible	Nutrient-rich garden soil, sunny, overwinter under cool conditions, do not water until shoot appears, do not transplant often, leave bowls and pots on the terrace or embed them in the soil.
Oxalis tetraphylla Good luck leaf, lucky clover	Dark pink with yellow eye, summer, 6 to 8 in.	IV, in groups, 1 in., also in containers	Undemanding as regards the soil, sunny or semi-shaded, remove in IX and overwinter at 37 to 41°F; also suitable for growing in pots.
Ranunculus asiaticus Persian buttercup	White, yellow, pink-red, VII to IX, 12 to 24 in.	III to IV (V), in groups, 2 to 2 ½ in.	Nutrient-rich, well-aerated soil, sunny, best to water bulbs 12 hours before planting, overwinter bulbs under cool and dry conditions.
Rhodohypoxis baurii Red star, rosy posy	White, vivid pink and light red, V to VIII, 4 in., also higher-growing varieties	IV to V, 4 in.	Rather sandy soil, not too nutrient-rich and not too dry during the growing period, overwinter bulbs under cool and almost dry conditions, also winter hardy in mild locations; suitable for rock gardens and planting in bowls.
Sprekelia formosissima Jacobean lily	Carmine-red, VII, 12 in.	V, Bulb TIP must be just covered with soil, also in containers	Permeable, humic soil, warm, sheltered site, also suitable for balcony boxes, frost-free, overwinter under initially warm, later cooler conditions at around 54°F.
Tigridia pavonia Peacock flower, tiger flower,	White, yellow, pink, and red colors, throat speckled, VII to IX, 16 to 24 in.	L. IV, in groups, 3 to 4 in., also in containers	Permeable, nutrient-rich garden soil, sunny, water well during the growing period, remove from soil in the fall and overwinter as for gladioli.
Zantedeschia elliottiana Altar lily, arum lily	Whitish to intense pink, also yellow, VIII to IX, up to 32 in.	E. V, in groups, 3 to 4 in.	Nutrient-rich, humic soil, sunny or out of direct sun, uniformly moist, overwinter tubers in dry peat; suitable for cut flowers and flowerbeds.

Table 25. Annual and Biennial Flowers

Some of the plants listed here are in fact herbaceous perennials; in other words, they are perennial plants in their native habitats. However, since they are generally not winter hardy in Zones 4–8, they are listed here as annuals.

BOTANICAL NAME ENGLISH NAME SPECIES	FLOWER COLOR, ONSET OF FLOWERING (MONTH), HEIGHT	SOWING LOCATION, MONTH	PLANTING TIME (MONTH), SPACING	REQUIREMENTS AND SPECIAL REMARKS
Ageratum houstonianum Flossflower	Blue colors, also white, L. V, 6 to 24 in.	Hothouse, E. II	After M. V, 6 × 6 to 8 × 8 in.	Warm, permeable garden soil, sunny, flowers from spring until the onset of frost, also suitable for planting larger areas; *Lonas annua*, the African daisy or yellow ageratum, is similar.
Agrostemma githago Corn cockle	Light crimson, red-violet, VI, up to 3 ¼ ft.	Directly on site, spring	8 × 10 to 10 × 12 in.	Nutrient-rich garden soil, sunny, very richly flowering, until VIII; for summer beds.
Alcea rosea Hollyhock	White, yellow, pink, red, black-red, L. VII, 32 to 60 in. (or higher)	Cold frame, also seedbed outdoors, V to VI	VII to VIII, 24 × 20 in.	Nutrient-rich loamy soil, sunny, flowers only in the year after planting (biennial), does not tolerate winter wetness; effective as solitary plant, but also in groups.
Amaranthus caudatus Love lies bleeding	Inflorescences and leaves red, VII, also fall, 24 to 35 in.	Cold frame, E. IV or in V directly on site	L. V, 20 × 16 in., low 16 × 12 in.	Nutrient-rich, light garden soil does not tolerate wetness, sunny, flowers from high summer to the fall; solitary and in groups.
Antirrhinum majus Snapdragon	All colors except blue, VII, 8 to 12 in., 16 to 20 in., and 24 to 32 in.	Cold frame, E. III to E. IV	From L. IV, 8 × 8 to 10 × 10 in.	Nutrient-rich garden soil, sunny, tall varieties sheltered from the wind, low varieties also for area coverage, also suitable for balcony boxes; popular cut flower.
Arctotis venusta African daisy, blue-eyed African daisy	Yellow, orange, copper-colored, scarlet, L. VI, 16 to 20 in.	Cold frame, E. III to E. IV	L. V, 10 × 10 in.	Permeable, warm garden soil, not wet; sunny, sheltered; for groups or colorful flowerbeds, also for suitable for cut flowers.
Bassia (syn. *Kochia*) *scoparia* 'Trichophylla' Belvedere, burning bush, summer cypress	Foliage light green, red-colored in the fall, flowers inconspicuous, 24 to 35 in.	Cold frame, E. IV, directly on site, L. IV	After M. V, 10 to 24 in.	Not too dry, as nutrient-rich as possible garden soil, sunny or out of direct sun; suitable as annual hedge, but also for solitary plants.
Begonia Semperfloren Cultorum Group Fibrous rooted begonia, succulent begonia	White, pink to red, M. to L. V, 4 ¾ to 10 in.	Hothouse, XII to II	After M. V, 4 × 6 to 6 × 8 in.	Fresh, humic garden soil, shady or out of direct sun; particularly low-growing varieties are suitable for planting large areas, also for balcony boxes and bowls.
Bellis perennis Daisy, English daisy	White, pink to dark red, E. IV, 6 in.	Cold frame, VI to VII	L. VIII to E. IX or IV, 6 × 8 in.	Medium garden soil, sunny or out of direct sun, flowers only in the year after sowing, protect with brushwood in harsh situations.
Calendula officinalis Pot marigold, ruddles, Scotch marigold	Yellow to orange, single to double, L. V, 16 to 32 in.	Directly on site, III to IV or IX	E. V, 8 × 12 in.	Any garden soil, sunny or out of direct sun, self-seeds easily, thin out lower-growing varieties; for teas and ointments, also suitable for cut flowers.

BOTANICAL NAME ENGLISH NAME SPECIES	FLOWER COLOR, ONSET OF FLOWERING (MONTH), HEIGHT	SOWING LOCATION, MONTH	PLANTING TIME (MONTH), SPACING	REQUIREMENTS AND SPECIAL REMARKS
Callistephus chinensis China aster	All colors, single to double, VII, 8 to 32 in.	Cold frame, from L. III	M. V, 8 × 10 to 10 × 12 in.	Nutrient-rich garden soil, sunny, change site annually (wilting diseases), suitable for plant groups; cut flowers.
Campanula medium Canterbury bells, cup-and-saucer plant	Blue, white, pink, single to double, VI, 28 to 40 in.	Cold frame, VI, also seedbed outdoors	VII to VIII, 12 × 16 in.	Humus- and nutrient-rich garden soil, sunny, in harsh situations provide winter protection with brushwood, solitary plants or in groups; popular for colorful floral bouquets.
Celosia argentea var. *cristata* Cockscomb	Golden-yellow, orange, red, to violet, VII, 8 to 14 in.	Under glass, III to E. IV	L. V, 10 × 10 in.	Light, humic soil, warm, keep fairly dry after seedling emergence; suitable for balcony boxes or group plantings.
Centaurea cyanus Bachelor's button, cornflower	Blue, pink, white, fall sowing V, spring sowing VI, up to 3 ¼ ft.	Directly on site, fall or spring	8 × 10 in.	Nutrient-rich garden soil, sunny, very richly flowering, for summer beds, lower-growing varieties also for balcony boxes; nectar source for bees.
Clarkia unguiculata Elegant clarkia, mountain garland	White, salmon, pink, orange, red, double, VII, 20 to 24 in.	Directly on site, from L. III	8 × 10 in.	Light, humic, not too infertile garden soil, sunny or out of direct sun; also suitable for cut flowers.
Cleome hassleriana (syn. *spinosa*) Spider plant	Pink, red, white, VI to X, 16 to 40 in.	Hothouse, III	L. V, 16 × 16 in.	Permeable, nutrient-rich, almost dry soil, sunny, as solitary plant or in groups; also suitable for long-lasting cut flowers; nectar source for bees.
Cobaea scandens Cup-and-saucer vine, Mexican ivy	Blue-violet, also white, VII, up to 16 ft.	Greenhouse/ cold frame, III	M. V, 16 × 20 in.	Nutrient-rich humic soil, warm, sunny; attractive flowering climbing plant.
Consolida Larkspur 1. *C. ajacis* 2. *C. regalis*	White, pink, blue, and car-mine-red, VI, 20 to 48 in.	Directly on site, III/IV or IX	8 × 8 in.	Nutrient-rich, somewhat moist, calciferous garden soil, sunny, tall varieties should be shel-tered from the wind, also suitable for individual plants; decorative vase plant.
Convolvulus tricolor Dwarf morning glory	Blue, white, and pink color shades, VI, 12 in.	Directly on site, IV to M. V	8 × 8 in.	Permeable, not too nutrient-rich and not too acidic soil, sunny warm site; for colorful flowerbeds.
Coreopsis tinctoria Annual morning glory, tickseed	Yellow, golden-yellow, red, VI, 12 to 40 in.	Cold frame, L. III to M. IV, directly on site, L. IV	8 × 8 in.	Light, humic garden soil, sunny; tall species for flowerbeds, low-growing species as edging, also suitable for cut flowers.
Cosmos bipinnatus Garden cosmos, Mexican aster	White, pink, purple-pink, red, VII, 24 to 40 in.	Cold frame, L. III to E. IV	L. V, 14 × 14 in.	Damp garden soil, sunny, no waterlogging; for flowerbeds, also solitary, attractive cut flower.

BOTANICAL NAME ENGLISH NAME SPECIES	FLOWER COLOR, ONSET OF FLOWERING (MONTH), HEIGHT	SOWING LOCATION, MONTH	PLANTING TIME (MONTH), SPACING	REQUIREMENTS AND SPECIAL REMARKS
Dianthus Carnation, pink 1. *D. barbatus*, Sweet William 2. *D. caryophyllus*, Carnation, Gillyflower 3. *D. caryophyllus*, Carnation, clove pink 4. *D. chinensis*, Annual pink	1. Pink, red, also white, multi-colored, VI, 14 to 20 in. 2. White to dark red, VI, 12 to 14 in. 3. White, yellow, pink, red, VII, 14 to 16 in. 4. White, pink, red, multicolored, VII, 8 to 14 in.	1. and 2. Seed-bed outdoors, VI/VII 3. Under glass, I/II 4. Cold frame, III to IV	1. and 2. L. VII to E. VIII 3. IV to 4. E. V; 1. to 3. 10 × 10 to 10 × 12 in. 4. 8 × 10 in.	Permeable, nutrient-rich, somewhat calciferous, not too wet soil, also sandy loam soil, no fresh stable manure, apply mineral fertilizers during growth, protect from mice and rabbits; for colorful flowerbeds, popular cut flowers; 1. and 2. Biennials, also perennials, winter protection required; 3. and 4. Annuals.
Digitalis purpurea Foxglove	White, pink to red, VI to VIII, 32 to 48 in.	Seedbed out-doors, V to VI, directly on site, V to VII	E. VIII, 12 to 16 in.	Any garden soil, sunny or semi-shaded, mostly self-seeding; effective planted next to trees and shrubs, but also solitary.
Dorotheanthus bellidiformis Livingstone daisy	White, yellow, orange, pink, carmine-red, VI, to 4 in.	Under glass, III, later plant in small pots	L. V, 6 × 6 to 8 × 8 in.	Warm, dry, sandy humic, not too nutrient-rich soil, sunny, flowers up until the onset of frost; for flower carpets and edging.
Erysimum (syn. *Cheiranthus*) Wallflower 1. *E. ×allionii* (annual), Siberian wallflower 2. *E. cheiri* (biennial)	1. Orange-yellow, VIII, 10 to 12 in. 2. Yellow to dark brown, scarlet, crimson-violet, L. IV, 12 to 24 in.	1. Directly on site, III 2. Cold frame or seedbed outdoors, V/VI	VII to VIII, 10 × 10 to 12 × 12 in.	Humus- and nutrient-rich soil, as calciferous as possible, sunny; prized, fragrant vase decora-tion; double dwarf varieties for balcony boxes, pots, and bowls; also suitable as medicinal plant; 1. Also biennial, also double; 2. Often perennial as well, winter protection required.
Eschscholzia californica California poppy	White to yellow, orange, pink, and carmine-red, from VI, 12 to 16 in.	Directly on site, L. III to E. IV	8 × 10 in.	Permeable light garden soil, sunny, brings color into the garden; for beds or edging; sowing L. IX also possible, then flowering in the following year from L. V.
Euphorbia Spurge 1. *E. heterophylla*, Japanese poin-settia, Mexican fire plant 2. *E. marginata*, Snow on the mountain	Decorative because of the whitish green upper leaves in particular, from VII, 24 to 32 in.	Cold frame, L. III, or directly on site, L. IV	After M. V, 8 × 10 in.	Permeable garden soil, sunny, often self-seed-ing, latex poisonous; for colorful flowerbeds, also suitable for cut flowers.
Gaillardia pulchella Annual gaillardia, firewheel	Yellow, scarlet to wine-red, also bicolored, from VI, 16 to 20 in.	Cold frame, E. IV	M. V, 10 × 10 in.	Not too moist, somewhat calciferous, not nitro-gen-rich soil, sunny, rich- and long-flowering; for colorful flowerbeds, also as cut flowers.

BOTANICAL NAME ENGLISH NAME SPECIES	FLOWER COLOR, ONSET OF FLOWERING (MONTH), HEIGHT	SOWING LOCATION, MONTH	PLANTING TIME (MONTH), SPACING	REQUIREMENTS AND SPECIAL REMARKS
Gazania Treasureflower	White cream, yellow, orange, brown-red, from L. VI, 8 to 16 in.	Under glass, L. II to E. III, later plant in small pots	M. to L. V, 8 × 8 to 12 × 12 in.	Permeable, nutrient-rich soil, sheltered, warm site, flowers close up in the afternoon and on dull days, in central Europe cultivated as annuals only.
Glebionis (syn. *Chrysanthemum*) *segetum* Corn marigold	White to golden-yellow, VII, 16 to 24 in.	Cold frame, from II, or directly on site, IV to V	After M. V, 10 × 8 in.	Deep, medium warm garden soil, no water-logging; do not over-fertilize with nitrogen; suitable for group plantings, also for cut flowers.
Gypsophila elegans Baby's breath	White, also pink, from VII, 16 to 20 in.	Directly on site, III to IV	8 × 8 in.	Permeable, as calciferous as possible, not too moist garden soil, sunny; suitable for floral bouquets.
Helianthus Sunflower 1. *H. annuus* 2. *H. debilis*, Beach sunflower	1. Yellow, brown, red, also double and bicolored, from VII, 20 to 100 in. 2. Yellow to bronze and copper, from VII, 20 to 60 in.	Directly on site, from M. IV, up to 5 grains per site	16 × 24 in.	Nutrient-rich, humic soil, sunny, leave only one plant at each sowing site, solitary, also for planting up fences; decorative in large vases placed on the floor; kernels can be used as birdseed; nectar source for bees.
Iberis umbellata Annual candytuft	White to pink and crimson-violet, from VI, 8 to 12 in.	Directly on site, III/IV, 6 × 6 in.	6 × 6 in.	Medium humic garden soil, sunny, cutting back after flowering will lead to a second florescence; also suitable for edging; when sown in L. IX, flowers in the following year from L. V; nectar source for bees.
Impatiens Busy Lizzie, balsam 1. *I. balsamina*, garden balsam, rose balsam 2. *I. walleriana*, 3. Busy Lizzie	1. White, yellow, blue, violet to crimson-red, from L. VI, 20 to 28 in. 2. White to pink, orange, and scarlet, from L. VI, 6 to 28 in.	Under glass, from L. III to M. IV	After M. V, 1. 12 × 12 in., 20 × 20 in.; 2. 8 × 10 in.	Humic, nutrient-rich garden soil; 1. For colorful flowerbeds in a sunny situation; 2. Also semi-shaded, underplanting under trees, also the north side of the house; both also available as pot plants and in numerous varieties.
Ipomoea tricolor Flying saucers, heavenly blue morning glory	Sky-blue, white center, flower edge initially red, from L. VII, 32 to 48 in.	Greenhouse, III	L. V, 40 to 24 in.	Permeable, warm, humic, nutrient-rich soil, sunny, sheltered site; leave to spread over trellises or wires.
Ismelia (syn. *Chrysanthemum*) *carinata* Painted daisy	White to yellow and copper-red (also bicolored), VI, 20 to 24 in.	Cold frame, from II, or directly on site, IV to V	After M. V, 10 × 8 in.	Deep, medium warm garden soil, no water-logging; do not over-fertilize with nitrogen; suitable for group planting, also for cut flowers.
Lathyrus odoratus Sweet pea	All colors, from VI, 40 to 70 in.	Directly on site, from L. III	Lay 3 to 4 grains individually every 10 in.	Deep soil, as calciferous as possible, sunny, remove seed heads continually, since otherwise flower development will decline, spreads over latticework and fences; also suitable for cut flowers.

BOTANICAL NAME ENGLISH NAME SPECIES	FLOWER COLOR, ONSET OF FLOWERING (MONTH), HEIGHT	SOWING LOCATION, MONTH	PLANTING TIME (MONTH), SPACING	REQUIREMENTS AND SPECIAL REMARKS
Lavatera trimestris Rose mallow	Pink, also salmon and white, VII until the onset of frost, 20 to 35 in.	Directly on site, IV to V	20 × 16 in.	Not too wet soil, sunny, long flowering time, also suitable for cut flowers; nectar source for bees.
Linum grandiflorum Red flax, scarlet flax	Blood-red, from VI, 12 to 16 in.	Directly on site, L. IV	6 × 6 in.	Permeable, warm, sufficiently moist soil, sunny; also suitable for cut flowers; 'Rubrum' even darker.
Lobelia erinus Edging lobelia, trailing lobelia	Blue color shades, also white and crimson-pink, from M. V, 4 in.	Under glass, II to III	M. V, 4 × 6 in.	Permeable, medium garden soil, sunny or out of direct sun, cut back following main flowering elicits a second florescence; for hanging loblias.
Lobularia maritima Sweet Alison, sweet alyssum	White, pink, violet to carmine-red, from VI, 2 ½ to 6 in., also up to 12 in.	Directly on site, M. IV, 6 × 6 in.	6 × 6 in.	Light to medium garden soils, as calciferous as possible, sunny, cut back after main florescence, then remontant; also for edging.
Matthiola incana Brompton stock, stock, ten-week stock	All colors, single to double, from L. VI, 14 to 35 in.	Cold frame, III/IV	M. IV, 4 × 6 to 12 × 12 in.	Nutrient-rich, sandy humic loam soil, no fresh stable manure, sunny, select smaller planting width for single-shoot varieties; suitable for cut flowers.
Mimulus ×hybridus Monkey flower, musk	Yellow, orange, pink, red, striped, spotted, from VI, 8 to 12 in.	Under glass, III, later plant out in small pots	L. V, 8 × 8 in.	Damp garden soil, sunny if sufficient moisture available, may not dry out; in climatically favorable situations can grow wild on pond edges.
Myosotis sylvatica Wood forget-me-not	Blue to dark blue, also white and pink, E. V, 6 to 14 in.	Seedbed outdoors, VI/VII	L. VIII to E. IX, or IV, 8 × 8 in.	Damp, sufficiently moist garden soil, light shade; similar, but larger and flowering from VI, is *Cynoglossum*, the hound's tongue (sow in III/IV).
Nemesia Nemesia	White, yellow to orange and red, also bluish, VI, 8 to 12 in.	Cold frame, E. IV, also directly on site, from L. IV	After M. V, 8 × 6 in.	Permeable, humus-rich, loose garden soil, sufficient moisture, sunny, cutting back after the initial flowering elicits a second florescence; also suitable for cut flowers.
Nigella damascena Love-in-a-mist	Double, blue, white, also pink, from VI, 16 to 18 in.	Cold frame or directly on site, from E. IV, or IX	10 × 8 in.	Undemanding, medium, not acidic garden soil, sunny; cut flowers can be kept for 1 week.
Papaver Poppy 1. *P. nudicaule*, Iceland poppy, Icelandic poppy 2. *P. rhoeas*, Corn poppy, field poppy, Flanders poppy	1. White, yellow, orange, red, from VI, 12 to 20 in. 2. White, pink, red, also double, from VI, 24 to 28 in.	Directly on site, from L. III, also IX	1. 10 × 6 in. 2. 12 × 10 in.	Damp, permeable, nutrient-rich, calciferous soil, sunny, remove seed heads for a longer florescence; for summer flowerbeds; for cut flowers cut as buds only, will keep for several days.

BOTANICAL NAME ENGLISH NAME SPECIES	FLOWER COLOR, ONSET OF FLOWERING (MONTH), HEIGHT	SOWING LOCATION, MONTH	PLANTING TIME (MONTH), SPACING	REQUIREMENTS AND SPECIAL REMARKS
Penstemon Penstemon	White, pink, red, purple, from VII, 20 to 32 in.	Under glass, II to III, later plant out in smalls pots	L. V, 14 × 12 in., with root ball	Damp, permeable, humic garden soil, sunny; for colorful beds, cut flowers will keep for several days.
Phacelia tanacetifolia Lacy phacelia, blue tansy	Light to violet-blue, from VI, 24 to 35 in.	Directly on site, III to VI	8 × 6 in.	Undemanding as regards the soil, not too wet, sunny; can be used as planting for infertile areas; nectar source for bees.
Phlox drummondii Annual phlox	All colors, from L. VI, 8 to 12 in.	Cold frame, III/IV	M. V, 8 × 8 in.	Permeable, warm garden soil, water when dry, vivid colors; also suitable for rock gardens.
Portulaca grandiflora Common portaluca, moss rose, rose moss	White, yellow, orange, red, crimson-red, from VII, 4 to 6 in.	Cold frame, E. IV, prick out into pots following seedling emergence	L. V, 8 × 6 in.	Dry, sandy humic, not nutrient-rich soil, sunny, rots easily in wet conditions; suitable for rock gardens and dry stone walls.
Reseda odorata Common mignonette	Greenish yellow with copper-red to pink-red, from VII, 12 to 16 in.	Directly on site, M. IV	8 × 8 in.	Nutrient-rich, humic, medium garden soil, will also tolerate light semi-shade; young plants are easily infested with flea beetles, which should be combatted immediately; annual fragrant plant; nectar source for bees.
Rudbeckia hirta Black-eyed Susan	Golden-yellow to bronze and mahogany-red, from VII, 24 to 40 in.	Cold frame, III/IV	From M. V, 10 × 10 in.	Permeable, damp garden soil, warm site; removing stalks after flowering will prolong the flowering time, annual species only; also suitable for solitary plantings.
Salpiglossis sinuata Painted tongue, salpiglossis	Colorful, white, yellow, brown, red, violet, from L. VI, 24 to 32 in.	Cold frame, E. IV, or directly on site, E. V	After M. V, 10 × 8 in.	Well-tilled, not too acidic garden soil, sunny, prone to fungal diseases in wet years; also suitable as individual plants.
Salvia splendens Scarlet sage	Scarlet, from VI, 8 to 14 in.	Under glass, II, then prick out into 2 ¾ in. pots	After M. V, 10 × 10 in.	Nutrient-rich medium garden soil, sunny, best to buy plants, often infested with red spider mites during dryness, remove died-off inflorescences regularly.
Sanvitalia procumbens Creeping zinnia	Yellow with dark center, from VI, 4 to 6 in.	Cold frame, E. IV, directly on site, IV to V	M. V, 6 × 10 in.	Permeable humic garden soil, warm site; not too wet; good ground cover, also suitable for rock gardens.
Scabiosa atropurpurea Mournful widow, sweet scabious	White, pink, red, blue, dark crimson, also yellow, from VII, 16 to 24 in.	Cold frame, L. III to M. IV	After M. V, 12 × 10 in.	Permeable nutrient-rich garden soil, sunny, cut flowers only when fully flowering, since otherwise they will not keep; also for solitary plantings.
Schizanthus ×wisetonensis Butterfly flower	White, purple, pink, and light or dark flecked, from VII, 8 to 12 in.	Cold frame, III, or directly on site, IV	After M. V, 8 × 12 in.	Fresh humic, not too wet, calciferous garden soil, sheltered warm site; also suitable as pot plant.

BOTANICAL NAME ENGLISH NAME SPECIES	FLOWER COLOR, ONSET OF FLOWERING (MONTH), HEIGHT	SOWING LOCATION, MONTH	PLANTING TIME (MONTH), SPACING	REQUIREMENTS AND SPECIAL REMARKS
Tagetes Marigold 1. *T. erecta* 2. *T. patula* 3. *T. tenuifolia*	Yellow to orange, from VII; 1. Double, 18 to 28 in. 2. and 3. Also brown-red, double and single, 6 to 14 in.	Cold frame, III to IV	After M. V; 1. 12 × 12 in.; 2. and 3. 8 × 10 in.	Undemanding, medium, not too moist garden soil, sunny; also for balcony boxes and bowls; trimming died-off flowers extends the florescence; only weakly fragrant varieties of 2. are suitable for cut flowers.
Tanacetum (syn. *Chrysanthemum*) *parthenium* Feverfew	Yellow and white, double, VI, 12 to 24 in.	Cold frame, from III, or directly on site, IV to V	M. V, 10 × 10 to 12 × 12 in.	Deep, medium garden soil, no wetness, sunny; for cottage gardens, perennial beds, and flower borders; prized vase decoration.
Tropaeolum majus Nasturtium 1. Low-bushy varieties 2. Climbing varieties	Yellow to orange and red, from L. VI; 1. 8 to 12 in. 2. 6 ½ to 10 ft.	Directly on site, E. V, lay 3 to 4 grains in a bunch every 8 in.	After M. V, 8 × 10 in., also 12 in.	No heavy or wet garden soil, richly flowering in the sun, climbing varieties grow on wires, also as hanging plants, or lying prone on the ground; leave only the most vigorous of the young plants planted in bunches standing.
Ursinia anethoides	Orange-yellow with crimson-red, VI, 14 to 16 in.	Directly on site, L. IV	10 × 8 in.	Warm, sandy loam soil, sunny, suitable for attractive cut flowers and as underplanting for roses.
Verbena Vervain 1. *V. rigida* 2. Varieties	1. Purple-blue, from VI/VII, 6 to 16 in. 2. White, pink, scarlet, blue, from VI/VII, up to 16 in.	Under glass, III, later plant out in small pots	After M. V, 8 × 8 to 12 × 12 in.	Humus-rich warm garden soil, sunny, better to buy plants; for rock gardens, also balcony boxes and bowls.
Viola Pansies, violets 1. *V. cornuta*, Horned pansy 2. *V. ×wittrockiana*	All colors, mono- or bicolored, from III/IV, 4 in.	Seedbed outdoors, VI to M. VII	E. IX or III/IV, 6 × 8 in.	Undemanding, not too wet or dry garden soil, sunny; 1. Often self-sown; 2. Suitable as a colorful spring-flowering plant for balcony boxes and troughs, also for gravesite planting.
Zinnia Zinnia 1. *Z. angustifolia* 2. *Z. elegans*	1. Brown-red with yellow, from VII, 12 to 16 in. 2. All colors except blue, from VII, 12 to 32 in.	Cold frame, E. IV	M. to L. V, 8 × 8 in. to 12 × 12 in.	Humic, warm, nutrient-rich garden soil; sensitive to fungal diseases in wet and cold years, change site annually if possible; suitable for cut flowers for colorful summer bouquets.

Table 26. Annual Dry Flowers and Dry Grasses

Dry flowers and dry grasses are cut in full flowering, bundled, hung with the flowers facing downward, and dried slowly in a shady, airy place.

BOTANICAL NAME ENGLISH NAME SPECIES	FLOWER COLOR, ONSET OF FLOWERING (MONTH), HEIGHT	SOWING LOCATION, MONTH, REMOVAL	PLANTING TIME (MONTH), SPACING	REQUIREMENTS AND SPECIAL REMARKS
Briza maxima Greater quaking grass	Yellowish white spikes, from VI, up to 16 in.	Directly on site, M. IV, thin out to 6 × 8 in.	6 × 8 in.	Undemanding, not too wet soil, sunny, cut stalks just before maturity and hang up to air-dry in a shady place.
Bromus sterilis Barren brome, poverty brome	Loose spikes, from VII, up to 24 in.	Directly on site, E. IV, thin out to 6 × 6 in.	6 × 6 in.	Undemanding, not too wet soil, sunny; cut stalks just before maturity, cut everything back, since the brome spreads wild easily.
Gomphrena globosa Globe amaranth	White, pink, and crimson, from VI, 6 to 12 in.	Cold frame, L. III	L. V, 10 × 10 in.	Warm, humus-rich soil, sunny sheltered; also suitable as border plant.
Lagurus ovatus Hare's tail grass	Velvety-soft false spikes, from VII, 10 to 16 in.	Cold frame, M. IV, directly on site, M. IV	M. V, 8 × 6 in.	Undemanding, not too wet soil, sunny, plant in bunches; for nature gardens, also for colorful flowerbeds.
Limonium sinuatum Sea lavender	White, yellow, pink, red, and blue colors, from VII, 24 to 35 in.	Cold frame, M. II to E. IV	After M. V, 10 × 12 in.	Warm, permeable nutrient-rich soil, sunny; also suitable for colorful flowerbeds, also freshly cut in vases without water.
Psylliostachys (syn. *Limonium*) *suworowii* Statice	Pink-red, from VII, 32 in.	Cold frame, M. II to E. IV	After M. V, 10 × 12 in.	Warm, permeable, nutrient-rich soil, sunny; also for colorful flowerbeds; also freshly cut in vases without water.
Rhodanthe (syn. *Helipterum*) *manglesii* Paper daisy	Yellow, pink, crimson, red, from VI, 10 to 16 in.	Cold frame, M. IV	M. V, 8 × 6 in.	Light, humic, rather acidic soil, sunny open site; for drying, cut only once the flowers have developed a good color.
Xeranthemum annuum Common immortelle	White, pink, crimson, double, from VII, 20 to 24 in.	Directly on site, L. IV, thin out to 10 × 8 in.	10 × 8 in.	Loose, light sandy soil, sunny; more vivid colors when the flowers are dipped in a dilute (1:10) hydrochloric acid solution after cutting.
Xerochrysum (syn. *Helichrysum*) *bracteatum* Paper daisy, straw daisy	White, yellow, orange, pink, red, also violet, from VII, 28 to 35, also 12 in.	Cold frame, M. III to E. IV	After M. V, 10 × 10 in.	Warm, permeable, humic soil, sunny; also suitable for colorful beds; for drying, cut when the first bracts spread out (provided the flower still forms a ball).
Zea mays Ornamental corn	Cobs with colorful grains, yellow, brown, orange, violet, 60 to 70 in.	Directly on site, E. V, lay 3 or 4 grains in bunches, thin to 12 × 12 in.	12 × 12 in.	Nutrient-rich, damp, not too dry soil, sunny, especially vigorous growth with additional watering and fertilizer application; suitable as visual barrier; cut and dry once the grains have developed their full color.

Table 27. Plants for Balcony Boxes and Pots, Also for Terraces (Not Winter Hardy or Grown as Annuals)

BOTANICAL NAME ENGLISH NAME SPECIES	PLANTING TIME (MONTH), ONSET OF FLOWERING (MONTH), PLANT REQUIREMENT (PLANTS/LINEAR YARD)	SOIL REQUIREMENTS AND SPECIAL REMARKS
Ageratum houstonianum Flossflower	M./L. V, M./L. V, 5 to 7	Light, humic soil, somewhat sheltered site, flowers almost until the onset of frost if the died-off flowers are removed continually, flowers different shades of blue, also white and purple.
Anagallis tenella Bog pimpernel	M. V, M. V, 5 to 6	Garden soil or potting mixture, sunny to out of direct sun, keep moderately moist, apply fertilizer regularly, richly flowering, flowers vivid salmon-red.
Begonia Semperflorens Cultorum Group Wax begonia	After M. V, M. V, 5 to 7	Light, nutrient-rich, humic potting mixture, better out of direct sun than in full sun, flowering up until the first frost, keep sufficiently moist, removing wilted flowers will ensure a richer florescence, flowers white, pink, and red, also bicolored.
Begonia Tuberhybrida Group Tuberous begonia	After M. V, L. V, 4 to 5	Light, nutrient-rich, humic potting mixture, out of direct sun to light semi-shade, not windy, provide support for large-flowered varieties, flowers red, orange, yellow, white, single, also fringed or double.
Bellis perennis Daisy, English daisy	E./M. III, III, 5 to 7	Garden soil or potting mixture, sunny to out of direct sun, water thoroughly in periods of dryness, apply fertilizer sparingly, removing wilted flowers will ensure a longer florescence, flowers single, double, white, pink, red.
Calceolaria integrifolia Slipper flower	M./L. V, L. V/E. VI, 4 to 5	Potting mixture or compost earth, full sun, but no hot and dry south-facing site (east- or west-facing is better), always water abundantly, otherwise easily infested by aphids or greenhouse whitefly, apply fertilizer sparingly and often, remove died-off flowers for a longer florescence; flowers yellow.
Cuphea ignea Mexican cigar plant	M. V, IV to V, 4 to 5	Humic, loose potting mixture, mostly raised as annuals (plant out in pots also in the fall and overwinter at 59°F), sunny to semi-shaded, keep uniformly moist, apply fertilizer sparingly and often in summer, protect from hot midday sun and desiccating wind; flowers red and yellowish white.
Dahlia Dahlia, Mignon dahlias only	After M. V, L. VI, 4 to 5	Permeable soil, provide abundant water and fertilizer, sunny, buy young plants, low-growing varieties; flowers in all colors except blue.
Dianthus caryophyllus Carnation, gillyflower	M./L. IV, VI, 3 to 5	Humic, not acidic soil, high air humidity, tolerates sun, east-or west-facing sites are better, apply fertilizer sparingly, overwinter under light and frost-free conditions, shoot length up to about 3 ¼ ft., flowers red, pink, also yellow.
Diascia barberae Twinspur	V, VI, 4 to 5	Permeable soil, sunny, always keep moderately moist, no waterlogging, growth semi-pendulous, long-flowering, in many colors and varieties.
Dorotheanthus bellidiformis Livingstone daisy	After M. V, VI, 6 to 8	Warm, sandy-humic soil, full sun, too much water leads to rotting, apply minimal fertilizer, varieties in pastel colors, white, yellow, orange, pink, and carmine-red, also bicolored.
Fuchsia Fuchsia	M./L. V, L. V, 4 to 5	Humic, nutrient-rich soil, semi-shaded, sunny only if sufficiently moist, suitable for north-facing sites, not suitable for hot, dry, or windy places, overwinter at around 41°F and not in completely dry conditions, use predominantly hanging fuchsias.

BOTANICAL NAME ENGLISH NAME SPECIES	PLANTING TIME (MONTH), ONSET OF FLOWERING (MONTH), PLANT REQUIREMENT (PLANTS/LINEAR YARD)	SOIL REQUIREMENTS AND SPECIAL REMARKS
Impatiens walleriana Busy Lizzie	After M. V, L. V/E. VI, 5 to 6	Humic, fertile potting mixture, semi-shaded, sufficiently moist, apply fertilizer sparingly and continually, no dry hot sites, also suitable for north-facing sides, cut back severely from time to time, flowers dish-shaped, white, pink, red, also white/red and double.
Lantana camara Lantana	M. V, M. V, 4 to 5	Humic potting mixture, warm sunny site, water sufficiently, apply fertilizer every 2 weeks, cut back long shoots severely, overwinter under cool, airy, and light, only moderately moist conditions, flowers white, pink, yellow, orange, orange-red, purple, darker when flowers begin to wilt.
Lobelia erinus Edging lobelia, trailing lobelia	After M. V, M./L. V, 6 to 7	Permeable, humic soil, water copiously, apply fertilizer sparingly and continually, sunny to light shade, hanging form, shoot lengths up to 12 in., flowers blue, blue with white "eye," white, carmine-red.
Myosotis sylvatica Forget-me-not	E./M. III, III to VI, 5 to 7	Potting mixture or garden soil, uniformly moist, not wet, bright to light semi-shade, flowers die off quickly on hot sites in full sun, flowers light to dark blue, white, pink to carmine-pink.
Osteospermum ecklonis African daisy, Vanstaden's river daisy	M. V, V to VI, 4 to 5	Permeable soil, sunny, mostly utilized as annuals, but the plant is a perennial and can be overwintered under light and cool conditions, cut back severely in early spring, can also be propagated by cuttings.
Pelargonium Peltatum Group Ivy-leaved geraniums	M. V, E./M. V, 4 to 5	Nutrient-rich potting mixture or garden soil, full sun to light semi-shade, water uniformly, apply fertilizer weekly until L. VIII, plant at an angle to minimize risk of breakage, overwinter under light, frost-free, and nearly dry conditions, flowers pink, salmon, red, carmine-red.
Pelargonium Zonale Group Zonal geraniums	M. V, IV, 4	Nutrient-rich potting mixture or garden soil, full sun to light semi-shade, water uniformly, apply fertilizer weekly until L. VIII, flowers white, pink, salmon, red, violet-red.
Petunia Petunia	After M. V, L. V, 4 to 5	Nutrient-rich potting mixture or garden soil, full sun to light semi-shade, water and apply fertilizer uniformly, remove died-off flowers for a longer florescence, cut back as well, flowers white, pink, red, bluish to blue-violet, also bicolored.
Plectranthus forsteri 'Marginatus' Swedish ivy	M./L. V, summer, 4	Potting mixture or well-rotted compost earth, full sun to light semi-shade, keep moderately moist, apply fertilizer sparingly, long and pendulous with decorative leaves, leaves green with creamy-white edge, flowers inconspicuous, whitish, overwinter under fairly dry conditions at around 50°F.
Salvia splendens Scarlet sage	M./L. V, E./M. V, 4 to 5	Potting mixture or humic garden soil, full sun without wind, water regularly and apply weak fertilizer, remove died-off inflorescences, flowers vivid red, also pink and violet.
Scaevola saligna Fairy fan flower	M./L. V, E. V, 4	Potting mixture, full sun to light semi-shade, uniformly moist, no waterlogging, subsequent fertilizer applications promote florescence, flowers violet with a light "eye."
Tagetes patula French marigold	M. V, V, 5	Potting mixture, full sun, long-flowering until first frost, use only low-growing varieties of *T. erecta* and *T. patula*.

BOTANICAL NAME ENGLISH NAME SPECIES	PLANTING TIME (MONTH), ONSET OF FLOWERING (MONTH), PLANT REQUIREMENT (PLANTS/LINEAR YARD)	SOIL REQUIREMENTS AND SPECIAL REMARKS
Thymophylla (syn. Dyssodia) tenuiloba Dahlberg daisy, golden fleece	M./L. V, M./L. VI, 5	Potting mixture or humic garden soil, full sun, warm site, water regularly but keep only moderately moist, apply fertilizer sparingly, only around 6 in. high but spreading growth, flowers pure yellow with orange center.
Tropaeolum majus Nasturtium	E. V, L. V/E. VI, 3	Humic potting mixture, advance planting E. IV, also direct sowing, lay 3 or 4 grains every 6 to 8 in., thin out later, water regularly, not too wet, attach climbing varieties to support structure or use hanging ones, not suitable for windy sites, full sun, flowers yellow, orange, red.
Verbena Vervain	M. V, L. VI, 5	Potting mixture or humic garden soil, warm site, water regularly, not too wet, removed wilted flowers for a longer florescence, flowers white, pink, red, purple, and blue, also with white "eye."
Viola Pansy 1. *V. cornuta*, horned pansy 2. *V. ×wittrockiana*	III, III, 5 to 7	Garden soil or potting mixture, sunny to out of direct sun, water plentifully when dry, apply weak fertilizer, remove wilted flowers for a longer florescence—until planting with summer flowers, many varieties: white, yellow, orange, wine-red, light to dark blue, unicolored, also with dark spot.

Table 28. Tub Plants, Plants for Winter Gardens, Flower Windows, and Rooms (Not Winter Hardy)

Details regarding light conditions refer to adult plants. Young plants must always be protected from strong sun to begin with, along with plants that have been freshly moved and those which have been taken from the overwintering room and placed outdoors. In spring and summer, all plants that are growing under glass must be protected from the hot midday sun. Temperatures given are mostly what is optimal for the plants. However, many tub plants, including palms, will also tolerate lower temperatures in winter.

BOTANICAL NAME ENGLISH NAME SPECIES	OPTIMAL TEMPERATURE (IN °F), LIGHT, FLOWERING TIME	SOIL REQUIREMENTS AND OTHER REMARKS
Abutilon Flowering maple, Indian mallow	59 to 75, winter 41 to 50, sunny, variable	Nutrient-rich humic soil, water well in summer, water less in cold conditions in winter, apply fertilizer regularly from III to VIII; cut back heavily in spring; suitable for light, cool rooms.
Acacia Acacia, mimosa 1. *A. dealbata*, Silver wattle 2. *A. floribunda* 3. *A. retinodes*	Winter 41 to 54, sunny; 1. Winter, also summer 2. and 3. Winter	Loamy potting mixture, water moderately in winter in cold conditions, in summer plentifully, apply fertilizer sparingly in spring and summer only; if necessary, cut back heavily after flowering; suitable as tub plants for large containers, terraces, and winter gardens.
Acalypha hispida Red hot cat's tail	64 to 75, out of direct sun, I to X	Humic, permeable soil, high air humidity, uniform substrate moisture; suitable for extended flower windows, and winter gardens.
Adiantum Maidenhair fern	54 to 76, out of direct sun to semi-shaded	Humic soil, high air humidity, small containers, uniform substrate moisture; for display cabinets, extended flower windows, and winter gardens.
Aechmea Aechmea	54 to 76, sunny to semi-shaded, variable	Coarse, humic plant substrate, high air humidity, always add water to the leaf-tanks, old rosettes die off slowly after flowering, hard-leaved species such as *A. chantinii*, *A. fasciata*, and *A. recurvata* are suitable for rooms, soft-leaved species such as *A. fulgens* are suitable for higher air humidity; all are suitable for flower windows and winter gardens.
Aeonium Aeonium	60 to 77, sunny	Permeable, sandy-loamy soil, moderately moist, in winter cool and light, in summer outdoors; for light rooms.
Agapanthus campanulatus African lily	64, winter 39 to 46, full sun, VII to IX	Loamy-humic soil, water plentifully in summer, apply fertilizer often, light to semi-shaded, moderately moist; tub plant for the balcony and terrace.
Agave americana Agave, century plant	70, winter 41 to 46, sunny, out of direct sun	Sandy-loamy soil, in winter light and almost dry; large-growing species are suitable as tub plants for the terrace and balcony, smaller species for rooms.
Aglaonema commutatum Chinese evergreen	64 to 72, winter not below 60, out of direct sun to shaded	Humic soil, not too large pots, uniformly moist, apply a little fertilizer often; leafy plant, for rooms, flower windows, and flower gardens, also suitable as underplanting and for hydroculture.
Albizia Albizia *A. julibrissin*, pink siris, silk tree *A. lophantha* (syn. *Paraserianthes lophanta*), plume albizia	32 to 75, sunny, VIII to IX	Sandy-humic potting mixture, always moderately moist, sensitive to wetness, but no root ball dryness, suitable as an indoor plant in the first year only, overwinter in cool and light conditions; plant larger specimens in climatically favorable areas; prune frequently as tub plant, can also be planted out in winter gardens.
Allamanda cathartica 'Hendersonii' Golden trumpet	64 to 72, winter not below 59, sunny, summer	Humic potting mixture, always moderately moist, air humidity not too low, apply fertilizer weekly from IV to IX, cut back in spring before new growth, older plants need support; attractive tub plant for warm winter gardens.

BOTANICAL NAME ENGLISH NAME SPECIES	OPTIMAL TEMPERATURE (IN °F), LIGHT, FLOWERING TIME	SOIL REQUIREMENTS AND OTHER REMARKS
Aloe species Aloe	Winter 46 to 59, sunny to out of direct sun	Humic, permeable soil warmer than century plants, water well in summer, in winter nearly dry, not too large pots; large-growing species such as *A. arborescens* and *A. ferox* for the terrace and balcony in summer, small-growing species such as *A. aristata* and *A. variegata* for rooms.
Ananas Pineapple 1. *A. comosus* 2. *A. nanus*	60 to 75, plenty of light, flowering variable	Humic, permeable soil, all tolerate dry air, sunny, 'Variegatus' semi-shaded, not too large pots, water generously in summer, apply fertilizer sparingly, the leaf tufts of pineapple fruits can be left to develop roots in bark substrate; *A. nanus* with an infructescence around 14 in. high, hardy, decorative indoor plant.
Anthurium Flamingo flower, tail flower 1. *A. andreanum* hybrids 2. *A. scherzerianum* hybrids	Light, not sunny; 1. 60 to 72, I to XII 2. Winter not below 54, I to V	Friable, humic plant substrate, good pot drainage, never completely dry, high air humidity through frequent spraying, substrate moderately moist in winter; cover aerial roots on extended shoots with moss; 1. Especially suitable for winter gardens, small-growing, and 2. Also for flower windows, rooms, and large display cabinets.
Aphelandra squarrosa Saffron spike, zebra plant	64 to 75, winter not below 60, out of direct sun to semi-shaded, VI to X	Humic soil, uniformly moist, not wet, a little drier after flowering; if the leaves fall off, the plant is standing too wet; apply a little fertilizer regularly in spring and summer, keep a lookout for red spider mites and scale insects in particular; suitable for windows, display cabinets, flower windows, and winter gardens.
Araucaria heterophylla Norfolk Island pine	Winter 41 to 54, light, no direct sun in summer	Humic, somewhat loamy soil, in winter airy, cool, water moderately, spray often, in summer uniformly moist, apply a little fertilizer regularly, replant in spring; suitable as a tub plant for the terrace or balcony.
Arbutus unedo Strawberry tree	Winter frost-free, sunny, XI to XII	Humic, somewhat loamy potting mixture, water moderately in winter and generously in summer, apply fertilizer occasionally until VIII; tub plant, suitable for the terrace, balcony, and winter garden.
Argyranthemum frutescens Boston daisy, marguerite	In winter 41 to 50, sunny, summer	Nutrient-rich humic, well-drained potting mixture, water moderately in winter and generously in summer, apply fertilizer frequently until VIII, cut back in spring; suitable for the terrace and winter garden.
Asparagus Ornamental asparagus 1. *A. declinatus* (syn. *crispus*), Basket asparagus 2. *A. densiflorus* (syn. *aethiopicus*) 'Sprengeri', Sprenger's asparagus, 'Myersii', Myers' asparagus 3. *A. setaceus* (syn. *plumosus*), Asparagus fern	1. and 2. 8 to 72, light, sunny 3. 59 to 75, semi-shaded; summer	Humic garden or compost soil, replant before new growth, in summer water regularly and apply fertilizer sparingly, in winter keep cool, light, and drier; 1. and 2. Undemanding, not suitable for excessively warm rooms, from XI to E. III keep cool and almost dry for more vigorous new growth in spring; 3. Moister air, more warmth (also in winter), also suitable as climbing plant for large flower windows and in winter gardens.
Aspidistra elatior Bar-room plant, cast-iron plant	39 to 75, out of direct sun to semi-shaded	Loamy-humic soil, undemanding, water uniformly, never wet, apply fertilizer sparingly until VIII; robust tub plant, also suitable for sites with poor light.
Asplenium nidus Speenwort	64 to 75, winter not below 57, out of direct sun to semi-shaded	Friable humic, lime-free soil, no large containers, high air humidity, frequent spraying (rainwater), never dry, no waterlogging, apply fertilizer sparingly from III to VIII; suitable for large flower windows and winter gardens, young plants also suitable for display cabinets, suitable for hydroculture.

BOTANICAL NAME ENGLISH NAME SPECIES	OPTIMAL TEMPERATURE (IN °F), LIGHT, FLOWERING TIME	SOIL REQUIREMENTS AND OTHER REMARKS
Aucuba japonica Japanese aucuba, spotted laurel	37 to 75, out of direct sun to semi-shaded	Loamy-humic soil, undemanding, tolerates light frost, also thrives outdoors in a winegrowing climate, water uniformly, never wet, apply fertilizer sparingly until VIII; robust tub plant, also suitable for sites with poor light.
Begonia Elatior Group Begonia	64 to 23, winter not below 60, light, no full sun, variable	Humic, nutrient-rich potting mixture, not too dry and fresh air, water regularly and apply fertilizer sparingly, but be careful in lower temperatures; flowers single and double, white, pink, red, yellow, suitable for rooms and airy winter gardens.
Begonia Rex Cultorum Group King begonia, rex begonia	59 to 73, light, not sunny, variable	Sandy humic soil, uniformly moist, moderately warm in winter, apply fertilizer sparingly; many species and varieties for rooms, flower windows, display cabinets, and winter gardens, leaves often colored; other king/rex begonias: *B. bowerae, B. ×corallina, B. ×credneri, B. ×erythrophylla, B. manicata, B. masoniana, B. metallica, B. ×phyllomaniaca, B. ×verschaffeltii*, etc.
Billbergia Billbergia	59 to 73, out of direct sun, spring, variable	Humic, coarse and loose plant substrate, water regularly, fill large leaf-tanks with water, apply fertilizer sparingly during growth, keep drier in winter; suitable for rooms, flower windows, and winter gardens.
Bougainvillea glabra Paper flower	Winter 46 to 54, sunny, summer	Nutrient-rich, somewhat loamy potting mixture, water moderately in winter and generously in summer, apply fertilizer often, tie up older plants, cut back excessively long shoots; suitable as tub plant for light, airy winter gardens.
Browallia speciosa Sapphire flower	59 to 75, light, summer to fall	Humic potting mixture, keep plant substrate uniformly moist, best raised afresh each year from seeds or cuttings (cut in summer); suitable for light windowsills, also as balcony plant.
Brugmansia arborea (syn. *Datura arborea*) Angel's trumpet	Around 72, winter 39 to 54, sunny, V to X	Nutrient-rich, loamy-humic soil, water generously in spring and summer, apply fertilizer from IV to VIII, in winter cool, nearly dry and dark (will then lose leaves), in lighter conditions for new growth in spring; tub plant; all plant parts are poisonous.
Cacti Many genera and species	Winter 41 to 50, full sun, variable	Permeable, humic, loamy-sandy soil, in winter nearly dry, cool, and very light; a wide diversity of growth forms, flowers, and thorns; for light windowsills, in summer also on balconies.
Calceolaria Slipper flower	46 to 60, light, out of direct sun, III to V	Potting mixture or compost earth, full sun but no hot or dry south-facing side, care in a cool and airy place allows the annual plants to be kept for longer, applying fertilizer sparingly promotes bud development, keep a lookout for aphids and greenhouse whitefly; for cool rooms.
Callistemon citrinus Crimson bottlebrush	54 to 73, sunny, VI to VIII	Loamy rhododendron potting soil, water uniformly, apply fertilizer sparingly until VIII, does not tolerate lime, use rainwater only; overwinter in light conditions and at 54°F; tub plant.
Camellia japonica Common camellia	57 to 64, light, no full sun, I to IV	Sandy peat soil or camellia soil (commercially available), replant every 2 to 3 years after flowering; once the annual shoots have ripened (VI to VII), spray only (rainwater), water sparingly, but do not allow to dry out, water more generously after buds appear, uniformly moist, apply fertilizer sparingly every week from spring to fall; 37 to 46°F is sufficient up to flowering, 59°F at most; bud drop due to variable light levels, high temperatures, dry or wet root ball; suitable for cool, airy rooms and winter gardens.
Campanula Bellflower (hanging) 1. *C. fragilis* 2. *C. isophylla*	54 to 64, winter not below 46, out of direct sun; 1. VI to VII 2. VII to IX	Potting mixture or compost earth, undemanding, cool, airy, water regularly but only a little in winter, replant after cutting back (just above the soil) in spring, moderate fertilizer application in spring and summer, propagation by division and cuttings; hanging plant for airy winter gardens, rooms, and balconies.

BOTANICAL NAME ENGLISH NAME SPECIES	OPTIMAL TEMPERATURE (IN °F), LIGHT, FLOWERING TIME	SOIL REQUIREMENTS AND OTHER REMARKS
Capsicum annuum Cerasiforme Group Ornamental pepper	54 to 68, sunny	Humic potting mixture, uniformly moist, dryness leads to leaf drop, sow afresh each year at room temperature; decorative fruits from summer to fall, predominantly red.
Caryota mitis Burmese fishtail palm	Winter not below 60, sunny	Humic garden soil, uniformly moist, in winter moderately moist, light, and not too cold; tub plant.
Chamaedorea elegans Parlor palm	Winter 60 to 64, out of direct sun to semi-shaded	Humic potting mixture, keep moderately moist, does not tolerate wetness, often prone to pest infestation in dry air; low-maintenance pinnate palm for semi-shaded places in the winter garden.
Chamaerops humilis European fan palm, Mediterranean fan fern	57 to 73, sunny, also light shade	Sandy-loamy potting mixture, water plentifully in summer and sparingly in winter in cool conditions, overwinter in light and cool conditions; robust, small-growing palm suitable as tub plant for light rooms or winter gardens, also outdoors in summer.
Chlorophytum comosum Spider plant	41 to 72, light to shady, summer half-year	Potting mixture or humic compost earth, undemanding, airy, water regularly, no waterlogging, propagation by means of offsets from the inflorescence; suitable as pot and hanging plants for rooms, winter gardens, and balconies.
Cissus Grape ivy, treebine 1. *C. alata* (syn. *rhombifolia*), grape ivy 2. *C. antarctica*, kangaroo vine 3. *C. discolor*, rex begonia vine	All light, out of direct sun to semi-shaded; 1. and 2. 60 to 72, winter not below 46 3. Over 64	1. and 2. Loamy-humic, nutrient-rich soil; green-leaved hanging plants, also suitable for trellises, rooms, and winter gardens; 3. Loose, nutrient-rich, humus-rich soil, high air humidity; creeping, leaves green, silvery marbled to a considerable extent, undersides red; suitable for warm rooms, especially for flower windows and winter gardens; water all species moderately in winter, replant annually, apply fertilizer regularly in spring and summer.
Citrus Citrus tree (grapefruit, lime, mandarin, orange, lemon)	Winter not below 41, sunny	Acidic, permeable, somewhat loam-containing soil, in summer water generously, in winter water only a little when cool, keep low through cutting back in spring; small-fruiting varieties are suitable for growing, including crosses with *Fortunella* (kumquat); for rooms or winter gardens, also as tub plants.
Clivia miniata Kaffir lily	50 to 72, out of direct sun to light semi-shade, II to V	Potting mixture or humic compost earth, not too large pots, undemanding, replant every 2 to 3 years after flowering (without damaging the roots); to enable flowering, include a resting period from M. IX to L. XI at 50 to 59°F and with a fairly dry plant substrate; for rooms, winter gardens, and in a room for an open flower window.
Codiaeum variegatum Croton	Not below 59, light, out of direct sun to light semi-shade	Humic potting mixture, warm, moist air, soil always moderately moist, apply only a little fertilizer, leave colors from yellowish green to yellowish greenish red, plentiful light leads to intense colors; for flower windows, winter gardens, and warm rooms.
Coffea arabica Coffee	54 to 72, light, out of direct sun, VIII to X	Loamy-humic potting mixture, water generously in summer and moderately in winter, apply a little fertilizer regularly, flower white, fruit red, also orange; for rooms and winter gardens.
Columnea Columnea 1. *C. gloriosa* 2. *C. microphylla*	59 to 73, out of direct sun 1. IX to V 2. III to VIII	Coarse, humic, sandy potting mixture or compost earth, water generously in summer, otherwise water moderately, do not wet leaves in the sun (spot formation), apply fertilizer sparingly in the summer, keep cooler at 54 to 59°F to enable flowering in the fall; attractive hanging plant, for flower windows, winter gardens, and display cabinets.

BOTANICAL NAME ENGLISH NAME SPECIES	OPTIMAL TEMPERATURE (IN °F), LIGHT, FLOWERING TIME	SOIL REQUIREMENTS AND OTHER REMARKS
Cordyline fruticosa (syn. *terminalis*) Cabbage tree	Not below 64, very light, but out of direct sun	Humic, sandy potting mixture, higher air humidity, spray often, water uniformly, apply light fertilizer regularly in summer; for rooms, display cabinets, and winter gardens.
Crassula ovata Baby jade, jade plant	50 to 75, sunny, late winter to early spring	Permeable, sandy-humic soil, good drainage, always keep only moderately moist, water a little more only in very high temperatures, overwinter under cool conditions, then nearly dry, flower white (on older specimens only); decorative indoor plant.
Crossandra infundibuliformis Firecracker flower	Around 60 to 77, very light, but protect from hot midday sun, V to IX	Humic, damp soil, not too dry air; evergreen sub-shrub, up to 20 in. high, mostly raised as annuals (propagation through head cuttings in spring), overwintering also possible (light and warm), then severe cutting back in early spring; 'Fortuna' flowers orange-colored, 'Lutea' flowers golden-yellow, 'Mona Wallhead' flowers salmon-colored.
Cryptanthus Earth star bromeliad	64 to 72, semi-shaded	Permeable, sandy-humic soil, warm and moist, also in winter; for display cabinets and bottle gardens.
Curcuma Curcuma, turmeric	60 to 72, sunny, summer	Sandy-humic potting mixture, always keep slightly moist, no dry air, plant retracts its leaves in the winter, remove tuber from pot, overwinter in dry conditions from 60 to 64°F, plant in L. II, put in a light and warm place, water only very sparingly until the leaves appear, flowers large and pink; attractive tub plant for light rooms and winter gardens, in summer also in sheltered places outdoors.
Cyclamen persicum Florist's cyclamen	50 to 59, plenty of light, no full sun, VIII to IV	Sandy-humic potting mixture, the warmer the site, the lighter, reduce water applications after flowering, from VII/VIII water a little more again and maybe replant, also apply fertilizer once the roots have filled the pot, do not water the tuber directly, no water in the saucer; for cool rooms and winter gardens.
Cyperus Galingale, umbrella grass *C. alternifolius* *C. haspan*	54 to 72, does not need to be out in the lightest place	Potting mixture or compost earth, always add water to the saucer or cachepot, transplant in spring; propagation: leaf tuft sprouts roots readily in water; for rooms, winter gardens, and flower windows; *C. haspan* is smaller with respect to all plant parts.
Cyrtanthus elatus Fire lily	57 to 72, winter 41 to 50, light, out of direct sun, VI to IX	Sandy-loamy, humic earth, in winter keep only moderately moist, very small pots, bulbs must be only half-embedded in the soil; for light windowsills, but not in full sun.
Dieffenbachia seguine (syn. *maculata*) Dumb cane, mother-in-law's tongue	64 to 73, light to light semi-shade	Humic, nutrient-rich potting mixture, water regularly, no waterlogging, spray and apply fertilizer often; other species also available; for rooms, flower windows, and winter gardens, also for hydroculture.
Dracaena fragans (syn. *deremensis*) Dragon tree	59 to 73, light, not full sun	Sandy-humic potting mixture, avoid waterlogging, replant older specimens every 2 to 3 years, not too large pots, water regularly, apply fertilizer lightly; for rooms, flower windows, and winter gardens, also for hydroculture.
Echeveria Echeveria	41 to 64, plenty of light, sunny	Humic, sandy potting mixture or compost earth, water moderately, almost dry in winter, propagation by leaf cuttings; for light windowsills, balconies, in summer also outdoors.
Epiphyllum Orchid cactus	Not below 50 to 59, sunny, summer	Humic, sandy compost earth, not too large containers, water moderately, keep only very slightly moist in winter, in cool overwintering dry, protect from midday sun; for rooms, winter gardens, and balconies.

BOTANICAL NAME ENGLISH NAME SPECIES	OPTIMAL TEMPERATURE (IN °F), LIGHT, FLOWERING TIME	SOIL REQUIREMENTS AND OTHER REMARKS
Epipremnum Devil's ivy 1. *E. aureum*, Devil's ivy, golden hunters robe 2. *E. pinnatum*, tongavine, variegated philodendron	64 to 73, light to nearly shaded, leaf decoration	Humic potting mixture, keep uniformly moist and warm, also in winter, spray often, apply fertilizer sparingly, hydroculture is a good option (often falsely offered commercially as *Scindapsus*!); hanging plant, for rooms, flower windows, and window gardens.
Episcia cupreata Basket plant	64 to 75, semi-shaded, V to X	Humic soil, uniformly moist, high air humidity, apply a little fertilizer often; suitable as underplanting in display cabinets, bottle gardens, and for closed flower windows.
Eriobotrya japonica Japanese medlar, loquat, nispero	50 to 75, sunny, IX to X	Sandy-loamy, humic earth, keep uniformly moderately moist in summer, does not tolerate any root ball dryness, in winter light, cool, and only moderately moist; evergreen tub plant.
Eucalyptus gunnii Cider gum	In winter 35 to 50, sunny, leaf decoration	Humic, fertile potting mixture, rapidly growing, accordingly regular cutting back required, best in the spring, overwinter in a cool, light, and airy place, water plentifully in summer, almost dry in winter; tub plant.
Erythrina crista-galli Cockspur coral tree	54 to 75, winter not below 46, sunny, VIII to IX	Sandy-loamy, humic soil, water uniformly, apply fertilizer sparingly until VIII, place completely dry in winter quarters, cut back annual shoots, can be overwintered under almost dark conditions; splendidly flowering tub plant.
Euphorbia Spurge 1. *E. milii*, Crown of thorns, Christ thorn 2. *E. pulcherrima*, Christmas plant, lobster plant, Mexican flameleaf, poinsettia	1. 54 to 72, light, sunny, variable 2. 60 to 73, out of direct sun, XI to I	1. Sandy potting mixture or compost earth, water moderately, in winter keep in light, cool, and nearly dry conditions, suitable for light rooms; 2. Humic potting mixture with bark humus, water generously during flowering time, no wetness, since otherwise leaf fall will result, apply fertilizer often, suitable for rooms and warm winter gardens; both in varieties with red, pink-colored, and white bracts.
×*Fatshedera lizei* Aralia ivy	Winter 41 to 54, out of direct sun to nearly shaded, leaf decoration	Humic potting mixture or compost earth, air not too dry, water generously in summer and moderately in winter, cut back often if need be; cross between Japanese fatsia and ivy; suitable for rooms, winter gardens, and balconies.
Fatsia japonica Japanese fatsia, glossy-leaved paper plant	Winter 46 to 59, out of direct sun to semi-shaded, leaf decoration	Humic potting mixture or compost earth, in winter as light as possible, air not too dry, water only moderately, in summer water generously and apply fertilizer sparingly, do not cut back; suitable for rooms and winter gardens.
Ficus Fig 1. *F. aspera* 2. *F. benjamina*, Benjamin fig, tropic laurel, weeping fig 3. *F. carica*, fig 4. *F. cyathistipula* 5. *F. elastica*, Rubber plant, rubber tree 6. *F. lyrata*, Fiddle-leaf fig 7. *F. pumila*, Climbing fig, creeping fig 8. *F. rubiginosa*, Port Jackson fig, rusty fig 9. *F. natalensis* subsp. *leprieurii* (syn. *triangularis*), Natal fig	60 to 72, in, winter not below 57 (6. not below 50), out of direct sun to semi-shaded, leaf decoration	Coarse humic soil, good drainage, always water moderately only, more generously if very warm, wetness around the roots and standing in cool conditions leads to leaf fall; some species with white and colored leaves; suitable for rooms, flower windows, and winter gardens; 1. Warm with moist air, thin leaves up to 8 in. long with hirsute undersides with white, light green, and dark green patterning, large figs already present on young plants; 2. Small leaves, overhanging shoots; 3. As tub plant in the winter keep in cool, nearly dry conditions, figs edible; 4. Decorative indoor plant, rough leathery leaves; 5. Best-known rubber plant, 'Decora' with better branching; 6. Large leathery, violin-shaped leaves, young plants already have fruits (walnut-sized); 7. Small-leaved, climbing; 8. Hirsute medium-sized leaves, 'Variegata' with yellow-speckled edge, grows well in hydroponics containers; 9. Leaves almost triangular, 'Variegata' with colorful foliage.

BOTANICAL NAME ENGLISH NAME SPECIES	OPTIMAL TEMPERATURE (IN °F), LIGHT, FLOWERING TIME	SOIL REQUIREMENTS AND OTHER REMARKS
Fittonia verschaffeltii Nerve plant	60 to 82, almost shady	Humic soil, uniformly moist, high air humidity, leaves green, also intense red ('Pearcei') or white ('Argyroneura'); suitable for underplanting in display cabinets, flower windows, and bottle gardens.
Gardenia jasminoides (syn. *augusta*) Cape jasmine	54 to 72, out of direct sun to semi-shaded, VII to X	Humic, somewhat acidic soil with bark substrate, uniformly moist, a cooler location is favorable in winter, but then water only a little, flowers wax-like with a wonderful fragrance; suitable for rooms and winter gardens.
Gasteria species Gasteria	41 to 64, light, also sunny	Sandy potting mixture, tolerates dry air and temperature fluctuations, in winter keep in an airy and almost dry place (wetness leads to root rot); suitable for light rooms, balconies, in summer also outdoors.
Gerbera Transvaal daisy, many varieties	60 to 75, sunny (protect against hot midday sun, especially under glass), IV to IX	Permeable humic soil, always moderately moist, no dry air, overwinter under light and cool conditions, susceptible to rot if kept too wet and cool, also gray rot if not enough fresh air; short-stalked varieties suitable as indoor plants (winter garden, flower windows), long-stalked varieties suitable for cut flowers.
Grevillea Spider flower 1. *G. banksii* 2. *G. robusta* 3. *G. thelemanniana*	Winter 43 to 59, sunny, later summer, leaf decoration	Loamy-humic soil, protected from strong midday sun, moderately moist in winter; suitable as tub plant, only *G. thelemanniana* already flowers as a small shrub, the others as leafy plants; 1. Bluish foliage; 2. Leaves pinnate, dark green, undersides silver-gray; 3. Spidery foliage, flowers red.
Guzmania Guzmania	59 to 73, out of direct sun to semi-shaded	Friable humic soil, uniformly moist, in winter somewhat drier, always fill leaf-tanks with water, high air humidity; suitable for flower windows and winter gardens, small-growing species also suitable for display cabinets.
Gynura aurantiaca Purple velvet plant	64 to 75, out of direct sun, IX to X	Humic potting mixture, higher air humidity, keep uniformly but moderately moist, also in winter, apply fertilizer sparingly in summer; suitable for rooms, winter gardens, and display cabinets.
Haemanthus albiflos Elephant's tongue, paintbrush	50 to 75, sunny, VII to X	Sandy-humic, permeable soil, moderately moist, also nearly dry for brief periods (not during flowering), in winter keep cool and water only sporadically, transplant only seldom, flowers white; splendidly flowering, robust indoor plant.
Hedychium gardnerianum Kahila ginger lily	50 to 75, sunny, L. VII/E. IX	Humic, fertile potting mixture, good drainage, uniform substrate and high air humidity, in winter keep cool, fairly dry, and light at 50 to 59°F; splendidly flowering gingerwort plant suitable as large, rare tub plant for the winter garden, in summer also outdoors.
Heliotropium arborescens Cherry pie, heliotrope	Winter 41 to 50, sunny, V to IX	Humic potting mixture, water plentifully in summer and little in winter, around 3 ¼ ft. high, flowers violet-blue with vanilla fragrance; tub plant, was already popular in terraces and winter gardens three generations ago, as annuals also suitable as summer flowers and in balcony boxes.
Hibiscus rosa-sinensis Chinese hibiscus, rose of China	54 to 72, light and sunny, III to X	Nutrient-rich soil, water generously during flowering, keep moderately moist in winter, replant every 2 to 3 years, cut back severely in spring, low air humidity leads to pest infestation; for airy rooms, winter gardens, and balconies.
Hippeastrum Amaryllis	60 to 72, light, sunny to out of direct sun, I to V	Nutrient-rich soil, water uniformly, apply a little fertilizer weekly until late VIII, then keep drier for ripening; from X to XII, keep completely dry at 60 to 68°F, removed wilted leaves, replant once new buds are visible, water when the buds are ½ to ¾ in. in size; for rooms and winter gardens.
Hoya carnosa Waxplant	59 to 72, winter not below 50, out of direct sun to semi-shaded	Compost earth or potting mixture, in winter keep cool from 50 to 59°F and moderately moist for a rich florescence, replant every 2 to 3 years, do not remove old inflorescences, develops new flowers continuously; for climbing frames in rooms and winter gardens.

BOTANICAL NAME ENGLISH NAME SPECIES	OPTIMAL TEMPERATURE (IN °F), LIGHT, FLOWERING TIME	SOIL REQUIREMENTS AND OTHER REMARKS
Hydrangea macrophylla Hortensia, lace cup hydrangea	41 to 64, out of direct sun, III to VI (VIII)	Rhododendron potting soil, water generously, apply fertilizer often, do not apply nitrogen from VIII, blue coloration from iron-containing bog soil or alum salts, do not cut in the fall, cut back by two-thirds following flowering; for airy rooms, balconies, and terraces.
Impatiens Balsam, busy Lizzie 1. New Guinea Group 2. *I. walleriana*	57 to 60, out of direct sun, I to XII	Sandy-humic, fertile potting mixture, water and apply fertilizer regularly, under-cooling in winter leads to rot, only sparsely flowering at excessively dark sites, cut back in spring or propagate by means of cuttings in water, also annual culture through sowing or young plants; for balconies and airy, not air-dry rooms.
Jacaranda mimosifolia Jacaranda	59 to 75, sunny to out of direct sun, also light shade, leaf decoration	Humic, fertile potting mixture generally drops leaves in winter, then keep only moderately moist in a cool place; sow as an annual indoor plant in II with a soil temperature of more than 68°F or as a perennial tub plant for the winter garden (flowering in very large specimens only).
Justicia brandegeeana (syn. *Beloperone guttata*) Shrimp plant	Winter 54 to 64, sunny, variable, often all year round	Compost earth for potting mixture, keep cool and moderately and moderately moist in winter for a rich florescence, water plentifully in summer; attractive pot plant for light, cool rooms or winter gardens, in summer outdoors as well.
Kalanchoe blossfeldiana Kalanchoe, flaming Katy	54 to 72, Winter not below 46, full sun II to IV, variable	Annually raised plants in potting mixture, uniformly moist, never keep wet, also keep as light as possible; rewarding flowering plants for rooms; succulent plants in sandy-loamy humic soil, care similar to that for cacti; for succulent collections, other kalanchoe species are also available, as well as bryophyllum (*Bryophyllum*); all tolerate warmth; for light rooms.
Lagerstroemia indica Crape myrtle	Winter 39 to 46, full sun, VIII to X	Sandy-loamy, humic soil, water uniformly, apply fertilizer sparingly until VIII, place almost dry in winter quarters, cut back annual shoots severely to overwinter in darker conditions; tub plant.
Laurus nobilis Laurel	Winter 32 to 50, sunny to semi-shaded	Sandy-loamy soil, older specimens will tolerate light frost for brief periods, water sparingly in winter, otherwise uniformly, apply fertilizer sparingly until VIII, overwinter under light conditions or darker if need be; evergreen tub plant, kitchen spice.
Ledebouria socialis Silver squill	50 to 73, sunny to out of direct sun, IV to VI	Permeable, sandy potting mixture, undemanding, water less under cool conditions and more when warm, leaves appear from small bulbs; small, up to 6 in. high, robust indoor plant.
Livistona australis Australian fan palm, cabbage palm	57 to 73, sunny, also light shade	Sandy-loamy potting mixture, water well in summer, but only a little in winter in a cool site, overwinter under cool and light conditions; robust palm suitable as tub plant for large, light rooms or winter gardens.
Lycianthes rantonnetii (syn. *Solanum rantonnetii*) Blue potato bush, Paraguay nightshade	Winter 41 to 50, sunny, out of direct sun, VII to X	Nutrient-rich, humic soil, always water uniformly in spring and summer, apply fertilizer until VIII, in winter keep light, cool, and only moderately moist, cut back lightly in early spring; richly flowering tub plant.
Lytocaryum (syn. *Micro-coelum*) *weddellianum* Weddel palm	64 to 68, out of direct sun	Humic potting mixture, always keep uniformly moist and warm, also in winter, higher air humidity required; suitable as tub plants for winter gardens.
Maranta leuconeura Prayer plant	64 to 75, not below 57, out of direct sun to semi-shaded	Humic potting mixture, always keep uniformly moist, never too wet or dry, loves higher air humidity, apply fertilizer sparingly in summer; suitable for rooms, display cabinets, flower windows, and winter gardens.

BOTANICAL NAME ENGLISH NAME SPECIES	OPTIMAL TEMPERATURE (IN °F), LIGHT, FLOWERING TIME	SOIL REQUIREMENTS AND OTHER REMARKS
Metrosideros excelsa New Zealand Christmas tree, pohutukawa	50 to 75, sunny, V to VI	Humic potting mixture, keep uniformly moist at all times, apply fertilizer until IX, less moist for a brief time before the start of flowering in spring, in winter light, cool, and moderately moist (too much warmth inhibits flower development), flowers red, from around the third growing year; attractive tub plant.
Monstera deliciosa Swiss cheese plant	60 to 77, light, out of direct sun to semi-shaded, leaf decoration	Humic, nutrient-rich soil, uniformly moist, never wet, high air humidity, infestation with red spider mites if air too dry, temperature-tolerant, do not cut off aerial roots; for light rooms and winter gardens, small-growing forms also for flower windows.
Musa Banana 1. *M. acuminata* 'Dwarf Cavendish', Dwarf banana 2. *M. sikkimensis*, Darjeeling banana	Sunny; spring/summer 1. 64 to 75, up to 2 m high 2. Up to 75, up to 4 m high	Humic, sandy-loamy soil; 1. Water uniformly, also in winter, protect from hot midday sun in spring and summer, in winter keep in a light, airy place, no dry air, propagation by offsets at the base of the mother plant (if these have their own roots, cut them off), fruit small, strong flavor; for large, light rooms and winter gardens; 2. Grow from seed at 68 to 77°F, a long process, later with vigorous growth, overwintering as tub plant in frost-free, light, and airy conditions; in the case of specimens planted outdoors, cut the plant above the ground after the first frost, protect the root zone from frost and wetness, and the plant will put forth shoots again in spring; fruits develop only after continuous cultivation.
Myrtus communis Common myrtle	Winter 35 to 60, full sun, VI to IX	Humic, sandy-loamy soil, always water uniformly, in winter not too moist if kept in a cool place, apply fertilizer sparingly until VIII, overwinter under light conditions, cut back older plants lightly in spring; evergreen tub plant.
Neoregelia Nest bromeliad	59 to 75, sunny to semi-shaded	Coarse, permeable, humic plant substrate; uniformly moist, always fill leaf-tanks with water; for rooms, flower windows, winter gardens, small-growing species such as *N. ampullacea*, *N. pygmaea*, and *N. roethii* suitable for display cabinets.
Nephrolepis exaltata Boston fern, sword fern	59 to 73, winter not below 50 to 54, out of direct sun to semi-shaded	Humic, loose potting mixture, always keep uniformly moist, sensitive to excessively dry air, keep cooler in winter, apply fertilizer sparingly in summer; suitable for rooms, flower windows, and winter gardens.
Nerium oleander Oleander	Winter 35 to 59, full sun, VI to IX	Humic, sandy-loamy soil, water generously in summer, apply fertilizer until III, in winter keep moderately moist, cool, and light, tub plant (leaves poisonous).
Nidularium Bird's-nest bromeliad	60 to 73, out of direct sun to semi-shaded	Friable, permeable, humic soil, uniformly moist, never wet, loves high air humidity, always fill leaf-tanks with water; for rooms, flower windows, winter gardens, and display cabinets.
Pachypodium lamerei Madagascar palm	50 to 79, sunny	Permeable, sandy-loamy soil, always only moderately moist, in winter keep nearly dry in a somewhat cooler place, replant at least every 2 years; suitable for light rooms and warm winter gardens.
Pachystachys lutea Golden candle, lollipop plant	64 to 73, not below 59, out of direct sun to semi-shaded, III to X	Humic, nutrient-rich soil, keep uniformly moist, wetness or dryness leads to leaf fall, repot after flowering, apply fertilizer often in summer, higher air humidity, keep a lookout for red spider mites and greenhouse whitefly; suitable for rooms, flower windows, and winter gardens, also display cabinets.
Pandanus tectorius (syn. *veitchii*) Screw pine	64 to 75, not below 60, plenty of light, also sun after suitable acclimatization	Sandy-humic potting mixture, water generously in summer, do not cut off aerial roots but guide them into the earth (buttress roots), replant every 2 to 3 years, plant grows very tall; suitable for light rooms and winter gardens.
Passiflora caerulea Blue passionflower	50 to 68, light, spring or summer	Sandy loam-containing humus soil, keep uniformly moist, leaf fall if dry, cut back by a third in III, put in a warmer place, and then water more generously, keep a lookout for mealybugs and red spider mites in particular; grow on trellises and support frames; suitable for windowsills and winter gardens.

BOTANICAL NAME ENGLISH NAME SPECIES	OPTIMAL TEMPERATURE (IN °F), LIGHT, FLOWERING TIME	SOIL REQUIREMENTS AND OTHER REMARKS
Pelargonium 1. Scented begonias 2. Grandiflorum Group, Regal begonias	1. 54 to 72, sunny, summer 2. 54 to 75, light, no full sun, IV to VI (VII)	1. Humic garden soil, always keep only moderately moist, in winter nearly dry in a cooler place, lemon fragrance (also mint, eucalyptus, and others); 2. Nutrient-rich, sandy-humic potting mixture or compost earth, keep moderately moist in summer and winter, maintain in an airy place, keep a lookout for greenhouse whitefly in particular; 1. and 2. Suitable for rooms and winter gardens.
Peperomia Radiator plant 1. *P. argyreia*, Watermelon peperomia 2. *P. obtusifolia*, Baby rubber plant	1. 60 to 73, not below 57, out of direct sun to semi-shaded 2. 64 to 72, out of direct sun	1. Sandy-humic soil, moist to moderately moist, never wet, keep drier in winter replant in summer, leaves in rosettes or on long shoots, single, also in whorls; suitable for display cabinets, rooms, winter gardens; 2. Conifer needle soil or sandy-humic soil, moderately moist, ovate, fleshy leaves, different yellow-green spotted varieties.
Pericallis ×*hybrida* Senecio Cruentus Group Cineraria, florist's cineraria	46 to 59, needs plenty of light, II/IV	A cool, airy site allows the annual plants to be kept for longer; applying fertilizer sparingly promotes the flowering of all buds; keep a lookout for aphids and greenhouse whitefly in particular; no subsequent cultivation possible; suitable for light cool rooms and winter gardens.
Philodendron Philodendron	64 to 75, not below 60, out of direct sun to semi-shaded, leaf decoration	Sandy-humic, nutrient-rich potting mixture and compost soil, uniformly moist, not wet; many different, upright, hanging, and creeping species, also on a moss pole; suitable for rooms, flower windows, winter gardens, and display cabinets.
Phoenix Date palm 1. *P. canariensis*, Canary Island date palm 2. *P. dactylifera*, Date palm 3. *P. roebelenii*, Miniature date palm, pigmy date palm	1. 59 to 75, sunny 2. 57 to 75, sunny 3. 64 to 72, out of direct sun	1. Fertile, sandy-loamy, humic soil, keep light and cool in winter, water moderately, in summer generously; tub plant; 2. Sandy-loamy, humic soil, in winter light and cool, water moderately, in summer generously, mostly raised from seed, can be grown only as young plants; tub plant; 3. Sandy-humic potting mixture or compost earth, uniformly moist, maintain indoors all year round; for light rooms and winter gardens.
Pilea Artillery plant 1. *P. cardierei* 2. *P. involucrata* (syn. *spruceana*)	Out of direct sun to semi-shaded; 1. 54 to 64 2. 64 to 72	Humic compost earth or potting mixture, in winter in light conditions, moderately moist, in summer spray and apply fertilizer often, cut back in spring, propagation by cuttings (sprouting roots in water); suitable for rooms, flower windows, and display cabinets.
Piper Pepper 1. *P. nigrum* 2. *P. ornatum*	60 to 75, out of direct sun to semi-shaded	Sandy-humic potting mixture, uniformly moist, not wet, apply fertilizer often in summer, sensitive to undercooling and dry air; suitable as underplanting, also creeping, in display cabinets, flower windows, and winter gardens.
Platycerium Elkhorn fern, staghorn fern	57 to 75, winter not below 54, out of direct sun to semi-shaded	Friable humic plant substrate, dipping in water once per week is better than watering, apply fertilizer occasionally, easily maintained in a lath basket, tolerates temperature fluctuations, replant if required; suitable as a hanging plant in rooms and winter gardens, or tied up to an epiphyte stem.
Plectranthus scutellarioides (syn. *Coleus blumei*) Coleus	54 to 72, light, sunny, leaf decoration	Potting mixture or humic compost earth, sunny, leaf color fades in the shade, water and apply fertilizer regularly; suitable for light windowsills, winter gardens, and balconies.

BOTANICAL NAME ENGLISH NAME SPECIES	OPTIMAL TEMPERATURE (IN °F), LIGHT, FLOWERING TIME	SOIL REQUIREMENTS AND OTHER REMARKS
Plumbago auriculata (syn. *capensis*) Cape leadwort	50 to 75, sunny, VI to IX	Sandy-humic, fertile potting mixture, water uniformly in summer, keep moderately moist in winter in a cool place, train on trellis, apply fertilizer until VIII, otherwise cut back before overwintering, flowers light blue, white, pink; richly flowering tub plant for light rooms.
Primula Primel 1. *P. malacoides*, Baby primrose, fairy primrose 2. *P. obconica*, German primrose	50 to 64, out of direct sun to semi-shaded 1. I to III 2. I to XII	Humic, sandy-loamy soil, cool, airy, and light; 1. Buy plants new every year; 2. Uniformly moist, not wet, apply fertilizer frequently in summer, replant following flowering in spring or summer, keep a lookout for chlorosis (see **TABLE 32**); both in numerous varieties and color shades for rooms and winter gardens that are not too warm.
Pteris cretica Ribbon fern	54 to 64, out of direct sun to semi-shaded	Humic soil, uniformly moist, higher air humidity, apply fertilizer occasionally in summer, replant annually, not too large pots, propagate through division; suitable for cool rooms, flower windows, and winter gardens.
Punica granatum Pomegranate	Winter 35 to 59, full sun, VII to VIII	Humic, sandy-loamy soil, water generously in summer, apply fertilizer until VIII, in winter cool, nearly dry, and dark (mostly loses its leaves), acclimatize to sun slowly with new growth in spring; red-flowering tub plant, the small-growing 'Nana' is suitable as richly flowering pot plant.
Rhapis excelsa Bamboo palm, ground rattan cane, lady palm	50 to 72, out of direct sun, also light shade	Sandy-loamy potting mixture, water plentifully in summer, only a little in winter when in a cool place, overwinter under cool and light conditions; robust, compact palm suitable as a tub plant for large rooms or winter gardens, also outdoors in summer.
Rhipsalidopsis ×*graeseri* Easter cactus	Winter 50 to 57, light, still semi-shaded, III to V	Friable humic soil, water moderately, never wet, from XI to I keep cool and fairly dry (for flowering to begin), not too large pots, breeds available in different shades of red; for rooms and winter gardens.
Rhipsalis Mistletoe cacti	60 to 72, out of direct sun	Orchid potting soil, warm and only moderately moist, also in winter, but high air humidity; suitable for rooms with not too dry air, also for closed flower windows and warm winter gardens.
Rhododendron Simsii Group Indoor azalea	Winter 41 to 60, out of direct sun, still semi-shaded, XII to V	Rhododendron potting soil, keep uniformly moist, never let root balls dry out (best dip in water), does not do well in warmth but does love higher air humidity, remove leaf shoots at the buds, cut back after flowering; for cooler rooms and winter gardens, in summer both airy and light in the room or garden.
Rosa Dwarf roses (see TABLE 13)	41 to 75, sunny, early summer to fall	Sandy-humic potting mixture, keep uniformly moist, best kept outdoors in summer, in winter light, cool, and moderately moist, use only varieties that are resistant to pests and diseases; for light rooms, balconies, and winter gardens.
Rosmarinus officinalis Rosemary	Winter 35 to 59, sunny, IV to V	Loamy-humic soil, water plentifully in summer, apply fertilizer until VIII, in winter water moderately, nearly dry, and not more than 59°F light and airy, replant in spring only if necessary; slow-growing tub plant.
Saintpaulia African violet	60 to 75, out of direct sun to semi-shaded, I to IX	Humic, loose soil, keep uniformly moist, apply fertilizer frequently in summer, florescence richer following a brief dry period, replant often, yellowish spots through water on the leaves in sun, keep a lookout for tarsonemid mites; suitable for rooms, display cabinets, and flower windows.
Sansevieria trifasciata Bowstring hemp, mother-in-law's tongue, snake plant	59 to 72, out of direct sun to semi-shaded, leaf decoration	Sandy-loamy, humic soil, water sparingly (only when the soil is dry), water even less often in winter, tolerates dry air but not cold air when ventilated in winter, not too large pots; suitable for rooms and winter gardens, also for hydroculture; 'Laurentii' growth form like the species, leaves with golden-yellow edges, 'Hahnii' small-growing in rosettes.

BOTANICAL NAME ENGLISH NAME SPECIES	OPTIMAL TEMPERATURE (IN °F), LIGHT, FLOWERING TIME	SOIL REQUIREMENTS AND OTHER REMARKS
Saxifraga stolonifera Mother-of-thousands, strawberry geranium	Winter frost-free, out of direct sun to nearly shaded	Humic soil, keep in an airy place, no dry warmth, uniformly moist, no containers; delicate hanging plant suitable for rooms and flower windows; 'Tricolor' warmer at 59 to 64°F.
Scadoxus (syn. *Haemanthus*) 'König Albert' Blood flower	59 to 72, out of direct sun to semi-shaded, IV to V	Sandy-humic compost earth, water less from IX on, keep almost dry during the winter dormant period, older leaves are shed with new growth in spring, replant seldom, renew the upper third of the soil every year with the start of new growth, flowers vivid vermilion-red; splendidly flowering indoor plant, can also be grown outdoors in summer.
Schefflera Ivy tree, umbrella tree	54 to 75, winter not below 50, sunny, also semi-shaded	Sandy-loamy humic soil, replant every 2 to 3 years, water regularly, never let the root ball dry out, apply fertilizer sparingly and in summer only, higher air humidity, in winter cool; outdoors in summer, also suitable for cool, light rooms (*S. elegantissima* somewhat warmer) and winter gardens.
Schlumbergera Christmas cactus	50 to 64, out of direct sun to semi-shaded, XI to I	Humic soil, water regularly, not wet, from IX (until buds appear) light, nearly dry and cool, nights 50 to 59°F, then keep moister again, when buds are present do not modify site any further if possible, since buds may fall otherwise, after flowering cool and drier, replant in spring; Christmas-flowering plant for rooms and winter gardens.
Scindapsus pictus Scindapsus	68 to 72, light to nearly shady, leaf decoration	Humic potting mixture, keep uniformly moisty and warm, also in winter, does not tolerate dry air, spray frequently (*Epipremnum* is often falsely offered commercially under this name!); hanging plant, for closed flower windows, winter gardens, and display cabinets.
Sedum morganianum Burro's tail, donkey's tail	60 to 77, sunny	Permeable, sandy-humic soil, moderately moist, drier in winter in a cool place, leaves fall easily after being touched; hanging plant for light rooms.
Selaginella Lesser club moss	64 to 72, semi-shaded	Humic potting mixture, keep uniformly moist and warm, also in winter, does not tolerate dry air; for closed flower windows, display cabinets, and bottle gardens.
Sinningia Florist's gloxinia	64 to 77, out of direct sun to semi-shaded, IV/VIII	Humic soil, drier after flowering, overwinter tubers under dry conditions (at 64°F) after the leaves have turned yellow; preferably buy plants when they are flowering, can be kept for several years, place tubers in pots from II, better from IV, barely cover with earth, water moderately, keep moister following sprouting shoots, later apply fertilizer weekly; attractive flowering plant for warm rooms.
Solanum Eggplant, nightshade, potato 1. *S. capsicastrum*, False Jerusalem cherry 2. *S. melongena*, Eggplant, aubergine 3. *S. pseudocapsicum*, Jerusalem cherry, Madeira winter cherry	59 to 72, sunny, V, decorative fruits	Sandy-humic potting mixture, keep uniformly moist and warm, water plentifully in summer, a sheltered site outdoors promotes fruiting; 1. and 3. Round red, also white or yellow-colored fruits, sow from III, cut back seedlings, annual, or overwinter under cool and light conditions; suitable for sunny windowsills or sheltered sites outdoors; 2. Mostly as annual indoor plants with attractive violet flowers and white ovate fruits, up to 20 in. high, sow from I to VI.
Soleirolia soleirolii Angel's tears, baby's tears, Irish moss, mind your own business	41 to 72, out of direct sun to semi-shaded, leaf decoration	Humic soil, keep uniformly moist, some water can be left standing in the saucer, replant rarely (only if plant needs to be divided); ground cover in flower windows and bottle gardens, also for north-facing windows.

BOTANICAL NAME ENGLISH NAME SPECIES	OPTIMAL TEMPERATURE (IN °F), LIGHT, FLOWERING TIME	SOIL REQUIREMENTS AND OTHER REMARKS
Sparmannia africana African hemp	43 to 60, out of direct sun to semi-shaded, I to III	Potting mixture or humic compost earth, in summer water generously and apply fertilizer often, in winter keep in a light and airy place and only moderately moist; however, does not tolerate any root ball dryness; cut back after flowering; attractive white flowers; suitable for cool rooms, in summer also outdoors (light shade).
Spathodea campanulata African tulip	50 to 75, sunny, summer	Potting mixture or humic compost earth, fast growing, water regularly, in winter keep cooler and water less frequently, keep lower by cutting back, can be sown all year round, large pinnate leaves, flowers orange-red; tub plant.
Stenocarpus sinuatus Firewheel tree	50 to 75, light shade, VII to VIII	Permeable humic compost earth, evergreen, fast growing, water regularly, in winter keep cooler and water less frequently, keep lower by cutting back, can be sown all year round, flowers with orange-red filaments; suitable as tub plant for greenhouses, winter gardens, or in a sheltered place outdoors in summer.
Strelitzia reginae Bird of paradise	Winter 46 to 60, full sun, II to VIII	Nutrient-rich, humic soil, in summer water uniformly, apply fertilizer up until IX, overwinter under light, cool, and dry conditions; decorative tub plant, in summer also outdoors, also planted out in winter garden.
Streptocarpus Cape primrose	54 to 72, out of direct sun to semi-shaded, III to X	Sandy-humic soil, in winter moderately moist when kept in a cool place, water more frequently in warm rooms, also apply fertilizer sparingly; rewarding flowering plant for rooms, flower windows, and winter gardens.
Syngonium podophyllum American evergreen, arrowhead vine	64 to 72, out of direct sun to nearly shaded, leaf decoration	Humic, nutrient-rich soil, water uniformly, not too low humidity, in summer apply fertilizer often but sparingly; hanging and creeping, also varieties with colorful leaves for winter gardens, rooms, and flower windows.
Tibouchina urvilleana Glory bush, purple glory tree	Winter 46 to 54, sunny to out of direct sun, VIII to V	Rhododendron potting soil, water uniformly, no lime-containing fertilizer, in summer in a sheltered place outdoors, overwinter under airy, light, and cool conditions, cut back frequently as young plant; tub plant, also planted out in winter gardens.
Tillandsia Air plant	60 to 77, sunny	Friable, permeable, humic soil, uniformly moist, never wet, high air humidity, in species with leaf-tanks, fill the leaf-tanks with water, attach species without leaf-tanks to bark pieces with little or no plant substrate, then spray or dip in water (rainwater) often; suitable for rooms, flower windows, winter gardens, and display cabinets.
Trachycarpus fortunei Chusan palm	39 to 75, sunny	Humic soil, in summer water plentifully, in winter sparingly, overwinter under cool and light conditions, seed propagation; suitable as tub plant.
Tradescantia Spiderwort 1. *T. fluminensis*, Wandering sailor 2. *T. spathacea*, Boat lily, Moses-in-the-boat 3. *T. zebrina*, Wandering Jew	1. and 2. 54 to 72, winter not below 50, out of direct sun to semi-shaded, variable 3. 54 to 73, out of direct sun to semi-shaded	1. and 2. Humic, nutrient-rich compost earth or potting mixture, keep uniformly moist, easily propagated by shoot tips in a pot, flowers appear sporadically, *T. spathacea* (formerly *Rhoeo spathacea*) with shell-like bracts; hanging plant for warm or cooler rooms; 3. Humic, nutrient-rich compost earth or potting mixture, uniformly moist, in winter not below 54 to 59°F, leaves with two silver longitudinal stripes (formerly *Zebrina pendula*, "zebra plant"), easily propagated in a pot by means of shoot tips; hanging plant for warm or cooler rooms.
Viburnum tinus Laurustinus	Winter 32 to 50, sunny, late fall to spring	Humic, nutrient-rich compost earth or potting mixture, in summer water plentifully, in winter sparingly, overwinter under light and cool conditions; tub plant, in summer also outdoors, also winter hardy in climatically favorable regions.
Vriesea splendens Flaming sword	59 to 75, out of direct sun to semi-shaded	Friable, permeable, humic soil, keep uniformly moist, never wet, higher air humidity, always fill leaf-tanks with water; suitable for rooms, flower windows, and display cabinets.

Table 29. Orchids for Rooms, Winter Gardens, and Small Greenhouses

For most of the species listed below, there are numerous hybrids (and cultivars) that are just as suitable for growing, in many cases even more so. Otherwise note:

GENUS, SPECIES	CULTIVATION	GROWTH HEIGHT	FLOWER COLOR	FLOWERING TIME
Brassavola nodosa Lady-of-the-night orchid	Tempered, marked resting period	Low	Yellow, white, labellum with red dots	Summer, fall
Brassia verrucosa	Tempered, moderate resting period	Medium-large	Green, spotted, labellum white, green warts	Spring, summer
Brassocattleya 1. Large-flowered 2. Flowers stellate	Warm/tempered	1. Medium-large to large 2. Low to medium-large	1. White, with pink and red, white/carmine-red 2. White, yellow, pink, carmine, also spotted	1. Winter, spring 2. Winter to summer
Cattleya intermedia	Tempered/warm, moderate resting period	Medium-large	Whitish to pink, crimson-red in front	Spring, summer
Cattleya labiata	Warm/tempered, marked resting period	Medium-large	Light carmine-red, labellum crimson-red	Fall
Coelogyne tomentosa (syn. *massangeana*)	Tempered/warm, moderate resting period	Medium-large to large	Creamy yellow, labellum with brown patterning	Early summer, fall
Cymbidium mini-hybrids	Tempered, marked resting period	Medium-large to large	Yellowish, greenish, reddish, whitish	Late winter, spring
Dendrobium 1. *D. kingianum* 2. Nobile hybrids	1. Tempered/cool 2. Warm/tempered, marked resting period	1. Small to medium-large 2. Medium-large	1. Pink, white 2. Light carmine-red, labellum with red-brown patterning	Spring
Epidendrum ciliare	Tempered, moderate resting period	Medium-large	Linden-green, white labellum	Fall, winter
Laelia purpurata (syn. *Cattleya purpurata*)	Tempered, moderate resting period	Medium-large to large	Light carmine-red, labellum crimson-red	Spring, summer
Laeliocattleya	Tempered	Medium-large to large	White with red, pink, carmine-red	Spring, also variable
Maxillaria picta (syn. *Brasiliorchis picta*)	Tempered	Medium-large	Yellow, brown spots	Fall/winter to spring
Miltonia hybrids Pansy orchid	Tempered, moderate resting period	Medium-large	White, pink, red, yellow, labellum patterned	Summer
Odontioda hybrids	Tempered, moderate resting period	Medium-large	Pink, red, darker patterning	Variable
Odontocidium hybrids	Tempered, moderate resting period	Medium-large, seldom large	Mostly red-brown, labellum mostly yellow	Variable

GENUS, SPECIES	CULTIVATION	GROWTH HEIGHT	FLOWER COLOR	FLOWERING TIME
Oncidium 1. *O. flexuosum,* (syn. *Cyrtochilum flexuosum*), Dancing doll orchid 2. *O. forbesii,* (syn. *Gomesa forbesii*) 3. *O. ornithorhynchum*	1. Tempered, moderate resting period 2. Tempered, moderate resting period 3. Tempered	Medium-large	1. Yellow, brown to red-brown patterning 2. Brownish red, yellow patterning 3. Pink	Summer, fall
Paphiopedilum hybrids	Tempered/warm, slight resting period	Medium-large	Variable, yellow, greenish, white, red	Variable
Phalaenopsis hybrids	Warm, slight resting period	Medium-large	Variable, white, pink, carmine-red, yellow	Variable
Prosthechea fragans (syn. *Encyclia fragrans*)	Tempered, marked resting period	Medium-large	Creamy white, labellum with carmine-red stripes	Spring, summer
Rhynchostele bictoniensis (syn. *Odontoglossum, Rossioglossum*)	Tempered	Medium-large	Yellow/brown	Spring
Sophrocattleya hybrids	Tempered	Small to medium-large	Predominantly red, also carmine-red and pink-red	Variable
Stanhopea tigrina	Tempered	Medium-large	Creamy yellow/red-brown	Early summer
Vanda hybrids	Warm/tempered, high air humidity, plenty of light	Medium-large to large	Pink, red, blue, white, creamy yellow	Variable
Vuylstekeara hybrids	Tempered, moderate resting period	Medium-large, more seldom large	Variable, white, red/orange patterning	Variable

Slight resting period = slightly or hardly reduced temperature and substrate moisture;
Moderate resting period = somewhat lower temperature and only moderately moist plant substrate;
Marked resting period = more markedly reduced temperature, almost dry plant substrate.

Table 30. Orchids for the Garden

These days, it is both a matter of course and generally known that native orchids are strictly protected and may not be removed from the wild. In recent times, many orchids have been artificially propagated and bred for growing in gardens and are commercially available. Specific soil conditions are recommended for successful growing. In short, these are:

a. Site sunny to out of direct sun, sandy-loamy soil with calcareous rocks and some humus;

b. Site semi-shaded, sandy-loamy soil, plenty of humus with rocks for aeration;

c. Site sunny to semi-shaded, marshy to boggy, acidic soil with bark humus or raw humus from conifer needles (or also chopped-up conifer twigs and branches).

GENUS, SPECIES	SOIL REACTION AND WINTER HARDINESS	SITE AND VEGETATION CONDITIONS	HEIGHT (IN.), FLOWERING TIME
Bletilla striata Chinese ground orchid	Calcicolous, winter hardy	a. Also humic garden soil, moderately, moist	12 to 20, IV to VII
Calopogon tuberosus Grass pink	Calciphobous, winter hardy	c. Sunny, moist to wet	10 to 16, V to VI

Cypripedium
Lady's slipper
1. *C. calceolus*
2. *C. macranthos*
3. *C. parviflorum*
4. *C. reginae*
	1. Calcicolous
	2. Calcicolous
	3. Calciphpbous
	4. Calciphobous
	   All need light winter protection
		1. - b.
		   Semi-shaded, moderately moist
		2. - a.
		   Semi-shaded, moderately moist
		3. - b.
		   Semi-shaded, moderately moist
		4. - c.
		   Semi-shaded, moist to wet
			1. 12 to 28, V to VI
			2. 12 to 16, IV to VII
			3. 12 to 16, V to VIII
			4. 20 to 24, VI to VIII

Epipactis 'Sabine' Helleborine	Neutral to calcicolous, light winter protection required	b. Out of direct sun, moderately to uniformly moist	24 to 32, VI to VIII
Pleione limprichtii Indian crocus	Neutral, winter hardy	a./b. Semi-shaded, moderately moist	4 to 6 I (II), III to IV
Pogonia ophioglossoides Snakemouth orchid, rose pogonia	Calciphobous, winter hardy in favorable climates	c. Sunny, moist to wet	12 to 16, VI to VII

Table 31. The Most Important Ornamental Plant Pests

When combating pests with domestic remedies such as a soap solution (rinse with clear water afterward), spirit, nettle fertilizer tea, and so on, apply the remedy several times and repeat at brief intervals. Only when this proves ineffective, or in cases of severe infestation of many plants in the stand, should approved insecticides—that are otherwise not harmful to useful animals—be applied.

The preparations are mostly sprayed. Some have a systemic action in that they are taken up via the roots and transported to all parts of the plant in the sap flow. In this way, pests that cannot be reached directly by spraying are also targeted, as well as those which have protective defenses, such as scale insects. These remedies are also supplied as pesticide sticks.

Commercially available useful animals for biological control such as predatory mites, assassin bugs, parasitic wasps, and species of different nematodes, hoverflies, and lacewings can be used both outdoors and in winter gardens, closed flower windows, large plant display cabinets, and greenhouses.

PEST NAME	DAMAGE; DESCRIPTION OF PEST	PREVENTIVE MEASURES; CONTROL
Aphids (greenfly) On nearly all ornamental plants	Leaves wither or curl up; green, yellow, also black, wingless or winged insects, sucking mainly on new shoots.	As a preventive measure, wash off indoor plants often or spray them repeatedly with water in dry air; in cases of infestation, wash off indoor plans with a soap solution, in the garden spray plants with nettle fertilizer tea, deploy useful insects (such as lacewing larvae, ladybugs, assassin bugs, hoverflies, gall midges, and predatory wasps).
Garden rose tortrix (moth)	Leaves and shoot tips spun together in a web-like structure, leaves stuck to one another; light green, about ¾ in. long caterpillars feed on the buds and shoot tips.	Regular checks; collect the caterpillars until VII; they then pupate, producing new butterflies in VII (these lay eggs from which the destructive caterpillars hatch in the spring), destroy affected shoots in large stands.
Greenhouse whitefly, whitefly On many indoor and tub plants, also in the garden	Sticky secretions, yellow dots and spots on the leaves, the roughly 1⁄16 in. whitish animals fly up when the plant is touched; immobile larvae present on the leaf underside.	Avoid excessive fertilizer application for indoor and garden plants, avoid excessive warmth and humidity in rooms, greenhouses, and winter gardens; remove the larvae by mechanical means, deploy useful insects (predatory wasps, lacewing larvae, assassin bugs), spray with insecticides that are not harmful to useful animals only in cases of severe infestation.
Leaf miner (moth) On lilac, privet, forsythia, snowberry, ash tree	Gray flecks initially, then rolled-up leaves, later brown color; brown moth with white stripes, whitish green caterpillars up to ¼ in. long.	Collect caterpillars repeatedly and dispose of them with the household waste; predatory wasps lay their eggs in the larvae.
Leaf-rolling wasp	Leaves rolled into tubes; these mostly contain the 1⁄8 in. long caterpillars.	Regular checks, destroy affected leaves, the caterpillars migrate into the soil from VII /E. VIII.
Lily beetle On lilies, crown imperial, and fritillary	Eaten-out spots on leaves; red, shiny beetles, up to 1⁄8 in. in size, yellowish gray larvae.	Collect the beetles (which make a crowing sound), wash off the larvae with water (they will not develop further on the ground).
Mealybugs On indoor, tub, and garden plants	White, wax-like, water-repellent woolly cocoon or web; sucking larvae and adult insects especially present in the leaf axils.	Optimal site conditions for garden, indoor, and tub plants; in minor infestations, remove mechanically with wooden sticks, wash off with soap solution, deploy useful animals in the garden (larvae of the Australian ladybug or hoverfly larvae), in extreme cases spray with insecticides that are not harmful to useful animals.
Mole crickets In beds with seedlings and young plants	Young plants and seedlings wilt from digging damage, the larvae feed on shoots and roots; yellowish brown insect up to 2 in. long, lives underground during the day.	Natural enemies are birds and moles; destroy broods in their chambers, catch crickets with glasses embedded in the ground (with the opening flush with the soil), and release them into the wild.

PEST NAME	DAMAGE; DESCRIPTION OF PEST	PREVENTIVE MEASURES; CONTROL
Psyllids (jumping plant lice) On boxwood, wallflowers, and others	Sticky secretions (attract ants), bud drop; greenish yellow winged animals, greenish larvae.	Protect the psyllids's natural enemies such as spiders; remove lice from affected leaves by mechanical means, deploy parasitic wasps and lacewing larvae.
Red spider mites On many indoor and tub plants, also in the garden on roses, etc.	Yellowish dots on the leaves, in severe infestation leaf undersides with a white spun cocoon or web; yellowish or reddish animals 1/64 in. long (larvae and fully grown insects).	Avoid dry air in rooms, winter gardens, and overwintering rooms, spray often, protect ladybugs in the garden; wash off indoor plants repeatedly with a soap solution, deploy predatory mites in the garden, winter garden, and greenhouse, spray with insecticides that are not harmful to useful animals only in cases of severe infestation.
Root lice On summer flowers, indoor plants and tub plants	Growth disturbances, leaf yellowing; woolly wax secretions on the roots, and 1 ¼ in. size yellowish lice.	Ensure sufficient and uniform soil moisture, protect ground beetles; dip the roots of indoor plants in a soap solution (remember to rinse afterward) or wash out roots thoroughly and set them in new soil; in the garden, spray with nettle fertilizer tea.
Rose leafhopper	Yellowish white-speckled leaf upperside; light green (flightless) insects are present on the leaf underside, along with larvae (the eggs overwinter in the bark of young shoots).	Do not destroy natural enemies such as spiders; remove larvae by mechanical means or destroy affected leaves, also wash with soap solution or spray with nettle fertilizer tea; in large stands, deploy predatory mites or assassin bugs, and also nematodes, or, if necessary, combat with insecticides that are not harmful to useful animals.
Rose shoot sawfly, rose tip-infesting sawfly (two species)	Wilting of the shoot tips, boreholes, often white bore meal; yellowish white, ⅖ in. long larvae present inside the shoots.	Regular checks, the larvae already migrate into the soil in L. VI; destroy affected leaves (cut back into the healthy portion).
Scale insects On indoor and tub plants	Disfigured leaves, sticky secretions; fully grown animals have a brown armor and are immobile, younger animals are lighter and mobile.	Optimal site, proper care, regular checks; wash repeatedly with soap solution (including the leaf undersides), mechanical removal with wooden sticks, maybe additionally deploy predatory wasps.
Sitka spruce louse On conifers	Whitish yellow dots on the needles, brown coloration, needles later drop; green lice up to 1/16 in. long (similar to aphids).	Check in early spring (use a magnifying glass); deploy useful animals such as lacewings or hoverflies, also ladybugs or their larvae; in cases of severe infestation or presence on several trees, spray with insecticides that are not harmful to useful animals.
Slugs In the garden, greenhouse, and winter garden	Signs of eating, especially on delicate plant parts and young plants, also flower buds; red, brown, or gray mollusks ¾ to 3 in. long, without a shell.	Natural enemies such as hedgehogs and toads should be protected in the garden, do not water in the evenings (slugs are active at night and love moisture), erect slug-proof fences, in greenhouses place wood shavings (young lettuce plants) or cotton wool (orchid buds) around endangered plants; in the greenhouse and winter garden deploy toads, also catch slugs with beer in shallow bowls, set up upturned flowerpots in the garden (collect the slugs in the evening or morning), special slug baits are also an option.
Tarnished plant bugs On carnations, cherry laurel, China asters, chrysanthemums, dahlias, hydrangeas, roses, and others	Leaves and shoot tips deformed; animals six-legged, flat, up to ⅖ in. long, gray, brownish, green, also multicolored.	Major infestation possible in hot, dry summers; collect animals, in cases of severe infestation in the early morning hours when the animals are not yet moving around.

PEST NAME	DAMAGE; DESCRIPTION OF PEST	PREVENTIVE MEASURES; CONTROL
Thrips, thyanopter On amaryllus, azaleas, busy Lizzie, carnations, cyclamens, dragon arum, flamingo flowers, gladioli, lilies, ornamental asparagus, roses, umbrella grass, and others	Leaves have a silvery shine and later drop, along with twisted growth deformities of the shoots; black insect, around $1/82$ in. long, causing damage by sucking, larvae whitish.	In the case of indoor plants, ensure moist air, wash off leaves often, especially the undersides, or spray the entire plant, keep cooler in winter, in very dry conditions, briefly spray tubers to be overwintered, such as gladioli; in infestations of indoor plants, wash off with a soap solution; in the garden, on balconies, and in winter gardens, deploy predatory mites or assassin bugs; in the garden, also spray with nettle fertilizer tea.
Vine/cyclamen/ apple/raspberry/ strawberry weevil On many tub plants, also rhododendrons	Holes chewed in leaves; nocturnally active, flightless beetles, up to ½ in. long, yellowish white or light brown larvae live in the soil and feed on the roots.	Protect hedgehogs in the garden (they feed on the beetles); collect the beetles, examine the earth for larvae, deploy predatory nematodes against the larvae, potentially wash out with irrigation water.
Voles	Chewed and devoured flower bulbs, tunnels that are oval in cross-section are present just beneath the soil surface; rapid increase in the brownish rodents, nearly 8 in. long (including tail).	When tulip bulbs are available for the animals to feed on, they will only seldom take bait; domestic remedies include garlic cloves and rags soaked in diesel; a "vole frightener" (a device that releases vibrations or shock waves) is highly suitable.
Wireworms On moist soil, also on lawns	The click beetle larvae feed on the roots, tubers, or bulbs, and the plants wilt; orange-colored animals ½ to ¾ in. long	Examine root balls; attract the animals with slices of raw potato or carrot (press into the soil) and destroy them; frequent hoeing also disturbs the wireworms.

Table 32. The Most Important Ornamental Plant Diseases

Here, too, the same applies as for the introduction to **TABLE 31**; try combating the problem with conventional methods first and apply plant protectants only when these methods fail, and the infestation continues to worsen. If the plants are kept under optimal conditions and appropriate sites have been selected, the incidence of pests and diseases will be greatly reduced or almost absent. Healthy plants are well able to defend themselves against the diseases that pests often transmit.

Fungicides are helpful against fungal diseases. These can kill the fungi or inhibit their impact by disrupting their metabolism. Essential oils, which are present in many plants, can kill or inhibit fungal growth. Accordingly, infusions, in other words soaking plant parts in water, oil, or alcohol and applying them to affected plants, can inhibit fungal growth effectively. An example is a horsetail infusion: soak 1 lb. of horsetails in 5 quarts of water for 2 to 3 hours. The effect is enhanced by bringing the solution to a boil, letting it cool, filtering it, and repeatedly applying it diluted, or (in very severe infestations) undiluted, to the diseased plants. Garlic and chive infusions also have an antifungal effect: Pour 1 quart of boiling water over 2 oz. garlic (finely chopped) or leave 2 oz. of chives to soak in 1 quart of water for one day.

DISEASE NAME	DAMAGE	PREVENTIVE MEASURES; CONTROL
Black spot On roses	Yellowish, brown, or black spots with serrated borders on the leaves, which turn yellow and fall off	Protect rose foliage from moisture; destroy affected leaves.
Black spot disease On Christmas roses	Irregularly distributed, sharply delineated black spots on the leaf uppersides and undersides that lead to the death of the leaves	Sheltered place, damp, loamy soil, neutral to weakly alkaline, no waterlogging, apply fertilizer only sparingly; destroy affected plant parts.
Chlorosis (disruption of iron balance) Common in primroses, gardenias, azaleas, hydrangeas, etc.	Whitish yellow discolored leaves or leaf parts, the leaf ribs often stay green	Use only well-rotted plant substrate and no lime-containing irrigation water, avoid cold and wet on the roots; loosen the plant substrate (crumb structure) to facilitate iron uptake by the root tips, or replant in fresh substrate (pH value neutral to slightly acid, depending on the plant species).
Clematis wilt	Plants wilt suddenly and die for no apparent reason during full growth	Not too heavy soil, not too much moisture, plant at a sufficient depth, and provide shade for the lower plant parts.
Dahlia virus	Deformed, spotted, gray-green leaves, stunted (dwarf) growth and small flowers	Pest control, especially of sucking insects (disease transmission); destroy affected plants with tubers (dispose of them with the household waste).
Downy mildew	Mold-like fungal growth on the leaf undersides, brownish to dark violet spots on the uppersides	High soil moisture and air humidity along with poor light facilitate fungal growth; destroy affected leaves, spray repeatedly with diluted fresh milk, disinfect garden tools and plant containers.
Gladiolus rot On gladioli	Brown to black, paint-like, shiny spots on the tuber skins, with sunken patches underneath with a raised edge, paint-like secretions	Improve heavy, wet soil with sand, replant gladioli on the same site only after 5 years; destroy affected tubers along with their progeny, as well as recognizably diseased plants with reddish brown spots on the leaves that turn into blackish rotting patches.
Gray mold On snowdrops, cyclamens, tulips, etc.	Spring growth deformed and covered with whitish fungal growth or mold	Ensure optimal care, not too moist, removed died-off plant parts; keep plant drier, cut off diseased plant parts and destroy immediately.
Hard and dry rot On gladioli	Brownish to red-brown spots on the leaves, sunken, dark brown to black patches on the tubers, which shrink and become mummified in severe cases of infestation	Do not store tubers too warm in winter, check regularly for discoloration, switch site every year; destroy diseased tubers.
Leaf blight and burn On gladioli	Discolored leaves that turn yellow prematurely, leaf burn also infects tubers	Plant in a different place every year, not too densely, good nutrition; dispose of affected leaves, and dispose of affected tubers when removing them from the ground.

DISEASE NAME	DAMAGE	PREVENTIVE MEASURES; CONTROL
Leaf spot Frequently on dahlias	Yellowish, brown, gray, reddish, or blackish spots on the leaves, often with a dark border	Plant in a sunny, open site, no waterlogging or dryness, check constantly; remove affected leaves.
Powdery mildew	Gray-white, mealy covering (fungal network) on the leaf upperside, later the shoot tips and buds are also affected	Remedy cultivation errors, such as overly dense stands and unbalanced fertilizer application; destroy affected plant parts, spray repeatedly with diluted fresh milk, disinfect garden tools and plant containers.
Red fire disease On amaryllis	Red-brown, distended, also fissured patches on the flower stalk, leaves, and bulb skins, deformation and death of the leaves, also disfigured buds and flowers	Avoid excessive temperatures, do not keep excessively wet, provide plenty of fresh air, destroy diseased plant parts; additionally, apply warm water treatment to the bulbs for about 2 hours at 109°F.
Root rot (damping-off) On seedlings and cuttings	Roots turn brown or red and die off; the rot often spreads to the base of the stalk	Use disinfected soil for propagation by sowing and cuttings, airy warm sites, not too much moisture; destroy diseased plants.
Root rot and collar rot On gladioli	Plants wilt and die; rot spreads from the base of the bulb or from the root bases	Not too wet sites, good water drainage, no excess nitrogen fertilizer application; destroy diseased plants or flower bulbs, save the plant by taking cuttings of healthy plant parts.
Rust fungus On snapdragons, sweet Williams, roses, geraniums, fuchsias, house leeks, silver fir, etc.	Rust-red to brown sori, mostly on the leaf undersides, spreading over wide areas, on the leaf uppersides frequently as yellowish, translucent spots	Avoid moist garden places or waterlogging, water on the leaves facilitates the spread of the disease; spray repeatedly with nettle fertilizer tea, destroy affected plant parts and diseased plants.
Sclerotial disease On orchids	Plants often pale green, wilt and dry out, on diseased places yellowish, later dark brown, persistent fungal body around $1/82$ in. in size	Avoid excessively high temperatures and excessive moisture; destroy diseased plant parts, replace substrate completely.
Sclerotial disease On tulips	Bulbs produce only weak new shoots in spring or not at all, shoot often covered in fungal network, bulb reddish gray with dry rot	Switch planting site every 2 to 3 years; destroy diseased bulbs.
Soil fungi	On underground plant parts, freshly germinated seedlings, or young plants, there are dark colorations and rot visible on the root collar, and the roots die off	Optimal site conditions, no excessive fertilizer application, especially nitrogen; destroy diseased plants.
Sooty mold	Black, crustose layer on the leaves	Combat aphids, also greenhouse whitefly, since fungi establish themselves on their sticky secretions; wash off with soap solution, destroy severely affected leaves or plant parts.
Stem rot On azaleas	Brown discoloration of stem right above the soil, bark decays, leaves yellow, brown, ultimately black and withered	Avoid large temperature fluctuations, do not apply excess fertilizer, when transplanting do not set the plant deeper in the soil than it had been before; destroy affected plants.
Storage rot On gladioli tubers and dahlias	Base of the affected tubers can be pressed in, tuber brown and soft, often with sunken patches covered in mold	Do not bring moist, injured, or diseased tubers into winter storage, do not store too closely together, check regularly during winter and ventilate on frost-free days; destroy affected tubers.
Wilting diseases On China asters, cyclamens, gladioli, carnations, zinnias, etc.	Sudden wilting of the plant, especially on warm days, followed by yellowing of the leaves, with brown discoloration on the root collar or a layer of mold and orange-red discoloration of the leaf veins (nerves)	Plant wilting disease–resistant varieties, supply sufficient potassium and lime for the soil, no excessive nitrogen fertilizer application, no excessive moisture, do not plant too densely; in cases of infestation, destroy the entire plant stand, change of site essential.

ILLUSTRATION CREDITS

INDEX

Aaron's beard, 335
Abeliophyllum distichum, 322
Abies, 256, 328, 334
Abies balsamea 'Nana', 334
Abies concolor, 328
Abies koreana, 334
Abies lasiocarpa var. *arizonica*, 328
Abies nordmanniana, 328
Abies procera 'Glauca', 328
Abies veitchii, 328
Abutilon, 96, 383
Abyssinian gladiolus, 279
Acacia / acacia, 383
Acacia dealbata, 383
Acacia floribunda, 383
Acacia retinodes, 383
Acaena magellanica, 349
Acalypha hispida, 383
acaricides (miticides), 37
Acer campestre, 331
Acer japonicum 'Aconitifolium', 322
Acer palmatum, 334
Achillea, 343, 349
Achillea ageratifolia, 349
Achillea chrysocoma, 349
Achillea clypeolata, 349
Achillea filipendulina, 343
Achillea millefolium, 343
Achillea ptarmica, 343
Achillea tomentosa, 349
Achillea umbellata, 349
acidanthera, 370
acidified soil, 12, 121, 182, 295, 309
acid-loving plants, 13, 295
Aconitum, 253
Acorus calamus, 357
Actaea species, 145, 343
Actinidia, 340
Actinidia arguta, 340
Actinidia kolomikta, 340
Adam's needle, 348
adderwort, 357
Adenium obesum, 40
Adiantum, 38, 300, 383
Adiantum pedatum, 364
Adonis amurensis, 58
Adonis vernalis, 349
adpressa aurea English yew, 337
Aechmea / aechmea, 35, 40, 99, 383
Aeonium / aeonium, 40, 176, 383
Aethionema, 349
Aethionema armenum, 349
Aethionema grandiflorum, 349

Aethusa cynapium, 182
African daisy, 124, 256, 372, 381
African hemp, 40, 96, 97, 299, 395
African lily, 383
African tulip, 395
African violet, 97, 261, 393
Agapanthus campanulatus, 383
Agave / agave, 34, 40, 383
Agave americana, 383
Ageratum / ageratum, 124, 128, 174, 178, 256
Ageratum houstonianum, 372, 380
Aglaonema / aglaonema, 35
Aglaonema commutatum, 383
Agrostemma, 257
Agrostemma githago, 372
air plants, 99, 395
Ajuga, 349
Ajuga genevensis, 349
Ajuga reptans, 349, 355
Akebia quinata, 340
Alaska fern, 365
Alberta spruce, 329
Alberta white spruce, 329
Albizia / albizia, 383
Albizia julibrissin, 289, 383
Albizia lophantha, 383
Alcea, 195, 240
Alcea rosea, 145, 372
Alisma plantago-aquatica, 132, 357
Alison, 87, 310, 349
Allamanda cathartica 'Hender-sonii', 383
Alleghany service berry, 322
allergic reactions, 184
Allium aflatunense 'Purple Sensa-tion', 366
Allium / allium, 239, 366
Allium christophii, 366
Allium giganteum, 366
Allium karataviense, 366
Allium moly, 145, 366
Allium oreophilum, 366
Allium schubertii, 366
allotment gardens. *See* communi-ty (allotment) gardens
Aloe species / aloe, 40, 384
alpine aster, 350
alpine avens, 351
alpine bells, 355
alpine currant, 332
alpine phlox, 352
alpine plants, 82, 278

alpine rose, 326
alpine violets, 37
Alstroemeria, 366
Alstroemeria aurea, 366
Alstroemeria ligtu × *Alstroemeria haemantha* with varieties, 366
Alstroemeria ligtu hybrids, 366
altar lily, 371
Althaea officinalis, 145
alumroot, 355
Alyssum, 87, 349
Alyssum moellendorfianum, 349
Alyssum montanum, 349
Alyssum saxatile, 145, 350
Alyssum saxatilis, 350
Amaranthus caudatus, 372
amaryllis, 36, 137, 242, 389, 403
Amelanchier, 322
Amelanchier laevis, 322
Amelanchier lamarckii, 322
American evergreen, 395
American maidenhair, 364
Amorpha, 130
Amstelveen barberry, 334
Amur pheasant's eye, 58
Amur silver grass, 363
Amur stonecrop, 354
Anagallis, 177
Anagallis tenella, 380
Ananas, 384
Ananas comosus, 384
Ananas nanus, 384
Anaphalis triplinervis, 349
Androsace, 349
Androsace primuloides, 349
Androsace sarmentosa, 349
Anemone / anemone, 310, 343, 366
Anemone apennina, 366
Anemone blanda, 366
Anemone coronaria, 258, 370
Anemone hupehensis, 134, 253
Anemone hupehensis var. *japonica*, 343
Anemone sylvestris, 343
Anemone tomentosa, 343
angel's tears, 394
angel's trumpet, 34, 135, 258, 385
animals, useful, 24–25, 145–148, 183–184, 246, 318
annual candytuft, 122–123, 375
annual climbing plants, 92–93

annual dry flowers and dry grasses, 379 (table)
annual gaillardia, 374
annual larkspur, 123
annual morning glory, 373
annual phlox, 377
annual pink, 170, 374
annuals, cool-season, 131, 257
annual savory, 117
annual sun marigold, 124
annual sweet alyssum, 123
Antennaria dioica, 349
Anthemis marschalliana, 349
anthracnose, 320
Anthurium, 384
Anthurium andreanum hybrids, 384
Anthurium scherzerianum hybrids, 384
Antirrhinum, 92, 131, 170
Antirrhinum majus, 372
Apennine windflower, 366
Aphelandra, 35
Aphelandra squarrosa, 384
aphids (greenfly), 95, 146, 196, 201, 228, 318, 399
apple tree, 101, 325
aquatic plants, 89–90, 91–92, 132, 220, 287, 357–359 (table)
Aquilegia, 82, 145, 343
Arabis, 349
Arabis ×*arendsii*, 349
Arabis caucasica, 349
Arabis procurrens, 349
aralia ivy, 179, 388
Araucaria araucana, 129, 328
Araucaria heterophylla, 129, 384
arborvitae, 333, 336, 337
Arbutus, 134, 280
Arbutus unedo, 384
Arctanthemum arcticum, 349
Arctotis venusta, 372
Argyranthemum frutescens, 135, 384
Aristolochia, 81, 276
Aristolochia macrophylla, 340
Arizona cork bark fir, 328
Armeria maritima, 350
arolla pine, 330
aromatic herbs. *See* herbs
arrowhead, 359
arrowhead vine, 395
artillery plant, 392
arugula, 251
arum lily, 371

Asarina, 93
Asarum, 121
Asarum europaeum, 355
Asiatic poppy, 195, 346
Asiatic water plantain, 357
asparagus
    asparagus dams, 75, 113–114
    fertilizing, 75, 114, 150,
      191–192, 306
    harvesting, 74, 113–114, 160
    hoeing, 214
    pests and diseases, 114, 192,
      272, 318, 320
    planting / sowing, 26, 73–74,
      114, 285, 309, 311, 312
    white, 73, 75, 113, 191, 272
Asparagus (ornamental), 384
Asparagus aethiopicus
    'Myersii', 384
    'Sprengeri', 384
Asparagus crispus, 384
Asparagus declinatus, 384
Asparagus densiflorus
    'Meyerei', 137
    'Myersii', 384
    'Sprengeri', 137, 384
asparagus fern, 137, 384
Asparagus plumosus, 137, 384
Asparagus setaceus, 137, 384
Aspidistra elatior, 135, 384
Asplenium nidus, 384
Asplenium scolopendrium, 364
Asplenium trichomanes, 364
"assassin" bugs, 146
Aster alpinus, 87, 350
Aster amellus, 343
Aster / aster, 134, 145, 310, 343, 350
Aster dumosus, 87, 350
Aster novae-angliae, 343
Aster novi-belgii, 343
Aster tongolensis, 343
Astilbe ×*arendsii*, 343
Astilbe / astilbe, 13, 87, 220, 278,
    343
Astilbe chinensis var. *pumila*, 343
Athyrium, 364
Athyrium filix-femina, 364
Athyrium niponicum 'Metallicum',
    364
Atlantic cedar, 328
Atlas cedar, 328
aubergine, 149, 307, 312, 394
aubretia, 350
Aubrieta deltoidea, 350
Aucuba, 280
Aucuba japonica, 134, 135, 385
auricula, 353
Aurinia saxatilis, 145, 350
Australian fan palm, 390
autumn catchfly, 354

autumn crocus, 134, 240, 366
avens, 345, 351
Azalea / azalea, 322, 326
    as acid-loving, 13
    fertilizing, 96
    indoor azalea, 37, 38, 393
    north-facing placement, 135
    pests and diseases, 401, 402,
      403
    post-flowering care, 96
    water requirements, 38, 242

Babiana stricta, 370
baboon flower, 370
baby jade, 387
baby primrose, 393
baby rubber plant, 392
baby's breath, 345, 351, 375
baby's tears, 394
bachelor's button, 373
balcony boxes, 95, 201, 380–382
    (table)
balcony plants, 241
Balkan blue grass, 363
Balkan daphne, 335
Balkan windflower, 366
balloon flower, 347
balsam, 375, 390
bamboo palm, 393
banana, 175, 258, 391
barbed wire, 143
barberry, 81, 322, 331, 334
bark humus, 11, 13, 205, 207, 221,
    288
bark mulch, 13
barren brome, 379
bar-room plant, 384
basil, 167, 216, 312
basket asparagus, 384
basket plant, 388
Bassia scoparia 'Trichophylla',
    125, 372
bay, 280
bay tree, 34, 139, 224
beach sunflower, 375
beans, 65, 177, 308, 309, 318, 320.
    See also broad (fava) beans;
    bush beans; climbing
    beans
bean tree, 325
bearberry cotoneaster, 87, 334
bearskin fescue, 362
beauty bush, 325
bed measuring stick, 21
beds
    double or triple digging, 14,
      264–265
    flowerbeds, 119
    raised beds, 266
    tools for preparing, 17–18, 21

vegetable beds, 10, 21, 30,
    48–49
beebalm, 346
beech, 117, 118, 276, 296
beer in pest control, 102–103
bees, 145, 246
beetle hotel, 147
beets
    fertilizing, 306
    harvesting, 271–272, 315
    planting / sowing, 28, 75, 113,
      191, 232, 309, 312, 315
    storing, 271
begonia, 385
    extending bloom, 257
    fertilizing, 177
    fibrous rooted begonia, 372
    indoor, 203
    king begonia, 385
    leaf cuttings, 97
    leaf loss and light require-
      ments, 298
    overwintering, 32–33, 263, 280
    planting, 94, 111, 135, 174, 177
    rex begonia, 385
    succulent begonia, 372
    tuberous begonia, 94, 135, 174,
      263, 370, 380
    wax begonia, 380
Begonia Elatior Group, 385
Begonia Rex Cultorum Group,
    203, 298, 385
Begonia Semperflorens Cultorum
    Group, 174, 175, 178, 372,
    380
Begonia Tuberhybrida Group,
    370, 380
bellflower, 25, 60, 139, 310, 343,
    350, 385
Bellis, 95, 131, 221
Bellis perennis, 240, 372, 380
belvedere, 372
Benjamin fig, 35, 388
Berberis, 81, 322, 331, 334
Berberis buxifolia, 130, 322, 331
    'Nana', 331
Berberis candidula, 334
Berberis ×*frikartii* 'Amstelveen',
    334
Berberis gagnepainii var. *lanceifolia*,
    322
Berberis julianae, 322
Berberis ×*stenophylla*, 322
Berberis thunbergii, 331
    'Atropurpurea', 322, 331
    'Atropurpurea Nana', 334
Berberis verruculosa, 331
Bergenia, 278
Bergenia cordifolia, 343

berry bladder fern, 364
betony, 354
Bieberstein's crocus, 240
biennials, 181, 240, 288, 372–378
    (table)
bigleaf hydrangea, 324
Billbergia / billbergia, 40, 385
bindweed, 182
biotopes, 287
bird of paradise, 261, 395
birds
    birdbaths, 92, 144, 246
    blue tits, 22, 24, 64, 284
    cat predation, 64, 144
    feeders and feeding, 9, 22–24,
      246, 284
    nesting boxes, 21–22, 64, 144,
      246
    retaining natural food sourc-
      es, 23
    usefulness, 21–22, 145, 147–148
Birds Canada, 23
bird's eye, 354
bird's nest bromeliad, 391
birthwort, 81, 276
bishop's hat, 121, 355
bishop's mitre, 355
Bistorta affinis, 350
Bistorta officinalis, 357
black bean aphids, 158, 190
black broom, 335
black-eyed Susan, 55, 93, 377
black hellebore, 345
black pine, 330
black root, 348
black salsify (viper's grass)
    fertilizing, 214, 232, 306
    harvesting, 272, 315
    hoeing, 160, 214
    planting / sowing, 53, 72–73,
      309, 315
    powdery mildew, 191, 321
    winter protection, 285
black spot disease, 80, 172, 402
bladder senna, 256
blanket flower, 344
blazing star, 345
Blechnum, 364
Blechnum penna-marina, 364
Blechnum spicant, 364
bleeding heart, 134, 310, 344
Bletilla striata, 175, 398
blood flower, 137, 394
blue alpine daisy, 350
blue atlas cedar, 328
bluebeard, 145, 322, 334
bluebell, 220
blue-eyed African daisy, 372
blue-eyed Mary, 356
blue fescue, 362

blue flag, 357
blue hound's tongue, 124
blue lungwort, 356
blue oat grass, 94
blue passionflower, 391
blue poppy, 195
blue potato bush, 390
blue spiraea, 334
blue spruce, 329
blue star juniper, 129, 336
blue tansy, 145, 377
boat lily, 395
bog arum, 357
bog bean, 358
bog pimpernel, 380
bok choy (pak choi), 212–213,
    230–231, 306, 312, 315
borage, 117, 118, 167, 194, 312
boron deficiency, 113, 115, 320
Bosnian pine, 330
Boston daisy, 384
Boston fern, 300, 391
Boston ivy, 240–241, 341
    'Veitchii', 241
Botrytis paeoniae, 170
bottlebrush bush, 280
bottle gardens, 39
Bougainvillea / bougainvillea, 175,
    258, 299
Bougainvillea glabra, 299, 385
boundaries in garden design, 142,
    143, 274
Bouteloua gracilis, 362
bowstring hemp, 40, 139, 259, 393
box honeysuckle, 332
boxleaf holly, 331, 335
boxwood, 131, 148, 276, 331, 400
boxwood hebe, 335
branches, growing plants on,
    297–298
brandy bottle, 358
bridewort, 31, 57, 310, 327, 333
British Hedgehog Preservation
    Society, 183
British Trust for Ornithology, 23
Briza, 125
Briza maxima, 379
broad (fava) beans
    as catch crop, 160
    fertilizing, 112, 158, 190, 306
    harvesting, 190, 315
    pests, 158
    planting / sowing, 52, 70, 309,
        315
    watering, 158, 190
    yield, 158
broccoli, 65, 104, 148, 208, 306, 315
bromeliads, 35, 38, 40, 99, 281, 298
Brompton stock, 376
Bromus sterilis, 379

broom, 134, 323, 335
Browallia speciosa, 385
brown rot, 229, 321
Brugmansia, 34, 135, 175, 258
Brugmansia arborea, 385
Brunnera macrophylla, 355
brushwood protection, 24, 32, 148,
    278, 297
Brussels sprouts
    diseases, 320, 321
    fertilizing, 160, 214, 306
    harvesting, 296, 315
    hoeing, 214
    planting / sowing, 67, 150,
        159–160, 191, 309, 312, 315
    watering, 214
Buddleja, 81, 130, 145, 276, 288, 322
Buddleja alternifolia, 322
Buddleja davidii, 322
Buddleja ×weyeriana, 322
bugbane, 145, 343
bugle, 349, 355
Buglossoides, 355
bulbocodium, 369
bulbs and tubers, generally
    digging and storing, 199–200,
        205, 220, 278
    diseases, 43, 200, 287
    non-winter-hardy bulb and
        tuber plants, 370–371
        (table)
    planting, 171, 200, 239, 252
    winter-hardy perennial bulb
        and tuber plants, 366–369
        (table)
bulrush, 359
Burkwood's daphne, 335
Burmese fishtail palm, 386
burning bush, 125, 326, 344, 372
Burro's tail, 394
bush beans, 148–149, 184–185,
    208–209
bush (dwarf) beans, 306, 315
bush roses, 127
bushy aster, 343, 350
busy Lizzie, 54, 175, 177, 375, 381,
    390
Butomus umbellatus, 357
buttercup, 359
butterflies, 145
butterfly bush, 81, 130, 145, 276, 322
butterfly flower, 377
butterwort, 356
buttonbush, 322
button snakeroot, 345
button squash, 165, 306, 315
Buxus, 276
Buxus sempervirens
    'Blauer Heinz', 331
    'Suffruticosa', 331

cabbage / cabbage species. See also
    savoy cabbage
    Chinese cabbage, 209, 229,
        247, 267, 306, 312, 316
    crop rotation, 108, 159, 160,
        209, 251, 311
    fertilizing, 109, 229
    harvesting, 230, 270, 285
    pests and diseases, 165, 201,
        214, 230, 318, 320, 321
    planting / sowing, 108–109,
        156, 191, 310
    red cabbage, 108–109, 191,
        214, 270, 307, 309, 313, 317
    storing, 270
    watering, 229
    white cabbage, 75–76, 109,
        215, 270, 308, 310, 314, 317
    winter cabbage, 270
cabbage gall weevil, 108, 166, 230
cabbage moth, 318
cabbage palm, 390
cabbage root fly, 104, 108, 318
cabbage tree, 387
cabbage white butterfly, 201, 318
cacti, 39, 97, 176, 258, 385
Calamagrostis ×acutiflora, 362
calamus, 357
Calceolaria, 178, 385
Calceolaria integrifolia, 380
Calendula, 123, 257
Calendula officinalis, 372
calico bush, 325
California lilac, 31, 130, 322
California poppy, 124, 374
Calla palustris, 357
Callistemon, 280
Callistemon citrinus, 385
Callistephus, 92
Callistephus chinensis, 373
Calluna, 173
Calluna vulgaris, 145, 334
Calocedrus decurrens, 328
Calochortus, 370
Calopogon tuberosus, 398
Caltha palustris, 92, 357
Calycanthus floridus, 322
camass (or camas), 239, 366
Camassia, 239, 366
Camassia cusickii, 366
Camassia quamash, 366
Camellia / camellia, 37, 38, 96, 175,
    242, 258, 290
Camellia japonica, 385
Campanula, 343, 350, 385
Campanula carpatica, 350
Campanula cochleariifolia, 350
Campanula fragilis, 60, 139, 385
Campanula isophylla, 60, 139, 385
Campanula latifolia, 343

Campanula medium, 195, 240,
    288, 373
Campanula persicifolia, 343
Campanula portenschlagiana,
    350
Campanula poscharskyana, 350
Campanula rotundifolia, 134
campion, 346, 348, 354
Campsis, 340
Campsis radicans, 340
Campsis ×tagliabuana, 340
Canadian hemlock, 330, 337
Canary Island date palm, 392
candelabra primrose, 353
candytuft, 33, 122–123, 128, 310,
    352, 375
Canna / canna lily, 94, 174, 263, 279
Canna indica, 370
Canterbury bells, 195, 240, 373
Cape jasmine, 389
Capeland African hemp, 40
Cape leadwort, 393
Cape primrose, 179, 395
capers, 234
Capsicum annuum Cerasiforme
    Group, 386
Carex, 362
Carex grayi, 362
Carex morrowii 'Variegata', 362
Carex pendula, 362
Carex sylvatica, 121, 355
Carlina acaulis ssp. caulescens,
    350
carline thistle, 350
carnation, 350, 374, 380
    cutting back, 59
    light requirements, 178
    overwintering, 33, 34, 281
    pests and diseases, 254, 400,
        403
    planting / sowing, 132, 170,
        240, 310
Carolina allspice, 322
carpet broom, 335
Carpinus, 276
Carpinus betulus, 30, 58, 81, 274,
    331
carrion flower, 40
carrot fly, 112, 159, 201, 318
carrots
    early, 52, 69, 306
    fertilizing, 115, 212, 306
    harvesting, 52, 189, 315
    late, 306
    overwintering, 270
    planting / sowing, 52, 69,
        111–112, 157, 189, 212, 309,
        315
    using row covers, 112, 159
    yellowing, 166

Caryopteris, 145
Caryopteris ×*clandonensis*, 334
    'Grand Bleu', 322
    'Heavenly Blue', 334
Caryota, 36
Caryota mitis, 386
cascade roses, 80, 338
cast-iron plant, 384
catchfly, 346, 348, 354
caterpillars, 145, 228
cathedral bells, 40
catmint, 128, 352
catnip, 219
cat's foot, 349
cattail, 359
Cattleya, 98, 396
Caucasian campion, 354
Caucasian fir, 134, 328
cauliflower
    fertilizing, 108, 148, 184, 247,
        306
    frost protection, 104, 247
    harvesting, 104, 184, 315
    pests and diseases, 104, 319,
        320, 321
    planting / sowing, 65, 67,
        103–104, 184, 208, 309, 312,
        315
    watering, 110, 184
Ceanothus, 31, 130, 322
Ceanothus ×*delilianus* 'Gloire de
    Versailles', 322
Ceanothus fendleri, 322
Ceanothus impressus 'Victoria', 322
Cedrus atlantica
    'Glauca', 328
    'Glauca Pendula', 328
Celastrus orbiculatus, 340
celeriac (root celery)
    diseases, 320, 321
    fertilizing, 187, 306
    harvesting, 268
    low temperature sensitivity,
        73
    planting / sowing, 155, 309,
        312, 315
celery
    bleaching process, 247
    diseases, 187
    fertilizing, 184, 187, 207, 211
    harvesting, 268, 316
    low temperature sensitivity,
        73
    planting / sowing, 148, 184,
        187, 312, 316
    storing tubers, 26, 269
celery scurf
Celosia argentea var. *cristata*, 373
Centaurea, 278, 344
Centaurea cyanus, 257, 373

Centaurea dealbata, 344
Centaurea macrocephala, 344
Centaurea montana, 344
century plant, 383
Cephalanthus occidentalis, 322
Cephalotaxus, 129
Cephalotaxus harringtonia 'Fasti-
    giata', 129
Cerastium, 350
Cerastium grandiflorum, 350
Cerastium tomentosum, 350
Ceratophyllum submersum, 90, 357
Cereus, 176
Ceylon cinnamon, 224
Chaenomeles, 323
Chaenomeles japonica, 323
    'Cido', 323
Chaenomeles speciosa
    'Exima', 323
    'Nivalis', 323
Chaenomeles ×*superba* 'Andenken
    an Karl Ramcke, 323
Chamaecyparis, 130, 328, 334
Chamaecyparis lawsoniana, 328,
    331
Chamaecyparis nootkatensis 'Pen-
    dula', 328
Chamaecyparis obtusa, 87, 334
    'Nana Gracilis', 87
Chamaecyparis pisifera, 334
Chamaecytisus purpureus, 334
Chamaedorea, 36
Chamaedorea elegans, 386
Chamaerops, 36, 175, 280
Chamaerops humilis, 278
chamomile / chamomile family,
    125, 196, 349
chard, 67–68, 111, 306, 309, 316
cheddar pink, 171, 350
Cheiranthus cheiri, 95
chenault coralberry, 327
cherry apple, 57
cherry laurel, 81, 130, 256, 288,
    326, 400
cherry pie, 389
cherry tree, 31
cherry twigs, 299
chervil, 77, 166, 194, 217, 234, 250,
    273, 312
Chiastophyllum oppositifolium, 355
chickens, 102
chicory, 28, 49, 149, 209, 267, 273,
    306, 316
Chile pine, 129, 328
chili pepper, 235
China aster, 92, 201, 310, 373,
    400, 403
China fir, 328
Chinese chives, 54
Chinese evergreen, 383

Chinese fountain grass, 363
Chinese ground orchid, 175, 398
Chinese hibiscus, 96, 135, 258,
    299, 389
Chinese juniper, 129, 329
Chinese silver grass, 363
Chinese windmill palm, 36, 134,
    280, 289
Chinese wisteria, 341
Chinese witch hazel, 324
Chionanthus virginicus, 288
Chionodoxa, 239, 366
Chionodoxa forbesii, 366
Chionodoxa sardensis, 366
chippers and shredders, 11
chives, 73, 117, 217, 251, 273, 306,
    312, 316
Chlorophytum, 97, 139
Chlorophytum comosum, 386
chlorosis, 402
chocolate vine, 340
Christmas cactus, 40, 260, 394
Christmas plant, 388
Christmas rose, 33, 278, 293, 297,
    345, 402
Christmas star, 298
Christ thorn, 388
chrysanthemum, 134, 200, 253,
    310, 344
Chrysanthemum carinata, 375
Chrysanthemum ×*grandiflorum*,
    200, 253, 344
Chrysanthemum parthenium, 378
Chrysanthemum segetum, 375
Chusan palm, 395
cider gum, 388
Cimicifuga, 145, 343
cineraria, 392
Cinnamomum aromaticum, 224
Cinnamomum cassia, 224
Cinnamomum verum, 224
Cinnamomum zeylanicum, 224
cinnamon, 224
cinquefoil, 353
Cissus, 139, 386
Cissus alata, 179, 386
Cissus antarctica, 386
Cissus discolor, 386
Cissus rhombifolia, 179, 386
×*Citrofortunella microcarpa*, 135
Citrus / citrus, 386
    fertilizing, 222
    overwintering, 224, 258, 299
    as tub plant, 34, 135, 175
    watering, 179, 222, 224
citrus tree (grapefruit, lime, man-
    darin, orange, lemon), 386
Clarkia unguiculata, 373
cleaning plants, 298
Clematis alpina, 342

Clematis / clematis, 81, 130–131,
    276, 288, 340, 342 (table)
clematis wilt, 402
Cleome hassleriana, 373
Cleome spinosa, 373
Clethra alnifolia 'Rosea', 323
cliff maids, 352
cliff stonecrop, 354
climbing beans, 115, 161–162, 192,
    307, 316, 320
climbing clematis, 81
climbing fig, 35, 297, 388
climbing hydrangea, 80–81, 340
climbing lily, 176, 279, 370
climbing nasturtium, 166, 176
climbing plants, generally, 92–93,
    143, 198, 340–341 (table)
climbing roses, 80, 127–128, 218,
    338
Clivia, 60, 137, 259
Clivia miniata, 179, 386
clove pink, 374
clovers, 65
clubroot, 11, 230, 320
club rush, 359
Cobaea scandens, 55, 92, 176, 373
cockscomb, 373
cockspur coral tree, 200, 258, 289,
    299, 388
Codiaeum variegatum, 386
Coffea arabica, 386
coffee, 386
cogon grass, 362
Colchicum, 366
Colchicum autumnale, 240
cold frames
    constructing, 47–48
    maintaining, 16, 228, 294
    packing heated, 49–50
    planting / sowing, 28, 49, 66,
        92
    raising young plants in, 50
    transportable, 48
    ventilating, 66, 104–105, 296
cold whiskey plant, 325
coleus, 96, 139, 392
Coleus blumei, 96, 139, 392
Colorado beetle, 182
Colorado fir, 328
Colorado spruce, 329
columbine, 82, 134, 145, 310, 343
Columnea / columnea, 386
Columnea gloriosa, 386
Columnea microphylla, 386
Colutea, 256
common arrowhead, 359
common beech, 331
common box, 331
common broom, 323
common camellia, 385

common chickweed, 142, 182
common elder, 327, 332
common fennel, 107
common fumitory, 182
common garden peony, 346
common holly, 331
common hornbeam, 30, 58, 81, 274, 276, 331
common immortelle, 379
common ivy, 335, 340
common juniper, 129, 329
common lilac, 327
common mallow, 145
common mignonette, 377
common myrtle, 391
common pearl bush, 324
common peony, 346
common polypody, 356, 365
common spindle, 324
common spruce, 329
common thrift, 350
common triteleia, 369
common water moss, 132
common yarrow, 343, 349
common yew, 330, 333
community (allotment) gardens, 28, 142, 169, 251
compact Bosnian pine, 330
compost and composting, 11–13, 15, 102, 266
compost heaps, 11, 102, 123, 207, 246, 266
compost thermometer, 29, 54
coneflower, 145, 278, 347
conifer branches as protective covering, 287–288
conifers, 32, 128, 173, 237–238, 256, 327–330 (table)
Consolida ajacis, 373
Consolida / consolida, 123, 257, 373
Consolida regalis, 373
container plants
    frost effects, 94, 134, 175, 257–258, 280, 288
    overwintering, 34, 135, 280
Convallaria majalis, 134, 355
Convolvulus tricolor, 124, 373
coppicing, 56
coral bells, 310, 351
Cordyline fruticosa, 387
Cordyline terminalis, 387
Coreopsis, 134, 145, 198, 253, 344
Coreopsis grandiflora, 344
Coreopsis tinctoria, 373
Coreopsis verticillata, 344
corkscrew hazel, 323
corky spindle, 324
corn, ornamental, 379. See also sweet corn
corn buttercup, 182

corncockle, 257, 372
cornel, 323
cornelian cherry, 323, 331
cornflower, 257, 373
Cornish heath, 335
corn lily, 174, 370
corn marigold, 375
corn poppy, 376
Cornus, 323
Cornus alba, 323
Cornus florida, 323
Cornus kousa, 57, 323
Cornus mas, 323, 331
Corsican pine, 330
Cortaderia selloana, 94, 173, 287, 362
Cortusa matthioli, 355
Corydalis cava, 145
Corydalis / corydalis, 145, 353, 356
Corydalis lutea, 353, 356
Corylopsis spicata, 323
Corylus, 33, 323
Corylus avellana
    'Aurea', 57, 323
    'Contorta', 323
Corylus maxima 'Purpurea', 57, 323
Cosmos bipinnatus, 373
Cotoneaster acutifolius, 331
Cotoneaster adpressus, 334
Cotoneaster bullatus, 323
Cotoneaster / cotoneaster, 256, 323, 331, 334
Cotoneaster dammeri, 87, 334
Cotoneaster dielsianus var. dielsianus, 331
Cotoneaster divaricatus, 331
Cotoneaster horizontalis, 323
    'Saxatilis', 334
Cotoneaster microphyllus, 323
Cotoneaster salicifolius 'Parktep-pich', 334
cottage gardens, 25
cottage peony, 346
couch grass, 14, 82, 182, 265
cowslip, 347, 353
craneberry, 351
crape myrtle, 134, 280, 390
Crassula, 40
Crassula ovata, 179, 387
Crataegus laevigata 'Paul's Scar-let', 323
cream bush, 324
creeping and climbing woody plants, 340–341 (table)
creeping clematis, 81
creeping cotoneaster, 334
creeping English yew, 337
creeping fig, 35, 297, 388
creeping jenny, 356
creeping juniper, 336

creeping phlox, 352
creeping snapdragon, 93
creeping zinnia, 123, 178, 377
cretan brake, 300
crimson bottlebrush, 385
crimson magnolia, 325
crinum, 370
Crinum ×powellii, 370
Crocosmia, 126, 279
Crocosmia ×crocosmiiflora, 366
Crocus / crocus, 58, 134, 220–221, 227, 239, 240, 281, 366
Crocus speciosus, 240
crop rotation, 25–26, 26–27, 311 (table). See also planting / sowing under specific plant names
crossanda, 258
Crossandra infundibuliformis, 387
cross-leaved heath, 335
croton, 386
crowfoot, 359
crown imperial, 145, 240, 367
crown of thorns, 40, 388
cruciferous species, 251
Cryptanthus, 387
Cryptomeria japonica, 328, 334
cucumbers
    fertilizing, 186, 187, 210, 307
    growing in cold frames, 106–107, 152
    harvesting, 154, 210–211, 229, 316
    house cucumbers, 105–106, 150–151, 186, 210
    pests and diseases, 319, 320, 321
    planting / sowing, 105, 152–154, 309, 312, 316
    pruning or thinning, 152, 153–54, 186
    varieties, 153, 210
    watering, 186–187, 210
    wind protection, 154
    yields, 152, 186, 210
cucurbit (gourd) plant family, 169
Culver's root, 348
Cunninghamia lanceolata, 328
cup-and-saucer vine, 55, 92, 176–177, 373
Cuphea ignea, 178, 380
×Cuprocyparis leylandii, 328, 331
Curcuma / curcuma, 387
curly kale
    fertilizing, 248, 307
    harvesting, 28–29, 51, 185, 263, 268, 316
    planting / sowing, 150, 186, 210, 309, 316
    winter protection, 296

currant, 332
cushion pink, 354
cushion plant, 197
cushion spurge, 351
cutleaf lace shrub, 327, 333
cut-leaved mallow, 145
cutworms, 147, 166, 318
Cyclamen coum, 279, 367
Cyclamen / cyclamen, 96, 202, 260, 279, 281, 290, 367, 403
Cyclamen hederifolium, 279, 367
Cyclamen persicum, 260, 387
Cyclamen purpurascens, 279, 367
Cymbalaria, 355
Cymbalaria muralis, 355
Cymbalaria pallida, 355
Cynoglossum, 124
Cyperus, 96, 139, 175, 202, 258, 387
Cyperus alternifolius, 387
Cyperus haspan, 387
Cyperus longus, 357
Cypripedium, 175, 398
Cyrtanthus, 36, 137, 179
Cyrtanthus elatus, 387
Cystopteris bulbifera, 364
Cytisus, 323, 335
Cytisus decumbens, 335
Cytisus ×kewensis, 335
Cytisus nigricans 'Cyni', 335
Cytisus ×praecox, 81, 276, 323
Cytisus scoparius, 323

daffodil, 199, 239, 252, 253, 310, 368, 369
Dahlberg daisy, 178, 382
Dahlia / dahlia, 370, 380
    extending bloom, 255
    leaf spot, 403
    overwintering, 32–33, 55, 263, 278
    planting, 133, 310
    removing flowers, 241
    staking, 181, 197
dahlia virus, 402
daisies, 95, 131, 221, 240, 372, 380
danica arborvitae, 337
Daphne blagayana, 335
Daphne ×burkwoodii, 335
Daphne cneorum, 81, 335
Daphne / daphne, 31, 57, 59, 256, 335
Daphne mezereum, 323
Darjeeling banana, 391
Dasiphora fruticosa, 332, 337
date palm, 36, 299, 392
Datura arborea, 385
David's lily, 368
dawn redwood, 329
daylily, 310, 345
deadheading, 198, 202–202

deciduous plants, defined, 30
decorative apple, 325
deer fern, 364
Delphinium, 198, 344
Deschampsia cespitosa, 362
desert candle, 239–240, 367
desert rose, 40
Deutzia / deutzia, 31, 57, 310, 323, 335
Deutzia gracilis, 335
Deutzia ×*hybrida* 'Mont Rose', 323
Deutzia ×*magnifica*, Showy deutzia, 323
Deutzia scabra 'Candidissima, 323
devil's ivy, 97, 139, 202, 203, 222, 388
Dianthus, 33, 350, 374
Dianthus barbatus, 240, 374
Dianthus caryophyllus, 59, 132, 170, 178, 240, 374, 380
Dianthus chinensis, 170, 374
Dianthus deltoides, 350
Dianthus gratianopolitanus, 171, 350
Dianthus microlepis, 350
Dianthus petraeus, 350
Dianthus plumarius, 171, 344
Diascia barberae, 380
Dicentra eximia, 350
Dicentra spectabilis, 134, 344
Dictamnus, 257
Dictamnus albus, 344
Dieffenbachia / dieffenbachia, 35, 130, 139, 203, 222
Dieffenbachia maculata, 387
Dieffenbachia seguine, 387
Digitalis, 55, 195, 240
Digitalis purpurea, 374
Dimorphotheca, 124
Diplotaxis tenuifolia, 251
diseases
    control by crop rotation, 25, 320, 321
    of ornamental plants, 402–403 (table)
    plant protection from, 201
    in vegetable gardens, 320–321 (table)
Disocactus, 176
display cabinets, 39
dittany, 257, 344
diversity. *See* near-natural gardens
Dodecatheon meadia, 350
dog fennel, 349
dog nettle, 182
dog's tooth violet, 367
donkey's ears, 59, 369
donkey's tail, 40, 394
Doronicum, 145
Doronicum orientale, 344

Dorotheanthus bellidiformis, 374, 380
Douglas fir, 330
Douglas phlox, 352
Draba, 350
Draba aizoides, 350
Draba bruniifolia, 350
Draba haynaldii, 350
Dracaena deremensis, 387
Dracaena fragans, 387
dragon tree, 97
drooping sedge, 362
dropwort, 344
drumstick primrose, 347
Dryas octopetala, 351
Dryas ×*suendermannii*, 351
drying flowers, 171, 255–256, 296
Dryopteris, 364
Dryopteris erythrosora, 364
Dryopteris filix-mas, 364
dry stone walls
    constructing, 58, 82–84, 88
    maintaining, 122
    plantings, 84, 133, 171
    winter protection, 32, 278
duck potato, 359
dumb cane, 97
dusty miller, 170, 353
Dutchman's pipe, 340
dwarf Alberta spruce, 336
dwarf balsam fir, 328, 334
dwarf banana, 391
dwarf blue spruce, 336
dwarf Bosnian pine, 330
dwarf euonymus, 335
dwarf forsythia, 335
dwarf golden English yew, 337
dwarf golden Japanese yew, 337
dwarf holly, 335
dwarf juniper, 336
dwarf morning glory, 124, 373
dwarf purple willow, 332
dwarf roses, 80, 339, 393
dwarf Russian almond, 337
dwarf Scotch pine, 336
dwarf Siberian pine, 336
dwarf spurge, 182
dwarf tomatoes, 115
dwarf white spruce, 336
Dyer's broom, 324
Dyssodia tenuiloba, 382

earth star bromeliad, 38, 387
earthworms, 265–266
earwigs, 146, 196, 221
Easter cactus, 40, 179, 393
eastern flowering dogwood, 323
eastern hemlock, 330, 337
eastern red cedar, 329
east-facing sites, 178

East Indies aster, 343
Eccremocarpus scaber, 93
Echeveria / echeveria, 40, 176, 179, 387
Echinacea, 145
Echinacea purpurea, 344
Echinopsis, 176
Echinops ritro, 344
edelweiss, 352
edge stones, 45–46
edging lobelia, 376, 381
eggplant, 394
    fertilizing, 210, 307
    growing in cold frames and foil houses, 150
    harvesting, 210, 229, 268
    planting / sowing, 104, 149–150, 185, 312
    pruning, 209–210
    watering, 186
Eichhornia crassipes, 357
Elaeagnus multiflora, 331
elder, 332
elderberry, 145, 327, 332
elder tree, 246
elegant clarkia, 373
elephant's tongue, 137, 389
elkhorn fern, 392
Elymus repens, 182
emerald fern, 137, 147
endives. *See* winter endives
English daisy, 372, 380
English hawthorn, 323
English holly, 293, 331
English ivy, 335, 340
English lavender, 336
English yew, 330, 333
Enkianthus campanulatus, 324
Epimedium, 121, 355
Epimedium pinnatum subsp. *colchicum*, 355
Epimedium pubigerum, 355
Epipactis 'Sabine', 398
Epiphyllum, 40, 387
epiphytes, 38, 40, 297, 299
Epipremnum, 97, 139, 202, 203, 388
Epipremnum aureum, 388
Epipremnum pinnatum, 388
Episcia cupreata, 388
Eranthis hyemalis, 58, 145, 221, 367
Eremurus, 239, 367
Erica, 173, 335
Erica carnea, 33, 145, 335
Erica gracilis, 257
Erica herbacea, 335
Erica tetralix, 335
Erica vagans, 335
Erigeron, 145, 198, 344
Eriobotrya, 134
Eriobotrya japonica, 135, 280, 388

Eruca sativa, 251
Eryngium, 82
Eryngium bourgatii, 344
Erysimum, 374
Erysimum ×*allionii*, 374
Erysimum cheiri, 95, 195, 240, 288, 374
Erythrina, 175
Erythrina crista-galli, 258, 289, 299, 388
Erythronium, 367
Erythronium dens-canis, 367
Erythronium tuolumnense, 367
Eschscholzia, 124
Eschscholzia californica, 128, 374
Eucalyptus gunnii, 388
Eucomis, 370
Euonymus, 256, 324, 335
Euonymus alatus, 324
    'Compactus', 335
Euonymus europaeus, 324
Euonymus fortunei, 335
    'Emerald Gaiety', 335
Euonymus japonicus 'Marieke', 129
Euonymus nanus var. *turkestanicus*, 335
Euonymus phellomanus, 324
Euphorbia, 351, 374, 388
Euphorbia capitulata, 351
Euphorbia epithymoides, 351
Euphorbia exigua, 182
Euphorbia heterophylla, 374
Euphorbia marginata, 374
Euphorbia milii, 40, 351, 388
Euphorbia myrsinites, 351
Euphorbia palustris, 357
Euphorbia polychroma, 351
Euphorbia pulcherrima, 298, 388
European beech, 331
European cranberrybush, 327
European fan palm, 36, 175, 280, 386
European hornbeam, 331
European larch, 329
European wild ginger, 355
evening primrose, 346
evergreen broad-leaved trees, 128, 173, 220, 237–238, 275
evergreen container plants, 34
evergreen grasses, 94
evergreen plants, defined, 30
evergreen shrubs, 57, 129, 198–199, 220, 297
evergreen trees, 57, 129, 198–199, 297
evergreen viburnum, 337
Exochorda racemosa, 324

Fagus, 276
Fagus sylvatica, 331

fairy fan flower, 381
fairy primrose, 393
Fallopia baldschuanica, 81, 198, 276, 340
false buck's beard, 343
false cypress, 87, 130, 328, 334
false indigo, 130
false Jerusalem cherry, 394
false mallow, 348
fan-leaved water crowfoot, 359
fan palm, 36, 134, 280, 289
Fargesia murieliae 'Simba', 362
×*Fatshedera lizei*, 179, 388
Fatsia japonica, 179, 388
Faucaria, 40
fava beans. *See* broad (fava) beans
feather grass, 363
feather reed grass, 362
February daphne, 323
fences
    for animal pest control, 102
    as boundaries, 142, 143
    constructing, 46–47
    maintaining, 16, 228, 284
fennel. *See* Florence fennel
fernleaf peony, 346
ferns, 125, 299–300, 364–365 (table)
fertilizers and fertilizing, 14–16, 306–308 (table)
fescue, 362
Festuca, 362
Festuca gautieri, 362
Festuca glauca, 362
Festuca valesiaca, 362
feverfew, 378
Ficus, 35, 203, 260, 388
Ficus aspera, 388
Ficus benjamina, 35, 388
Ficus carica, 35, 289, 388
Ficus cyathistipula, 388
Ficus elastica, 35, 388
Ficus lyrata, 35, 388
Ficus natalensis subsp. *leprieurii*, 388
Ficus natalensis subsp. *triangularis*, 388
Ficus pumila, 35, 297, 388
Ficus rubiginosa, 388
fiddle-leaf fig, 35, 388
field clover, 182
field maple, 331
field poppy, 376
fig, 289, 297, 388
Filipendula, 344
Filipendula rubra, 344
Filipendula vulgaris, 344
fingerleaf rodgersia, 347
fir, 129, 237, 256, 328, 334
firecracker flower, 387

fire lily, 36–37, 179
firethorn, 326, 332
firewheel, 374
firewheel tree, 395
fishtail palm, 36, 386
Fittonia, 38
Fittonia verschaffeltii, 389
five finger, 353
five finger fern, 364
five-leaf akebia, 340
flag, 268, 345, 357, 368
flag root, 357
flaky juniper, 336
flaming Katy, 40, 390
flamingo flower, 384
flaming sword, 395
Flanders poppy, 376
fleabane, 145, 198, 344, 345
flea beetles, 109, 123, 159, 165, 201, 318
fleece flower, 350
fleeces, 103, 147, 150, 154, 190
Florence fennel
    fertilizing, 230, 307
    harvesting, 211, 230, 316
    night frosts, 268
    planting / sowing, 107, 155, 313, 316
    watering, 187
    'Zefa Fino', 107
florist's cineraria, 392
florist's cyclamen, 260, 387
florist's gloxinia, 259, 394
flossflower, 174, 178, 372, 380
flower bulbs. *See* bulbs and tubers; *specific flowers*
flowering allium, 239
flowering almond, 31, 33, 57, 173, 326
flowering currant, 57, 145, 326, 332
flowering maple, 383
flowering plants
    annual and biennial flowers, 372–378 (table)
    annual dry flowers and dry grasses, 379 (table)
    dividing and replanting, 197, 245, 253
    extending bloom, 257–258
    fall-flowering, 125, 134
    native, 121–122, 134
    single-flowering varieties, 25, 134
    spring-flowering, 197
    summer-flowering, 54–55, 82, 92, 95, 122, 125, 170–171, 257
flowering quince, 30, 57, 58, 323
flowering rush, 357
flowering shrubs, 31, 43, 59, 198

flowering twigs, decorative use, 33, 299
flower meadow, 121–122
flowers, removing withered, 201–202
flower windows, 34–35, 136, 139, 178, 383–395 (table)
fly honeysuckle, 332
flying saucers, 375
foil
    air bubble foil, 49, 51, 105
    bags, 97, 223
    houses / tents, 53, 66, 105, 110, 151, 247
foil pond lining, 89, 91
Fontinalis antipyretica, 90, 132
Fontinalis antipyretica var. *gigantea*, 357
fool's parsley, 182
forget-me-not, 358, 381
    planting / sowing, 95, 131, 221, 240, 310
    winter protection, 32, 288
Forsythia / forsythia, 324, 331
    flowering indoors, 33, 299
    'Melee d'Or', 335
    pests, 399
    pruning / cutting back, 30, 31, 58
    selecting, 57, 81
    soil requirements, 310
Forsythia ×*intermedia*, 324, 331
    'Spectabilis', 331
    'Weekend', 331
Forsythia ovata, 324
four o'clock plant, 370
foxglove, 25, 55, 195, 240, 374
fox's grape fritillary, 367
foxtail barley, 125
foxtail fern, 137
foxtail lady, 367
foxtail lily, 239–240
fragrant snowflake, 350
Freesia / freesia, 133, 254
French lilac, 327
French marigold, 381
fringe tree, 288
Fritillaria, 367
Fritillaria imperialis, 145, 240, 367
Fritillaria meleagris, 239, 367
Fritillaria michailovskyi, 367
Fritillaria uva-vulpis, 367
fritillary, 367
frogs and toads, 183–184
frost
    black frost, 13
    containers and water lines, 64, 266, 284
    effect on germination, 278
    effects on birds, 23, 284

    effects on container plants, 94, 134, 175, 257–258, 280, 288
    effects on pond fish, 287
    fall-planted perennials forced up by, 57–58, 59, 94, 122
    frost-free rooms, 34
    frost-sensitive plants, 174
    protecting newly planted or sown plants, 103
fruiting barberry, 81
Fuchsia / fuchsia, 380
    cutting back, 60, 136
    extending bloom, 257
    fertilizing, 177
    overwintering, 34, 281, 299
    planting / sowing, 177, 201
Fuchsia magellanica var. *gracilis*, 324
Fumaria officinalis, 182
fungal cultures, 167

Gaillardia, 344
Gaillardia pulchella, 374
galane, 346
Galanthus, 239, 367
Galanthus elwesii, 367
Galanthus nivalis, 58, 367
galingale, 96, 357, 387
Galinsoga parviflora, 182
Galium odoratum, 355
Galium tricornutum, 182
gallant soldier, 182
gall midges, 146
Galtonia candicans, 367
garden auricula, 347, 353
garden balsam, 177, 375
garden cosmos, 373
garden cress, 166, 194, 273, 307, 313
Gardenia augusta, 389
Gardenia / gardenia, 40
Gardenia jasminoides, 389
garden lupine, 346
garden phlox, 346
garden pink, 350
garden rose tortrix (moth), 172, 399
gardens, establishing, 10
garland flower, 81, 335
garland wreath, 327
garlic, 77, 116, 166, 234, 313
Gasteria species / gasteria, 40, 389
Gazania, 375
Genista, 335
Genista lydia, 335
Genista pilosa, 335
Genista tinctoria, 324
gentian, 134, 278, 351
Gentiana, 134, 278, 351

Gentiana acaulis, 134, 351
Gentiana septemfida var. *lagodechiana*, 134, 351
Gentiana sino-ornata, 134, 351
Geranium cinereum subsp. subcaulescens, 351
Geranium / geranium, 351
    cutting back, 59–60, 136
    cuttings, 243
    extending bloom, 257
    overwintering, 34, 59, 281
    planting / sowing, 54, 136, 177, 201
    removing flowers, 201
    rust fungus, 403
Geranium pratense, 145
    'Rozanne', 145
Geranium sanguineum, 351
Gerbera, 389
German primrose, 36, 393
Geum, 351
Geum coccineum, 351
Geum ×*cultorum*, 345
Geum montanum, 351
giant allium, 366
gillyflower, 374, 380
ginkgo, 328
Ginkgo biloba, 328
Gladiolus callianthus, 279
Gladiolus / gladiolus, 370
    Abyssinian (or fragrant) gladiolus, 279
    bulblets, 255
    bulbs, 32–33, 254–255, 279, 286
    flowering, 93–94, 255
    overwintering, 32–33, 55, 263, 279, 286
    pests and diseases, 196, 254, 286, 402, 403
    planting, 93–94, 125–126, 196, 310
    propagation, 255
    use as cut flowers, 255
    watering, 196
Gladiolus hybrids, 370
Gladiolus murielae, 279, 370
Glebionis segetum, 375
Gleditsia triacanthos, 331
globe amaranth, 379
globeflower, 278, 348
globe thistle, 344
globe tulip, 370
Globularia cordifolia, 351
Gloriosa / gloriosa, 176, 279, 370
Gloriosa superba, 176, 370
glory bush, 258, 395
glory flower, 93
glory of the snow, 239, 366
glossy-leaved paper plant, 388

glove flower, 134
gloxinia, 60, 92–93, 222, 259, 394
Glyceria maxima 'Variegata', 362
golden alyssum, 145, 350
golden candle, 298, 391
golden chain tree, 31, 57, 81, 325
golden clematis, 342
golden club, 358
golden English yew, 337
golden flax, 352
golden fleece, 178, 382
golden hardhack, 326, 332, 337
golden hazel, 323
golden hunters robe, 388
golden leaf hazel, 57
golden polypody, 300
golden rain tree, 81, 325
goldenrod, 348
golden shield fern, 364
golden star, 369
golden trumpet, 383
golden tuft, 350
Gomphrena globosa, 379
good luck leaf, 371
grama grass, 362
grape hyacinth, 220, 227, 239, 368
grape ivy, 139, 179, 386
grass clippers and trimmers, 21
grass clippings, 182
grasses
    annual dry flowers and dry grasses, 379 (table)
    ornamental grasses, 125, 362–363 (table)
grassnut, 369
grass paths, 120
grass pink, 398
gray mold, 170, 402
greater bellflower, 343
greater bird's foot trefoil, 358
greater quaking grass, 379
greater spearwort, 359
greater water-moss, 357
great white trillium, 369
great wood-rush, 362
greenfly, 196, 228
greenhouse growing, 28, 38–39, 50–51, 247
greenhouse whitefly, 146, 147, 222, 319, 399
green manuring, 15
green moor grass, 363
Greenovia, 176
greenweed, 335
Grevillea, 389
Grevillea banksii, 389
Grevillea robusta, 389
Grevillea thelemanniana, 389
gromwell, 355
ground beetles, 146

ground coverings (mulches), 175, 182, 276
ground rattan cane, 393
guelder rose, 327
Guzmania / guzmania, 40, 99, 389
Gynura aurantiaca, 389
Gypsophila, 351
Gypsophila cerastioides, 351
Gypsophila elegans, 375
Gypsophila paniculata, 345
Gypsophila repens, 351

Haemanthus albiflos, 137, 389
Haemanthus 'König Albert', 137, 394
hairy greenwood, 335
Hakonechloa macra 'Aureola', 362
hakone grass, 362
Halesia carolina, 324
Hamamelis, 33, 59, 81, 324
Hamamelis ×*intermedia* 'Ruby Glow', 324
Hamamelis japonica, 324
Hamamelis mollis, 324
hanging plants, 139, 202
hard and dry rot, 286, 402
hard fern, 364
hard rush, 358
hard shield fern, 365
hardy fuchsia, 324
hardy kiwi, 340
harebell, 134
hare's foot fern, 300
hare's tail grass, 125, 379
harlequin flower, 126
harping Johnny, 348
Hart's tongue fern, 364
hazelnut, 323
hazel shrubs, 57
headed cabbage. *See* cabbage
heart-leaf bergenia, 343
heart-leaved globe daisy, 351
heath, 335
heather species / heather, 87, 96, 145, 173, 220, 257
heath garden, 87
heath pearlwort, 353
heavenly blue morning glory, 375
Hebe armstrongii, 335
Hebe buxifolia, 335
Hebe / hebe, 87, 335
Hedera, 38, 81, 121, 130, 202, 256, 276
Hedera helix, 179, 240, 340, 355
    'Conglomerata', 335
hedge fern, 365
hedgehog Norway spruce, 336
hedgehogs, 147, 183, 246
hedge maple, 331
hedge mustard, 251

hedge nettle, 354
hedges
    conifer species, 236
    cutting back for density, 276
    deciduous, 30, 275, 276
    evergreen, 130, 275
    freestanding vs. trimmed, 81, 274–275
    planting, 81, 199, 275–276
    pruning, 30, 58, 199
    recommended trees and shrubs for, 331–333 (table)
    uses, 143, 274
hedge veronica, 87, 335
Hedychium gardnerianum, 389
Helenium, 198, 345
Helen's flower, 198, 345
Helianthemum, 134, 253, 351
Helianthus, 123, 375
Helianthus annuus, 375
Helianthus debilis, 375
Helianthus decapetalus, 345
Helichrysum bracteatum, 379
Helictotrichon sempervirens, 94, 362
Heliocereus, 176
Heliopsis helianthoides, 345
heliotrope (or turnsole), 175, 257, 258, 389
Heliotropium, 258
Heliotropium arborescens, 389
Helipterum manglesii, 379
helleborine, 398
Helleborus niger, 33, 278, 297, 345
    'Praecox', 33, 297
Hemerocallis, 345
Hepatica, 351
Hepatica nobilis, 351
Hepatica transsylvanica, 351
herbs, generally
    about, 184
    annual, 26–27, 194
    fertilizing, 79, 118, 194
    growing in window boxes, 118
    harvesting, 184
    light requirements, 26
    perennial, 26, 32, 58–59, 79, 116, 194
    planting / sowing, 26–27, 118, 136, 312–314 (table)
    raised beds, 266
    for tea infusions, 296
herbs, wild, 25, 182
herringbone cotoneaster, 323, 334
Heuchera, 351
Heuchera micrantha 'Palace Purple', 351
Heuchera micrantha sanguinea, 351
Heuchera sanguinea 'Splendens', 351
×*Heucherella tiarelloides*, 355

hiba, 129
hibiscus, 57, 288, 324
Hibiscus rosa-sinensis, 96, 135, 175, 258, 299, 389
Hibiscus syriacus, 57, 288, 324
Hieracium ×rubrum, 351
Himalayan bistort, 350
Himalayan blue poppy, 346
Himalayan cowslip, 358
Himalayan meadow primrose, 353
hinoki cypress, 334
Hippeastrum, 36, 137, 242, 389
Hippophae, 130
Hippuris vulgaris, 90, 357
hoeing, 53, 69, 103, 142, 197, 207
hollowroot, 145
holly, 81, 256, 288, 325, 331
hollyberry cotoneaster, 323
holly grape, 332
hollyhock, 25, 145, 195, 240, 372
Holodiscus discolor, 324
honey locust, 331
honeysuckle, 256, 276, 332, 341
hoof and horn meal, 15
hoop petticoat, 369
hops, 340
Hordeum jubatum, 125
hornbeam, 30, 58, 81, 274, 276, 331
horned pansy, 378, 382
horseradish, 77–78, 189, 212, 270, 285, 309
hortensia, 390
Hosta tardiflora, 355
hot peppers, 296
house entrances, 135
house leek, 354
houseplants. *See* indoor plants
hoverflies, 146
Hoya, 139
Hoya carnosa, 389
Humulus lupulus, 340
humus, 11, 25–26
hyacinth, 367
    hyacinth jars, 37, 259
    planting, 37, 60, 253
    spreading, 220–221
    winter flowering, 37, 259, 290, 298
Hyacinthoides hispanica, 367
Hyacinthus orientalis, 367
hybrid St. John's wort, 335
hybrid tea roses, 80
hybrid yew, 330
Hydrangea anomala, 80
Hydrangea anomala subsp. *petiolaris*, 81, 340
Hydrangea / hydrangea, 13, 80–81, 87, 137–138, 179, 324, 400, 402

Hydrangea macrophylla, 137–138, 179, 324, 390
Hydrangea paniculata, 31
    'Grandiflora', 324
hydroponic growing, 138–139
Hypericum, 81, 276, 335
Hypericum calcinum, 335
Hypericum ×moserianum, 335
Hypericum patulum, 324

Iberis, 33, 122, 128, 352
Iberis saxatilis, 352
Iberis sempervirens, 352
Iberis umbellata, 375
Icelandic (Iceland) poppy, 221, 376
ice plant, 348
Ilex, 81, 256, 288, 331
Ilex aquifolium, 293, 325, 331
Ilex crenata
    'Fastigiata', 331
    'Stokes', 335
Impatiens, 375, 390
Impatiens balsamina, 177, 375
Impatiens New Guinea Group, 390
Impatiens walleriana, 54, 175, 177, 375, 381, 390
Imperata cylindrica 'Red Baron, 362
imperial lewisia, 352
Inca cucumbers, 169–170
Incarvillea compacta, 352
Incarvillea / incarvillea, 352
Incarvillea mairei, 352
incense cedar, 328
Indian azalea, 179
Indian crocus, 175, 398
Indian mallow, 96, 383
Indianshot, 370
indicator crops, 53, 69–70, 73, 115
indoor plants
    cleaning, 178–179
    cutting back, 96
    with diseased roots, 136
    fertilizing, 35, 95–96, 138, 139
    growing under glass, 38–39
    grown from cuttings, 96, 97
    humidity, 297
    hydroponic culture, 138–139
    light levels, 38, 178, 242, 281, 289
    "oversummering" outdoors, 179, 202–203, 260
    pests, 139, 203, 242, 289, 400
    replanting, 36, 136, 259
    south-facing windows, 136, 178
    sun damage, 95, 136, 139

temperatures, 35, 178, 259–260
    watering, 35, 139, 179, 202, 223, 281, 289
insect habitats, 134, 147
insects, useful, 24–25, 145–148, 183, 318
Inula ensifolia, 352
Inula orientalis, 345
Ipheion uniflorum, 367
Ipomoea, 92
Ipomoea tricolor, 375
Iris barbata, 220
Iris bucharica, 239, 357
Iris danfordiae, 239
Iris ensata, 357
Iris histrioides, 239
Iris histrioides var. *reticulata*, 368
Irish moss, 353, 394
Iris ×hollandica, 279, 368
Iris / iris, 345, 357, 368
    Barbata Nana Group (Miniature Dwarf Bearded), 352
    bearded iris, 219–220
    Bukhara iris, 368
    bulb iris, 239
    Dutch iris, 279–280, 368
    dwarf irises of the Bartiris group, 352
    flag iris (or yellow flag), 92, 357
    horned iris, 368
    Japanese iris / Japanese water iris, 357
    planting, 219–220, 310
    rabbit-ear iris, 357
    shallow-flowered iris, 357
    Siberian iris, 220
    varieties, 197
Iris laevigata, 357
Iris pseudacorus, 92, 357
Iris reticulata, 239, 357
Iris sibirica, 220
Iris versicolor, 357
Ismelia, 375
Italian aster, 343
Italian cress, 251
Italian honeysuckle, 341
Italian starwort, 343
Ithuriel's spear, 369
ivy, 355
    cuttings, 202
    as a ground cover, 121
    growing on house walls, 240–241
    growing on moss poles, 222
    growing under glass, 38
    planting, 276
    as a suggested plant, 81, 130
    watering, 179

ivy-leaved cyclamen, 279
ivy-leaved geraniums, 381
ivy tree, 179, 222, 258, 394
Ixia, 174, 370
Ixiolirion / ixiolirion, 252, 368
Ixiolirion tataricum, 368

jacaranda, 390
Jacaranda mimosifolia, 390
Jacobaea maritima, 170
Jacobean lily, 279, 371
Jacob's ladder, 347
jade plant, 179, 387
Japanese anemone, 253, 343
Japanese aucuba, 385
Japanese barberry, 331, 334
Japanese cedar, 328, 334
Japanese cowslip, 353
Japanese creeper, 341
Japanese dogwood, 57, 323
Japanese euonymus, 129
Japanese fatsia, 179, 388
Japanese holly, 331, 335
Japanese iris, 357
Japanese ivy, 341
Japanese lady fern, 364
Japanese lantern, 256, 347
Japanese larch, 329, 336
Japanese maple, 322, 334
Japanese meadowsweet, 327, 333, 337
Japanese medlar, 135, 280, 388
Japanese pachysandra, 356
Japanese pieris, 326
Japanese plum yew, 129
Japanese poinsettia, 374
Japanese primrose, 353
Japanese quince, 323
Japanese radishes, 232
Japanese reed grass, 362
Japanese rose, 277, 325, 332, 339
Japanese sedge, 362
Japanese shield fern, 364
Japanese show flower, 335
Japanese skimmia, 337
Japanese spirea, 31, 327, 333, 337
Japanese spurge, 356
Japanese stephanandra, 327
Japanese stone pine, 336
Japanese toad lily, 369
Japanese water iris, 357
Japanese wisteria, 341
Japanese witch hazel, 324
Japanese yew, 129, 135
jasmine twigs, 299
Jasminum nudiflorum, 33, 59, 80, 81, 299, 325
Jerusalem artichoke, 102
Jerusalem cherry, 135, 394
Jesuit's nut, 359

Jew's mallow, 332
Juncus inflexus, 358
juneberry, 322
juniper, 129, 329, 336
juniper berries, 129
Juniperus, 329, 336
Juniperus chinensis, 129, 329
Juniperus chinensis ×*Juniperus sabina*, 329
Juniperus communis, 129, 329
Juniperus communis var. *saxatilis*, 336
Juniperus horizontalis, 336
Juniperus ×*pfitzeriana*, 329, 332
Juniperus sabina, 129, 329
Juniperus squamata, 336
    'Blue Star', 336
Juniperus virginiana, 329
Justicia brandegeeana, 298, 390

kaffir lily, 60, 137, 179, 259, 386
kahila ginger lily, 389
Kalanchoe blossfeldiana, 40, 179, 390
Kalanchoe / kalanchoe, 97, 390
Kalanchoe pinnata, 40
Kalmia angustifolia, 336
Kalmia latifolia, 81, 129, 325
kangaroo vine, 386
Kerria japonica, 325
    'Pleniflora', 325
Kerria / kerria, 325
Kew broom, 335
kingcup, 357
kiwi fruit, 340
knapweed, 278, 344
Kniphofia, 134, 253
Kniphofia uvaria, 345
knives, gardening, 18
knotweed, 350
kobushi magnolia, 325
Kochia, 372
kohlrabi
    'Blauer Speck', 188
    diseases, 320
    fertilizing, 108, 109, 155, 248, 307
    growing in foil houses or greenhouses, 50–51, 108, 110
    harvesting, 269, 316
    moisture fluctuations, 188
    planting / sowing, 65, 67, 155, 187–188, 211, 309, 316
    tuber-like growths, 230
    watering, 155
Kolkwitzia amabilis, 325
kolomikta, 340
Korean fir, 328, 334

Korean forsythia, 324
Korean lilac, 327

Labrador violet, 354
Laburnum, 31, 57, 81, 325
Laburnum anagyroides, 325
Laburnum ×*watereri* 'Vossii', 325
lace cup hydrangea, 390
lace shrub, 327
lacewings, 146, 196, 201, 222
lacy phacelia, 377
ladybugs (ladybirds), 128, 146, 183, 228
lady fern, 364
lady palm, 393
lady's cypress, 175, 398
Lagerstroemia indica, 134, 280, 390
Lagodekhi crested gentian, 351
Lagurus ovatus, 125, 379
Lake Constance forget-me-not, 358
lamb's lettuce (corn lettuce)
    fertilizing, 114, 307
    growing in cold frames, 247, 296
    harvesting, 316
    planting / sowing, 210, 245, 247, 309, 311, 313, 316
    winter protection, 272
Lamiastrum, 355
Lamium galeobdolon, 121, 355
    'Florentinum', 355
Lantana camara, 381
Lantana / lantana, 60, 176, 221, 381
larch, 30, 329
large-flowered trillium, 369
large-growing / large-leaved plants, 222, 298
Larix, 329
Larix decidua, 329
Larix kaempferi, 329
    'Wolterdingen', 336
larkspur, 134, 198, 257, 344, 373
Lathyrus odoratus, 93, 198, 375
lattice structures, 175–176
laurel, 134, 280, 326, 390
laurel tree, 139, 224
Laurus, 134, 280
Laurus nobilis, 34, 139, 224, 390
laurustinus, 280, 395
Lavandula angustifolia, 336
Lavatera trimestris, 124, 376
lavender, 25, 77, 145, 167, 235, 273
lavender cotton, 337
lavender mountain lily, 252
lawnmowers, 20–21
lawns
    establishing, 119–120
    flowers in, 239
    lawn care, 20–21, 121, 199, 278

plant alternatives to, 121–122, 355–356 (table)
    rolled or ready-made, 120–121
    tools for maintaining, 20–21
Lawson's cypress, 328, 331
Laxmann's bulrush, 359
leadwort, 175, 280
leaf-rolling wasp, 172, 399
leaf spot disease, 187, 320, 403
leatherleaf viburnum, 327
Ledebouria socialis, 390
leeks
    fertilizing, 213, 231, 307
    frost protection, 29
    harvesting, 29, 271, 316
    heeling in, 271, 285
    hoeing, 213
    planting / sowing, 70, 112, 158, 190, 309, 313, 316
    taste, 29, 54
    watering, 213
legume family, 65
lemon balm, 116, 167, 194
lemon tree, 224
Lenne's magnolia, 325
Leontopodium, 352
Leontopodium alpinum, 352
Leontopodium souliei, 352
leopard plant, 145, 346
leopard's bane, 145, 344
Leptinella squalida, 352
lesser bulrush, 359
lesser club moss, 394
lesser glory of the snow, 366
lettuce. *See also* lamb's lettuce
    Asian lettuces, 113
    Batavia lettuce, 110, 214, 306, 312, 315
    butterhead, 72, 113, 315
    curly, 113, 214
    early varieties, 212
    fertilizing, 191, 307, 308
    growing in cold frames, 51–52
    growing in foil houses or greenhouses, 51, 68, 110
    harvesting, 113, 214, 248, 316
    iceberg lettuce, 68, 110, 160, 188, 307, 316
    leaf lettuce, 72, 113, 214, 315
    oak-leaved, 113, 307, 315
    pests and diseases, 51, 188, 319, 320, 321
    planting / sowing, 72, 110–111, 160, 188, 212, 214, 230, 316, 317
    red-leaved varieties, 111
    romaine (cos), 113, 160, 191, 214, 308, 317
    soil requirements, 110, 309
Leucanthemum, 345

Leucanthemum maximum, 198, 345
Leucojum, 368
Leucojum aestivum, 368
Leucojum vernum, 239, 368
Lewisia cotyledon, 352
Leyland cypress, 328, 331
Liatris spicata, 345
Ligularia, 145, 346
Ligularia ×*hessei*, 346
Ligularia przewalskii, 346
Ligustrum, 30, 50, 81, 256, 275, 276, 332
Ligustrum obtusifolium var. *regelianum*, 332
Ligustrum ovalifolium, 130, 332
    'Aureum', 332
Ligustrum vulgare 'Atrovirens', 130
lilac, 31, 56, 57, 81, 173, 310, 327, 399
lilies, 25, 134, 251–252
Lilium candidum, 239, 251, 368
Lilium davidii var. *willmottiae*, 368
Lilium lancifolium, 238, 368
Lilium martagon, 368
Lilium regale, 368
Lilium speciosum, 368
Lilium tigrinum, 368
lily leek (lilyleek), 145, 366
lily of the Incas, 366
lily of the valley, 134, 355
lily-of-the-valley bush, 326
lime
    adding to soil, 12, 160, 161, 265
    intolerant plants, 81, 87, 96, 111, 132, 163
lime-containing fertilizers, 81, 96
lime-containing water, 41, 98, 222
limequat, 135
limestone saxifrage, 353
Limonium, 256
Limonium sinuatum, 379
Limonium suworowii, 379
Linaria, 355
Lincoln's weed, 251
Linum flavum, 352
Linum grandiflorum, 376
Lithospermum purpurocaeruleum, 355
littleleaf cotoneaster, 323
littleleaf mock orange, 336
livelong, 348
liverleaf, 351
Livingstone daisy, 374, 380
Livistona, 36
Livistona australis, 390
Lobelia erinus, 178, 376, 381
Lobelia / lobelia, 174, 175, 177, 178
lobster plant, 298, 388
Lobularia maritima, 123, 376

lollipop plant, 298, 391
Lonas annua, 124, 256
London pride, 353, 356
long beech fern, 364
Lonicera, 256, 276, 332, 341
Lonicera ×brownii 'Dropmore
      Scarlet', 341
Lonicera caprifolium, 341
Lonicera ×heckrottii, 341
Lonicera japonica, 341
Lonicera ledebourii, 325
Lonicera nitida 'Elegant', 332
Lonicera pileata, 336
Lonicera ×tellmanniana, 341
Lonicera vulgare
      'Atrovirens', 332
      'Lodense', 332
Lonicera xylosteum, 332
loosestrife, 346, 358
loquat, 134, 135, 280, 388
Lotus uliginosus, 358
lovage, 194, 250
love-in-a-mist, 257, 376
love lies bleeding, 372
lucky clover, 371
lupine, 25, 55, 65, 82, 310
Lupinus, 55, 82
Lupinus polyphyllus, 346
lutea, 353
Luzula, 362
Luzula nivea, 362
Luzula sylvatica, 362
Lychnis, 346
Lycianthes rantonnetii, 258, 390
Lydia broom, 335
Lysichiton, 358
Lysichiton americanus, 358
Lysichiton camtschatcensis, 358
Lysimachia nummularia, 356
Lythrum, 346
Lythrum salicaria, 346
      'Robert', 358
Lythrum virgatum, 346
Lytocaryum, 36, 179, 390
Lytocaryum weddellianum, 390

mace sedge, 362
Madagascar palm, 36, 391
Madeira winter cherry, 394
Madonna lily, 239, 251, 368
madwort, 87, 349
Magellan barberry, 130, 331
Magnolia kobus, 325
Magnolia liliiflora 'Nigra', 325
Magnolia / magnolia, 57, 81, 325
Magnolia ×soulangeana, 57, 325
Magnolia stellata, 57, 325
mahonia, 81–82, 135, 256, 325
Mahonia aquifolium, 325, 332
maidenhair fern, 38, 300, 383

maidenhair spleenwort, 364
maiden pink, 350
male fern, 364
mallow family, 40, 145
Maltese cross, 348
Malus, 325
Malus hybrids, 57
Malva alcea, 145
Malva moschata, 145
Malva neglecta, 145
Malva sylvestris, 145
manure, 15, 102, 206–207, 265
manzanita, 280
Maranta leuconeura, 390
mare's tail, 357
marguerite, 135, 384
marigold, 25, 92, 134, 171, 296,
      310, 378
mariposa tulip, 370
marjoram, 54, 166, 217, 250, 313
marsh mallow, 145
marsh marigold, 357
marsh spurge, 357
martagon lily, 368
marvel of Peru, 370
Matricaria chamomilla, 196
Matteuccia, 364
Matteuccia pensylvanica, 364
Matteuccia struthiopteris, 364
Matthiola, 132, 170
Matthiola incana, 376
Maule's quince, 323
meadow bistort, 357
meadow cranesbill, 145
meadow rue, 348
meadowsweet, 344
mealybugs, 95, 146, 399
Meconopsis, 195
Meconopsis betonicifolia, 195, 346
Meconopsis cambrica, 195
Mediterranean fan fern, 386
Mediterranean plants, 224
Mediterranean sea holly, 344
melons, 111, 156–157, 186, 188–189,
      212, 230, 307
Menyanthes trifoliata, 358
Metasequoia glyptostroboides, 329
Metrosideros excelsa, 391
Mexican aster, 373
Mexican cigar plant, 178, 380
Mexican fire plant, 374
Mexican flameleaf, 388
Mexican ivy, 373
Meyer lilac, 327
mezereum, 323
mice, 30, 49, 200, 246, 269, 270
Michaelmas daisy, 134, 343
Michael's flower, 367
microbiota, 129, 336
Microbiota decussata, 129, 336

Microcoelum, 36
Microcoelum weddellianum, 179,
      390
mignon dahlia, 380
mignonette, 122
Miltonia, 98, 396
mimosa, 383
Mimulus ×hybridus, 376
mind your own business, 394
miniature date palm, 392
miniature gardens, 59, 94
mint, 116
Mirabilis jalapa, 370
Miscanthus, 363
Miscanthus floridulus, 363
Miscanthus sacchariflorus, 363
Miscanthus sinensis, 363
Missouri evening primrose, 352
mistletoe cacti, 393
miyamatatabi, 340
mock orange, 57, 81, 326, 332
mole cricket, 147, 319, 399
moles, 49, 144–145, 147
Molinia, 363
Molinia arundinacea, 363
Molinia caerulea, 363
moly, 145, 366
molybdenum, 321
Monarda, 346
monkey flower, 376
monkshood, 253
Monstera, 35, 222
Monstera deliciosa, 391
montbretia, 126, 279, 366
moor grass, 363
Morina longifolia, 346
morning glory, 92
Moses-in-the-boat, 395
mosquitoes, 206
moss, 121, 223
moss campion, 354
moss phlox, 352
moss pink, 352
moss poles, growing plants on,
      222
moss rose, 178, 377
mossy saxifrages, 353
mother-in-law's tongue, 97, 393
mother-of-thousands, 394
moth orchid, 242
mountain avens, 351
mountain currant, 332
mountain garland, 373
mountain juniper, 336
mountain laurel, 81, 129, 325
mountain pine, 336
mournful widow, 377
mouse ear, 350
mullein, 134, 280
muriel bamboo, 362

Musa, 175, 258, 391
Musa acuminata, 391
Musa sikkimensis, 391
Muscari species, 239, 368
mushrooms, 117–118, 167–169, 194,
      217, 235–236, 274
musk, 376
musk mallow, 145
muskmelons, 156
Myers' asparagus, 384
Myosotis, 95, 131, 221, 240, 288
Myosotis palustris, 358
Myosotis rehsteineri, 358
Myosotis sylvatica, 376, 381
myrtle, 34, 175, 179, 280, 299
Myrtus, 175, 280
Myrtus communis, 299, 391

naked ladies, 240, 366
Narcissus bulbocodium, 369
Narcissus cyclamineus, 59, 369
Narcissus / narcissus, 310, 368–369
narrow-leaved inula, 352
nasturtium, 26–27, 117, 118, 166,
      194, 233–234, 378, 382
natal fig, 388
National Audubon Society, 23
native plants, 121–122, 134
near natural garden pond, 90
near-natural gardens, 25, 134
nectar-producing plants, 145
needle grass, 363
nematodes, 147
Nemesia / nemesia, 376
Neoregelia ampullacea, 38
Neoregelia / neoregelia, 35, 38,
      99, 391
Neoregelia pygmaea, 38
Nepeta, 128, 352
Nepeta ×faassenii, 352
Nepeta nervosa, 219, 352
Nephrolepis, 300
Nephrolepis exaltata, 391
nerine, 371
Nerine bowdenii, 371
Nerium, 175, 280
Nerium oleander, 224, 299, 391
nerve plant, 389
nest bromeliad, 391
netting. See wire netting, uses
nettle fertilizer tea, 15, 95
New England aster, 343
New Zealand brass buttons, 352
New Zealand burr, 349
New Zealand Christmas tree, 391
New Zealand spinach, 75, 161, 215,
      307, 313, 316
Nidularium, 99, 391
Nigella, 257
Nigella damascena, 376

nightshade, 394
nispero, 388
nitrogen-fixing capability, 15, 65, 188, 209
nitrogen requirements for vegetable species, 306–309 (table)
noble fir, 328
noble roses, 80
Nootka cypress, 328
Nordic lemon, 323
Norfolk Island pine, 37, 129, 384
north-facing sites, 135, 178
Norway spruce, 329
Nuphar lutea, 90, 358
Nymphaea, 358, 360–361
Nymphoides peltata, 358

oat grass, 94, 362
obedient plant, 347
ocean spray, 324
Oenothera fruticosa, 346
Oenothera macrocarpa, 352
Olea, 134, 280
oleander, 34, 175, 224, 280, 299, 391
olive, 134, 280
Omphalodes verna, 356
Oncidium, 98, 397
onion fly, 194, 201, 319
onions
    conoisseur selections, 54
    fertilizing, 115, 193, 216, 307, 308
    harvesting, 233, 245, 250, 316
    pests and diseases, 166, 319
    planting / sowing, 53, 76, 105, 309, 316
    seed onions, 193, 307
    Spanish onions, 53, 105, 193, 216, 308
    storing, 273
    yellow onions, 233
Onoclea sensibilis, 364
Opuntia fragilis, 352
Opuntia / opuntia, 176, 352
Opuntia phaeacantha, 352
orchid cacti, 39, 40, 387
orchids
    dormancy, 289
    fertilizing, 96
    growing in branches, 298
    low-maintenance hybrids, 41
    obtaining, 175
    orchids for rooms, winter gardens and small greenhouses, 396–397 (table)
    orchids for the garden, 175, 398 (table)
    sclerotial disease, 403

small-growing, 38, 99
soil requirements, 98, 398
watering, 98, 260, 289
winter-hardy, 175
Oregon cedar, 328, 331
Oregon grape, 332
Oriental bittersweet, 340
Oriental cherry, 326
Oriental garlic, 54
Oriental poppy, 346
Ornithogalum umbellatum, 369
Orontium aquaticum, 358
orpine, 348
Osmunda, 364
Osmunda cinnamomea, 364
Osmunda regalis, 364
Osteospermum, 124
Osteospermum ecklonis, 381
ostrich fern, 364
Oxalis tetraphylla, 133, 371
oxeye / oxeye daisy, 25, 134, 345
oxlip, 36, 258, 347

Pachyphytum, 176
Pachypodium lamerei, 36, 391
Pachysandra, 121
Pachysandra terminalis, 356
Pachystachys lutea, 298, 391
Pacific Island silver grass, 363
Paeonia, 170, 346
Paeonia lactiflora, 346
Paeonia officinalis, 346
Paeonia ×suffruticosa, 325
Paeonia tenuifolia, 346
paigles, 347
paintbrush, 389
painted daisy, 375
painted tongue, 377
paleleaf barberry, 334
palms, 34, 35–36, 175, 179, 222, 224
pampas grass, 94, 173–174, 287, 362
Pandanus, 139, 202
Pandanus tectorius, 391
Pandanus veitchii, 391
panicle hydrangea, 31, 324
Panicum virgatum, 363
pansy, 378, 382
    as outdoor container plant, 95
    planting / sowing, 131, 221, 240
    seedlings, 55, 403
    winter protection, 32, 288
Papaver, 257, 376
Papaver nudicaule, 221, 376
Papaver orientale, 346
Papaver rhoeas, 376
paper daisy, 124, 256, 379
paper flower, 385
Paphiopedilum, 98, 397

Paraguay nightshade, 390
Paraserianthes lophanta, 383
parlor palm, 386
parsley (curly), 70, 250, 273, 307, 309, 313, 316. *See also* root parsley
parsnips, 27, 69–70, 189, 265, 271, 313, 317
Parthenocissus, 81, 276, 341
Parthenocissus quinquefolia, 341
Parthenocissus tricuspidata, 240
    'Veitchii', 241, 341
pasque flower, 134, 145, 353
Passiflora caerulea, 179, 391
passionflower, 179
paths, 19, 44–45, 151–152
paving stones, 84, 121
peach-leaved bellflower, 343
peacock flower, 279, 371
pea moth, 319
pearly everlasting, 349
pear rust, 129
peas
    fertilizing, 65, 112, 307
    harvesting, 210, 317
    plant family, 65
    sowing, 66, 93, 309, 311, 313, 317
    split peas, 65
    sweet peas, 65, 93
    wrinkled peas, 65, 104
pea shrub (or pea tree), 256
peat, 11, 13, 132
peat walls, 175
Pelargonium, 54, 392
Pelargonium Grandiflorum Group, 392
Pelargonium Peltatum Group, 381
Pelargonium Zonale Group, 381
pendulous sedge, 362
Penicillium bulb rot, 287
Pennisetum alopecuroides, 363
Penstemon hartwegii 'Picotee Red, 346
Penstemon / penstemon, 377
peony, 25, 240, 310, 346
Peperomia, 38, 260, 392
Peperomia argyreia, 392
Peperomia obtusifolia, 392
peppermint, 116, 194, 217, 234–35, 273–274
    'Multimentha', 116
peppers, 52, 157, 213, 231, 234, 271, 273, 307
peppers, hot, 296
peppers, ornamental, 386
perennials
    dividing and replanting, 82, 197, 238, 245, 278
    fall-blooming, 253

fall-planted forced up by frost, 57–58, 59, 94, 122
fertilizing, 131, 194
growing at pond edges, 132
low, shade-loving, 121, 355–356 (table)
ornamental grasses, 362–363 (table)
perennial herb gardens, 32, 58–59
planting / sowing, 14, 54–55, 82, 125, 170, 174, 199
protecting tall, 197
for rock gardens, 349–354 (table)
seed propagating, 55
sensitive, 253
winter-hardy, 198, 343–348 (table)
winter protection, 79
Pericallis ×hybrida Senecio Cruentus Group, 392
Persian buttercup, 258, 281, 371
Persian onion, 366
Persian violet, 281, 290, 367
Peruvian lily, 366
pesticides, 206
pests
    acquiring knowledge about, 24
    important ornamental plant pests, 399–401 (table)
    important pests in vegetable gardens, 318–319 (table)
    plants in pest control, 26, 201
    prevention and control, 24–25, 318–319, 399–401
    useful animals, 24–25, 145–148, 183–184, 318, 399
Petunia / petunia, 54, 175, 177, 201–202, 222, 381
Pfitzer juniper, 329, 332
phacelia, 145
Phacelia tanacetifolia, 145, 377
Phalaenopsis, 41, 98, 242, 397
Phalaris arundinacea 'Picta', 363
Phegopteris connectilis, 364
Philadelphus, 57, 81, 326
Philadelphus coronarius, 326
Philadelphus ×lemoinei 'Erectus', 326, 332
Philadelphus microphyllus, 336
Philadelphus ×purpureomaculatus 'Belle Étoile, 326
Philadelphus ×virginalis, 326
    'Girandole', 326
    'Schneesturm', 326
Philodendron / philodendron, 392
    cuttings, 97, 202
    growing on branches or poles, 222, 260

hydroponic culture, 139
remaining inside all year, 203
supporting, 222
temperature fluctuations, 35
watering, 260
Phlebodium aureum, 300
Phlomis samia, 346
Phlox douglasii, 352
Phlox drummondii, 377
Phlox paniculata, 346
Phlox / phlox, 134, 145, 278, 310, 352
Phlox stolonifera, 352
Phlox subulata, 352
Phoenix, 392
Phoenix canariensis, 36, 299, 392
Phoenix dactylifera, 36, 299, 392
Phoenix roebelenii, 36, 392
pH values in ponds, 132
pH values of important cultivated
plants, 309–310 (table).
See also planting / sowing
under *specific plant names*
Phyllitis scolopendrium, 364
Physalis, 256
Physalis alkekengi var. *franchetii*,
347
physic, 348
Physostegia virginiana, 347
Phytophthora, 229
Phytoseiulus, 146
Picea, 256, 329, 336
Picea abies, 329, 336
'Echiniformis', 336
'Pygmaea', 336
Picea glauca 'Conica', 336
Picea glauca var. *albertiana* 'Con-
ica', 329
Picea omorika, 329
Picea pungens, 329
'Glauca Globosa', 336
Picea pungens, 329
pickerel weed, 358
Pieris japonica, 326
pigmy date palm, 392
Pilea, 392
Pilea cardierei, 392
Pilea involucrata, 392
Pilea spruceana, 392
pimpernel, 177
pincushion flower, 82, 347
pine, 256, 330, 336
pineapple, 384
pineapple flower, 370
pineapple fruits, 281
pineapple mint, 116
pink, 171, 344, 350, 374
pink lily leek, 366
pink siris, 289, 383
Pinus, 256, 330, 336
'Smidtii', 330

Pinus cembra, 330
Pinus heldreichii 'Compacta Gem',
330
Pinus mugo subsp. *mugo*, 336
Pinus nigra, 330
Pinus parviflora, 330
Pinus pumila, 336
Pinus strobus, 330
Pinus sylvestris 'Watereri', 336
Piper, 392
Piper nigrum, 392
Piper ornatum, 392
Plantago nivalis, 352
plant damage, causes and prevention, 24–25
planting / sowing, generally
advance planting, 54–55, 92
crop rotation, 25–26, 26–27,
311
dibbling method, 20, 53
digging trenches, 14
intensive planting, 26
plants grown on open land,
315–317 (table)
preparing soil in winter, 48
spacing, 25
tools, 17–18, 20
vegetables and aromatic
herbs, 312–314 (table)
Platycerium, 179, 298, 392
Platycodon grandiflorus, 347
Plectranthus forsteri 'Marginatus',
381
Plectranthus scutellarioides, 96,
139, 392
Pleione limprichtii, 175, 398
Plumbago, 175, 280
Plumbago auriculata, 393
Plumbago capensis, 393
plume albizia, 383
plum yew, 129
Pogonia ophioglossoides, 398
pohutukawa, 391
poinsettia, 298, 388
poisonous plants, 40, 176, 195,
240, 256, 293, 297
Polemonium caeruleum, 347
pollinators, 145, 246
Polygala chamaebuxus 'Purple
Passion', 336
Polygonatum ×*hybridum*, 347
Polygonum aubertii, 81, 198, 276,
340
polypod ferns, 300
Polypodiaceae, 300
Polypodium, 365
Polypodium interjectum, 365
Polypodium vulgare, 356, 365
polypody, 365
Polystichum, 365

Polystichum aculeatum, 365
Polystichum setiferum, 365
pomegranate, 134, 135, 280, 289,
299, 393
ponds and pools. *See also* aquatic
plants; swamp pools
algae, 132
for children, 90
construction and uses, 89–91
edge plantings, 132
fish, 206, 287–288
maintaining, 92, 220, 283
Pontederia cordata, 358
poppy, 257, 310
poppy anemone, 258, 370
Port Jackson fig, 388
Portulaca grandiflora, 178, 377
potatoes, 10, 155, 307, 309
potatoes, early, 67, 107, 187, 211,
229
potato pests and diseases, 183,
187, 229, 319
Potentilla, 353
Potentilla atrosanguinea, 353
Potentilla aurea, 353
Potentilla fruticosa, 326, 332, 337
Potentilla megalantha, 353
Potentilla nitida, 353
Potentilla ×*tonguei*, 353
pot marigold, 123, 257, 372
pot plants, 11, 13, 202
poverty brome, 379
powder puff tree, 258
powdery mildew, 123, 171–172,
191, 403
prairie cord grass, 363
prairie evening primrose, 352
prairie mallow, 348
prayer plant, 390
predatory mites, 146–147
predatory wasps, 146, 147, 228
prettyface, 369
prickly pear, 352
prickly shield fern, 365
primel, 393
primrose, 36, 95, 258, 302, 310, 347,
353, 358
Primula, 95, 347, 353, 358, 393
Primula auricula, 353
Primula beesiana, 353
Primula cortusoides, 353
Primula denticulata, 347
Primula elatior, 36, 258, 347
Primula florindae, 358
Primula japonica, 353
Primula juliae, 347, 351
Primula littoniana, 358
Primula malacoides, 36, 393
Primula marginata, 353
Primula obconica, 36, 393

Primula ×*pubescens*, 347, 353
Primula rosea, 353
Primula vialii, 358
Primula vulgaris, 36, 258, 347
privet, 30, 81, 130, 256, 275, 276
privet honeysuckle, 336
propagation
aquatic and swamp plants,
357–359 (table)
cuttings, 96–97
flowering perennials, 55, 82,
197, 245, 253, 278
indoor plants, 96–97
self-seeding plants, 195, 221
prostrate broom, 335
Prunella, 353
Prunella grandiflora, 353, 356
Prunella ×*webbiana*, 353
pruning tools, 18
Prunus, 31, 33, 326
Prunus laurocerasus, 81, 130, 256,
288, 326
Prunus serrulata, 326
Prunus tenella, 337
Prunus triloba, 57, 173
'Plena', 326
Pseudofumaria, 353, 356
Pseudofumaria lutea, 356
Pseudolysimachion, 347
Pseudolysimachion longifolium, 347
Pseudolysimachion spicatum, 347
Pseudotsuga menziesii var. *glauca*,
330
Psylliostachys suworowii, 171, 379
Pteris, 300
Pteris argyraea, 300
Pteris cretica, 300, 393
Pteris cretica var. *albolineata*, 300,
393
Pulmonaria angustifolia 'Azurea',
356
Pulsatilla, 353
Pulsatilla halleri, 353
Pulsatilla pratensis, 134
Pulsatilla vulgaris, 145, 353
pumpkins, 156, 188, 230, 248, 307,
309, 317
Punica, 280, 289
Punica granatum, 134, 135, 299, 393
purple broom, 334
purple coneflower, 344
purple giant filbert, 57
purple glory tree, 395
purple leaf barberry, 331, 334
purple-leaved hazel, 323
purple loosestrife, 346, 358
purple moor grass, 363
purple primrose, 347
purple velvet plant, 389
purple willow, 332

Puschkinia / puschkinia, 239
Puschkinia scilloides, 369
pussy willow, 135, 327
pygmy Norway spruce, 336
Pyracantha coccinea, 326, 332
    'Red Column', 332
    'Soleil d'Or', 332

quaking grass, 125, 379
quamash, 239, 366
Queensland arrowroot, 370

rabbits, 16, 33, 254, 284
radiator plant, 260, 392
radicchio, 158–159, 190, 213, 231, 271, 307, 313, 317
radishes. *See also* red radishes
    fall and winter varieties, 190–191, 213, 232, 271, 317
    fertilizing, 232, 307
    growing in greenhouses, 51
    harvesting, 271, 317
    planting / sowing, 53, 112, 190, 213, 309, 317
    rat tail radishes, 169
    watering, 112, 191
rainwater for indoor plants, 179
rainwater tanks, 206
rakes, 17, 19
Ranunculus, 359
Ranunculus aquatilis, 359
Ranunculus arvensis, 182
Ranunculus asiaticus, 258, 281, 371
Ranunculus circinatus, 90, 359
Ranunculus lingua, 359
red-berried elder, 332
red cedar, 130, 330, 333, 337
red elderberry, 332
red flax, 376
red hot cat's tail, 383
red hot poker, 134, 253, 345
red juniper, 329
red radishes
    fertilizing, 71, 159, 191, 308
    growing in cold frames or greenhouses, 51, 53, 66, 248
    harvesting, 68, 190, 248, 317
    as indicator crop, 53, 69–70, 73
    pests, 165, 318
    planting / sowing, 53, 159, 190, 248, 309, 317
    watering, 112, 159
red spider mites, 37, 95, 182, 289–290, 319
red star, 371
redvein enkianthus, 324
reed canary grass, 363
reedmace, 359
reed sweet grass, 362

regal lily, 368
Reseda, 122
Reseda odorata, 377
rex begonia vine, 386
Rhapis excelsa, 393
Rhipsalidopsis, 40
Rhipsalidopsis ×graeseri, 179, 393
Rhipsalis, 40, 393
Rhizobium, 65
Rhodanthe manglesii, 124, 256, 379
Rhododendron / rhododendron, 326
    fertilizing, 81
    humidity and shade, 130
    'Praecox', 59, 326
    removing spent flowers, 173
    soil requirements, 13, 87, 295, 310
    watering, 81, 198–199
    winter protection, 32, 288
Rhododendron simsii, 179
Rhododendron Simsii Group, 393
Rhodohypoxis baurii, 371
rhubarb
    fertilizing, 72, 159, 185, 214, 308
    frost protection, 29
    harvesting, 72, 185
    planting / sowing, 26, 71, 248–249, 309, 313
    rootstocks, 29, 285
    sprouting, 29
Rhus typhina, 326
ribbon fern, 300, 393
ribbon grass, 363
Ribes, 332
Ribes alpinum 'Schmidt', 332
Ribes sanguineum, 57, 145, 326, 332
rice button aster, 343, 350
Robinia hispida, 326
rockcress, 349
rocket, 251
rock gardens
    design and construction, 86, 88
    perennials for, 349–354 (table)
    shrubs for, 334–337 (table)
    soil and substrate, 86
    winter protection, 32, 278
rock jasmine, 349
rock pink, 350
rock rose, 134, 253, 310, 351
Rodgersia aesculifolia, 347
Romanesco broccoli, 104
Roman fennel, 107
root parsley, 70, 250, 317
root rot, 321, 403
Rosa canina, 218
Rosa dwarf roses, 393

Rosa rubiginosa, 338
Rosa rugosa, 277, 339
Roscoea cautleoides, 369
rose acacia, 326
rose balsam, 375
rose daphne, 335
rose mallow, 124, 376
rosemary, 135, 224, 299, 393
rose moss, 377
rose of China, 299, 389
rose of Sharon, 335
rose pogonia, 398
roses
    bed roses, 80, 339
    'Charmant', 135
    classification by use, 80
    climbing roses, 128, 195–196, 338
    colors, 80
    'Compassion', 128
    diseases, 171–172, 402, 403
    dwarf roses, 339
    fertilizing, 196, 218
    grafting, 218–219, 241
    miniature, 135
    overwintering, 127, 135
    pests, 128, 172, 196, 400, 401
    planting, 80, 126–128, 127, 277, 310
    in pots, 135
    pruning / cutting back, 18, 31, 56, 79, 195, 218
    removing withered flowers, 195–196
    shrub roses, 80, 339
    species roses, 338
    'Super Dorothy', 135
    'Super Excelsa', 135
    supports, 127
    underplanting, 128, 135
    variety selection, 80, 128, 338–339 (table)
    wild roses, 339
    wind protection, 195
    winter protection, 32, 79, 135, 277
rose shoot sawfly, 172, 400
rosette saxifrages, 353
Rosmarinus officinalis, 224, 299, 393
rosy posy, 371
rowan tree, 246
row covers, 52, 75, 112, 159
royal fern, 364
rubber plant, 35, 203, 260, 388
rubber tree, 388
rucola, 251
Rudbeckia, 278, 347
Rudbeckia fulgida var. *sullivantii*, 347

Rudbeckia hirta, 377
Rudbeckia nitida, 347
ruddles, 372
rue, 196
Rumex acetosella, 182
Russian arborvitae, 336
Russian statice, 171
Russian vine, 31, 81, 198, 276, 340
rusty fig, 388
rutabagas (swedes), 150, 188, 212, 229, 248, 269, 308
Ruta graveolens, 196

saffron spike, 384
sage, 54, 174, 346
sage (culinary), 78, 116, 167, 194, 235, 273
Sagittaria, 359
Sagittaria latifolia, 359
Sagittaria sagittifolia, 359
Saintpaulia, 38, 97, 261, 393
Salix caprea 'Pendula', 135, 327
Salix purpurea, 332
    'Gracilis', 332
    'Nana', 332
sallow, 327
salpiglossis, 377
Salpiglossis sinuata, 377
salt cedar, 288, 327
Salvia, 54
Salvia nemorosa, 347
Salvia splendens, 377, 381
Sambucus, 332
Sambucus nigra, 327, 332
Sambucus racemosa, 332
sand rocket, 251
sanicle, 356
Sanicula europaea, 356
Sansevieria, 40, 139, 260
Sansevieria trifasciata, 393
Santolina chamaecyparissus, 337
Sanvitalia procumbens, 123, 178, 377
sapphire flower, 385
Satureja, 196
saucer magnolia, 57, 325
savin juniper, 329
savory, 117, 196
savoy cabbage
    fertilizing, 308
    harvesting, 270, 317
    planting / sowing, 31, 75–76, 109, 191, 215, 309, 314, 317
Sawara cypress, 334
Saxifraga, 353, 356
Saxifraga agina subulata, 353
Saxifraga ×arendsii, 353
Saxifraga axifraga, 353
Saxifraga callosa, 353
Saxifraga cochlearis, 353

Saxifraga cuneifolia, 353, 356
Saxifraga longifolia, 353
Saxifraga paniculata, 353
Saxifraga stolonifera, 394
Saxifraga trifurcata, 353
Saxifraga umbrosa, 353, 356
saxifrage, 353, 356
Scabiosa, 82
Scabiosa atropurpurea, 377
Scabiosa caucasica, 347
scabious, 347
Scadoxus 'König Albert', 137, 394
Scadoxus multiflorus subsp. *katharinae*, 137
Scadoxus puniceus, 137
Scaevola saligna, 381
scale insects, 95, 146
scarlet flax, 376
scarlet runner bean, 177, 308
scarlet sage, 377, 381
Schefflera, 34, 135, 175, 179, 222, 394
Schizanthus ×*wisetonensis*, 377
Schlumbergera, 40, 179, 260, 394
Schoenoplectus, 359
Schoenoplectus lacustris, 359
Schoenoplectus tabernaemontani, 359
Sciadopitys verticillata, 330
Scilla, 239, 369
scindapsus, 394
Scindapsus pictus, 394
Scirpus, 359
Scotch broom, 323
Scotch heather, 334
Scotch marigold, 372
screw pine, 139, 202, 391
sea buckthorn, 130
sea holly, 82
seakale beet, 25
sea lavender, 256, 379
sedge, 362
Sedum, 40, 348, 354
Sedum acre, 354
Sedum album, 354
Sedum cauticola, 354
Sedum hybridum, 348
Sedum morganianum, 40, 394
Sedum selskianum, 354
Sedum spectabile, 348
Sedum spurium, 354
Sedum telephium, 348
seedlings, 28, 40, 55, 116
seeds
  collecting and storing, 55
  frost / cold germinators, 278
  obtaining, 27, 48
  viability testing, 27–28
Selaginella / selaginella, 38, 394
selfheal, 353, 356
Sempervivum, 176, 354

Senecio cineraria, 170
sensitive fern, 364
Septoria, 187
serviceberry, 322
Sesleria heufleriana, 363
shade perennials, 122, 355–356 (table)
shade saxifrages, 353
shamrock, 133
shasta daisy, 198, 345
sheep laurel, 336
sheep sorrel, 182
shield-leafed saxifrage, 353
shooting star, 350
showy Chinese gentian, 351
showy Japanese lily, 368
shrimp plant, 390
shrubby cinquefoil, 326, 332, 337
shrubby milkwort, 336
shrubs. *See also* hedges
  attractive species and varieties, 81, 322–327 (table)
  broad-leaved trees and shrubs, 322–327 (table)
  evergreen, 57, 129, 198–199, 220, 297
  fertilizing, 241, 276
  flowering, 31, 59, 198
  planting, 14, 57, 65, 122, 128, 276
  pruning or cutting back, 30–31, 56, 277
  for rock gardens and small gardens, 334–337 (table)
  sensitive ornamental, 276
  in tubs, 241
  watering, 199, 245, 277
Siberian bugloss, 355
Siberian iris, 220
Siberian mountain lily, 252
Siberian pine, 336
Siberian stonecrop, 348
Siberian wallflower, 374
sickles, 21
Sidalcea, 348
Silene, 348, 354
Silene acaulis, 354
Silene chalcedonica, 348
Silene schafta, 354
Silene viscaria 'Plena', 348
silk tree, 289, 383
silver bell, 324
silver-edged primrose, 353
silver feather grass, 363
silver fir, 403
silver lace vine, 31, 81, 198, 276, 340
silver ragwort, 170
silver squill, 390
silver wattle, 383
Sinningia, 259, 394

Skimmia japonica 'Rubella', 337
skin irritation, 184
skunk cabbage, 358
slender deutzia, 335
slipper flower, 178, 380, 385
slipper orchid, 98
slugs, 102–103, 147, 183, 203, 229, 266, 319, 400
small flower tamarisk, 327
small-leaved ivy, 38
smoothies, 296
snails, 102
snakemouth orchid, 398
snake plant, 40, 139, 260, 393
snake's head fritillary, 239, 367
snapdragon, 131, 170, 310, 372
sneezeweed, 198, 345
snow
  avoiding snow breakage, 32
  harvesting in, 247
  protective aspects, 13, 130, 285, 287, 288, 296
  tilling snow-covered soil, 14, 30
snowball bush, 327
snowberry, 256, 327
snowdrop, 58, 59, 220, 239, 281, 367
snowdrop tree, 324
snowflake, 368
snow on the mountain, 374
snow water, 264, 278
snowy wood rush, 362
soft hornwort, 357
soft shield fern, 365
soil
  acidic or alkaline indicators, 182
  acidified, 12, 121
  arable soils and their characteristics, 305 (table)
  double digging or triple digging, 14, 264–265
  "good gardening soil" defined, 305
  improving, 10–11
  maintaining, 142
  pH values, 295, 309–310 (table)
  potting compost, 13
  preparing for sowing, 48
  soil exhaustion, 25
  steam-sterilizing, 284
soil requirements. *See also* planting / sowing under *specific plant names*
  for balcony boxes, pots and terraces, 380–382 (table)
  pH values, 295, 309–310 (table)

  for tub plants, winter gardens, flower windows, 383–395 (table)
Solanum, 135, 394
Solanum capsicastrum, 394
Solanum melongena, 394
Solanum pseudocapsicum, 394
Solanum rantonnetii, 390
solar yellow, 355
soldier beetles, 146
Soleirolia, 38
Soleirolia soleirolii, 394
Solidago, 348
Solomon's seal, 347
Sonchus arvensis, 182
soot, 13
southern lady fern, 364
south-facing sites, 95, 111, 135, 136, 150, 178
South Japanese white pine, 330
sow thistle species, 182
Spanish bluebell, 367
Spanish marigold, 370
Sparaxis, 126
Sparmannia, 96, 97
Sparmannia africana, 40, 179, 299, 395
Spartina pectinata 'Aureomarginata', 363
Spathodea campanulata, 395
spear grass, 363
speedwell, 347, 354
speenwort, 384
spider flower, 389
spider ivy (or spider plant), 97, 139, 373, 386
spiders, 146
spiderwort, 395
spiked loosestrife, 346, 358
spike winter hazel, 323
spinach
  fertilizing, 114, 232, 308
  harvesting, 317
  planting / sowing, 75, 215, 232, 245, 249, 309, 314, 317
  winter protection, 272
spindle, 256, 324, 335
Spiraea, 31, 145, 327, 333
Spiraea ×*arguta*, 327
Spiraea japonica
  'Anthony Waterer', 31, 327
  'Little Princess', 327, 337
Spiraea ×*vanhouttei*, 327
spirea, 145
split peas, 65
spoonleaf yucca, 348
spotted laurel, 134, 135, 280, 385
spreading cotoneaster, 331
Sprekelia, 279
Sprekelia formosissima, 371

Sprenger's asparagus, 384
spring adonis, 349
spring snowflake, 220, 239
spring starflower, 367
springtails, 242
sprinklers, 19
spruce, 226, 256, 329
spurge, 121, 145, 374, 388
squash, 156, 188, 248, 307, 309, 317
squill, 220, 239, 369
Stachys byzantina, 354
staff vine, 340
staghorn fern, 38, 179, 298, 392
staghorn sumac, 326
Stapelia, 40
star magnolia, 57, 325
star of Bethlehem, 369
star of Persia, 366
star thistle, 278, 344
statice, 379
Stellaria media, 142, 182
Stenocarpus sinuatus, 395
Stephanandra, 327
Stephanandra incisa, 327, 333
Stephanandra tanakae, 327
sticky catchfly, 348
Stipa, 363
Stipa barbata, 363
Stipa capillata, 363
Stipa pennata, 363
St. John's wort, 81, 276, 324, 335
stock, 132, 170, 310, 376
stone cress, 349
stonecrop, 348, 354
stone walls, 32
storage rot, 33, 55, 287, 403
Stratiotes aloides, 359
strawberry geranium, 394
strawberry tree, 134, 280, 384
strawberry weevil, 147, 401
straw daisy, 92, 255–256, 379
straw mats, 49, 50, 51, 105, 107, 168, 194
Strelitzia reginae, 261, 395
Streptocarpus, 179, 395
striped squill, 369
succulents, 40, 176
suet, 24
sugarloaf, 193, 233, 272–273, 308, 317
sugar peas, 65
summer cabbage fly, 190
summer cypress, 372
summer flowers, 54–55, 92, 94, 95, 122, 170–171, 257, 288
summer hyacinth, 367
summer phlox, 346
summer savory, 167, 201, 216, 250, 314
sundials, 89

sunflower, 123, 375
sunflower seeds, 255
sunflower species, 102
sun rose, 134, 253, 351
swamp plants, 357–359 (table)
swamp pools, 32, 92, 132, 239, 287
swede midge, 104, 319
Swedish ivy, 381
sweet Alison, 376
sweet alyssum, 376
sweet briar, 339
sweet corn, 154, 165, 193, 216, 249, 308
sweet galingale, 357
sweet mock orange, 326
sweet myrtle, 357
sweet pea (ornamental), 93, 198, 375
sweet pepper bush, 323
sweet scabious, 377
sweet viburnum, 327
sweet violets, 134
sweet William, 240, 374
sweet woodruff, 355
Swiss cheese plant, 222, 391
Swiss stone pine, 330
switch grass, 363
sword fern, 300, 391
sword lily, 345, 357, 368
Symphoricarpos, 256, 327
Symphoricarpos albus var. laevigatus, 327
Symphoricarpos ×chenaultii, 327
Syngonium podophyllum, 395
Syringa, 31, 57, 81, 327
Syringa meyeri 'Pink Perfume', 327
Syringa ×vulgaris, 327

tables, about, 303–304
Tagetes, 26, 92, 171, 175, 257, 378
Tagetes erecta, 378
Tagetes patula, 378
Tagetes tenuifolia, 378
tail flower, 384
tall grasses, 94
tall moor grass, 363
tamarisk, 57, 81, 288, 327
Tamarix, 57, 81, 288, 327
Tamarix parviflora, 327
Tamarix ramosissima, 327
Tanacetum, 378
Tanacetum coccineum, 348
tank bromeliads, 35
tansy, 348
tara vine, 340
tarragon, 76–77
Taxus, 236, 330, 337
Taxus baccata, 330, 333
'Adpressa Aurea', 337

'Repandens', 337
'Summergold', 337
Taxus cuspidata 'Nana', 337
Taxus cuspidata var. cuspidata, 330
Taxus cuspidata var. nana, 129, 135, 337
Taxus ×media, 330
teesdale violets, 182
ten-week stock, 376
terraces, plants for, 176, 380–383 (table)
Teucrium chamaedrys, 333, 354
Thalictrum aquilegiifolium, 348
thermocomposters, 246
thinleaved sunflower, 345
threadworms, 146
thrift, 350
thrips, 196, 201, 289, 318, 401
Thuja, 130, 330
Thuja occidentalis, 330, 337
'Danica', 337
'Ellwangeriana', 333
'Teddy', 337
Thuja plicata 'Atrovirens', 330
Thujopsis, 129
Thunbergia alata, 55, 93
thyme, 78–79, 167, 235, 354
Thymophylla tenuiloba, 178, 382
Thymus, 354
Thymus pseudolanuginosus, 354
Thymus serpyllum, 354
Tiarella cordifolia, 356
Tibouchina, 175, 258
Tibouchina urvilleana, 395
tickseed, 134, 145, 198, 253, 344, 373
tiger flower, 133, 279, 371
tiger grass, 363
tiger jaws, 40
tiger lily, 238, 368
Tigridia, 133, 279
Tigridia pavonia, 371
Tillandsia / tillandsia, 298, 395
toadflax, 355
toadshade, 369
tomatoes
about, 227
bush tomatoes, 164
dwarf tomatoes, 163
fertilizing, 162, 163, 192, 193, 215, 308
growing in foil houses or greenhouses, 105, 115
harvesting, 317
house tomatoes, 162–163, 192
pests and diseases, 232, 319, 320, 321
pinching back, 162–163, 164, 192, 232–233
pinching off, 215

planting / sowing, 105, 115, 163, 164, 309, 317
staking, 163–164
temperatures, 162
tying up, 162–163
watering, 162
tongavine, 388
tools, maintaining, 16, 294
topinambur, 102
torch lily, 134, 253, 345
Trachycarpus, 36, 134, 280
Trachycarpus fortunei, 395
Tradescantia ×andersoniana, 348
Tradescantia fluminensis, 395
Tradescantia spathacea, 395
Tradescantia / tradescantia, 139, 179, 395
Tradescantia zebrina, 395
trailing lobelia, 376, 381
Transvaal daisy, 389
Trapa natans, 359
treasure flower, 375
treebine, 386
tree hydrangea, 324
tree peony, 325
trees
adjusting surrounding terrain, 86
attractive trees and shrubs, 81, 322–327 (table)
conifers, 32, 128, 173, 236, 237–238, 256, 327–330 (table)
evergreen, 57, 129, 198–199, 297
evergreen broad-leaved, 128, 173, 220, 237–238, 275
landscape uses, 57
planting, 14, 57, 65
thinning or cutting back, 56
in tubs, 241
winter pruning, 30
trellises, building, 294–295
trellises, planting, 176–177
Tricyrtis hirta, 369
Trifolium arvense, 182
Trillium, 369
Trillium grandiflorum, 369
Trillium sessile, 369
trinity flower, 369
Triteleia, 369
Triteleia ixioides, 369
Triteleia laxa, 369
Trollius, 278, 348
Trollius chinensis, 348
Trollius europaeus, 348
Tropaeolum majus, 378, 382
tropic laurel, 388
troughs, 59, 95
trumpet creeper, 340
trumpet gentian, 134, 351

Tsuga canadensis, 330, 337
    'Nana', 337
    'Pendula', 337
tub plants
    decorative use, 135, 280
    fertilizing, 139
    frosts and cold snaps, 94–95,
        134–135, 258, 280
    Mediterranean, 224
    not winter hardy, 383–395
        (table)
    overwintering, 34, 95
    pests and diseases, 95, 222,
        399, 400, 401
    planting, 95, 134–135
    relocating to outdoors, 135,
        141, 175
    soils, 118
    sun damage, 139, 383
    transplanting, 241
    trees and shrubs, 139, 241
    watering, 34, 95, 222
    winter light requirements,
        289, 299
tufted hairgrass, 362
tulip, 369
    diseases, 402, 403
    low-growing varieties, 259
    planting, 59, 171, 239, 252, 253,
        310
    use as cut flowers, 133
    watering died-off, 60
    winter flowering, 259, 290,
        298
Tulipa, 369
tumbleweed onion, 366
tuna, 352
Turkestan allium, 366
turkey corn, 350
Turk's cap, 368
turmeric, 387
turnip, 67, 150, 188, 212, 229, 248,
    269, 308
turnip root fly, 319
twinberry honeysuckle, 325
twinspur, 380
two row stonecrop, 354
Typha, 359
Typha angustifolia, 359
Typha latifolia, 359
Typha laxmannii, 359
Typha minima, 359

umbrella grass, 96, 139, 202, 258,
    387
umbrella pine, 330
umbrella tree, 179, 222, 258, 394
Ursinia, 125
Ursinia anethoides, 125, 378
Urtica urens, 182

Vallota, 36, 137, 179
Vanstaden's river daisy, 381
variegated philodendron, 388
vegetable clamps, 29, 54, 117, 269,
    285, 296
vegetable peas, 65
vegetables, generally
    fall-growing species, 247
    heeled-in, 30
    main / aftercrop pairings, 26
    seeds and seedlings, 27–28
    storing, 296
    varieties, 28
    wilting, 165–166
    wind-sensitive species, 165
Veitch fir, 328
Veitch's silver fir, 328
Venus' slipper, 98
Verbascum, 280
Verbena, 175, 177, 378, 382
Veronica, 354
Veronica armena, 354
Veronica prostrata, 354
Veronicastrum virginicum, 348
Verticillium wilt, 201
vervain, 378, 382
very slender feather grass, 363
vetches, 25, 65, 134, 198, 310
Vial's primrose, 358
Viburnum carlesii, 327
Viburnum davidii, 337
Viburnum opulus 'Roseum', 327
Viburnum plicatum f. *tomentosum*,
    327
Viburnum rhytidophyllum, 327
Viburnum tinus, 280, 395
Viburnum / viburnum, 31, 33, 57, 327
Vinca minor, 356
Viola, 378, 382
Viola canina, 134
Viola cornuta, 278, 382
Viola labradorica, 354
Viola odorata, 134
Viola rupestris, 182
Viola ×wittrockiana, 55, 95, 131, 221,
    240, 288, 378, 382
violet, 310, 378
Virginia creeper, 81, 276, 341
voles, 145, 246, 266, 401
Volga fescue, 362
Vriesea, 40, 99
Vriesea splendens, 395
Vuylstekeara hybrids, 98, 397

wake robin, 369
Waldsteinia geoides, 356
Waldsteinia ternata, 356
Waldsteinia / waldsteinia, 121, 356
wallflower, 95, 195, 240, 310, 374
wall germander, 333, 354

wallpepper, 354
wandering Jew, 395
wandering sailor, 395
Warminster broom, 81, 276, 323
warty barberry, 331, 334
water aloe, 359
water and watering
    amounts, 144
    lime-containing water, 41, 98,
        222
    rainwater for indoor plants,
        179
    rainwater tanks, 206
    spraying vs., 144
    tap water, 98, 144, 186, 189,
        281
    tools, 19, 64, 223–224, 228,
        266
    vacation watering of indoor
        plants, 223–224
    water containers, 64, 206, 284
    water lines, 284
    water supply, 64
    water table, 10
    wicking procedure, 224
water arum, 357
water buttercup, 359
water chestnut, 359
water crowfoot, 359
water fringe, 358
water gladiolus, 357
water hyacinth, 357
water lilies, 33, 132, 287, 360–361
    (table)
watermelon peperomia, 392
water plaintain, 132
water soldier, 359
water trefoil, 358
wax flower, 139
waxplant, 389
weather monitoring, 21
Weddel palm, 36, 179, 390
weed horsetail, 182
weeds, 19, 82, 103, 142, 182, 265, 278
weegbree, 352
weeping blue atlas cedar, 328
weeping Canadian hemlock, 337
weeping fig, 388
Weigela / weigela, 31, 57, 327, 333
Welleseley yew, 330
western red cedar, 330
west-facing sites, 178
wetlands, 13, 92, 132. *See also*
    swamp pools
wheelbarrows and carts, 19
white alder, 323
white asparagus, 73, 75, 191, 272,
    285
white butterflies, 214
white dogwood, 323

white fir, 328
white forsythia, 322
white lily, 239, 368
white mallow, 145
white peony, 346
white pine, 330
white spiderwort, 348
white stonecrop, 354
white trillium, 369
Whitlow grass, 350
whorlflower, 346
wild bergamot, 346
wild crocus, 58
wild ginger, 121
wild roses, 56, 80, 339
wild sage, 347
willow bell, 343
willow leaf cotoneaster, 334
windbreaks, 274
windflower, 253, 343, 366, 370
windmill palms, 280
window boxes, 94–95, 118, 176,
    178, 201
winged spindle, 256, 324, 335
winter aconite, 58, 145, 221, 367
winter chrysnthemum, 253
winter creeper, 335
wintercress, 29
winter endives
    "bleaching" process, 249
    fertilizing, 233, 308
    growing in cold frames or
        greenhouses, 216, 233
    harvesting, 249
    monitoring in storage, 285
    planting / sowing, 193,
        215–216, 233, 311, 313, 316
    storing, 272
winter gardens
    avoiding heat buildup, 22
    cleanliness and hygiene, 95
    plants, 176, 259, 383–395
        (table), 396–397 (table)
    temperature and ventilation,
        34
wintergreen broad-leaved trees
    and shrubs, 256
wintergreen perennials, 278, 287
wintergreen plants, defined, 30
winter-hardy plants
    on balconies and terraces, 34,
        288
    flowering herbaceous peren-
        nials, 343–348 (table)
    orchids, 175
    perennial bulbs and tubers,
        366–369 (table)
winter heath, 33, 145, 335
winter jasmine, 33, 59, 80, 81,
    299, 325

winter protection, 283, 296, 297
wire netting, uses
    containing leaves, 246
    pest control, 33, 49, 102–103,
        254, 269
    plant support, 66, 143, 175
wireworms, 146, 166, 319, 401
Wisteria floribunda, 341
Wisteria sinensis, 341
Wisteria / wisteria, 31, 81, 198,
    276, 341
witch hazel, 33, 43, 59, 81, 299, 324
woadwaxen, 335
wood, shredding, 31
wood ash, 13, 265
wood fibers, 13, 55, 175
wood forget-me-not, 376
woodland sage, 347

wood lily, 369
wood-rush, 362
wood sedge, 121, 355
woundwort, 354
wrinkled peas, 65, 104

Xanthocyparis nootkatensis, 328
Xeranthemum annuum, 379
Xerochrysum, 92, 255, 379
Xerochrysum bracteatum, 379

yellow ageratum, 124, 256
yellow archangel, 121, 355
yellow flag, 92, 357
yellow flax, 352
yellow floating heart, 358
yellow-flowering marsh marigold,
    92

yellow fumitory, 353, 356
yellow pheasant's eye, 349
yellow pond lilly, 358
yellow sage, 136
yellow skunk cabbage, 358
yellow water lilly, 358
yew, 236–237, 330, 333, 337
yucca, 97
Yucca filamentosa, 348

Zantedeschia elliottiana, 371
Zea mays, 379
zebra plant, 384
zebra rush, 359
Zinnia / zinnia, 92, 171, 310, 378,
    403
zonal geranium, 381
zucchini, 115, 164–165, 308, 317